JEFFERSON AND HAMILTON

THOMAS JEFFERSON
By Nancy Clifton M. Randolph after Thomas Sully

JEFFERSON
AND
HAMILTON

*The Struggle for Democracy
in America*

CLAUDE G. BOWERS

with illustrations

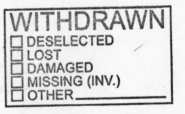
HOUGHTON MIFFLIN COMPANY BOSTON

The Riverside Press Cambridge

PREFACE

All American history has since run along the lines marked out by the antagonism of Jefferson and Hamilton. Our history is sometimes charged with a lack of picturesqueness because it does not deal with the belted knight and the moated grange. But to one who considers the moral import of events, it is hard to see how anything can be more picturesque than the spectacle of these two giant antagonists contending for political measures which were so profoundly to affect the lives of millions of human beings yet unborn.

JOHN FISKE

IT is the author's purpose, in developing the stirring story of the Plutarchian struggle of Jefferson and Hamilton, to show that without belted knights the period was picturesque and dramatic. The extraordinary men who gave and took lusty blows did not, as some would have us think, confine themselves to calm academic discussions of elemental principles. The dignified steel engravings of the participants, with which we are familiar, give no impression of the disheveled figures seen by their contemporaries on the battle-field.

This battle-field was rich in movement and color. There was tragedy and pathos, much of comedy, something of the grotesque. Here we shall meet marching mobs, witness duels and fist-fights, turbulent mass meetings, public dinners in groves and taverns, hangings in effigy, and champions of democracy in the galleries of theaters, pelting the aristocrats in the pits, and coercing the orchestras into playing 'La Marseillaise.' It was in the midst of such scenes as these that Jefferson and Hamilton fought the battle of the fundamentals.

The struggle of these two giants surpasses in importance any other waged in America because it related to elemental differences that reach back into the ages, and will continue to divide mankind far into the future. The surrender at Yorktown ended one phase of the Revolution, but it was not complete until, after twelve years of nationhood, it was definitively determined that this should be not only a republic, but a democratic republic. That was the real issue between Jefferson and Hamilton.

The passions of the period still persist, and much of myth has been built up by idolaters and enemies about both leaders. It has seemed possible to the author to tell the story of their struggle with complete justice to both. The part each played in the creation of the Nation was essential. It has been the purpose to depict these two men and their associates as they really were in the heat of controversy, neither sparing their weaknesses nor exaggerating their virtues; to paint them as men of flesh and blood with passions, prejudices, and human limitations; to show them at close quarters wielding their weapons, and sometimes, in the heat of the fight, stooping to conquer; and to uncover their motives as they are clearly disclosed in the correspondence of themselves and friends. This has necessitated the demolishment of some fashionable myths, when myths have obstructed the view to truth.

The facts as here set forth throw a vivid light on the causes of the collapse of the Federalist Party, which, in the average of its leadership, was, perhaps, the most brilliant, and certainly the most attractive, in American history. Men of wonderful charm they were, but they were singularly lacking in an understanding of the spirit of their times and country. They fell, as we shall find, because they neither had nor sought contact with the average man, and sternly set themselves against the overwhelming current of democracy.

Even so, we shall find an explanation of their distrust of popular government in the illiteracy of the times, the exaggerated notions of freedom that prevailed, and the levity with which so many looked on financial obligations. It is easier to understand the Hamiltonian distrust of democracy than to comprehend the faith of Jefferson — a faith of tremendous significance in history. Quite as remarkable as his faith was the ability of Jefferson to mobilize, organize, and discipline the great individualistic mass of the towns, the remote farms along the Savannah, the almost unbroken wilds of the Western wilderness. With a few notable exceptions, he was forced to rely for assistance on lieutenants pathetically inferior to the group of brilliant men who sat on the Federalist board of strategy. He won because he was a host within himself, capable of coping single-handed against the combined geniuses of the opposition in the field of practical politics.

A liberal use has been made of the newspapers of the period; not only of the descriptions of actual events, but of the false rumors and stories that entered into the creation of the prejudices that always play their part in the affairs of men. In determining why a given result was forced by public opinion, it is no more necessary to know what the truth was than to know what the people who formed that opinion thought the truth to be.

Along with the struggles in Congress, the bickerings in streets, coffee-houses, and taverns, the actions of mobs and mass meetings, it has been thought important to show the part 'society' played in the drama — for it was a significant part. This was inevitable in a clear-cut fight between democracy and aristocracy. The elegant home of Mrs. Bingham was scarcely less identified with the Federalists than was that of Lady Holland with the English Whigs, or that of Madame Rolland with the party of the Gironde. The pettings which the Otises and Harpers there received after the battles in the House were very real rewards to men of their temperament. The part played by men and women of fashion in the politics of the time will appear in the ostracism of Democrats from their charmed circle, when even Jefferson, snubbed, was driven for solace to the solitude of the library of the Philosophical Society.

Throughout the struggle we shall find the forces well defined — aristocracy against democracy, and sometimes we shall see it illustrated with theatrical exaggeration, as when the Philadelphia aristocrats of the army that marched against the Whiskey Boys, on prancing horses and in broadcloth uniforms, paraded their ragged, weather-beaten prisoners of the frontier through the fashionable streets for the delectation of the ladies at the windows.

It is impossible to treat of this period without giving to John Adams a place apart. He was in some respects a tragic figure, and, though ludicrously vain and often all but clownish in small things, we shall have occasion to admire and respect his independence and courageous subordination of his personal fortunes to the service of humanity and country in making the peace with France. If at times the mere recitation of his personal weaknesses seems like ill-natured ridicule, it should be borne in mind that this is necessary to the explanation of why a statesman and patriot, so able and deserving, was so unfortunate in his public career.

The purpose of the author is not to make out a case for or against democracy, but to show how it came to the Republic, sometimes blundering and making a fool of itself on the way; to re-create, if possible, an heroic, picturesque, and lusty age; to make the men of the steel engravings flesh and blood; to stage the drama of a day when real giants trod the boards.

CLAUDE G. BOWERS

CONTENTS

Original cover design by William Barss

ILLUSTRATIONS

JEFFERSON AND HAMILTON

CHAPTER I

DAYS OF COMEDY

I

WHEN Fisher Ames, exuberant over his unhorsing of Samuel Adams, and eager to try his lance on others, reached New York to take his place in the House of Representatives, he was disgusted to find few indications that a new government was about to be established. Wandering about the narrow, crooked streets he encountered few colleagues. That was the beginning of his cynicism.

A week after the date set for the opening of Congress but six Senators had appeared, and a circular letter was sent to the others urging their immediate attendance. Two weeks more and neither House nor Senate could muster a quorum.[1] Ames could see little improvement on the 'languor of the old Confederation,' but expected an organization of the House within a day or two. A Virginian, lingering in Philadelphia with a slight indisposition, was expected momentarily and the Representatives from New Jersey were on the way. But there was nothing definite on which to base such fair hopes of the Senate.[2] The next day Madison wrote Washington in a similar vein.[3] This seeming indolence or indifference was the subject of pessimistic conversations among the members in town as they meandered about the streets. Revenue was being lost — 'a thousand pounds a day'; credit was going; the spirit of the new experiment was sinking. 'The people will forget the new government before it is born,' wrote Ames. 'The resurrection of the infant will come before its birth.'[4] Already petty jealousies and ambitions were manifesting themselves, with much

[1] Pickering (Wingate to Pickering), II, 447.
[2] Ames, I, 31.   [3] *Writings*, I, 450.   [4] Ames, I, 31, 32.

intriguing for the honor of being messengers to notify the President and Vice-President of their election.[1] The little city was overrun with job-hunters. Even before the gavel fell on the first session, there were discussions of removing the capital elsewhere because of 'the unreasonable expense of living,' in New York.

It was not until April 2d, almost a month late, that a quorum was formed in the two houses. The following day George Washington was elected President, John Adams Vice-President, and messengers started for Mount Vernon and Braintree. Confronted by the most momentous governmental task in history, the men on whom fell the burden of creating a new nation had consulted their personal convenience about starting. It was not a promising beginning.

II

If the lawmakers had been derelict, the people of New York had not. They at least appreciated the possibilities of a capital. The task of designing Federal Hall in which Congress was to meet had been entrusted to L'Enfant — who was to win undying fame by planning the city of Washington—and he had done his work well — some thought too well. Ames was rather delighted over the fact that it had cost '20,000 pounds York money,' but Ames was a lover of luxury, and the more democratic Wingate, while conceding that the city had 'exerted itself mightily,' was afraid it had done so 'excessively.'[2] In truth there was dignity and beauty in the stately arches and the Doric columns, in the lofty vestibule paved with marble and lighted from an ornate dome, in the design and decorations of the chambers, with their graceful pilasters and their crimson draperies. There was richness enough to disturb the republican souls of members from the rural districts and the small towns.[3] Among the members who sat down amidst these surroundings were a number who were nationally known and brilliant, but the majority were comparatively obscure and mediocre. Looking over his colleagues, the enthusiastic and impressionable Ames found himself 'less awed and terrified' than he had expected; for while it was 'quite a republican assembly' because 'it looks

[1] Pickering (Wingate to Pickering), ɪɪ, 447.   [2] Ames, ɪ, 31; Pickering, ɪɪ, 447.
[3] *Republican Court*, 120–22; *Story of a Street*, 101.

like one,' he could see few 'shining geniuses.'[1] To the more ex-
perienced Madison, the outlook was not so pleasing. 'I see on the
list of Representatives a very scanty proportion who will share in
the drudgery of business,' he wrote.[2]

III

After a triumphant journey, constantly interrupted by ovations
and addresses, by the thunder of artillery, the clatter of cavalry,
and the ringing of bells, John Adams reached the city, took his
seat beneath the canopy of crimson velvet in the Senate and began
his reign. The ceremony and adulation of his progress from Braintree had gone to his head. Almost immediately he began to mimic
the manners and parrot the language of the Old World court
circles, until even the aristocratic Ames was moved to regret his
'long absence' from the country because of which he had 'not so
clear an idea of the temper of the people as others who have not
half his knowledge in other matters.'[3]

With the approach of Washington, the Senate, partly under the
inspiration of Adams, began to grapple soberly with the problem
of form and titles. Even before the arrival of Adams, when every
one was 'busy in collecting flowers and sweets . . . to amuse and
delight the President . . . on his arrival,' the prosaic Roger Sher-
man had 'set his head to work to devise some style of address
more novel and dignified than "Excellency."' There was an
ominous growl from the skeptics who doubted the propriety, and
some ribald laughter from the wits. A caricature had even appeared under the caption 'The Entry,' representing the President
on an ass, and in the arms of his man Billy Humphreys, who was
shouting hosannas and birthday odes, while the Devil looked on
with the comment:

> 'The glorious time has come to pass
> When David shall conduct an ass.'[4]

It was to require more heroic treatment than this, however, to
cool the senatorial ardor for high-sounding names. Even before
Adams had been elected, he had participated in serious discussions
in Boston as to whether the President should be called 'Majesty,'
or 'Excellency,' or nothing at all. Of course the Senators and Re-

---

[1] Ames, I, 32–34.   [2] *Writings*, I, 450.   [3] Ames (to Minot), I, 41–42.
[4] *Republican Court*, 122, note.

presentatives should be given the honest English title of 'Most
Honorable,' for Major Russell in the 'Centinel' had been doing
that all along. But the time for decision had come. The President
was approaching. It had been decided that on his arrival at the
Senate Chamber for his inauguration, he was to be met at the door
by Adams, conducted to a chair, and informed that both houses
were ready to attend him when he took the oath. But how should
he be addressed? Should it be as 'Mr. Washington,' 'Mr. President,' 'Sir,' 'May it please your Excellency,' or what? Adams
took his troubles to the Senate. Should it be as 'Excellency,' as in
the army? Adams was free to admit that he preferred it to 'Mr.
President,' which 'would put him on a level with the Governor of
Bermuda.'

There were Senators who instantly caught the importance of
the point. One proposed the appointment of a committee to
determine.[1] But these troubles came, not singly, but in battalions.
What was Mr. Adams to do when Washington was in the Chamber? He did not know whether the framers of the Constitution
'had in view the two Kings of Sparta or the two Consuls of Rome
when they formed it.' He could not tell whether the architect of
the building, in making his chair wide enough for two, had the
Constitution before him. He was Vice-President — but he was
also President of the Senate. 'When the President comes into the
Senate, what shall I be?' he asked plaintively. 'I cannot be President then. I wish gentlemen to think what I shall be.'

It was a solemn moment. Adams, with an air of distress, sank
into his chair. The silence was depressing. The leveler from the
frontier of Pennsylvania, Maclay, found 'the profane muscles of
his face in tune for laughter,' but controlled himself. Ellsworth, a
practical man, was seen feverishly turning the pages of the fundamental law. At length he rose to announce the result of his research. It was clear enough that wherever the Senate was, 'there,
sir, you must be at the head of them.' But — 'here he looked
aghast as if some tremendous gulf yawned before him' — but
'further, sir, I shall not pretend to say.'[2]

Thus the great day arrived to find the Senate caught unawares
by a new crisis. Adams had just risen to explain that Washington
would probably address the Congress, and to ask instructions as to

[1] Adams's explanation, *Works*, VIII, 511–13.   [2] Maclay, 2–3.

'how I shall behave.' It was a congenial subject for discussion. Lee of Virginia rose to explain the ways of the Lords and the Commons. Izard of South Carolina, who had been educated abroad and wished it understood, told how often he had been in the Houses of Parliament. Lee had observed that, while the Lords sat, the Commons stood. True, admitted Izard, but there were no seats for the Commons. Adams here interrupted to tell the Senate how often he too had been in Parliament. Old Carroll of Carrollton, who lived like a lord, but did not think like one, grumblingly suggested that it did not matter what the English did.

And just then — consternation!. The Clerk of the House was at the door! How should he be received? The discussion was feverishly resumed. Lee, getting his cue from the Commons again, was sure that he should be met at the door by the Sergeant-at-Arms with his mace on his shoulder. Confusion worse confounded — the Speaker and members of the House were now at the door! Members left their seats in their embarrassment, the doors were opened, the House filed in. Some one had blundered![1]

Meanwhile, with increased animation, the debate over the title for the President was resumed. Of course there should be titles, said Lee. Venice, Genoa, Greece, Rome — all had them. Ellsworth began to find virtue in kings; Izard was impressed with the antiquity of kingly government. Old Carroll, grumbling — or laughing — as usual, did not care for kings. But the President's title — what should it be? Ellsworth thought 'President' common. Adams eagerly added that there were 'presidents of fire companies and cricket clubs.' 'Excellency?' — suggested by Izard. 'Highness?' — proposed by Lee. 'Elective Highness?'[2]

At length it was settled — 'His Highness the President of the United States and Protector of the Rights of the Same.' Adams was disgusted. 'What will the common people of foreign countries; what will the soldiers and sailors say to "George Washington, President of the United States"? They will despise him to all eternity.'[3]

The rabid republicans began to laugh. Speaker Muhlenberg dubbed Maclay, 'Your Highness of the Senate.' Maclay himself, usually sardonic, grew facetious in debate, and thought the title satisfactory if the President was really high 'and gloriously greased

[1] Maclay, 7–10. [2] Ibid., 22–24. [3] Ibid., 25–27.

with a great horn of oil' to make him conspicuous. Even Robert
Morris complained that the Congress was also 'Protector of the
Rights of the People.'[1] But alas, it was a case of love's labor lost,
for when the ponderous title reached the House, James Madison
quietly announced that the Constitution had given the head of the
State a title — 'President of the United States'; and so it has been
from that day to this.

The more thoughtful had witnessed the tempest in a teapot with
some misgivings. Madison thought the success of the Senate plan
would have 'given a deep wound to our infant Government';[2]
and Ames thought it 'a very foolish thing to risk much to secure'
and wished 'that Mr. Adams had been less disguised.'[3] But they
who continued for twelve years to refer to 'the court' were not
content. A correspondent of Fenno's 'Gazette,' the 'court journal,'
continued to plead for 'titles of distinction' and to pray piously
that Congress would 'not leave the important subject to chance,
to whim, caprice, or accident.'[4]

IV

In the midst of these acrimonious discussions of the flubdubbery
of ceremonials, and with Adams proposing that the Sergeant-at-
Arms be called 'Usher of the Black Rod,'[5] Washington reached
New York. A black mass of humanity awaited him in the rain at
the water-front, peered down upon him from roofs and windows.
The roaring of cannon and the pealing of bells apprized the crowd
that the ornate barge the city had provided to 'waft His Excellency across the bay'[6] had been sighted. The thirteen pilots in
white uniforms who manned the barge were conspicuous as it
moved on to the accompaniment of cheers to the Wall Street
wharf. As it swept alongside the landing, bands on the banks
joined in the noisy welcome of the cannon and the bells. When
Washington, in a plain suit of blue and buff, rose to descend 'the
stairs covered with crimson trapping, the shouts of the populace
drowned the combined noises of the mechanical devices.'[7]

Declining the use of carriages, he proceeded with his party and
the committee on foot down Wall Street to Pearl, then Queen,

---

[1] Maclay, 37.   [2] *Writings*, I, 470–71.   [3] Ames, I, 46.
[4] June 3, 1789.   [5] Maclay, 31.   [6] *Daily Advertiser*, April 24, 1789.   [7] *Ibid.*

and up the full length of that then fashionable thoroughfare, which boasted a sidewalk that would accommodate three walking abreast, to the house prepared for him on Cherry Street. The crowd followed, men, women, and children, masters and men. There at the house they left him; and a few moments later he returned down Pearl Street to the home of Governor George Clinton to dine. That night the houses of the city were illuminated. The monarch had entered his capital. To the masses he was the maker of a nation; to the world of fashion he was the creator of a court.[1]

The day of inauguration found the city fluttering with flags, colorful with decorations, Wall Street fairly screaming with the spirit of festivity. Wreaths and flowers hung from windows. A reverential throng packing Wall, Broad, and Nassau Streets watched the great man enter the Hall; and a few minutes later he appeared upon the balcony of the Senate Chamber — a gallant figure in deep brown, 'with medal buttons, an eagle on them, white stockings, a bag and sword'[2] — to take the oath.

The keen eyes of Alexander Hamilton surveyed the scene from his home across the street.

Thence back to the Senate Chamber where the inaugural address, in trembling hands, was read with difficulty because of the shaking paper. The erratic but loyal Maclay was pained to find that his hero was not 'first in everything.'[3] Thence back to the house on Cherry Street.

Never had the little city been so picturesquely and brilliantly illuminated as on that night of general rejoicing. Transparent paintings shone all over the town — that at the bottom of Broadway 'the finest ever seen in America.'[4] It was a beautiful evening, 'and no accident cast the smallest cloud upon the retrospect.'[5]

A few evenings later, an inaugural ball was given by the Assembly in their rooms on Broadway above Wall Street. The President 'was pleased to honor the company with his presence,'[6] and 'every pleasure seemed to be heightened' as a result.[7] There, too, was 'His Excellency the Vice-President,' and members of Congress with their families, officers of the army, the Ministers of France

---

[1] *Story of a Street*, 221.   [2] Maclay, 7–10.   [3] *Ibid.*
[4] *Gazette of the United States*, May 2, 1789.   [5] *Ibid.*
[6] *Ibid.*, May 8, 1789.   [7] *Daily Advertiser*, May 8, 1789.

and Spain. 'Joy, satisfaction and vivacity was expressed on every countenance.'[1] Each lady, passing the ticket-taker, was presented with a fan made in Paris, with an ivory frame containing a medallion portrait of Washington in profile. 'A numerous and brilliant collection of ladies' it was, according to the impressionable reporter, all dressed 'with a consummate taste and elegance.'[2]

Society awoke that night to the fact that a nation had been created and a capital established on the Hudson, and it fairly titillated at the prospect of the gayety of a 'court.'

V

Now let us take a turn around the city and familiarize ourselves with the setting of the drama. It will not take long, for the little city of thirty-five thousand was compactly built. Broadway, the most promising and pretentious of the thoroughfares, was paved only to Vesey Street — beyond that, mud. The houses, most of them modest, were surrounded by gardens. From the west side of Broadway to the west side of Greenwich, the town was well built up from Bowling Green to Reade. Beyond that, only the hospital and a few widely scattered houses. On the east side, building extended as far north as Broome. Were we on a shopping expedition we should seek Nassau and William, the heart of the retail district, passing on the former many attractive homes including that of Aaron Burr. Were we bent on a promenade, to meet the ladies and the dandies, we should betake ourselves to Wall, where, notwithstanding the auctioneers, the shoemakers, the grocers, the tailors, the confectioners, the peruke-makers, we should pass handsome homes. Perhaps we should jostle the statesmen emerging from the boarding-houses along the way.

These narrow, crooked streets we should find more tolerable by day than by night. The street lamps were at wide intervals and frequently unlighted. If we escaped a highwayman in the night, we should be lucky to escape the mud of the poorly paved sidewalks, and if we did not bruise our shins by collision with the town pumps, we should be fortunate not to stumble over a pig. Off somewhere in the darkness we should probably hear the curses of some unfortunate wanderer fallen over an obstruction, the

[1] *Daily Advertiser*, May 8, 1729.   [2] *Gazette of the United States*, May 9, 1789.

grunting of hogs rooting in the gutters, the barking of innumerable dogs.[1] The long line of negroes bearing burdens toward the river might pique our curiosity did we not know that they were the sewage carriers of the city doing their nightly routine work.

Even by day we should find traveling not without its risks, for many of the streets were torn up for improvements.[2] Thus 'the Hon. Mr. Huger,' thrown from his sedan chair and painfully bruised, lays claim to immortality in the pages of Maclay [3] and in the yellowing sheets of Fenno's journal.[4] Faring forth in search of the political celebrities, we should not have far to go, for most were herded in boarding-houses. Hamilton lived comfortably at Broad and Wall Streets, Burr around the corner on Nassau. Jefferson was soon realizing his dream of comfort on Broadway after living in a little house in Maiden Lane. Randolph, the Attorney-General, had found a modest place in the country for two hundred and fifty dollars with 'an excellent pump of fresh water.'[5] Knox was living beyond his means on Broadway, and Adams was at Richmond Hill. But most of the lawgivers found boarding-houses more congenial to their purses. Thus, within a few steps on Great Dock Street we should find Robert Morris, Caleb Strong, Pierce Butler, Fisher Ames, and Theodore Sedgwick; in Maiden Lane, James Madison; on Smith Street, Charles Carroll, and on Water Street, Oliver Ellsworth.

Turning from the celebrities to the lowly and the base, we could visit the slave market which was then active, for there were more than two thousand negroes in bondage in the city. While the orators at Federal Hall were speaking reverently of liberty, the hammer of the auctioneer was knocking down negro girls to the highest bidder, and the local papers were running 'rewards' for the capture of runaway slaves.[6] Were we in the mood to walk to the end of the pavement on Broadway, we could regale ourselves, in the grove where the City Hall now stands, with a view of the gallows enshrined in a Chinese pagoda where the executioners competed successfully at times with the debaters in attracting the

[1] Governor Page complained bitterly of hogs and mud. *Memorial History*, III, 48.
[2] The *Daily Advertiser* advertises the specifications April 13, 1789.
[3] Maclay, 90.
[4] *Gazette of the United States*, June 27, 1789.
[5] *Memorial History*, III, 47.
[6] *Daily Advertiser*, March 6, 1789.

curious. There, too, stood the whipping-post.[1] In the midst of so much that was grim, little wonder that the statesmen resented the frequent ringing of funeral bells. 'The gentlemen from the country complain exceedingly of this noisy, unmeaning and absurd custom,' wrote 'A Citizen' to his favorite paper. 'This is the moment to abolish it, and give an evidence of a disposition to please them.'[2] But it is not of record that the 'gentlemen from the country' were permitted to interfere with the privileges of the dead.

Were we to turn from these grim specters to amusement, we could get a conveyance at one of the city's six livery stables to carry us into the country to the Florida tea-gardens on the North River; thence to Perry's on the present site of Union Square, or to Williamson's, near the present site of Greenwich and Harrison.[3] But were our mood of darker hue, we could find no dearth of entertainment at the taverns. When Congress quarreled and struggled at Federal Hall, and Washington dwelt on Cherry Street, one hundred and thirty-one taverns were licensed in the city to which flocked all manner of men. There, with liquor or ale, we could enjoy a cock-fight and pick the winner, or gather about the table and gamble at cards. Laborers, loafers, sailors, criminals infested these dives, and if we preferred cleaner company, we might get an invitation to the Black Friars, the one social club in the city.[4] Or, if more intellectual entertainment were desired, it could be found in the wooden building painted red on John Street, a stone's-throw from Saint Paul's Church where Washington had his pew, where the Old American Company regaled the people of the pit, the boxes, and galleries with the plays of Shakespeare, Sheridan, Goldsmith, Garrick, and some of indifferent merit.[5] Here 'The Father,' by William Dunlap, the historian of the American theater, had its first presentation — a notable event, since Washington, a spectator, was seen to laugh at the comedy.[6] Indeed, his health permitting, the President was frequently seen in his box which bore the arms of the United States, and the press was not amiss in keeping the public informed when the great man went to the play.[7] He had been in the house on Cherry Street but a few days, when,

---

[1] *Memorial History*, III, 45.   [2] *Daily Advertiser*, April 15, 1789.
[3] *New York in 1789*, 117.
[4] *Memorial History*, III, 65; *New York in 1789*, 117–20.
[5] *New York in 1789*, 172–75.   [6] *Ibid.*, 176.   [7] *Ibid.*, 178.

disregarding the frowns of the purists, he went to see the 'School
for Scandal.' Two days before, the 'Daily Advertiser' had gayly
hinted of the prospective visit. 'It is whispered that "The School
for Scandal" and "The Poor Soldier" will be acted on Monday
night for the entertainment of the President,' it said. And then it
added, by way of gentle admonition to the players: 'Mrs. Henry
ought on this occasion to condescend to give passion and tenderness to Maria. . . . Mrs. Henry ought to act Norah and improve
the delightful farce by the melody of her voice. Mrs. Henry ought
to take no offense at the suggestion.'[1] We may be sure it was a fes-
tive occasion, for Fenno's 'court journal' said that 'there was a
most crowded house and the ladies, who were numerous, made a
most brilliant appearance.'[2] One sour Senator in the presidential
party did not take kindly to the play. 'I think it an indecent
representation before ladies of character and virtue,' he wrote —
and there were ladies in the party![3] The President, however, was
pleased to go again quite soon to see 'The Clandestine Marriage,'
again subjecting 'ladies of character and virtue' to temptation,
for Mrs. Morris and Mrs. Knox were with his party when 'Mrs.
Henry and Mrs. Morris played with their usual naïveté and uncommon animation' due to 'the countenance of such illustrious
auditors.'[4]

Other forms of entertainment, all too few, were not neglected
by the celebrities. 'The President and his Lady and family and
several other persons of distinction were pleased to honor Mr.
Bowen's wax-works exhibit with their company at 74 Water Street'
— looms among the announcements of the 'court journal.'[5]

VI

Nor were the entertainments dependent wholly upon the residents and governmental dignitaries. The little city was bravely
simulating the airs of a real capital. The social climbers, hearing
of the 'court,' flocked to town from the four corners with their
wives and daughters.[6] The cost of living mounted alarmingly, and
the rental of suitable houses was prohibitive to many. Oliver

[1] May 9, 1789.   [2] *Gazette of the United States*, May 13, 1789.   [3] Maclay, 31.
[4] *Gazette of the United States*, June 6, 1789.
[5] *Ibid.*, September 19, 1789.
[6] *Story of a Street*, 112.

Wolcott, hesitating about accepting a place paying fifteen hundred
dollars a year, had been assured by Ellsworth that a house could be
had for two hundred dollars, wood for four dollars a cord, hay for
eight dollars a ton, but that marketing was twenty-five per cent
higher than at Hartford.[1] But soon after his arrival, the discouraged official was writing his father that 'the expense of living here
will be greater than I had imagined.'[2] The leading tavern, on the
west side of Broadway, near Cedar, was a modest establishment
with immodest prices.[3] And to make matters worse, 'society' had
set a giddy pace.

We are especially interested in this society because Jefferson, on
his arrival, was shocked at its unrepublican tone. The inner or
select circle did not number more than three hundred.[4] A French
traveler was impressed with its tendency to luxury, its love of
grandeur, and ostentatious display. 'English luxury,' 'English
fashions,' the women in 'the most brilliant silks, gauzes, hats, and
borrowed hair,' the men, more modest as to dress, but taking
'their revenge in the luxury of the table' and in smoking cigars
from the Spanish islands.[5] The Loyalist families were forward in
asserting their social prerogatives in the shadow of the Republican
'Court.' Did they not have money and the prestige of having
wined and dined and danced with the officers of His Majesty in the
days of the occupation? None more conspicuous than the Henry
Whites with a fine house on Wall Street, with one son in His
Majesty's army, another a rear admiral in His Majesty's navy.
About the Misses White — 'so gay and fashionable, so charming
in conversation, with such elegant figures' — the young blades
gathered like moths about the flame. Giddy were the parties
there, the men Beau Brummels in the extreme of fashion, and out
of the few fugitive pictures we catch a glimpse of Mrs. Verplanck
dancing a minuet 'in hoop and petticoats,' and a young beau
catching cold from 'riding home in a sedan chair with one of the
glasses broken,' after partaking too freely of hot port wine.[6]

Balls and teas there were aplenty, but 'society' preferred to
dine and talk. Hamilton in his home on Wall Street gave frequent
dinners insinuating when not boldly proclaiming his doubts of the

[1] Gibbs, I, 22.   [2] Ibid., I, 43.   [3] New York in 1789, 19.   [4] Ibid., 119
[5] Warville, 96–97.   [6] Republican Court, 210, note.

people. Van Breckel, the Dutch Minister, entertained lavishly, making his dining-room the resort of the little foreign circle — and every one tried to keep up the pace.

It was the pace that killed — financially. The Henry Knoxes then began their journey toward bankruptcy, living elaborately on Broadway, maintaining horses and grooms, five servants, and giving two dinners a month. Almost a ninth of his salary went for wine alone. What with his own hair-dressing, and that of the expansive Lucy, who wore her hair, after the extreme fashion, 'at least a foot high, much in the form of a churn bottom upward,' the family account with Anthony Latour, hair-dresser, was no small matter,[1] and his annual deficit was a third of his salary.

Nor was the Secretary of War unique. The social life was a hectic swirl of calls, teas, entertainments. 'When shall I get spirit to pay all the social debts I owe?' wrote one lady of quiet tastes.[2] It was harvest-time for the dressmakers, the jewelers, the hairdressers. The ball given in compliment to Washington by the French Minister called for special costumes, for there were 'two sets of Cotillion Dancers in complete uniforms; one set in that of France and the other in Buff and Blue,' while the ladies were 'dressed in white with Ribbands, Bouquets and Garlands of Flowers answering to the uniforms of the Gentlemen.'[3] And so with other functions equally gay.

But after all, the 'court' had come to town, and if there was no Majesty on Cherry Street, it was not because the 'court set' did not pretend it so. The illusion of vanity was fostered by the snobbery of Fenno of the 'court journal.' When Madame Washington arrived, 'conducted over the bay in the President's barge rowed by thirteen eminent pilots in handsome white dress,' the editor enumerated the ladies who had 'paid their devoirs to the amiable consort of our beloved President.' There were 'the Lady of His Excellency the Governor, Lady Sterling, Lady Mary Watts, Lady Kitty Duer, La Marchioness de Brehan, the ladies of the Most Honorable Mr. Langdon, and the Most Honorable Mr. Dalton ... and a great many other respectable characters.'[4] This was too

---

[1] Brooks, *Knox*, 217–18.
[2] Mrs. Iredell; McRee, *Iredell*, II, 296–97.
[3] *Gazette of the United States*, May 16, 1789.   [4] *Ibid.*, May 30, 1789.

much for 'A Republican' who worked off his fury in a scornful letter to the opposition paper referring to the 'tawdry phraseology,' to the 'titular folly of Europe's courts,' and suggesting that we 'leave to the sons and daughters of corrupted Europe their levees, Drawing Rooms, Routs, Drums, and Tornedos.'[1] It was to require more than this, however, to jar the high-flying Fenno from the clouds, and his readers were soon informed that 'His Excellency the Vice-President, His Excellency the Governor of the State, and many other personalities of the greatest distinction will be present at the theater this evening.' It was not for nothing that the pedagogue pensman from Boston had launched his paper with the hope 'that the wealthy part of the community will become patrons of this publication.'[2] The 'inconveniency of being fashionable' was impressed upon one Senator on finding a colleague, who, having 'set up a coach,' and, embarrassed in his plans by the irregular adjournments, was wont to sit alone in the Chamber 'in a state of ennui' as much as 'two or three hours' waiting for his carriage 'to take him three or four hundred yards.'[3]

But while there was much of this ridiculous affectation, society was not without its charms; for Mrs. Hamilton had her days for receiving, and her drawing-room was brilliant, and all the more interesting because her vivacious sister, Mrs. Church, just back from London, bringing with her 'a late abominable fashion of Ladies, like Washwomen with their sleeves above their elbows,' was there to assist.[4] And all the men were not on stilts, for it is on record that the congressional delegation from Pennsylvania would occasionally break through the 'court circle' to dine from three to nine, and indulge in 'a scene of beastial badness' with Robert Morris proving himself 'certainly the greatest blackguard in that way.'[5] There was the usual small gossip to bring the soarers to earth. The cream served at the table of Mrs. Washington was not the best. Mrs. Morris had been compelled to 'rid herself of a morsel' of spoiled food there, but 'Mrs. Washington ate a whole heap of it.'[6] Mrs. Knox amused the Mother Grundys because so fat, and

---

[1] *Daily Advertiser*, June 19, 1789.
[2] *Gazette of the United States*, April 15, 1789.
[3] Maclay, 257–58.
[4] Wharton, *Salons, Colonial and Republican*, 53.
[5] Maclay, 266.   [6] *Ibid.*, 73–74.

her blundering misuse of words caused much tittering behind fans and much whispering among her friends.

But it was on the Wall Street promenade that the gossips depended for their choicest morsels. The Wall Street of that day was just beginning to displace Pearl as the abode of fashion. True, there were a few business houses, a tavern, a fashionable caterer, a jeweler, but from Broadway to Pearl there was a row of substantial residences in which dwelt people of importance. It was there in the promenade that the political celebrities were encountered, but more appealing to the gentlemen of pleasure were the fine ladies who passed in their finery — gay silks and satins — walking or taking the air luxuriously in their sedan chairs. The cronies of Dan McCormick, the unsnared and lordly entertainer, who gazed out of the windows of his House of Gossip at Number 39, and from his front steps surveyed the parade with the eyes of connoisseurs, must have been trying to the modesty of the timid — but perhaps none such passed that way. If they laughed over the latest blunders of Mrs. Knox as she hove into sight like a huge ship in full sail, and made merry over the sister of the French Consul as she was borne luxuriously along in her sedan chair, we may be sure that they were appreciative of the pretty. And these crowded the narrow street for the promenade, quite as much bent on amusement and flirtation as the men about town on the steps of the House of Gossip.

For it was an age of gallantry, the men quite as vain as the women dared be, and there, in addition to political celebrities, paraded the local blades of society in their white buzz wigs, their three-cornered hats, and silver shoe buckles. Here the elegant Hamilton in banter with a blushing belle, there the courtly Burr bowing over the hand of a coquette unafraid of the fire, and yonder Dr. John Bard, who prescribed pills for the fashionable, pounding the pavement with his heavy cane as he walked along smiling a bit sardonically upon his patients. And, swinging along like a symphony, a dandy in a scarlet coat with mother-of-pearl buttons, a white silk waistcoat embroidered with colored flowers, black satin breeches, white silk stockings, and a cocked hat, an Irish miniature painter out for an airing and to give the ladies a treat. Here — on Wall Street — was Vanity Fair.[1]

[1] *Story of a Street*, 112, 114–17, 121.

Albeit the Vice-President had not then become the social head
of the Nation, society liked nothing better than an invitation to
Richmond Hill, the home of Adams, a mile and a half from the
city. Even Abigail was delighted, for her home reminded her 'of
the valley of Honiton in Devonshire,' with its avenue of forest
trees, its shrubbery, its green fields, its pastures full of cattle, and
the Hudson 'white flecked with sails.'[1] Here at the dinner-table
statesmen and their wives and the social leaders contrived to talk
like ladies and gentlemen of the court, and Jefferson thought in a
language foreign to a republic. But good talk it was, and good
dinners, we may be sure, even though the French Consul did take
his cook to Richmond Hill with the explanation that he had had
experience with New York dinners.[2] There was enough elegance at
Richmond Hill to encourage the Adams coachman to put on airs
that offended the groundlings as he drove through the streets.

VII

But it was about the 'court' on Cherry Street that the interest of
society centered. It was a plain brick mansion with five windows
looking out on Cherry Street and as many on Franklin Square.
The furniture was plain, and Madame Washington had sent by
sea from Mount Vernon numerous articles of luxury and taste —
pictures, vases, ornaments presented by European admirers. Here
the first President in the first days of the Republic received visitors, gave dinners and receptions, consulted with his Cabinet.
The following year he moved to a more commodious house on
Broadway below Trinity Church.

The great man had entered upon his physical decline when he
assumed the Presidency, and many found him changed — 'pale,
almost cadaverous,' his deportment 'invariably grave,' his sobriety barely stopping short of sadness. Even at Mrs. Washington's drawing-rooms, when beautiful girls swarmed about him,
his face never softened to a smile.[3] It is more than probable that
he was not a little bored by the artificial restraints imposed upon
him by his advisers on etiquette who had aristocratic notions of

---

[1] Richmond Hill, at present site of Charlton and Varick Streets.
[2] *Letters of Mrs. Adams* (to Mrs. Shaw), II, 201; (to Thomas Brand-Hollis), II, 205.
[3] Ames (to Minot), I, 34; Maclay, 375; *Familiar Letters*, 86–89.

the dignity of his position. Both Hamilton and Adams were responsible for planning his isolation from the people. Did citizens
seek a meeting? This was a matter for the chamberlain or gentle-
man-in-waiting. Should he give public entertainments? Not at all
— only small dinners. Could he make calls? Very guardedly, and
with 'few attendants,' but formal visits should be reserved for the
rare occasions when 'an Emperor of Germany or some other sovereign should travel in the country.' [1] Thus it came to pass that he
found himself with a 'court chamberlain' in the flamboyant
Colonel Humphreys, who reveled in ceremony, and on one occasion moved Parson Weems's perfect man to profanity. [2] When the
erstwhile host of Fraunces Tavern was selected as the presiding
deity of the kitchen, he appeared in the papers as 'Steward of the
Household.' [3] He too tried the great man's patience and outraged
his sense of economy by serving a shad early in the season that had
cost two dollars, and the royal fish was devoured by the 'Steward
of the Household' in the kitchen. [4]

But on state occasions the highfaluting notions of his advisers
prevailed, and he rode forth in regal magnificence in the finest
coach ever seen in America, a marvelous thing in shape and color,
decorated with cupids and festooned with flowers. Thus he lumbered through the streets drawn by four horses except when
driving to Federal Hall, when six were necessary.

And so they who dreamed of royal pomp were pleased with the
progress made, and at the dinner tables wagging tongues dwelt
ecstatically on the advantages of monarchical government, and
Fenno's 'court journal' began the publication of 'The Discourses
of Davila,' by the Vice-President. Thus, when Jefferson arrived
the following spring to meet society at the dinner tables, he was
filled with 'wonder and mortification' to find that 'politics was
the chief topic, and a preference for kingly over republican government . . . evidently the favorite sentiment.' [5]

But we may be sure that no such sentiments were heard at the
President's dinners, which appear to have been dull, formal, and
silent enough. No fault could be found with the food, drink, or

[1] Adams, *Works*, VIII, 491–92. [2] Thayer's *Washington*, 180–81.
[3] *Gazette of the United States*, May 6, 1789. [4] *Republican Court*, 149, note.
[5] *Autobiography*, Ford, I, 171.

service. Even the gout-pestered Maclay found one of these dinners 'the best of the kind I was ever at,'[1] and the more easily
pleased Iredell was immensely delighted with the wine.[2] But such
silence, such solemnity! 'The most solemn dinner ever I sat at,'
wrote Maclay. 'Not a health drank, scarce a word said until the
cloth was taken away.' Then Washington filled his glass and
solemnly drank to the health of each of his guests by name. Then
'everybody imitated him, and such a buzz of "health, sir," and
"health, madame," and "Thank you, sir," and "Thank you, Madame," never had I heard before.' Then another prolonged silence
— and the ladies retired — and the dinner was over.[3] Months
later, Maclay dined at the President's again. 'The President
seemed to bear in his countenance a settled aspect of melancholy,'
he wrote. 'No cheering ray of convivial sunshine broke through
the cloudy gloom of settled seriousness.' The great man was evidently bored — much company forced upon him that he would
gladly have shunned. Cold, serious to melancholy, silent, he sat
and 'played on the table with a knife and fork like a drum stick.'
So it was at the previous dinner when, retaining his fork as the
cover was removed, he 'played with the fork, striking on the edge
of the table with it.'[4]

Here we may leave him playing on the table with his fork, and
turn to the proceedings at Federal Hall.

VIII

Madison soon verified his fear that few members of Congress
could be relied upon for constructive work. Then, as ever after,
this fell to the industrious few, of whom Madison himself was by
odds the most dependable and wise. Petty ceremonies and formalities continued to disturb the serenity of some. When a member took exception to the reference in the minutes to a Presidential message as a 'most gracious speech,' as imitative of the parlia-
mentary references to addresses from the throne, Adams was all
but shocked to suffocation. As for himself he preferred 'a dignified
and respectable government,' but the point was pressed and the offensive words erased.[5] Receiving a letter addressed to him as 'His

---

[1] Maclay, 138.   [2] Iredell, II, 138.   [3] Maclay, 138.
[4] Ibid., 138, 206.   [5] Ibid., 101.

Excellency,' Adams took the sense of the Senate on the propriety of opening it. Robert Morris dryly remarked that their Majesty, the people, could write as they wished, and that crisis passed.[1] When a Bishop was mentioned in the minutes as 'Right Reverend,' and Maclay snorted his disapproval, Adams, in righteous wrath, informed him that 'the government will never be properly administered until titles are adopted in the fullest manner.'[2]

But all the while James Madison, constructive, profound, was seeking to drag his colleagues of the divine afflatus from the clouds to the working of the untilled field. Money was needed — more even than titles — and precious time was being squandered. In an earnest appeal, he begged for the postponement of the consideration of a permanent fiscal system in the hope of persuading the suppliants for tariff aid to wait awhile. But it was of no avail. Privilege entered the halls of Congress in the very beginning. When, at length, a measure was framed, the merchants of New York, Philadelphia, and Boston made common cause to hold it back. They had ordered heavily in anticipation of such a law and were determined to prevent its enactment until their goods arrived. The whole thing smacked of scandal. The merchants had already added the amount of the duties to the price of the goods on their shelves, increasing their profits while depriving the Government of the necessities of life. With the Government starving for revenue, the mercantile interest, with the aid of members, held it off until July 4th, and then it was passed with the proviso that it should be inoperative until August 1st. Many, says a noted historian, thought this 'the first instance of a series in which the action of government turned in favor of the moneyed class.'[3]

The creation of the executive departments next called forth acrimonious discussions. Should the finances be in the hands of a man or a commission? Where could be found a single man capable of such a task? The Republic would be endangered were one man to have command of three or four millions. Then, too, the Cabinet was liable to be looked upon by the President as of more consequence than the Senate. A system of favoritism would be established, and oligarchy confirmed, the liberties of the people

[1] Maclay, 38.   [2] Ibid., 50.   [3] Bassett, The Federalist System.

destroyed.[1] And the power of removal — who should possess that? Some wanted to lodge the power in the President, others in the Senate. Madison favored the former.[2] But others could not see it that way. What! exclaimed one statesman, give the power to the President? Why, 'ministers would obtrude upon us to govern and direct the measures of the legislature and support the influence of their master.' A new Walpole would arise.[3] 'Good God,' cried another, 'authorize in a free republic . . . by your first act, the exertion of a dangerous royal prerogative in your Chief Magistrate!'[4] The result was the striking out of the authorization of the President to remove on the ground that it was implied in the Constitution. Madison took this view, and it was to rise against him in his later battles with Hamilton over the implied powers.

This jealousy between the executive and legislative departments soon found some justification in the action of Washington himself. It was late in the summer of the first year that he appeared in the Senate with General Knox to get 'advice and consent' to some propositions respecting a treaty with the Southern Indians. With cold dignity he took his place beside Adams, with Knox near at hand. The latter passed him a paper which he, in turn, gave to Adams, who began to read. The windows were up and the purport was all but lost in the rumble of carriages on Wall Street.

'Do you advise and consent?' asked Adams.

A Senator suggested that in a matter of importance new to the Senate, it was the duty of Senators first to inform themselves. Storm-clouds appeared on the presidential countenance. Some one moved postponement of action on the first article, then the second — and third. Finally, the motion was made that the whole be referred to a senatorial committee.

Up Washington 'started in a violent fret.' The motion defeated the purpose of his coming. He had brought along the Secretary of War who knew all that it was necessary for the Senate to know. The reference to the committee would mean delay and time was pressing. Then, making a virtue of necessity, he agreed to the postponement, and withdrew 'with sullen dignity.'

[1] Gerry, *Annals*, May 20, 1789.   [2] *Writings* (to Randolph), I, 471–73.
[3] Jackson, *Annals*, I, 486–89.   [4] Page, *Annals*, I, 548–52.

'I cannot be mistaken,' wrote a Senator that evening in his boarding-house, 'the President wishes to tread on the necks of the Senate. Commitment will bring the matter to discussion, at least in the committee, where he is not present. He wishes us to see with the eyes and hear with the ears of his Secretary only. The Secretary to advance the premises, the President to draw the conclusions, and to bear down our deliberations with his personal authority and presence. . . . This will not do with Americans.'[1]

This fear, accentuated by the incident referred to, was to grow into a conviction a little later, when a more domineering and masterful figure than Washington or Knox appeared upon the scene. By many his advent had been eagerly awaited. To the leaders his identity was known, for the genius of Alexander Hamilton as a financier had been established, and his ambition was surmised.[2] His aspirations were supported by the mercantile interests generally, and the political forces they controlled. Even they who were to become his political enemies were favorable to his selection — preferring him to John Jay, who was considered. There is something of irony in the letter written to Jefferson by Madison to the effect that Hamilton was 'best qualified for that species of business, and on that account would be preferred by those who know him personally.'[3]

To most he promised to be a successful administrator of finance, and only the few among his intimates foresaw his rapid rise to the brilliant leadership of a powerful party. Certainly there could have been but few to take alarm on reading in the 'Daily Advertiser' on September 12, 1789, the simple announcement of one of the most momentous events in the political history of the country:

The President of the United States has been pleased to make the following nominations of Officers for the Department of the Treasury:

Alexander Hamilton, Esq. of this city, Secretary.

Nicholas Everleigh, Esq. of South Carolina, Comptroller.

And the Senate of the United States having taken the said nominations into consideration were pleased to advise and consent to the same.

[1] Maclay, 128–31.   [2] Iredell (Lowther to Iredell), II, 258–59.
[3] *Writings*, I, 471–73.

CHAPTER II

HAMILTON: A PORTRAIT

I

THE genius for whom the Nation had been waiting, who walked briskly and with a martial air[1] into the Treasury, and sat down at the almost effeminate mahogany desk with the women's faces carved upon the legs, to bring order out of chaos, looked the leader. Not that he was of commanding stature, for he was but five feet seven in height, with a figure of almost boyish slimness. It was rather in his soldierly erectness and the dignity of his bearing that he impressed. If his carriage suggested the camp, the meticulous care of his dress hinted of the court, for he was something of an elegant in his attire. We have one striking picture of him in a blue coat with bright buttons, the skirts unusually long, with a white waistcoat, black silk small-clothes, white silk stockings;[2] another in fine lace ruffles.[3] It is quite impossible to think of him as unfit for an instant summons to a court levee or a ladies' drawing-room, albeit Wolcott, who saw him first in his office, thought him 'a very amiable plain man.'[4] It was an age of frills and fancies among the men of the aristocracy and his very conservatism would have dissuaded him from the slightest departure from the conventions.

It was his head and features that denoted the commander. His well-shaped, massive, and symmetrical head, with its reddish fair hair turned back from his forehead, powdered and collected in a queue behind, was not so likely to attract attention as his pronounced features. These were unique in that rarest of all combinations of beauty and strength. He was handsome enough to be attractive to women, with his fair complexion and almost rosy cheeks, his well-moulded lips, and dark, almost violet, deep-set eyes that could smile as sweetly and seductively as any gallant's.

[1] Warville, 102. [2] *Familiar Letters*, 236–37.
[3] Oliver, 114. [4] Gibbs, I, 22.

And yet these lips could be firm and stern, and the soft, mirthful eyes could freeze and flash. If women were to observe the softer nature, the politicians were to note the man of relentless will disclosed in the firm, strong jaw. Graceful and debonair, elegant and courtly, seductive and ingratiating, playful or impassioned, he could have fitted into the picture at the Versailles of Louis XV, or at the dinner table at Holland House. No one born in the atmosphere of courts could have looked the part more perfectly.

And yet, such was his origin that the envious Adams could sneer at him as 'the bastard brat of a Scotch pedlar,' [1] and it was not without reason that Gouverneur Morris, meditating his funeral oration, and his 'illegitimate birth,' contrived a mode 'to pass over this handsomely.' [2] Even the sympathetic researches of Mrs. Atherton have failed to lift the mystery of his origin and family. All we know is that he was born of an irregular relation, without the intervention of the clergy, [3] between an unprosperous Scotch merchant of the West Indies and a brilliant and beautiful daughter of the French Huguenots. Even his parentage by the man named Hamilton was doubted, on circumstantial evidence, by so ardent a friend as Pickering, who thought he had found the father in a physician. [4] Whoever the father — and the Pickering Papers are not convincing — there is no doubt that Hamilton inherited his genius from his brilliant, passionate, high-strung mother.

Nor does the mystery end with his birth. Pickering was half persuaded that the mother lived into the manhood of her son, but the church records at Saint Kitts bear out the claims of the family that she died in 1768. It is not easy to account for the rather morbid relations later between Hamilton and his father and brother. Both appear to have been a worthless sort. For years Hamilton was ignorant of his father's whereabouts, which does not appear to have bothered him much. [5] Later there was some correspondence looking to a possible reunion in America, out of which nothing came. [6] At intervals money passed from the great man in America to the indigent old man in the West Indies, [7] but at no time does it appear that Hamilton had any thought of visiting his father in

[1] *Autobiography*, 278.   [2] Morris, *Diary*, II, 456.
[3] Oliver, 15.   [4] See Appendix, Lodge, *Alexander Hamilton*.
[5] *Works*, IX, 405–06; letter to brother.   [6] *Ibid.*, X, 109.   [7] *Intimate Life*, 3.

the isle of his childhood. It was a long cry from the squalid life in the West Indies to Mrs. Bingham's drawing-room, and the genius turned his back upon the past.

II

There is nothing so inexplicable in this amazing man as the precocity of his genius. There is a suggestion of it in the younger Pitt, but he had sat from infancy at the feet of Chatham. To the easy-going natives of his natal isle this passionate, fiery-tempered, supersensitive boy, dreaming of power, must have seemed an exotic. As a mere child he appeared to sense that his field of conquest lay across the sea. He was planning a career while his companions were absorbed in childish games. His early range of knowledge and reading was remarkable. In his passion for literature he was unconsciously moulding one of the weapons for his successful assault on fame; through the pages of Plutarch he was lifting himself above the drab slothful surroundings to the companionship of the great.

Sometimes fate was serving his destiny when he felt himself a captive beating against his cage. Thus, in the counting-room at Santa Cruz he was mastering business methods and absorbing the commercial spirit on which he was later to predicate his philosophy of government.[1] The business letters he wrote were preparations for the framing of his 'Report on the Public Credit.' Even then it was a peculiarity of his genius that he could write on business matters without clipping the wings of his fancy. He seemed born with a mastery of words, a rare gift of expression. When a hurricane swept the islands the description he wrote for a paper became the talk of the West Indies. Only a little while before he was rebelling against the 'groveling ambition of a clerk,' and passionately writing that he 'would willingly risk his life but not his character to elevate his station.' These were the aspirings of a boy not yet thirteen. 'I shall conclude by saying, I wish there was a war.' Here we have a vivid light upon his character.[2]

The description of the hurricane made his fortune. Dreaming of rising by the sword, it was his pen that rallied friends who raised the money to send him to America for an education. Through all

[1] *Life*, by son, I, 4.   [2] Fiske, I, 104–05.

his days he was to aspire to glory through the sword, little knowing that he was winning immortality with his pen.

The Little Corsican touching the soil of France, the little West Indian landing in America — there is a striking analogy: both dreaming of martial glory in the land of strangers; both obsessed with a morbid ambition sustained by the rarest powers of application.

The records of the years preceding the Revolution are but vague, though we get glimpses of the genius forging his weapons in the boy at the grammar school at Elizabethtown poring over books till midnight, to rise at dawn to continue his studies in the quiet of a near-by cemetery; practicing prose composition; writing an elegy on the death of a lady; composing the prologue and the epilogue of a play,[1] and, at Kings College (Columbia), amazing his companions by the energy of his mind, and puzzling pedestrians by talking to himself as he walked for hours each day under the great trees of Batteau (Dey) Street.[2] Here, too, an occasional display of the eloquence of maturity, enriched by the glow of genius, set him apart.

Then came the Revolution. 'I wish there was a war!' cried the boy of thirteen. And war came to find the lad of nineteen as eager to seize its opportunities as was the Corsican youth when ordered to clear the streets of Paris.

III

The war was to prove his genius, not as a soldier, but as a writer and constructive thinker on governmental matters. He was a natural journalist and pamphleteer — one of the fathers of the American editorial. His perspicacity, penetration, powers of condensation, and clarity of expression were those of a premier editorial writer. These same qualities made him a pamphleteer without a peer. That he would have shone with equal luster in the reportorial room of a modern paper is shown in his description of the hurricane, and in his letter to Laurens picturing vividly the closing hours of Major André.[3] From the moment he created a sensation, with 'A Farmer Refuted,' in his eighteenth year, until, in the closing months of his life, he was meeting Coleman surreptitiously

---

[1] *Life*, by son, I, 10.   [2] *Ibid.*, 22.   [3] *Ibid.*, 263–74.

in the night to dictate vigorous editorials for the New York 'Evening Post' he had established,[1] he recognized his power. No man ever complained more bitterly of the attacks of the press; none ever used the press more liberally and relentlessly to attack.

In 'A Farmer Refuted,' the maturity of the thought, the severity of the reasoning, the vigor of the onslaught, the familiarity with history and governmental processes displayed, denoted the hand of one seasoned in controversy. The sprightliness, wit, humor, sarcasm, suggested more than talent. The evident joy in the combat, with the air of assurance, was that of the fighter unafraid. These are the qualities that were to run through all of Hamilton's literary work. Nowhere in the literature of invective is there anything more vitriolic than the attack on a war speculator and profiteer, under the signature of 'Publius.'[2] This tendency to bitter invective will appear, as we proceed, in Hamilton's attacks on Jefferson and Adams.

But usually he appealed to reason, and then he was at his best. Thus, in 'The Continentalist,' urging a more perfect union and a more potent government, and in his letter to James Duer,[3] we are impressed with the writer's intimate knowledge of conditions, his constructive instinct, his vision.[4] And thus, especially do these appear in 'The Federalist' — one of the most brilliant contributions to the literature of political science in the world's history. It will be impossible to comprehend the genius of Hamilton, his domination of his party, and his power, despite his unpopularity with the masses, without a foreknowledge of his force with the pen. It was his scepter and his sword.

IV

His power as an orator was unsurpassed in any assembly that called it forth, but with very few exceptions he did not appear before the multitude. He swayed the leaders and won them to his leadership. There was little of fancy in his speeches, scarcely any appeal to the emotions, but he spoke with enthusiasm and an intensity of conviction. Force, clearness, fire — 'logic on fire' — and a rapid fusillade of impressively directed facts — with these he usually

[1] Payne's *Journalism*, 191–92.
[2] *Works*, I, 202.   [3] *Ibid.*, I, 213–39.   [4] *Ibid.*, I, 243–87.

swept all before him. The comparatively few speeches which have come down to us fail to explain his power. The stories of audiences moved to tears are scarcely in keeping with the absence of the slightest attempts at pathos or appeals to the emotions. Kent, who heard him in court, recalled, long after Hamilton was dead, 'the clear, elegant and fluent style, and commanding manner.'[1] Physically, he was far from imposing, but it is easy to imagine the virility of his manner, the flash of his conqueror's eye. In the New York Convention called to pass on the Constitution, it was the force and persuasiveness of his arguments that converted a hostile majority. Later Congress was to refuse him permission to present personally his reports on the ground that he might unduly sway its judgment; and Jefferson was to resent his interminable and passionate 'harangues' in the Cabinet room. But these exhibitions of his eloquence advanced his political career by impressing the leaders with the brilliancy of his intellect.

V

It is significant that, while he was not vain of his power as a writer and orator, he lived and died firmly convinced of his genius as a soldier. In the earliest of his letters we have his longing for a war. His son and biographer was impressed with the fact that, 'while arms seemed to be his predominant passion, the world was at peace.'[2] He never faced the prospect of a war without seeing an opportunity for distinction. At a time when he abhorred the French Revolution, and all associated with it, he wrote of Napoleon as 'that unequalled conqueror, from whom it is painful to detract.'[3]

Was he a military genius? We have nothing on which to base a judgment. In the Revolution we see him attracting the attention of Washington by his military alertness on the heights of Harlem. At Monmouth we see his horse shot under him as he dashes into the fray with a recklessness that looked to the commander like a courting of death. Throughout his services in the military household of Washington, where he became all but indispensable in a secretarial capacity and in diplomacy, he chafed under the conviction that his place was in a position of command. One of his friends

[1] *Life*, by son, II, 277.   [2] *Ibid.*, I, 69.   [3] *Works*, VI, 276.

declared that 'the pen of our army was held by Hamilton; and for dignity of manner, pith of matter, and elegance of style, General Washington's letters are unrivaled in military annals,' but the youthful Hamilton felt that he should have been the army's sword.[1] The vision of the renown of the military conqueror was ever before him. The war was an opportunity for glory, and he was missing it. 'I explained to you candidly my feelings in respect to military reputation,' he wrote Washington when seeking a separate command, 'and how much it was my object to act a conspicuous part in some enterprise that might perhaps raise my character as a soldier above mediocrity.'[2] At Yorktown he took desperate chances in an effort for renown.[3] We shall find him leaving the Treasury to command soldiers sent to put down the western insurrection, with no possible occasion for it beyond his preference for the saddle and the sword. And when war with France loomed large, we shall find him resorting to importunity and intrigue to get the command over the protest of the President.

Was Hamilton a Napoleon? He thought himself of the race of military masters. He had the courage, the coolness under fire, and the audacity, but nothing that he did disclosed more genius than was shown by Aaron Burr. Had the chance come, he might have justified his own high pretensions as a military genius — but it did not come. He died with his boyhood ambition to command great armies unrealized — and undimmed.[4]

VI

His association of a strong military establishment with a strong and stable government was due in large measure to his temperament. He was essentially an aristocrat. From the moment of his arrival in America, he cultivated only the élite. His most partisan biographer has painted his portrait in a sentence — 'His sympathies were always aristocratic, and he was born with a reverence for tradition.'[5] There is nothing more contradictory in his career than the lowliness of his origin and his inherent passion for the lofty. This charity student moved in mansions as to the manor born. He had lived on terms of comparative intimacy with the

[1] *Life*, by son, I, 69. [2] *Ibid.*, I, 318. [3] *Ibid.*
[4] Lodge, 26. [5] Oliver, 27.

aristocratic Washington of the camp, with Lafayette who brought something of the flavor of Old World aristocracy, and he married into one of the proudest of the manorial families, but his love of grandeur was inherent. He luxuriated in.elegant society and fine houses, loved fine laces as an adornment, and, without having ever seen the interior of a gallery, at least affected a partiality for the fine arts, collecting such prints as his purse permitted, painting some himself, and advising Mrs. Washington in the purchase of paintings.[1]

His ideal of government was the rule of 'gentlemen' — the domination of aristocrats; on the theory that these, with a certain prestige to maintain, were more jealous of their honor and above the vulgar strivings for mere place.[2] Thus it was impossible for him to conceive of a strong and capable government over which the aristocracy did not have sway.[3] Long before the Constitutional Convention we find him writing Morris on financial matters, setting forth the importance of creating an alliance between government and men of wealth.[4] One of his most enthusiastic panegyrists has illustrated his ideal: 'The nearest approach to it is the popular conception of the empire of Japan — a mass of intelligent humanity, reckless of their lives, yet filled with the joy of life, eager for distinction, hungry for success, alert, practical and merry; but at the same time subordinate, humbly and piously subordinate, to a pure abstraction.'[5] But this abstraction had to be aristocracy — never democracy; for he believed that democracy could only lead to anarchy.[6] Temperamentally hostile to democracy in the beginning, maintaining that attitude to the end, he never appreciated and always despised public opinion, and in 1794 he frankly confessed to Washington that he 'long since learned to hold public opinion of no value.'[7] This distrust of the people, contempt for democracy, and reliance on strong government supported by wealth, and, if need be, sustained by standing armies, were carried by him into the Constitutional Convention and there proclaimed with all the tremendous force of his personality.

---

[1] *Intimate Life*, 47.   [2] Oliver, 161–62.   [3] Lodge, 177–78; Oliver, 163–64.
[4] Oliver, 86.   [5] *Ibid.*, 263.   [6] *Ibid.*, 376.   [7] *Works*, VI, 457.

Unless we divest ourselves of the Hamiltonian myths in reference to the Constitution, an intelligent comprehension of his
political character will be impossible. We must rid ourselves of
the fallacious notion that he was satisfied with the Constitution
or believed it adequate. No one contributed more mightily to
making the Constitutional Convention possible. In the preliminary convention at Annapolis, no one did more to crystallize sentiment for it, and it was his persuasive pen that wrote the history-
making address there determined upon. About his dining-table
in New York he did yeoman service in coaxing skeptical and reluctant members of Congress to call a convention. There, under a
simulation of gayety, his eloquence and wit and banter made
converts of the most stubborn — a service of immeasurable
value.[1]

But in the Convention itself he played no such part as is popularly ascribed to him. After the presentation of his own plan in the
early stages, he played an inconspicuous part, and much of the
time he was not only absent from the Convention, but out of the
State. This was not because of indifference to the event, but to a
realization that he could accomplish nothing for his plan.[2]

This plan was a direct contradiction of that which was adopted.
There is nothing conjectural about that fact — the records are
indisputable. We have the plan, the brilliant five-hour oration in
its behalf, the brief from which he spoke. These have come down
to us, not from his enemies, but from his partial biographers, his
son the editor of his 'Works,' and the report of Madison on the
authenticity of which he himself passed. This plan provided for
the election of a President for life; for Senators for life or during
good behavior, and by electors with a property qualification; and
for the crushing of the sovereignty of States through the appointment by the President of Governors with a life tenure and the
power to veto any act of the State legislatures, though passed
unanimously. Not only was the President enabled under this plan
to negative any law enacted, but he had the discretionary power
to enforce or ignore any law existing.[3] Though his President,

[1] Oliver, 149.   [2] Fiske, 120; Lodge, 58.   [3] Beck, 75.

serving for life, was not called a king, he was to be armed with more arbitrary power than was possessed by the King of England. His English eulogist does not overstate when he says that 'what he had in mind was the British Constitution as George III had tried hard to make it,' and failed because the English people would not tolerate it.[1] This interpretation of Hamilton's purpose is reënforced by another of his most brilliant disciples who asserts that 'Hamilton's governor [President] would have been not dissimilar to Louis XIV and could have said with him, "L'état c'est moi." ... Thinly veiled, his plan[2] contemplated an elective king with greater powers than those of George III, an imitation House of Lords, and a popular House of Commons with a limited tenure.'[3] Even so this plan confessedly fell far short of his conception of an ideal government. In the brief for his speech[4] we are left in no doubt as to his partiality for a monarchy, in which the aristocracy should have a special power. 'The monarch ... ought to be hereditary, and to have so much power that it would not be his interest to risk much to acquire more.' As for the aristocracy, 'they should be so circumstanced that they can have no interest in a change.'[5] We should be 'rescued from the democracy.'[6] As to the republican form of government — 'Republics are liable to corruption and intrigue,'[7] and, since 'a republican government does not admit of a vigorous execution, it is therefore bad.'[8]

Later, in one of his few discussions, he said that 'those who mean to form a solid republican government ought to proceed to the confines of another government.'[9] His republic, and in his great speech he had conceded that no other form would be accepted by the people, 'was to be an aristocratic as distinguished from a democratic republic, and the power of the separate States was to be effectually crippled.'[10] In one of his brief Convention talks he said of the States that 'as States he thought they should be abolished.'[11] Even after the Constitution had been adopted, he believed that one of the objects of administration should be 'to acquire for the federal government more consistency than the Constitution seems to promise for so great a country,' to the end that it 'may triumph

---

[1] Oliver, 156. [2] *Works*, I, 347–69. [3] Beck, 76.
[4] *Life*, by son, II, 487. [5] *Ibid.*, 487. [6] *Ibid.*, 488. [7] *Ibid.*
[8] *Ibid.* [9] *Ibid.*, 516. [10] Lodge, 60. [11] *Works*, I, 404.

altogether over the state governments and reduce them to an utter subordination, dividing the large States into simpler districts.'[1] Such were the ideas urged by Hamilton in the forceful five-hour speech which Gouverneur Morris thought the most brilliant intellectual exhibition he had ever witnessed. After this exhaustive exposition, he took but little part. Toward the close he explained his comparative silence: 'He had been restrained from entering into the discussions by his dislike of the scheme of government in general.'[2] This distaste did not diminish as the Convention closed its labors, and he accepted the Constitution in the end 'as better than nothing.'[3] His motive for joining in recommending it to the people is conclusively shown in his last Convention utterance: 'No man's ideas are more remote from the plan than my own are known to be; but is it possible to deliberate between anarchy and convulsion on one side, and the chance of good to be expected from the plan on the other?'[4]

Nor did he ever lose faith in his own plan, or gain confidence in the Constitution which was adopted.[5] Just before retiring from the Cabinet he avowed himself a monarchist who had 'no objections to a trial being made of this thing of a republic.'[6] Two years before his death he wrote bitterly to Morris of his support of a Constitution in which he had never had faith 'from the beginning,' in which he described it as 'a frail and worthless fabric.'[7] And the night of his death, when his bosom friend and confidant was meditating the funeral oration he was to deliver on the steps of Trinity Church, he wrote in his diary, 'He was in principle opposed to republican and attached to monarchical government, but then his opinions were generally known and have been long and loudly proclaimed. His share in the forming of our Constitution must be mentioned, and his unfavorable opinion cannot therefore be concealed.'[8]

If, however, he was a tremendous factor in making any Constitutional Convention possible, he was to be even more essential in securing the ratification of the document he disliked — and it is here that he rises to the pinnacle of patriotic statesmanship, and

[1] Gordy, I, 70.   [2] *Works*, I, 417.   [3] *Ibid.*
[4] *Works*, I, 420.   [5] Lodge, 62–63.
[6] Statement to Tench Coxe quoted by Jefferson, *Works of Jefferson*, Ford, I, 338.
[7] Letter to G. Morris, *Works*, x, 425.   [8] Morris, *Diary*, II, 456.

earns the eternal gratitude of the Republic. When on that summer day, on a packet floating lazily down the Hudson, he subordinated his personal preferences to the public good, and sat down
to the writing of the first number of 'The Federalist,' he reached
the very acme of his greatness. Had he done nothing else, his fame
would have been as eternal as the Nation he helped to make.
Thus does he take his rightful place among the greatest nation-
builders of all time.

VIII

The qualities of strength and weakness accounting for the successes and failures of his political leadership are easily found in an
analysis of his character. As is true of most genius, his was three
fourths hard work. From his earliest boyhood he had learned the
value of system. Nothing was permitted to disturb the programme
by which he regulated his days and nights. We may surmise that
he was his own most relentless taskmaster from the rules he wrote
for the guidance of his favorite son. This almost monastic schedule denotes the system by which he governed his own life.[1] He
never completed his education, and the exactions of politics and
his profession never made him a stranger to his library. Here,
surrounded by his family, he ministered to an insatiable mind.
Never tiring of the classics, he kept pace with the printing-press,
and Mrs. Church rummaged about the book-stalls of London to
supply him with all the new worth-while publications. Thus the
'Wealth of Nations' was in his hands as soon after its appearance
as a boat could cross the sea.[2] His manner of study was intensive,
absorbing, and he fairly lashed his mind and memory to their
allotted tasks. Walking the floor while reading and studying, it
was a comment of his friends that with equal exertion he could
have walked from one end of the country to the other.[3]

Quite as remarkable as the intensity of his application was his
abnormal capacity for sustained exertion. He thought nothing of
sitting over a paper 'until the dawn dimmed his candles.'[4] Talleyrand's comment on finding lights in his office in the early morning
is famous. It was not unusual for him to ponder a problem long

---

[1] *Works*, x, 480.   [2] *Intimate Life*, 75.
[3] *Life*, by son, i, 398.   [4] Parton's *Jefferson*, 358.

and earnestly until he had thought it through, then to retire to sleep regardless of the hour of the night, and after a while to arise, refresh himself with a cup of strong coffee, seat himself at his table, and work on with great rapidity for six, seven, or eight hours without rest. The resulting product of his pen was so perfect, we are assured, such was his felicity of expression, that it seldom required revision.[1]

This tenacity was one of the factors in his leadership. He was never a fair-weather fighter. Opposition only whetted his appetite for battle. Nor was he easily discouraged. Explaining to a friend who wished to carry the news to New York of the situation in the Poughkeepsie Convention, that the members stood two to one against the ratification of the Constitution, he concluded with grim emphasis: 'Tell them the Convention shall never rise until the Constitution is adopted.'[2]

Along with this tenacity, he had an illimitable moral courage which made it easy for him to fight for a cause without counting the cost. The real Hamilton is seen in his defense of the persecuted Tories at the close of the Revolution; in his fighting his way through a mob eager for the blood of the Tory president of Columbia College to hold it at bay with his indignant eloquence; in his letter to Jay against the destruction of the notorious Rivington Press by a mob.[3] This reverence for law and the constituted authority was the mainspring of his political character, and he always had the moral courage to stand for both when cowardice would have recommended compromise.

To these qualities must be added another which gave character to his leadership — he was personally honest. Called to a station where he might easily have enriched himself, as did many of his friends, he retired to private life poorer than when he entered the public service. Small wonder that Talleyrand was astounded at such disinterestedness and restraint. There was no affectation in his letter lamenting his inability to succor some immigrants from France. 'I wish I was a Crœsus; I might then afford solid consolation to these children of adversity, and how delightful it would be to do so. But now, sympathy, kind words, and occasionally a din-

---

[1] *Familiar Letters*, 236–37.   [2] Oliver, 177–78.
[3] *Works*, x, 3; letter to King.

ner are all that I can contribute.' And at the time he wrote great fortunes had been built on the financial system he had created. So impeccable was he in this regard that his great political protagonist, writing an estimate of his character in the calm of his closet, recorded him as 'disinterested, honest and honorable in all private transactions.'[1] Profound as a thinker, exhaustive as a student, moving in eloquence, powerful with the pen, logical in his reasoning, constructive in his methods, tenacious in the advancement of his plans, possessed of the courage of his convictions, personally honest in public and private action, he possessed qualities of leadership that drew high-minded men about, and to, him. But he unhappily had the weakness of his strength that was to operate disastrously upon his political fortunes. It is impossible to understand his ultimate failure as a leader without a reference to his temperamental deficiencies.

IX

As a party leader he was singularly lacking in tact, offensively opinionated,[2] impatient and often insulting to well-meaning mediocrity, and dictatorial. He did not consult — he directed. He did not conciliate — he commanded. In the Cabinet he was to offend Jefferson early because Hamilton 'could not rid himself of the idea that he was really the prime minister.'[3] It was not diplomatic to order Adams back to his post of duty in Philadelphia in the manner of one addressing a subordinate. Nor was it considerate to write to McHenry, who adored him, and was doing the best his limited ability would permit: 'Pray take a resolution adequate to the emergency and rescue the credit of your department.'[4] These outbursts of impatience and this intolerance of weakness were forgiven by the strong, but treasured against him by smaller and more envious minds, and the time was to come when, with his field marshals loyal, he was to have few colonels and captains, and practically no privates. He was a failure in the management of men, and only his superior genius made it possible for him to dominate so long.

There was much of egotism and some vanity behind this dicta-

---

[1] Jefferson's *Anas*, i, 180. [2] Morris, *Diary*, ii, 456.
[3] Lodge, 156. [4] *Works*, x, 354.

torial disposition. This was inherent and incurable. The lowliness of his origin, the phenomenal rapidity of his rise, the homage
properly paid him for the brilliancy of his youthful efforts with
voice, pen, and sword, all tended to convince him of his superiority. No one knew or lamented his egotism more than men who
loved him. Morris went weeping from his death-bed to write his
intimate opinion in his diary that he was 'vain and opinionated.'[1]
Cabot, who clung to him like a lover, wrote him frankly: 'I am
bound to tell you that you are accused by respectable men of egotism.'[2] A descendant and biographer concedes his vanity, taking
issue with Hamilton's son who had foolishly, but naturally, denied
it in his biography.[3] His self-sufficiency is evident in his letter to
Laurens: 'It is my desire to preserve myself free from particular
attachments, and to keep my happiness independent of the ca-
prices of others.'[4] But were we without these confessions from his
friends, we should find them in his letters. What more amazing
and amusing than his letter to Schuyler explaining with gusto and
some swagger his quarrel with Washington.[5] Even at the age of
twenty-three and while serving in a secretarial capacity to one of
the foremost figures of all time, he was placing himself on an
equality at least with Washington and writing glibly of 'what we
owed to each other.' This spirit of self-exaltation was to drive
many of the minor leaders of his party from him, and to lead him,
in the end, to the supreme folly of his pamphlet attack on Adams
which was hopelessly to cripple, if not completely destroy, his
influence.

Even more serious than his flamboyant egotism was his queer
lack of judgment in the handling of men. It was an irreparable
blunder to force the election of his father-in-law to the Senate
from New York over Chancellor Livingston who had superior
claims. It was a temporary triumph that drove one of the most
powerful families in the State into the ranks of his enemies.[6] Only
the most execrable taste can pardon the undignified writing of
anonymous attacks on a colleague of the Cabinet.[7] His blunder in
the case of the Schuyler election could be excused by his lack of

---

[1] Morris, *Diary*, II, 456.   [4] *Life*, by son, I, 236.   [6] Lodge, 81.
[2] Cabot, 298–300.   [5] *Ibid.*, 233.   [7] *Ibid.*, 144.
[3] *Intimate Life*, 48.

political experience, but his most sympathetic biographer admits that 'middle age instead of ripening his judgment, warped it.'[1] His was a nature of eternal youth, and in many respects the indiscretions of boyish exuberance cursed him to the end.

If these personal weaknesses were to weaken him with the leaders of the second rank, his unpopularity with the rank and file was to come from his lack of sympathy for, and understanding of, the American spirit. No one realized it more than he. In justice it must be said that he honestly tried to suppress his doubts of America; but in moments of depression he burst forth with expressions that bear the marks of long incubation. 'Am I a fool — a romantic Quixote — or is there a constitutional defect in the American mind?' he wrote King. 'Were it not for yourself and a few others I would adopt the reveries of De Paux, as substantial truths, and could say with him that there is something in our climate which belittles every animal, human or brute.'[2] And toward the close of his life he wrote Morris: 'Every day proves to me more and more that this American world was not made for me. You, friend Morris, are a native of this country, but by genius an exotic. You mistake if you fancy that you are more of a favorite than myself, or that you are in any sort upon a theatre suited to you.'[3] This touch of the exotic, of which he himself was painfully conscious, was not lost upon his political enemies. 'Thus ignorant of the character of this nation, of Pennsylvania, and of his own city and State of New York, was Alexander Hamilton,' wrote Adams.[4] But it was left for another to discover the real secret of his confusion as to the American character — he had never known the spirit, or had the training, of the New England town meeting.[5] A marvelous genius, he thought in terms of world politics at a time when America was creating a new spirit and system of her own. It was not to weaken his work as the creator of credit, but it was to dim his vision as an American leader.

x

If he possessed traits that made him thoroughly hated by some, he had other qualities that bound his friends to him with bonds of

[1] Oliver, 40. [2] *Works*, x, 90–91. [3] *Ibid.*, x, 425–26.
[4] *Works*, x, 123–26; letter to Lloyd. [5] Parton's *Jefferson*, 355.

steel. He commanded affection because he was himself affectionate. His letters to his wife were uniformly tender and playful. He
was idolized by his children. His comrades in the army loved him
because he not only shared their hardships, but at times helped
them to necessities out of his own all but empty pockets. He was
sensitive to the sufferings of many refugees in Philadelphia and
New York, and he would often direct his wife to send money and
delicacies to the women and children.[1] We have many instances of
his generosity, like his attempt to spare André the humiliation of
the scaffold, and his letter to Knox protesting against the execution of British officers in retaliation for the murder of an American.[2]
Among the young French officers he was idolized because of his
merry disposition and the cleverness and brilliancy of his conversation. While prone to hold aloof from the mass, he was a 'good fellow' among those whom he considered his social equals. In social
assemblies of both sexes he fairly sparkled with boyish enthusiasm.[3] In stag affairs, where he was immensely popular, we may
be sure that he was nothing of a prude. It is not of record that he
often drank to excess, but like most men of his time he loved his
wine, and we have it on the best authority that he sometimes took
a wee bit too much.[4] On these convivial occasions he could always
be prevailed upon to sing his one and only song:

> 'We're going to war, and when we die
> We'll want a man of God near by,
> So bring your Bible and follow the drum.'

His one serious weakness was an inordinate fondness for women
which was to involve him in the one serious scandal of his career.
It was McHenry who wrote to Pickering, another friend: 'Far be
it from me to attempt to palliate his pleasures, the indulgence in
which Mr. Hamilton himself publicly lamented.'[5] It was Otis
who wrote of his 'liquorish flirtation' with a married woman at a
fashionable dinner party.[6] It was Lodge who, in touching on his
overpowering passions, refers to his 'relations, which had an un-
enviable notoriety.'[7] It is Oliver who says that 'his private short-

---

[1] *Intimate Life*, 46.   [2] *Works*, ix, 256–58.   [3] *Familiar Letters*, 236–37.
[4] Morison's *Otis* (to Mrs. Otis), i, 141–43.   [5] Cabot, 204–05.
[6] Morison's *Otis*, i, 141.   [7] Lodge, 272.

comings cannot be denied,'[1] and that 'in private life Hamilton was not always vigilant.'[2] It is the historian of 'The Republican Court' who records that 'it is true that Hamilton was something of a roué.'[3] And it was reserved for a descendant to remind us of the story of the alleged relations with the celebrated Madame Jumel, who, in old age, made an unsuccessful attempt to live with Aaron Burr,[4] and of the gossip, which he discredits, that his relations with his sprightly sister-in-law, Mrs. Church, were more tender than they should have been.[5] This same descendant, writing with professional authority, explains these moral delinquencies on the theory that, like other men of genius and great intelligence, he was prone to 'impulsively plunge into the underworld in obedience to some strange promptings of their lower nature.'[6]

And yet, such are the strange inconsistencies of the temperamental — nothing could have been more beautiful than his home life. His endearing traits are evident in the passionate devotion of all who knew the Hamilton of the hearth. If the ties that bound Angelica Church to him were not more tender than they should have been, her letters indicate something akin to love.[7] His wife, who must have suffered tortures over the confessions of the Reynolds pamphlet, clung to him with a faith born perhaps of an understanding of how much he must have resisted. If he sometimes broke his vows, there can be no doubt that the shrine of his heart was at his hearth.

'Colonel Beckwith tells me that our dear Hamilton writes too much and takes no exercise, and grows fat,' wrote Angelica Church to Mrs. Hamilton from London. 'I hate both the word and the thing, and I desire you to take care of his health, and his good looks.'[8] Here we have the suggestion of another frailty which makes all the more notable the intensity of his sustained efforts and the magnitude of his achievements — the delicacy of his health. The first, and possibly the last, medical service rendered by McHenry on becoming a member of Washington's military family was to prescribe for Hamilton and make suggestions as to his diet. Early in the war he who was never robust contracted a malarial infection from which he suffered every summer through-

---

[1] Oliver, 76.   [2] *Ibid.*, 381.   [3] Griswold, 173.
[4] *Intimate Life*, 55.   [5] *Ibid.*, 56.   [6] *Ibid.*, 60.   [7] *Ibid.*, 259.   [8] *Ibid.*, 73.

out his life.[1] His correspondence is sprinkled throughout with references to his health.[2] While in no sense an invalid, the magnitude and multiplicity of his labors despite a chronic physical disability measure the power of mind over matter and indicate something of his unyielding will.

XI

In view of the sincere or simulated interest in religion shown by Hamilton where political interests were involved, it would be interesting to know just what he thought and felt. The records here are slight. During his youth he passed through the period of religious exaltation not uncommon in the average life. Not only was he attentive to public worship, but he prayed fervently and with eloquence in the seclusion of his room.[3] About this time he wrote a hymn, 'A Soul Entering into Bliss,' which is said to have had some literary merit.[4] We hear no more concerning his religious fervor for many years until he pretended, if he did not feel, an intense indignation against the revolutionary reaction aimed at the church establishment in France. He was shocked that 'equal pains have been taken to deprave the morals as to extinguish the religion of the country.'[5]

A few years more, and, with the fall of his party, he outlined to Bayard a 'Plan of Conduct' for Federalists with a view to its rehabilitation, and proposed an association to be denominated 'The Christian Constitutional Society,' having for its objects 'the support of the Christian Religion' and 'the support of the Constitution.'[6] This hints strongly of the Old World idea of the union of Church and State. In Connecticut the clergy had been the shock troops of Federalism, and it is quite possible that the political advantage of an alliance between the Church and his party appealed to Hamilton.

At any rate, he was a member of no church. One of his descendants assures us that 'he was a man of earnest, simple faith, quite unemotional in this respect, so far as display was concerned, but

[1] *Intimate Life*, 17.
[2] *Works*, v, 61 (to Washington); x, 256 (to William Smith); x, 275 (to King); x, 343 (to Pickering).
[3] *Life*, by son, reminiscences of Troup, i, 10.   [4] *Ibid.*
[5] *Works*, vi, 276.   [6] *Ibid.*, x, 432–37.

his belief was very strong'[1] Strong as it was, it never led him to the altar.

Leaving his idol's death-bed, Oliver Wolcott wrote his wife that 'Colonel H. in late years expressed his conviction of the truths of the Christian Religion, and his desire to receive the Sacrament — but no one of the clergy who have yet been consulted will administer it.'[2] At length, life ebbing away, a bishop consented after being earnestly solicited the second time. Thus in his dying hour, Hamilton declared: 'It has for some time past been the wish of my heart, and it was my intention to take an early opportunity of uniting myself to the church.' The natural deduction from the meager information we have is that his intensive political and professional activities and consuming ambitions gave him little time to meditate on religion. He certainly never gave it the consideration of his greatest political opponent whom his party attacked as an enemy of Christianity. But he used the Church, whenever possible, to advance his political views — and with effect.

Quite as problematical as his religious feeling was his attitude toward Washington. It was the policy of the Federalists to capitalize politically the popularity of the man of Mount Vernon, and they succeeded, as we shall find, to a marked degree. Even so, some of Hamilton's most partial biographers[3] have commented on the absence of any deep affection between the two, and Dr. Hamilton is not convincing with his observation that his ancestor signed his letters to Washington, 'Very affectionately.'[4] As a matter of fact none of his letters to Washington denote real affection. This would be more impressive, however, but for the singular absence of the note of affection in all his political correspondence. But in one of his letters we find the very opposite of either affection or admiration. This was his letter to General Schuyler on the occasion of Hamilton's withdrawal from Washington's military family, and it does not speak well for the reliability of his son's biography that he deliberately mutilated the letter. It was in this that he wrote that he had found his chief 'neither remarkable for delicacy or good temper' and complained of his 'self love.'

[1] *Intimate Life*, 334.   [2] *Ibid.*, 406.
[3] Oliver and Sumner.   [4] *Intimate Life*, 261.

Here we have the confession that 'for three years past I have felt no friendship for him and have professed none.'[1]

In his letter to Lear, the secretary, when Washington died he probably came perilously near to summing up his attitude in a sentence: 'I have been much indebted to the kindness of the General, and he was an Aegis very essential to me.' And then, the significant postscript: 'In whose hands are his papers gone? Our very confidential situation will not permit this to be a point of indifference to me.'[2]

Such a man was Hamilton, a Colossus, brilliant, fascinating, daring, and audacious — a constructive statesman of the highest order, a genius of the first rank, with all the strength and the weaknesses of genius. Such the man who sat down at the mahogany desk to write the documents that were to give credit to a nation and a programme to a party.

[1] *Works*, IX, 232–37.   [2] *Ibid.*, X, 356–57.

CHAPTER III

HAMILTON IN THE SADDLE

I

THERE was quite enough in the picture of the handsome, penniless Hamilton, at the age of thirty-two, striding upon the national scene with the air of a conqueror to undertake the solution of the problem on which the existence of the young Republic depended, to appeal to the popular imagination. The mystery and romance of his history, the dash in his manner, the shimmer of his genius, interested all and fascinated many of his contemporaries. The audacious gayety with which he faced his task imparted a feeling of confidence to those who did not know, as many did, just what was in his mind. He set to work with an enthusiasm that smacked of inspiration, for it was a task to his taste.

With the startling effect of a magician at his tricks he created the machinery of his complicated department, selected his assistants with discrimination, trained them with meticulous care in their duties, outlined his plans for revenue immediately required, and sat down with joy to the preparation of his 'Report on the Public Credit,' which was to proclaim the public faith and establish the Nation's credit.

The mere presence of this youthful figure at the mahogany desk commanded confidence. Here was a man who was primarily interested in the rights of property, who believed in the sanctity of contracts and had the courage of his convictions. Even as he was writing his 'Report,' he loomed large as the man of the hour. His close associates foresaw the nature of his recommendations. The mercantile and financial interests plumed themselves upon a triumph. Within a month after his appointment a contemporary rhymester put in verse the counting-room conception of the man:

> '... young Hamilton's unshaken soul
> The wayward hosts of anarchy control —
> And while the Senate with his accents rung
> A full conviction followed from his tongue.' [1]

---

[1] *Daily Advertiser*, October 9, 1789.

His plans, given in confidence to some, were soon whispered among the politicians and the merchants of New York, Philadelphia, and Boston, and the market price of public securities in the cities rose fifty per cent two months before Congress convened.

It was not until in early January that the 'Report' was read in House and Senate. His wish to present it personally was denied, not by his political enemies as his partial biographers contend, but by the supporters of his plan.[1] In the galleries of the House eager speculators were closely packed. They overflowed and filled the lobbies. Some were drawn by mere curiosity, some were the original creditors who had waited long for their reward, but the greater number were speculators, who, in anticipation of such a recommendation, had bought freely of the skeptical holders at ridiculously low prices. Not a few of these poured forth into Wall Street at the conclusion with the exhilarating knowledge that a fortune was within their grasp.

In the Senate the 'Report' was heard in secret and in 'awful silence,' for the elder statesmen met behind doors closed and locked. Most of these listened with approval, but the rheumatic Maclay, who had been puzzled for some time with 'the extraordinary rise in public securities,' wrote that night in his journal that Hamilton 'recommends indiscriminate funding, and, in the style of the British Minister, has sent down his bill.' There were some complaints that 'a committee of speculators in certificates could not have formed it more to their advantage.' In truth, 'it occasioned many serious faces,' and Maclay himself was 'struck of a heap.'[2] But the prevalent note was one of jubilation. In New York, enthusiasm in the coffee-houses; in Boston, 'great applause';[3] in other commercial cities, Philadelphia, Charleston, Baltimore, approbation, with reprobation for objections.[4]

All men of honor sympathized with the purpose of discharging the debt. The repudiationists were among the ignorant and the vicious. Few at the moment found fault with the funding system, though some would have preferred a speedy liquidation through the sale of the public lands. Then — suddenly — a low murmur

---

[1] Gerry and Clymer, both supporters of the *Report*, objected. *Annals*, January 9, 1790.
[2] Maclay, 177.   [3] *Writings, J. Q. Adams*, I, 49.
[4] *Connecticut Gazette*, February 19, 1790.

of protest, followed by acrimonious attacks. Thousands of the original creditors had been 'swindled' out of their certificates for a song — were these, who rendered Revolutionary services, to be taxed to ensure exorbitant profits to the speculators? Why should the Federal Government assume the debts contracted by the separate States — debts unevenly distributed? And what was the purpose of the proposal that the Government should be prohibited from paying more than two per cent of the principal a year? The indignation of the insurgents, at first a glimmer, became a flame. The greater part of the certificates were in the hands of the prosperous who had taken advantage of the necessities of the original holders — Revolutionary soldiers, small farmers, hard-pressed country merchants. The funding system would tax all the people to pay to the rich a hundred cents on the dollar for evidence of debts that had cost them fifteen and twenty. With the people taxed to pay the interest — it was proposed to perpetuate the debt. Thus, for generations, perhaps, as many reasoned, the Government would operate for the enrichment of the few already rich, and the masses would pay the piper.

Had Hamilton been disposed to frankness, he would have smiled his acknowledgment of the charge. One of his biographers has conceded that through this system he hoped to 'array property on the side of the Government,' by giving it a financial interest in the Government, and 'to assure to the property of the country a powerful influence upon the Government.'[1] Having 'been unable to introduce a class influence into the Constitution by limiting the suffrage ... with a property qualification,' he hoped through his financial system to accomplish his purpose in another way.[2]

There was nothing diabolical in the plan — coming from one who looked upon the masses as lawless and unfit for self-government. His obsession was a strong, stable government — and to sustain it he required the interested devotion of the propertied class. The astonishing thing is that the comparatively crude Maclay from the wilds of Pennsylvania and the leather-lunged James Jackson from sparsely settled Georgia should have caught the full significance of it all before it dawned on Jefferson and

[1] Lodge, 90–91.   [2] Ibid.

Madison. The latter thought the 'Report' 'well digested and illustrated,' and 'supported by very able reasoning,' but after a while he, too, was depressed with the injustice to the original creditors who 'were most instrumental in saving their country,' and concluded there was something 'radically wrong in suffering those who rendered a bona fide consideration to lose seven eighths of their dues, and those who had no particular merit toward their country to gain seven or eight times as much as they advanced.'[1]

II

Meanwhile, speculation was manifesting itself with incredible audacity and mendacity. The greater part of the securities in the hands of original creditors were in the hands of soldiers, farmers, and merchants in the remote interior. To most of these, they had come to mean so much worthless paper. No telegraph could flash the news into the back country of Georgia and North Carolina that Congress was about to legislate to par the promises to pay. Weeks or months would pass before the proceedings in New York could be known and comprehended by holders of the paper living in the woods of the Carolinas or on the banks of the Savannah. Poor, and mostly ignorant, they had no correspondents in the coffee-houses to write them of the activities at Federal Hall; and even if they had, it required weeks for a letter to reach them.

But members of Congress knew what to expect — for they were the actors in the drama; and their friends, the capitalists and merchants of the cities, knew — for they had been informed. The unscrupulous and adventurous soldiers of fortune on the scene comprehended the opportunity at a glance. The day after the 'Report' was read, the city buzzed with the gossip of the speculators. One Senator, making calls in the congressional circle, found it almost the sole topic of conversation. He heard that Robert Morris of the Senate, who had been consulted by Hamilton, 'must be deep in it, for his partner ... had one contract for $40,000 worth.' It was whispered that 'General Heister had brought over a sum of money for Mr. Morris for this business.' Senator Langdon, it was noted, was living with a Mr. Hazard 'who is an old and intimate friend of Mr. Morris,' and he admitted that he had 'fol-

[1] Madison's *Writings* (letter to Pendleton), I, 507–09.

lowed buying certificates for some time past.' 'Ah,' said the visiting Senator, 'so you are one of the happy few who have been let in on the secret' — and Mr. Hazard seemed abashed. It was understood that Representative Fitzsimons of Philadelphia was likewise concerned in the business.

Four days after the 'Report' was read, 'expresses with very large sums of money on their way to North Carolina for purposes of speculation in certificates' splashed and bumped over the wretched winter roads, the drivers lashing the straining horses. Two fast-sailing vessels, chartered by a member of Congress who had been an officer in the war, were ploughing the waters southward on a similar mission — and this scandalous proceeding was to be mentioned frequently in the subsequent debates. 'I really fear,' wrote Maclay, 'the members of Congress are deeper in this business than any others.'[1] Whether they were deeper or not, they were deep enough, and numerous enough to hold the balance of power in the body that legislated the certificates to par. These ranged from Robert Morris, the chief legislative agent of Hamilton in the Senate, to Fisher Ames, who was his most eloquent defender in the House.[2] In later years Jefferson was to record in justice to Ames that his speculative activities had been greatly exaggerated and that he had acted as an agent in the enterprises of his Boston friends, Gore and Mason.[3]

So thoroughly did this money-madness take possession of the minds of men that even the puritanic John Quincy Adams was to write his father, without a homily, that by September of 1790, Christopher Gore, the richest lawyer in Massachusetts, and one of the strongest Bay State members of Hamilton's machine, had 'made an independent fortune in speculation in the public funds'; and that other leaders of the bar[4] had 'successfully engaged in speculation' by playing at 'that hazardous game with moneys deposited in their hands' by clients at a distance. They took the chance of becoming 'masters of sums to an equal amount before

---

[1] Maclay, 179. The member of Congress who sent the vessels was Jeremiah Wadsworth of Connecticut.

[2] Professor C. A. Beard makes a conclusive case against both in his *Economic Origins of Jeffersonian Democracy*.

[3] *Works of Jefferson*, I, 354.

[4] Mr. Amory, H. G. Otis, and William Wetmore.

they have been called upon for payment.'[1] Maclay thought 'there is no room to doubt but that a connection is spread over the whole continent on this villainous business.'[2] Everywhere men with capital — and a hint — were feverishly pushing their advantage by preying on the ignorance of the poor. Thus, paper held for years by the private soldiers was coaxed from them for five, and even as low as two, shillings on the pound by speculators, including leading members of Congress, who knew that provision for the redemption of the paper had been made.

In all this, Hamilton had no part and no responsibility beyond having made indiscreet disclosures of which his friends availed themselves, and through buying and selling through his agents in New York and Philadelphia for his brother-in-law.[3] Just how he viewed the scandalous proceedings in the earlier stages we do not know. They were not without defense from his supporters. The obsequious John Fenno took notice of the gossip with a defense of speculation in the 'Gazette.' Were not moneyed men 'the props of the infant credit of the United States?'[4] The dark insinuations of the gossips, the criticism of the 'rabble,' we may be sure caused Hamilton no concern. Surveying the field at the beginning of the battle, he must have been content. He saw the financiers, the commercial interests of the large centers, including the speculators, enlisted under his banner. The influential Society of the Cincinnati, composed of Revolutionary officers, men of means who had been able to hold on to their paper, gave dignity to his cause. With its compact organization in every State, and its system of correspondence, it was an engine of tremendous power. The social and intellectual circles were flying his flag. He looked upon his work and called it good.

III

With the first discussion in the House, it was apparent that speculation was to play a conspicuous part in the debates. The speculators packed the galleries, overflowed into the lobby, causing the complacent Theodore Sedgwick of Massachusetts, himself

[1] *Writings of J. Q. Adams*, I, 56–59.   [2] Maclay, 177–78.
[3] Beard's *Economic Interpretation*, 104–12.
[4] *Gazette of the United States*, 'Common Sense,' January 30, 1790.

a speculator, to insist that the 'ardent expectations of the people on this subject want no other demonstration than the numerous body of citizens assembled within these walls.' The effect was different on the pugnacious Jackson of Georgia. 'Since this Report has been read,' he shouted, with a contemptuous glance at the eager gallery,'the spirit of speculation . . . has arisen and been cherished by people who had access to information the Report contained, that would have made a Hastings blush to have been connected with, though long inured to preying on the vitals of his fellow man. Three vessels, sir, have sailed within a fortnight from this port freighted for speculation.'[1]

The unctuous Sedgwick was melting suavity. Speculation within reasonable bounds was not bad, but action should be taken with all possible speed to stop it; and the troublesome Jackson returned to the attack — this time on New York City. He wished to God Congress had met in the woods and out of the neighborhood of a populous town. The gallant veterans, driven by economic necessity to the wilderness, were being robbed by these speculators of the pittance a grateful country had bestowed. Since the assumption of State debts was proposed, why not postpone action until the various legislatures could express the sentiment of the States? 'Then these men may send out other vessels to countermand their former orders; and perhaps we may yet save the distant inhabitants from being plundered by these harpies.'[2]

This line of attack had not been anticipated, and Hamilton was not the man to take anything for granted. His well-groomed figure was seen moving nervously about the lobbies of Federal Hall, within a few days after the commencement of the debate. One of his enemies observed that he 'spent most of his time running from place to place among the members.'[3] In the evenings he gathered his more influential supporters about him at his home. At his table he brought his most seductive charms to bear upon the doubting. Time was all-important and indefinite delay might be fatal.

With the thunder of Jackson's ugly charges reverberating through the streets, taverns, coffee-houses, Hamilton was 'moving heaven and earth for his funding system.' The commercial in-

[1] *Annals*, January 28, 1790.   [2] *Ibid.*   [3] Maclay, February 1, 1790.

terests and the members of the Cincinnati hastened to join the lobby, which began to seek out the wavering or the doubtful in their lodging-houses. A fashionable minister found his way to the quarters of Speaker Muhlenberg and Senator Maclay to extol the policies of the dynamic young Secretary, and 'argued as if he had been in the pulpit.' Time, too, for a redoubling of effort, for there were rumors that Madison, the strongest man in the House, had been unpleasantly impressed with the fast-sailing vessels and the expresses jolting over the roads southward. A bitter attack had appeared in one of the papers which gossip ascribed to the popular George Clinton.[1]

In the House — still harping were the foes on speculation, when with a benevolent expression Sedgwick rose with saccharine urbanity to regret the vice of speculation, and declare himself 'totally disinterested,' albeit he was financially concerned. It was only his distress over speculation that admonished him to speedy action to minimize the evil. It was really unfortunate that so much heat had been engendered. After all, were not 'a great and respectable body of our citizens creditors of the United States?' It would be tragic were these animosities to create 'factions among the people.'

'A danger there?' bellowed Jackson, the incorrigible infant terrible. 'Do not gentlemen think there is some danger on the other side? Will there not be grounds for uneasiness when the soldier and the meritorious citizen are called upon to pay the speculator more than ten times the amount they ever received from him for their securities?'[2]

Meanwhile the fight was spreading from Federal Hall to the newspapers where congressional courtesy imposed no restrictions on the temper. Sinister stories were finding their way into print. 'Several officials in conjunction with Robert Morris and wealthy contractors "were" at the bottom of this new arrangement.' If it succeeded, Robert Morris would benefit $18,000,000, Jeremiah Wadsworth would profit $9,000,000 and Governor George Clinton would make $5,000,000.[3]

It was under these conditions, with the speculators packing the

[1] Maclay, 194.   [2] *Annals*, February 10, 1790.
[3] *New York Daily Advertiser*, February 13, 1790.

galleries, with the lobbyists, legitimate and illegitimate, buzzing through the corridors, with the most amazing rumors floating about the streets, that James Madison, who had remained silent heretofore, rose in a crowded House to fire the first gun in the Jeffersonian war on the financial policies of Alexander Hamilton.

IV

Here was a man at whom the Federalist leaders dare not sneer. A stranger, looking down from the gallery, would have been at a loss to understand the deference with which members hung upon his words. His personal appearance was disappointing. The short little man dressed in sober black, with a bald head, and a little protuberant in front, whose lower limbs were slight and weak,[1] was surely not meant to ride on the whirlwind and direct the storm. The impression of physical weakness he conveyed did belie the fact. In the mild blue eyes there was much to suggest the meditative philosopher, nothing to hint of the fighter. His voice was so weak that even in the cozy little chamber he could scarcely be heard.[2] He spoke in low tones, without gesture or excitement, almost like a man communing with himself in the seclusion of his closet. And yet he commanded a hearing vouchsafed to few. It was the triumph of character.

Here, too, was a man with a background second to none in the infant Republic. An ailing body had obsessed him in youth with the premonition of an early death, and, feeling the futility of entering on any pursuit, he had sought consolation in his books. He not only consumed, he assimilated. He not only read, he thought. Thus he became something more than a learned man — he developed into a political philosopher 'worthy to rank with Montesquieu and Locke.'[3] At the time he rose to propose an amendment to Hamilton's plan there was not a man in America who was his peer in the knowledge of constitutional law or history. Nor was there a man, either, whose support Hamilton more eagerly coveted. Even the jealous Ames conceded him to be 'our' first man,' consoling himself for the concession with the comment

[1] *Familiar Letters*, 108.
[2] *Gazette of the United States*, April 15, 1790.   [3] Fiske, 187.

that 'I think him too much of a book politician and too timid in
his politics,' and that 'he speaks decently as to manner and no
more.'[1]

But the ill-natured jealousy of the more ornamental Ames
failed to take account, as most of his colleagues did, of the important practical use to which he had put his knowledge of the battles
he had fought and the victories he had won. No one in either
branch of Congress or at the head of any of the departments had
approached his services in the framing of the Constitution. It was
his genius that conceived the Virginia plan which became the
basis of the agreement. At many critical junctures his speeches
had dissipated the gathering darkness with their light. His pen,
unknown to many at the time, had recorded the story of the
Convention. His contributions to 'The Federalist' had been quite
as important, if not so numerous, as those of Hamilton; and the
fight he waged in the Virginia Convention for ratification was
quite as Titanic and conclusive as that of Hamilton in New York,
but with this difference — Hamilton was confronted by Melanc-
thon Smith, while Madison had to cross swords with Patrick
Henry, with the powerful George Mason and the accomplished
Pendleton.

He was not an orator of frills and fancies, magnetic and dramatic, appealing to the passions and emotions, but he was formidable in debate. In the speeches of none of his contemporaries is
found such erudition, more driving logic, such tact and moderation of statement, or greater nobility of sentiment, fairness, justice. If they are a bit heavy in their sobriety, the occasion called
for something remote from theatrical frivolity. His grace was in
his reasoning, not his rhetoric — and yet his style would have given
him a foremost place at Saint Stephen's.

It is not surprising that such a man should not have been a
favorite with the crowd. There was a diffidence in his manner,
a formality and precision in his method, a quiet dignity in his
bearing that discouraged familiarity. He was too absorbed in his
work to fit in with the social festivity of his time. Only at his own
table and among his intimates did he appear in the rôle of 'an
incessant humorist' and 'keep the table in roars of laughter over

[1] Ames (letter to Minor), I, 35.

his stories and his whimsical way of telling them.'[1] Even his letters read like state papers. But there were a few, greater than Ames, who appreciated him. These were the three most important personages of his time — Washington, Hamilton, and Jefferson.

Washington consulted him and made use of his pen. Hamilton cultivated him. Jefferson loved him as a son. His relations with the latter were no less than beautiful. Through many years they constantly interchanged visits, corresponded regularly, and traveled together whenever possible. A strikingly incongruous pair they must have seemed as they plodded along country roads together, or rode to and from Philadelphia together in Jefferson's carriage — the tall, thin, loose-jointed, and powerful master of Monticello, and the short, frail, bald-headed Madison. But the incongruity was in their physical appearance only, for they had much in common — a common sweetness of disposition, a common code of political principles and morals, a common liberality of views, and a common passion for knowledge. The older man paid tribute to his protégé's qualities long after both had passed from active public life: his 'habits of self-possession which placed at ready command the rich resources of his luminous and discriminating mind'; his language 'soothing always the feelings of his adversaries by civilities and softness of expression'; his 'pure and spotless virtue which no calumny has ever attempted to sully' — all qualities that made him a congenial companion for the philosopher who shared them in a large degree.[2] Observing Jefferson's happiness at the inauguration of his successor, a lady who knew them both intimately wrote what all who knew them felt: 'I do believe father never loved a son more than he loves Mr. Madison.'[3] But when Madison rose that cold February day to make his first attack on Hamilton's programme, he acted on his own volition and without consultation with the man who was to be his chief.

V

The character of Madison's speech in favor of discrimination between the original holders and the purchasers of securities was

---

[1] *First Forty Years of American Society, Family Letters of Mrs. Margaret Bayard Smith,* 61.

[2] *Works of Jefferson,* Ford, I, 86.   [3] Mrs. Smith, 63.

not so open to attack as that of the impulsive and loose-thinking Jackson. He began in a manner to conciliate his hearers, matching Hamilton in his insistence on the sanctity of the debt and the necessity for its discharge. The question is — to whom is the money due? There could be no doubt in the case of the original holders who had not alienated their securities. The only rival pretensions were those of the original holders who had assigned and the present holders of the assignments.

'The former may appeal to justice,' he said, 'because the value of the money, the service or the property advanced by them has never been really paid to them. They may appeal to good faith, because the value stipulated and expected is not satisfied by the steps taken by the Government. The certificates put in the hands of the creditors, on closing their settlements with the public, were of less value than was acknowledged to be due; they may be considered as having been forced on the receivers. They cannot therefore be adjudged an extinguishment of the debt. They may appeal to the motives for establishing public credit, for which justice and faith form the natural foundation. They may appeal to humanity for the sufferings of the military part of the creditors who never can be forgotten while sympathy is an American virtue.'

Admitting that the purchaser also had a claim, he proposed a plan designed, as he thought, to do justice to both — to pay the original holder in full, and, where there had been an assignment, the assignee to receive the highest market value and the original holder whatever remained over.[1] The plan spread consternation. At the Knoxes' dinner table that night, where members of Congress and diplomats were gathered, it was almost the sole topic of conversation. In the coffee-houses, where the speculators gathered about their mugs, Madison was denounced as a dreamer and an enemy of public faith. The more cautious regretted the insurmountable difficulties of the scheme. This was felt by Madison as the one legitimate argument in opposition, and writing Jefferson three days later he made the admission with the suggestion that 'they might be removed by one half the exertions that will be used to collect and color them.'[2] It was not until four days later that the Hamiltonian leaders attacked the plan with their heavy artil-

[1] *Annals*, February 11, 1790.   [2] Madison's *Writings*, I, 507.

lery. One by one they rushed to the assault. 'It is not pretended,' cried Sedgwick, 'that any fraud or imposition has been practiced' — which is precisely what was charged. If the original holders lost, it was their own fault. It was too bad. He really sympathized with their misfortunes. But business was business. There was 'no fraud on the part of the holder,' echoed Laurance of New York — who knew that the town was humming with the charge. At any rate, 'the general opinion of men of property is in favor of it.' No public bodies like Chambers of Commerce were against the Hamilton plan. As for 'the people' — newspapers and pamphlets could not be taken as expressive of public opinion. William Smith of Charleston had heard few advocates of discrimination 'in society.' As for the newspapers, they appeared on both sides. And why so much sympathy with the original holders?

It was reserved for Ames, whose friend Gore was getting rich on speculation, to take a stouter stand. Why should not 'the seller who sold for a trifle be taxed to pay the purchaser?' he asked. 'He certainly ought to fare as other citizens do. If he has property, then the plea of necessity is destroyed; if he has none, then his taxes will be a mere trifle.' And public opinion against it? Then 'all the more duty on Government to protect right when it may happen to be unpopular; that is what Government is framed to do.' Away with maudlin sentiment — it was not the function of the State to 'rob on the highway to exercise charity.'[1]

Meanwhile the commercial organizations of the larger towns were summoned to the field against discrimination, and they responded — even in Richmond. 'It is the natural language of the towns,' wrote Madison, 'and decides nothing.'[2] As the debate proceeded, Wall Street swarmed with the curious who could not get into the House where the speculators packed the galleries, and lined up deep behind the railing in the rear of the chamber. Petitions began to pour in. Passions rose. 'I do not believe the crowd in the gallery consists of original holders,' shouted one speaker with a contemptuous glance at the covetous group bending over the railing.[3] Soldiers! 'Poor soldiers!' sneered Wadsworth — he who had sent the two fast-sailing vessels to the South — 'I am tired of

[1] *Annals*, February 15, 1790.   [2] *Writings* (to Randolph), I, 512.
[3] White, *Annals*, February 16, 1790.

hearing about the poor soldiers. Perhaps soldiers were never better paid in any part of the country.'[1]

Two days later, Madison returned to the attack in a speech unusually spirited for him. Only when he had parted with his self-respect 'could he admit that America ought to erect the monuments of her gratitude, not to those who saved her liberties, but to those who had enriched themselves on her funds.' It was his last effort. He had spent himself to the utmost. A spectator entering the House late in the day found him 'rather jaded.'[2] He had incurred the hate of the Hamiltonians without having consolidated all the opposition in favor of his plan.

Three days later — it was Sunday — that extreme democrat Senator Maclay, who was indifferent to Madison's plan because opposed to funding altogether, sat down in his boarding-house and framed a plan of his own looking to the extinguishment of the debt through the sale of public lands. Having satisfied himself, he went forth in search of Thomas Scott, his colleague. But 'shame to tell it — he a man in years and burdened with complaints — had lodged out and was not home yet.' Pity that 'a good head should be led astray by the inordinate lust of its concomitant parts.' At length the old 'roué' was found, and he urged that it be submitted to Madison at once.

The next day found Maclay indignantly chafing at Madison's lodging-house because it was 'a long time' before he appeared. As the radical from Pennsylvania read his plan, it seemed to him that Madison 'attended to no one word, being so much absorbed in his own ideas.' Maclay handed him the paper, and Madison handed it back without glancing at it. Alas, thought the radical, 'his pride seems of the kind that repels all communications.'[3] It was not an easy task to organize the forces of Democracy.

The next day Madison's plan was voted down. It was found long afterward that of the sixty-four members of the House, twenty-nine were security-holders.

VI

One thing, however, had been accomplished — the public interest had been awakened. The tongue of criticism had been

[1] White, *Annals*, February 16, 1790.   [2] Maclay, 199.   [3] *Ibid.*, February 22, 1790.

loosened. The man in the street began to hold forth. It was all beyond him — as problems of finance were beyond Madison himself; but he could understand that a policy had been adopted that would be advantageous to the rich, profitable to the speculator, and mean loss to the common soldier. In the commercial centers of the cities Madison became anathema. Young Adams reported to his father that in Boston 'Mr. Madison's reputation has suffered from his conduct,' albeit so respectable a character as Judge Dana had adopted Madison's views.[1] The immediate reaction through letters to the papers was so bitter that Fenno was moved to a homily under the caption, 'Honor Your Rulers,' in which he pointed to such outrageous derelictions as expressions of doubt concerning the propriety of the proceedings of Congress.[2] These expressions had gone far beyond a mere questioning of the wisdom of Congress. 'A War Worn Soldier' thought it 'happy there is a Madison who fearless of the blood suckers will step forward and boldly vindicate the rights of the widows and orphans, the original creditors and the war worn soldier.'[3] Another 'Real Soldier' described 'the poor emaciated soldier, hungry and naked, in many instances now wandering from one extreme part of the country to another. . . . But thank God there lives a Madison to propose justice. . . .'[4] An uglier and more pointed note was struck by 'A Farmer' in Pennsylvania. 'Would it not be a good regulation,' he wrote, 'to oblige every member of Congress . . . to lay his hand on his heart and to declare that he is no speculator; and that he did not come forward to claim for himself the price of the blood or the limb or the life of the poor soldier?'[5] Another wrote to 'gentlemen who by superior wealth have monopolized the public securities' that if honor and public faith called for the maintenance of the paper at par then, there was more occasion for it 'when they were in the hands of those poor people to whom they were justly due, who had implicitly pinned their faith on your sheaves.'[6] 'An Old Soldier' recalled Washington's pledge to see justice done the common soldier. 'Ample means are said to be now about to be provided, not for their relief, but to enable eight or nine hundred per

---

[1] *Writings, J. Q. Adams*, I, 49. [2] *Gazette of the United States*, June 12, 1790.
[3] *Centinel*, February 24, 1790. [4] *Ibid.*, March 20, 1790.
[5] *Pennsylvania Gazette*, copied in *Maryland Gazette*, February 26, 1790.
[6] Boston, *Independent Chronicle*, March 4, 1790.

cent gain on the purchase money of the speculator.'[1] 'Ah well,' wrote 'A Citizen' of Boston, 'Madison, Jackson and others in favor of discrimination in funding the public debt have probably immortalized their memories.'[2]

Their letters probably reflect the talk among the workers on the wharves, the pioneers on the fringe of the forests, the gossips of the taverns. Rightly or wrongly, a spirit of resentment had been aroused — a feeling in the breast of many that their interests were being subordinated by the Government. This sentiment was to grow and to increase the trouble of Hamilton in the next step toward the adoption of his funding system.

VII

With the easy victory, however, the Hamiltonians entered with gayety upon the next step — the Assumption of the State debts — determined to rush it through. On the very night of the day discrimination was defeated, the Pennsylvania delegation, on the suggestion of Robert Morris, met at the lodgings of Representative Fitzsimons of Philadelphia to 'consider' the matter of Assumption. One glance convinced the keen-eyed Maclay that the meeting was for ratification, not for consideration purposes. 'By God,' swore Morris, 'it must be done!' George Clymer, another of the Hamilton Reliables, bubbled with enthusiasm over the advantage that would accrue to Pennsylvania. Maclay was embarrassed by the almost affectionate comradery of some of his colleagues. Why should the delegation not hold weekly social sessions and work in harmony? Fitzsimons's lodgings would be the very place to meet. Yes, agreed Morris, and they could have wine and oysters.[3]

A few days later Muhlenberg, returning to Maclay's lodgings from a levee at the presidential mansion, declared with intense emphasis that the State debts must be assumed — which impressed the suspicious Senator as 'the language of the Court.'[4]

But it was not to be so simple as all that. Assumption, argued many, would but extend the scope of the operations of the hated speculators. It was another move to mortgage the Government to

---

[1] Boston, *Independent Chronicle*, March 25, 1790. [2] *Ibid.*, April 15.
[3] Maclay, 202. [4] *Ibid.*, 205.

the capitalists. The greater part of the speculating gentry were in the North; they would soon accumulate all the State certificates of the South into their own hands and one section would be paying taxes to increase the fortunes of a favored class in another.

There was another reason for the revolt of the Southerners — which, reversed, would have operated quite as powerfully on the Northerners. The States with the largest unpaid debts were in the North, Massachusetts with the greatest debt of all. Virginia, which led the opposition, had liquidated most of her debt. There is nothing inexplicable in the objections of the Virginians, who had paid their debt, to being taxed to help pay the debt of Massachusetts and Connecticut.

This was appreciated by many in the North, and a citizen of Stockbridge, Massachusetts, writing for a New York paper, thought it unfair. If the 'leveling system' was vicious as applied to men, it was quite as bad when applied to States. Then, too, 'the public creditors, the most opulent part of the community, would, by this means, be detached from the interest of the State Governments and united to that of the general Government.' This aimed at the annihilation of the State Governments and the perpetuation of the debt.[1] Thus an attack began on the general policy of funding, taking an ugly form, appealing to class prejudices. 'A number of drones are brought into society and the industrious bee is forced to furnish them with all the honey of its search.'[2]

But this opposition from the unimportant meant nothing to Hamilton. In those days, and for many days to come, it was only necessary to know what Oliver Wolcott [3] said or wrote to know what his master thought. Writing his father about this time, Wolcott gives us sketchily the operations of Hamilton's mind. This matter of assumption was connected with 'the engine of government.' Since 'the influence of the clergy, the nobility and the army' was impossible, 'some active principle of the human mind can be interested in the support of the Government.' It would never do to have 'civil establishments,' but there was an influential class in existence — the moneyed class. They could and

---

[1] *New York Advertiser*, February 20, 1790.
[2] *Ibid.*, February 22, 1790.   [3] Comptroller of the Treasury.

should be bound by interest to the general Government. What more 'active principle' of the human mind than the desire for wealth? And if the capitalists looked to the Federal rather than to the State Governments for their money, what better 'engine of government' than that? 'For these reasons,' wrote Wolcott, 'I think the State debts should be assumed.' True, it would make the debt of the United States 'inconvenient,' the taxes would be 'burdensome,' and 'will appear to be just only to those who believe that the good attained is more important than the evil which is suffered.'[1]

It was fear of the effect of these 'burdensome taxes' on the popularity of the Federal Government that led some men, including `Madison, into opposition.[2] Some of the Hamiltonians were alarmed, fearing that 'such bold politics are unfitted to . . . the infant resources' of the young Republic.[3] Every enemy of Assumption was not hostile to the central Government, but all who were jealous of the sovereignty of the States were in opposition. Rufus King, the brilliant and virile Hamiltonian leader in the Senate, was convinced that in New York 'the anti-federalists think that the advantages to be derived to the State from the retention of that debt are so great and important that they stand ready to accede to any terms which the creditors may propose.'[4] About the same time the unreconciled Patrick Henry was writing James Monroe that 'it seems to be a consistent part of a system I have ever dreaded,' and that the 'subserviency of Southern to Northern interests are written in Capitals on its very front.'[5]

Such was the atmosphere in which the second battle began.

VIII

On the opening of the debate one champion of Assumption [6] let the cat out of the bag with the statement that 'if the general Government has the payment of all the debts, it must of course have all the revenue, and if it possesses the whole revenue, it is equal, in other words, to the whole power.' 'Yes,' cried the irrepressible Jackson in stentorian tones, 'if it lulls the Shays of the

---

[1] Gibbs, I, 43.　　　[2] Madison's *Writings* (to Jefferson), I, 511.
[3] McRee, *Iredell* (from Senator Johnson), II, 286; (from William R. Davie), II, 281, note.
[4] King, I, 385.　　　[5] Henry, II, 459.　　　[6] Stone of Maryland.

North it will rouse the Sullivans of the South' — and the fight was on.

Almost immediately Assumption became confused with the whole system of funding, and a week after Madison had made his argument against the former, he was compelled to return to a defense of the latter, not as something he desired, but as a necessity imposed by unescapable conditions. Madison was too much of a statesman to be a demagogue.

Very soon, Maclay, watching the proceedings in the House with ferret eyes, thought he observed 'the rendezvousing of the crew of the Hamilton galley.' He found that 'all hands are piped to quarters.' The plan to force a vote on March 8th was abandoned toward evening, and that night he heard it was to await the arrival of Representative Vining of Delaware, and to give Hamilton time 'to prepare him properly.'[1]

There was some mystery about Vining, and wild rumors were afloat that some one had said that he would give the new arrival a thousand guineas for his vote. 'A thousand guineas,' snorted Maclay, with a twinge in his gouty knee,' they could get him for a tenth that sum.'

Meanwhile, there was feverish activity among Hamilton's supporters in Congress and out. Government officials left their desks to become lobbyists. The clergy turned politicians and solicited. The speculators were active. The members of the Cincinnati were mobilized and marched. Two Congressmen, one lame, the other sick, were carried to the House to meet a possible emergency. Another, planning to leave town, was ordered to his post.[2] The friends of Assumption were becoming uneasy. Letters in opposition were pouring in from men like Doctors Rush and Logan of Philadelphia and were being peddled about by Maclay to members of the Pennsylvania delegation. Alas, that he should have found 'a woman in the room' with old man Scott again.[3]

These activities so wrought upon the nerves of Robert Morris that he sought a new avenue of approach to his erratic colleague. Would Maclay join Morris in some land speculations? The former was suspicious, but interested.[4] For several days Morris talked

[1] Maclay, 208. [2] Ibid., 209. [3] Ibid., 212. [4] Ibid., 214.

land—the play continuing for eleven days. The debate was becoming bitter. The able, bitter-tongued Ædanus Burke of South Carolina made a ferocious attack on Hamilton, and the lobbies, coffee-houses, streets, buzzed with talk of a duel.[1]

The distress among Hamilton's friends increased. In the Senate, shut off from the curious eyes of the public, feelings could be manifested with some abandon. Ellsworth and Izard 'walked all the morning back and forward.' Strong of Massachusetts and Paterson of New Jersey 'seemed moved but not so much agitated.' King 'looked like a boy who had been whipped.' And the hair on Schuyler, a heavy speculator and father-in-law of Hamilton, 'stood on end as if the Indians had fired at him.'[2]

But courage was revived, and there was unwonted activity. Most of Washington's household joined the lobby—Humphreys, Jackson, and Nelson, his secretaries — and were particularly attentive to Vining. This was the result of a caucus of Hamilton's supporters the night before when the decision was reached to risk a vote.

Three days later, the chance was taken, and Hamilton lost by two votes. The scene was dramatic. Sedgwick made an ominous speech and, on being called to order, took his hat and left. 'A funeral oration,' sneered Maclay. When he returned he seemed to have been weeping. Even the eyes of the self-contained Fitzsimons 'were brimming full' as he went about 'reddened like scarlet.' Clymer, 'always pale,' was 'deadly white,' his lips quivering. But 'happy impudence sat on Laurance's brow.' Wadsworth, who was financially interested, 'hid his grief under the rim of a round hat,' and Boudinot,[3] another speculator, left his distress naked to his enemies — 'his wrinkles rose in ridges and the angles of his mouth were depressed and assumed a curve resembling a horse shoe.'[4]

The speculators poured out of the galleries and into the coffeehouses and taverns to relieve their feelings with oaths over a mug. The air was electric — and cause enough. Many speculators or their agents had been scouring the back country of the Carolinas and Georgia for months buying up State securities on the assump-

---

[1] Maclay, 227, 230.
[2] *Ibid.*, 234.
[3] Elias Boudinot of New Jersey.
[4] Maclay, 237.

tion that they would be funded. They had bet on a sure thing —
and lost.

IX

For a moment the friends of Assumption appeared to lose interest in the new Government. Some acted as though the experiment launched by the Constitution had failed and was not worth a
ceremonious burial. The interest of Congress lagged, and in the
Senate, where the Assumptionists were strongest, business was
practically abandoned. In less than an hour after it was called to
order, Rufus King would move an adjournment.[1] It was a gloomy
and cold April — the distant hills and even the house-tops covered
with snow.[2] 'The Eastern members talk a strange language,'
wrote Madison to Monroe. 'They avow, some of them at least, a
determination to oppose all provisions for the public debt which
does not include this, and intimate danger to the Union from a
failure to assume.'[3] Senator Johnson of North Carolina found 'the
gentlemen who are in favor of assumption . . . very sore and impatient under their defeat.'[4] Not a few of the Federalists began to
speak and write pessimistically of the doubtful value of the Government. From his library at Beverly, George Cabot could see the
danger of 'division, anarchy and wretchedness,'[5] and if the States
seized the opportunity to 'provide honestly for their creditors . . .
the general government would be ruined irrevocably.' But the
thing that pained Cabot most was the attitude of Madison. Had
he changed his principles?[6]

In the Hamiltonian press the comments were funereal. Fenno's
paper teemed with indignant protests and savage attacks on the
State 'demagogues' who were 'hankering after popularity at
home.'[7] 'Americanus,' paying tribute to Hamilton and his funding
plan, found it 'wantonly destroyed' and 'in broken pieces at the
several shrines of ambition, avarice and vanity.'[8]

Yet all the scribes were not similarly depressed. A writer in the
'New York Journal,' describing the birth and death of Assumption,
worked the advocates of the measure into a frenzy. He pictured it

---

[1] Maclay, 248. [2] Ibid., 250.
[3] Writings, I, 517. [4] McRee, Iredell, II, 286.
[5] Lodge, Cabot, 35–36. [6] Ibid. (to Goodhue), 37.
[7] Gazette of the United States, April 21, 1790. [8] Ibid., April 24, 1790.

as 'the bastard of Eastern speculators who have lost their puritanic manners' — the 'brat' having been brought into the world 'by the dexterous application of the forceps.' Thus it was injured by the 'violence of the delivery,' but 'Dr. Slop' had hoped to save it by having it bathed 'in Yankee rum.' 'The unfortunate child was presented to the baptismal font by Granny Fitzsimmons; and Mr. Sedgwick, who is gifted with canting talents, officiated as priest, baptized the infant, and his name stands on the parish books as Al—ex—der Assumption.' But alas, 'the child of promise who would have redeemed the Eastern States from poverty and despair is now no more.'[1]

But Hamilton was not despairing — he had just begun to fight.

X

It was under these conditions that an event of tremendous import occurred. On Sunday a stage-coach lumbered up to the tavern on Broadway, and a tall, travel-worn man emerged and entered the hostelry. Momentous as was the meaning of his arrival, it claimed but scant notice in the papers of the city.

'On Sunday last, arrived in this city, Thomas Jefferson, Esq., Secretary of State for the United States of America.'[2]

There is nothing in the press or the correspondence of the time to indicate the slightest appreciation of the significance of this accession to governmental circles. No doubt Madison was among the first to greet him, but of this we have no evidence. For two weeks Jefferson had been upon the road from Richmond, resting a day at Alexandria where an eighteen-inch snow caused him to send his carriage on by water and take the public stage. The roads were wretched and there was little opportunity for restful sleep. Occasionally the long-legged traveler left the stage to mount his horse for exercise. Thus he rode to the field of battle.

XI

As Hamilton surveyed the wreckage of the field, he saw an opportunity. There was another bitter battle pending over the selection of the site of the permanent capital. Might he not bar-

[1] *Centinel*, June 19, 1790.   [2] *Daily Advertiser*, March 24, 1790.

gain a bit and trade enough votes for Assumption? The site of the capital was a matter of indifference to him. No sentimental ties bound him to any State or community. No dust sacred to him rested anywhere in American soil. He was ready to go with any group that could contribute enough votes to make Assumption sure. Philadelphia — New York — the Susquehanna — Baltimore — the Potomac — a mere bagatelle to him. In the fact that it was more than that to others he saw his chance. Could the Virginians or the Marylanders who had opposed Assumption pay him in votes for a capital at Georgetown, or even Baltimore? Could Robert Morris whip the stubborn Pennsylvanians into line for a capital in Philadelphia or on the Susquehanna? True, Washington favored Georgetown, but that meant nothing to Hamilton if Georgetown could not bring Assumption. It is a myth of history that he was tenderly considerate of the wishes of his chief: the facts to sustain it do not appear. Far more important to him was the fact that Madison and Carroll favored Georgetown. They had votes.

The intense bitterness over the struggle called for infinite diplomacy and sagacity in negotiation. The papers of the country were filled with ill-natured letters on the fight which was no more in evidence in Congress than in the bar-rooms of the competing cities. Ames, like Hamilton, cared little about the site if he could but get Assumption, and was disgusted with the 'despicable grog-shop contest, whether the taverns in New York or Philadelphia shall get the custom of Congress.' Sedgwick had become a 'perfect slave to the business,' and 'Goodhue frowned all day long and swears as much as a good Christian can . . .'[1]

By early June the bargaining stage had been reached. One day Tench Coxe, of the Treasury, and Jackson, one of Washington's secretaries, called at the lodgings of Fitzsimons and Clymer with the bald proposition to trade the permanent residence to Philadelphia for enough Pennsylvania votes to pass Assumption. Taking this as a hint from Hamilton, Robert Morris wrote him that early the next morning he should be taking a walk on the Battery, and if any propositions were open he would be very glad to have the Secretary of the Treasury join him in his constitutional. Thus,

[1] Ames (to Dwight), I, 79–80.

long before many of the statesmen had enjoyed their coffee, Hamilton and Morris paced up and down at the deserted Battery. With Walpolean directness, Hamilton went to the point. He needed one vote in the Senate and five in the House. If Morris could assure him these, he could give assurance, in return, that the permanent residence would be given to Germantown or the Falls of the Delaware. Morris promised to consult his colleagues — but how about the temporary residence for Philadelphia? After thinking it over, Hamilton sent word that he would not think of bargaining on the temporary residence.[1] For several days these negotiations continued. The Pennsylvanians moved with a deliberation that tried Hamilton's patience. A few days later he threatened his Philadelphia friends with the possibility of the New-Englanders going to Baltimore or the Potomac.[2]

Meanwhile, Hamilton had been thinking seriously of Jefferson. They met as strangers, knowing one another well by reputation. Their feelings were friendly. There were innumerable reasons why they should ultimately fly at each other's throats, but that was in the future. One June day they met at the presidential mansion on Broadway, and, leaving at the same time, Hamilton saw his opportunity.

There was a picture for an artist to paint — Hamilton and Jefferson, arm in arm, walking along Broadway discussing the possibilities of a bargain. With all the persuasiveness of his eloquence, Hamilton dwelt on the very real danger of disunion if Assumption failed. With subtle diplomacy he seemed to throw himself trustfully on Jefferson's mercy. A great struggle for independence — a promising young nation — and was all to be lost? The South wanted the capital, the North wanted Assumption — could there not be a common meeting-ground? Jefferson would see.

A dinner at Jefferson's table in the house on Broadway. Men from the South about the board. The topic — the pending bargain. A little later, Hamilton was informed that an agreement could be reached. The word was passed along the line. Even Madison satisfied himself that, since Assumption could not be prevented, the bargain might as well be made — but if there had

[1] Maclay, 292.   [2] Ibid., 299.

been no bargain there would have been no Assumption. A few nights later the Pennsylvania delegation entertained both Hamilton and Jefferson at dinner. The latter impressed one guest with his 'dignity of presence and gravity,' Hamilton with his 'boyish giddy manner.' Whatever may have been the cause of the gravity of Jefferson, there was reason for the giddiness of Hamilton — he had won![1]

XII

The attempt of Jefferson in later life to explain his part in the bargain over Assumption, with the assertion that he had been deceived by Hamilton, is in the nature of an alibi created after the crime. He was not a simple-minded rustic, and his correspondence previous to the bargain shows that he had given serious consideration to Assumption. He had been in daily contact with Madison who had led the fight against it. A meticulously careful student of the press, he unquestionably was familiar with every objection to Assumption and funding which he afterward offered. He had undoubtedly read Madison's argument which had been published a month after he reached New York. As late as June 20th, he was writing Monroe that, unless the quarrel over Assumption and the residence was settled, 'there will be no funding bill agreed to, our credit will burst and vanish, and the States separate, to take care, every one of itself.' Much as he would prefer that the States pay their own debts, he could see 'the necessity of yielding to the cries of the creditors . . . for the sake of the Union, and to save it from the greatest of all calamities, the total extinction of our credit in Europe.'[2] Here was justification enough for his action without resorting to the fanciful story of his deception by Hamilton. 'The question of assuming the State debts has created greater animosities than I ever yet saw,' he wrote Dr. Gilmer a week after his letter to Monroe.[3] Thus he knew precisely how the lines were drawn. Perhaps he did not appreciate at the moment the political advantage of appearing on the side of the opposition, — but he was not deceived. Nor was Madison imposed upon. He accepted the bargain because 'the crisis demands the spirit of accommodation,'

[1] Maclay, 310.
[2] *Works*, Ford, VIII, 42–45.   [3] *Ibid.*, VIII, 52.

albeit he wished it 'considered as an unavoidable evil and possibly not the worse side of the dilemma.'[1]

With many, however, the triumph of Assumption meant placing Hamilton and his followers in an impregnable position; this, too, was the idea of the Hamiltonians and great was their rejoicing. When the measure passed the Senate, members of the lower House were packed behind the iron railing, the smiling faces of Ames and Sedgwick conspicuous among them. To the extremists in the opposition it seemed the end. 'I do not see that I can do any good here and I think I had better go home,' wrote Maclay. 'Everything, even to the naming of a committee is prearranged by Hamilton and his group of speculators.'[2] And the Hamiltonians, who had raged over the satirical article on the birth of Assumption, made merry over a verse in Fenno's journal:

> 'The wit who bastardized thy name
> And croaked a funeral dirge
> Knew not how spotless was thy fame
> How soon thou would'st emerge.'[3]

When Congress adjourned, Hamilton, rejoicing in his triumphs, turned gayly to the next step in his programme, with more powerful influences behind him than he had ever had before.

[1] *Writings* (to Monroe), i, 522.   [2] Maclay, 332.
[3] *Gazette of the United States*, August 25, 1790.

CHAPTER IV
PREMONITIONS OF BATTLE

I

HAMILTON was at the high tide of his popularity and power when Congress next convened in Philadelphia. His funding system had established the Nation's credit, and the genius and daring of the brilliant young man of thirty-three were on every tongue. The 'Maryland Journal' claimed 'respectable authority' for the assertion that in Quebec he was 'supposed equal to the celebrated Mr. Pitt, and superior to the Prime Minister of any other court in Europe.'[1] Among the merchants and people of wealth and property he was acclaimed the savior of the State. Everywhere he was the idol of the aristocracy.

And, in the saddle, he was riding hard. Although his was the second position in the Cabinet, he thought of himself as the Prime Minister. Washington was a constitutional monarch. The other members of the President's official family were his subordinates. His policies were the policies of the Government, and to question them was hostility to the State. In the Cabinet meetings his manner was masterful to a degree. Considering himself Prime Minister, he felt no delicacy about interfering in the departments of his colleagues. Even Knox, who adored him, resented his determination to make all the purchases for the Department of War. When the War Secretary resisted, Hamilton had a compliant Congress pass a law giving him that privilege — an absurdity that continued as long as he was in the Cabinet.[2] The soft-spoken, mild, and courteous Jefferson, who preferred the ways of conciliation and persuasion, observed the dictatorial airs of his masterful young associate with a surprise that hardened to distaste.

But the feeling awakened among the masses by the failure to discriminate in the matter of the securities, and by Assumption, was increasing in intensity. The common soldier had not profited by these policies. The farmer and the mechanic could see no bene-

[1] February 25, 1791.   [2] Brooks, *Knox*, 213.

fit to themselves, but among speculators, some of them members of Congress, they observed evidence of new-found wealth. These were building finer houses, riding in coaches where they had previously walked, and there was an ominous rumbling and grumbling beneath the surface, to which the Hamiltonians were oblivious or indifferent. After all, this was merely the whining of the ne'er-do-wells of the taverns and the illiterates of the farms.

The work was only begun, and there could be no turning back now. The assumption of the State debts called for the tapping of new sources of revenue. This would increase the burdens of the people, but what would they have? They could not eat their cake and have it too — could not have a strong government without paying the price. Utterly unmindful of the complaining of the people of no importance, Hamilton turned resolutely to his task and prepared his excise tax for the consideration of Congress.

II

In raising money to meet the obligations of Assumption, it was the purpose of Hamilton to resort to direct taxation as little as possible, and to make luxuries bear the burden. This directed his attention to the domestic manufacture of spirits — a luxury to some, but a very real necessity to others. This was particularly true in the States where distilleries were plentiful. That it would call forth a protest from some quarters, he had no doubt, and he rejoiced in the certainty of combat. Strong man that he was, he went forth in shining armor to establish the right of the Government to an internal revenue. He knew that excise taxes were obnoxious, albeit necessary, and he sought the chance to vindicate the right of the Government to do the necessary, unpopular thing.

Instantly the challenge was accepted in Pennsylvania where whiskey stills abounded in the Alleghanies. Some of the State's representatives in Congress were instantly on their toes, denouncing the plan as arbitrary and despotic. In the Legislature, Albert Gallatin, a remarkable young man, soon to prove himself the only member of the opposition capable of coping with Hamilton in the field of finance, framed a reply, denouncing the plan as 'subversive of the rights, liberty and peace of the people.' In the midst of excitement — for the Legislature sat in Philadelphia — the reply was debated and adopted by an overwhelming majority.

But the opposition was comparatively weak. Jefferson and Madison were hostile to the principle, but there had been a bargain on Assumption to which they were parties. They could not deceive themselves as to the necessity. If Jefferson raised a finger to prevent the passage of the bill, he covered his tracks. Even Giles, soon to become the most vehement leader of the Jeffersonian party, at first looked upon it with some favor. Madison could see no escape.

Among the masses throughout the country, however, the obscure orators were busy in the bar-rooms, on the streets, and at the crossroads. The character of the discussion among the people is indicated in imaginary conversations by a writer in a Baltimore paper. A friend of the excise fares forth into the streets and meets its enemies. 'An outrage!' cried one. 'Had we not gone to war with England on a tax?' 'Ah,' but, says the defender, 'then we were taxed by another country and without representation, while here we tax ourselves through our chosen representatives.' 'Yes,' but, says Rumor, 'under the excise act men can break into the people's houses.' 'Wrong,' says the defender; 'the law provides no such arbitrary power.' 'But,' persists the enemy, 'we shall be eaten up by excise officers.' 'Silly,' says the defender; 'numerically these officials will be unimportant.' Then the defender encounters one candid enemy of the measure. 'I hate the excise,' he cries, 'because it strengthens the Government by providing effectually for its necessities; and the Government which lays it because it is a Government of vigor.' Whereupon the defender praises him as an honest man.[1]

The moment the Excise Bill was presented in the House, the ever alert Jackson was ready with a motion to strike out the essential part of the first clause. 'The mode of taxation was odious, unequal, unpopular, and oppressive, more particularly in the Southern States,' where under the hot Southern skies spirituous liquors were more than salutary — they were necessary. Why deprive the masses of 'the only luxury they enjoy'? Why impose upon the American people an excise that had been odious in England from

[1] *Maryland Journal*, February 11, 1791.

the days of Cromwell, and which had been reprobated by Blackstone?

Yes, added an indignant Virginian,[1] 'it will convulse the Government; it will let loose a swarm of harpies, who, under the domination of revenue officers, will range through the country, prying into every man's house and affairs, and like a Macedonian phalanx bear down all before them.' The mercantile interests were paying their duties with promptitude? He was tired of these encomiums. 'The increase in the revenue has served to enhance the value of the public securities, of which it is well known they hold a very considerable portion.'[2]

On the second day, Madison went on record as opposed to the principle and in favor of the measure. The only question to be considered was the necessity for the revenue — and that was indisputable. He personally would prefer direct taxes, but the majority of the people were against them. Of all forms of the excise, that on ardent spirits impressed him as the least objectionable.

But, demanded Jackson, disappointed at Madison's failure to join in the assault, why not other taxes — taxes on salaries, pensions, lawyers? Because, answered Laurance, the Assumption calls for revenue, and this is the best way to raise it. True, added another,[3] and he had 'not found a single person against it' — and this in Philadelphia where the Legislature was sitting! What! exclaimed Timothy Bloodworth of North Carolina, why 'people to the southward universally condemn the tax.' Yes, indeed, contributed another, especially in North Carolina, 'where the consumption of ardent spirits is ten times greater than in Connecticut.'

Up rose Sedgwick in conciliatory mood. He was not impressed with 'the considerations of morality,' and could not think that the tax 'would be attended with any sensible inconvenience.' There certainly was no thought of using military force in its collection. And then it was that Giles, who, next to Madison, was the most fervent and able of the Jeffersonians, astonished many by giving his hearty approval to the tax as necessary 'to the honor, peace and security' of the country.[4]

---

[1] Josiah Parker.   [2] *Annals*, January 5, 1791.
[3] Samuel Livermore.   [4] *Annals*, January 6, 1791.

Thus for days the debate continued with its reiterations, until a new note was struck with a proposed amendment, aimed at Hamilton whose audacious methods and successive successes were causing grave concern in some quarters, to prohibit revenue agents from interfering in elections. These officers in their work, said Samuel Livermore, 'will acquire such a knowledge of persons and characters as will give them great advantage and enable them to influence elections to a great degree.' 'Impolitic in respect to law, repugnant to the Constitution, and degrading to human nature,' protested Ames. It would prevent self-respecting men from taking the places, added Sedgwick. When the vote was taken, the amendment was defeated with both Madison and Giles voting against it.

It was not until the House took up the duration of the tax that the great battle began, and under the leadership of Giles, who had hitherto given it his support.[1] But Madison was not impressed, and in the vote on placing a limitation on the operation of the bill he was found with the Hamiltonians — and there he stood on the final vote.

Even in the Senate the attempt to defeat the measure was continued, and while Hamilton was strongest in that body, the energetic young Secretary took nothing for granted. It was not enough that the committee considering the bill had been packed with his supporters; he took personal charge. For several days he walked briskly into the room and took his place at the table, after which the doors were closed and locked. The worried Maclay, who was preparing the case against the measure on behalf of the distillers, sensed a conspiracy. When Adams hastened an adjournment of the Senate while the committee was sitting, the victim of the gout put him down as 'deep in the cabals of the Secretary.'[2] Preparing a list of distillers who would be affected, on which to base an argument, Maclay knocked at the committee room. The door opened and the eager eye of the Senator caught a glimpse of Hamilton at the table before Robert Morris closed it, as he stepped outside. With his suspicions confirmed, the gruff old Democrat left his papers with his colleague and turned away. 'I suppose no further use was made of it,' he commented.[3] When the bill passed four

---

[1] *Annals*, January 11, 1791. [2] Maclay, 385. [3] *Ibid.*, 385.

days later, he thought 'war and bloodshed ... the most likely consequence'; and concluded that 'Congress may go home' since 'Mr. Hamilton is all-powerful and fails in nothing he attempts.'[1]

The same conclusion had been reached by Jefferson before. Just after the passage of the bill, he was writing a friend of his fears of the effect of the policies of the Treasury upon the people. Even though they were right, 'more attention should be paid to the general opinion.' The excise had passed — the Bank Bill would pass. Perhaps the only corrective for 'what is corrupt in our present form of government' would be an increase in the membership of the House 'so as to grant a more agricultural representation which may put that interest above that of the stock jobbers.'[2]

Jefferson had reached the end of his patience, and was preparing to challenge the pretensions, policies, and power of his ardent and dictatorial young colleague.

III

It was inevitable that a national bank should be a feature of Hamilton's financial system. Long before a national government loomed large as a probability, he had conceived the plan, and with the temerity of youthful audacity had solemnly outlined it in letters to Robert Morris.[3] With the opportunity before him, he moved with confident strides to his purpose, and the day after his recommendation of an excise reached Congress, his 'Report on the Bank' was read. His rare familiarity with the principles of finance, the history of banking, and the banking experiences of nations made his 'Report' a persuasive document.[4] Its adoption was as inevitable as its submission. He was on the very peak of his power. Commerce and wealth in all the cities were saluting him, for his policies were in their interest, and the professional and intellectual class had been won by the dazzling success of his daring undertakings. In House and Senate he numbered among the registers of his will the greater part of the strong and the brilliant. Somehow, too, the impression was prevalent that he was the favorite instrument through which Washington wrought his plans. If

---

[1] Maclay, 387.   [2] Jefferson's *Works*, VIII, 123.
[3] *Works*, III, 319–41; 342–87.   [4] *Ibid.*, 388–443.

the small farmers and the mechanics seemed acquiescent, it only meant that they were inarticulate — but inarticulate they were as this dashing figure moved on from triumph to triumph with a shouting multitude of merchants, lawyers, politicians, and speculators in his wake.

Thus, when the Bank Bill reached the Senate, Maclay expressed the general feeling in the comment that 'it is totally in vain to oppose this bill.'[1] Ten days later, he was all the more convinced at a dinner where he met Morris and sat between two 'merchants of considerable note,' and observed, on mentioning the Bank, that they were 'magnetically drawn to the contemplation of the moneyed interest.'[2]

If the bill passed the Senate without a conflict, it was not to get through the House without a skirmish which was to mark, as some historians think, the definite commencement of party warfare.

The House debate was brief but sharp, though pitched upon a higher plane than some preceding discussions. There was some questioning of the necessity of a bank; some criticism of the monopolistic features of the bank proposed; but Madison, who spoke at the beginning, furnished the dominant theme in his challenge to the constitutionality of such an institution. There was certainly no specific authorization of congressional power in the Constitution. This was conceded by Hamilton, who boldly evoked the doctrine of implied powers. It required no abnormal perspicacity to foresee the unlimited possibilities of these. Here was something read into the Constitution that would, rightly or wrongly, have made its ratification impossible had it provided a specific grant of such power. Hamilton and many of his lieutenants had been frankly dissatisfied with the powers that had been conceded by the people; and here was an opening for the acquisition of power that the people would have refused. This to-day — what to-morrow?

When Madison rose to oppose the Bank, we may be sure that it was after many intimate conversations with Jefferson. He spoke in low tones and with his customary dignity and precision and without abuse, and his argument was not susceptible to an easy assault. After all, 'the Father of the Constitution' knew something about his child.

[1] Maclay, 364.   [2] Ibid., 369.

'The doctrine of implication is always a tender one,' he said. 'The danger of it has been felt by other governments. The delicacy was felt in the adoption of our own; the danger may also be felt if we do not keep close to our chartered authorities. . . . If implications thus remote and thus multiplied may be linked together, a chain may be formed that will reach every object of legislation, every object within the whole compass of political economy.' More than that — 'It takes from our constituents the opportunity of deliberating on the untried measure, although their hands are also to be tied by the same terms.' More still — 'it involves a monopoly which affects the equal rights of every citizen.'[1]

On the next day Fisher Ames made his defense of the doctrine of implied powers. The argument of Madison had impressed him as 'a great speech,' but steeped in 'casuistry and sophistry.' He thought Madison had wasted his time, however, in reading the debates on constitutional powers in the various State ratifying conventions — not at all to the purpose. 'No man would pretend to give Congress the power,' he wrote, 'against a fair construction of the Constitution.'[2]

But the clever Ames had no intention of making such a frank admission on the floor. He was a practical man and he defended the Hamiltonian doctrine with eloquence and vigor.[3] With these two speeches, the debate might as well have closed, but it continued long enough to permit the Hamiltonian Old Guard to say their pieces. Giles argued and Jackson raved in opposition, and the measure passed with a margin of nineteen votes.

It is significant that nineteen of the twenty votes in opposition were those of Southern members, the only Northerner in the list being Jonathan Grout of Massachusetts, a Democrat, who did not return to the next Congress. Like preceding Hamiltonian measures, this meant the concentration of the financial resources of the country in the commercial North to the disadvantage of the agricultural South. But this was not the only reason. With the Southerners, among whom banks were a rarity, and the Westerners, to whom they were as meaningless as the canals on Mars, the advan-

[1] *Annals*, February 2, 1791.   [2] Ames (to Dwight), I, 94.
[3] *Annals*, February 3, 1791.

tage of such an institution was not felt. In both sections anything that hinted of monopoly was abhorrent. Thus, in addition to the constitutional difference, there was an economic conflict that was sectional in its nature.

IV

But the battle was not yet won. The conflict was transferred to the Cabinet, for Washington was not at all convinced that there was no constitutional prohibition. Not only did he withhold his signature till the last minute, but there are reasons to believe that he had a veto in mind almost to the end. For Madison, with whose part in the framing of the Constitution he was familiar, he had a profound respect. Having discussed the bill with Jefferson informally, Washington requested written opinions from both Jefferson and Randolph, the Attorney-General. Both were in complete accord with the conclusions of Madison. The opinion of Jefferson, expressed with all his force of reasoning, was a powerful challenge to the doctrine of implied powers.[1]

It was at about this time that Washington summoned Madison to the Morris house, which served as the Executive Mansion in Philadelphia, to invite a fuller expression of his views. The great man listened in silence, and Madison thought with sympathy, while the little giant of the Constitutional Convention, out of the wealth of his learning and experience, poured forth his reasons for opposition. Not once, but several times, the little figure of Madison must have been seen entering the Morris house in those days of suppressed excitement, for there were numerous conferences. As the ten-day period followed for the affixing of the presidential signature was drawing to an end, and Washington requested his friend to reduce his objections to writing, Madison assumed that it was a veto message he was asked to frame. Nor was it a far-fetched assumption, for on more than one occasion the President had made use of Madison's pen.[2]

Meanwhile the Hamiltonians, at first puzzled, became alarmed. From the temper of their talk in Philadelphia, Madison was convinced that in the event of a veto they were ready for open opposition to Washington, backed by the wealth and influence of the

---

[1] Jefferson's *Works*, III, 145–53.　　[1] Madison's *Writings*, III, 171.

powerful.[1] Ugly, silly stories, reflecting upon the great personage
on whom the Hamiltonians found it profitable to claim a monopoly,
were set afloat.   Fisher Ames gave currency in Boston to the theory that Washington was influenced by the fear that the establishment of a financial capital in Philadelphia would prevent the removal of the political capital to the banks of the stream that
washed the boundary of Mount Vernon.[2] If some discretion was
used in Philadelphia, where the grumbling was confined to the
fashionable drawing-rooms, no such circumspection was observed
in New York, where the meanest motives were ascribed to the
President, and among the speculators and Tory sympathizers
open threats were made. Madison heard, while there a little later,
that 'the licentiousness of [these] tongues exceeded anything that
was conceived.'[3] This struggle marked a definitive break in the
relations of Hamilton and Jefferson. The dictatorial disposition of
the former would brook no opposition, and he was temperamentally incapable of a differentiation between political opposition
and personal hostility. The fact that Jefferson, in response to a
command from Washington, had written an opinion against the
Bank could bear only one interpretation — 'asperity and ill humor
toward me.'[4] The fact that Washington accepted Hamilton's
view, did not, however, shake Jefferson's faith in the President,
and in defeat nothing so ill-tempered escaped him as flowed in a
stream from the Federalists when threatened with defeat. Within
a month after Hamilton had won his fight, Jefferson, in commenting to a friend on what he conceived to be a dangerous trend, wrote
that 'it is fortunate that our first executive magistrate is purely
and zealously republican' — the highest praise he could bestow.[5]

The press was not verbose in its comments on the bill, albeit
Freneau fought it in the 'Federal Gazette.'[6] The 'Pennsylvania
Gazette' was ungraceful in defeat. Denouncing the Bank as 'a
proposition made to the moneyed interest,' it commented on its
'preparations to subscribe,' and found 'the terms . . . so advantageous that no equal object of speculation is perhaps presented in
any quarter of the globe.'[7] Fenno offered his best in a verse:

[1] Madison's *Writings*, III, 171.   [2] Ames (to Minot), February 17, 1791.
[3] Madison's *Writings* (to Jefferson), I, 534–35.
[4] Hamilton's *Works* (letter to Carrington), IX, 513–35.
[5] Parton, II, 1.   [6] Dustin's *Freneau*, 160.   [7] May 11, 1791.

'The States as one agree that this is right
Let pigmy politicians rave and write.'[1]

Thus the First Congress closed its labors with no little rhapso-
dizing in the press over the results. A New York paper offered an
epitaph of glorification,[2] which a Boston paper condensed into the
simple comment that it had 'established public confidence and
credit, reconciled the jarring interests of discontented States, and
cemented the people in the bonds of harmony, peace and love.'[3]

One man, at least, had cause for jubilation. In two years Hamilton had risen to a position of commanding power, proved his
genius in constructive statesmanship, accomplished everything he
had set out to do, made himself the idol of the wealthy and the
powerful, the recognized leader of the influential commercial
class, the acknowledged head of a brilliant and militant party.
His friends were comparing him to Pitt, then in the heyday of his
power — and he was only on the threshold. So great was the enthusiasm in commercial circles that he made a special trip to New
York to accept the homage of the Chamber of Commerce at a
reception, to linger a week among his worshipers, and to return to
Philadelphia reinvigorated by the wine of idolatry pressed to his
lips.[4] At that moment he was on the top of the world.

v

Meanwhile, Jefferson and Madison drove out of Philadelphia
together on one of those journeys of recreation during which politicians so often plan the strategy of war. Historians have found
more in this journey than is to be discovered in the record. The
trip through New England probably had no other object than that
of pleasure and enlightenment. The relations of these two men
were beautiful and went far beyond a mere congeniality in political
opinions. There was a marked similarity in their characters. Both
scholarly in their tastes, the books that interested one were certain
to appeal to the other. Here were two men whose spirits were in
accord. It is easy to think of them as sitting the candle out in converse about the winter fire, or as sitting far into the night in silence,

[1] *Gazette of the United States*, April 6, 1791.
[2] *Daily Advertiser*, February 25, 1791.
[3] *Independent Chronicle*, March 10, 1791.   [4] *New York Daily Advertiser*, July 19, 1791.

each finding pleasure in the mere presence of the other. Such a relationship had grown up through the years. They thought alike, found similar enjoyment in agricultural pursuits, and in the many little things of common life.

'What say you,' wrote Jefferson just before the beginning of the much-discussed journey, 'to taking a wade into the country at noon? It will be pleasant above head at least, and the party will finish by dining here. Information that Colonel Beckwith[1] is coming to be an intimate with you, and I presume not a desirable one, encourages me to make a proposition which I did not venture as long as you had your agreeable congressional society about you; that is to come and take a bed and plate with me. . . . To me it will be a relief from the solitude of which I have too much; and it will lessen your repugnance to be assured that it will not increase my expenses an atom. . . . The approaching season will render this situation more agreeable than Fifth Street, and even in the winter you will not find it disagreeable.'[2] It required no assiduous and cunning cultivation by Jefferson to wean Madison away from Hamilton. The relations of the first two far antedated those of the last. Madison had agreed with Hamilton on the necessity for a more permanent and substantial union. They had fought together for the ratification of the Constitution, but such were their temperamental differences that the breach which quickly appeared was inevitable when it came to the determination of the policies of that union. While Jefferson was still in Paris, Madison, without consulting his friend, was foreshadowing the policy of the future Jeffersonian party in his fight for discrimination against England in the revenue measure of the first congressional session. He proposed discrimination between the original creditors and the speculators before he had the opportunity to discuss the subject with Jefferson. If there was an accord with the latter, it was due less to the influence of one upon the other than to the similarity of their thinking. The little man with the mild, almost shy expression, who rode out of Philadelphia with Jefferson that spring of 1791, was much too big to have been led around by the nose by any of his contemporaries.

As early as the spring of 1791, the names of the two were asso-

---

[1] British Agent.   [2] *Domestic Life*, 197–98. Jefferson was living in the country.

ciated in the minds of many as the prospective leaders of a party that would challenge the purposes of the Federalists. Answering a series of articles in the 'Maryland Journal,' some one advised the author of how to make his opinions worth while. 'Keep always before your eyes the steps by which Jefferson and Madison have gradually ascended to their present preëminence of fame. Like them you must devote your whole leisure to the most useful reading. Like them you must dive into the depths of philosophy and government.'[1] Thus they were already associated in the public mind, and there was some whispering among the Federalist leaders when they set forth in their carriage.

Bumping and splashing over the rough tree-lined roads those spring days, they unquestionably discussed the political situation, but these discussions were only the continuation of others that had been proceeding throughout the previous fall and winter. If politics was the object of the journey, they were both remarkably successful in covering their tracks. There is nothing in the letter Jefferson wrote his daughter Mary to indicate anything more than a pleasure jaunt.[2] In a letter to his other daughter, Martha, we hear much of fishing for speckled trout, salmon, and bass, of the strawberries in bloom, of vegetation and agricultural conditions — but nothing of politics.[3] To his son-in-law he wrote descriptions of historic places, of botanical objects and scenery, and of running foul of the blue law in Vermont prohibiting traveling on Sunday.[4] The one reference to the journey in the correspondence of Madison merely says that 'it was a very agreeable one, and carried us through an interesting country, new to us both.'[5] In none of these letters do we find a single reference to politics or politicians.

Something is made of the call of the travelers on Burr and Livingston when in New York, and on Governor Clinton at Albany; but their conduct would have been suspicious only if they had failed to observe the ordinary amenities of social life in calling upon the leading public characters in the towns through which they passed. Still we may safely surmise that they found time while waiting for the fish to bite to exchange views on the necessity of organizing an opposition to the Federalists. It is even possible

[1] *Maryland Journal*, March 22, 1791.   [2] *Domestic Life*, 199.   [3] *Ibid.*, 201.
[4] Jefferson's *Works*, VIII, 205.   [5] Gay's *Madison*.

that out of these conversations on country roads actually sprang the Democratic Party, but there is no evidence.

VI

On his return to Philadelphia, Jefferson found himself the center of a remarkable newspaper controversy. Fascinated by the beauty of Marie Antoinette, Edmund Burke of England had written his bitter attack, not only on the excesses of the French Revolution, but upon its democratic principles as well. It was the fashion in those days to conceal a hate of democracy under the cloak of a simulated horror over the crimes of the Terrorists. Thomas Paine had replied to Burke with his brilliant and eloquent defense of democracy, 'The Rights of Man.' In American circles where democracy was anathema, and even republicanism was discussed with cynicism, the Burke pamphlet was received with enthusiasm. It was not until some time later that 'The Rights of Man' reached New York, albeit its nature was known and there had been a keen curiosity to see it. Early in May, Madison had promised Jefferson to secure a copy as soon as possible. He understood that the pamphlet had been suppressed in England, and that Paine had found it convenient to retire to Paris. 'This,' he wrote, 'may account for his not sending copies to friends in this country.'[1] At length a single copy arrived and was loaned by its owner to Madison, who passed it on to Jefferson. He read it with enthusiasm. Here was a spirited defense of democracy, and of the fight the French were waging for their liberties; here an excoriation of the prattle in high social and governmental circles of the advantage, if not necessity, for titles of nobility. Here was not only an answer to Burke, but to John Adams, whose 'Discourses of Davilla' had been running for weeks in Fenno's paper, and had been copied extensively in other journals with a similar slant. Jefferson was immensely pleased.

Before he had finished with it, the owner had called upon Madison for its return, as arrangements had been made for its publication by a Philadelphia printer. It was agreed that Jefferson should send it directly to the print shop, and in the transmission he wrote a brief explanation of the delay, and added: 'I am extremely pleased to find it will be reprinted here, and that something is at

[1] Madison's *Writings*, I, 534.

length to be publicly said against the political heresies which have sprung up among us. I have no doubt our citizens will rally a second time round the standard of "Common Sense."'

To this note he attached so little importance that he kept no copy. With astonishment he found that the printer had used his note as the preface, with his name and official title as Secretary of State. The general conviction that the word 'heresies' was meant to apply to the Adams papers sufficiently indicates the popular interpretation of their trend. The storm broke.

Major Beckwith, the British Agent, hastened to express his pained surprise to Washington's Secretary at the recommendation by the Secretary of State of a pamphlet which had been suppressed in England. The secretary was sufficiently impressed by the scandalized tone of the aristocratic society of Philadelphia, which was usually lionizing some degenerate members of the European nobility, to write his chief in detail. When Randolph dined with Mrs. Washington, Lear retailed it to him, and the suggestion was made that Jefferson should know. Thus there was something more than a tempest in a teapot. Everywhere men were partisans of the pamphlets of Burke or Paine, the aristocrats on one side, the democrats on the other, the stoutest of the republicans everywhere delighted with 'The Rights of Man.' This was true in even the small towns and the villages of far places. One traveler passing through Reading was surprised to find the two pamphlets the 'general topic of conversation,' and he was assured of the delight that awaited him in the reading of Paine's.[1] All too long had the Americans been drugged with Fenno's deification of the upper classes — with John Adams's 'Discourses' on the necessity of 'distinctions' — and here was old 'Common Sense' back again in the old form slashing the aristocrats fore and aft. The press responded to the popular demand, and everywhere 'The Rights of Man' was being published serially to be eagerly read by the thousands who had not seen the pamphlet. But it was not all one-sided. If the 'Painites' wrote furiously in some papers, the 'Burkites' were prolific in Fenno's and a few others. In the fashionable drawing-rooms a poll would have shown a decided preference for the defender of aristocracy who had wept so eloquently over the woes of a frivolous

[1] Graydon, 375.

Queen. Nowhere was Burke so popular and Paine so loathed as in the home of Adams, the Vice-President. 'What do you think of Paine's pamphlet?' asked Dr. Rush, to whom society was cooling because of his democratic tendencies. The second official of the Republic hesitated as if for dramatic effect, and then, solemnly laying his hand upon his heart, he answered, 'I detest that book and its tendency from the bottom of my heart.' Indeed, most of the Federalists were frankly with Burke. 'Although Mr. Burke may have carried his veneration for old establishments too far, and may not have made sufficient allowance for the imperfections of human nature in the conflict of the French Revolution,' wrote Davie to Judge Iredell, 'yet I think his letter contains a sufficient amount of intelligence to have rescued him from the undistinguishing abuse of Paine.'[1]

With most of the Federalist leaders in sympathy with Burke, few ventured to attack Paine in the open. Not so with Adams who was spluttering mad over the Jefferson 'preface.' He was positive that the publication of Paine's pamphlet in this country had been instigated by his former colleague at Paris.[2] To him the pamphlet of Paine, the 'preface' of Jefferson, the acclaim for both on the part of the people was but a devilish conspiracy of Jefferson's to pull him down. 'More of Jefferson's subterranean tricks.' And with this conviction, John Quincy Adams, the son, then in Boston, took up a trenchant pen to write the articles of 'Publicola' for the 'Centinel,' sneering at the Jeffersonian note to the printer, assailing Paine and democracy, and stoutly defending the governmental forms of England. So well did he discharge his filial duty that his articles were published in pamphlet form in England by the friends of Burke, and many of the Federalist papers reproduced them as they appeared.

Then the newspaper battle began in earnest. Many indignant democrats rushed to the attack of 'Publicola' with all the greater zest because of the belief that 'Publicola' was none other than 'Davila' himself. 'America will not attend to this antiquated sophistry,' wrote one, 'whether decorated by the gaudy ornaments of a Burke, the curious patch-work of a Parr to which all antiquity must have contributed its prettiest rags and tatters, or the homely

[1] McRee, *Iredell*, ii, 335.   [2] Adams, *Adams*, i, 454.

ungraceful garb which has been furnished her by Mr. John Adams.'[1] Another suggested that 'Publicola' would soon cease to write since 'the time for the new election is approaching,' although the 'Discourses' might be continued without danger since 'dullness, like the essence of opium, sets every reader to sleep before he has passed the third sentence.'[2] As for 'Publicola,' his letters were 'being brought forward to persuade the people that an hereditary nobility, and, of consequence, high salaries, pomp and parade are essential to the prosperity of the country.'[3] In Boston, where the letters were appearing, 'Agricola' and 'Brutus' began spirited replies in the rival paper.[4] Other writers, with less grace and force, joined in the fray. Who are to constitute our nobility, demanded 'Republican,' our moneyed men — the speculators? If so 'Dukes, Lords and Earls will swarm like insects gendered by the sun,' and the worn-out soldier who had been tricked out of his paper would have the satisfaction of 'bowing most submissively to their lordships while seated in their carriages.'[5]

But Adams was not without his defenders. 'An American' declared that all the abuse was 'designed as a political ladder by which to climb.' Miserable creatures! 'Ages after the tide of time has swept their names into oblivion, the immortal deeds of Adams will shine on the brightest pages of history.'[6] 'The Ploughman' indignantly resented the insinuation that Adams had written the 'Publicola' letters. In truth, 'his friends consider Dr. Adams as being calumniated' by having such sentiments ascribed to him.[7] To all the 'hornets' that were buzzing about Adams, Fenno felt he could be indifferent, for they had no stings. They were merely nonentities trying to give consequence to their scribblings by appearing to be answering the Vice-President.

Meanwhile, Jefferson was keenly enjoying the turmoil. We wish it were possible to trace it all to his contrivance, for nothing could have served his purpose better. To have foreseen that the writing of a few simple lines would have awakened the militant republicanism of the country and have aroused the democratic impulses of the inert mass would have been complimentary to his

[1] *New York Daily Advertiser*, July 8, 1791.
[2] *Ibid.*, July 9, 1791.
[3] *Ibid.*, July 14, 1791.
[4] *Independent Chronicle*, June 23, 1791.
[5] *Ibid.*, July 7, 1791.
[6] *Ibid.*, August 26, 1791.   [7] *Ibid.*

political genius. But this is not the only instance where a clever politician with the reputation of a magician has stumbled forward. There is no doubt that Jefferson was astonished and embarrassed on learning that the printer had made an unauthorized use of his personal note. He admitted to Washington that he had Adams's writings in mind, but that nothing was more remote from his thoughts than of becoming 'a contributor before the public.' However, he was not impressed with the reflections on his taste. 'Their real fear,' he added, 'is that this popular and republican pamphlet . . . is likely . . . to wipe out all the unconstitutional doctrines which their bellwether, Davilla, has been preaching for a twelve-month.' [1] This explanation was enough for Knox, who wrote accordingly to Adams,[2] but not enough for Jefferson who sent a frank explanation to Adams with an expression of regret. In generous mood, the latter accepted the explanation with the protestation that their old friendship was 'still dear to my heart,' and that 'there is no office I would not resign rather than give a just occasion for one friend to desert me.' [3]

Madison, to whom Jefferson had sent a similar explanation, had assumed that there had been a mistake or an imposition, but he could see no reason for indignation on the part of Adams or his friends. 'Surely,' he wrote, 'if it be innocent and decent for one servant of the public to write against its government, it cannot be very criminal or indecent in another to patronize a written defence of the principles on which that Government is founded.' [4]

However much Jefferson may have regretted the unauthorized use of his letter, he rejoiced in its effect. He wrote Paine that the controversy had awakened the people, shown the 'monocrats' that the silence of the masses concerning the teachings of 'Davilla' did not mean that they had been converted 'to the doctrine of king, lords and commons,' and that they were 'confirmed in their good old faith.' [5] The incident had established Jefferson in the public mind as the outstanding leader of democracy, had set the public tongue to wagging on politics again. More was involved in the pamphlets of Burke and Paine than differences over the French Revolution. The keynote of Burke's was aristocracy and privilege;

---

[1] Jefferson's *Works*, VIII, 192.   [2] Adams, *Works*, VIII, 503.   [3] *Ibid.*, 505.
[4] Madison's *Writings*, I, 535.   [5] Jefferson's *Works*, VIII, 223.

that of Paine's was democracy and equal rights. The former was the gospel of the American Federalists; the latter the covenant of the American Democracy. Studying the reactions with his characteristic keenness, Jefferson was convinced that the time was ripe to mobilize for the inevitable struggle.

VII

'What do you think of this scrippomony?' Jefferson wrote to Edward Rutledge in the late summer. 'Ships are lying idle at the wharfs, buildings are stopped, capital withdrawn from commerce, manufactures, arts and agriculture to be employed in gambling, and the tide of public prosperity . . . is arrested in its course. . . . I imagine that we shall hear that all the cash has quitted the extremities of the nation and accumulated here.'[1] As he wrote, Jefferson had before him the report of the craze which had just reached him in a letter from Madison in New York. 'Stock and scrip the sole domestic subjects of conversation . . . speculations . . . carried on with money borrowed at from two and a half per cent a month to one per cent a week.'[2]

Men grown reckless with the frenzy of the intoxication were resorting to fraud to rob the Government, many taking out administration papers for deceased soldiers who had left no heirs. 'By this knavery,' wrote Madison at an earlier period, 'a prodigious sum will be unsaved by the public, and reward the worst of its citizens.' And suppose one of the clerks of the account offices is not proof against the temptation?[3]

By the middle of the summer (July 10th) Bank stock had risen as much in the market in New York as in Philadelphia with the feeling that there was a certainty of gain. A scramble had set in 'for so much public plunder.' The meticulously scrupulous Madison, with his lofty notions of official propriety, was shocked to find 'the members of the Legislature who were most active in pushing this job openly grasping the emoluments.' Schuyler, the father-in-law of Hamilton, was to be the head of the directors of the Bank 'if the weight of the New York subscribers can effect it.' Stock-

[1] Jefferson's *Works*, VIII, 232.
[2] Madison's *Writings*, I, 540.
[3] *Ibid.*, I, 534.

jobbing monopolized all conversation. The coffee-houses buzzed with the gamblers.[1]

Meanwhile, from the high-placed to the ordinary scamp, men maddened, by the money-itch, were resorting to ordinary crime to get possession of public paper. In some places clever counterfeiters were driving through the country under the pretext of examining securities with the idea of purchase and cleverly exchanging the worthless for the real.[2] In the South and in the remote parts of Maine, swindlers were scouring the woods for State notes, lying to the uninformed and ignorant about their value, and getting them for a song. 'What must be the feelings of the widow and orphan,' wrote a correspondent of a Philadelphia paper, 'when they find themselves thus defrauded of a great part of their little all, and that, not unlikely, the earnings of their late husbands and fathers, who died in the service of their country, by these pests of society who ought to be despised?'[3] But greed knew no shame. An appalling picture: members of Congress feathering their nest through their legislative acts, counterfeiters robbing the unwary, common crooks stealing from the Government by posing as the administrators of the dead, and distinguished members of the Boston Bar, like Otis and Gore, speculating with their clients' money without their knowledge or consent.

So sinister was the situation that notes of warning began to appear in the newspapers. The 'Pennsylvania Gazette' found that speculators had 'turned raving mad, and others so agitated that they appear on the borders of insanity.'[4] Fenno tried vainly to restore sobriety to the drunk — for Hamilton himself was shocked and not a little concerned.[5] Better be careful about parting with Bank scrip, warned the 'New York Daily Advertiser.' Efforts were being made to buy up all the scrip in the city 'and for this purpose a powerful combination was formed . . . on Saturday night to reduce the price.'[6] Beware of another South Sea Bubble, warned 'Centinel' in the same paper. 'The National Bank stock has risen so high, so enormously above its real value, that no two transactions in the annals of history can be found to equal it . . .'[7]

[1] Madison's *Writings*, I, 538.   [2] *Maryland Journal*, February 15, 1791.
[3] *Pennsylvania Gazette*, September 7, 1791.   [4] August 17, 1791.
[5] Hamilton's *Works* (to King), I, 402.   [6] August 8, 1791.   [7] August 9, 1791.

From Boston came similar stories of the madness. All the while the New York papers were publishing day-by-day quotations on the scrip.[1] By August 15th the mania was at its height. 'It has risen like a rocket,' wrote an amused scribbler. 'Like a rocket it will burst with a crack and down drops the rocket stick. What goes up must come down — so take care of your pate, brother Jonathan.'[2] The craze was becoming ridiculous. The sane and the honest looked upon it as a spectacle. Above the angry cries in the market-place rang the laughter of the observers who kept their heads. Some put their scoffing into verse:

> 'What magic this among the people,
> That swells a Maypole to a steeple?'[3]

Suddenly the bubble showed signs of bursting. A New York bank stopped discounting for some of the speculators. Messengers hurried forth with the ominous news, horses' hoofs hammering the Jersey roads to Philadelphia, where there was consternation and a falling-off in buying.[4] Pay-day had not yet come, but it was on the way, and men began to regain their senses.

Then came the emergence of the political phase. 'Does history afford an instance,' asked one observer, 'where inequality in property, without any adequate consideration, ever before so suddenly took place in the world? or the basis of the power and influence of an Aristocracy was created?'[5] A Boston paper commented significantly on the ease with which the mere opening and closing of the galleries of Congress could serve the purposes of speculation. 'How easily might this be done should any member of Congress be inclined to speculate.'[6]

Thus the talk of a 'corrupt squadron' in the First Congress was not the invention of Jefferson — it was the talk of the highways and the byways, the coffee-houses and the taverns, and we find it recurring in the correspondence of the public men of the period.

---

[1] August 13, 1791. 'Scrips sold last night: Cash 212–202–210–206; 10 days, 216, 217½, 214; 30 days, 223, 212, 215; 45 days, 216; 60 days, 219; Sept. 10, 224; Deliver and pay December 1, 235; Deliver October 1 and pay January 1, 242; Monday next, 207; Tuesday, 215½, 217, 210.' (*New York Daily Advertiser.*)

[2] *Daily Advertiser*, August 15, 1791.   [3] *New York Daily Advertiser.*

[4] *Daily Advertiser*, August 17, 1791.

[5] *New York Daily Advertiser*, September 21, 1791.

[6] *Independent Chronicle*, September 1, 1791.

Everywhere sudden fortunes sprang up as if by magic. There was a rumbling and grumbling in the offing. With the people thinking more seriously of Madison's fight for discrimination, he began to loom along with Jefferson as a prospective leader against the 'system.' With the discovery that the law had been violated in the subscription of more than thirty shares, it was hoped that it would 'draw the attention of Madison . . . immediately on the meeting of Congress' and that 'the whole proceedings . . . be declared nugatory.'[1]

Then came the election of Bank directors in the fall, and indignation flamed when the prizes went to leaders in the Congress that had created the Bank — to Rufus King, Samuel Johnson of North Carolina, William Smith of South Carolina, Jeremiah Wadsworth of the 'fast sailing vessels,' John Laurance of New York, William Bingham of Philadelphia, Charles Carroll of Carrollton, George Cabot, Fisher Ames, and Thomas Willing, the partner of Robert Morris.

Members of Congress had speculated heavily and profitably on their knowledge of their own intent in legislation; they were owners of bank scrip of the Bank they created, and their leaders were on the board of directors. There was talk among the people of a 'corrupt squadron,' and Jefferson did not invent the term; he found it in the street and used it. Though Hamilton, scrupulously honest, was not involved in proceedings that were vicious, if not corrupt, many of his lieutenants were, and that, for the purposes of politics, made an issue.

But Hamilton was in the saddle, booted and spurred, and riding hard toward the realization of his conception of government, followed by an army that fairly glittered with the brilliancy of many of his field marshals, and which was imposing in the financial, social, and cultural superiority of the rank and file; an army that could count on the greater part of the press to publish its orders of the day, and on the beneficiaries of its policies to fill its campaign coffers. And it was at this juncture that Jefferson began the mobilization of an army that would seem uncouth and ragged by comparison. The cleavage was distinct; the ten-year war was on.

[1] *Independent Chronicle*, August 18, 1791.

As a preliminary to the story of the struggle, it is important to know more of the character and methods of the man who dared challenge Hamilton's powerful array and something of the social atmosphere in Philadelphia where the great battles were fought.

CHAPTER V

THOMAS JEFFERSON: A PORTRAIT

I

IN the personal appearance of Thomas Jefferson there was little to denote the powerful, dominating leader and strict disciplinarian that he was. Unlike Hamilton, he did not look the commander so much as the rather shy philosopher. The gruff Maclay, on seeing him for the first time, was disappointed with his slender frame, the looseness of his figure, and the 'air of stiffness in his manner,' while pleased with the sunniness of his face.[1] He was of imposing height, being more than six feet, and slender without being thin.[2] All contemporaries who have left descriptions refer to the long, loosely jointed limbs, and none of them convey an impression of grace. His hair, much redder than that of Hamilton, was combed loosely over the forehead and at the side, and tied behind. His complexion was light, his eyes blue and usually mild in expression, his forehead broad and high. Beneath the eyes, his face was rather broad, the cheek-bones high, the chin noticeably long, and the mouth of generous size. The casual glance discovered more of benevolence than force, more of subtlety than pugnacity. Nor, in that day of lace and frills, was there anything in his garb to proclaim him of the élite. His enemies then, and ever since, have made too much of his loose carpet slippers and worn clothes, and the only thing they prove is that he may have had the Lincolnian indifference to style. Long before he made his 'pose' in the President's house for the benefit of the groundlings, we find a critic who was to be numbered among his followers complaining because his clothes were too small for his body.[3] The truth, no doubt, is that he dressed conventionally, because men must, and was careless of his attire.

Certain it is that when she first met him, Mrs. Bayard Smith, who had been unduly impressed with the Federalist references to the 'coarseness and vulgarity of his manners,' was astonished at

[1] Maclay, 272.   [2] *Familiar Letters*, 148.   [3] Maclay, 272.

the contradiction of the caricature by the man. 'So meek and mild, yet dignified in his manners, with a voice so soft and low, with a countenance so benign and intelligent' she found him.[1] In truth there was enough dignity in his manner to discourage the stranger on a first approach, as Tom Moore found to his disgust. Even Mrs. Smith thought his 'dignified and reserved air' chill at first;[2] and a French admirer who made a sentimental journey to Monticello thought him somewhat cold and reserved.'[3] 'The cold first look he always cast upon a stranger'[4] appears too often in the observations of his contemporaries to have been imaginary.

As some have found fault with his dress, others have criticized a slovenly way of sitting — 'in a lounging manner, on one hip commonly, with one of his shoulders elevated much above the other';[5] while another — a woman too — was charmed at the 'free and easy manner' in which he accepted a proffered chair.[6] The natural deduction from the contradictions is that he seated himself as comfortably as possible with little regard to the picture in the pose. There is a manifest absurdity in the idea that the man who moved familiarly in the most cultured circles of the most polished capital in Europe could have been either impossible in dress or boorish in manner.

But there is one unpleasant criticism of his manner that cannot be so easily put aside — a shiftiness in his glance which bears out the charge of his enemies that he was lacking in frankness. The most democratic member of the first Senate, meeting him for the first time, was disappointed to find that 'he had a rambling vacant look, and nothing of that firm collected deportment which I expected would dignify the presence of a Secretary or Minister.'[7] Another found that 'when speaking he did not look at his auditor, but cast his eyes toward the ceiling or anywhere but at the eye of his auditor.'[8] This weakness was possibly overemphasized, for he was notoriously shy.

Aside from this, there is abundant evidence that there was an ineffable charm in his manner. One who objected to his 'shifty glance' was favorably impressed with 'the simplicity and sobriety'

[1] Mrs. Smith, 6.   [2] *Ibid.*, 6–7.   [3] Liancourt, III, 157.
[4] Parton on the Moore incident, III, 115–19.   [5] Maclay, 272.
[6] Mrs. Smith, 6–7.   [7] Maclay, 272.   [8] *Familiar Letters*, 149.

of his deportment, and found that while 'he was quiet and unob-
trusive . . . a stranger would perceive that he was in the presence
of one who was not a common man.'[1] He was free of the affectations of pedantry, courteous and kindly, modest and tolerant.
Thus he appeared to excellent advantage in conversation, and,
with one exception, all who knew him and have left their impressions found him an entertaining and illuminating talker. Maclay,
who was certainly not the most competent of judges, thought his
conversation 'loose and rambling,' and yet admitted that 'he scattered information wherever he went, and some even brilliant sentiments sparkled from him.'[2] It is probable that the gout-racked
radical confused conversation with set speeches, and quite as possible that on this particular occasion, when Jefferson was meeting
with a curious senatorial committee, he was not inclined to tell all
he knew.

Certainly the polished nobleman, familiar with the most intellectual circles of Paris, who found his 'conversation of the most
agreeable kind,' and that he possessed 'a stock of information not
inferior to that of any other man,' and 'in Europe . . . would hold a
distinguished rank among men of letters,' was quite as competent
a judge as the Senator from the wilderness of Pennsylvania.[3]
Among men his manner of conversation was calm and deliberate,
without the Johnsonian *ex-cathedra* touch, and yet he 'spoke like
one who considered himself as entitled to deference.'[4] Among
friends, and particularly women, he appears to have been deferen-
tial and captivating in his tactful kindness. Then when, 'with a
manner and voice almost femininely soft and gentle,' he 'entered
into conversation on the commonplace topics of the day,' at least
one woman found that 'there was something in his manner, his
countenance and voice that at once unlocked [her] heart.'[5]

Such was the Jefferson seen superficially by his contemporaries.

II

Those who prefer to think of Jefferson as an aristocrat, born to
the purple, who departed from the paths of his fathers, refer only
to the maternal ancestry. The American founder of this branch

---

[1] *Familiar Letters*, 148. [2] Maclay, 272. [3] Liancourt, III, 157.
[4] *Familiar Letters*, 148. [5] Mrs. Smith, 6-7.

of the family liked to think of himself as the descendant of gentlemen of title and of the half-brother of Queen Mary. Jefferson preferred to dismiss this claim on the aristocracy with the statement that his mother's family traced 'their pedigree far back in England and Scotland, to which let every one ascribe the faith and merit he chooses.' From the Randolphs he probably inherited his love of beauty, his fondness for luxury, but they failed utterly to transmit to him any aristocratic notions of government. There was a reason — his father was a middle-class farmer, and it was from him and his early environment that he received his earliest and most lasting political impressions.

This father was no ordinary man. Physically a giant, he was big in mind and strong in character. By the light of the log fire in the evenings, he was wont to read Shakespeare, Swift, and Addison to his family. An ardent Whig with advanced democratic ideas, he as a magistrate manifested sympathy for the plain people.[1] His thousand acres at Shadwell were in the wilderness and on the frontier, and his son was as much a Westerner in his boyhood as is the boy of Idaho to-day, for the West is a relative term.

This Western boy at the most impressionable age was sent to school in Louisa County, which was then the hot-bed of radical democracy and Presbyterian dissent. The natives about him were in buckskin breeches and Indian moccasins, and, with no coat over their rough hunting shirts, they covered their heads with coonskin caps. It was a long cry from the polished circles of Boston, New York, and Philadelphia to this typical Western scene; if one was the East, the other was the West. The small proprietor farmers lived in crude cabins, and theirs was the hard lot of the pioneer. Thus Jefferson's training was that of the Westerner.[2]

The boy was father to the man. When he entered college at Williamsburg, he found himself in the headquarters of the aristocracy, for there, at the capital, the lords of the land had their winter homes where lavish hospitality was displayed. Into this society Jefferson was thrown, and he moved therein as to the manor born — at heart a Western man with Eastern polish.[3] It was not for nothing that there was Randolph blood in his veins.

[1] Randall, I, 14.
[2] Dodd, *Statesmen of the Old South*, 3–4.   [3] *Ibid.*, 9.

Even as he moved among the hard-drinking, fox-hunting imitators of the English squires, his sympathies were enlisted in the growing democratic movement of the small farmers among the upper rivers, the tobacco-growers, the hunters and trappers of the Alleghany slopes. The western counties, then the western frontier, had been populated by the Scotch-Irish and Germans — earnest, hard-working, hard-thinking men, who wrestled with nature as with their consciences, built churches in the woods, and school-houses in the clearing. These men were democrats, and their cause became the cause of Jefferson even while he was in college. Volumes have been written to explain Jefferson, but it was reserved for Professor William E. Dodd to do it in a paragraph:

It is not difficult . . . to see how the great principle of Jefferson's life — absolute faith in democracy — came to him. He was the product of the first West in American history; he grew up with men who ruled their country well, who fought the Indians valiantly. . . . Jefferson loved his backwoods neighbors, and he, in turn, was loved by them.[1]

If in college he was confirming his faith in democracy, born of his schooling in the land of the small farmers, he was burnishing his weapons for the fight. It is significant that he disliked Blackstone and liked Coke because he found the former a teacher of Toryism and the latter a reflector of the philosophy of the Whigs. His training in the law was thorough, for he studied under George Wythe, with whom both Marshall and Clay received their legal schooling. The friendship of Professor Small encouraged his natural spirit of toleration and investigation; and at the 'palace' of Francis Fauquier, the gay and brilliant royal governor — 'a gentleman of the school of Louis XV translated into England by Charles II, and into English by Lord Chesterfield'[2] he formed his literary tastes and learned the virtues of literary style. Thus assiduous in his studies, reasonably circumspect in his morals, and profiting immeasurably by contact with superior minds, he was receiving an intensive preparation for his future labors. In the seclusion of his room he communed with Coke and Milton, Harrington and Locke, and the time was to come when his most notable literary production was to disclose, in word and phrase, the influence of the latter. Locke, not Rousseau, was the well from

[1] Dodd, *Statesmen of the Old South*, 23.   [2] Parton's *Jefferson*, I, 27.

which he drew; and there is no sillier assertion in history than that his democracy was born of association with the men of the French Revolution.

III

Long before there were levelers in France, Jefferson was a leveler in Virginia; and because he was a leveler in Virginia, the reactionaries who resented his reforms were afterward to charge his democracy to the influence of the levelers of Paris. His democracy was inherent, in part inherited from a pioneer father. His dislike of the aristocratic system amounted to a prejudice, and he could not bear the novels of Scott because of his detestation of the institutions of medieval times.[1] Having written the Declaration of Independence in the house of a bricklayer, he declined a reëlection to Congress to enter the House of Burgesses in Virginia to revamp the institutions of the State along democratic lines. When he finished his work there, he had made himself one of the foremost democrats of all times — and the French Revolution was still in the distance.

The Virginia system had been made for caste society; the landed aristocracy were as much a caste as that in England — minus the titles. They had the same love of land, the same obsession that the alienation of any part of their possessions was treason to the family. Through the system of entail, the lands and slaves of the aristocracy could be passed on down through the generations, proof against the extravagance and inefficiency of the owners and the attacks of creditors. The law of primogeniture was designed to serve the same general end of preventing the disruption of the great estates. With a fine audacity, Jefferson sallied forth quite gayly to attack them both. Even Henry thought this was radicalism gone mad. Pendleton was more hurt than outraged. The aristocratic members of his mother's family looked upon him as a matricide. Undaunted by the hate engendered, he put his hand to the plough and kept it there until he had ploughed the field and prepared it for a democratic harvest. His friend Pendleton begged a compromise on primogeniture giving the eldest son a double share of the land. 'Yes,' replied the leveler, 'when he can eat twice

[1] Randall, III, 448.

the allowance of food and do double the allowance of work.' It was his purpose to eradicate 'every fibre of ancient or future aristocracy.'[1] The outraged landed aristocracy never forgave him. He was the first American to invite the hate of a class, and from the beginning he turned his back on the aristocracy and made his appeal to the middle-class yeomanry.[2] All this was behind him when he went to Paris before the Revolution there began. There the tall, slender American in the elegant house on the Grande Route des Champs Élysées, with its extensive gardens and court, was an impressive figure. 'You replace Doctor Franklin, I hear,' said Vergennes, the Minister of Foreign Affairs. 'I succeed him,' Jefferson replied; 'nobody could replace him.' There could have been no more ingratiating reply, for his predecessor had been greatly admired and loved.

No one could have found the conversation of the salons and dinner tables more congenial. His manners were those of a man of the world, and he shared the French fondness for speculative talk, and the French knack of spicing gravity with frivolity. Even his table tastes were similar. He ate sparingly and preferred the light wines. Both his natural hospitality and his respect for the dignity of his position spread the reputation of his lavish table; and while he gave no great parties, gay and frequent dinners were the rule. Lafayette ran in and out constantly; members of the diplomatic set found Jefferson's house an agreeable meeting-place; the young French officers who had served in America liked his company, and De la Tude, the wit, who had served thirty-five years in prison for writing an epigram on Pompadour, enlivened many an evening with his reminiscences. American tourists were captivated by his civilities, introductions to celebrities, itineraries for profitable trips. Like Franklin before him, he charmed the beautiful women of the court with his wit and humor, and the eloquence of his conversation. He loved the promenades and shops, and was constantly alert for something unusual to send his friends at home — rare books for Madison, Monroe, and Wythe, a portable table for Madison, an artistic lamp for Lee. And yet he was far from an elegant idler, and his days were laboriously passed; mornings at his office, afternoons given to country walks, evenings to society, art,

---

[1] *Autobiography*, i, 77.   [2] Fiske, 148.

music. He found time for elaborate and illuminating reports that are models in diplomatic literature and which exacted tribute from even John Marshall. Feeling frequently the need of absolute seclusion for his work, he had rooms in the Carthusian Monastery on Mount Calvary where silence was enjoined outside the rooms, but where he had the privileges of the garden.

'I am much pleased with the people of this country,' he wrote a lady. 'The roughness of the human mind is so thoroughly rubbed off with them, that it seems one might glide through a whole life without a jostle.'[1] And in another letter, the same impression: 'Here it seems a man might pass a life without encountering a single rudeness.'[2] But if he loved the society of Paris, he was not, like Morris, seduced into an acceptance of its system. His passion for democracy did not permit him to judge the happiness of a nation by the luxuries of the court and aristocracy. He struck out into the country to judge for himself of the condition of the peasants, looked into the pots on the fire to see what they ate, felt their beds to see if they were comfortable. He inquired into the wages and the working conditions of the artisans of the cities — and his conclusions were unavoidable, of course. 'It is a fact,' he wrote, 'in spite of the mildness of their governors, the people are ground to powder by their form of government. Of twenty million people supposed to be in France, I am of opinion there are nineteen million more wretched, more accursed in every circumstance of human existence than the most conspicuously wretched individual in the whole United States.'[3] And to another: 'I find the general fate of humanity here most deplorable. The truth of Voltaire's observation offers itself perpetually, that every man here is either the hammer or the anvil.'[4] He was shocked by a system that dedicated the sons of peasants as cannon fodder in remote wars precipitated by the whims of a prostitute; that winked at the debauchery of their wives and daughters; that gave men to the Bastile for the expression of a criticism; that crushed the people with intolerable taxation to sustain the luxury of a few; that forced the poor to live on food not fit for a stray dog in a city slums, and which awed the masses into submission to such conditions by the

[1] *Works* (to Mrs. Trist), v, 151.   [2] *Ibid.* (to Bellini), v, 151.
[3] *Ibid.* (to Mrs. Trist), v, 81–82.   [4] *Ibid.* (to Bellini), v, 151–54.

bayonets of the soldiery. This was the France of which he thought in the day when his sympathy with the Revolution was to damn him with the Federalists' taunt of 'Jacobin' and 'anarchist.'

Such being his observations and views, he rejoiced in the popular awakening in the dawning days of the Revolution. Witnessing the meeting of the Assembly of the Notables, a fascinated spectator of the razing of the Bastile, listening, deeply moved, to the audacious eloquence of Mirabeau, he wrote, with the joy of the reformer, to Washington that 'the French nation has been awakened by our Revolution.' It was in those days that Gouverneur Morris, the friend of Hamilton, was accustomed to drop in on Jefferson for a chat on the situation, and their friendly disagreements were soon to appear in a party division in America. 'He and I differ,' wrote Morris in his diary, 'in our system of politics. He with all the leaders of liberty here is desirous of annihilating distinctions of order.'[1] And yet he was not hostile to the King or the monarchy. He hoped for reforms, freely granted. Louis he found 'irascible, rude, very limited in his understanding,' with 'no mistress,' but governed too much by the Queen — 'devoted to pleasure and expense, and not remarkable for any other vices or virtues.'[2] As the storm-clouds lowered and the easy-going monarch remained inert, he became less tolerant. 'The King, long in the habit of drowning his cares in wine, plunges deeper and deeper. The Queen cries but sins on. The Count d'Artois is detested.'[3] And a month later: 'The King goes for nothing. He hunts one half the day, is drunk the other, and signs whatever he is bid.'[4]

As the future Terrorists ascended from the cellars and descended from the garrets, and occasional riots gave premonitory signs of the bloody days ahead, he reported to Jay that the rioting was the work of the 'abandoned banditti of Paris,' and had no 'professed connection with the great national reformation going on.'[5]

All this time he was being constantly consulted by Lafayette and the moderate leaders who were to become the members of the attractive but unfortunate party of the Gironde. They even met at his dinner table to make plans, without notifying him of their

---

[1] Morris, *Diary*, I, 101.
[2] *Domestic Life* (letter to Madison), 155; *Works*, I, 131–38.
[3] *Domestic Life* (letter to Adams), 156.   [4] *Ibid.* (to Jay), 156.
[5] *Ibid.* (to Jay), 159.

intent, and his voluntary explanation to the Minister was received with the expression of a hope that he might be able to assist in an accommodation of differences. He did, in fact, propose a plan, which, had it been accepted, might have saved the monarchy. It was his suggestion that Louis step forward with a charter in his hands, granting liberty of the person, of conscience, of the press, a trial by jury, an annual legislature with the power of taxation, and with a ministry responsible to the people.[1] These associations and these views are conclusive as to the absurdity that he was permeated with the theories of Jacobinism and brought them back to the United States. He was the same kind of Jacobin as Lafayette. His interest was the interest in democracy and popular rights that he had taken with him when he sailed for Europe. Mirabeau was still laboring to save the monarchy with reforms when Jefferson returned to America on leave.

IV

Jefferson was a humanitarian ahead of his time. His humanity spoke above the passions of the Revolution in his letter to Patrick Henry against the mistreatment of the German prisoners. 'Is an enemy so execrable,' he wrote, 'that though in captivity his wishes and comforts are to be disregarded and even crossed? I think not. It is for the benefit of mankind to mitigate the horrors of war as much as possible.'[2] These captives, interned near Monticello, came to love the master on the hill for his efforts to lighten the burdens of their captivity.[3] A little later, in the Virginia Legislature, we find him opposing the death penalty except for treason and murder, and the policy of working convicts on the highways and canals. 'Exhibited as a public spectacle,' he wrote, 'with shaved heads and mean clothing, working on the highroads produced in the criminals such a prostration of self-respect, as, instead of reforming, plunged them into the most desperate and hardened depravity.'[4] It was novel then to hear men speaking of reform instead of punishment.

That this humanitarian impulse was not confined to people at a

---

[1] *Works* (letter to Lafayette), VII, 370; (to De St. Etienne), VII, 370–72; (the Charter), VII, 372–74.

[2] *Ibid.*, IV, 72.   [3] *Ibid.* (to De Unger), IV, 138–39.   [4] *Autobiography*, I, 72.

distance is shown in his relations to his own servants, both the employees and the slaves. A woman of fashion commented on 'the most perfect servants at the White House' during his eight years there and the significant circumstance that 'none left.'[1] But we must turn to his relations with his slaves to find him at his best. One picture will suffice. It is on the occasion of his return to Monticello from his French mission. At the foot of the hill all the slaves in their gaudiest attire are assembled to greet him. The carriage appears down the road. The slaves, laughing, shouting, rush forward to welcome him, unhitch the horses to draw the carriage up the steep hill, some pulling, some pushing, and others huddled in a dark mass close around the vehicle. Some kiss his hands, others his feet, and it is long after he reaches the house before he is permitted to enter. This was long before the day when correspondents with cameras pursued public men and demonstrations were staged.[2] Here was a master who loved his slaves.

Nor can there be any possible doubt as to his hostility to slavery. One of the features of his Virginia reforms was abolition. While he failed, he never doubted that ultimately the chains would fall. 'Nothing is more certainly written in the book of fate than that these people are to be free,' he wrote in his 'Autobiography.'[3] A little later, referring to his strictures on slavery in his 'Notes on Virginia,' he expressed a desire to get them to the young men in the colleges. 'It is to them I look, to the rising generation, and not to the one now in power, for these great reformations.'[4] Declining membership in a society for abolition in France on the ground that his official status would make improper a demonstration against an institution his own people were retaining, he said that 'it is decent of me to avoid too public a demonstration of my wishes to see it [slavery] abolished.'[5] Without any of this evidence, his hostility to slavery would be irrefutably established by the Ordinance of the Northwest Territory, in the handwriting of Jefferson in the archives of the Nation, prohibiting slavery in any of the States that might be carved therefrom after the year 1800.

[1] Mrs. Wharton, 391.   [2] Parton's *Jefferson*, I, 344.   [3] Vol. I, 77.
[4] *Works*, V, 3–4: letter to Chastellus.   [5] *Ibid.*, VI, 428: to Warville.

V

Such is the persistency of falsehood that Jefferson has come down to us vaguely as an atheist and an enemy of the Christian religion. Since this charge is to play a part in the political story we are about to tell, it calls for some attention. He was brought up in the Church of England, and his earliest recollection was of saying the Lord's Prayer when his dinner was delayed.[1] He planned at least one church and contributed to the erection of others, gave freely to Bible Societies, and liberally to the support of the clergy. He attended church with normal regularity, taking his prayer book to the services and joining in the responses and prayers of the congregation. No human being ever heard him utter a word of profanity. During the period of his social ostracism by the intolerant partisans of Philadelphia, he passed many evenings with Dr. Rush in conversation on religion.[2] 'I am a Christian,' he once said, 'in the only sense in which Jesus wished any one to be — sincerely attached to his doctrines in preference to all others.' On one occasion when a man of distinction expressed his disbelief in the truths of the Bible, he said, 'Then, sir, you have studied it to little purpose.'[3] While the New England pulpits were ringing with denunciations of this 'infidel,' and old ladies, unable to detect the false witness of the partisan clergy, were solemnly hiding their Bibles to prevent their confiscation by the 'atheist' in the President's House, he was spending his nights in the codification of the 'Morals of Jesus,' and through the remainder of his life he was to read from this every night before retiring.[4] In his last days he spent much time reading the Greek dramatists and the Bible, dwelling in conversation on the superiority of the moral system of Christ over all others. In his dying hour, after taking leave of his family, he was heard to murmur, 'Lord, now lettest Thy servant depart in peace.'[5]

The reason for the myth created against him is not far to seek. Just as the landed aristocracy of Virginia pursued him with increasing venom because of his land reforms, the clergy hated him

[1] Randall, i, 17.   [2] *Ibid.*, iii, 556–58; letter to Rush.
[3] *Ibid.*, 671–76.
[4] *Ibid.*; also see *The Thomas Jefferson Bible*, edited by Henry Jackson.
[5] Randall, iii, 547.

for forcing the separation of Church and State. When he made the fight for this reform, it was a crime not to baptize a child into the Episcopal Church; a crime to bring a Quaker into the colony; and, according to the law, a heretic could be burned. If the latter law was not observed, that compelling all to pay tithes regardless of their religious affiliations and opinions was rigidly enforced. This outraged Jefferson's love of liberty. The Presbyterians, Baptists, and Methodists, who were making inroads on the membership of the Established Church, were prosecuted, and their ministers were declared disturbers of the peace and thrown into jail like common felons. Patrick Henry and his followers fought Jefferson's plan for a disestablishment — but he won.[1] The 'atheist' law, which was never forgiven by the ministers of Virginia and Connecticut, was simple and brief:

No man shall be compelled to frequent or support any religious worship, place or ministry whatsoever, nor shall be enforced, restrained, molested or burdened in his mind or goods, nor shall otherwise suffer on account of his religious opinions or belief; but all men shall be free to profess, and by argument to maintain, their opinions in matters of religion, and the same shall in no wise diminish, enlarge, or affect their civil capacities.

Here we have the secret of the animus of the clergy of the time — but there were other reasons. In his 'Notes on Virginia' he did not please the orthodox, and Dr. Mason, a fashionable political minister of New York City, exposed him in the pulpit, holding him up to scorn as a 'profane philosopher' and an 'infidel.' Discussing the theory that the marine shells found on the high mountains were proof of the universal deluge, Jefferson had rejected it. 'Aha,' cried Mason, 'he derides the Mosaic account'; he 'sneers at the Scriptures' and with 'malignant sarcasm.' When Jefferson, referring to the tillers of the soil, wrote that they were 'the chosen people of God if ever He had a chosen people,' and referred to Christ as 'good if ever man was,' the minister charged him with 'profane babbling.'[2]

His view of creation is set forth in a letter discussing a work by Whitehurst. He believed that a Supreme Being created the earth and its inhabitants; that if He created both, He could have

[1] Dodd, *Statesmen of the Old South*, 36.   [2] Randall, iii, 620–22.

created both at once, or created the earth and waited ages for it
to get form itself before He created man; but he believed that
it was created in a state of fluidity and not in its present solid
form. This was his infidelity. He probably did not believe that
Jonah was swallowed by the whale — and that was enough to
damn him. But if he was not a Christian, the pulpits are teem-
ing with atheists to-day.[1]

VI

We have seen that Hamilton had no faith in the Constitution,
but did yeoman service for its ratification; we have the charge
that Jefferson was hostile to both; and the truth is that he was
hostile to neither and favorable to both. The evidence is overwhelming.

When the new form of government was under consideration,
he proposed 'to make the States one in everything connected with
foreign nations, and several as to everything purely domestic,' and
to separate the executive, legislative, and judicial branches.[2] He
was bitterly hostile to any plan based on the monarchical idea, and
advised its friends 'to read the fable of the frogs who solicited
Jupiter for a King.'[3] When the Convention met, he wrote Adams
that it was 'really an assembly of demigods,' but regretted that
they began their deliberations 'by so abominable a precedent as
that of tying up the tongues of the members.'[4] His first impressions of the completed document were unfavorable. In a letter to
Adams he complained of the reëligibility of the President.[5] To
another correspondent he complained that the proposed system
would merge the States into one without protecting the people
with a bill of rights.[6]

Writing to Madison, he went more into detail, balancing the
good against the bad. He liked the separation of the departments,
endorsed the lodging of the power of initiating money bills with
the representatives of the people, and was 'captivated with the

<hr>

[1] *Works*, VI, 11–15; to Charles Thompson.

[2] *Ibid.*, 227–29 (to Edward Carrington); 269–71 (to J. Blair).

[3] *Ibid.*, 296–301 (to Benjamin Hawkins and George Wythe); 231–32 (to Count Del
Vermi).

[4] *Ibid.*, 285–89; to John Adams.   [5] *Ibid.*, 368.

[6] *Ibid.*, 378–83; to William Carmichael.

compromise of the opposite claims of the great and little States';
but he insisted that a bill of rights 'is what the people are entitled
to against every government on earth, general or particular, and
what no just government should refuse or rest in inference.' Pro-
fessing himself 'no friend to a very energetic government' as 'always oppressive,' he added that should the people approve the Constitution in all its parts he should 'concur in it cheerfully in hopes
that they will amend it whenever they think it works wrong.' [1]

Little more than a month later he had become an ardent friend
of ratification. 'I wish with all my soul,' he wrote, 'that the nine
first Conventions may accept the Constitution; because this may
secure to us the good it contains, which I think great and important. But I equally wish that the four latest Conventions, whichever they may be, may refuse to accede to it till a declaration of
rights is annexed.' [2]

When the Massachusetts Convention accepted with 'perpetual
instructions to her Delegates to endeavor to secure reforms,' he
was delighted,[3] and the same day he wrote another correspondent
of his pleasure at the progress made toward ratification. 'Indeed
I have presumed that it would gain on the public mind as I confess it has on my own.' [4] When South Carolina acted, he wrote
E. Rutledge his congratulations. 'Our government wanted brac-
ing,' he said. 'Still we must take care not to run from one extreme
to another; not to brace too high.' [5] When the requisite nine States
had ratified, he wrote Madison in a spirit of rejoicing. 'It is a good
canvas on which some strokes only want retouching. What these
are I think are sufficiently manifested by the general voice from
North to South which calls for a bill of rights.' [6]

After the ratification, he wrote Madison in praise of 'The Federalist,' describing it as 'the best commentary on government
ever written,' and admitting that it had 'rectified' him on many
points.[7] In the same vein he wrote to Washington, expressing the
hope that a bill of rights would be speedily added.[8] In the spring of

[1] *Works*, vi, 385–93.
[2] *Ibid.*, 425–27. I have the authority of Josephus Daniels for a tradition in North Carolina that such a letter in the hands of Willie Jones was responsible for the failure of the first
Convention there to ratify. The letter is apparently lost.
[3] *Ibid.*, vii, 26–30; to Carmichael.   [4] *Ibid.*, 36–39; to Colonel Carrington.
[5] *Ibid.*, 79–88.   [6] *Ibid.*, 93–99.   [7] *Ibid.*, 183–87.   [8] *Ibid.*, 223–31.

1789 he wrote another that the Constitution was 'unquestionably the wisest ever yet presented to men.'[1] And after the Bill of Rights had been added, he wrote to Lafayette that 'the opposition to the Constitution has almost totally disappeared' and that 'the amendments proposed by Congress have brought over almost all' of the objectors.[2]

Years afterward, when he wrote his 'Autobiography,' he reviewed his reactions on the document: 'I received a copy early in November,' he wrote, 'and read and contemplated its provisions, with great satisfaction. ... The absence of express declarations, ensuring freedom of religious worship, freedom of the press, freedom of the person under the uninterrupted protection of the Habeas Corpus & trial by jury in civil as well as in criminal cases excited my jealousy; and the reëligibility of the President for life I quite disapproved. I expressed freely in letters to my friends, and most particularly to Mr. Madison and General Washington, my approbations and objections.'[3] His recollections were true to the facts as conclusively shown in the correspondence to which reference has been made.

He was no more opposed to the Constitution and its ratification than he was an atheist.

VII

This brings us to Jefferson the creator and leader of a party, and his methods of management. Here he was without a peer in the mastery of men. He intuitively knew men, and when bent upon it could usually bend them to his will. He was a psychologist and could easily probe the minds and hearts of those he met. In his understanding of mass psychology, he had no equal. When a measure was passed or a policy adopted in Philadelphia, he knew the reactions in the woods of Georgia without waiting for letters and papers. This rare insight into the mass mind made him a brilliantly successful propagandist. In every community he had his correspondents with whom he communicated with reasonable regularity, doing more in this way to mould and direct the policies of his party than could have been done in any other way. Seldom has there lived a more tireless and voluminous letter-writer. With

[1] *Works*, VII, 319–24.   [2] *Ibid.*, VIII, 10–13.   [3] *Autobiography*, I, 118.

all the powerful elements arrayed against him, he appreciated the importance of the press as did few others. 'I desired you in my last to send me the newspapers, notwithstanding the expense,' he wrote a friend from Paris.[1] Believing that the people, in possession of the facts, would reach reasonable conclusions, he considered newspapers a necessary engine of democracy. 'If left to me,' he once wrote, 'to decide whether we should have a government without newspapers, or newspapers without a government, I should not hesitate for a moment to prefer the latter.'[2] There is not a scintilla of evidence to confute his stout contention that he never wrote for the papers anonymously, but the evidence piles mountain high to prove that he constantly inspired the tone of the party press.

In his personal contacts he was captivating — a master of diplomacy and tact, born of his intuitive knowledge of men. Perhaps no better illustration of his cleverness in analyzing men can be found than in his letter to Madison on De Moustier, a newly appointed French Minister to the United States. 'De M. is remarkably communicative. With adroitness he may be pumped of anything. His openness is from character, not affectation. An intimacy with him may, on this account, be politically valuable.'[3]

In his leadership we find more of leading than of driving. He had a genius for gently and imperceptibly insinuating his own views into the minds of others and leaving them with the impression that they had conceived the ideas and convinced Jefferson. To Madison this was a source of keen delight.[4] Jefferson was the original 'Easy Boss.' His tact was proverbial. He never sought to overshadow or overawe. Inferior men were not embarrassed or depressed in his presence. He was amazingly thoughtful and considerate. In a company he instinctively went to the assistance of the neglected. Thus at a dinner party, a guest, long absent from the country, and unknown to the diners, was left out of the conversation and ignored. In a momentary silence, Jefferson turned to him. 'To you, Mr. C., we are indebted for this benefit —' he said, 'no one deserves more the gratitude of his country.' The other guests were all attention. 'Yes, sir, the upland rice which you sent from Al-

---

[1] *Works*, v, 147; to F. Hopkinson.   [2] *Ibid.*, vi, 55–58; to Carrington.
[3] *Ibid.*, 335–36.   [4] Randall, i, 404–05.

giers, and which thus far succeeds, will, when generally adopted by
the planters, prove an inestimable blessing to our Southern States.'
After that the neglected guest became the lion of the dinner.[1]
Thoughtfulness in small things — this entered not a little into
Jefferson's hold on his followers.

It was at the dinner table that he planned many of his battles.
He did not care for the stormy and contentious atmosphere of a
caucus. He was not an orator. In the Continental Congress he
was disgusted by the 'rage for debate.' [2] Later he was to find his
lot in the Cabinet intolerable because he and Hamilton were
constantly pitted against each other 'like cocks in a pit.' He was
not afraid of a fight, but the futility of angry controversy repelled
him. It was this which made him a delightful dinner host — all
controversial subjects that might offend were taboo. If his position
were warmly controverted, he changed the subject tactfully. It
was never the opposition that interested him, but the reason for it;
and with rare subtlety he would seek to obliterate the prejudice,
if it were prejudice, or to remove the misunderstanding if it were
ignorance of facts. Thus he won many victories through a seeming
retreat.[3]

Unescapable quarrels and separations were minor tragedies to
him. He long sought to get along with Hamilton. He advised his
daughters to be tolerant of disagreeable people and acted on his
own advice. Fiske has explained him in a sentence: 'He was in no
wise lacking in moral courage, but his sympathies were so broad
and tender that he could not breathe freely in an atmosphere of
strife.' [4] Thus considerate of his foes, he never hurt the sensibilities
of his friends through offensive methods. He liked to gather his
lieutenants about him at the table and 'talk it out' — each man
free to give his views. Here he ironed out differences, dominating by the superiority of his intellect and fascinating personality
while appearing singularly free from domination.

In his power of self-control Jefferson had another advantage
over his leading political opponents. There was something uncanny in his capacity to simulate ignorance of the hate that often
encompassed him. To the most virulent of his foes he was the pink

---

[1] Mrs. Smith, 389.   [2] *Autobiography*, I, 90.
[3] Randall, II, 403–04.   [4] Fiske, 154.

of courtesy. He mastered others by mastering himself. And because he was master of himself, he had another advantage — he kept his judgment clear as to the capacity and character of his opponents. One may search in vain through the letters of Hamilton for expressions other than those of contemptuous belittlement of his political foes. Jefferson never made that mistake. He conceded Hamilton's ability and admired it. Visitors at Monticello, manifesting surprise at finding busts by Ceracchi of Hamilton and Jefferson, facing each other across the hall, elicited the smiling comment — 'opposite in death as in life.' There never would have been a bust of Jefferson at 'The Grange.' Through the long years of estrangement with Adams, Jefferson kept the way clear for the restoration of their old relations. Writing Madison of Adams's faults, he emphasized his virtues and lovable qualities. When the bitter battles of their administrations were in the past and a mutual friend wrote that the old man at Quincy had said, 'I always loved Jefferson and always shall,' he said, 'That is enough for me,' and set to work to revive the old friendship. Thus the time came when in reply to Jefferson's congratulations on the election of John Quincy Adams in 1824, Adams wrote: 'I call him our John because when you were at the Cul de Sac at Paris, he appeared to me to be almost as much your boy as mine.'[1] This capacity for keeping his judgment clear of the benumbing fumes of prejudice concerning the qualities of his enemies was one of the strong points of his leadership.

This does not mean that in practical politics Jefferson was a 'Miss Nancy' or a 'Sister Sue.' This first consummate practical politician of the Republic did not consider it practical to underestimate the foe, nor to dissipate his energy and cloud his judgment by mere prejudices and hates. He was not an idealist in his methods, and this has given his enemies a peg on which to hang the charge that he was dishonest. He was an opportunist, to be sure; he never refused the half loaf he could get because of the whole loaf he could not have. He trimmed his sails at times to save his craft — and this was wisdom. He compromised at the call of necessity. He was hard-headed and looked clear-eyed at the realities about him. He was cunning, for without cunning he

[1] Adams, *Works*, x, 414.

could not have overcome a foe so powerfully entrenched. He was as elusive as a shadow, and this has been called cowardice — but it was difficult to trap him in consequence. His antipathy to the frontal attack has often been referred to with contempt, but, leading a large but unorganized army against one of tremendous power, he preferred the methods of Washington in the field — which was to avoid the frontal attack with his ragged Continentals against the trained and disciplined army. Because of these conditions he was given to mining. When apparently quiescent, he was probably sowing discord among his foes — his part concealed. This was hateful to the Federalists — just as the tactics of Frederick were hateful to the exasperated superior forces against him.

Jefferson was the most resourceful politician of his time. For every problem he had a solution. He teemed with ideas. These were his shock troops. If he seemed motionless, it was because by a nod or look he had put his forces on the march. Like the wiser of the modern bosses, he knew the virtue of silence. When in doubt, he said nothing. When certain of his course, he said nothing — to his foes. It was impossible to smoke him out when he preferred to stay in. In the midst of abuse he was serene. And he was a stickler for party regularity.[1] He appreciated the possibilities of organization and discipline. When money was needed for party purposes, his friends would receive a note: 'I have put you down for so much.' When the party paper languished, he circulated subscription lists among his neighbors, and instructed his friends to imitate his example. He was never too big for the small essential things, and he was a master of detail — very rarely true of men of large views. His energy was dynamic and he was tireless. He never rested on his arms or went into winter quarters. His fight was endless. The real secret of his triumph, however, is found in the reason given by one of his biographers: 'He enjoyed a political vision penetrating deeper down into the inevitable movement of popular government, and farther forward into the future of free institutions than was possessed by any other man in public life in his day.'

[1] *Works*, III, 358; to Duane.

VIII

No American of his time had such versatility or such diversified interests. He was asked to frame the Declaration of Independence because of his reputation as a writer. Adams has told the story: 'He brought with him a reputation for literary science and a happy talent for composition. Writings of his were handed about [1] remarkable for their peculiar felicity of expression.' It was the 'Summary View' which elicited the admiration of Edmund Burke. A more ambitious effort, his 'Notes on Virginia' were written during the fatal illness of his wife, and while he was confined to the house two or three weeks by a riding accident.[2] It was a valuable contribution to the natural, social, economic, and political history of the State, with a number of eloquent passages and fascinating pages.

He had an artistic temperament, loved music, and at the beginning of his career we find him busy planning his garden at Monticello, and practicing three hours a day on his loved violin, under the instructions of an Italian musician. His hospitality to the Hessian prisoners is partly explained by a mutual love of music. Returning from an absence to find 'Shadwell,' his early home, in ashes, he inquired anxiously about his books. 'Oh, my young master,' exclaimed the distressed slave, 'they were all burnt, but we saved your fiddle.' [3]

Loving art in all its forms, he was fond of the company of artists. It was he who arranged in Paris for Houdon to go to America to make the statue of Washington.[4] He entertained Trumbull in the French capital, accompanying him to Versailles to see the King's art collection, and urged him to remain in Paris and study.[5] He was delighted with architectural beauty and lingered about the masterpieces. From Nesmes, he wrote enthusiastically to a woman friend: 'Here I am, Madame, gazing whole hours at the Maison Quarree, like a lover at his mistress. This is the second time I have been in love since I left Paris. The first was with a Diana at the Chateau de Laye-Epinaye in Beaujolais, a delicious morsel of sculpture, by M. A. Soldtz. This you will say was in rule, to fall in

---

[1] *A Summary View*, and *A Reply to Lord North.*   [2] *Domestic Life*, 58.   [3] *Ibid.*, 43.
[4] *Works*, v, 33; 42; 59.   [5] *Ibid.*, 400–01.

love with a female beauty; but with a house. No, Madame, it is not without a precedent in my own history. While in Paris I was violently smitten with the Hotel de Salm.'[1] When the Capitol at Richmond was in contemplation, he urged the construction of the most beautiful edifice possible as a model to be emulated in other buildings; drew some plans himself; examined those of Hallet, was captivated with those of Thornton, and urged their acceptance. 'Simple, noble, beautiful,' he wrote home.[2]

And yet, so many-sided was this man, that he was a utilitarian and scientist as well as artist. In Europe he was thought a philosopher, and Humboldt came to America to pass many hours under his roof. A perusal of his letters discloses the intensity and range of his interests. He was entranced with clocks, and we find him writing David Rittenhouse reminding him of 'a kind promise of making me an accurate clock,'[3] and later to Madison of a watch he had made for himself and inquiring if his friend wished one.[4] He summoned a Swiss clock-maker to Monticello who died on the mountain and is buried in the enclosure with his patron. He put the noted Buffon to rout in Paris on points in natural history.[5] Admiring the red men, he spent years collecting their vocabularies.[6] When in Paris he heard that an Arabic translation of Livy had been found in Sicily, and importuned the *chargés des affaires* of Naples to make inquiries, and was much excited to hear that such a translation had been found 'and will restore to us seventeen of the lost books.'[7] In the midst of the political diversions and social distractions of Paris he found time to write at length on the 'latest discoveries in astrology.'[8] As early as the summer of 1785, when Pilatre de Rozière made his fatal attempt to cross the English Channel in a balloon, we find him eagerly discussing the possibilities of the aeronautical science.[9] A newly invented lamp pleased him and he sent one to a friend from Paris.[10] The use of steam in the operation of grist mills interested him and he found time to witness the test.[11] Even the absorbing drama of the French Revolution in its early stages did not lessen his interest in Paine's iron bridge, and he attended its exhibition,[12] and finding the in-

[1] *Works*, vi, 106; *Domestic Life*, 109.   [2] *Works*, ix, 17–19.   [3] *Ibid.*, iv, 42.
[4] *Ibid.*, v, 180.   [5] *Ibid.*, 244–45; vi, 20–23.   [6] *Ibid.*, vii, 267–70.
[7] *Ibid.*, 73–79.   [8] *Ibid.*, v, 244–45.   [9] *Ibid.*, 22–24.
[10] *Ibid.*, 294–95.   [11] *Ibid.*, 294–95; vi, 11–15.   [12] *Ibid.*, vii, 113–16.

ventor hesitating between 'the catenary and portions of a circle,'
he sent to Italy for a scientific work by the Abbe Mascheroni.[1]
Fascinated by inventions, he was, himself, the inventor of a
plough.

IX

Interested as he was in art and inventions, his heart was with
the country life and the farmer's lot. He was never happier than
when, in the early morning, mounted on one of his beloved horses,
he rode over his broad acres at Monticello, observing with a per-
ennial zest the budding of the trees in spring, the unfolding of the
flowers, the ripening of the harvest. Wherever he was, throughout
his life, he longed for the house he had made on the hill, the broad
fields, the family circle and the servitors and slaves. There he was
lord of the domain. If he employed Italian gardeners, they con-
formed to his ideas. If he had a supervisor, it was he himself who
determined what should be planted and where — where the or-
chards should be, what trees should be set and their location; and
even the vines and shrubs, the nuts and seeds, the roots and bulbs
claimed his personal attention. Even his hogs were named, and
when one was to be killed, he designated it by name.[2] There, too,
he lived in an atmosphere of affection. There he had taken his
bride, a woman of exquisite beauty, grace, and loveliness; there his
children had been born, and there, all too soon, their mother died.
He was passionately devoted to her and there was no successor. To
the daughters who were left he became both a father and a mother,
resulting in an intimacy seldom found between father and daughters. In Paris he would not permit even his trusted servant to do
their shopping, reserving that duty for himself. Always patient,
never harsh, and ever sympathetic, he was the ideal parent.[3]

Though he did not remarry, he was fond of the society of women
and they of his. The few letters to women that have been preserved are masterpieces of their kind, sprightly, playful, sometimes
beautiful. His relations with the women of the Adams family are
shown in a note to John Adams's married daughter, written from
Paris: 'Mr. Jefferson has the honor to present his compliments to
Mrs. Smith and to send her the two pair of corsets she desired.

[1] *Works*, VII, 241–44.   [2] Watson, 114.   [3] Randall, I, 481.

He wishes they may be suitable, as Mrs. Smith omitted to send her measure. Times are altered since Mademoiselle de Samson had the honor of knowing her; should they be too small, however, she will be so good as to lay them by a while. There are ebbs as well as flows in this world. When the Mountain refused to go to Mahomet, he went to the Mountain.' [1] In Paris he formed a few cherished friendships with women, notably with Mrs. Cosway, Italian wife of an English painter, a woman of charm, beauty, and intellect, with whom he corresponded. One of his letters, the dialogue between the Head and the Heart on her departure for England, is unique and sparkling.[2] He appreciated the exquisite Mrs. Bingham whom he met in Paris, and his chiding letters to her after her return to America must have pleased that artificial lady immensely.[3] He was a friend of the Comtesse De Tesse whose mind he admired, [4] and of Madame De Corney whose beauty attracted him. 'The Bois de Boulogne invited you earnestly to retire to its umbrage from the heats of the sad season,' he wrote her gallantly. 'I was through it to-day as I am every day. Every tree charged me with this invitation.' [5]

Such was Thomas Jefferson who took upon himself the organization of the forces of democracy, when its enemies were in the saddle, booted and spurred, and with a well-disciplined and powerful army at their back. None but an extraordinary character could have dared hope for victory, and he was that, and more. Democrat and aristocrat, and sometimes autocrat; philosopher and politician; sentimentalist and utilitarian; artist, naturalist, and scientist; thinker, dreamer, and doer; inventor and scholar; writer and statesman, he enthralled his followers and fascinated while infuriating his foes.

[1] *Domestic Life*, 78.   [2] *Ibid.*, 87–89.
[3] *Works*, vi, 81–84.   [4] *Ibid.*, 102–06.   [5] *Ibid.*, 145–46.

CHAPTER VI
THE SOCIAL BACKGROUND

I

'IF New York wanted any revenge for the removal,' wrote Mrs. Adams to her daughter soon after reaching Philadelphia, 'the citizens might be glutted if they could come here, where every article has been almost doubled in price, and where it is not possible for Congress and the appendages to be half as well accommodated for a long time.'[1] Reconciliation for the removal was not complete several months later when Oliver Wolcott wrote his father complaining that 'the manners of the people are more reserved than in New York.'[2] Even so he had 'seen nothing to tempt [him] to idolatry,' after having seen 'many of their principal men,' and he had no apprehensions of 'self-humiliating sensations' after a closer acquaintance.'[3] It was not with unrestrained enthusiasm that the officials took up their residence in the greater city, with its population of more than 60,000. 'The Philadelphians,' according to the indignant comment of Jeremiah Smith, 'are from the highest to the lowest, from the parson in his black gown to the fille de joie or girl of pleasure, a set of beggars. You cannot turn around without paying a dollar.'[4]

To the visitor entering by coach on Front Street and rumbling up to the City Tavern the prospect did not seem so black as to those who received their first impressions from the water-front. These beheld 'nothing . . . but confused heaps of wooden store houses, crowded upon each other' — and, behind the wharves, Water Street, narrow, shut in by the old bank of the river, dirty, filthy, stinking.[5] Could he have looked down upon the city from some convenient hill, he would have found something to revive his drooping spirits in the compactness of the town and the substantial character of the houses. The principal streets of the period were Front, Second, Third, and Fourth, and beyond Sixth there

---

[1] *Mrs. Adams's Letters*, II, 207.   [2] *Republican Court*, I, 56.   [3] *Ibid.*, I, 64.   [4] *Ibid.*, 253.
[5] Weld, I, 5–6.

were scarcely any habitations. No one thought of building on Arch or Chestnut Streets west of Tenth, where the land was thickly dotted with frogponds.[1] Practically all of business and fashion was to be found east of Fourth Street, and the visitor or official sojourner could congratulate himself on the ease with which he could get about from place to place. An English tourist, observing that with the exception of Broad and High Streets the thoroughfares were not more than fifty feet in width, found them suggestive of 'many of the smaller streets of London except that the foot pavement on either side is of brick instead of stone.'[2]

If the filth of the odorous water-front, the narrowness of the streets, and the frogponds on the outskirts, so audible in the night, were depressing, the houses, attractive, and in many instances architecturally pretentious, hinted of comfort and solidity if not of opulence. The fact that almost all were constructed of brick was not lost upon the travelers.[3] In the more congested districts these houses had a shop on the first floor.

The streets, with their red-brick foot pavements and rows of trees, making them fragrant after summer rains, and drearily murmurous in the winter winds, were paved with pebbles in the middle,[4] with a gutter made of brick or wood, and lined with strong posts to protect the area of the pedestrians.[5] The trees, mostly buttonwood, willow, and Lombardy poplars, had been brought over from Europe some years before by William Hamilton.[6] At frequent intervals town pumps offered refreshment to the thirsty, or, in the night, an accommodating hanging-post for the inebriate staggering home from one of the popular taverns.[7] Not without its charm was a walk through the streets of Philadelphia in the days when Hamilton and Jefferson were exchanging shots, with the poplars and willows to shut off the sun, the pumps to minister to the comfort, and with most of the houses offering to the view a garden filled with old-fashioned flowers — lilacs, roses, pinks, and tulips, morning-glories and snowballs with gourd vines climbing over the porches. In the case of the more imposing mansions there were more elaborate gardens with rare flowers and

---

[1] *Republican Court*, 256; *Annals of Philadelphia*, I, 225.   [2] Twining, 44.
[3] Wansey, 184; Liancourt, IV, 91; Weld, I, 8; Twining, 45.
[4] Liancourt, IV, 91; Weld, I, 7–8.   [5] Warville, 187.
[6] Scharf, II, 875.   [7] Warville, 187.

shrubbery, but in many of these wealth claimed its privilege and shut off the view from the common folk who could only catch the fragrance.[1]

The visitor on public business bent found all the governmental centers close together. If interested in the debates at Congress Hall, erected for the purpose at Sixth and Chestnut Streets next to the State House, the smallest child could direct him. If a person of no special importance, he could find his way into the commodious gallery of the House, and, looking down upon the chamber, a hundred by sixty feet, with its three semi-circular rows of seats facing the Speaker's rostrum — 'a kind of pulpit near the center'[2] — could find Ames busy at his circular writing-desk, Madison on his feet or Sedgwick in conference with a lobbyist. If fortunate he might be admitted to the space on the floor beneath the gallery. But it was not so easy to penetrate to the more sacred precincts of the Senate on the floor above where the self-constituted guardians of the covenant and the rights of property held themselves aloof from the gaze of the vulgar. Perhaps, if he really prized the privilege, he might look down from some point of vantage on the State House Garden where the statesmen were wont to take the air and compose their thoughts.

Did he have business with Jefferson? It was only a little way to the three-story brick residence at High and Eighth Streets which had been taken over for the purposes of the State Department. With Hamilton? It was but a few steps to the old Pemberton mansion near Chestnut and Third, with its well-cultivated garden in the rear where the indefatigable human dynamo worked far into the night.[3] With the President? It was but a short distance from Jefferson's office to the Morris house.

At the time Washington moved in, the Morris house was one of the most distinguished in the city, a dignified and impressive brick mansion, with two large lamps in front, and with ample gardens to proclaim it the abode of a personage of consequence. It was under its roof that Washington had lived as the guest of Morris while presiding over the Constitutional Convention. It was not without difficulties and annoyances that the house was taken over. The banker was lustily praised by his friends for his sacrifice in

[1] Scharf, ii, 875.   [2] Wansey, iii.   [3] Lippincott, 36–37.

abandoning his home, but it appears to have been a sacrifice similar to that of managing the finances of the Revolution. One writer questioned whether 'giving up a house of moderate dimensions for 700 pounds a year can be deemed a great sacrifice ... when ... the President was accommodated in this city [New York] with a much more elegant house at 400 pounds per annum.'[1] Even Washington, who was Morris's intimate friend, was distressed at the difficulty in persuading him to fix the rental, and wrote Lear that he could not understand the Senator. He would be willing to pay as much as he paid in New York, and even more if there was not clear extortion. The owner finally fixed the rental at three thousand dollars a year.[2] Thus Washington moved in, and there the Presidents lived until the capital was moved to Washington.

There, if properly presented, the visitor might call to receive the rather cold, stately bow of Washington or even drink a cup of tea with Mrs. Washington. In the case of a levee, he was sure to be welcome. But if his social status did not suffice to justify the crossing of the threshold, he might, if he were patient, see the great man as he drove forth in his ornately decorated coach; or, better still, see him emerge on foot with his secretaries, Lear and Jackson, one on either side, with cocked hats on their heads, the aides a little in the rear. If he had the temerity to follow at a respectable distance, he would have been surprised, perhaps, to find that the President did not converse with his secretaries while on his walks.[3]

II

It was not joy unconfined to be interned in any of the hotels or taverns of Philadelphia at any time while it was the capital. In the journals of tourists who sojourned there we encounter no enthusiastic encomiums, even for O'Eller's, which owes something of its glamour in perspective to the fact that the Assembly dances were held in its ballroom. It was infinitely better, at any rate, than the Sign of the Sorrel Horse on Second Street, which comes down to us as a 'bad one.'[4] The City Tavern, scene of numerous political demonstrations, concededly one of the best, would have been bet-

[1] New York letter to *Maryland Journal*, November 19, 1790.
[2] *Republican Court*, 341.   [3] *Ibid.*, 366.   [4] Davis, *Travels*, 40–41.

ter rid of vermin that infested the beds.[1] The London Tavern, which had its days as the 'principal hotel,' was 'deficient in comfort' even at its best,[2] and the Indian Queen distinguished itself as the scene of a doleful robbery when some of Ames's colleagues lost their linen, and thirty thousand dollars in securities, and he escaped only because his name on his trunk assured the 'partial rogues' that 'nothing was to be got by taking it away.'[3] In 1794, the Golden Lion or the Yellow Cat at Eighth and Filbert Streets was a favorite because of its well-drawn beer and porter; and the visitor, pushing through the smoke-laden air to drink malt liquor from a pewter mug, would, likely as not, find Governor Mifflin or General Knox of the Cabinet enjoying their mugs along with the mechanics and clerks.[4] But it was not necessary to sleep in the beds of the Yellow Cat to quaff its liquors, and after a brief experience with the taverns the tourist would be likely to follow the example of Thomas Twining and seek more comfortable and sanitary quarters in some of the numerous rooming-houses that catered particularly to members of Congress. The choicest of these resented the idea that they were other than the private houses of gentlemen accommodating political personages — this particularly true in the case of Francis, the Frenchman, at whose house on Fourth Street, Vice-President Adams had a room.[5] In these private rooming and boarding-houses, in which the majority of the celebrities lived, an abundant table, clean agreeable rooms, and the congenial companionship of colleagues made an appeal. At Francis's the head of the table was reserved for Adams, and all the ceremonial forms were scrupulously observed, although he frequently had his meals served in his rooms. It was not until he had escaped from the Indian Queen and found lodgings 'at the house of Mrs. Sage that Ames began 'to feel settled and at home.'[6] This hiving had its comedies, sometimes its scandals, and occasionally its romances, as on the day Senator Aaron Burr took James Madison to call upon the winsome daughter of his landlady, and history was made in the candlelit parlor of the boarding-house.

Quiet and home-like, at least, these boarding-houses of our early statesmen, and if they had no bars, they were in close proximity to

---

[1] Wansey, III.   [2] Twining, 31.   [3] Ames, I, 88–89.
[4] Scharf, II, 985.   [5] Twining, 31–34.   [6] Ames, I, 83–89.

many that were of good repute. The members of the Legislature sometimes were known to discuss important measures at Geisse's Tavern over the mugs,[1] were wont, on adjournment, to linger at Mr. O'Eller's for his incomparable punch,[2] and to celebrate the ending of a session with an evening of conviviality at 'Mr. Burns tavern on Tenth Street.'[3] Gentlemen riding along the banks of the Schuylkill could seldom resist the impulse to dismount at the tavern of Metz — for these drinking-houses were kindly placed among a people intolerant of puritanism.[4]

Going forth into the streets to mingle with the common people was a revelation to the polished tourist from the old lands. Here they found nothing of the humility of the lowly to which they were accustomed. The mechanics and common laborers took the theory of equality seriously. One traveler found 'the lower sort of people' lacking in good manners [5] and observed that a well-dressed stranger, asking a polite question, was almost certain of an impudent answer.[6] These were the men who were to man the societies fashioned after those of the Parisian radicals, to rally passionately to the support of the French Revolution, and to supply Jefferson with his shock troops — and sometimes shocking troops — in his fight for the democratization of the Republic.

These, too, in their desperate striving for equality were moved to imitations of the spendthrift practices of the rich. Even the servants and the negroes gave elaborate balls which Liancourt found 'destitute of the charming simplicity of the fêtes of our peasants.' [7] The women appeared in dresses beyond their means; the laborer and his lady rode in coaches to the dance, where an elaborate supper was served, with liquid refreshments. Sundays found the public-houses of the environs packed with the men of the factories and shop, borne thither, with their families, in chairs. There was much drinking and spending with gambling on the fights arranged for their delectation.[8] At Harrowgate Gardens, two miles out on the New York road, and Gray's Gardens on the Schuylkill, they flocked to drink tea or liquor, to dance, promenade, or flirt, and on summer nights the young men of all stations

---

[1] Hiltzheimer's *Diary*, 167.   [2] *Ibid.*, 201.   [3] *Ibid.*, 205.   [4] *Ibid.*, 205.
[5] Weld, I, 29.   [6] *Ibid.*, I, 30.
[7] Liancourt, IV, 108–09.   [8] *Ibid.*

were lured to them by the promise of romance. Even the grave and reverend statesmen could not, in all cases, resist the call. Gay and wicked some must have thought the scene — with the painted women of the town a bit brazen in their fishing for men. 'We have Eves in plenty, of all nations, tongues and colors,' wrote Oliver Wolcott to his wife from Gray's Gardens where he had taken refuge from the yellow fever, 'but do not be jealous — I have not seen one yet whom I have thought pretty' — leaving her to imagine the possibilities should one such appear.[1] And yet, pleasure-loving as the population was, the nights were reasonably quiet. About the time the city assumed the dignity of a capital, there was little to disturb the tranquillity of the night after ten o'clock beyond the voice of the watchman, or the footsteps of some nighthawk wending his way by the light of the street-lamps 'placed like those in London.'[2] But five years later, a visitor who recalled that in 1794 it was unusual to meet any one at night, or to hear any noises after eleven o'clock, found that the nocturnal annoyances continued far later into the night.[3]

It was by day, however, that the city made its best impression. The luxury-loving people, the wealth and extravagance of the social leaders insisting upon London and Parisian styles, the commercial traditions of the community gave to its shopping district an elegance found nowhere else in America. The houses of the importers and wholesalers, some maintaining their own ships, were found, for the most part, on Front and Water Streets. When in the spring and autumn the ships came in, and the great boxes of English dry-goods were stretched along the pavement of Front between Arch and Walnut Streets to be opened, it was a thrilling event to the Philadelphians. Fluttering about them were the retail merchants — for most of these in the days of the city's political preëminence were women — exclaiming ecstatically over the contents. Soon the goods were transferred to the shops, which even a Frenchman found 'remarkable for their neatness'[4] — due, no doubt, to the sex of the proprietors. What more fascinating than to stand before the great show windows — something new — at Mrs. Whiteside's fancy dress-goods shop, with exquisite cloths and

[1] Gibbs, I, 561. [2] Warville, 187.
[3] Liancourt, IV, 99. [4] Warville, 183.

dresses hung full length and festooned to best advantage after the manner of Bond Street, London. Did it add anything to the appeal to know that the proprietress had come from London? Alas, no doubt. Thither the ladies from the mansions drove in their carriages to make their purchases, and thence, perhaps, for something more, to the South Second Street store of the smiling Mrs. Holland, and then on, perchance, to Mrs. Jane Taylor's at the Sign of the Golden Lamb.[1] And then, having ministered to the materialistic yearnings of vanity, as like as not milady directs the coachman to stop at Bell's British Book Shop on Third Street, near Pearl, lest the lord and master, in placing his order with his London agent, overlooked something she would not miss.

An easy, patrician life for some of these Philadelphians, but not for all. The workman receiving a dollar a day and board, and with the smallest houses on the outskirts renting for three hundred dollars a year, found it far from a frolic to make both ends meet. The middle-class employees of the stores and industries, paying from eight to twelve dollars a week for board, without wine, candles, or fire, could have found little to interest them in Mrs. Whiteside's show windows, for, while the clerks were courteous and the merchant polite, the cost of her goods was far in excess of that on Bond Street.[2] But it is not with these of the more humble order that we are concerned just now. It is quite possible that the curious Jefferson, who had a habit of prying into the living conditions of 'people of no importance,' may have wondered how these lived, but the social environment of the majority of the statesmen was far removed from the common people. It is with the world of fashion that we are concerned.

III

No society in America could have been less in harmony with the spirit of democracy, for nowhere was class consciousness and caste pride more pronounced. 'Those who constitute the fashionable world are at best a mere oligarchy, composed of a few natives and as many foreigners,' wrote Otis to his wife.[3] 'I might have believed myself in an English town,' said Viscount de Chateaubriand.[4] An

[1] Wharton, *Salons*, 71. [2] Liancourt, IV, 101.
[3] Otis, I, 128. [4] Scharf, II, 907.

Englishman noted that 'amongst the upper circles... pride, haughtiness, and ostentation are conspicuous; and it seems that nothing could make them happier than that an order of nobility should be established, by which they might be exalted above their fellow citizens, as much as they are in their own conceit.'[1] A French nobleman could not escape the observation that 'the English influence prevails in the first circles and prevails with great intolerance.'[2] And Otis, who liked the tone himself, was much impressed with the discovery that 'the women after presentations to the court of George III or Louis XVI transplanted into Philadelphia society the manners of the English aristocracy and the fashions of Paris.'[3] During the days of the British occupation, the cream of society had reveled with the British officers, and many of these had resumed their places in the society of the republican capital without abandoning their former views. This English tone was to be felt by Jefferson a little later when his sympathy with the French Revolution was to enter into his policies. From the beginning these pro-English aristocrats were to draw political lines in social intercourse, and in time Otis was to record that 'Democratic gentlemen and their families, no matter how high their social qualifications, were rigidly ostracised by the best society.'[4] Along with this went a rather vulgar deification of the dollar, and, strangely enough, a lack of polite hospitality to the stranger. 'What is justly called society,' wrote Liancourt whose ideas had been fashioned at Versailles, 'does not exist in this city. The vanity of wealth is common enough.' The picture he paints is not a pretty one. It shows a flamboyant rich man flauntingly displaying 'his splendid furniture, his fine English glass, and exquisite china,' to the stranger invited to come to 'one ceremonious dinner,' and then dismissing him for another who had not 'seen the magnificence of the house, nor tasted the old Madeira.' This, we are told, was the routine for all who came from Europe — 'philosophers, priests, literati, princes, dentists, wits and idiots.' But alas, 'the next day the lionized stranger is not known in the street except he be wealthy.'[5] However much they may have fallen short in manners, they yielded nothing to Versailles in dress. This 'elegance of dress' astonished

---

[1] Weld, I, 21.   [2] Liancourt, IV, 105.   [3] Otis, I, 126.
[4] Morison, *Otis*, I, 126.   [5] Liancourt, IV, 104–05.

Chateaubriand, and Liancourt was amazed at 'the profusion and luxury' in 'the dresses of their wives and daughters.' At balls, 'the variety and richness of the dresses did not suffer in comparison with Europe.' The brilliant note was assiduously sought in costumes, and there was much copying of the subjects of Gainsborough and Sir Joshua Reynolds. One foreigner noting the 'immense expense on their toilet and head dress' thought it 'too affected to be pleasing.'[1] But by common consent these grand dames and belles were beautiful, with their sparkling eyes, graceful forms, and the brilliancy of their complexions.

If this aristocracy was neglectful of the stranger who had no golden key to its interest, it was not because of a dearth of entertaining. Here there was a hectic activity — dinners, dances, breakfasts, teas, parties enough to satisfy the most insatiate passion for such excitement. Throughout the season the great houses were ablaze with light, and if, as Mrs. Adams complained, there was much the same company in all, it was congenial company, and the intimacy of the contact allowed a familiarity that sometimes verged on the *risqué*. In less than a month after her arrival, Mrs. Adams was appalled at 'the invitations to tea and cards in the European style,'[2] and was complaining that she 'should spend a very dissipated winter if [she] were to accept one half the invitations, particularly to the touts or teas and cards with even Saturday night . . . not excepted.'[3] A little later Aaron Burr was being swamped with 'many attentions and civilities — many invitations to dine, etc.'[4] If Burr declined, as he wrote his wife, the handsome young Otis, who loved the company of women, was not so coy. 'I have dined once with Cuttling at Mrs. Grattan's,' he wrote home, 'once at Yznardi's [Spaniard who spent much time in Philadelphia] in great stile; and yesterday in the country with Jonathan Williams [nephew of Franklin]. I am engaged for next Christmas with Mrs. Powell, but with nobody for the Christmas after next.'[5]

At these functions — heavy drinking — flirting — *risqué* talk. Even a German was shocked to find that at public dinners each

[1] Warville, 190.   [2] Mrs. Adams's *Letters* (to Mrs. Smith), II, 211.   [3] *Ibid.*, II, 213–14.
[4] Davis, *Burr*, I, 303.
[5] Morison, *Otis*, I, 128–29.

person would often consume six bottles of Madeira.[1] Only Burr
was hard to satisfy. 'I despair of getting genuine Trent wine in
this city,' he wrote Theodosia. 'There never was a bottle of real
unadulterated Trent imported here for sale. Mr. Jefferson, who
had some for his own use, has left town.'[2] But if there was no
Trent, Madeira flowed in streams, beer and ale, punch and whiskey
and champagne could be had for the asking, and there was asking
enough, even at parties and dinners. Even Hamilton, who drank
with moderation, sometimes became 'liquorish' at the table, and
on one occasion made rather free with another man's wife to the
husband's indignation until mollified with the assurance of his
spouse that she 'did not like him at all.' Even so, thought the
irate husband, Hamilton 'appears very trifling in his conversation
with ladies.'[3] And 'trifling' indeed must have been much of the
talk.

Thus it was at a dinner at Clymer's, a leading member of the
House. Present, Otis, the Binghams, the Willings — the top
cream of the aristocracy. Aha, cried the vivacious sister of Mrs.
Bingham, referring to the host's newly acquired stomacher, and
mentioning the touching case of the Duke of York, recently
married to the Duchess of Württemberg who was compelled to cut
a semi-circle out of his table to give access to his plate. Mrs.
Bingham coyly expressed sympathy for the Duchess. (Bursts of
laughter and applause.) But Clymer, not to be outdone, turned to
his married sister with the comment that he would 'soon be able to
retort this excellent jest on her.' (Renewed laughter and more applause.) It was an hilarious occasion, the applause 'would have
done credit to a national convention' and 'Miss Abby and Miss
Ann did not disguise their delight nor their bosoms.'[4] On now to a
dinner at Harrison's, who married a sister of Mrs. Bingham, where
one of the guests, 'after rallying Sophia . . . upon her unfruitful-
ness,' led to a 'natural but not very flattering transition' which
'introduced Mrs. Champlin and her want of prolific qualities as a
seasoning for the Canvas Backs.'[5] But let us hurry on to a third
dinner, with Hamilton, his vivacious sisters-in-law, Mrs. Church
and Miss Schuyler. A lively company! Mrs. Church, 'the mirror

[1] Scharf, II, 910 (from Bulow). [2] Davis, Burr, I, 376.
[3] Morison, Otis, I, 141–43. [4] Ibid., I, 135. [5] Ibid., I, 135.

of affectation,' who is 'more amusing than offensive' because so affable and free from ceremony; and, still more lively, Miss Schuyler 'a young wild flirt from Albany, full of glee and apparently desirous of matrimony.' Mrs. Church drops her shoe bow, Miss Schuyler picks it up and fastens it in Hamilton's button-hole with the remark, 'I have made you a knight.' 'But what order?' asks Mrs. Church, 'he can't be a knight of the garter in this country.' 'True, sister, but he would be if you would let him.'

Wine, women and song — such the spirit in some of the great houses in moments of *abandon*. But it would be unfair to leave the impression these incidents would convey. There were brilliant men of vast achievement, and women of extraordinary charm and cleverness moving behind these curtained windows. Let us meet them in the mansion of Mrs. Bingham — the uncrowned queen of the Federalist group — the woman without a peer.

IV

None of the three capitals of the country have produced another social leader of the cleverness, audacity, and regality of Mrs. William Bingham. During the eight years of the domination of the Federalists, of whom her husband was one of the leaders, there was no public character of the first order who did not come under the influence of her fascination. By birth, environment, nature, and training she was fitted to play a conspicuous part in the social life of any capital in the world. The daughter of Willing, the partner of Robert Morris, she was the favored of fortune. Some years before her birth, her father, inspired by sentimental motives, built the mansion on Third Street in which she was born, and patterned it after the ancestral home in Bristol, England. There, surrounded by all the advantages of wealth, her beauty unfolded through a happy childhood. The pomp and pride of great possessions did not imbue her with a passion for republics or democracy. She was destined to play a part in a rather flamboyant aristocracy, and was as carefully perfected in the arts and graces of her sex as any princess destined to a throne. In the midst of the Revolution, in her sixteenth year, she married William Bingham who combined the advantages of wealth, social position, and a capacity for political leadership.

She was only twenty, when, accompanied by her husband, she went abroad to captivate court circles with her vivacity, charm, and beauty. At Versailles, the gallants, accustomed to the ways and wiles of the most accomplished women of fashion, were entranced. At The Hague, where she lingered awhile, the members of the diplomatic corps fluttered about the teasing charmer like moths about the flame. In the court circles of England she suffered nothing in comparison with the best it could offer, and the generous Abigail Adams, thrilling to the triumph of the young American, found her brilliancy enough to dim the ineffectual fires of Georgiana, Duchess of Devonshire. Five years of familiarity with the leaders in the world of European fashion and politics prepared her to preside with stunning success over the most famous political drawing-room of the American capital.

It was after their return from Europe that Mrs. Bingham moved into the imposing mansion on Third Street built on the ample grounds of her childhood home. All the arts of the architect, landscape gardener, and interior decorator had been drawn upon to make a fit setting for the mistress. The garden, with its flowers and rare shrubbery, its lemon, orange, and citron trees, its aloes and exotics, was shut off from the view of the curious, only mighty oaks and the Lombardy poplars visible above the wall — 'a magnificent house and gardens in the best English style.'[1] The furnishings were in keeping with the promise of the exterior. 'The chairs in the drawing-room were from Seddon's in London of the newest taste, the back in the form of a lyre, with festoons, of yellow and crimson silk,' according to the description of an English tourist. 'The curtains of the room a festoon of the same. The carpet, one of Moore's most expensive patterns. The room papered in the French taste, after the style of the Vatican in Rome.'[2] The halls, hung with pictures selected with fine discrimination in Italy, gave a promise not disappointed in the elegance of the drawing-rooms, the library, the ballroom, card-rooms, and observatory.[3] To some this extravagant display of luxury was depressing, and Brissot de Warville, who was to return to Paris to die on the guillotine as a leader of the ill-fated party of the Gironde, held the mis-

---

[1] Wansey, 136.   [2] *Ibid.*, 136.
[3] Wansey; Twining; Lippincott; *Republican Court;* Scharf, II, 911.

MRS. WILLIAM BINGHAM

tress of the mansion responsible for the aristocratic spirit of the town. It was a pity, he thought, that a man so sensible and amiable as Bingham should have permitted a vain wife to lead him to 'a pomp which ought forever have been a stranger to Philadelphia.' And all this display 'to draw around him the gaudy prigs and parasites of Europe,' and lead 'to the reproach of his fellow citizens and the ridicule of strangers.'[1] But if the French republican was shocked, even so robust a democrat as Maclay was so little offended that he was able to write after dining at the mansion that 'there is a propriety, a neatness, a cleanliness that adds to the splendor of his costly furniture and elegant apartments.'[2]

And 'the dazzling Mrs. Bingham,' as the conservative Abigail described her,[3] what of her? The elegance and beauty which has come down to us on canvas prepares us for the glowing descriptions of contemporaries. Hers was the type of patrician beauty that shimmered. She was above the medium height and well-formed, and in her carriage there was sprightliness, dignity, elegance, and distinction. Sparkling with wit, bubbling with vivacity, she had the knack of convincing the most hopeless yokel introduced into her drawing-room by the exigencies of politics that she found his personality peculiarly appealing. Daring at the card-table, graceful in the dance, witty in conversation even though sometimes too adept with the naughty devices of a Congreve dialogue, inordinately fond of all the dissipations prescribed by fashion, tactful in the selection and placing of her guests at table, she richly earned the scepter she waved so authoritatively over society.[4] What though she did sometimes stain her pretty lips with wicked oaths, she swore as daintily as the Duchess of Devonshire, and if she did seem to relish anecdotes a bit too spicy for a puritanic atmosphere, she craved not the privilege of breathing such air.[5]

Hers the consuming ambition to be the great lady and to introduce into American society the ideas and ideals of Paris and London. Did Jefferson gently chide her for her admiration of French women? Well — was she not justified? Did they not 'possess the happy art of making us pleased with ourselves?' In their conver-

---

[1] Warville, 190.   [2] Maclay, 366.   [3] *Mrs. Adams's Letters*, II, 211.
[4] *Republican Court*, 291–302.   [5] Morison, *Otis*, I, 135.

sation could they not 'please both the fop and the philosopher?'
And despite their seeming frivolity, did not these 'women of
France interfere with the politics of the country, and often give a
decided turn to the fate of empires?' In this letter to the man she
admired and liked, while loathing his politics, we have the nearest
insight into the soul of the woman.[1]

But these graver ambitions were not revealed to many who observed her mode of life, her constant round of dissipations, her
putting aside the responsibilities of a mother, leaving her daughters to their French governesses until the tragic elopement of
Marie with a dissipated nobleman, and the apprehension of the
pair after their marriage at the home of a milliner in the early morning. Hers were not the prim notions of the average American of
her time. It was Otis, not she, who was shocked to find Marie so
thinly dressed in mid-winter that he was 'regaled at the sight of
her whole legs for five minutes together,' and wondered 'to what
height the fashion would be carried.'[2] Swearing, relating *risqué*
stories, indulging in dissipations night after night, shaming her
motherhood by her affected indifference or neglect, the fact remains
that the breath of scandal never touched her until the final scene
when in her early thirties they bore her on a stretcher from the
home of her triumphs in the vain hope of prolonging her life in
the soft air of the Bermudas.

And so to her dinners, dances, parties, the clever men of the
Federalist Party flocked, with only a sprinkling of Jeffersonians,
for, though Jefferson himself could always count on a gracious
reception from the hostess, he was not comfortable among the
other guests. Always the best was to be had there — and the
newest. Did she not introduce the foreign custom of having servants announce the arriving guests, to the discomfiture of Monroe?

'Senator Monroe,' called the flunky.

'Coming,' cried the Senator.

'Senator Monroe' — echoed a flunky down the hall.

'Coming as soon as I can get my greatcoat off,' promised the
Senator.

But we may be sure that no expression of amusement on the
face of the beaming Mrs. Bingham added to his embarrassment.

[1] *Domestic Life*, 98–100.   [2] Morison, *Otis*, I, 137.

'A very pretty dinner, Madame,' said the intolerable Judge Chase, after looking over the proffered repast, 'but there is not a thing on your table that I can eat.'

An expression of surprise or resentment on the hostess's face? Not at all. What would the Judge relish? Roast beef? Very well — and a servant received his orders and soon hurried back with beef and potatoes to be gluttonously devoured and washed down with a couple of bottles of stout ale instead of French wines.

'There, Madame,' said the Judge, made comfortable, 'I have made a sensible and excellent dinner, but no thanks to your French cook.'

And he never knew from the lady's pleased expression that she thought him an insufferable bore.

Such the woman whose home was to be to the Hamiltonians what Madame Roland's was to the Girondists, and Lady Holland's to the English Whigs. Now let us peep into the drawing-room and observe the men and women who bowed to her social scepter.

V

In deference to Mrs. Bingham we shall permit the servant to announce these visitors as they arrive.

'Mr. and Mrs. Robert Morris.'

No doubt about their importance, for he was as intimate with Washington as she with Mrs. Washington, and such was her intimacy that she was frequently referred to as 'the second lady in the land.' It was she who accompanied Mrs. Washington from Philadelphia to New York after the inauguration, and during the spring and autumn the two might frequently be seen under the trees at 'The Hills,' the Morris farm near the city, enjoying the view of the river and such pastoral pictures as were offered by the imported sheep and cattle grazing on the rolling hills. Of Mrs. Morris it was said that 'so impressive is her air and demeanor that those who saw her once seldom forgot her.'[1] She had dignity, tact, and elegance, and, like Mrs. Washington, no respect for 'the filthy democrats.' She was a thorough aristocrat. Her husband, banker, merchant, Senator, was of imposing height, his merry blue eyes, clear complexion, and strong features denoting some-

[1] *Republican Court*, 309.

thing of his significance; and he had the social graces that captivate and hold. His wealth alone would have made him a commanding figure in the society of the time and place. Some generations were to settle on his grave before he was to appear as the
martyr who had sacrificed a fortune to liberty, for there was a
different understanding in his day.[1] A natural aristocrat, ultra-
conservative because of his business connections and great possessions, if he was tolerant of the experiment in republicanism,
he took no pains to conceal his contempt of democracy — in
Senate or drawing-room.

'Mrs. Walter Stewart.'

Another of the intimate circle of the Washingtons who dwelt
in a fine house next door to the Morrises, she was one of the
most brilliant and fascinating women with whom Mrs. Bingham
liked to surround herself. A long way she had traveled from her
girlhood home as the daughter of Blair McClenachan, the ardent
democrat who was to help burn Jay's Treaty, welcome Genêt, and
to follow Jefferson, for she was the wife of the rich General Stewart,
and had been seduced by the glitter of the aristocracy. Like Mrs.
Bingham, she had had her fling with the nobility in London, Paris,
Berlin, and Rome, and had returned to open her house for some of
the most elaborate entertaining of her time. In striking beauty,
conversational charm, and a caressing manner, she rivaled Mrs.
Bingham at her best. About her dinner table the leaders of the
Federalist Party were frequently found.[2]

'Mrs. Samuel Powell.'

An interesting lady, 'who looks turned fifty,'[3] enters to be
greeted by the hostess as 'Aunt.' A courteous, kindly woman,
almost motherly in her manner, she talks with the fluency and
ease to be expected of the mistress of the famous house on 'Society Hill.'[4] No one of Mrs. Bingham's guests who has not prome-
naded on summer evenings in the Powell gardens, the walks lined
with statuary.[5]

'General and Mrs. Knox.'

An impressive figure, the Secretary of War, his height carrying

[1] Oberholtzer's *Life* (Major Armstrong's letter to General Armstrong), 70; Governor
Reed to General Green, 70.
[2] *Republican Court*, 314.   [3] *Mrs. Adams's Letters*, ii, 211.   [4] *Ibid.*
[5] *Early Philadelphia*, 38.

the two hundred and eighty pounds not ungracefully, his regular Grecian nose, florid complexion, bright, penetrating eyes giving an attractive cast to his countenance. They who know him best suspect that he enjoys too well the pleasures of the table, but love him for a kindliness that temper cannot sour, a sincerity and generosity that know no bounds, a gayety that his dignity cannot suppress — a fine sentimental figure with a Revolutionary background. What though he had been a bookseller before he eloped with a lady of quality, he was too keenly appreciative of the advantages of aristocracy to have much patience with the queer notions of Tom Jefferson, whom he liked. He rubbed his shins when Hamilton stumbled over a chair.

And Mrs. Knox — she must have been a dashing belle in her romantic youth, for despite her enormous weight, she was still handsome with her black eyes and blooming cheeks.[1] Passing her girlhood in the Loyalist atmosphere of an aristocratic home, she had never become reconciled to the impertinence of the people, and even during the war her adoring Henry had been moved to warn her against sneering openly at the manners and speech of the people of Connecticut. 'The want of refinement which you seem to speak of is, or will be, the salvation of America,' he wrote.[2] But hers was the more masterful nature and his democracy was to capitulate to her aristocracy in the end.[3] But — whither goes the lady from the drawing-room so quickly? Ah — of course, it is to the card-room, for was it not the gossip that 'the follies of a gambling wife are passed on to the debits of her husband?'[4] In the morning, no doubt, she will run in on Mrs. Washington at the Morris house, for they are very close.

'Mr. and Mrs. Alexander Hamilton.'

What a romantic picture he makes in the finery that sets him off so well — brilliant eyes sparkling, eloquent lips smiling, a courtly figure bending over the hostess's hand. Only a moment for the lightest kind of banter with the ladies, and he is off to the Pemberton mansion to work far into the night. Mrs. Hamilton will linger a little longer, an appealing type of woman, her delicate face set off by 'fine eyes which are very dark' and 'hold the life and energy of

---

[1] Drake, *Knox*, III.   [2] Brookes, *Knox*, 60.   [3] *Ibid.*, 264.
[4] Steiner, *McHenry* (Williamson to McHenry), 196–97.

the restrained countenance.'[1] Hamilton had found her in the Schuyler homestead at Albany, 'a brunette with the most good-natured, dark lovely eyes,'[2] gentle, retiring, but in the home circle full of gayety and courage. Weeks and months sometimes found her missing from the social circle, for with her, in those days, life was just one baby after another.

'Mr. and Mrs. Oliver Wolcott, and Miss Wolcott.'

A pleasing personality was that of the handsome protégé of Hamilton, breathing the spirit of jollity, given to badinage, capable, too, of serious conversation on books and plays. He loses himself in the lively throng, but his infectious laughter is as revealing of his presence as the bell of Bossy in the woods. But we are more interested in his companions. Mrs. Wolcott was all loveliness and sweetness, grace and dignity, and such was the appeal of her conversation that one statesman thought her 'a divine woman'; another, 'the magnificent Mrs. Wolcott'; and the brusque Senator Tracy of her State, on being assured by a condescending diplomat that she would shine at any court, snorted that she even shone at Litchfield.[3] Even so the eyes of the younger men are upon Mary Ann Wolcott, sister of the Federalist leader, a pearl of her sex, combining an extraordinary physical beauty with opulent charms, and a conversational brilliance unsurpassed by any woman of the social circle. Very soon she would marry the clever, cynical Chauncey Goodrich and take her place in official society in her own right. The Wolcotts, we may be sure, read Paine's 'Rights of Man' with amazement and disgust.

'Mr. and Mrs. Theodore Sedgwick.'

A magnificent type of physical manhood, the face of one accustomed to command and sneer down opposition; a woman of elegance and refinement, typical of the best New England could offer in a matron.

'Pierce Butler.'

A handsome widower this man, maintaining an elegant establishment in Philadelphia, who affected to be a democrat, and carefully selected his associates from among the aristocracy, a South Carolinian with a certain reverence for wealth.

---

[1] Wharton, *Salons*, 54.   [2] *Intimate Life*, 95.
[3] Gibbs, I, 161; *Queens of American Society*, 35.

'Mrs. William Jackson.'

An equally charming but less beautiful sister of the hostess, now wife of one of Washington's secretaries, a favorite at the Morris mansion, and with no time for thinking on the grievances of the yokels and mechanics — an American prototype of the merry ladies of Versailles before the storm broke.

Among the foreign faces we miss the tall figure of Talleyrand whose Philadelphia immoralities shocked the French Minister, and whose affairs with a lady of color [1] excluded him from the Bingham drawing-room. But there is Viscount de Noailles who had proposed the abolition of feudal rights in the early days of the French Revolution; and Count Tilley, the dissipated roué planning an elopement with his hostess's daughter with the connivance of her French governess; and Brissot de Warville, enlightened political idealist of France soon to fall beneath the knife of Robespierre. There, too, the Duc de La Rochefoucauld-Liancourt who was redolent of courts, and the Baring brothers of London, bankers, soon to marry the Bingham girls.

A veritable Vanity Fair, many clever, some brilliant, most skeptical of republics, idolatrous of money and distinctions, and few capable of discriminating between anarchy and democracy. Such was the social atmosphere of the capital when the fight to determine whether this should be a democratic or aristocratic republic was made.

VI

We have an English-drawn picture of an evening at the British Legation with many American guests gathered about the blazing fire. The Consul is 'descanting on various subjects, public and private, as well as public and private characters, sometimes with unbecoming levity, sometimes with sarcasm even more unbecoming.' An English guest was afraid that such talk 'could hardly fail to be offensive to . . . many of the guests and to the good taste of all.' But could this English gentleman have listened in on the conversations at Mrs. Bingham's, Mrs. Morris's, or Mrs. Stewart's, he might have concluded that these reflections on certain public characters were altogether pleasing to the principal figures in the

[1] Probably Madame Grand; *Intimate Life.*

society of the capital.[1] And could he have returned a little later to find society chuckling over the display in the windows of a newspaper office of the pictures of George III, Lord North, and General Howe, he might have decided that there was a pronouncedly pro-English party in America. Had he driven about the environs, among the hills, and along the banks of the rivers, he would have seen country houses of the aristocracy — Lansdowne, the seat of the Binghams; Bush Hill, where the Adamses lived at first; Woodford, and other country places to suggest similar seats in his own land. And had he been meandering in the neighborhood of Horsehead's or Chew's Landing, seven or nine miles out, he might have been startled at the familiar English picture of gentlemen in bright coats, the pack in full cry after the fox.[2] And having made these observations he could have found some extenuation in the conversation in the British Minister's house.

The snobbery of class consciousness entered into even the Dancing Assembly which held forth at frequent intervals at O'Eller's, in a ballroom sixty feet square, with a handsome music gallery at one end, and the walls papered after the French style.[3] The suppers at these dances were mostly liquid,[4] and, since it is on record that on hot summer days ladies and gentlemen could count on a cool iced punch with pineapple juice to heighten the color, it may be assumed that the Assembly suppers were a success.[5] The fact that the young ladies sometimes took two pair of slippers, lest they dance one out, hints of all-night revels.[6] And the expulsion from membership of a young woman who had dared marry a jeweler tells its own tale.[7] At the theater, which was usually crowded,[8] the aristocrats and democrats met without mingling, for the different prices put every one in his or her place, and if wine and porter were sold between acts to the people in the pit 'precisely as if they were in a tavern,'[9] the aristocracy paid eight dollars for a box,[10] and an attaché, in full dress of black, hair powdered and adjusted in the formal fashion, and bearing silver candlesticks and wax candles, would meet Washington at the entrance and conduct him with much gravity to the presidential box, festooned with red drapery,

---

[1] Twining, 39.
[2] Lippincott, 212.
[3] Wansey, 132.
[4] Agnes Repplier, 135.
[5] Wansey, 131.
[6] Wharton, *Salons*, 157.
[7] Lippincott, 282.
[8] Liancourt, iv, 109.
[9] Weld, i, 24.
[10] Hiltzheimer, 204.

and bearing the United States coat of arms.[1] 'The managers have been very polite to me and my family,' wrote Mrs. Adams. 'The actors came and informed us that a box is prepared for us. The Vice-President thanked them for their civility, and told them he would attend whenever the President did.'[2] On these occasions, when the highest dignitaries of the State attended, a stranger, dropped from the clouds, would have scarcely thought himself in a republic. At the theater he would have found a military guard, with an armed soldier at each stage door, with four or five others in the gallery, and these assisted by the high constables of the city and police officers.[3] There was no danger threatening but the occasion offered the opportunity for pompous display so tempting to the society of the city.

At first the statesmen had to content themselves with the old Southwark Theater, which was dreary enough architecturally, lighted with oil lamps without glasses, and with frequent pillars obstructing the view.[4] But the best plays were presented, by good if not brilliant players, and the aristocracy flirted and frolicked indifferent to the resentful glances of the poorer classes in less favored seats. It reached the climax of its career just as the new theater was about to open with the then celebrated tragic actress, Mrs. Melmoth — and soon afterward, the new Chestnut Street Theater opened its doors and raised its curtain. The opening was an event — the public entranced. Two or three rows of boxes, a gallery with Corinthian columns highly gilded and with a crimson ribbon from capital to base. Above the boxes, crimson drapery — panels of rose color — seats for two thousand. 'As large as Covent Garden,' wrote Wansey, 'and to judge by the dress and appearance of the company around me, and the actors and scenery, I should have thought I had still been in England.'[5] And such a company! There was Fennell, noted in Paris for his extravagance, socially ambitious, and handsome, too, with his six feet of stature, and ever-ready blush, about whom flocked the literary youth of the town. Ladies — the finest trembled to his howls of tragedy and simpered to his comedy. There, too, was Harwood, who had married the granddaughter of Ben Franklin — a perfect gentle-

[1] Lippincott, 118.   [2] *Mrs. Adams's Letters* (to Mrs. Smith), ii, 213.
[3] Scharf, ii, 967.   [4] Lippincott, 119.   [5] Wansey, 126–27.

man; and Mrs. Oldmixon, the spouse of Sir John, the 'beau of Bath,' who divided honors in his day with Nash and Brummel; and Mrs. Whitlock, whom her admirers insisted did not shine merely by the reflected glory of her sister, Mrs. Siddons.

Quite as appealing to both aristocrat and democrat was the Circus at Twelfth and Market Streets, established in 1792 by John Ricketts whose credentials to society were in his erstwhile connection with the Blackfriars Bridge Circus of London. Washington and Martha occasionally witnessed the performances, quite soberly we may be sure, and the 'court party' thus got its cue if any were needed. The proprietor riding two horses at full gallop, Signor Spinacuta dancing daringly on a tight rope, a clown tickling the risibilities of the crowd and mingling Mrs. Bingham's laughter with that of Mrs. Jones, her washwoman, women on horseback doing stunts, and a trained horse that could leap over other horses without balking — such were the merry nights under the dripping candles.[1]

Then there was Bowen's Wax Works and museum of curiosities and paintings and the museum of Mr. Peale — and under the same roof with the latter the reading-room of the Philosophical Society, where Jefferson was to find a sanctuary in the days when he was to be anathema in the fashionable drawing-rooms.

Frivolity, extravagance, exaggerated imitation of Old-World dissipations, could scarcely have been suited to Jefferson's taste; but when he wished for society of another sort he could always run in on Rittenhouse to discuss science, or on Dr. Rush who mixed politics with powders, or, better still, he could drive out to 'Stenton,' the beautiful country house of Dr. James Logan and his cultured wife, approached by its glorious avenue of hemlocks. There he could sit under the trees on the lawn or walk in the old-fashioned gardens or browse in the fine library. There before the huge fireplace in the lofty wainscoted rooms he could sit with the Doctor and discuss the aristocratic tendencies of the times — and this he frequently did. Despite his democracy, Jefferson lived like an aristocrat. He had found a place in the country near the city where the house was 'entirely embosomed in high plane trees with good grass below,' and there, on warm summer days, he was wont

[1] Scharf, II, 952.

to 'breakfast, dine, write, read, and entertain company' under the trees. Even in its luxury, his was the home of the philosopher. It was under these plane trees that he worked out much of the strategy of his political battles.[1] Such was the social background for the struggle of Hamilton and Jefferson — with little in it to strengthen or encourage the latter in his fight.

[1] *Domestic Life* (to Martha), 221-22.

CHAPTER VII
JEFFERSON MOBILIZES

I

WHEN Jefferson assumed the task of organizing the opposition to the policies of the Federalists all the forces most susceptible to organization and intelligent direction were arrayed upon the other side. The commercial interests, constituting Hamilton's shock troops, had their organizations in all the larger towns and in a crisis could be speedily mobilized in the smaller. The various Chambers of Commerce were Federalist clubs that could be summoned to action on a day's notice. The financial interests, always in close formation when not sleeping on their arms, could be ordered to the front overnight. The live-wire speculators whose fortunes had sprung up magically were on their toes to do battle for the system that had enriched them, and eager to do the bidding of the magician who had waved the wand. The greater part of the intellectuals, lawyers, doctors, professors, preachers, were enthusiastic champions of Hamiltonian policies — and because of their prestige these were powerful factors in the moulding of opinion. And, most serious of all, from Jefferson's point of view, the major portion of the press was either militantly Hamiltonian or indifferently democràtic. In the drawing-rooms were heard the sentiments of the Chambers of Commerce — in glorification of materialism.

The rich, the powerful, and their retainers among the men of the professions, were bound to the Federalist by a common interest in property and a common fear of the masses. Since the policies of Hamilton were frankly in the interests of the commercial classes, their supporters were found largely in cities and towns of the commercial North — within easy reach. A word from the chief to his leaders in the capital — Ames and Cabot of Massachusetts; King, Schuyler, and Lawrence of New York; Wolcott and Ellsworth of Connecticut; Morris, Bingham, and Fitzsimmons of Pennsylvania; Dayton of New Jersey; McHenry of Maryland;

FISHER AMES

ROBERT GOODLOE HARPER

GEORGE CABOT

GOUVERNEUR MORRIS

Smith and Harper of South Carolina — a word from these to the commercial leaders in their States, and from these a word to those under obligations to them — the small merchants operating on credit — and the coffee-houses buzzed, the Chambers of Commerce acted, editors plied their pens, preachers thundered from pulpits, and even at the social functions they danced and flirted in the war paint of the party.

As Jefferson surveyed the field, he observed that his great antagonist's organization was but a consolidation of organizations previously existent — and these imposing in their representation of wealth, intellect, and social prestige. Hamilton could snap his fingers, and the merchants came; could lift his hand, and the officers of the Cincinnati were in the saddle; could wave his wand, and Fenno, Russell, and other potent editors would instantly do his bidding, and the preachers of New England scarcely waited for the sign to pass the devil by to damn democracy.

But Jefferson had his eye on other forces, numerically stronger, if less imposing. The farmers, comprising ninety per cent of the Nation, were resentful of policies that pampered the merchant and left them out in the cold. The private soldiers of the Revolution, less respected then than when Webster made his Bunker Hill address, were embittered because their securities had gone for a song while speculators had waxed wealthy on the sacrifice. The more robust republicans were shocked at the aristocratic affectations of their rulers and the tone of the Federalist press. The excise law was hated in the remote sections, and unpopular with the masses everywhere. The doctrine of implied powers had alarmed the friends of State sovereignty. There was an undercurrent of feeling, which Jefferson, with ear marvelously keen for rumblings, caught, that laws were passed for the few at the expense of the many. And it was being bruited abroad that in high quarters there was a disposition to cultivate England to the neglect of France. Everywhere through the South and West there was a bitter resentment of government by and for the East.

Including all, and more important than any single one, there was a fervent spirit of democracy running through the land, while the Federalist leaders were openly denouncing the democrats. 'Looking simply at the field of American history,' says Professor

Anson D. Morse, 'it would be just to enumerate among the causes of the Democratic Party all influences which from the beginning of the colonial period carried forward at a really marvelous rate the democratization of the American character.'[1] The country was really democratic before there was a party of democracy. Jefferson knew it; Hamilton never suspected it, or, suspecting, determined to override the sentiment. Therein lies the original cause of the ultimate triumph of Jefferson, and the evidence that the Federalist Party was foredoomed to ultimate failure.

But how to reach, galvanize, vitalize, organize this great widely scattered mass of unimportant, inarticulate individuals — that was the problem that confronted Jefferson. Ninety-five per cent of the people lived in the country or in villages. Communication was difficult. There were for them no Chambers of Commerce, no coffee-houses, no Faneuil Halls. Thousands had no idea what was going on outside the boundaries of their isolated farms and villages. If the masses in the cities were in sympathy with democracy — and they were — comparatively few of these were permitted to vote. Under the John Jay Constitution of New York, as late as 1790, only 1303 of the 13,330 male residents of voting age in New York City were allowed to vote with the property qualification deliberately designed for their disfranchisement.[2] In Vermont alone, of the New England States, no property qualification attached to the suffrage, albeit in New Hampshire any male paying tax, however small, was qualified. In Massachusetts, Rhode Island, and Connecticut great numbers were excluded by their poverty. Thus, in the beginning, the thousands of hewers of wood and drawers of water in the towns and cities of the North were lost to all practical purposes. But all of the common folk were not disfranchised, and they who had the vote were splendid material for a militant organization. They had a genius for practical politics when under the orders of a drill master, and were not too fastidious for the grime and sweat of the polling-places. One of these was worth a dozen dandies from Mrs. Bingham's circle on election day.[3] There was abundant material for a party — if it could be assembled and coordinated.

[1] *Parties and Party Leaders*, 156–57.   [2] Alexander, 15.
[3] Biddle, *Autobiography*, 246.

II

As Jefferson's mild eye surveyed the field, he found in almost every State local parties, some long in existence, fighting for popular rights as they understood them; but their fights had been waged on local issues. The party he was to create was to fight in precisely the same cause—on the national field. Here, then, was something already at hand. Why not consolidate these local parties into one great national organization, and broaden the issue to include the problems of both State and Nation? The local leaders? Why not make them field marshals in command of the Massachusetts division, the North Carolina division, Pennsylvania and Maryland divisions?

The philosopher-politician took up his pen, for he had learned in the organization of the Revolution what could be done through correspondence. Out under the plane trees he was to sit at his table writing — to Sam Adams, to Rutledge, to John Taylor, to Willie Jones. Under his roof and at his table conferences with Madison, Monroe, Giles, Bloodworth, became commonplace. 'Oh, I should note that Mr. Jefferson, with more than Parisian politeness, waited on me at my chamber this morning,' wrote Maclay. 'He talked politics, mostly the French difference and the whale fishery.' [1] A very cautious approach, we may be sure, for the master politician and psychologist thoroughly understood the little vanities, prejudices, and weaknesses of that singularly suspicious democrat. Quite different would have been a conversation with Gallatin or Monroe. Taking an inventory of prospective lieutenants in the States, and comparing the material with that against him, he could not but have realized his disadvantage. Brilliant men are prone to flutter about the rich and powerful, and nothing succeeds like success with the strong. No chance for him to ride to war surrounded by such scintillating company as that which encircled Hamilton — but here and there was a man who shimmered in the sun.

In Massachusetts, home of Ames, Cabot, and Sedgwick, Jefferson could count on two men who surpassed any of this famous group in service in the making of the Republic, but, strange as it

[1] Maclay, 397.

may seem in perspective, old Sam Adams and John Hancock were not in good standing with the staid business men of Boston. Their republicanism was too robust, their devotion to the principles of the Declaration too uncompromising for the materialists, who appeared, for the most part, on the battle-field after the fight was won, to claim the fruits of the victory. Sam Adams had lost his race for Congress to Fisher Ames who had dallied with his books when the ragged Continentals were struggling in the field. When the clever politicians of the Essex Junto exchanged letters, these erstwhile Revolutionary heroes of the dark days were seldom mentioned with respect; but they had their following in the streets and among those who had shared in the perils they had faced. Upon these two Jefferson could rely.

But there were others, more active and militant in the Boston of those days in the building of the party of democracy. Foremost in the fight, and most annoying to the ruling oligarchy, was the brilliant Dr. Charles Jarvis, who was a powerful orator [1] whose social status, on a par with that of Otis, raised him above the condescension or contempt of the moneyed aristocracy, and whose ability was beyond the reach of disparagement.[2] Through many years of leadership in the legislature he 'had made the rights of man his pole star.' [3] No one did so much to organize and vitalize the masses, for he could pass from the legislative hall to the public platform without any diminution of power. As in the former he could match the best in argument, on the latter no one knew better how to direct the storm.' Jarvis's electioneering influence in this town is very great,' wrote John Quincy Adams to his father.[4]

As a file leader, organizer, agitator, he had powerful support in the robust, rough-hewn rope-maker, Ben Austin, who wrestled under the rules of catch-as-catch-can, mingled with the element that Ames and Cabot considered vulgar, and under the signature of 'Honestus' dealt telling blows in letters that the mechanic could understand. 'Rabid essays,' they were — judged by the standard of the élite.[5] Sam Adams, John Hancock, Austin, and Jarvis — these were the Jeffersonian leaders in the Old Bay State. Less

---

[1] Thomas, I, 21.   [2] Morison, *Otis*, I, 52.
[3] Quoted from *Independent Chronicle*, by Robinson, 10.
[4] J. Q. Adams, *Works*, I, 191.   [5] Morison, *Otis*, I, 52.

aggressive, but often valuable, was James Sullivan, orator, leader of the Bar, letter-writer and pamphleteer, whose vigorous mind, powers of application, and indomitable courage were to render yeoman service.

In the other New England States the democrats were less fortunate. In Connecticut, ruled with an iron hand by an oligarchy of preachers, professors, and reactionary politicians, the prospects were dark enough, but even there the Jeffersonians found a leader capable of coping with the best of the opposition in the hard-hitting, resourceful Abraham Bishop, who was a veritable scandal and stench to the gentlemen of the cloth and of the counting-room. Nowhere in America was such an amazing combination of Church and State. Election days were celebrated with religious services, and the sermons were party harangues, described by the irreverent Bishop as consisting of 'a little of governor, a little of Congress, much of politics, and a very little of religion — a strange compote, like a carrot pie, having so little ingredients that the cook must christen it.'[1] The ruling Council of the State was so organized that the system was an impregnable stronghold beyond the reach of the people. Nowhere on American soil anything so un-American or unrepublican. It did its work behind doors closed and barred. The Congregational clergy were the Cossacks of Connecticut Federalism, laying the lash of their furious denunciation on the backs of critics. It required more than a majority to rule under this system, and more than ordinary courage to challenge its pretensions.[2] The good Doctor Dwight of Yale was busy damning democrats to perdition. A little later Gideon Granger and Ephraim Kirby were to take their place beside Bishop, and with the aid of the 'American Mercury' of Hartford and the 'New London Bee' to give blow for blow. But the fighting was against desperate odds, the Federalists strongly entrenched on a steep hill, the ascent to which could be raked with canister.

'The masses are disfranchised,' cried Bishop. 'Yes, poor porpoises,' sneered Noah Webster the Federalist who was soon to become editor of a New York paper launched by Hamilton.[3] But Bishop and his little coterie were fighters, and Jefferson took them to his heart.

[1] *Connecticut in Transition*, 190–91.   [2] *Ibid.*, 193–97.   [3] *Ibid.*, 222.

In New Hampshire, Jefferson had to bide his time. Among the members of the Senate no one had a better record of unselfish Revolutionary service than John Langdon. Practical, hard-headed, unimaginative, a lover of money, he had accumulated some wealth in mercantile pursuits. Fond of company, pleasing and unaffected in his manner, impressive in appearance, his senatorial toga became him well.[1] When Hamilton's financial plans were pending, he gave them his support, and, alas, profited not a little, but from the beginning the keen-eyed Jefferson discerned the traits that were ultimately to separate him from the Hamiltonians. Within two years Langdon had assumed the leadership of the Jeffersonians in New Hampshire, but as late as 1798, according to the recollection of a famous Jacksonian, 'with the exception of Langdon and a few sterling patriots there could not be said to be in this State a party favorable to the principles of Thomas Jefferson.'[2]

In Vermont the situation was somewhat similar, albeit the opportunities there were greater in the absence of a property qualification for the vote. There, too, was Matthew Lyon, of whom we shall hear much, whose fanatical devotion to democracy was a heritage from a father who had paid the penalty of his patriotism on the gallows in Ireland; whose hatred of aristocracy was but a reaction to the memory of his days of poverty. Possessing a genius for business, and succeeding, he was irresistibly drawn to politics, where his Celtic humor, his energy, impetuosity, and sincerity surrounded him with friends. His radicalism became a flaming torch that lighted up the granite hills. Not for nothing was he born in the land of the Donnybrook Fair, for he loved a fight or a frolic, and he was to have much of both. Enlisting in the Jeffersonian fight in the beginning, he was to fight unceasingly, take blows, and know the degradation of a cell. There was a degree of felony in democracy in the New England of the last days of the eighteenth century.

In Rhode Island, Jefferson sought vainly for an effective leader, though the field was fertile because of the lingering hostility to centralization and the poverty and debts of the people.

Leaving New England, the leader found much to interest him

[1] *Republican Court*, 49.   [2] Isaac Hill, quoted by Robinson, 29.

in New York. There was that sturdy, indomitable champion of State rights, and inveterate enemy of aristocracy, George Clinton, an uncompromising republican of Cromwellian audacity and decision, with an unequaled hold on the confidence and affections of the people. There, too, were the Livingstons, mortally offended by the political stupidity of Hamilton in defeating the brilliant Chancellor's aspirations for the Senate. Had this numerous and powerful family a conference one night to discuss the affront and to emerge a unit in opposition?[1] Whatever the cause, the effect was clear — the Livingston clan was only too eager to join the insurgents, and this was not lost on the astute politician of Monticello. Chancellor Robert R. Livingston, convincing orator, erudite lawyer, profound statesman, fascinating personality, possessing the glamour of wealth and tradition so important to a Jeffersonian leader in New York with its commercial princes and barons of the soil — here was a man to be cultivated with all the finesse of which Jefferson was capable. The master of Monticello could speak the language of the master of the New York manor house.

And Burr? Just what Jefferson expected of Burr is a mystery unsolvable. He appreciated his brilliancy and professional prestige, but were the penetrating eyes blind to the weaknesses of character? Just a little while before Burr had joined with Hamilton against Clinton, and Federalist votes had sent him to the Senate. There, to be sure, he had arrayed himself on the popular side, but could he be relied upon? He had played a lone hand, holding aloof from the Clintonians and the Livingstons, and dining often at the table of Hamilton; but that he was singled out for assiduous cultivation we may be sure. No one was closer to Jefferson than Dr. Rush when, in the early fall of 1792, the latter wrote a wheedling note to Burr. 'Your friends everywhere,' wrote the Doctor, 'look to you to take an active part in removing the monarchical rubbish of our government. It is time to speak out or we are undone.'[2] Previous to this, Jefferson had been most courteous in permitting the charming Senator from New York to examine papers in the archives of the State Department until Washington interposed.[3]

Clinton, Livingston, and Burr — a triumvirate that caught Jefferson's fancy; but he was interested in opportunities in New York

---

[1] Hammond, I, 107.   [2] Davis, *Burr*, I, 316–17.   [3] *Ibid.*, I, 331.

having no direct connection with any of the three. The less imagi-
native Maclay had seen in a parade of the Sons of Tammany only
'a grotesque scene,' with the members 'in Indian dresses,' and
while he had addressed them at a dinner he had concluded that
'there is some kind of a scheme' which was 'not well digested as
yet.'[1] Jefferson made it his business to learn more. He found that
the strange organization was an answer, in part, to the Cincinnati
which stood, in the popular mind, for aristocracy; that it was rabidly republican and wholly democratic; that it sympathized with
the revolutionists in France, and resented the property disqualifi-
cations of our own Revolutionary soldiers for the suffrage, while
the wealthy, notoriously friendly to England when these soldiers
fought, were being accorded political recognition and place. Here
was a society after his own heart, here a method to make the
masses felt — a combination and coördination of their efforts. All
over the land the hundreds of thousands of inarticulate, unimportant, ineffective, commonplace friends of democracy, and in one
city these had been given a voice, an arm, a rostrum. It was not
'grotesque' to Jefferson. He did not join these imitation red men
in their wigwam, nor drink of their ale, but John Pintard the chief
became his friend and idolater, and with him the great man talked.
The non-partisan society grew more and more democratic, soon
intensely partisan, and at Tammany dinners the welkin rang to
the toast to 'Thomas Jefferson.' New York became a cock-pit
from the start.

But when the Jeffersonian board of strategy turned to New
Jersey, the problem was more difficult. No outstanding leader,
strong in the faith, stood ready to mount and ride. There, true,
the Janus-faced Jonathan Dayton was ready to flirt with any force
that might serve his personal ends. He was a speculator — and
worse. Supporting and profiting from the Hamilton policies, he
smiled on the Jeffersonians significantly.

In Pennsylvania there was the nucleus of a party and virile men
to lead it — men like Mifflin, who, despite his drunkenness, was
popular and a power; like Maclay, who had the force that intense
conviction brings in spite of temperamental handicaps; men like
Alexander J. Dallas, aggressive, daring, able; men utterly unfit for

[1] Maclay, 260.

ALBERT GALLATIN

EDWARD LIVINGSTON

WILLIAM BRANCH GILES

JAMES MADISON

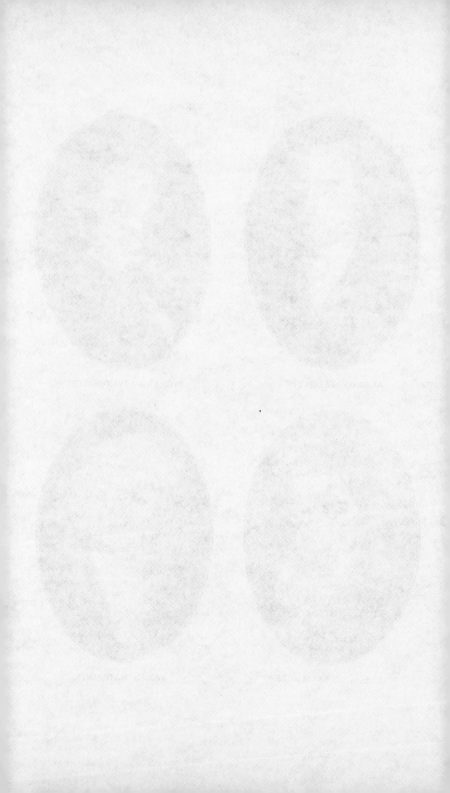

the rough-and-tumble combats of practical politics whose characters and abilities made them potent in the fight — like Rush the physician, Rittenhouse the scientist, Logan the philosopher, and, looming above the tops of the Western forests, a young giant and genius, Albert Gallatin.

In Delaware, nothing; in Maryland, John Francis Mercer, fighter and intriguer, sapper and miner, agitator and organizer, with whom democracy was a religion, Hamilton a devil, and Jefferson a saint. In Virginia, a sparkling galaxy, Madison, Monroe, the accomplished Pendleton, the resourceful Giles, the extraordinary John Taylor of Caroline.

In North Carolina, Jefferson found a leader cut from his own pattern, an aristocratic democrat, a radical rich man, a consummate politician who made the history that lesser men wrote without mentioning his name, Willie Jones of Halifax. His broad acres, his wealth, his high social standing were the objects of his pride, and he lived in luxury and wore fine linen while the trusted leader of the masses, mingling familiarly with the most uncouth backwoodsman, inviting, however, only the select to partake of the hospitality of his home. There was more than a touch of the Virginia aristocrat of the time in his habits — he raced, gambled, hunted like a gentleman. Like Jefferson he was a master of the art of insinuation, a political and social reformer. He loved liberty, hated intolerance, and prevented the ratification of the Constitution in the first State Convention because of the absence of a Bill of Rights. There he exerted a subtle influence that was not conspicuous on the floor. If he was neither orator nor debater, he was a strategist, disciplinarian, diplomat, who fought with velvet gloves — with iron within. A characteristic portrait would show him puffing at his pipe in the midst of his farmer followers, suggesting, insinuating, interspersing his political conversation with discussions of the crops, farming implements, hunting dogs, horses. An Anthony in arousing the passions by subtle hints, he was an Iago in awakening suspicions.[1] Here was the man with the stuff that Jefferson required, generous and lovable in social relations, in politics relentless, hard as iron. He was the Jefferson of North Carolina — 'a man ... the object of more hatred and more adora-

[1] McRee, *Iredell*, II, 232, 239; Dodd, *Macon*, 38.

tion than has ever since lived' in that State.[1] Nor did he stand alone
without assistants, for there was Nathaniel Macon, honest, intense,
man of the soil who loved his few acres, his dogs and horses, and
his class; and there was Timothy Bloodworth whose fierce adherence to democracy and fanatical hatred of privilege may have
been a poignant reflection of his poverty. Jones, the aristocratic
lord of many acres; Macon the representative of the small farmer;
Bloodworth the artisan, smithy at the forge, watchmaker, wheel-
wright, as well as preacher, doctor, and cultivator of the soil: his
radicalism was born in suffering and in suffering he had grown.[2]

In Georgia, Jefferson had equal cause for satisfaction. There
were small farms, poor industrious men, ardent republicans, with
the frontiersmen's natural democracy and the debtors' suspicions
of concentrated wealth allied with governmental power. And there
to lead them was James Jackson, idol of the people, a boisterous,
impassioned orator whose eloquence often gave more heat than
light. Historians have been prone to sneer at him, but this man
who came as a child from Devonshire in England to take his place
three years later in the army of Washington, and to receive the
keys of Savannah from the British ten years after his arrival, was
something more than an upstart. He who refused the governorship of his State when twenty-one, and six years after leaving his
English home, to take his chances in the field, was scarcely an object for jest. He was a power as a leader and was to strike Titan
blows in the cause that Jefferson nationally led.[3]

In South Carolina, dominated by rich commercial Charleston,
Jefferson long looked in vain for a leader for his cause. A friend of
the Pinckneys and the Rutledges, they held aloof or joined their
fortunes with Hamilton. Only toward the close did Charles Pinckney, the most eloquent, resourceful, and magnetic of his family,
part company with his cousins to lunge and lash with gusty joy for
the man of Monticello.

Such were the leaders on whom Jefferson was dependent in
welding the popular parties in the various States into a strong
national army marching in step, with a common policy and purpose.

---

[1] Dodd, *Maccon*, 51.   [2] McRee, *Iredell*, II, 233.
[3] Senate Docs., vol. 56, 61st Congress, 2d Session, 755.

III

Had Jefferson been even richer than Hamilton in brilliant leaders, he would not have made the latter's fatal blunder of assuming them to be enough. He was too much the practical politician to be impressed with a brilliant staff of officers — without privates. He set out to arouse the masses, mobilize, drill, and lead them. Above all, it was his intention to lead. Within a year, Ames was to observe with desperation and disgust the divisions among the Federalists and to comment that 'Virginia moves in a solid column . . . the discipline of the [Jefferson] party is as severe as the Prussian' and 'deserters are not spared.'[1]

The first necessity was to get the men to discipline. A vast number of the masses had no conception of their political power and were indifferent to the vote. Thousands over the country were disfranchised by property qualifications, and one of the prime purposes of the new party would be to break these down. The immediate problem was to awaken the interest of those who, having the vote, did not appreciate the privilege. With many of these, this was due to the lack of political consciousness; with others, to the feeling that it was useless for the unimportant to attempt to influence governmental action. To the latter it would be necessary to prove the possibilities of the concerted action of large numbers of uninfluential men — and there was the Society of Tammany pointing the way. No squeamishness in the mobilization either — the possession of the vote was enough. Soon, very soon, strange, disturbing things would be seen even in New England — cabinetmakers, shoemakers, mechanics perking up on politics, with evidence of organization here and there. Federalist leaders would soon be complaining that organization was conspiracy against the 'government.' In New Hampshire they would be calling those uniting for political action 'insurgents.' The insolence of the Jeffersonians appealing to the people for support would be frowned upon as degrading. 'Of course,' said a Massachusetts paper, 'there can be but two parties in a country — the friends of order and its foes.'[2]

And such people! The very riff-raff that one would never invite

[1] Ames (to Dwight), I, 136–37.　　　　[2] Robinson, 53.

into one's parlor — 'desperate, embarrassed, unprincipled, disorderly, ambitious, disaffected, morose men.'[1] Were not these the propertyless who wasted their earnings in a grogshop?[2] And who were these petty agitators? Who but 'Jacobins' holding forth 'in the bar-rooms of Rhode Island and Vermont and trying to stir up opposition.'[3] Wretched offal after all — but what a pity that Jefferson should countenance, least of all cultivate, such people. 'Mr. Jefferson appears to have shown rather too much of a disposition to cultivate vulgar prejudices,' wrote Wolcott, and 'accordingly he will become popular in the ale-houses.'[4]

Miserable 'Jacobins!' Disreputable clowns of the bar-rooms! And such unthinkable methods! Here — there — everywhere, when a few men could be gathered together, some one appeared to deliver free lectures on practical politics. And such subjects! 'Discipline'; 'How to Make Men Follow their File Leaders.'[5]

IV

In arousing and consolidating the widely scattered democrats, Jefferson instantly appreciated the importance of a national newspaper to the end that the farmer in Georgia, the planter in Virginia, the frontiersman in western Pennsylvania, the mechanic in Boston, the shopmen of Rhode Island, and the reds of Tammany sipping their ale in the New York tavern, might all talk the same language at the same time. True, the Jeffersonians were not without able editorial support. There was Thomas Greenleaf pounding away vigorously in the 'New York Journal'; Thomas Adams hammering merrily in the Boston 'Independent Chronicle'; and in Philadelphia, Benjamin Franklin Bache was making a mild show of opposition in his 'Pennsylvania Daily Advertiser.' But these were independent supporters, not 'organs,' and it was an 'organ' that was needed — something to meet the Hamilton organ which was becoming increasingly offensive to the democrats.

In estimating the sincerity of the simulated shock of the Federalists when the Secretary of State encouraged the establishment of a paper to support his principles, it is well to bear in mind that the

[1] Robinson, 55.
[2] Quoted from David Daggett's pamphlet, by Purcell in *Connecticut in Transition*, 225.
[3] *Centinel*, August 22, 1792.   [4] Gibbs, i, 73.
[5] Robinson, quoting from *American Mercury*, 9.

Secretary of the Treasury had done precisely the same thing two years before. Then, as always, politicians were shocked at the turpitude of their opponents. Just how John Fenno came to establish the 'Gazette of the United States' is an impenetrable mystery. He was in his thirty-eighth year when he appeared at the home of Rufus King, perhaps the ablest of Hamilton's supporters, with a letter of introduction from Christopher Gore, a member of the inner council of Boston Federalism who afterward waxed wealthy on speculation in the funds. The record is meager as to Fenno's previous career beyond the revelation that he was born in Boston and taught for several years in the Old South Writing School. In the letter to King, we have the assurance of Gore that Fenno's 'literary accomplishments are very handsome'; that Gore had known him long and could testify that 'his honor and fidelity are unquestionable; and, strangely enough, that 'his talents as the editor of a public paper are unrivaled in this commonwealth.' As Benjamin Russell was then editing the 'Columbian Centinel,' the tribute would seem strained but for the intimation that the strength and sparkle of that able journal was due to Fenno's contributions; and since the 'Centinel' suffered no apparent loss on his leaving Boston, even this theory seems absurd.

If his origin is a mystery, the purpose of his call on King was made clear enough in the letter of introduction. The 'unrivaled' editor sought encouragement for the establishment of a newspaper through arrangements for 'obtaining the patronage of Congress' in the printing of its journals and official papers. If something of the sort could be arranged, Gore was positive that Fenno would prove 'capable of performing essential service in the cause of Federalism and good government.'[1]

The conversation was evidently agreeable, assurances of some sort were manifestly given, and within a few weeks the 'Gazette of the United States' was making its appearance. That Hamilton, who was intimately identified with King, was consulted, we may be sure; and within four years the relations between Fenno and Hamilton were so confidential that the former felt no hesitancy in appealing in a letter to the latter for a loan of two thousand dollars. Months before, the editor had submitted a schedule of his

[1] King, *Works*, I, 357.

debts and credits to the head of the Treasury. The two had talked over the financial difficulties of the paper. The appeal for the loan was not lightly brushed aside. Hamilton wrote to King of the troubles of 'poor Fenno,' and proposed that if King would raise a thousand dollars in New York, he would himself undertake to raise a similar amount in Philadelphia. It is to be assumed that the money was raised, for the paper continued to appear. It is significant that in his letter to Hamilton, the editor wrote as one who had rendered faithful service and was entitled to consideration.[1]

From the beginning Fenno had liked to think of himself as the editor of 'the court journal.' Possessing considerable merit, it is impossible to turn its yellowing pages even now without being oppressed with a sense of sycophancy and snobbery. There was a fawning on wealth and kow-towing to power in most of the leading articles. The tone was pronouncedly pro-English and all Hamiltonian. Democracy was anathema. The critics of the policies of the leader of the Federalists were inciters to disorder. All the influence of the Federalist leaders was exerted to throw all possible governmental patronage into his office.

Hamilton had his paper before Jefferson got his own.[2] It was to meet these conditions that James Madison and Governor Henry Lee conceived the notion of persuading Philip Freneau, 'the poet of the Revolution,' to establish a newspaper in Philadelphia. This fiery petrel of democracy was eking out a mere existence on a New York newspaper when Madison, who had been his roommate at Princeton, made the proposal. This was due in part to personal affection and the feeling that the poet's sufferings and losses in the Revolution entitled him to some consideration, but in large measure to the purity of his republicanism and his zeal for the popular cause. 'I entertained hopes,' wrote Madison later, 'that a free paper, meant for general circulation, and edited by a man of genius of republican principles and a friend of the Constitution, would be some antidote to the doctrines and discourses circulated in favor of Monarchy and Aristocracy.'[3] With the view to giving some slight protection to a precarious enterprise, Madison sought a clerkship for his college friend in one of the governmental de-

[1] King, *Works*, I, 501–02.   [2] Payne, *History of Journalism*, 155.
[3] *Writings*, I, 569–70.

partments. Nor was it to Jefferson that he first applied.[1] The outcome, however, was the offer of a clerkship of foreign languages in
the State Department at a salary of two hundred and fifty dollars a year. He accepted, went to Philadelphia, and established
the 'Federal,' or 'National Gazette.'

The leaders of the new party were plainly pleased with the
prospect. Jefferson himself did not scruple to solicit subscribers
among his Virginia neighbors. Henry Lee, who was to desert to the
enemy later, sent in subscriptions through Madison, in a letter rejoicing because the paper 'is rising fast into reputation,' and lamenting because of the precariousness of its arrival.[2] 'His paper
in the opinion here,' wrote Madison acknowledging Lee's letter,
'justifies the expectations of his friends, and merits the diffusive
circulation they have endeavored to procure it.'[3]

The Philadelphians awoke with a start to find that an entirely
new note had been struck in political journalism. Within a few
weeks, the 'Federal Gazette' was being extensively copied in the
papers over the country. Bache in his 'Advertiser' caught something of Freneau's fire and audacity, and began to take a firmer,
bolder tone. Fenno found himself forced to defend himself and
his friends in almost every issue. Men and even women scanned
its columns eagerly and with emotions determined by their political prepossessions. Within a few months the poet-editor was
being hotly debated by the two leading papers of Boston. 'As all
the friends of civil liberty wish at all times to be acquainted with
every question which appears to regard the public weal,' said the
'Independent Chronicle,' 'a great number of gentlemen in this
and neighboring towns have subscribed for the Federal Gazette
published by Mr. Philip Freneau at Philadelphia; and it is hoped
that Freneau's Gazette, which is said to be printed under the eye of
that established patriot, Thomas Jefferson, will be generally taken
in the New England States.'[4] What! wrote a correspondent in the
'Centinel,' is this an avowal that Jefferson is the real editor? A
paper hostile to religion and government! 'Surely T. Adams
ought to be well founded in his affections before he brings forward
Mr. Jefferson as the patron of such a Gazette.'[5]

---

[1] *Writings*, I, 569–70. [2] Rives, *Madison*, III, 194, note. [3] *Writings*, I, 543
[4] September 6, 1792. [5] September 12, 1792.

Within a short time Freneau had aroused the savage rage of the
Federalist leaders and the zealous loyalty of the democrats everywhere. Here was a man who was not awed by power, and, brush-
ing aside mild criticism and vapory innuendoes, struck hard and
mentioned names. Soon the Jeffersonian farmers in Georgia were
talking what he was writing, and Jeffersonian editors generally
were following his lead. In the bar-rooms of Rhode Island men of
no consequence were reading the paper aloud over their mugs, and
David Rittenhouse in the library of the Philosophical Society was
chuckling over its vicious thrusts. Just then 'friends of the Constitution' among the Federalists began to regret a certain provision in the Bill of Rights and to begin the slow incubation of the
Sedition Law. That incomparable political preacher, Timothy
Dwight, began to denounce papers as the 'vice' of the people in
the new settlements, and another pious gentleman of the cloth
thundered from the pulpit: 'Many of you in spite of all the advice
and friendly warnings of your religious and political fathers have
taken and continue to take and read Jacobin papers, full of all manner of mischief and subtlety of the Devil.'[1] The hand-to-hand
fighting of Hamilton and Jefferson was forced by the lusty blows
of Freneau, who deserves to be something more than a name in
the Plutarchian struggle.

V

Philip Freneau had richly earned the right to hold and express
opinions concerning the destiny of his country. Many years before the Revolution, his Huguenot ancestors had come over from
France, and for years his was a well-known name in the best
circles of New York City where he was born. His childhood had
been passed on the thousand-acre estate of his father near the
battle-field of Monmouth, in a fine old mansion fashioned after
the colonial style, with a great hall running through it, and large
porticoes commanding a view of a beautiful country. The house
was served by many domestic slaves. Near by rose Beacon Hill,
thickly timbered, and from the peak could be seen the lower bay
and the blue waters of the Atlantic. There his early childhood was
passed under the tender care and training of a mother of rare in-

[1] Robinson, 70, note.

telligence. From her he caught a love of poetry, and of the things of which poetry is made. The spirit of his liberty-loving ancestors was strong within him. He had all the impulsiveness, the fighting courage of the Gael. When not at his studies, he wandered alone into the woods and upon the hill where he could brood dreamily upon the mystery of the sea. On the site where the battle of Monmouth was to be fought, he began the study of Greek and Latin in his tenth year. Even as a child he had a hot passionate hatred of oppression, an unfathomable contempt for hypocrisy, and an ardent love of beauty. All this he put into childish verse.

When he entered Princeton (Nassau Hall), great events were beginning to unfold. The patriots of Massachusetts, protesting against an English law, had been declared rebels, the leading offenders had been ordered across the sea for trial, the troops of General Gates had marched into Boston. The college was a hotbed of sedition. That superb patriot, John Witherspoon, was president, and among the students who gathered in the evening in the room that Freneau shared with Madison, were 'Light Horse' Harry Lee, Aaron Burr, William Bradford, destined to close an exceptionally promising career as a member of Washington's Cabinet, and Brockholst Livingston.

Nothing that Freneau ever said or did in after-life that was not foreshadowed at Princeton can be found. His tongue was sharp, and his pen dripped the vitriol of satire. He wrote much verse, and long before the Declaration of Independence, he had a hatred of kings. Even thus early in his 'Pyramid of Kings,' he made profession of his democracy.

> 'Millions of slaves beneath their labors fainted,
> Who were here doomed to toil incessantly,
> And years elapsed while groaning myriads strove
> To raise this mighty tomb — and but to hide
> The worthless bones of an Egyptian king.'

Under the encouragement of Witherspoon, all the patriotic fire within him burst into flame.

Long before Washington, Adams, or Franklin were dreaming of a republic and absolute independence, this was his dream. During the time he was supposed to be poring over Coke and Blackstone, he was feverishly plying his pen writing political articles for the press. He was a rebel by nature. He wrote deliberately to arouse a burning hatred of tyranny and a militant love of liberty. He sang the songs of hate, and read and studied the Roman and French satirists to perfect himself in the art he was to use so effectively later. When the war began he threw himself into the struggle. A pathetic little figure, this — a mere wisp of a boy charging on ahead to smash the connection with England, only to find that the other patriots had no such thought. They were fighting for rights within the empire, not for independence. Even then he was too radical for his times or the comfort of his associates. They were thinking of rights, and he of liberty — and in sheer disgust he sailed away to Jamaica.

There was the illusion of liberty on the sea and there was beauty and poetry, and there was opportunity, too, to prepare himself for the part he was to play a little later. It was always his joy to be prepared. On that voyage he perfected himself in the science of navigation. In the languorous air of Santa Cruz he luxuriated in the beauties of nature at its richest, and sought to transcribe to paper all he saw and felt. He had an irresistible impulse for creation — a poet's passion for expression.[1] But even here he was a rebel born to protest. Slavery at its worst was all about him — and he hit it hard in his descriptions.

It was while a guest of the Governor of Bermuda, writing love sonnets to the fair daughter of his host, that the news came of the Declaration of Independence. This was the sort of rebellion Freneau could understand, and he hurried home to find that a battle had been fought at his very door, and that the cushions of the Tennant church he had attended had been stained with blood. Instantly he took out letters of marque and reprisal from the Continental Congress, and put to sea to battle with the British ships. Plunging patriotically with all his means he had a ship built for his own use, named it the *Aurora*, and sought the enemy. In a battle his ship was struck, and it was as a prisoner on the deck of an enemy vessel that he saw his ship, his fortune, sink beneath the waves. The rest was torture and a living death. The *Scorpion* on which he was confined was a miserable old hulk converted into a prison ship, reeking with foul smells and rank disease, and into

[1] 'The Beauties of Santa Cruz,' and 'The House of Night.'

this he was packed where the accommodations were not fit for swine. One by one he saw his fellows perish from disease and neglect, listened in the night to their shrieks of pain and dying groans. When verging on death, he was transferred to the *Hunter* which some sardonic soul had dubbed a 'Hospital Prison Ship.' Its horrors have come down to us in his own poems with its bitter execration of the Hessian doctor.

> 'Here uncontrolled he exercised his trade,
> And grew experienced by the deaths he made;
> By frequent blows we from his cane endured
> He killed at least as many as he cured.'

At length he was exchanged. Leaving the vessel with a raging fever, with pains in his joints that made walking a torture, he turned toward home, going through the woods 'for fear of terrifying the neighbors with [his] ghastly looks.'[1] This was the background against which he was to view Washington's policy of neutrality in the war between France and England. He hated England from that hour to his death.

Broken in health almost beyond hope of redemption, his ship sunk, his money gone, the war still on, he turned to his other weapon and took up the pen. 'The Prison Ship' helped to fire the patriots shivering about the cold camps. The poem of contemptuous imprecation, in imitation of Horace, on the treason of Arnold, fanned their wrath. That on the victory of Paul Jones heartened the downcast. Poem followed poem, copied throughout the country, many published on strips of paper and distributed through the army. Some were posted in conspicuous places where they could be committed to memory. Paine wrote 'The Crisis' in prose, Freneau wrote of the crisis in verse; both were a tonic for the wavering. Even Washington did not then speak of him as 'that rascal Freneau,' and that characterization even from Washington cannot rob him of the glory of having been 'the Poet of the Revolution' who gave his health, his entire fortune, almost his life, and all his heart to the cause of liberty.

The close of the war found him in New York barely existing on crumbs from the table of an editor. His was a familiar figure in the

[1] *Life,* 129.

Merchants' Coffee-House at Wall and Water Streets where leading men congregated. The problem then was to get the necessities of life, and literary work was not then included among the means. This was the condition in which Madison found him. He knew the story of his poet friend, and thus it came about that the plan was made for the 'Federal Gazette.' He was ideally fitted for the task. It called for one who could write in the language of the people, could wield a scorpion lash, whose heart was in the cause — and no greater master of invective was in view, no keener satirist. He required no tutoring, and he would accept no orders. He was a rebel still, a radical, a crusader for democracy, who looked with amusement on 'aristocracy,' with hatred on monarchy. He was an original thinker, a breaker of idols, an iconoclastic genius. He had the wit, the keenness, the quickness, the felicity of his French blood, the stern firmness of the Huguenot mind. He was a gusty warrior with a lusty blade and he kept it shining in the sun.

Soon Philadelphia found him a familiar figure in its streets — a rather little man with slightly stooped shoulders, thin yet muscular, who walked briskly like one who knew where he was going. In his office at his work he was more imposing, for there one could note the high intellectual brow, the dark gray deep-set eyes that sometimes blazed under the slightly drooping lids. Usually pensive in repose, his face lighted with animation when he talked. His manners were courteous and refined and women found him interesting and gallant. Nor was this democrat a Marat in dress — he wore the small-clothes, the long hose, the buckled shoes, and cocked hat, long after others had accepted less picturesque fashions. He had no vanity, no ambition for place or power, and no fear of either. He wore no man's collar and he was no man's man. He was a law unto himself.

CHAPTER VIII

THE GAGE OF BATTLE

I

THERE was little in the reception of Hamilton's famous 'Report on Manufactures' during the congressional session of 1791–92 to foreshadow the part it was to play in American politics. Bristling with facts and figures laboriously assembled, the plea for protection and bounties for manufacturers was plausibly presented. Foreseeing the hostility of the farmers, the most persuasive arguments were reserved for them. The diversification of industry would increase the demand for the products of the farm; the elimination of foreign competition would decrease the cost of manufactured goods; and the certainty of immigration would prevent any labor shortage with agriculturists. Better still, the factories would afford the farmers an opportunity to put their wives and children to work in the mills.[1] Four sevenths of the employees of the cotton mills of England were women and children, and many of the latter of 'tender age.'[2] In the making of nails and spikes young boys were able to do the work.[3] As to the constitutional objection, that was disposed of by the doctrine of implied powers.

The newspapers, including Freneau's, ran the report in full, but nothing came of it for the moment. No one was shocked at the idea of working women and children of tender age. After a while a writer in Freneau's paper warned that a new field was being opened 'for favoritism, influence and monopoly.'[4] Madison wrote to Pendleton that 'if Congress can do whatever in their discretion can be done with money . . . the Government is no longer a limited one.'[5] But this 'Report' resulted in less controversy than any that had preceded. There was no storm — just a bare stirring of the leaves.

But Hamilton was not content to allude to brighter worlds — he led the way. Long before, he had been impressed with the in-

[1] Hamilton's *Works*, IV, 91.   [2] *Ibid.*   [3] *Ibid.*, 166.
[4] *National Gazette*, June 18, 1792.   [5] *Writings*, I, 545.

dustrial possibilities of beautiful Passaic Falls in New Jersey, midway between New York and Newark at the very door of the market. Just how long he was in interesting moneyed men in his ambitious plans for a great national manufactory there, we do not know. But even before the publication of his 'Report,' he had personally appeared with others interested before the New Jersey Legislature to 'elucidate anything that may appear obtuse' in the request for a charter.[1] It was only a little trip from Philadelphia to Trenton. Then, one summer day, a group of men appeared at the Falls to purchase land and select the precise sites for the various mills, and the small but masterful figure of Hamilton was the center of the group. All sorts of things would be manufactured, cotton mills predominating, and it would become — this city of Paterson — the industrial capital of the Republic. Major l'Enfant was summoned to the task of making this industrial beehive beautiful, and he responded.[2] Soon there were grumblings among the farmers, outraged because the charter that Hamilton's influence had secured gave the company the right to dig canals on any man's land. The other manufacturers were indignant because the new factory was to be free from taxation for ten years, and its employees were to be excused from military services except in cases of dire necessity. 'A Manufacturer' wrote a vehement protest, mentioning Hamilton by name, and denouncing the act of the legislature as vicious beyond comparison.[3] Soon the Philadelphia papers were advertising that the five letters 'To the Yeomanry,' in pamphlet form, complaining of the privileged nature of the corporation and of the part played by Hamilton, could be had at the various stores of the city.

But Hamilton was not concerned with the grumblings of the groundlings, for he was at high tide. In New York men had subscribed for a portrait of him by Trumbull, and the subscription lists 'were still open in the coffee-house.'[4] He had become the idol of the most powerful class. A little later, Trumbull's work completed, 'the best that ever came from his pencil,' it was placed temporarily in the old city hall in New York.[5] The obscure boy

[1] *National Gazette*, November 14, 1791.
[2] Spooner's *Vermont Journal*, July 31; *National Gazette*, July 14, 1792.
[3] *National Gazette*, September 8, 1792.   [4] *Ibid.*, January 2, 1792.
[5] *Philadelphia Advertiser*, July 6, 1792.

from the West Indies had become an institution in the city of his
adoption. Even so Hamilton was ever vigilant. He had not liked
the Freneau project from the start, and he was watching it like a
hawk.

II

When the poet-journalist took an office on High Street and began the publication of his paper, there was little to justify grave
apprehensions. In his first issues the editor had pledged himself to
the support 'of the great principles on which the American Revolution was founded,' and while this smacked of the jabberings
of Sam Adams, Hancock, and Jefferson, it was probably only a
gesture. The tone of the early editions was temperate, almost
academic. The ordinary reader must have thought it harmless
enough, but Hamilton, who used the press effectively himself,
examined the articles more critically. There were phrases creeping in, innocently, perhaps, that Fenno would have scorned. The
idea that 'public opinion sets the bounds to every government,
and is the real sovereign of every free one,' [1] would never have
soiled the pages of the 'Gazette of the United States.' The little
essays on politics and government were sprinkled all too freely
with these disturbing suggestions. Only an essay on 'Nobility' —
but why make it the vehicle for the thought that 'the downfall of
nobility in France has operated like an early frost toward killing
the germ of it in America.' [2] With Fenno chiding the critics of
officials, what more unfortunate than Freneau's assertion that
'perpetual jealousy of the government' is alone effectual 'against
the machinations of ambition,' and his warning that 'where that
jealousy does not exist in a reasonable degree the saddle is soon
prepared for the back of the people.' [3] A defense of parties coupled
with a denunciation of privilege,[4] stiff criticism of ministerial inefficiency apropos of the St. Clair expedition; forceful protests
against the excise law; [5] and then an article by 'Brutus' on the
funding system which could not be ignored — these were bad
enough. That system, said 'Brutus,' had given undue weight to
the Treasury Department 'by throwing the enormous sum of fifty

[1] *National Gazette*, December 19, 1791.   [2] *Ibid.*, January 19, 1792.
[3] *Ibid.*, January 16, 1792.   [4] *Ibid.*, January 23, 1792.
[5] *Ibid.*, by H. H. Brackenridge, February 9, 1792.

million dollars into the hands of the wealthy,' thus attaching them to all the Treasury measures 'by motives of private interest.' Having combined the great moneyed interest, it had been made formidable by the Bank monopoly. Out of it all had come the 'unlimited excise laws and imposts' that 'anticipated the best resources of the country and swallowed them all up in future payments.' Because the certificates had fallen to the wealthy, 'the industrious mechanic, the laborious farmer and poorer classes generally are made tributary to the latest generation.' [1] Rights of property? Yes — but there is property in rights.[2] Be loyal to the Union? Yes, but who are the enemies of the Union? 'Not those who favoring measures which, pampering the spirit of speculation, disgust the best friends of the Union.' 'Not those who promote unnecessary accumulations of the debts of the Union.' Not those 'who study by arbitrary interpretations and insidious precedents to pervert the limited government of the Union into a government of unlimited discretion.' [3]

With Freneau hitting his stride, the Federalists began to lose their patience. Soon the 'United States Chronicle' of Providence learned that the 'very extraordinary productions' were probably 'the work of some foreigners who wish to reduce the funds in order to purchase.' [4] The 'Centinel' of Boston warned that Freneau's paper was 'supported by a junto for electioneering purposes' and was filled with 'the most absurd misrepresentations of facts, or falsehoods highly injurious to the prevailing character and principles of our government and people.' [5]

But it took the articles of 'Sidney' to force the fighting. These were open attacks on Hamilton and his principles and were written with a punch. He assailed the House for abdicating its power to originate money bills to the Secretary of the Treasury. To delegate that duty was to lie down on a job. And such 'reports'! Arguments! Pleas! Sophistries! Thence to the major attack. 'If we admit that the Secretary is a fallible mortal, and, however great his capacity may be, that he is liable to mistakes or to be imposed upon, or, in range of hypothesis, if we suppose these possible cases, that his political principles do not correspond with

---

[1] *National Gazette*, March 15, 1792.		[2] *Ibid.*, March 29, 1792.
[3] *Ibid.*, April 2, 1792.		[4] *Ibid.*, February 9, 1792.		[5] *Ibid.*, July 18, 1792.

the genius of the government, or with public opinion; or that he embraces the interests of one class in preference to the interests of the other classes, — I say admitting any or all of these circumstances to be possible, then the ministerial mode of influencing the deliberations of Congress practiced since the change of the government, is more dangerous than even that which is pursued but loudly complained of in Britain.'[1] These attacks by Sidney continued with painful regularity, and Freneau's paper became a scandal in the best-regulated families in Philadelphia. Others joined in the fray. 'A Citizen' from a remote section, who had visited the capital to 'know more of men and measures,' speedily convinced himself that many members of government 'were . . . partners with brokers and stock jobbers, and that the banking schemes have been too powerfully and effectually addressed to their avarice.'[2] 'Centinel' warned that 'the fate of the excise law will determine whether the powers of government . . . are held by an aristocratic junto or by the people.'[3] With the pack in hot pursuit of his idol, Fenno rushed to the defense with a denunciation of the 'mad dogs' and 'enemies of the government.' Ah, replied Freneau, welcoming the fight, 'I will tell a short story that will put the matter in a proper light. A pack of rogues once took possession of a church . . . held in high veneration by the inhabitants of the surrounding district. From the sanctuary they sallied out every night, robbed . . . all the neighbors, and when pursued took shelter within the hallowed walls. If any one attempted to molest them there, they deterred him from the enterprise by crying, "Sacrilege," and swearing they would denounce him to the inquisition as a heretic and an enemy of the Holy Mother Church.'[4] And Freneau persevered in his perversity. Right joyously he returned to the scandal of speculation. 'It is worthy of notice that no direct denial has ever appeared of the . . . multiplied assertions that members of the general government have carried on jobs and speculations in their own measures even while those measures were depending.'[5]

[1] *National Gazette*, April 23, 1792. [2] *Ibid.*, May 3, 1792. [3] *Ibid.*, May 7, 1792.
[4] *Ibid.*, May 10, 1792. [5] *Ibid.*, January 4, 1792.

III

An interesting picture was presented the day after the appearance of this attack: Emerging from the doorway of the Morris house was a distinguished party. Washington himself, sober and stately, with his matronly spouse; Hamilton, alert and suave, with little Betty; and a tall, loose-jointed man of pleasing aspect whom spectators instantly recognized as Jefferson. Entering carriages they drove away to visit Mr. Pearce's cotton manufactory. No one knew better than Washington that a crisis had been reached in the relations of his ministers. But a few days before he had sat pondering over a letter from Jefferson. It dealt with the reason for the growing distrust in government, the fiscal policy of Hamilton, the disposition to pile up debt, the corruption in Congress — and it announced a determination to retire from the Cabinet.[1] Washington, greatly distressed, had earnestly importuned him to remain. He had agreed to stay on awhile, but the quarreling was becoming intolerable.

At the factory the little party entered, pausing to examine the machinery and comment upon it, Hamilton the irreproachable gentleman, courteous, amusing, pleasant, Jefferson observing all the amenities of the occasion. It was their last social meeting in small company. But if Washington, who had invited them, hoped thus to persuade them to drop their quarrel, he was foredoomed to disappointment. The cause of their disagreement was elemental and eternal. They returned to the Morris house after a pleasant diversion — and the fight went on.

IV

In early June, Fenno and Freneau were lashing each other with much shouting. But the editor of the Hamilton paper played constantly into the hands of his opponent. He lamented the appearance of a 'faction,' meaning party, because factions mean convulsions under a republican government. It would not be so serious if there were a king, because 'a king at the head of a nation to whom all men of property cling with the consciousness that all property will be set afloat with the government, is able to crush

[1] Jefferson's *Works*, VIII, 341–49.

the first rising against the laws.'[1] There must have been high glee among the cronies of Freneau in the office on High Street when they read it. 'King,' 'men of property' — Freneau could not have dictated the comment for his purpose better. 'Your paper is supported by a party,' charged Fenno. Yes, agreed Freneau, if 'by a party he means a very respectable number of anti-aristocratic, and anti-monarchical people of the United States.'[2] But, not to be diverted, the poet-editor returned persistently to his indictment. 'Pernicious doctrines have been maintained' — 'Members of Congress deeply concerned in speculating and jobbing in their own measures . . . have combined with brokers and others to gull and trick their uninformed constituents out of their certificates.'[3]

'The names — give us the names,' demanded Fenno. 'That reminds us,' said Freneau, 'of the impudence of a noted prostitute of London, who, having a difference with a young man, was by him reproached for her profligacy, and called by the plain name of her profession. . . . "I'll make you prove it or pay for it," said she. Accordingly, she sued the young man for defamation of character, and although half the town knew her character, yet nobody could prove her incontinency without owning himself an accomplice, and the defendant was lost for want of evidence and obliged to pay heavy damages. Thus it is when any man talks of speculators — "prove the fact, sir" — as if, indeed, the men who hired out the pilot boats and the brokers who negotiated the securities would come forward to expose their employers and themselves.'[4]

Thus with charge on charge, with sarcasm and satire, especially the latter, Freneau constantly increased the intensity of his assaults. These slashing and insidious attacks did not reach the citizens of Philadelphia only — they were copied far and wide. The paper itself went into every State. Men were discussing and quoting it on the streets, in the coffee-houses of New York, on the stage-coaches jolting between the scarcely broken forests of remote places, about the fireplace in the cabin in the woods. No one had followed it with greater rage than Alexander Hamilton. One day Fenno's 'Gazette' contained a short letter bearing the signa-

---

[1] *Gazette of the United States,* June 6, 1792. [2] *National Gazette,* June 21, 1792.
[3] *National Gazette,* June 21, 1792. [4] *Ibid.,* June 25, 1792.

ture 'T. L.,' which started the tongues to wagging all the way from O'Eller's grogshop to Mrs. Bingham's drawing-room.

Mr. Fenno: The editor of the National Gazette receives a salary from the Government. QUERE — Whether this salary is paid him for translations, or for publications, the design of which is to vilify those to whom the voice of the people has committed the administration of our public affairs — to oppose the measures of government, and by false insinuations to disturb the public peace?

In common life it is thought ungrateful to bite the hand that puts bread in its mouth; but if a man is hired to do it, the case is different.

Freneau's paper had become dangerous, Fenno was unable to meet its onslaughts, and thus, anonymously, Hamilton took up his pen.[1]

V

It was at this time that Hamilton first shocked his friends with the disclosure of his temperamental weakness that was to destroy his leadership. Persuaded that Freneau's journal was established for the primary purpose of wrecking him, he saw red, lost his customary poise and self-control, and, throwing discretion to the winds along with his dignity as a minister of State, he entered the lists as an anonymous letter-writer. We search in vain through the correspondence of his friends for evidence of approval.

The attack was met by Freneau with a certain dignity. Reproducing the 'T. L.' letter he wrote:

The above is beneath reply. It might be queried, however, whether a man who receives a small stipend for services rendered as French translator to the Department of State, and as editor of a free newspaper admits into his publication impartial strictures on the proceedings of government, is not more likely to act an honest and disinterested part toward the public, than a vile sycophant, who obtaining emoluments from government, far more lucrative than the salary alluded to, finds his interest in attempting to poison the minds of the people by propaganda and by disseminating principles and sentiments utterly subversive of the true republican interests of the country, and by flattering and recommending every and any measures of government however pernicious and destructive its tendency might be to the great body of the people. The world is left to decide the motive of each.[2]

[1] *Gazette of the United States*, July 25, 1792.   [2] *National Gazette*, July 28, 1792.

This controversy of mere journalists did not interest Hamilton. He was out gunning for bigger game. Thoroughly convinced that Jefferson was responsible for much of the contents of Freneau's paper, he hoped to draw his colleague into an open newspaper fight and, if possible, drive him from the Cabinet. The relations of the two Titans had been growing more and more hostile. They disputed across the table in the council room, and at rare times seemed at the point of blows. Hamilton knew Jefferson's opinions of his policies — and similar opinions were appearing in the paper edited by a clerk in his rival's office. Nor were they slovenly, superficial articles. They were the work of close observers and clever controversialists. Not only was he ignorant of the fact that many of these were the work of Madison, that Brackenridge wrote some, George Tucker, editor of the American edition of Blackstone, some,[1] but he ridiculously underestimated the capacity of Freneau. These articles were strong, stinging, effective, and therefore Jefferson wrote or dictated them. He would drag Jefferson into the arena and have it out.

Thus, in his letter of August 4, he contemptuously dismissed the editor as 'the faithful and devoted servant of the head of a party,' and launched his personal bitter attack on Jefferson. If he wished to attack 'the Government,' why didn't Jefferson resign? [2] 'Can he reconcile it to his own personal dignity, and the principles of probity, to hold an office under it, and employ the means of official influence in that opposition?' Besides, he was an enemy of the Constitution. He had been opposed to it and had written his objections 'to some of his friends in Virginia.' [3] Four days later, Freneau denied in an affidavit published in Fenno's paper that Jefferson had any connection with the 'National Gazette' or had written or dictated a line. The same day, in his own paper, he raised the curtain on Hamilton's *nom de plume*, with a comment that 'all is not right with certain lofty-minded persons who fondly imagined their ambitious career was to proceed without check or interruption to the summit of their wishes.' To which he added

[1] Austin, *Freneau*, 170, note.

[2] No one knew better than Washington that Jefferson would have resigned in the spring had he not been importuned to remain.

[3] One of these was Washington, to whom he made the objections mentioned in a previous chapter.

that 'the devil rageth when his time is short.'[1] In his letter of August 11th, Hamilton dismissed the denial unimpressively. At this moment he thought himself hot on the trail. Elias Boudinot, he recalled, had once told him of the part Madison had played. If he could get an affidavit from Boudinot! Acting on an impulse, he wrote him that 'a friend' was writing the attacks on Jefferson. He had mentioned the Boudinot conversation to that 'friend' who was anxious to have an affidavit. 'It is of real importance that it should be done,' he wrote. 'It will confound and put down a man who is continually machinating against the public happiness.'[2] But Boudinot does not appear to have had any stomach for the mess, albeit he, like every one else, must have known that the 'friend' was Hamilton himself. No affidavit was forthcoming.

While he was waiting vainly for the affidavit, an anonymous writer in Freneau's paper, referring to Hamilton's assaults, made a counter-charge. What about 'the immaculate Mr. Fenno'? Did he not have the printing of the Senate, 'the emoluments of which office are considerable?' Did he not 'enjoy exclusively the printing of the Treasury department where it seems he has rendered himself a particular favorite?' Was he not already 'making his approaches to another office on Chestnut Street [the Bank],' and in a fair way to secure 'if not already in possession of the business appertaining thereto?'[3]

On August 18th, Hamilton appeared again to sneer at Freneau's announcement that he would pay no attention to the charges until the author came forward to make them in the open. 'It was easily anticipated that he might have good reasons for not discovering himself, at least at the call of Mr. Freneau, and it was necessary for him to find shelter.'

Freneau's affidavit! scoffed a writer in Hamilton's organ. He had no faith in it. The editor had certainly not sworn upon the Bible. Had he taken the oath on Jefferson's 'Notes on Virginia'?[4]

But Hamilton was already discovered. No one there was in public life from Washington down who did not know the author. The amazing spectacle was the talk of the taverns and the dinner

[1] *National Gazette*, August 8, 1792.   [2] Hamilton's *Works*, x, 14–15.
[3] *National Gazette*, August 15, 1792.
[4] *Gazette of the United States*, August 25, 1792.

tables, and was beginning to assume the proportions of a scandal. Washington was shocked and aggrieved. He would stop it.

VI

On August 26th he tried his art of conciliation, appealing to both Hamilton and Jefferson, albeit, as he knew, the latter had not written a line. Both replied in September, Hamilton admitting the authorship of the articles, and declared his inability 'to recede now.' He had been forced to write. He had been 'the object of uniform opposition from Mr. Jefferson'; 'the object of unkind whispers and insinuations from the same quarter'; and he had evidence that the 'National Gazette' had been instituted by Jefferson 'to render me and all the objects connected with my administration odious.' He had been most patient. In truth, he had 'prevented a very severe and systematic attack upon Mr. Jefferson by an association of two or three individuals, in consequence of the persecution he brought upon the Vice-President by his indiscreet and light letter to the printer, transmitting Paine's pamphlet.' [1]

Jefferson replied that in private conversation he had 'utterly disapproved' of Hamilton's system, which 'flowed from principles adverse to liberty and calculated to undermine and demolish the Republic by creating an influence of his department over members of the legislature.' He had seen this influence 'actually produced' by 'the establishment of the great outlines of his project by the votes of the very persons who, having swallowed his bait, were laying themselves out to profit by his plans.' Then, too, Hamilton had constantly interfered with his department, particularly in relation to England and France.[2] As to Freneau, he hoped he 'would give free place to pieces written against the aristocratic and monarchical principles.' He and Fenno, he said, 'are rivals for the public favor. The one courts them by flattery, the other by censure, and I believe it will be admitted that the one has been as servile as the other has been severe.' Then, turning again to Hamilton: 'But is not the dignity and even decency of government committed when one of its principal Ministers enlists himself as an anonymous writer or paragraphist for either the one or

[1] Hamilton's *Works*, VII, 303–06.   [2] The evidence is conclusive on this point.

the other of them?' As for criticism of governmental measures, 'no government ought to be without censors; and where the press is free no one ever will. If virtuous, it need not fear the free operation of attack and defense. Nature has given to man no other means of sifting out the truth, either in religion, law, or politics. I think it is as honorable to government neither to know nor notice its sycophants, as it would be undignified and criminal to pamper the former and persecute the latter.' [1]

Thus ended Washington's attempt to intervene. Hamilton had refused to discontinue his attacks, and, within two days after replying to Washington's appeal, he was again appearing in the 'Gazette of the United States.'

VII

Even while Hamilton and Jefferson were writing their letters, the fight was proceeding merrily, if bloodlessly, in the papers. 'Aristides,' none other than Madison, had gone to the defense of his leader in an article in Fenno's paper on Jefferson's attitude toward the Constitution. No one was so well qualified to know, unless it was Washington himself. He had sat in the Convention, a leading figure, and listened to Hamilton's speeches and proposals, and had been in correspondence with Jefferson. It was not this defense that made Fenno restive. It was a pointed attack. 'It is said, Mr. Fenno, that a certain head of a department is the real author or instigator of these unprovoked and unmanly attacks on Mr. Jefferson — and that the time of that gentleman's departure from the city on a visit to his home was considered as best suited to answer the design it was intended to effect.' 'Unmanly attack' and an insinuation of cowardice! Fenno took the precaution to add a note warning that no further letters would be printed containing 'personal strictures' unless the name of the author was furnished 'in case of emergency.' Coffee and pistols — was it coming to that? [2] Freneau had no such concern, for on the same day a writer in his paper referred to the 'base passions that torment' Hamilton, and called upon the author of the anonymous articles to 'explain the public character who on an occasion well known to him, could

---

[1] Jefferson's *Works*, VIII, 394–408.
[2] *Gazette of the United States*, September 8, 1792.

so far divest himself of gratitude and revolt from the spirit of his station as to erect his little crest against the magnanimous chief who is at the head of our civic establishment, and has on many free occasions since spoken with levity and depreciation of some of the greatest qualities of that renowned character; and now gives himself out as if he were his most cordial friend and admirer, and most worthy of public confidence on that account.' [1]

Two days after refusing Washington's request for a cessation, Hamilton returned to the attack in answer to the charge of the 'National Gazette' that he had not liked the Constitution, and had pronounced the British monarchy the most perfect government. All this he stoutly denied. The records and debates of the Constitutional Convention were then under secrecy, and members who had heard his speeches were under the ban of silence. He felt safe. This is the most amazing letter of the series.

And so the dismal affair dragged on. Another letter appeared reiterating a connection between Jefferson and Freneau; another charging that Jefferson was opposed to the Constitution and against paying the public debt; still another complaining of Jefferson's interference with the Treasury Department. Then another on Jefferson and the Constitution, and finally, two months after Washington's appeal, demanding that Jefferson, who remained in the Cabinet on the earnest solicitation of Washington, withdraw. 'Let him not cling to the honor or emolument of an office, whichever it may be that attracts him, and content himself with defending the injured rights of the people by obscure or indirect means.'

Meanwhile, Jefferson had refused to be drawn into the controversy personally. The situation had become painful — the Philadelphia drawing-rooms lifting their brows at him. His official associations were unpleasant, but he never touched pen to a paper intended for publication. Only in his personal letters did he pour forth his bitterness against his colleague. 'The indecency of newspaper squabbling between two public Ministers,' he wrote Edmund Randolph, 'has drawn something like an injunction from another quarter. Every fact alleged . . . as to myself is false. . . . But for the present lying and scribbling must be free to those who

[2] *National Gazette*, September 8, 1792.

are mean enough to deal in them and in the dark.'[1] He had hoped
for an early retirement, and the attacks had indefinitely postponed
the realization of his desire. 'These representations have for some
weeks past shaken a determination which I had thought the whole
world could not have shaken,' he wrote Martha.[2] Meanwhile, the
small-fry partisans were busy in all the papers. The effect, on the
whole, had been favorable to Jefferson, making him the idol of the
democrats everywhere. 'It gives us great pleasure,' said a Boston
paper, 'to find that the patriotic Jefferson has become the object
of censure, as it will have a happy tendency to open the eyes of the
people to the strides of certain men who are willing to turn every
staunch Republican out of office who has discerning to ken the
arbitrary measures, and is honestly sufficient to reveal them.'[3]
To the 'Independent Chronicle' the 'slander and detraction' of
men like Jefferson seemed 'a convincing proof of the badness of
the cause behind it.'[4] The onslaught had in no wise weakened
Jefferson's faith in the effectiveness of the 'National Gazette.' The
smoke had not lifted from the field when he was rejoicing because
it was 'getting into Massachusetts under the patronage of Hancock and Sam Adams.'[5] Even Freneau found the democrats
rallying around him.

It is a Fact [wrote a correspondent] that immense wealth has been accumulated into a few hands, and that public measures have favored that
accumulation.

It is a Fact that money appropriated to the sinking of the debt has
been laid out, not so as most to sink the debt, but so as to succor gamblers
in the funds.

It is a Fact that a Bank law has given a bounty of from four to five
million dollars to men in great part of the same description.

It is a Fact that a share of this bounty went immediately into the
pockets of the very men most active and forward in granting it.

These, Mr. Freneau, are facts — . . . severe, stubborn, notorious facts.[6]

VIII

Thus Hamilton's remarkable attack had only whetted the appetite of the Jeffersonians for battle — and a national campaign was

[1] Jefferson's *Works*, VIII, 411.
[2] *Domestic Life*, 214–15; also letter to T. M. Randolph, *Ibid.*, 215.
[3] Quoted by Freneau, September 19, 1792.   [4] October 18, 1792.
[5] Randall, II, 102; to Randolph.   [6] *National Gazette*, October 20, 1792.

in progress. The unanimous reëlection of Washington was universally demanded, but why should the 'aristocratic' and 'monarchical' author of 'The Discourses of Davila' be chosen again? At any rate, efforts could be made to change the political complexion of Congress.

There were mistakes, blunders, tragedies, that could be used to affect public opinion. What more shocking than the humiliating collapse of the General St. Clair expedition against the Indians in the western country? Gayly enough had the unfortunate commander set forth with twenty-three hundred regular troops and a host of militiamen. There had been a scarcity of provisions and inadequate preparations. Hundreds of soldiers, consumed with fever, shaken with chills, had vainly called for medicine. Many died, hundreds deserted in disgust, and finally but fourteen hundred worn and weary, sick and hungry men remained to face the enemy. It was easy enough to blame St. Clair, and, as he passed through the villages en route to the capital, the people flocked about to hiss and jeer.

But why the lack of proper preparations? Why the insufficiency of the commissary? Even the officials in Philadelphia were prone to find extenuations for the failure of St. Clair. A correspondent of the Boston 'Centinel,' dining with some of the first official characters where the tragic collapse of the expedition had been discussed, found 'not one expression dropped to his prejudice.' [1] The Jeffersonians were aiming higher than St. Clair. There was Knox, Secretary of War — what had he to say in defense of the honesty of the army contractor, to the negligence of the quartermaster? The House investigating committee bore heavily on these two in its report — but who was responsible for the cupidity of the one and the inefficiency of the other? Soon the Jeffersonian press was attacking Knox with distressing regularity, picturing him as the 'Philadelphia Nabob.' [2] Was he not squandering public money on 'splendor' and 'extravagance'? Soon the more irresponsible of the gossip-mongers were whispering that he had profited financially. 'Infamous!' screamed the Federalist press. 'The public monies have never been in the hands of Mr. Knox.' [3] 'But who made ar-

[1] January 11, 1792.　　[2] *Independent Chronicle*, May 2, 1792.
[3] *Centinel*, June 9, 1792.

rangements with the dishonest contractor?' replied the Jeffersonians. 'Who selected the quartermaster who let the soldiers starve?'

All through the summer and autumn this was the talk in the taverns and coffee-houses, but with the bursting of the bubble of speculation a far more effective weapon of assault was at hand. To this inevitable outcome of the gambling mania Jefferson had looked forward with the utmost confidence. He had seen money 'leaving the remoter parts of the Union and flowing to [Philadelphia] to purchase paper'; had seen the value of property falling in places left bare of money — as much as twenty-five per cent in a year in Virginia. Extravagance, madness everywhere.[1] As a result in the remoter sections the hatred of the speculator had reached the stage of hysteria. 'Clouds, when you rain, bleach him to the skin,' prayed a Georgia paper. 'When you hail, precipitate your heaviest globes of ice on his ill-omened pate. Thunders, when you break, break near him, shatter an oak or rend a rock full in his view. Lightning, when you burst, shoot your electric streams close to his eyelids. Conscience, haunt him like a ghost. . . . Ye winds, chill him; ye Frost, pinch him, freeze him. Robbers meet him, strip him, scourge him, rack him. He starved the fatherless and made naked the child without a mother.'[2] Even the Worcester correspondent of the orthodox Boston 'Centinel' complained that 'as soon as one bubble bursts another is blown up' and 'we are in the way of becoming the greatest sharpers in the universe' — all 'assuredly anti-republican.'[3] When a town meeting was advertised for Stockbridge, a village wit penciled on the poster the purpose of the conference: 'To see if the town will move to New York and enter into the business of speculation.'[4] While publishing these letters and stories the Federalist organ in Boston did it with the sneer: 'They who are in — Grin. They who are out — Pout. They who have paper — Caper. They who have none — Groan.'[5]

Then in April, with the failure of Colonel Duer in New York the crash came. Many went to ruin in the wreckage, and New York became a madhouse, with business paralyzed, and Duer taking to

---

[1] Jefferson's *Works*, VIII, 315–18.   [2] *Independent Chronicle*, May 17, 1792.
[3] March 14, 1792.   [4] *Centinel*, March 28, 1792.   [5] March 14, 1792.

flight. He had been among the most favored of the beneficiaries of Hamilton's policies, rising from opulence overnight, and he was among the first to fall from their abuse. [1] The brutality and cowardice of the speculators intensified the general contempt for the tribe. 'Instead of exerting themselves to preserve some kind of moral character,' wrote a New York correspondent of the 'Maryland Journal,' 'they are endeavoring to lower themselves still more by descending to the mean level of fish women and common street boxers.' [2]

All this was viewed by Hamilton with indignation and concern. He had sought in every way to discourage the frenzy of speculation, and had used his office to protect the public wherever possible. But it began with the funding system — and with thousands that was enough. Instantly the Jeffersonian press was hot on the trail. 'Business has not been benefited by Hamilton's Bank,' declared the 'Independent Chronicle,' 'for a merchant can scarcely venture to offer his note for $100, while a speculator can obtain thousands for no other purpose than to embarrass commerce.' Look around and see who have obtained wealth. 'Speculators, in general, are the men.' Thus, 'the industrious merchant is forced to advance to the government thousands, while the gambling speculator is receiving his quarterly payments.' [3] A Maryland correspondent of Louden's New York 'Register' 'could not help thinking Mr. Madison's discriminating propositions would have prevented in great measure the exorbitant rage of speculation.' [4] Meanwhile, Fenno was denouncing the critics as 'anarchists' and enemies of the Government, which only intensified their rage. 'Our objection is not to paying off the debt,' protested an indignant critic, 'but to ... the excise, failure to discriminate, the play to speculation'; and if all who shared these views could be assembled it 'would make the greatest army that ever was on one occasion collected in the United States.' [5] In the 'Centinel,' Benjamin Russell was taking a lighter tone. 'The suffering yeomanry burdened with taxes? Why not simply eliminate all State and National debts and forget them?' [6] The storm?

---

[1] Pickering, letter to wife, III, 27.   [2] April 13, 1792.   [3] April 19, 1792.
[4] May 28, 1792.   [5] *Gazette of the United States*, October 10, 1792.
[6] 'Ironicus,' April 21, 1792.

What of it? 'The Six Per Cents, a first rate, belonging to the fleet commanded by Admiral Hamilton, notwithstanding several hard COUNTRY gales, and a strong lee current setting out of the Hudson and Delaware is still working to windward and bids fair to gain her destined port.'[1]

IX

With such attacks and counter attacks in the papers, the campaign of 1792 was fought, with the bitter gubernatorial battle between John Jay and George Clinton in New York setting the pace in the spring. The Federalists had set their hearts on the crushing of Clinton, and but for the frown of Hamilton, Burr might have joined them in the attempt.[2] The campaign was spectacular, and class feeling and prejudice played a part. Jay was an aristocrat by birth and temperament, and this gave the Clintonians their cue. Up, Plebs, and at 'em! An aristocrat against a democrat, the rich against the poor. Had not Jay said that 'those who own the country ought to govern it'? Had not Jay's Constitution disfranchised thousands on the score of their poverty? Were not the speculators, the stock-jobbers, the bankers, the gamblers, swindlers, and the forces of privilege supporting Jay?[3] The result was the election of Clinton, on a technicality,[4] and instantly there was an uproar, broken bones and bloody noses, coffee-house quarrels and blows, wild talk of a revolutionary convention and the seating of Jay with bayonets, and serious bloodshed was prevented only through the efforts of Hamilton, Jay, and King. Never had party feeling run so high, and several duels were fought in the course of a week.[5] The defeated or cheated candidate was accorded the acclamations due a conqueror on his journey from his judicial circuit to New York where he was given a testimonial dinner.[6] The democrats were none the less jubilant because of the questionable nature of their triumph, and at a dinner in honor of Clinton, the Tammany braves rose to the toast, 'Thomas Jefferson,' and gave their war-whoop.[7]

The bitterness in New York spread to various parts of the

---

[1] *Centinel*, March 17, 1792.   [2] Alexander, 50.   [3] *Ibid.*, 53.   [4] King's *Works*, I, 408–15.
[5] Bache's *General Advertiser*, July 19, 1792.   [6] *Ibid.*, July 13, 1792.
[7] Hammond, I, 72.

country where the Jeffersonians were fighting brilliantly, with clever strategy, to gain seats in the Congress. Some of the Federalists, who were to prove themselves generally inferior except in a smashing charge, and incapable of maintaining their morale in a siege or in reverses, were even then growing pessimistic. 'Perhaps you are not informed,' wrote George Cabot to Theophilus Parsons, 'that in Pennsylvania and New York the opponents are well combined and are incessantly active, while the friends discover a want of union and a want of energy.' [1] And Parsons, in melancholy mood, was convinced that the Government had 'seen its best days.' [2] Woe to the politician who enters the reminiscent stage when confronted by a virile opponent looking to the future. There was little in the New England of 1792 to depress the Federalists. Only a little evidence that among the working-men in Boston 'heresies' were making their way; only reports that 'itinerant Jacobins' were haranguing the curious in the bar-rooms of Rhode Island and Vermont; only the strange spectacle of 'drill masters' meeting with people of no property or importance to organize them to battle for democratic principles.[3] Only this, and a strange doctrine creeping into Vermont papers. In choosing members of Congress who should be selected? asked a 'Land Holder' of that State. 'What class of people should they represent? Who are the great body of the people? Are they Lawyers, Physicians, Merchants, Tradesmen? No — they are respectable Yeomanry. The Yeomanry therefore ought to be represented.' [4] In Maryland a ferocious fight was waged under the eyes of both Hamilton and Jefferson, for both were interested in the fate of Mercer who had slashed right lustily at the policies of Hamilton, making no secret of his belief that they were bottomed on corruption. He had vitalized the democrats of Maryland, extending his interest into districts other than his own, and arranging for candidates to oppose the sitting Federalists in the House. McHenry, who kept Hamilton informed of the progress of the fight, hoped to array the German Catholics against the obnoxious Mercer through the intervention of Bishop Carroll, whom he thought more influential than the better known Charles Carroll of Carrollton.[5] A man was em-

---

[1] *Life of Parsons*, 468–69.   [2] *Ibid.*, 467–68.   [3] Robinson, 9.
[4] Spooner's *Vermont Journal*, August 7, 1792.   [5] McHenry (to Hamilton), 136–37.

ployed by the energetic McHenry to circulate bills against Mercer, who fought back, and gave blow for blow. He was charged with having said that Hamilton had tried to bribe him in the Assumption fight; [1] that he was personally interested in the contract for supplying the western army, and privately engaged in the purchase of securities. This, Mercer was to disavow, and Hamilton's friends were to show that the conversation between the Marylander and the Secretary had been in the presence of company and in jest.[2] Even so we may assume that Mercer had painted the incident black. He let it be understood that Washington wished his re-election, and the celerity with which the President issued a denial was probably due to the importunity of Hamilton who did not scruple to use him without stint to further the cause of his party.[3]

In North Carolina the Jeffersonians, under the crafty leadership of picturesque Willie Jones, contested every inch of the ground, determined to retire all the Hamiltonians from Congress, and before the impetuosity of their charge the Federalists were forced to fight defensively and under a cloud.[4]

In the new State of Kentucky the Jeffersonians were thoroughly organized under the leadership of John Brown, a Virginian, educated at Princeton and at Jefferson's alma mater, who had fought through the War of Independence. 'Brown can have what he wants,' Madison wrote his leader in midsummer,[5] and he took the toga. In Virginia the Democrats were strongly in the ascendancy. The influence of Jefferson had been strengthened by the acquisition of Madison, and Hamilton, in the course of the campaign, wrote his famous letter to Colonel Edward Carrington attacking both in an effort to satisfy the Virginia Federalists of the justice of his own position, but it was blowing against a tornado.[6] An amazing campaign document — this letter.

Thus, in 1792, if the Jeffersonians had not yet perfected their organization, they had forced sporadic fighting, and the result of the congressional elections was greatly to strengthen them in the House.

---

[1] McHenry (to Hamilton), 137, note.
[2] *New York Daily Advertiser*, March 11, 1793, printed a letter from David Ross setting this forth in Hamilton's defense.
[3] McHenry, 138.
[4] Only one Federalist, William Barry Grove, was elected; Dodd's *Life of Macon.*
[5] Madison's *Writings*, I, 460–61.   [6] Hamilton's *Works*, IX, 513–35.

x

It was clear quite early that the Jeffersonians would not permit Adams's reëlection to go unchallenged. The press had teemed with controversial articles on his books for more than a year. As early as March his friends took up the cudgels in his defense. 'Homo' in the Boston 'Centinel' warned that 'a detestable cordon of desperadoes' were trying to destroy public confidence in Adams by vilification.[1] Within three months, Hamilton convinced himself that the opposition, in dead earnest, had concentrated on Clinton, and hastened to warn Adams, who was enjoying the placidity of his farm at Quincy.[2] It is interesting to observe that this plan to displace Adams was interpreted by Hamilton as 'a serious design to subvert the government.' If the candidacy of Clinton was annoying to Hamilton, the warning he received in September of the possible candidacy of Aaron Burr was maddening, and he fell feverishly to the task of denouncing the ambitions of this 'embryo Cæsar' in letters to his friends.[3] Clinton 'has been invariably the enemy of national principles,' he wrote General C. C. Pinckney in ordering a mobilization for defense in South Carolina, and as for Burr, he was a man of 'no principles other than to mount, at all events, to the full honors of the state, and to as much more as circumstances will permit.' Was Jefferson behind the conspiracy against Adams — Jefferson, that man of 'sublimated and paradoxical imagination, entertaining and propagating opinions inconsistent with dignified and orderly government?'[4] To John Steele in North Carolina he wrote in the manner of a commander, to inform him 'that Mr. Adams is the man who will be supported by the Northern and Middle States.' Of course, he had 'his faults and foibles,' and some of his opinions were quite wrong, but he was honest, and loved order and stable government.[5] Meanwhile, painful complications were threatened in Maryland where a number of notables[6] joined in a public letter rallying Marylanders to the support of Charles Carroll of Carrollton.[7] This gave James

---

[1] March 10, 1792.   [2] Adams, *Works*, VIII, 514.
[3] King's *Works*, I, 413, 427; Hamilton's *Works*, x, 19–20, 20–21.
[4] Hamilton's *Works*, x, 23–24.   [5] *Ibid.*, x, 27.
[6] Judge Samuel Chase, and Benjamin Stoddert, destined to a place in Adams's Cabinet among them.
[7] *Maryland Journal*, October 16, 1792.

McHenry, an idolater of Hamilton, and still tortured by a persistent, and, as yet, ungratified itch for office, his opportunity. He assumed the responsibility for whipping the rebels back into line. These signers of the Carroll letter had been imposed upon. The fight against Adams was a fight against the Constitution — in keeping with the plan of the enemies of government to drive able men from office. Had not Hamilton 'whose attachment to the Constitution is unquestionable' been assailed with virulence? Yes, from 'the master workman in his craft down to the meanest of his laborers,' all were engaged in the dirty work. Thus the submission of Carroll's claims at so late an hour wore 'a very doubtful and invidious aspect.' Was it done 'to get ten votes against Adams or to promote Carroll's election?' Was any one so foolish as to think that the Democrats in New York, Pennsylvania, and Virginia would desert Clinton? [1] This letter, signed by 'A Consistent Federalist,' was copied by all the Federalist papers of the country.

Meanwhile, Adams, lingering lovingly on his home acres, showed no inclination to return to Philadelphia, and it was reported that he might not appear to preside over the Senate until late in the session. This was an appalling lack of tact. Hamilton, assuming the rights of the leader, did not hesitate. 'I learn with pain that you may not be here until late in the session,' he wrote the loiterer behind the firing lines. 'I fear this will give some handle to your enemies to misrepresent. . . . Permit me then to say it best suits the firmness and elevation of your character to meet all events, whether auspicious or otherwise, on the ground where station and duty call you.' [2]

By November the press was hotly engaged in the controversy, but poor Fenno was to have trouble with his correspondents who were to convert his dignified journal into a cock-pit. Adams was both pelted and salved on the same page. His writings proved him a monarchist at heart, wrote 'Mutius.' [3] His writings would be appreciated more a century hence, said a defender in the same issue. Had he not already been vindicated on one point in the appearance of the 'gorgon head of party'? Freneau cleverly replied

[1] *Maryland Journal*, October 23, 1792.   [2] Hamilton's *Works*, x, 28–29.
[3] *Gazette of the United States*, September 26, 1792.

by quoting a laudatory article from an English paper paying tribute to the governmental notions of 'the learned Mr. Adams.' [1] Yes, wrote 'Cornucopia' in the 'Maryland Journal,' 'it will require the whole strength of the federalists to keep poor John Adams from being thrust out of the fold.' [2]

And 'poor John Adams' was not entirely happy in his defenders. Why not reëlect him, demanded 'Philanthropos' in a glowing tribute, for was he not 'a man of innocent manners and excellent moral character?' [3] 'Why not?' echoed a scribe in Albany. He was 'a reputed aristocrat, at the same time an honest man, the noblest work of God.' [4] From 'Otsego' came a more robust blow at Adams's enemies as 'the jacktails of mobocracy' seeking the defeat of 'the virtuous Adams' because he was against 'anarchy and disorder.' [5] Wrong, wrote 'Portius' the next day, advocating Clinton. 'Untinctured by aristocracy, and a firm republican, the patriots of America look to him.' [6] Titles, titles, sneered 'Condorcet.' 'This rattle which so peculiarly delights certain characters. . . . He never appears but in the full blaze of office, as if every place he went was a Senate, and every circle which he invited needed a Vice President.' [7] Thus, throughout the fall and early winter the lashing and slashing went on, but when the time came Adams was reëlected, albeit the result was a bitter humiliation to the proud, sensitive spirit of the victor. Where Washington had been unanimously reëlected, Adams had a margin of but twenty-seven votes. New York, Virginia, North Carolina, and Georgia had moved *en masse* into the Clinton camp, and Kentucky had cast her vote for Jefferson. Five States had gone over to the Jeffersonians, and the Federalists had been unable to get a unanimous vote in Pennsylvania. But if Adams was hurt, Hamilton could bear his pains, for the brilliant, dashing chief of the party preferred that the uncongenial man from Braintree should not become too perky.

Thus ended the first year of actual party struggle — Hamilton a bit soiled by his descent to anonymous letter-writing, Jefferson greatly strengthened by his silence under assault; the Hamilton-

[1] *National Gazette*, November 24, 1792.
[2] November 9, 1792.
[3] *Gazette of the United States*, December 1, 1792.
[4] *Ibid.*, January 5, 1793.
[5] Bache's *Daily Advertiser*, December 4, 1792.
[6] *Ibid.*, December 5, 1792.
[7] *Ibid.*, December 15, 1792.

ians triumphant, but not exultant over the reëlection of Adams, the Jeffersonians, having tasted blood, and tested their weapons, more than ever eager for combat and rejoicing in their congressional gains.

Hamilton had tried to drive Jefferson from the Cabinet, and failed. It was now the latter's turn.

CHAPTER IX

HAMILTON'S BLACK WINTER

I

THE winter of 1792–93 was notable in many ways. Not within the memory of the oldest inhabitant of Philadelphia had one so mild been known. As late as February there had been no interruption in the navigation of the Delaware, and the papers, making much of the catching of shad, were predicting that 'a considerable school may soon be expected.' In this, however, the sons of Ike Walton were to be disappointed, for a snowstorm and a northwester soon put an end to fishing.[1] Even so, the weather continued, for the most part, mild beyond the usual. Never had society adorned itself with more frills and furbelows, danced more feverishly, or pursued its pleasures with greater zest. The elegant new Chestnut Street Theater threw open its doors for the entertainment the mimic world can give, and the aristocracy, along with the plebeians, flocked to the play, despite the pouting of the uppish Mrs. Bingham who had been refused a box on her own terms. Even the venomous bitterness of the politicians failed to dim the lights of the great houses, albeit the followers of Jefferson were more and more given to understand that they were not wanted among the elect. The events, moving rapidly in France, were making a distinct cleavage here among the aristocrats and democrats. The members of the old French nobility, who had left their country for their country's good, were giving the tone to the most fashionable dinner tables. Out in the streets the 'people of no particular importance' were vulgarly vociferous over the trials and tribulations of the King and Burke's beautiful Queen — and the Jeffersonians were taking their tone from the howlings of this 'mob.'

It was evident from the moment Congress convened that a tremendous party struggle was impending. The incidents of the preceding summer had left their scars. The Jeffersonians were

[1] *National Gazette*, February 2, 1793.

embittered against Hamilton because of his anonymous attacks, and nothing could have done more to unsheathe their swords. The truce was over. Washington had permitted Hamilton to continue his attacks by disregarding his request; they would not now permit even Washington to interpose to save Hamilton from their assaults. The elections had given them a confidence they had not had before. The next Congress would not be so subservient to 'the first lord of the Treasury.' [1] The supercilious assumption of superiority on the part of the Federalist leaders would henceforth be resented. The war would begin in earnest.

The line the attack would take was shown early when Fitzsimons, one of Hamilton's henchmen in the House, offered a resolution calling for the redemption of so much of the public debt as the Nation had a right to redeem, and asking Hamilton 'to report a plan for the purpose.' This was in accordance with the custom which had grown up. From the moment he had taken office, Hamilton had considered the members of the House, constitutionally charged with the duty of framing money bills, as his automatons. He would determine upon the plans himself, prepare the bills, and call upon the House to pass them without too much discussion. He would manage the finances himself and he would not be plagued by foolish questions. For many months the committees to which his measures had been referred had been of his own choosing. They were his followers, and, not a few of them, beneficiaries of his policies.

The Fitzsimons Resolution was instantly challenged by the Jeffersonians as a rather high-handed proposal under a republican form of government, and Madison rose to suggest that the House should know the exact state of the finances before measures were taken for the reduction of the debt. After all, it was with the House, not with the Secretary of the Treasury, that money bills should originate. At any rate, the House could not act intelligently without having the facts in its possession. All too long had it been patient without definite reports.[2]

The feeling of the masses over the by-products of the funding system had by this time become deep-seated. Men who had voted to create the Bank had been made members of the board of

[1] Freneau's description.   [2] *Annals*, November 19, 1792.

directors. The ne'er-do-wells of yesterday were riding in coaches and building pretentious houses. Hamilton was urging bounties or protective duties for manufacturers one day and running over to the Falls of Passaic on the next to assist the directors of a corporation, that was to profit by his recommendations, in selecting the sites for the factories. Not a few honestly believed that he was personally profiting through governmental measures. Almost from the beginning, Senator Maclay had been suspicious of his integrity. This utterly false impression grew out of the positive knowledge that some of Hamilton's closest political associates were speculating in the securities. 'Hamilton at the head of the speculators, with all the courtiers, are on one side,' Maclay wrote in his diary.[1] Only a month before at Mount Vernon, where Washington had begged Jefferson to reconsider his determination to resign, the latter had charged the head of the Treasury with creating 'a regular system for forming a corps of interested persons who should be steadily at the orders of the Treasury.'[2] In 1790, William Duer retired from Hamilton's office to become the king of the money-chasers, and, going down to ruin in the financial crash of the preceding summer, was sending out dire threats of startling revelations from the debtors' prison. Many honest men were quite ready to believe that these threats were aimed at Hamilton.[3] It was under these conditions that a miserable creature by the name of James Reynolds, in prison for a crime against the Treasury, sought to blackmail his way out. He had papers in his possession to prove some financial transactions with Alexander Hamilton. An obscure person of a low order of mentality, he hinted at his use as a dummy in business in which a member of the Cabinet did not care to appear. These facts reached some members of Congress.

II

On December 15th, two sober-faced members of the House and one Senator filed into Hamilton's office in the Pemberton mansion. The Secretary knew them all and knew two of them as enemies. Frederick Muhlenberg had served as a Speaker in the first House

[1] February 15, 1790.   [2] *Anas* I, 235–37.
[3] Bassett, *The Federalist System.*

and was to resume that post in the third. A strong character, the recognized leader of the Germans, the foremost American Lutheran minister of his time, he had played a conspicuous part in the Revolution and in the constructive work that followed. Abraham Venable was a Representative from Virginia. The Senator was James Monroe whose fanatical devotion to Jeffersonian ideals and ideas had long since made him the object of Hamilton's contempt.

As they took seats facing the masterful little man at the desk, they had the manner of judges confronting a victim. None of them were finished in the art of tactful speech. Bluntly they blurted forth their mission — they had evidence of a mysterious connection between the Secretary of the Treasury and James Reynolds. What had Mr. Hamilton to say to that? Even under the least provocative circumstances, Hamilton was quick-tempered, and here was something to arouse the lion in him. For a moment he raged in his resentment. The visitors, a little moved, perhaps, stood their ground. They had papers and the right to an explanation. His fury having consumed itself, Hamilton realized that there was something to explain, and he was ready. Would they meet him at his house that night? They would. The three men rose, bowed, departed.

When they reached the Hamilton home that winter night, they found Oliver Wolcott, the protégé of the host, there before them. In the presence of these enemies it was wise to have one friend as a witness. The visitors were received with the courtly courtesy of which Hamilton was capable, and after they had found chairs about the table, he produced some papers of his own, spreading them out by the candlelight, before him. Then, quite calmly, and with an occasional touch of humor, he made a remarkable confession.

It was the old story of a great man's weakness. One summer day in 1791 a Mrs. Reynolds had appeared at his home with a pathetic story of her desertion by her husband and a plea for funds to enable her to return to her family in New York. Strangely enough, no description of this adventuress has come down to us, but it is a reasonable presumption that she was comely. The family of Hamilton was in the house. The master was moved. Naturally he would accommodate her, but at the moment he had no money with him. He would take her address and send or bring it in the evening. That night the gods looking down from Olympus might have seen one of their favorite earth-children furtively making his way through the dimly lighted streets, away from the fashionable quarter into the section of cheap boarding-houses. The woman received him in her room. It was the old story of Cæsar and Cleopatra, albeit this was a Cleopatra of the more vulgar sort. 'After that,' said Hamilton, 'I had frequent meetings with her at my own house, Mrs. Hamilton and her children being absent on a visit to her father.' [1] The comedy hurried on. At length he thought to bring it to a termination, and it was then that Mrs. Reynolds proved herself a mistress of her art. She was passionately in love. A separation would break her heart. Here, surely, was a violent attachment — perhaps it would be better to break off gradually. The lover was not lacking in the finer sensibilities, and then, too, his vanity was pleased.[2] With the continuance of the *amour*, Mrs. Reynolds, simulating a consuming passion, began to flood her *innamorato* with tender epistles.[3] The climax was on the wing. One day an hysterical note announcing the husband's discovery of her infidelity, and warning that, if no answer was forthcoming to the letter the Secretary would receive from the irate husband, Mrs. Hamilton would be informed. Would it not be wise to see him? Hamilton thought so and summoned Reynolds to his office. The cunning rascal had his story ready: the wife discovered writing a mysterious letter — a black messenger traced to the Hamilton house — the accused wife on her knees confessing all.[4] After negotiations the heartbroken husband decided that a thousand dollars would salve his wounded honor. 'And I will leave the town . . . and leave her to Yourself to do for her as you think proper,' he added.[5]

In the midst of these painful revelations, Muhlenberg and Venable declared themselves satisfied, but Hamilton insisted on telling the story to the end. Then followed the most amazing part of the tale. The husband invited his wife's lover to resume the *amour*. Hamilton was coy. Mrs. Reynolds added her plea in

[1] Hamilton's *Works*, VII, 389.   [2] Hamilton's expression, *Works*, VII, 391.
[3] *Ibid.*   [4] *Ibid.*, VII, 424.   [5] *Ibid.*, 427.

illiterate, pleading letters. The vanity of Hamilton was likewise persuasive, and the comedy was resumed. When he sought to escape notice by going by the back way, Reynolds was indignant. 'Am I a person of such a Bad carector [character] that you would not wish to be seen Coming to my house in the front way?' he wrote.[1] This should have put Hamilton on his guard, but he fell into the trap. A witness had been provided in another black-mailer, Clingman, who had been a clerk in Hamilton's office, and was an unspeakable scoundrel. Then more money was demanded. Mrs. Reynolds was again alarmed. Her husband was often mo-rose and beat her. At times he threatened to murder Hamilton. Loans were made. This, then, was the nature of the mysterious financial relations with Reynolds.

When the party rose to leave, Muhlenberg and Venable were apologetic — but not so James Monroe. He bowed stiffly, the sternness of his features unrelaxed, as the three passed out into the winter night. Hamilton had vindicated his official honor at a painful sacrifice. It was understood that the confession should be sacredly confidential, but in a sense he had lost. As he sat with Wolcott before the fire after his tormentors had departed, he real-ized that his enemies were out to wreck his official reputation. He may have had a premonition of the storm that was about to break.

III

Nine days after the scene enacted by candlelight in Hamilton's library, the bill authorizing the President to negotiate a loan of two million dollars to be applied to the reimbursement of a loan made of the Bank came up for consideration in the House. William B. Giles, who was now dividing the leadership of the Jeffersonians with Madison, was instantly on his feet with a request for post-ponement. Perhaps some method could be found without recourse to a new loan. It might be better to pay the loan by selling the stock the Nation owned in the Bank. The watchful Sedgwick was shocked at the suggestion. Dumping so much stock upon the market would reduce the price and not enough money would be realized to meet the country's obligation to the Bank. It was a mild premonitory skirmish.[2]

[1] Hamilton's *Works*, VII, 394.   [2] *Annals*, December 24, 1792.

Christmas Day brought an armistice, but the next day the discussion was resumed, with Madison taking a leading part. Why
was so much more to be borrowed than was demanded by the
Bank? To his personal knowledge a large sum was lying idle and
unappropriated in the Treasury. If this balance was appropriated
by the President, he wanted to know it. A delicate subject to
discuss, suggested Sedgwick. Not at all, thought Madison. It was
time for some 'candid explanation.' Was the appropriation lying
dormant in the Treasury, borrowed to meet the obligations to
France, being demanded by the country to which it was due? The
important question concerned the diverting of money appropriated to that specific purpose to the payment of Bank installments.
Could gentlemen justify themselves to their constituents for such
conduct? The debt to France was one of gratitude and justice,
and he wished the money could be sent thither on the wings of the
wind. True, the debt in whole was not yet due, but in the critical
condition of our benefactor, it would no doubt be particularly acceptable and he was opposed to the diversion of any part of it.[1]
Why two millions for the Bank? demanded Giles. True, two
hundred thousand dollars would be due the Bank on January 1st,
but why two millions? No one had offered an explanation of how
the money lying dormant was disposed of, or how it was intended
to dispose of it. No member rose to explain, and the bill was lost.

During the next month the lobbies, boarding-houses, taverns,
buzzed with discussions of the finances of the country. After all,
even the members of the House, presumed to be familiar with the
fiscal affairs of the Nation, knew scarcely anything. They had appropriated blindly. There was something uncanny in the silence.
Would the raising of the curtain disclose skeletons in the closet of
the Treasury? At any rate, the House had a right to the facts and
figures. Throughout the month Madison and Giles were frequently at the table or about the blazing fire at Jefferson's. Here
the campaign was planned. The fight should be forced into the
open on the floor of the House. Jefferson could not participate,
for manifest reasons, but he could direct. Madison could assist in
the preparation of the resolutions and in the debate. Giles, who
was a masterful debater, fearless and slashing in attack, could

[1] *Annals,* December 26, 1792.

sponsor the resolutions and lead in the assault. Because of the part he then played, it has been the fashion to dismiss him flippantly with a shrug and a sneer — but this is absurd. Giles of Virginia was unsurpassed by any American debater of his time.

IV

Giles was a veritable D'Artagnan of debate, a gusty, lusty Gascon transplanted to the tobacco-fields of Virginia, eager always for a fight or a frolic, and lightning-swift with his blade. A blustering fellow, true, quick to assert his rights and repel assault, he carried himself with a swagger that did not endear him to the Federalists, who rather plumed themselves on having a monopoly on that particular vice or virtue. But sneers at his ability are absurd. He who won the admiration of Patrick Henry,[1] commanded the confidence and respect of Jefferson, Madison, and Monroe, received the discriminating praise of Randolph of Roanoke,[2] and the reluctant tribute of Justice Story,[3] cannot be sneered from a respectable place in history by a wretchedly unfair caricature by a partisan English biographer of one of his enemies.[4]

The young Virginian who appeared in Philadelphia in the winter of 1790–91 was not prepossessing in appearance. Of average height, the fullness of his person conveyed the impression of a squat figure. His face, large, round, but colorless, bore none of the indications of genius, albeit there was something of virility in his brown eyes that harmonized with the robustness of his physique. One who knew him has recorded that he was of fair complexion,[5] but another who heard him frequently in debate commented on his dark color, and, since his hair and eyes were those of a brunette, we may accept the latter as more probable than the former.[6] All agree that he was careless in his dress, after the then prevailing Virginia manner,[7] although we have the record of one dramatic appearance in the Virginia Legislature, at the height of his renown, 'elegantly dressed in blue and buff' and with the Gascon touch of being 'booted and spurred, with a riding-whip in his hand.'[8] If there was nothing imposing or picturesque in his appearance, his man-

---

[1] Anderson, *Giles*, 6.
[2] Benton's *Thirty Years' View*, I, 682–83.
[3] *Life and Letters*, I, 158–59.
[4] Oliver's *Hamilton*, 292–94.
[5] *Familiar Letters*, 46.
[6] Justice Story, *Life and Letters*, I, 158.   [7] *Ibid.*
[8] Anderson, *Giles*, 65–66.

ners were such as to make him stand out conspicuously among his fellows. These were such as to impress the none too finished Maclay that 'the frothy manners of Virginia were ever uppermost.' It is easy enough to reconstruct the scene at Washington's table where Maclay met our Gascon, with Giles, the good liver, dwelling unctuously on Virginia canvasback ducks, Virginia hams, Virginia chickens, and the old Madeira, which was a little more mellow when drained from a Virginia glass in a joyous Virginia dining-room. Proud of Virginia was this provincial from the tobacco country, and proud as D'Artagnan himself of his physical prowess, for didn't he take more manual exercise than any man in New England? No place like the Old Dominion where the living was 'fast and fine,' where from noon to night the people drank wine or cherry bounce like gentlemen. Thus he thundered along, to the amazement of Maclay, who observed that 'he practiced on his principle every time the bottle passed.' [1] The picture is no doubt true, for Giles was racy of his native soil. The Amelia County of his early days was of the frontier, with all that that implies of the primitive vices and virtues. The sparsely settled country, with its miserable roads, lived very much to itself, and strangers who ventured among its inhabitants were treated coldly. The living was truly 'fast and fine' and rather loose, for the men were careless, indifferent to dress, heavy drinkers, inveterate smokers, their conversations picturesque with profanity; and they were fighters, too. Dumas's three immortals would have found it to their liking, and had they encountered young Giles at some crossroads tavern they would have taken him to their hearts. The spirit of independence flamed on every hearth, and the religious dissenters found it a happy hunting-ground.[2] It was in this atmosphere that Giles grew up. Like most of the Jeffersonian leaders, he was a frontiersman.

When he went to Princeton to complete his education, we get again the D'Artagnan touch. He set forth like a Virginia gentleman with his negro slave to serve him, no doubt kicking, cursing, and loving him all the way. Then followed a law course at William and Mary — and then a law office was opened in the little tobacco town of Petersburg. We are interested in this period of his career

[1] Maclay, 374.   [2] Anderson, *Giles*, 3.

only in that it throws light on his character and capacity. He favored the ratification of the Constitution, and, as a fascinated spectator of the debates in the Virginia Convention, formed a deep admiration for Madison. In the evenings he argued for ratification at the tavern, no doubt in the taproom. Hearing him one night, George Mason, a leader of the opposition, made the comment that 'he has as much sense as one half of us, though he is on the wrong side.'[1] He was not, then, an anti-Federalist on the Constitution.

Immediately on entering Congress at twenty-eight, he commanded attention, for he had a genius for congressional life. He became at once a giant in debate. When John Randolph, more cynic than flatterer, pronounced Giles the Charles James Fox of the House, he referred to the impression made by the Virginian in action. Fox was a student; Giles was not. Fox was capable of sustained research; Giles was not. Fox was a lover and reader of books, and Giles cared nothing for them. He bore a closer resemblance to Mirabeau or Danton in his methods, absorbing his knowledge from others in conversation. In the tavern, on the highway, at the dinner table, he was a tireless talker, and by provoking his friends into discussion he tested, corrected, and formed his impressions of events and measures. His mind absorbed like a sponge, his memory was retentive. The idea that Jefferson or Madison outlined his speeches for him is ludicrous. He merely assimilated what they said — and then gave it out more forcefully than either could in debate.[2]

It is impossible to reconcile the slurring references of some historians to his manner in debate with the speeches that speak for themselves on the musty pages of the 'Annals of Congress.' Here was a man speaking directly to a purpose. No critic need kill off his Roman consuls, for there were none. No craving here for a reputation for erudition. No mere rhetorical flourishes to confuse the sense. No theatrical appeals to the emotions. No verbosity at all — but 'a clear, nervous expression, a well-digested and powerful condensation of language,' which could make an impression on the scholarly Story. That great jurist, an unfriendly witness, could not hear him without admiration. 'He holds his

---

[1] Anderson, *Giles*, 8.   [2] Benton, I, 682.

subject always before him,' he wrote, 'and surveys it with un-
tiring eyes; he points his objects with calculated force and sustains
his positions with penetrating and wary argument. He certainly
possesses great strength of mind.' [1]

Having prepared himself to meet all comers, he thus dashed to
the combat. Having assimilated all that he had absorbed, his
native resourcefulness and ready command of good plain English
did the rest. He spoke with the forceful fluency which was the
best possible substitute for eloquence. A powerful voice, a virile
manner, compelled attention and respect. Did an enemy attack
him as he rushed along? He either crushed him with brutal
strength, or cleverly ducked the blow — and was on his way again.
Instinctively he knew when to strike and when to dodge. When
on the floor, he dominated the scene. This was the man, so much
belittled, whom Benton wrote down in cold deliberation as 'the
most accomplished debater which his country has ever seen.' This
the man selected in the conferences of Jefferson and Madison to
lead the attack on the Secretary of the Treasury.

v

During this period of waiting, with the gossips busy in the
taverns and the streets, Freneau was zealously seeking to create
the right atmosphere for the attack. With the Hamiltonians as-
cribing all prosperity to the policies of their chief, Freneau and
other editorial enemies were making much of the protest of
'Patriot,' who had been ruined through the abuse of these fiscal
policies.

The tale is true [it ran]. I loved my country. In 1775, my only son
fought on Bunker Hill. . . . His mother sent the chair down to carry him
home. She wiped the blood from his face and dressed the wound in his
breast. He died. My neighbor, Smallacre . . . said it was the proper reward for rebellion, but that a halter would have been more proper. I
persevered in the cause of freedom. Congress wanted money — I called
in my debts and sold all my land excepting forty acres. In . . . 1778 I had
12,000 in paper. I loaned the whole, and when they were consolidated at
forty for one I had a loan office certificate for $300. In 1784 the General
Court issued a large tax. As I could obtain neither the interest or principal of my loan office note I was obliged to sell it. My neighbor, Smallacre,

---

[1] Story, I, 158–59.

saved his property from the waste of a cause to which he was heartily opposed, and he appeared to buy my note at Three Shillings for Twenty. By this means I paid my State tax of Nine pounds, ten shillings and had four pounds left for town and parish taxes. As my son was dead I was content to be poor . . . My old chair and horse remained . . . My neighbor, Smallacre, has now become rich by purchase of public securities from people distressed as I was. He tells me that our Hancocks and our Sam Adams and those kind of men know how to pull down a government, but do not know how to build one.[1]

Prosperity? Yes, but for whom? demanded the enemies of Hamilton, poking the 'Patriot's' protest under the nose of his defenders. With the Hamiltonians crediting their idol with all the good things that had occurred, Freneau was moved to mirthful verse:

> 'Whales on our shores have run aground,
> Sturgeons are in our rivers found —
> Nay — ships have on the Delaware sailed,
> A sight most new.
> Wheat has been sown —
> Harvests have grown —
> On coaches now, gay coats of arms are borne
> By some who hardly had a cent before —
> Silk gowns, instead of homespun, now are seen,
> Instead of native straw, the Leghorn hat,
> And, Sir, 'tis true
> (Twixt me and you)
> That some have grown prodigious fat,
> And some prodigious lean.' [2]

This press crusade against Hamilton was carried on along with much laudation of Jefferson, inspired by the report of his decision to retire from the Cabinet. 'Mirabeau' heard with distress that 'the leader of democracy' wished to 'seek the peaceful shades' to 'solace himself with his favorite philosophy.' True, the sea had been made tempestuous for him, but 'the crew are his friends, and notwithstanding the endeavors of the officers to raise a mutiny to supercede him . . . his honest labor and firmness has frustrated their wicked intentions and he rides triumphant.' But with his retirement 'monarchy and aristocracy would inundate the coun-

---

[1] *National Gazette*, January 9, 1793, from *Boston Argus*.
[2] *Ibid.*, January 12, 1793.

try.'[1] Right, agreed 'Gracchus,' 'for though he has been in office near four years he has never assumed the insolence of it. His department has been that of a Republican and in no one action or expression has he manifested a superiority over his fellow citizens.'[2]

Hamilton and his followers had frankly sought to drive Jefferson from the Cabinet and failed; the plan was now complete for driving Hamilton himself into private life.

VI

On January 23d, the result of the deliberations of Jefferson, Madison, and Giles appeared when the latter rose in the House to present a set of resolutions calling upon the President to submit complete reports on the fiscal operations of the Government. To these the House was clearly entitled. Nor was there anything violent or outrageous in Giles's speech in which he explained them. The House had been legislating for four years 'without competent official knowledge of the state of the Treasury or revenue.' They had 'engaged in the most important fiscal arrangements,' and had 'authorized a loan of the Bank . . . for more than $500,000 when probably a greater sum of public money was deposited in the Bank.' They were now on the point of authorizing a further loan of $2,000,000 in the dark — and they were entitled to light. 'I conceive that it is now time for this information to be laid before the House.'[3] No one rose to object and the resolutions were adopted.

To Hamilton, who looked upon Congress as a meddlesome body, they appeared as something more than a bore. They were an imposition and an insult. He was entrusted with the financial arrangements, and all he asked was to be let alone. But he realized that such a lofty tone could not be publicly assumed. Suppressing his indignation, he set to work with meticulous care to prepare the fullest possible reports before the expiration of the congressional session. His enemies thought to burden him with a task that could not be performed in so short a time. Their strategy was to let the resolutions with their implications seep in on the minds of

[1] *National Gazette,* January 12, 1793, from *Boston Argus.*
[2] *Ibid.,* January 16, 1793.   [3] *Annals,* January 23, 1793.

the people throughout the ensuing summer; his cue was to thwart them in that purpose, to achieve the impossible, to meet the resolutions during the session, and win a triumph.

Not for him, that winter, the gala nights at the new Chestnut Street Theater, nor the dinners at the Binghams', nor the dances at the Stewarts', nor the felicities of the hearth with Eliza at his side. His place was at the Pemberton mansion, day and night, until the work was done. Oliver Wolcott and the clerks were doomed to the same drudgery. Far into the night the lights gleamed in the windows of the old house, and dark and deserted were the streets when the workers made their way to their various homes after dreary hours of poring over figures, assembling facts, and writing explanations.

Within twelve days, the first report, with elaborate tables containing the most minute details of transactions, was sent to the House. Two days later, the second report was done and in. A week more and the third was sent. Another six days, and the last was finished. The intense application, the late hours, the nervous strain, told perceptibly on Hamilton, who was never robust. The color left his cheeks when they were not flushed with excitement. His nights were all but sleepless. His waning strength was sustained by the driving force of his powerful mind. When it was over, even Wolcott found that his routine business had fallen behind and that he would 'be busy for some time to bring it up.' To his father he apologized for failure to answer letters. There was no time for letters. 'The winter . . . has required every exertion which I could make.' [1]

As these voluminous reports poured in upon the House in rapid succession, the Jeffersonians were amazed and the Hamiltonians beside themselves with joy. A startling intellectual feat, to be sure. 'I can recall nothing from the British Minister in all the conflicts of party equal to it,' wrote one admirer. 'Even Neckar's boasted account of the finances of France . . . is inferior, although that was the result of long study and elaborate preparation, and Hamilton's the work of a moment. Poor fellow, if he has slept much these last three weeks I congratulate him upon it.' [2] Wonderful reports, agreed the 'Centinel' of Boston. 'The manly unequiv-

[1] Gibbs, I, 89.   [2] *Gazette of the United States*, March 9, 1793.

ocable sentiments — the fair and accurate statements, and the judicious arrangements . . . must fix his character as a Patriot, a statesman, and an able and honest financier.' [1] Yes, added another, 'he will come forth pure gold.' [2]

But his enemies were not so much delighted. They read and studied the reports, complaining that the wizard of the speculators was up to his old tricks. A maze of words, interminable sophistries, columns of confusing figures, arguments instead of facts, and special pleading — no one could understand these reports — such the verdict of the rank and file. To which the Hamiltonians responded with a sneering verse:

> 'The Secretary makes reports
> When'er the House commands him;
> But for their lives, some members say,
> They cannot understand him.
> In such a puzzling case as this
> What can a mortal do?
> 'Tis hard for ONE to find REPORTS
> And understanding too.' [3]

But the leaders among the Jeffersonians were studying the reports and finding a few things that they could understand. Evidence of corruption they did not find, but they found technical violations of the law, an indifference on Hamilton's part to the clear intent of Congress in making appropriations — quite enough, as they thought, on which to continue the attack. Again Giles and Madison sat with Jefferson in his home going over the reports, and framing the second set of resolutions with which it was hoped to drive their enemy from the Cabinet.

VII

Three days before the end of the session, Giles presented his famous resolutions in condemnation of Hamilton's official conduct, based on the disclosures in his reports. It does not matter who originally wrote them. A scholarly historian [4] has produced proof of the part played by Jefferson. In the very nature of things

---

[1] *Centinel*, February 20, 1793.   [2] *Ibid.*, February 16, 1793.
[3] *Gazette of the United States*, February 23, 1793.
[4] Paul Leicester Ford, *The Nation*, September 5, 1895.

he must have had a part. Madison unquestionably made suggestions and possibly revamped the copy produced by Jefferson. Giles presented them, and they embodied the conclusions of the three outstanding leaders of the opposition.

These resolutions, intemperately denounced from the day of their appearance, set forth some novel theories, in view of the manner in which the Treasury had been administered, but, read in the light of the present regulations in the matter of appropriations, they are scarcely remarkable and not in the least vicious. They set forth that 'laws making specific appropriations of money should be strictly observed by the administrator of the finances'; that a violation of this rule was tantamount to a violation of the Constitution; and charged that Hamilton had violated the law passed August 4, 1790, making appropriations of certain moneys authorized to be borrowed in the following particulars, viz.:

First, by applying a certain amount of the principal borrowed to the payment of interest falling due upon that principal, which was not authorized by that or any other law.

Secondly, by drawing part of the same moneys into the United States without the instruction of the President.

They charged him with deviating from the President's instructions, with neglecting an 'essential duty' in failing to give Congress official information of his proceedings in the transactions of the foreign loans. More to the point, politically, was the charge that he 'did not consult the public interest in negotiating a loan with the Bank of the United States, and drawing therefrom $400,000 at five per cent per annum, when a greater sum of public money was deposited in various banks at the respective periods of making the respective drafts.' In conclusion, it was provided that a copy of the resolutions should be transmitted to Washington.

The main thing proved by the investigation was something that required no proof — that Hamilton had been managing the finances in the spirit of an autocrat, a little contemptuous of the rights of Congress, a little indifferent to the specific terms of the appropriations. These he had not hesitated to juggle to suit his own purposes. In so doing he had been guilty of technical violations of the law, but he had committed no crime. His hands were clean. Yet money intended for France had not been paid, and money not intended for the Bank had gone into its vaults. This was enough. Suspicion did the rest.

The most censurable feature of the attack was the introduction of the resolutions on the eve of adjournment. Jefferson, Madison, and Giles had no idea that they would or could be disposed of before Congress should automatically expire. Copies had gone to the papers of the four corners to be read by the people, and it is probable that it was the intent that they should have the summer and autumn to make their impression on the public mind. It was manifestly an unfair advantage. But the Hamiltonians had no thought of permitting any such delay. They were in a majority in the House. In the Pemberton house, by candlelight, the Treasury clan was summoned to a council of war, and they went forth to force the fighting to a speedy finish.

The reports had settled nothing with Hamilton's enemies. 'When Catullus[1] invited America to look through the windows of his breast and judge of the purity of his political motives, he did not invite in vain,' exulted 'Decius' in the 'National Gazette.'[2] Willing to meet his accusers? sneered 'Franklin.' 'Pardon me, sir, if I am one of those unbelievers, who, placing no confidence in any of your professions, do verily think that you neither wish, desire nor dare to meet full and fair inquiry. Have you asked it, sir?'[3] These jeers and exultant cries were intolerable. The vindication of the House must come speedily.

On the last day of February there was a preliminary skirmish, and on March 1st, the contending armies were marshaled for a decisive struggle. Sedgwick and the faithful Smith of South Carolina led off for Hamilton, and Giles followed for the Resolutions. Fitzsimons of Philadelphia and Laurance of New York City, both representatives of the commercial interests, attacked, and Mercer of Maryland replied. Boudinot defended Hamilton, and Madison rose to make the premier argument in condemnation of the policies of the Treasury; and Ames, the most brilliant of the Hamiltonian orators, who had been held in reserve for Madison, replied. Thus the day wore on, darkness fell, and the candles had long been lighted before the House adjourned for dinner. Seven

[1] Hamilton.   [2] February 20, 1793.   [3] *National Gazette*, February 27, 1793.

o'clock found the galleries packed, Senators upon the floor, favored spectators in the rear of the Chamber packed in close. The leading drawing-rooms were dark that night, for their mistresses looked down upon the drama of the black eyes and bloody noses. The struggle continued far into the night.

Here let us pause to catch the drift of the speeches. The supporters of Hamilton made the most of the failure to find any evidence of criminality. 'They present nothing that involves self-interest or pecuniary considerations. . . . Instead of anything being detected that would disgrace Pandemonium, nothing . . . which would sully the purest angel in Heaven.' Thus spoke Smith. No longer 'the foul stain of peculation,' but 'the milder coloring of an illegal exercise of discretion and a want of politeness in the Secretary of the Treasury,' said Barnwell.[1] What if a critical examination had revealed a deviation from the letter of the law, exclaimed Laurance. Was that an excuse for sounding 'the alarm from St. Croix to St. Mary's?' No corruption! cried Mercer, who had been forced to deny campaign charges he had made. 'I still entertain the opinion that there is corruption.' The House was in turmoil, and the Marylander was sharply called to order. On he plunged, recklessly fighting his way against calls to order.

No charge of corruption stained the lips of Madison, who moved on solid ground. There had been a technical violation of the law, and he proved it. There had been a disregard of the instructions of the President, and he showed it. He went thus far, no farther, and he hammered home the facts. 'I will not deny,' he said, 'that there may be emergencies in the course of human affairs of so extraordinary and pressing a nature as to absolve the Executive from an inflexible conformity to the injunctions of the law. It is, nevertheless, as essential to remember . . . that in all such cases the necessity should be palpable; that the Executive sanction should flow from the supreme source; and that the first opportunity should be seized for communicating to the Legislature the measures pursued, with the reasons of the necessity for them. This early communication is equally enforced by both prudence and duty. It is the best evidence of the motives for assuming the extraordinary power; it is a respect manifestly due to

[1] Of South Carolina.

the Legislative authority.' On this ground he stood, and there stood Giles.

The charges were dismissed by Ames, *ex-cathedra*-wise, with a shrug. What if there had been a juggling of the funds? 'It is impossible,' he said unblushingly, ' to keep different funds, differently appropriated, so inviolably separated as that one may not be used for the object of the other.' Nothing criminal had been proved.[1]

One by one the resolutions were taken up and overwhelmingly voted down — voted down even where Hamilton had admitted the charge and justified his acts. Before the last vote was reached, many of the members, worn by the excitement, the confinement, and fatigue, and confident of the result, deserted their posts and wandered forth into the winter night.[2]

VIII

Hamilton had sought, through his anonymous letters, to drive Jefferson from the Cabinet — and failed. Jefferson had tried, through this investigation, to drive Hamilton from public life — and failed. The struggle must go on. Each had caused the other some distress, each drawn a little blood, but neither had inflicted a serious wound.

With the adjournment of Congress, the skirmishing was taken up all over the country through the press. The Boston Federalists opened fire upon the 'Boston Argus.' It had published the resolutions, but not the Hamilton reports. The resolutions had been carried on the same mail that conveyed the vote of vindication, and the defeat of Giles had not been mentioned. Infamous![3] 'Marat' proposed satirical resolutions declaring 'highly reprehensible' every official 'who by integrity, talents, and important services . . . conciliates the esteem and affections of the people.' [4] Hamilton had come out pure gold, wrote a Philadelphian to a citizen of Rhode Island. 'The more it is rubbed, the more it will shine.' [5] A writer in the 'Connecticut Gazette' was moved to a frenzy of indignation. 'Dutch Republicans murdered De Witt

---

[1] *Annals,* February 27, March 1, 1793.   [2] *Centinel,* March 13, 1793.
[3] *Gazette of the United States,* March 23, 1793.   [4] *Ibid.,* March 20, 1793.
[5] *Centinel,* March 20, 1793.

and ate his heart. Republicans banished Aristides, the first, and condemned Socrates to Hemlock. And yet we have confined the punishment of eminent services and ability to attempts to degrade them from office by innuendoes, electioneering slanders, and newspaper detraction. This however may be the prelude to eating and banishing.'[1] A traveler in the Southern States wrote of the effect of the investigation in Virginia. It had 'opened the eyes of many who have hitherto been under the explicit direction of a certain would-be umpire of the United States.'[2] He found that prejudice had been created against Hamilton on the ground that he 'had not done as much as he ought to assist certain needy men to their claims for services,' but he was pleased to find that 'the unjust prejudice against the industrious patriot is decreasing daily.'[3]

Everything possible was done to make Hamilton's vindication a veritable triumph. When the Providence Society of New York met at Haut's Tavern for a dinner, the toast, 'The Secretary of the Treasury — may his distinguished talents and integrity command universal respect,' was received with shouts and the clicking of glasses.

But the Jeffersonians were unimpressed. 'After all,' they said, Hamilton 'acknowledges the freedom taken with appropriations and strives to work out an apology, rather than a justification.'[4] A week later, the 'National Gazette' presented an analysis of the vote of which the Jeffersonians were to make much. Vindication, indeed! — and by whom? Three were directors of Hamilton's National Bank. Fifteen or twenty were reputed to be stockholders in the same institution. 'Can these men be admitted as judges — men who in fact are parties to the cause?'[5] All over the land the Jeffersonians were making it uncomfortable for many members who had voted to vindicate, and the Kentuckians soon had Christopher Greenup begging for a suspension of judgment until he could explain.[6] 'Vindicated!' cried the Hamiltonians. 'Yes, and by whom?' answered the Jeffersonians. 'By Bank directors, by Bank stockholders who profited, by congressional speculators in the funds.'

[1] *Centinel*, March 21, 1793   [2] Jefferson.
[3] *New York Daily Advertiser*, April 6, 1793.
[4] *National Gazette*, March 20, 1793; 'Franklin.'   [5] *Ibid.*, March 27, 1793.
[6] *Kentucky Gazette*, September 7, copied in *Independent Chronicle*, October 21, 1793.

IX

Thus the Jeffersonians sought to explain their defeat and even turn it to account. The master mind among them expressed no surprise at the result. He drew up a list of the members who had voted the vindication, indicating which owned Bank stock and which speculated in the funds. When Jefferson journeyed back to renew his strength and courage on his beloved hill, others of his party followed. A little later there was a movement of the leaders to the country home of John Taylor of Caroline at Port Royal, Virginia, where the conferences were continued. Thither went Giles, Senator Hawkins of North Carolina, and Nathaniel Macon. The master of Port Royal was a remarkable character, an ardent Republican, an earnest champion of the agricultural interests, a robust, original thinker with something of the political philosopher, an able writer, a dignified though reluctant Senator. His mind ran much in the same groove with Jefferson's and Madison's, both of whom were anxious to enlist him more actively in their fight.

Just what occurred at the conferences that summer is not known. A few months later, however, the probable fruit of the discussions appeared in Philadelphia in the publication of a startling pamphlet, 'An Examination of the Late Proceedings of Congress Respecting the Official Conduct of the Secretary of the Treasury.' Here in an analysis of the vote the charge that interested parties had furnished the majority was not only made, but names were given. Of the thirty-five supporters of Hamilton, twenty-one were set down as stockholders or dealers in the funds, and three as Bank directors. Referring to the fervent declaration of Smith of Charleston that Hamilton was as free from taint 'as the purest angel in Heaven,' the author of the pamphlet commented that 'it is well known that [Smith] holds between three and four hundred shares in the Bank of the United States, and has obtained discounts, ad libitum.' As for Hamilton's reports, they contained vindications of his conduct 'in certain particulars relative to which no charge had been brought forward.' His explanation of the shuffling of appropriations was unimpressive. A deficiency in the appropriation? 'In such event it becomes his duty to state the fact simply and correctly to the Legislature, that they might, in turn, furnish

fresh and additional funds.' Hamilton had done nothing of the
sort. He had treated the House with contempt and violated the
law.

Here was clearly the answer of the Jeffersonians to the vote of
the House. It found its way to every city, town, and hamlet, to
the cabin in the Kentucky clearing, to the mansion of the master
of many slaves on the river James, to the pioneers about Fort Pitt
on the far frontier. John Taylor of Caroline had struck his blow.[1]

Thus the congressional battle merely served to accentuate the
differences of the parties. It marked, in great measure, the close
of the purely fiscal phase of the struggle. Neither Jefferson nor
Madison was qualified to cross swords with Hamilton in the field
of finance. Giles was hopelessly inadequate. A little later, a
Jeffersonian leader was to join them whose genius as a financier
would be as far above all the Federalists, save Hamilton alone, as
Hamilton was superior to Giles, but he was still waiting in the
wings for Fate to give the cue for his appearance.

Even as Taylor wrote, a new issue had appeared, made to order
for the purposes of Jefferson.

[1] An original copy is in New York Public Library.

CHAPTER X

ÇA IRA

I

UP to this time Jefferson had been fighting under a disadvantage. In the field of finance he was unable to cope on equal terms with his great protagonist. The mass of the people were not consciously concerned with the Hamiltonian policies, few comparatively had been swindled by the speculators, and, while they resented their neighbors' sudden acquisition of wealth, it was not easy to capitalize their discontent.

Then the French Revolution entered a more dramatic stage, captivating the imagination of the multitude. As the real significance of the struggle began to take form, with the crowned heads of the Old World marching in serried ranks under the leadership of Brunswick on the French frontier, the excitement was electric; and when they were turned back by the gallant resistance of the Revolutionists the floodgates of enthusiasm broke. One prolonged, triumphant shout went up from the masses. The 'people of no particular importance' somehow felt that the victory was theirs. They had been a little indifferent, these men of the shops, taverns, wharves, and the frontier, over the disputed financial and economic policies of their country, but they could understand the meaning of 'liberty, equality, fraternity.' It meant democracy. Thus the news of the French victories shook the bells in the New York steeples, Tammany celebrated with song, shout, and speech in her wigwam, and the bung was knocked out of the barrel of illiterate oratory in the beer saloons. These 'people of no importance' had been inarticulate, and they were moved to eloquence. They had found a cause they believed their cause — the cause of the people against privilege.[1] The enthusiasm swept over the country, and the scenes of riotous joy at Mr. Grant's fountain tavern in Baltimore [2] were imitated at Plymouth, Princeton, Fredericksburg, Norfolk, Savannah, Charleston, Boston, Philadelphia.

[1] *Centinel,* January 9, 1793.　　[2] *National Gazette,* December 26, 1792.

In Boston there was a salute of cannon at the castle, and a picturesque procession moved, fluttering French and American flags, bearing a roasted ox of a thousand weight for the barbecue and a hogshead of punch to wash it down, while girls and women waved from the windows, boys shouted from the roofs, and the frenzied throng roared approval to the eloquence of Charles Jarvis, the Jeffersonian leader, and to the Revolutionary poem by 'Citizen' Joseph Croswell.[1] The cheers of Boston were echoed back from Charleston, where the artillery boomed in the day, mingling its thunder with the bells of Saint Michael's. Only 'the pen of a Burke could describe the scene on State Street' packed with exultant humanity, with men looking down from the chimney-tops, while 'bevies of amiable and beautiful women' blessed the marchers with their smiles from the balconies of the houses.[2] On to Saint Philip's tramped the crowd for religious exercises, for these men were not anarchists or criminals, but decent citizens, moved to the depths by the defeat of the persecutors of France.[3]

And observing the unprecedented enthusiasm from his quiet corner, Thomas Jefferson rejoiced. At length the masses were politically awake, and the enemies of democracy had their answer.

II

The issues precipitated by the French Revolution had everything to do with American politics — inevitably so. There were sentimental reasons for the popular enthusiasm for the nation that had served America with men and money; and there were economic reasons for the opposition in the fact that the great merchants operated on English credit. But the political significance of the divisions soon to appear have been persistently written down, where they should be written up.

With some exceptions the Hamiltonian leaders were hostile to the purposes of the French Revolution from the beginning. Here was a rising of the people with a claim to power, and the keynote of Federalist policies was distrust of the people; here was defiance of 'authority,' and they were sticklers for constituted authority; here was a challenging of privilege, and they honestly believed in privilege; here was democracy, and they hated it. They were

---

[1] *Centinel*, January 26, 1793.   [2] *Ibid.*, January 30, 1793.   [3] Hazen, 165–69.

against it, just as Burke was against it, because it was an iconoclastic movement, a trampling on tradition. The death of the
King, the slaughtering by the guillotine, the stupidity and infamy
of Genêt, the intemperance of the American 'Jacobin clubs,' the
defiance of Washington's proclamation — on these they were to
seize to neutralize or destroy the popularity of the Revolution,
but it was the proclaimed principles of the Revolution that they
hated.

In the Senate, where the Hamiltonians were dominant, this was
evident from the beginning. As early as December, 1790, when
the resolutions of condolence adopted by the National Assembly
on the death of Franklin were submitted to the Senate, Adams,
in reading the letter from the President of that body which
accompanied them, referred sarcastically to the writer's titles,
apropos of the action of the Assembly in abolishing titles of nobility.[1] A few weeks later Oliver Ellsworth and Rufus King, the
ablest Federalists in the Senate, openly denounced the French, and
ridiculed their claims upon American gratitude, and when Maclay made indignant protest, Ellsworth, taking snuff, pretended
not to hear, Adams talked audibly with Otis the secretary, and
other Senators gathered in groups to talk aloud. As early as
February, 1791, the Hamiltonians in the Senate were in no mood
to listen to a defense of France.[2] Even the concession of a constitution by Louis XVI was resented by the senatorial fathers of
the Federalist persuasion. The more democratic House adopted
a reply praising 'the wisdom and magnanimity' shown in its
formation and acceptance, but when it reached the Senate,
George Cabot objected to the word 'magnanimity,' Ellsworth supported him, the Federalists voted accordingly, and it was stricken
out. 'Too many Frenchmen, like too many Americans, panting
for equality of persons and property,' grumbled Adams as early as
April, 1790.[3] 'We differed in opinion on the French Revolution,'
wrote Adams in retrospect to Jefferson many years later.[4] Adams
and Hamilton, King and Ellsworth, Cabot and Ames, Jay and
Bingham, looked with mingled cynicism and alarm upon the

---

[1] Maclay, December 10, 1790.
[2] *Ibid.*, February 26, 1791; Brown, *Ellsworth*, 212.
[3] Adams, *Works*, IX, 563–64.   [4] *Ibid.*, X, 12–13.

Revolution from the moment it began to take on a popular character and to aim at the destruction of privilege.

Jefferson was just as ardent in its support. He knew the miserable state to which the feudalistic institutions of the Bourbons had
reduced the masses of the people. He had seen justice bought and
sold in France on the auction block, the operations of the hideous
game laws that threw open the peasants' fields to the trampling
of the horses of the aristocracy, the bestial poverty of the poor,
the insulting of their wives and the debauching of their daughters,
with justice open-eyed and leering. He knew the wantonness of
Versailles, the drunkenness of the King, the profligacy of the
Queen, and he had no illusions as to the dignity of the law or
the righteousness of the authority in France. He had sat at the
table with some of the noblest minds in that country planning
the regeneration of a society that was rotten to the core.

But, more important to him, he was persuaded that the fate of
the American experiment was bound up with the success of the
French Revolution. From this opinion he was never to deviate one
hair's breadth.[1] In January, 1792, he had instructed the American
Minister in Paris that, if circumstances forced an expression as to
the French Government, it should be 'in conformity with the
sentiments of the great mass of our countrymen, who, having first
in modern times taken the ground of government founded on
the will of the people, cannot but be delighted at seeing so distinguished . . . a nation arrive on the same ground and plant their
standard by our side.'[2] A little later he reminded the American
Minister in London that 'we certainly cannot deny to other nations that principle whereon our government is founded, that
every nation has a right to govern itself internally under what
forms it pleases, and to change these forms at its own will.'[3]

Thus, Jefferson was in sympathy with the purposes of the French
Revolution, and the Hamiltonians were hostile. To Jefferson it
meant republicanism, democracy, the end of privilege — and he
wished it well; to the Hamiltonians it meant democracy — and
they wished it ill. When the despots of Europe combined to
crush it and force a degenerate king and court on the bowed backs

---

[1] *Works* (to George Mason), III, 123–25; (to Edward Rutledge), VIII, 232–34.
[2] *Ibid.*, 290–94.   [3] *Ibid.*, IX, 6–8.

of the people, Jefferson's heart was with the untrained boys rushing to the defense of the frontiers; the heart of the Hamiltonians was with the combination of the kings. And because the masses of the American people were in sympathy with the French, Jefferson rode on the crest of the wave in the closing days of 1792.

III

With the execution of the King, the political enemies of the Revolution, simulating shock, ventured into the open. Fenno eagerly seized upon the more graphic stories of the execution in the London papers and published them in full, and soon he was printing sympathetic poems on the event.[1] But the friends of the Revolution were not easily moved to compassion, and one of the theaters in Philadelphia revived the play 'Cato' to the noisy acclaim of frenzied partisans. The actors appeared before the curtain to sing 'La Marseillaise,' and the audience rose to join lustily in the chorus. Night after night this was repeated. The Pittsburgh 'Gazette' published a brutal pæan under the caption, 'Louis Capet has lost his Caput,' and this was copied throughout the country.[2] But these more savage bursts of glee did not meet with general approval, for when the news of Louis's fate reached Providence the people 'fell into an immediate state of dejection, and in the evening all the bells of the churches tolled.'[3] Many put on mourning, and 'Cordelia' announced her purpose to wear, in mourning for the martyred King, a black rose near the left breast, and 'entreated her dearly beloved sisters . . . to follow her example.'[4] For a time the reaction was so pronounced as to threaten the popularity of the Revolution, and it seemed that half the Nation had turned monarchists overnight.

The Democrats were infuriated to find that the reaction was not confined to the fashionable houses, but extended to the people in the streets. Even from New Bedford came the protest that 'the advocates of monarchy' and 'crocodile humanity defenders' were insisting that 'the succors from France . . . proceeded wholly from Louis,' and that he had really wished Frenchmen to be free.[5] A

---

[1] *Gazette of the United States*, April 13, May 18, 1793.
[2] *Ibid.*, April 17; *National Gazette*, April 20, 1793.
[3] *National Gazette*, April 10, 1793.   [4] *Centinel*, March 30, 1793.
[5] *Connecticut Gazette*, April 11, 1793.

citizen of Charleston was disgusted to see how 'the death of one man' could 'so affect the generality of the people' of his city. 'They burst forth in the most vehement invectives . . . against the whole French nation — forgetting the thousands that said king had directly or indirectly been the cause of their death.' [1] An 'Old Soldier' in Philadelphia was shocked to find that 'beer houses, taverns and places of public resort are filled with panegyrics upon the measures of the British administration, and our good allies, the French, are branded with every felonious epithet.' [2] And why all this fuss? Had not letters been received from one who had witnessed the execution with the assurance that 'everything was conducted with the greatest decency,' and had not the writer, traveling over France 'found the people quiet and generally approving of the public measures?' [3] Thus the debate raged in drinking-places, on the streets, in the highways, in the counting- and drawing-rooms — the enemies of the principles of the Revolution perking up and taking heart and seeming in the ascendant for a few days.

Meanwhile what of the leaders?

The Federalists were delighted with the reaction. Jefferson observed that the ladies of Philadelphia 'of the first circle are open-mouthed against the murder of a sovereign, and generally speak those sentiments which their more cautious husbands smother.' Tennant, the French Minister, at length 'openly hoisted the flag of monarchy by going into deep mourning for his prince,' and discontinued his visits to Jefferson, who interpreted it as 'a necessary accompaniment to this pious duty.' More significant to the keen-eyed politician was the observation that 'a connection between him and Hamilton seems to be springing up.' [4] Without indecent manifestations of pleasure over the King's death, Jefferson found some satisfaction with the tendency to render 'monarchs amenable to punishment like any other criminal.' [5] Madison was quite as unresponsive to pity. 'If he was a traitor he ought to be punished like any other man,' he wrote Jefferson.[6] If these clever politicians were not impressed with the cries of commiseration,

---

[1] *Connecticut Gazette*, April 18, 1793.   [2] *National Gazette*, April 20, 1793.
[3] *Connecticut Gazette*, May 2, 1793.
[4] Jefferson's *Works* (to Madison), IX, 33–35.   [5] *Ibid*. (to unknown), IX, 44–46.
[6] Madison's *Writings*, I, 576–77.

it was due to their appraisement of the noise. It was the first plausible and safe opportunity for the enemies of French democracy to denounce the movement they despised, and they made the most of it. Even so, for a few days the Hamiltonians were riding the crest of the wave.

Then another sea change.

IV

George III had joined the Coalition of the Kings, and the familiar redcoats were marching with the rest to crush the Revolution, and democracy. Here was something the masses could understand — monarchy against republicanism, autocracy and aristocracy against democracy, kings against people. The plain man of 'no particular importance' looked about to see the effect. Yes, the old Tories who had hobnobbed with the British officers while the ragged Continentals walked barefoot through the snows of Valley Forge were partisans of England — against France. The duty of the patriot was clear — France against England. The cry was spontaneous with the masses, and rent the heavens. Even then we owed a debt to Lafayette. Poor imbecile Louis was forgotten, the guillotine faded from the view. 'Ça Ira!' Even the children of Philadelphia had learned enough French to sing 'La Marseillaise,' and they sang it right lustily even before the windows of the Binghams. Did we not have a treaty with France that we had been glad to sign? Was not our own existence involved in the European struggle now? The Republic of France crushed by the allied monarchs to-day — our turn to-morrow.

And the partisans of England — who were they? The old American Tories, the rich merchants operating on English capital, the crooked speculators fawning on the money-lenders of Europe, the aristocrats kow-towing to the roués of a degenerate nobility in the homes of the moneyed aristocracy, the politicians who excluded the poor man from the polls.

The effect of the English declaration of war was magical. Again the old 'rabble' that precipitated the American Revolution poured into the streets, swarmed into the saloons, formed into processions and marched. And why not? England was still our enemy, impressing our seamen, retaining our western posts in defiance of the treaty, playing havoc with our commerce. Were the pioneers on the fringe of the western forests in daily danger of the tomahawk? England was responsible — so most of the argument ran. Now was the time to stand up and be counted — for the two republics or the Coalition of the Kings. Thus the reasoning, and it caught on and flashed and flamed like a conflagration sweeping the sun-parched grass of the plains.

To Hamilton this new burst of frenzied friendship for the French was alarming. Washington was at Mount Vernon. His immediate presence in Philadelphia was imperatively needed. He and he alone could stem the rising tide. It was setting in heavily against the English. On April 8th, Hamilton sat at his desk writing his chief a confirmation of the war between England and France with the sly comment that 'the whole current of commercial intelligence . . . indicates thus far an unexceptionable conduct on the part of the English Government toward the vessels of the United States.' This, he added, 'is received here with very great satisfaction as favorable to the continuance of peace . . . which may be said to be both universal and ardent.'

As his pen traveled over the paper the 'rabble' was shouting for war in the streets, and Jefferson was expressing the hope that the English interference with our vessels would 'not force us into war.' If he could only have looked over his rival's shoulder as he wrote!

Washington hastened back to Philadelphia.

v

He immediately gathered his Cabinet about him for a momentous decision. Genêt, young, dashing, audacious, had arrived in Charleston and would soon present his credentials as the Minister of the French Republic. He might even refer to the treaty in which we had pledged ourselves to guarantee the French possessions in the West Indies, and to throw open the ports of America to the prizes of the privateers of our ally while closing them to her enemies. It was a treaty we had been delighted to get, and now it rose to plague us — but there it was. Worse still, the people in the streets understood the nature of the pledge.

It was not Hamilton's way to concede to Jefferson a primacy where foreign relations were involved, and he had not been inactive while awaiting the return of Washington. Jay and King had been consulted particularly as to the receiving of Genêt. Neither could find any pretext for refusing to receive him; both thought he should be received with qualifications. Uppermost in the minds of all three was the treaty — the necessity of evading its obligations.[1] Having decided on the policy of Jefferson's department, Hamilton took no chances, and prepared the list of questions to be submitted to the Cabinet, which Washington copied in his own handwriting, but Jefferson was not deceived as to the authorship.[2] There were no illusions on Jefferson's part as to his position that April day in the room in the Morris house. There was Hamilton, eager, not a little domineering, who had prepared Washington's questions on which the Secretary of State had not been consulted; and Knox, big, pudgy, a bit flamboyant, complacent, and proud of his utter subserviency to Hamilton; and Randolph, with a legalistic mind capable of refining away any position he might take.

Should Genêt be received?

Yes, said Hamilton, with qualifications. Yes, said Jefferson, unqualifiedly. Yes, with qualifications, said Knox, dutifully echoing Hamilton, and, says Jefferson, 'acknowledging at the same time, like the fool he is, that he knew nothing about it.'[3] Randolph agreed with Jefferson.

Let him be received, said Hamilton, with the distinct understanding that we must reserve for future consideration the binding force of the treaties. There was no proof that Louis had been guilty, and evidence that the republicans in France had actually premeditated a plan to get rid of monarchical power.[4] There was no proof that the execution was an act of national justice, and all the courts in Europe held a different view.[5] In truth, 'almost all Europe . . . seems likely to be armed . . . with the intention of restoring . . . the royalty in the successor of the deceased monarch.'[6] If our treaty obligations proved disadvantageous, we should have the right to renounce them.[7] Respect the right of a nation to change its form of government? Yes. Receive its ambassador? Yes. But to throw our weight into the scale for the new republic

[1] King's *Works* (King to Hamilton), I, 439.
[2] *Anas*, I, 268.   [3] *Anas*, I, 268.
[4] Hamilton's *Works*, IV, 371.   [5] *Ibid.*, 372–73.   [6] *Ibid.*, 373.
[7] *Ibid.*, 374.

might be lacking 'in national delicacy and decorum.' [1] As to our obligations under the treaty, there were none, for France was waging an offensive war. The coalition of the monarchs to crush the republic forced the war? Perhaps — but France made the first formal declaration of hostilities.[2]

Jefferson approached the question from a diametrically opposite point of view. 'The reception of the Minister at all,' he said, 'is an acknowledgment of the legitimacy of their government; and if the qualifications meditated are to deny that legitimacy, it will be a curious compound which is to deny and admit the same thing.' The abrogation of the treaties? 'I consider the people who constitute a society as the source of all authority in that nation,' he said: 'as free to transact their common concerns by any agents they think proper; to change these agents individually, or the organization of them in form or function whenever they please; that all the acts done by these agents under the authority of the nation, are obligatory to them and inure to their use, and can in no wise be annulled or affected by any change in the form of government. . . . Consequently the treaties between the United States and France were not treaties between the United States and Louis Capet, but between the two nations of America and France; and the nations remaining in existence, though both of them have since changed their forms of government, the treaties are not annulled by these changes.' [3] All the Cabinet agreed to a proclamation forbidding Americans from participating in the war, to the unqualified reception of Genêt while holding the treaties in abeyance, and to the issuing of a proclamation.

With the appearance of the proclamation, the storm broke.

VI

This had seemed inevitable to Jefferson from the beginning.[4] Madison, then in Virginia, wrote that the proclamation 'wounds the national honor by seeming to disregard the stipulated duties to France,' and 'wounds the popular feeling by a seeming indifference to the cause of liberty.' [5]

---

[1] Hamilton's *Works*, IV, 385–86.
[2] *Ibid.*, 396–408.
[3] Jefferson's *Writings*, III, 226–43.
[3] Madison's *Writings*, I, 580–83; 584.
[4] Jefferson's *Works*, IX, 960–68.

The party issue was made. The Hamiltonians were sympathetic toward monarchical France, hostile to revolutionary France, friendly to England; the Jeffersonians were friendly to revolutionary France, hostile to the Bourbons, and unfriendly to the policy of Pitt in England. The heart of the Hamiltonians beat in tune to the martial steps of the Coalition of the Kings marching on the French frontier; that of the Jeffersonians was with the French peasants hurrying to defend their soil and revolution. And the overwhelming sentiment of the Nation was with Jefferson.

Instantly the Democratic masses saw in the coming of Genêt the opportunity for the manifestation of their feelings. There was much in the personality, appearance, and background of this ardent diplomat of the Gironde to explain the fervent enthusiasm with which he was received. Washington had been warned in advance by Morris, the Minister to France, that he was an 'upstart' — not a bad estimate, as it turned out, but the President had abundant proof that all the French republicans were upstarts.[1] He was not an upstart, however, in that he did not belong in the great world of high politics and society. For almost half a century his father had been in the Ministry of Foreign Affairs, and his celebrated sister, Madame Campan, had been one of the ladies of Marie Antoinette, of whom he had been a prime favorite. A familiar figure among the fashionable young dandies of Versailles, he had served for a while as the secretary of one of the brothers of the monarch. An extraordinarily brilliant youth, he had translated the 'History of Eric XIV' at the age of twelve, with historical notes of his own. Entering the diplomatic service, with the blessings of the Queen, he had served as attaché at the courts of Berlin, Vienna, London, and St. Petersburg. He spoke several languages with the fluency of a native. A romantic figure, this young man, handsome, elegant in manner, eloquent and entertaining in conversation, gracious, friendly, impulsive, with the virtues to neutralize the vices of his years.

If the reception he received in the aristocratic city of Charleston was enough to turn his head, it was nothing to the continuous ovation accorded him as he proceeded slowly on his month's

[1] Morris, *Diary*, ii, 26.

journey to Philadelphia. Farmers flocked to the rough roads to cheer him and offer him produce at a loss. In every town he was a conquering hero, and everywhere he was greeted with the strains of 'Ça Ira,' and orators paid tribute to France and the principles of its Revolution. The ringing of bells, the shouting of the multitude wearing liberty caps and waving French flags — such the sights and sounds that greeted him everywhere. Nor was this charming young diplomat pleasing to the Democratic rabble alone. At Baltimore, Justice Iredell of the Supreme Court was impressed with his 'fine open countenance, and pleasing unaffected manner.' [1] Federalist Iredell failed to find the 'upstart' who was so conspicuous to Federalist Morris.

As the reports of the continuous ovation dribbled into Philadelphia, Hamilton and the Federalists were alarmed and disgusted, Jefferson delighted. Here was proof that the people were sound in their republicanism. Better still, here were the masses making themselves felt in public affairs for the first time. Even better, they were casting aside the spirit of humility, and standing erect with their sovereignty under their hats. While Genêt was proceeding to the capital, Jefferson was writing joyously to Monroe of the 'old spirit of '76 rekindling the newspapers from Boston to Charleston' and forcing 'the monocrat papers . . . to publish the most furious philippics against England.' [2] And Madison was quite as pleased. He had hoped for a reception that would make 'the cant of the cities' and the 'cold caution of the Government' less offensive.[3]

Meanwhile, as Genêt approached, the Democrats in Philadelphia, suspecting that the Government hoped ' to prevent a joyful reception,' were determined to disappoint that hope. 'An Old Soldier,' in a stirring reminder of French services in the American Revolution, declared that 'if after such recollections you will hesitate to welcome their ambassador, I will mourn over the departed virtue of my country.' [4]

The appeal was not made in vain. Freneau and Bache in their papers were arousing the emotions of the people. The former was publishing Grey's speech in Parliament against going to war with

[1] McRee, *Iredell* (to his wife), ii, 386.   [2] Jefferson's *Works*, ix, 75–78.
[3] Madison's *Writings*, i, 578.   [4] *National Gazette*, April 27, 1793.

France. 'A shining character,' thought the editor.[1] He was also informing his readers that the news of our neutrality 'gave much satisfaction to the English nation.'[2] Meanwhile, the 'rabble,' embracing such characters as Rittenhouse, Dr. Hutchinson, and A. J. Dallas, was making preparations. The Minister would be met at Gray's Ferry, and every one who possibly could should go. The cannon on *L'Ambascade* would roar the announcements of the hero's approach early enough to permit all who wished to reach the Ferry in time.[3]

It was at this time that a strange rumor was floating about the streets, taverns, and beer-houses of the city. Count de Noailles had arrived in Philadelphia at nine o'clock on the night of May 3d, commissioned as Minister by the former Princes at Coblentz, and at a very late hour at night had been received by Washington at the Morris house where the two 'were in private conversation until near morning.' The Count had arrived — every one knew it. What sort of treachery was this? So this was the reason the Government was trying to discourage the reception to Genêt.[4] The people would see to that.

Thus, Genêt was met at Gray's Ferry by an immense throng with thunderous cheers — cheers that accompanied him all the way to the City Tavern. The streets packed, throbbing with joy. Looking out over the excited multitude, Genêt 'was quite overcome with the affectionate joy that appeared on every face,' according to a lady of Philadelphia who shared it. 'It is true,' she said, 'that a few disaffected persons did try to check the ardor of the people, but they had the mortification to find all their efforts blasted and were obliged themselves to join the general torrent and affect a cordiality . . . contrary to the feelings of their hearts.' A truly inspiring spectacle. 'It would be impossible, my dear, to give you any idea of the scene.'[5] Then followed the formal welcome. Resolutions were prepared at the home of Charles Biddle, were adopted enthusiastically at an immense meeting in the State

[1] *National Gazette,* April 27, 1793.   [2] *Ibid.,* May 4, 1793.
[3] *Ibid.,* May 15, 1793.
[4] Letter from Philadelphia 'from a gentlemen in the treasury department.' *Connecticut Gazette,* June 27, 1793.
[5] Letter from Philadelphia woman to a friend in Alexandria; *Connecticut Gazette,* June 20, 1793.

House yard — then on in a body to the City Tavern, Biddle leading the way and setting a merry pace. Ever and anon he received a frantic plea from Dr. Hutchinson, 'fat enough to act the character of Falstaff without stuffing,' to slow up, and with sardonic humor Biddle hurried on. The corpulent doctor reached the hotel in a state of complete exhaustion. But it was worth it. 'Ça Ira!' Long live the French Republic and damnation to its foes![1] Then the dinner at O'Eller's, the finest the city had ever seen, at four dollars a plate, with Genêt thrilling the diners by singing the French fighting song, the audience roaring 'Ça Ira,' liberty caps passing around, toasts fervent and fiery. 'What hugging and rugging!' grumbled a Philadelphian a quarter of a century later. 'What addressing and caressing! What mountebanking and chanting with liberty caps and the other wretched trumpery of sans-culotte foolery!'[2] When Genêt called on Jefferson, he was cordially received, but there was a drop in temperature when he presented his credentials to Washington, whose sober and restrained manner seemed cold to the Frenchman after the reception from the people. Worse still, he found portraits of Louis XVI and Marie Antoinette in the room. Enough, quite enough, had been done to turn the head of a stronger character than he. But the Philadelphia lady was right — many who hated the Revolution simulated enthusiasm, and one day Knox, Bingham, and other leading Federalists might have been seen going aboard *L'Ambascade* with Genêt to partake of a fraternal dinner.[3]

VII

Thus the popular protest against neutrality between England and France rose in a crescendo to a scream. Be patient with England? scoffed a Boston writer. What, with the western posts still held, the Indian wars, the impressment of American sailors on the sea?[4] The country's grievances against the English were mobilized and marched to the accompaniment of hisses. A resident of Pittsburgh wrote an open letter to Washington against neutrality. 'I doubt much whether it is the disposition of the United States to preserve the condition you enjoin. It may be the disposition of

[1] Biddle, *Autobiography*, 251.　　[2] Graydon, *Memoirs*, 381.
[3] *National Gazette*, June 1, 1793.　　[4] *Centinel*, April 20, 1793.

those who draw from funds but from no one else.'[1] Thus encouraged, 'Veritas' grasped his pen. 'I am aware, sir, that some court satellites may have deceived you' — not difficult to impose on a ruler 'particularly if so much buoyed up by official importance as to think it beneath his dignity to mix occasionally with the people.'[2] Freneau, who began to print a series of satirical poems attacking Washington, sardonically sent two copies of each issue to his desk. The great man fumed, fretted, occasionally burst into rage. 'Civic' launched his thunderbolts against 'incendiaries . . . who have lately outraged decency . . . by insulting Washington,'[3] and Fenno rushed to the defense with stupid denunciations of all critics as anarchists and traitors. The men in the streets jeered their disapproval.

Thus, the summer of 1793 was one of utter madness. Mechanics were reading the speeches of Mirabeau; clerks were poring over the reports of revolutionary chiefs; college students were finding Paine preferable to Virgil; and even the women were reading, with flushed cheeks, Barlow's 'Conspiracy of Kings.' Others too illiterate to read were stalking the narrow streets like conquerors, jostling the important men of the community with intent, and sneering at the great. Men were equal. The people's day had dawned. Down the streets swaggered the mob looking for lingering relics of royalty to tear or order down. A medallion enclosing a bas-relief of George III with his crown, on the eastern front of Christ's Church, caught its eye. Down with it! The church officials did not hesitate, but tore it down. On swept the mob in search of other worlds to conquer. Occasionally the lower element, drinking itself drunk, staggered out of the beer-houses to shout imprecations on a government that would not war on England.

Not wholly without provocation, these outbursts. Fenno's fulsome snobbery was disgusting to people of sense, and the English sailors in Philadelphia did not help. When four of these jolly tars attacked and all but murdered a lone French sailor without a rebuke from the city officials, Bache's paper warned that the friends of the French would 'take signal vengeance on such infamous banditti.' When, in New York, the aristocrats of the 'new and

[1] *National Gazette*, May 15, 1793   [2] *Ibid.*, June 5, 1793.
[3] *Gazette of the United States*, June 8, 1793.

elegant coffee-house' and the exclusive Belvedere Club were 'swallowing potent draughts to the annihilation of liberty,' notice was served that unless suppressed 'a band of Mohawks, Oneidas, and Senecas will take upon themselves that necessary duty — for Tammany was the very heart of the French movement in New York.[1] 'Ça Ira!' The people were the masters, and even in the theaters they went to dictate to managers and actors. When Hodkinson, a favorite actor, appeared, as his rôle required, in the uniform of a British officer, he was hissed. 'Take it off!' shouted the crowd; but when the quick-witted actor smilingly explained that he represented a bully, the jeers were turned to cheers.[2] On then with the play. The orchestras played 'La Marseillaise,' the galleries sang 'Ça Ira,' the managers shunted Shakespeare and Sheridan aside for 'Tyranny Suppressed,' 'Louis XVI,' and 'The Demolition of the Bastile.' In Boston, where the Federalists were firm, the Boston Theater continued to cater to their tastes, but even there the Haymarket drew the greater crowds with drama for the Democrats.

Everywhere liberty caps were worn and liberty poles were raised, and men and women became 'Citizen' and 'Citizeness,' while the Federalists roared their glee to keep up courage, making merry in their letters and through their papers at the expense of the 'citness':

> 'No citness to my name, I'll have, says Kate,
> Though Boston lads so much about it prate;
> I've asked its meaning, and our Tom, the clown,
> Says darn it 't means " woman of the town." ' [3]

From Hartford the witty Chauncey Goodrich wrote Wolcott that 'our citizenesses quite execrate their new name,' and that while 'they will have no objection to being called biped in common with men, if it can clearly be shown that term denotes nothing above the foot or ankle, but as it comes so near they are suspicious of mischief.' [4] What a world! What a world 'agog to be all equal to French barbers.' [5]

Then, suddenly, these Federalists ceased to grin, when Democratic Clubs, suggestive of those of Paris, appeared like magic

[1] Myers, *Tammany Hall*, 9.   [2] Hazen, 249.
[3] *Centinel*, March 16, 1793.   [4] Gibbs, i, 87.   [5] *Ibid.*

everywhere, differing according to the community and character of their leadership. It was not riff-raff in Philadelphia where David Rittenhouse was president, but it was sinister enough with its bold assertion that free men should 'regard with attention and discuss without fear the conduct of public servants.' [1] That at Norfolk summoned patriots to a courageous expression of their sentiments in answer to 'the tyrants of the world' united 'to crush the infant spirit of freedom' in France.[2] Strangely enough, they were nowhere so extreme as in Charleston where the 'Saint Cecilia Society' scorned the membership of plebeians or men in trade; and where Robert Goodloe Harper, fresh from the country and poor, rose rapidly to fame as the vice-president of the Jacobin Club, wearing a 'red rouge with great grace and dignity.' [3] And nowhere did they mean so much to the Jeffersonians as in New England where they were giving political importance to the masses. Even the Germans of Philadelphia organized to serve liberty and equality in their native tongue.[4]

The shrieks of protest from the Federalists against these clubs is inexplicable to the twentieth century. Like innumerable clubs for public purposes to-day, they were composed of the wise and foolish, the vicious and virtuous, but their purpose was to discuss and disseminate information on public affairs. Some then, as now, passed asinine resolutions, but that which alarmed the Hamiltonians was that they created power for the masses. Had not Fenno preached and preached that the masses were to be ruled and satisfied? The merchants should have their Chambers of Commerce; the financiers and even speculators could organize to influence public action — but what right had the 'man of no particular importance' to interfere?

In brief, these clubs were vicious because democratic. These 'demoniacal societies,' as Wolcott preferred to call them, were 'nurseries of sedition' because 'they are formed for the avowed purpose of a general influence and control upon measures of government.' [5] It was 'sedition' in those days for people of no special significance to hold views in opposition to the policies of their

[1] *National Gazette*, July 17, 1793.
[2] *Gazette of the United States*, June 15, 1793.
[3] Thomas, *Reminiscences*, I, 32.
[4] *National Gazette*, April 13, 1793.
[5] Gibbs (Governor Wolcott to son), I, 179.

rulers. It was the kind of sedition that Jefferson liked. From his home on the river he watched their organizations multiply and grow with a fond, hopeful interest. They were his Citizens' Training Camps where the army he was to lead to victory was being trained for political war.

VIII

Meanwhile, how fared neutrality on the part of England and France? On the part of Genêt, badly enough. Week by week some outrage was committed; and, worse still, the young fanatic was persuading himself of the propriety of his actions. The cheers in the streets convinced him that he could defy the President and appeal with safety to the people. He could hear the comparatively few extremists because they shouted loudest. Day by day he was becoming more intolerable. Devoted to the cause of revolutionary France, Jefferson sought to curb the impetuosity of its Minister in the interest of the cause, but toward the latter part of June he was plainly worried.[1]

The British were as arrogant and impudent. Outrages on American ships and the impressment of American seamen were almost daily occurrences, and protests to the Government in London brought no response.[2] Ships stopped, insulted, searched; cargoes confiscated; seamen seized, impressed, and thrown into jails; until Thomas Pinckney, the American Minister in London, was overwhelmed with his correspondence with Newgate Jail — for the poor wretches there were begging him for succor he could not give. He was met with a courteous smile and contemptuous indifference.'[3]

In American waters British as well as French were arming and equipping, and into American ports sailed English vessels with prizes taken in direct violation of the treaty with France. Then came the Orders in Council of June 8th ordering British ships to capture and take to British ports all vessels with foodstuffs destined for France.

On the day before this Order went into effect, a goodly company of English sympathizers met at Richardet's Tavern in Phila-

---

[1] Jefferson's *Works* (to Monroe), IX, 144.   [2] *Ibid.* (to Monroe), IX, 75–78.
[3] Pinckney, *Life of Pinckney*, 109.

delphia to celebrate the birthday of George III. An elegant dinner, unmarred by the presence of any part of the 'rabble,' with a guest list reading like a page from a Social Register. Enthusiasm bubbled, and 'Ça Ira' was not sung. The orchestra played 'God Save the King.' That monarch was toasted, and they toasted the Queen, and Hammond the British Minister, and Phineas Bond, the British Consul. They toasted Washington once and 'Neutrality' twice. And they brought a perfect evening to a close with another toast: 'The Red Coats and Wooden Walls of Old England.' [1] Fenno in the Federalist organ published a sympathetic account which was read with varying emotions from Mrs. Bingham's library to the beer saloon on Front Street. Even the soberest began to wonder if neutrality was one-sided. Nowhere was neutrality appealing to the masses as just, wise, or fair.

One June morning, Washington drove out of Philadelphia in a phaëton and pair for a fortnight's visit home,[2] and six days later the first of a brilliant and powerful series of articles by 'Pacificus' began to run in Fenno's paper. By the light of the candles, Hamilton was rushing into the breach with a pen that was mightier than a sword.

IX

No one doubted the identity of 'Pacificus.' None but the man in the Pemberton house was capable of such brilliancy, audacity, and dash in controversy. His purpose was twofold — to justify the Proclamation of Neutrality, and convince the people that they had greatly exaggerated the services of France in the Revolution. In the first paper he defended the constitutional right of the President to issue the Proclamation without a consultation with Congress. In the second he released the country from all treaty obligations on the ground that France was waging an offensive war. In the third he appealed to fear with the assertion that if we sought to serve our ally we should be forced to wage war on the sea against the combined fleets of the coalition. In the fifth he treated the claims of France on American gratitude as trivial and absurd.[3] In the sixth he paid a tribute to the stupid Louis, at-

[1] *Gazette of the United States*, June 8, 1793.
[2] Jefferson's *Works*, IX, 144–46.   [3] Hamilton's *Works*, IV, 467.

tacking the French people for executing their king. In the last he urged the timeliness and necessity of the Proclamation. Brilliant letters, mingling truth and sophistry, but readable — and they were read with mingled emotions. Society was enchanted, the 'mob' roared, and even Jefferson, who never made the Hamiltonian mistake of underestimating a foe, was concerned.

When 'Pacificus' was appearing, Jefferson was summering under his plane trees near Philadelphia, Madison was sweltering in his Virginia home, wishing nothing better than a release from political duties. As Jefferson sat under the trees with Fenno's paper before him, he instantly appreciated the necessity of a reply, and he ordered Madison to the task. Nothing could have been more distasteful to the mild little man suffering 'a distressing lassitude from the excessive and continued heat of the season,' and with avowed reluctance he undertook the task.[1] But in August, Madison's replies were running in all the papers — forceful, spirited, rapid in reasoning, making telling points with citations from Hamilton's articles in 'The Federalist.'[2] He denied the power of the President to declare a treaty no longer operative. Proof? The best — Hamilton's Number 75 of 'The Federalist.' Challenge the right of a nation to abolish an old government and establish a new? Why, it 'is the only lawful tenure by which the United States hold their existence as a nation.'

But the two sets of letters merely served to keep the discussion going. The papers were doing their part. 'This discussion must cease,' wrote Fenno. 'The Government has said we must be neutral and the people have no right to question its wisdom.' Freneau sniffed and snorted forth satirical articles on the infallibility of rulers.[3] No writer presuming to castigate the democrats was spared. 'Justice' was pouring forth indignant eloquence against them. Ah, sneered Freneau —

> 'Because some pumpkin shells and lobster claws
> Thrown o'er his garden wall by Braintree's Duke,[4]
> Have chanced to fall within your greedy jaws —
>
> .   .   .   .
>
> Because some treasury luncheons you have gnawed
> Like rats that play upon the public store . . .'[5]

---

[1] Madison's *Writings*, i, 586; 588; 591; 593–94; letters to Jefferson.
[2] *Ibid.*, i, 611–45.   [3] *National Gazette*, June 15, 1793.
[4] Adams.   [5] *National Gazette*, August 7, 1793.

The bitterness intensified with the heat of the summer. A satirical letter ascribed to a Tory in Philadelphia to one in London rejoicing over the turn American affairs had taken, went the rounds of the Democratic press. Washington was not spared. He 'is well surrounded, well advised.' Hamilton moved the correspondent to rapture — 'that great prop of our cause, that intrepid enemy of liberty.' Just read the third of the 'Pacificus' letters 'and judge . . . if there is anything criminal which honest Pacificus has not undertaken to defend.' [1]

'A blessed situation truly,' exclaimed 'Consistent Federalist,' referring to the recent Orders in Council. 'Camillus and Pacificus come forward and vindicate the lenity of Britain; continue to blast the French, and vent their spleen on the only nation that seems disposed to befriend us.' [2] 'Go on, then, Pacificus,' wrote 'Ironicus,' 'traduce the French nation and the combined powers of Europe will thank you for your assiduity.' [3] Soon the Democrats were grinning over the satirical announcement of the forthcoming book 'collected from the immortal work of Pacificus' on how to destroy free government by 'aristocracy and despotism.' [4]

x

But Hamilton could afford to disregard the attacks — he had Genêt working on his side. Never had conditions seemed so promising to the light-headed and hot-headed young diplomat than on July 4th, when he had licked his chops over the opportunity to decline an invitation to dine with the Cincinnati on the ground that he would not sit down at the same table with the Viscount de Noailles.[5] There were other celebrations in Philadelphia more to his taste.

It was at this moment that the brig *Little Sarah*, a French prize, was being rapidly converted into a privateer with the view to sending it to sea regardless of neutrality. Governor Mifflin sent his secretary, A. J. Dallas, scurrying through the midnight streets to Genêt's residence to order him to keep the vessel in port. The young fire-eater raved and ranted, and said strange things about

[1] *New York Daily Advertiser*, July 13, 1793.
[2] *Independent Chronicle*, September 12, 1793.   [3] *Ibid.*, November 11, 1793.
[4] *Ibid.*   [5] Biddle, 253.

appealing over the head of the President to the people. Jefferson, hearing of the incident, hurried in on Sunday from the country, listened to Genêt's cocky talk, attempted to reason with him without success, but left with the feeling that the ship would not be sent to sea before Washington's return from Mount Vernon.

The Cabinet met on Monday at the State House. Hamilton and Knox proposed establishing a battery on Mud Island and firing on the vessel if it sought to reach the sea. Hamilton vehemently denounced the French. Jefferson, having in mind his representations to England, was not at all sure that the violations of neutrality were on one side. He stoutly protested against any measure that might lead to war without a consultation with Washington.

Three days later the *Little Sarah* was still in Philadelphia and Washington returned. Hamilton and Knox were instantly on his neck. Jefferson, ill with fever, had prepared all the papers in the case for the President's use, marked them for 'instant attention,' left them on his desk, and retired to his home. Glancing at the papers, Washington sent a peremptory summons to Jefferson's office. Learning then of his absence, a note was sent to the sick man's home sizzling with indignation over Genêt's threat, and requiring Jefferson's opinion on procedure 'even before to-morrow morning, for the vessel may be gone.' Jefferson kept his temper — unless it is betrayed in the brevity and cold dignity of the reply: 'T. J. is himself of opinion that whatever is aboard of her of arms, ammunition, or men, contrary to the rules heretofore laid down by the President, ought to be withdrawn.'

It was after this that the *Little Sarah* put to sea.

The lunatic caperings of Genêt had been maddening to Jefferson, who instantly sensed the inevitable reaction against his party, and the ease with which the sophisticated reasoning of the Federalists could confuse, in the public mind, the cause of the French Revolution with the insolence of its Minister. Wherever his influence could be successfully exerted, he divorced his followers from the addle-brained diplomat who had become raving mad. To Madison he complained of the continued adherence of Freneau and Greenleaf to Genêt.[1] Dr. Hutchinson had informed

[1] Jefferson's *Works*, IX, 211–15.

him that 'Genêt has totally overturned the republican interest in Philadelphia.' Referring to the threat to appeal to the people over Washington's head, he added: 'I can assure you it is a fact.' [1]

Justifications for the fears of the leader under the plane trees were soon reaching him from Madison in Virginia, who had a plan afoot for the complete divorcing of Genêt from the Jeffersonian Party and from the cause of the French Republic. He prepared resolutions and arranged for their adoption in various county meetings in Virginia. One copy was sent to Edmund Pendleton of Caroline; Monroe was sent with another copy to Staunton. Still another went to Charlottesville.[2] The first of the county meetings to adopt the Madison Resolutions was at Caroline with Pendleton in the chair, and they were hurried to the newspapers throughout the country. They declared devotion to the Constitution, to the cause of peace, and to Washington, were warmly appreciative of the debt of gratitude to France, sympathetic toward her struggle for liberty, and denunciatory of the attempt to alienate the two republics and to drive the United States in the direction of monarchy and England.[3] They were sent to Washington, whose reply must have been galling to the English party with its laudation of France and the republican principle of government.[4] The Jeffersonian press gave the reply the widest possible publicity.

Thus, through July, August, and September the two parties contended over the threat of Genêt, each playing for advantage. Comparatively few extremists offered any excuse for the ruined Minister, who was despised by Jefferson and Madison for compromising their party and the cause of France. 'His conduct has been that of a madman,' wrote Madison to Monroe.[5] Even the Democratic Clubs followed the line laid down in Madison's Caroline Resolutions.

XI

Such was the inflammatory state of parties when on August 1st, Jefferson, Hamilton, Knox, and Randolph arrived at the Morris

---

[1] Jefferson's *Works*, IX, 211–15.
[2] Madison's *Writings*, I, 595–96; 596–97.
[3] *Ibid.*, I, 599; *Independent Chronicle*, October 10, 1793.
[4] *Independent Chronicle*, October 17, 1793.   [5] Madison's *Writings*, I, 601.

house to discuss with Washington the disposition to be made of Genêt.

Knox was not given to finesse when his passions were involved. 'Send him out of the country,' and without ceremony, he said. Publish all the correspondence in an appeal to the people before Genêt could carry out his threat, urged Hamilton. For forty-five minutes he spoke impassionedly, attacking Genêt, denouncing the Democratic Societies, assailing France. Jefferson, sitting in silence, thought it was an excellent 'jury speech.'

Randolph spoke in opposition to radical measures, and the meeting adjourned until the morrow.

The next day Hamilton again took the floor and spoke again for three quarters of an hour with unrestrained bitterness. As he sat down, Jefferson rose. He was not alarmed over the Democratic Clubs. They would die if left alone and would grow on proscription and persecution. Publish the facts and decisions of the President on the whole foreign controversy? Those decisions had been reached with divisions in the Cabinet — was it desired to proclaim that condition to the country? Was it desirable to injure our friend France with a stab, in the face of her enemies, the allied kings of Europe?

It was here that Knox broke in with references to Freneau's attacks on Washington. He had calculated the effect. The President flew into a rage, and the meeting adjourned because of the turmoil and excitement.[1] Determined to manage his own department, Jefferson thereupon sat down to the preparation of a letter to the American Minister in Paris, setting forth with scrupulous fairness and severity the antics of Genêt, and asking his recall. The sting to France was removed with an eloquent protestation of friendship. Hamilton at no time drew so damning and effective an indictment of Genêt, but all this was lost upon him because of the note of friendliness to France.[2]

Twelve days after the first meeting, the Cabinet again sat about the council table in the Morris house listening to the Jefferson draft. It was so unassailable that it was unanimously accepted — with one exception. Jefferson had referred to a possible conflict between the two republics as 'liberty warring on itself.'

[1] *Anas*, I, 305–08.   [2] Jefferson's *Works*, IX, 180–209.

Hamilton moved to strike out these words, Knox parroting his master's suggestion. Washington favored their retention, expressing the conviction that France, despite her blunders, was fighting for liberty; but Randolph voted with Hamilton and Knox against Washington and Jefferson, and the words were stricken out.[1]

In due time Genêt was recalled. That episode was over. Jefferson had won his fight to prevent a rupture with France — but it had cost him dearly.

XII

As early as May, Jefferson had been able to put his finger on the French and English parties in this country. With the English, the fashionable circles, the merchants trading on English capital, the supporters of the Treasury, the old Tory families; with the French, the small merchants, the tradesmen, mechanics, farmers, 'and every other possible description of our citizens.'[2] There was no doubt in his mind as to the position of the social circles of Philadelphia — he was made to feel it. The men were courteous in his presence, and he still dined occasionally with the Binghams and Robert Morris, though the ladies were but chillingly polite. The friend of the 'filthy democrats,' as Mrs. Washington is said to have called them, was, to them, beyond the pale. Mr. Hammond, the English Minister, was such a charming man! A few of the French noblemen, once numbered among the dissolute loafers of Versailles, were to be found frequently drinking Bingham's wine, paying courtly compliments to the women, and making love to the daughters of the house a bit clandestinely, as Mrs. Bingham was to find to her dismay a little later. Not a few of the social leaders had been 'presented' at court in both France and England, and they never recovered. Others looked forward to a possible presentation as the consummation of a life's ambition. Kings were adorable creatures, after all, and queens were as 'sweet queens' as Fanny Burney found hers, and the nobility was so elegant! As for the 'people' — were they not as the rabble who had cut off the head of the lovable Louis? And Jefferson was the enemy of kings, the idol of the rabble — and what was worse,

[3] Randall, II, 181.   [2] Jefferson's *Works*, IX, 87–89; to Madison.

their defender. The men thought his principles askew, but the women knew that his heart was black.

Thus it was fortunate that during the exciting summer of 1793, Jefferson could retire to the solitude of his murmuring plane trees and let society buzz. Even the Philadelphia streets were cold to him. Party feeling was running amuck. Old acquaintances pretended not to see each other as they passed. It was true everywhere. Even Noah Webster was complaining bitterly of this party narrowness in New York. 'Examine the detached clubs at the Coffee-House,' he wrote, 'there you will see persons of the same family associated. Go into the private families at dinner and on evening visits, there you will find none but people of the same party.' [1]

When Jefferson remained in town after leaving his office, he spent more and more time in the library of the Philosophical Society, at the home of Dr. Rush talking books more than politics, or he went to the welcome shade of 'Stenton,' where he was always sure of a cordial greeting from Dr. Logan and that incomparable Quakeress who was his wife. To Madison he opened his heart in the lament that he found 'even the rare hours of relaxation sacrificed to the society of persons . . . of whose hatreds I am conscious even in those moments of conviviality when the heart wishes most to open itself to the effusions of friendship and confidence, cut off from my family and friends . . . in short giving everything I love in exchange for everything I hate.' [2] The attacks on Washington, which society ascribed to the influence of Jefferson, made his position all the more unpleasant. Articles signed 'Democrat', or 'Veritas' foully assailing the President appeared in Federalists papers. The worst of these, Jefferson thought, were written by his enemies for the purpose of embittering decent men against his party. It was even whispered about that he was the author of the 'Veritas' letters, for Genêt, in an attempt to impress his Government with his own power, hinted that Jefferson had written them. The latter talked it over with Tobias Lear, the President's secretary, and made an investigation of his own, concluding that the author was William Irvine, a clerk in the Comptroller's office. 'I have long suspected this detestible game was playing by the

fiscal party to place the President on their side,' Jefferson wrote.[1]
It was manifestly absurd, but society preferred to believe it.

Unpleasant as was the attitude of the fashionable circles, it was
not so offensive to Jefferson as the constant quarreling and intriguing in official circles. He complained that he and Hamilton were
always against each other like cocks in a pit. He was never fond of
futile disputation. His own views were fixed, as were those of his
opponent. He was too much the philosopher to enjoy argumentation that accomplished nothing. Long before that summer he had
wanted to retire, and, as we have seen, had only been dissuaded
by the importunities of Washington, but he was now intolerably
tired of it all. Acknowledging a letter from a friend in Paris, he had
written, in reference to the 'oppressive scenes of business,' that
'never was mortal more tired of these than I am.' [2] Three months
earlier, he had promised his daughter Martha that the next year
they would 'sow [their] cabbages together.'

By July the situation was becoming unendurable. It was about
this time, when he was writing his notes to Hammond, the British
Minister, who was an intimate friend of Hamilton's, that Oliver
Wolcott, the mere shadow of his chief, was bitterly complaining
of Jefferson's 'duplicity of character' in treating Hammond
harshly.[3] These were the notes to which John Marshall gave the
highest praise in his 'Life of Washington,' but the observation of
Wolcott reflected the tone of society.

On July 31st, the philosopher-politician seated under his plane
trees might have read an attack upon himself in Fenno's paper
charging him with crimes against his country committed in such a
way as 'to keep him out of reach of the law.' [4] That very day he
sat down at his desk to write his resignation. Six days later, Washington drove out to Jefferson's country place, and out on the lawn
sought again to dissuade his Secretary of State from his purpose.
But he had had enough. With some bitterness, he told the President that 'the laws of society oblige me always to move exactly in
the circle which I know to bear me peculiar hatred . . . and thus
surrounded, my words are caught up, multiplied, misconstrued,
and even fabricated and spread abroad to my injury.' [4] Convinced

---

[1] Anas, I, 279.   [2] Domestic Life, 220.   [3] Gibbs, I, 122.
[4] Gazette of the United States, July 31, 1793.   [4] Anas, I, 311.

that Jefferson was unshakable, Washington discussed, with him, a possible successor. He favored Madison, but feared he would not accept, and then asked Jefferson's opinion of Jay and Smith, both rabid Hamiltonians. Jefferson asked him if he had ever thought of Chancellor Livingston. He had — but Hamilton was from New York. What did Jefferson know about Wolcott? 'I have heard him characterized as a very cunning man,' was the dry reply. It was finally agreed that Jefferson should remain on until January.[1]

XIII

August was a dreadful month in Philadelphia, a dry, deadening heat making the days and nights unbearable. Any one walking near Water Street was sickened by the fetid smells from the stinking wharves. Politically conditions were as depressing. The bitter party struggle went on. Even the heat and smells could not give it pause. Bache's paper published a letter describing Viscount de Noailles as 'a man who was employed by the late King of France to bribe the members of the Convention . . . and afterwards ran off with the money'; and the next day the nobleman, swords and pistols in his eyes, appeared to demand that the editor publish a denial and furnish the name of the author of the article. Thinking discretion the better part of valor, Bache gave 'Mr. Pascal, the Secretary of Genêt,' as the author and society expected a French duel — to be disappointed.[2] Genêt was hurrying off to New York to accept an ovation and the Hamiltonians began to lose faith in Washington, because he sat 'with folded arms' and let the Government 'be carried on by town meetings.' The Federalists were concluding that town meetings were a vicious influence. Meetings of Chambers of Commerce were different.[3] But it was reserved for Boston to give the Federalists their greatest shock when at the masthead of the French frigate *La Concorde*, appeared the names of eleven staid men of the city placarded as 'aristocrats,' and unfriendly to the French Republic. The charge was true, but here was something that smacked of the Terror in Paris. With the town seething with righteous wrath, a

[1] *Anas*, I, 313.　　　[2] *Philadelphia Daily Advertiser*, August 4, 1793.
[3] King's *Works*, I, 492–93.

committee boarded the vessel and demanded the removal of the placard. The officers expressed surprise that it was there, apologized, removed it. But the opportunity was too good to be lost. 'I wish to know what is to be their [the eleven citizens'] punishment, and who is to execute it,' wrote 'A Free American' in the 'Centinel.' 'Are they to suffer by the lamp post or by the guillotine here, or are they to be sent in irons to Paris to suffer there?' [1] Viewing the scene, as became a Cabot, from the vantage-point of aristocratic aloofness, George Cabot was alarmed. He wrote King of his 'amazement' at 'the rapid growth of Jacobin feeling.' Why had not the truth concerning France been told the people? Had she not 'obstructed our commercial views?' [2] Had Cabot unbent to the reading of the 'Independent Chronicle' of his city he might have understood the cause of the 'growth of Jacobin feeling.' It fairly teemed with the French and their Revolution. 'In case of distress whence is our succor to arise?' it demanded. 'Is there one among the combined powers contending against France on whose cordiality we could depend?' [3] Ask the soldier of our Revolution who helped win American independence. 'Who were the men who marched in columns to the capture of Cornwallis — or whose navy thundered the music of that defeat?' [4]

Then, with September, the reaper of Death stalked through the streets of Philadelphia.

XIV

It began with the filth and sickening smells of Water Street and spread like the deadly gas of modern battle-fields over the city. The poor of the congested quarters near the water-front fell like flies in winter. Soon it spread to the best residential sections. The evident inability of the physicians to cope with the disease increased the terror. Washington was ordered out of the city and hastened to Mount Vernon, and Knox took to precipitate flight.[5] Soon all the great houses were closed, and every one who could afford it abandoned his business and fled from the stricken city. Soon half the houses were abandoned, and they who remained

[1] August 10, 1793.   [2] Lodge, *Cabot*, 73.
[3] 'A Democrat,' August 19, 1793.   [4] 'Brutus,' August 26, 1793.
[5] Jefferson's *Works* (to Madison), IX, 227.

locked their doors, closed the windows, and lived in complete isolation as far as possible.[1]

Day and night the death-carts rumbled through the town and a covered wagon was kept busy conveying the sick to Bush Hill Hospital in the country — a dismal wagon with a bed, drawn by a weary horse.[2] With half the stores closed, the upward bound in the cost of provisions intensified the distress of the poor.[3] The streets were as those of a dead city, no one caring to brush against the black robe of the grim reaper that was taking such an appalling harvest. One observer looking down the street one day could not see a single soul.[4] Terror seized upon every one. Lifelong friends evaded one another like guilty creatures. Even the families of the stricken fled, leaving the suffering to die in barbarous neglect.[5] One man determined to remain in the city, but passing twelve corpses in the streets, he summoned a carriage and fled in horror.[6] Only the negroes seemed immune, and 'much to their honor, they . . . zealously contributed all in their power.'[7] And to accentuate the horror, the rumble of the death-cart, the cries of the dying, the groans of the abandoned, were mingled with the bold footsteps of the robbers making their way from one deserted mansion to another.'[8] Panic everywhere. A toothache, and the victim was on the verge of collapse from fright — it was the fever.[9] Timothy Pickering had a twinge, and off he hastened to the doctor to be bled, put on a starvation diet, and sent on long horseback rides into the country 'for pure air.' Many died literally from fear, and the horror of the scenes and sounds.[10]

When the death toll mounted from scores to hundreds, from hundreds to thousands, the neighboring villages and towns met to devise plans for keeping the Philadelphians away, and one of these threatened to receive them 'at the point of the bayonet.'[11] The hospitals were packed — two hundred Irishmen in the Naval Hospital alone.[12] Meanwhile the physicians were fighting coura-

---

[1] Gibbs (Wolcott to Washington), i, 112.   [2] Hiltzheimer's *Diary*, 195.

[3] McRee, *Iredell* (a servant to Iredell), ii, 401; King's *Works* (Wharton to King), i, 498.

[4] Biddle, 256.

[5] Pickering (to John Clark), iii, 55–58; Gibbs (Wolcott to father), i, 110.

[6] Biddle, 256.   [7] Gibbs, i, 110.

[8] McRee, *Iredell* (servant to Iredell), ii, 401.   [9] *Ibid.*, ii, 400.

[10] Pickering (to Clark), iii, 55–58.

[11] *Philadelphia Daily Advertiser*, August 27, 1793.

[12] McRee, *Iredell* (Duffield to Iredell), ii, 400.

geously, desperately, but blindly and futilely. Fisher Ames, who had a malicious humor, was amused at their plight and methods. 'All vouch success — none have it,' he wrote, 'and like Sangrado's patients they die for want of bleeding and warm water enough.' One doctor treated the disease as a plague — 'his patients died'; he adopted Rush's methods — 'they died.' He hit upon a combination of the methods — 'all died.' [1] Bache filled his columns with cures and suggestions, but the death-rate increased frightfully. It was impossible to keep a record. On October 20th, Wolcott wrote Washington that 'more than four thousand persons have died,' and the next day Pickering wrote him that 'about three thousand have died.' [2] As many as 517 were buried in the Potter's Field between August 19th and October 1st.[3]

The streets deserted, houses closed, death-like silence but for the rattle of burial wagons and the groans of the stricken, the tread of robbers in the night — the horrors deepened. No one understood the reason why — no one but Alexander Graydon, who thought it a grim visitation of God to purge the foul hearts of the Philadelphians because of their enthusiasm for French democracy. One of the democrats had fallen early, when Dr. Hutchinson paid his profession the honor of dying in the harness. One day he met a friend in the street and urged him to take his family and leave. Was the Doctor going? No, he felt it his duty to stay and serve the sick. Was he not afraid? Well, he thought he would probably fall a victim, and bade the friend farewell. A few days later he was dead — the greatest hero of the scourge.[4]

Meanwhile, Jefferson, living in the country, thought it his duty to go to the city every day, and did. And then Graydon's God made a blunder that must have made the angels weep — he struck Hamilton down with the blow that must have been intended for the Jacobin Jefferson.

Living two miles out in the country, Hamilton was stricken violently. Having given thought to the disease, he had conceived that cold water would be effective. He summoned Dr. Stevens and many attendants — 'the method being expensive' — and through cold water and bark he was cured.[5] 'Colonel Hamilton is

---

[1] Ames (to Minot), I, 130.   [2] Gibbs, I, 112; Pickering, III, 59.
[3] Hiltzheimer, 196.   [4] Biddle, 255.   [5] Ames (to Minot), I, 130.

ill of the fever but is recovering,' Jefferson wrote Robert Morris who had taken to flight.[1] By the time the country knew of Hamilton's peril he had recovered, and, with his family, had hastened to the Schuylers at Albany.

With the approach of winter the disease receded — died out.

XV

Even so, there was no disposition on the part of Congress to meet in the gloomy city, and November found the Government established temporarily in Germantown. The statesmen had to accommodate themselves to wretched quarters. Jefferson 'got a bed in the corner of a public room in a tavern,'[2] but it mattered little to him, for his time was short. As late as December 22d, Washington made a final effort to persuade him to remain. 'I hope it will be the last set at me to continue,' Jefferson wrote Martha.[3]

The publication of his correspondence with both Genêt and Hammond had raised him in the esteem of his worst enemies. No one then or since has pretended to the discovery of undue partiality in the treatment of the offenses of the two nations. In the field of foreign relations the papers of Jefferson during this period were as distinguished as those of Hamilton in the sphere of finance.

But he was to submit to Congress a final Report on Commerce which was to cut short his popularity with his enemies. 'The letting loose of the Algerines on us, which was contrived by England, has produced a peculiar irritation,' he wrote his daughter. 'I think Congress will indemnify themselves by high duties on all articles of British importation.'[4] Here he was referring to his Report.

In this notable document, which his party instantly adopted as a chart by which to steer, he laid down some broad general propositions which called for retaliation on England. If a nation placed high duties on our products, we should place high duties on its products, even to excluding articles that came into competition with our own. Where a nation prohibited American merchants or

[1] *Domestic Life*, 219.
[2] Jefferson's *Works* (to Madison), IX, 240; 253–54.
[3] *Domestic Life*, 226.   [4] *Ibid.*, 226.

agents from residing in parts of its domain, we could retaliate with propriety. If it refused to receive in our vessels any products but our own, we could adopt a similar regulation as to theirs. If it declined to consider any vessel as ours not built in our territory, the rule could work both ways. All this was accompanied with a report on our relative commercial intercourse with both England and France. The purpose was in harmony with the policy for which Madison had fought from the beginning.[1]

Leaving this as a legacy to his party, Jefferson prepared for his return to his beloved Monticello. The executive branch of the Government was to be turned over to the enemy, for no Jeffersonian considered Randolph, who succeeded Jefferson, as a party man. Better a complete separation and open opposition than a further pretense at an unworkable coalition of the two parties. And home was calling imperatively. His private affairs were in need of attention. His ten thousand acres had been neglected. His hundred and fifty-four slaves had not been properly directed. And there, on his serene hilltop, were his daughters, his grandchildren, his friends the books, the trees, the view over the valley at sunrise.

Bidding farewell to his friends and making ceremonious calls upon his foes, he set forth in his carriage for the southward on January 5th. He was going home. Soon the house he had planned on the hill would be in view, soon the negroes would be running down the hill road to meet the carriage, to touch his clothes, to kiss his hands. Soon he would be sitting at his own fireside — in rooms sacred to the memory of the woman for whom the house was built.

[1] Jefferson's *Works*, III, 261–83.

CHAPTER XI

HECTIC DAYS

I

SCARCELY had Jefferson reached his quiet hilltop when Madison submitted the resolutions based upon his chief's Commercial Report, and the English party was instantly in arms. These resolutions were more political than commercial and were clearly aimed at England in retaliation for her refusal to enter into a commercial treaty. The resentment against the English policy had been increasing rapidly, even John Quincy Adams finding the French ruling powers more favorable to the Western Republic than was the Ministry of Pitt.[1] Only in the commercial centers was there a disposition to suffer long and be kind for business reasons. The Chambers of Commerce were on their toes hissing; the Democratic Societies shouldered arms and marched to the tune 'Ça Ira.' The galleries of the House filled.

The Federalists met the Madison attack with a counter-charge from William Smith of Charleston, in an elaborate recitation prepared for his delivery by Hamilton. The Carolinian entered the fray with the breezy confidence born of the knowledge that a master mind was behind his utterances. No one was deceived. 'Every tittle of it is Hamilton's except the introduction,' Jefferson wrote Madison.[2] The strategy of the Smith-Hamilton speech was to divert attention from the political to the commercial phase, by showing that our business relations with England were more valuable than those with France. The next day Madison boldly proclaimed the political purpose of the resolutions.[3] Thereafter, with spectators packing the galleries, and almost suffocating the legislators by crowding onto the floor of the chamber, the forensic gladiators fought with more ferocity than finesse. Ames sowed trouble for himself with the amazing declaration that 'there is an amicable disposition on the part of Great Britain.'[4]

---

[1] J. Q. Adams, *Works* (letter to John Adams), I, 183–86.
[2] Jefferson's *Works*, IX, 281.
[3] *Annals*, January 14, 1794.   [4] *Ibid.*, January 15, 1794.

The English are 'as angry at us as we are at them,' said Dexter, warning of war. 'Ridiculous!' exclaimed Madison. 'What would Britain gain by war? Would it employ her starving manufacturers' or 'give employment to the vessels that formerly imported luxuries to America?' [1] But why these strange accusations against England? asked Ames. What are the specific facts? Facts? thundered Giles. She has 'subjected our vessels . . . to seizure and search'; she 'prevents our vessels from conveying to our friends and allies goods not contraband'; she is responsible for 'letting loose the pirates of the Barbary States upon our commerce.' [2] Tracy, Hamiltonian, could see no advantage we had received from the French treaty. At any rate, added Boudinot, we should 'not over-value the friendship of France.' [3] What, roared Giles, 'if a prophet in 1778 had foretold that in 1794 that question would have been triumphantly put in an American Congress . . . would not the prophecy have been deemed an imputation on the American character?'

But — blandly from Ames — what are our grievances against England? 'Is it necessary,' shouted Nicholas, Jeffersonian, 'to tell the gentleman of the hostilities of the savages on the frontier, of the murder of our citizens, and the plunder of our settlements?' [4] 'Only a set of resolutions on paper,' sneered Dayton. Is that our only or best weapon? Yes, answered Madison, 'we can make use of none against Great Britain more effectual than commercial weapons.' [5]

Thus day by day the debate dragged on. 'What recent injuries?' inquired Samuel Smith of Maryland, merchant. 'The recent proclamation respecting the stoppage of vessels of neutral nations, with all such excepted but the United States,' hotly answered Madison. 'Better accept excuses than fight battles,' warned Ames. Instantly Giles, whose passions slept with one eye open, was on his feet protesting against the idea 'that the mere exercise of our rights as an independent government is equivalent to a declaration of war.'

Thus the bitterness intensified, with personalities entering the discussions. One day the venerable Abraham Clark of New Jersey,

[1] *Annals,* January 23, 1794. [2] *Ibid.*
[3] *Ibid.,* January 24, 1794. [4] *Ibid.* [5] *Ibid.*

signer of the Declaration of Independence, sat open-mouthed while Smith of Charleston reiterated his views, and then, trembling with age and infirmities, declared that 'if a stranger were to come into this House he would think that Britain has an agent here.' Cries of 'Order!' 'Order!' Smith replied with a sneer at the old man's garrulity and years. With passions at white heat, the debate was postponed until the first Monday in March.

Meanwhile, out of doors the fight was being waged with spirit. In Boston, the 'Centinel,' organ of the Federalists, was making scurrilous attacks on Madison. He had been the counselor and abettor of Genêt — a corrupt tool of France since the embassy of Gerard.[1] He was the agent of France,[2] the tool of anarchists,[3] and he could have learned nothing about commerce in Virginia 'where no other commerce is transacted than buying and selling of negroes.'[4]

To these attacks the Jeffersonians responded with a call for a town meeting to act on the Madison Resolutions. Before a great crowd at the Old South Church a dramatic forensic scene was staged, the eloquent Jarvis leading for the Resolutions, the brilliant young Harrison Gray Otis for the opposition, until darkness forced an adjournment till the morrow when it was renewed until afternoon, when the question was indefinitely postponed. Otis had won the only victory possible in successfully filibustering against a vote.[5] At Portsmouth, New Hampshire, a mass meeting at the State House endorsed the Resolutions,[6] and to the astonishment of Madison a meeting was held in New York City at the instance of the Jeffersonians.[7] In Philadelphia, with Hamilton looking on from the wings, the merchants met to denounce the Resolutions, but after a demonstration in their favor the attempt to get a vote upon them was abandoned.[8]

But it was in Charleston that the rage of the populace over the pro-English utterances of Smith and Ames assumed the most virulent form. Men cursed them in the streets, denounced them in resolutions, burned them both in effigy. Bache, then the leading

[1] Madison's *Writings* (to Jefferson), II, 1–5.
[2] *Centinel*, February 19, 1794. [3] *Ibid.*, March 1, 1794.
[4] *Ibid.*, February 23, 1794. [5] Morison, *Otis*, I, 53.
[6] *Independent Chronicle*, March 3, 1794.
[7] Madison's *Writings* (to Jefferson), II, 1–5. [8] *Ibid.*, II, 5–6.

Jeffersonian editor, deprecated the burning. 'Sorry I am to see these English fashions adopted by free-born Americans.' [1] The cynical Ames's sense of humor left him unscorched by the flames. 'I am willing to have it believed,' he wrote, 'that as I come out of the fire undiminished in weight, I am pure gold.' [2] But it was more serious to Smith, for it was his constituents who consigned him to the fire. The publication and circulation of the speech he had not written had deepened the resentment. How much hotter might have been the flames had the mob foreseen the printing of an English edition with the boastful prefatory statement that it had driven the author of the Declaration of Independence from office![3] Indeed, the fortunes of the fight had turned, and the Hamiltonians, lately jubilant over Jefferson's embarrassment with Genêt, had troubles of their own. Wolcott was complaining that Hammond, the British Minister, was 'weak, vain and impudent,' [4] and even Ames was alarmed because he 'rails against the conduct of our Government, not ore rotundo, but with a gabble that his feelings render doubly unintelligible.' [5] By their speeches against Madison's Resolutions, the Federalists had inextricably entangled themselves with British policies, and it was the chatter of the streets and the gossip of the press.

> 'From the speechification of Sedgwick and Ames
>   Some might think that they both had drank deep of the Thames,
>   For " our dear Mother Country," the former stands forth
>   In strains that were worthy a pupil of North.' [6]

It was in this state of public opinion, and with Ames wailing that England was 'driving us to the wall,' that the news from the West Indies aroused the people to a white heat of fury and put them on the march.

II

In compliance with an Order in Council, the British had seized more than a hundred vessels and held them for condemnation. So appalling were the possibilities that even Bache made the an-

[1] *Philadelphia Daily Advertiser*, March 27, 28, 1794. [2] Ames, I, 137–38.
[3] Printed in London by John Stockdale, Piccadilly. [4] Gibbs, I, 133.
[5] Ames, I, 137–38. [6] *Philadelphia Daily Advertiser*, February 1, 1794.

nouncement in terms of measured moderation.[1] Ames no longer mentioned the 'amicable disposition' of the British, or inquired with a childlike innocence what England had done to offend the Americans. With war seemingly inevitable, the Hamiltonians were driven to the simulation of a warlike mood. The spirit of '76 burst into flames.

Under such conditions the debate on the Madison Resolutions was resumed. When the sneer of Ames and Parker that they bore 'the French stamp' was loudly hissed by enraged visitors in the galleries, the Federalists took to cover.[2] Extreme provocative measures were introduced and pressed. The demand for the sequestration of British debts led to vitriolic exchanges. 'That king of sea robbers!' That 'Leviathan which aims at swallowing up all that floats upon the ocean!' Boudinot, Hamiltonian, pleaded for 'calmness.'[3] Dexter denounced the proposal as the counsel of dishonor. 'English tool!' roared the raging streets.

Then came the Non-Intercourse Act, with the Federalists, off their high horse, literally begging for 'calm deliberation.' Even Sedgwick was in an importunate mood; but the measure was pushed with all the more determination and passed with most of the Hamiltonians against it.[4] Even when Fitzsimons fell into line, he was trounced by the press with the open charge that he had held out until his own brig 'had departed to our good English friends at Kingston . . . with a cargo of flour.'[5] Clearly the Hamiltonians had to conciliate the public in some way, and Sedgwick came forward with a plan for an army; and Madison denounced it as 'the old trick of turning every contingency into a resource for accumulating force in the government.'[6]

Out in the streets the people were on a rampage. Phineas Bond, the British Consul in Philadelphia, reported to Grenville that the Americans even resented the Orders in Council.[7] Worse still, he and Hammond the Minister could not even walk the streets without being subjected to 'menaces from knots of street politicians.'

---

[1] *Philadelphia Daily Advertiser*, March 24, 1794.
[2] *Annals*, February 28, 1794.   [3] *Ibid.*, March 27, 1794.
[4] *Ibid.*, April 21, 1794.
[5] *Philadelphia Daily Advertiser*, April 11, 1794.
[6] Madison's *Writings* (to Jefferson), II, 7–8.
[7] Bond's *Letters*, American Historical Association, *Report*, 1897, pp. 543–45.

The consul in Baltimore had been forced by threats of violence to take refuge in the capital.[1]

The democrats followed up every advantage. Where was the spirit of '76? 'Shall a paper system hold you in bondage?'[2] England would not dare, declared the Democratic Society of Philadelphia, but for the declaration of neutrality, interpreted as evidence of American cowardice.[3] And perhaps Smith of Charleston had given the English a wrong impression. Had he published his speech against the Madison Resolutions to show Americans he 'despises their opinion' or 'to prove to Great Britain that he has been a faithful friend?'[4]

Under such encouragement some French sailors in American ports became cheeky and chesty. In a Charleston theater one of these having insulted a woman and been roughly handled, hastened to his ship with the story of an assault by English sympathizers. His fellows sallied forth to avenge the insult, making accessions to their ranks on the way by spreading the fictitious story of the incident. Armed with cutlasses, they descended on the theater as the people were pouring out, in an indiscriminate attack which included the wrecking of some carriages and the wounding of a few horses. The alarm bells were rung, and citizens rushed to the battle.[5]

Everywhere people were steeling themselves for war. In New York a mass meeting, held at the Coffee-House[6] was belittled by Noah Webster, the Hamiltonian editor. Both he and Fenno were clamoring for negotiations. 'Why, to be sure, we must negotiate,' sneered Bache. '. . . The honor, the interest, the welfare of the United States are locked up in the funding system.'[7] Everywhere citizens were helping with fortifications. In New York the students of Columbia (King's) formally tendered their services,[8] the house carpenters gave their labor,[9] and other trades followed. The country boiled with excitement. The Nation was rushing into war. Hamilton and his associates put their heads together to devise a method to prevent it.

[1] Bond's *Letters*, American Historical Association, *Report*, 1897, p. 546.
[2] *Philadelphia Daily Advertiser*, April 13, 1794.   [3] *Ibid.*, April 14, 1794.
[4] *Ibid.*, May 21, 1794.   [5] *Ibid.*, April 5, 1794.
[6] *New York Journal*, March 22, 1794.
[7] *Philadelphia Daily Advertiser*, April 9, 1794.
[8] *New York Journal*, May 3, 1794.   [9] *Ibid.*, May 28, 1794.

III

The rage of the people could be held in check only by a definite action looking to the righting of wrongs, and since the last thing the commercial interests wanted was war, the only thing left was negotiation. Even though this finally failed, it might postpone the fatal day. The Federalists, in control, instinctively turned in the crisis to Hamilton as the safest man to negotiate. He above all was interested in preserving peace with England at all costs. His whole political system rested on the supremacy of the commercial element. He was the father of the national credit and it would collapse without the revenue from the imposts, the greater part of which came from English trade.

In the beginning no other name was considered in the Federalist conclaves for ambassador. 'Who but Hamilton would perfectly satisfy all our wishes?' wrote Ames.[1] A correspondent of Rufus King was writing about the same time that Hamilton's selection would give general satisfaction because he had 'the full confidence of the merchants and the people at large'; [2] and King was replying that he wished Hamilton 'may speedily go,' since 'then there would be some hope of our remaining at peace.' [3]

In truth, Hamilton's relations with England's representatives in America had been intimate. In the days of the agency of Colonel Beckwith, before a Minister was accredited, an intimacy had been established with Hamilton so close that Professor Bemis concludes that never afterward was Jefferson 'able to conduct his office with thorough independence.' [4] That intimacy continued until the arrival of the Minister, and in the meanwhile Hamilton figured in the Agent's confidential reports as 'No. 7.' [5]

The Minister, with more assiduity than ability, was George Hammond, a young man of twenty-seven, who immediately established similar relations with the Secretary of the Treasury. Soon we find him reporting to Lord Grenville that he preferred to make most of his communications privately to Hamilton and to have no relations with Jefferson that were not absolutely neces-

---

[1] Ames (to Gore), I, 139.
[2] King's *Works* (from Alsop), I, 159.   [3] *Ibid.*, I, 560.
[4] Bemis, 45.   [5] *Ibid.*, 65.

sary.[1] It is fair to say that in every crisis he found the opportunity to confer with the Secretary of the Treasury.[2] All this was known, in a general way, to the commercial element when it was urging Hamilton's appointment as ambassador, and suspected by the people at large. Thus, when the rumor of his prospective selection spread, there was a roar of protest. 'The object of a special embassy might as well be answered by commissioning Lord Grenville or Mr. Pitt,' wrote Bache.[3] In the meantime, Senator James Monroe had formally protested to Washington against the appointment. The opposition was due to the reason set down in the memorandum of Hamilton's warm friend, Rufus King: 'Colonel Hamilton did not possess the general confidence of the country.' [4]

It is easy to understand how hard it was for the Federalists to abandon their chief. Thrill enough there is, in the thought of Hamilton and Pitt seated across the table in one of the dingy little rooms in Downing Street — so similar in precocity, brilliancy, and genius.

One evening four men sat in the candle-lit room of Rufus King in Philadelphia. There was Oliver Ellsworth, a powerful figure before the Senate and Bar; George Cabot, in some respects a saner leader than Hamilton; Caleb Strong, whose strength was in common sense and toleration; and King, who was a monumental figure. It was agreed to make an effort for Hamilton, and Ellsworth was designated to call at the Morris mansion for the purpose. Washington did not commit himself. Whereupon Robert Morris was sent to reënforce the plea, but on learning that not only Hamilton and Jefferson were being considered, but Jay as well, he sensed the situation and veered to Jay. The result was that Jay was summoned and offered the post. He took it under consideration. The next day Jay was overrun with visitors. Hamilton urged his acceptance, having in the meanwhile written Washington withdrawing his own name from the list of aspirants.[5] King, Strong, Cabot, and Ellsworth followed, demanding Jay's acceptance as a duty. While Jay was deliberating, his party was thrown into a panic with the rumor that Madison was a possibility,

---

[1] Bemis, 104.   [2] Bemis, 105, 106, 147, 154; *Intimate Life*, 289.
[3] *Philadelphia Daily Advertiser*, April 7, 1794.   [4] King's *Works*, I, 517.
[5] Hamilton's *Works*, V, 114.

and that Monroe had encouraged a hope in Pierce Butler with a promise of the support of the Jeffersonians. Jay accepted.

IV

No one but Hamilton could have been more obnoxious to the Jeffersonians than John Jay. He was now verging on fifty, with a notable career behind him on which to base an opinion of his bias. In appearance he was amiable but unimpressive, with nothing in his manner to indicate his intellectual power.[1] Mrs. Adams's daughter was impressed with the 'benevolence stamped in every feature.' [2] Of commanding stature, he was slender, albeit well formed. He wore his hair down a little over his forehead, tied behind, and moderately powdered. Coal-black, penetrating eyes increased his pallor, for he was never robust. Kindly, gracious, courtly in social intercourse, he was sternly uncompromising where his integrity was involved. Politically, he was an aristocrat, with contempt for democracy, and an incurable distrust of the people. This, with his predominant devotion to the commercial interests, fixed his status among the Federalists. Upon the principles of the French Revolution he looked with abhorrence. 'That portion of the people,' he once wrote a friend, 'who individually mean well never was, nor until the millennium will be, considerable.' Others thought the masses too ignorant to act well, but it was reserved for Jay to say that they did not even mean well.

Few Americans then living were better qualified by experience for a diplomatic mission. At Madrid he had shown rare tact, infinite patience, and dignity in defeat, and he had helped negotiate the treaty of peace. It was unfortunate that he had, for a while, been Secretary of Foreign Affairs, for he had then made a secret report to Congress holding England justified in clinging to the western posts.[3] That secret was out.

In writing Jefferson of the appointment, Madison gave no indication of a probable opposition to Jay's confirmation. 'The appointment of Hamilton was likely to produce such a sensation,' he wrote, 'that to his great mortification he was laid aside and Jay named in his place.' [4] But behind closed doors the Senate engaged

---

[1] *Familiar Letters*, 59   [2] Pellew, 218.
[3] Bemis, 206–07.   [4] Madison's *Writings*, II, 12.

in a bitter battle over the confirmation. The opposition made much of the impropriety of naming a Justice of the Supreme Court, submitting in a resolution 'that to permit Judges of the Supreme Court to hold at the same time other offices emanating from and holden at the pleasure of the President is destructive of their independence, and that tending to expose them to the influence of the Executive is . . . impolitic.' According to Bache, the majority of the Senate subscribed to this reasoning and the scruples of enough for confirmation were overcome only by the assurances that Jay's 'delicacy and sense of propriety would certainly induce him to resign his office.' Eight persisted in opposition on the supposition that 'more was to be feared from Mr. Jay's avarice than was to be hoped from his delicacy or sense of propriety.' [1] By the suspicious Adams, who witnessed the struggle from the chair, the opposition was ascribed to the fear that a successful negotiation would interfere with plans for the elevation of Jefferson to the Presidency. On the surface, Jay's indifference to the navigation of the Mississippi, his mythical monarchical principles, his attachment to England and aversion to France, appeared explanatory of the hostility.[2]

The confirmation shifted the attack from the Senate to the streets. The Jeffersonians resented it as a purely partisan appointment, but the opposition 'out of doors' went deeper. Could no one be found outside the little coterie of office-holders? Was it the intent 'that certain characters should have a monopoly of power?' [3] The Democratic Society of Philadelphia bore down heavily on Jay's justification for the holding of the posts.[4] A frontiersman from western Pennsylvania denounced the appointment as evidence of indifference to the interest of the western country.[5] After Jay's report on the posts would it not be answer enough for Lord Grenville to quote Jay's own opinion 'on file in the Secretary's office'? [6] The Democratic Society of Washington, Pennsylvania, thought that 'no man but Washington . . . would have dared . . . to have insulted the majesty of the people by such departure from any principle of republican equality.' [7]

[1] *Philadelphia Daily Advertiser*, April 24, 1794.   [2] Adams, *Adams*, I, 472.
[3] *Philadelphia Daily Advertiser*, April 19, 1794.
[4] *Ibid.*, May 10, 1794.   [5] *Ibid.*, June 26, 1794.
[6] *New York Journal*, November 5, 1794.
[7] *Gazette of the United States*, July 25, 1794.

Disregarding the clamor of the 'rabble,' Jay had made preparations for an immediate departure, and without tendering his resignation as Chief Justice. The instructions he carried had been
prepared almost exclusively by Hamilton.[1] So intimately was the
economic policy of the Federalists connected with the relations to
England that these instructions had been determined upon at a
secret conference of Federalist leaders dominated by their chief.[2]
Thus, provided with instructions from a party conference, Jay set
sail on May 12th from New York. A thousand people assembled at
Trinity Church to escort him to the ship and give three cheers as
he went aboard. A salute was fired as he passed the fort. But,
wrote Greenleaf, 'the militia had refused parading to honor the
departure of our extraordinary Minister.'[3]

If the Federalists were pleased, the Jeffersonians were complacent and Madison wrote that Jay's appointment 'is the most
powerful blow ever suffered by the popularity of the President.[4]
But the Federalists regained confidence after several months of
unpopularity and depression — and it was now the Jeffersonians'
time to suffer again — for the Whiskey Boys were up in western
Pennsylvania.

v

The Whiskey Boys of the 'insurrection of 1794' have been pictured as a vicious, anarchistic, unpatriotic, despicable lot — and
they were nothing of the sort. These men were doing more for
America than the speculators of Boston and New York, for they
were hard-working conquerors of the wilderness, felling the
forests, draining the swamps, redeeming the land for the cultivation of man. Fortunately for America, they were a tough set.
These rough men in coarse raiment and coonskin, with muskets
on their shoulders, were not arrayed for a pose. They fought their
way against savage forces, subduing Nature while warding off the
blows of the tomahawk. Their lot was hard. No luxuries in the
log cabins where they fought, wrought, suffered in the Homeric
work of extending an empire and making it safe for the soft crea-

[1] Hamilton's *Works*, v, 115–19; draft of instructions, *ibid.*, 121–23; letter to Jay, *ibid.*,
123–28; Bemis, 210.
[2] Bemis, 212.   [3] *New York Journal*, May 14, 1794.
[4] Madison's *Writings* (to Jefferson), ii, 14–15.

tures of the counting-rooms and drawing-rooms who would ultimately follow. Newspapers they seldom saw, books scarcely at all, and most were illiterate. It was a long cry from these powerful figures with muscular arms and dauntless hearts to the perfumed dandies simpering silly compliments into the ears of the ladies at Mrs. Bingham's.

Within a radius of a hundred miles, there were but seventy thousand souls. Pittsburgh was a crude little village of twelve thousand people. Here they lived, shut off from the eastern country by the mountains, for the few passes and winding roads through the dense woods were too rough for vehicles. The little trade they carried on with the East was through the use of pack-horses. From the South they were shut off by savage tribes of red men. Here they were, left to shift for themselves by their Government, which manifested little interest in their welfare, but did not forget the taxes. Because there was no market for their grain, they were forced to convert it into alcohol, which was largely their medium of barter. Money was seldom seen, and the excise tax laid on their alcohol was payable only in money. No people in America received so little benefit from the Government, and none were hit so hard by the Excise Law. Perhaps these pioneers who thought themselves abused were ignorant, but there was an intellectual giant among them who knew they were abused. This was Albert Gallatin.

A mingling of comedy and pathos is the story of the insurrection. The masses were victims of a few demagogues,[1] but alas, these demagogues were working with a real grievance. Public meetings had not served to moderate the passions. Wise advisers, like Gallatin, were unable to control, and the extremists followed the more flamboyant and less scrupulous. The law was resisted, officials intimidated, prisoners released from custody by mobs, and farmers who informed revenue men of the location of stills read their mistake by the light of their burning barns. When Washington sought to suppress the insurrection through negotiations, it was too late, and the troops he summoned marched.

It was inevitable that politics should play a part. The Excise Law was Hamilton's child, born to meet the obligations of the Assumption.

[1] Madison's *Writings* (to his father), II, 16.

The Jeffersonians had opposed its passage, and Jefferson thought it 'an infernal law.' [1] Then, too, it was felt that Hamilton welcomed the opportunity to test the Federal power. There had been too much skepticism on that point, and he longed for a decisive contest with the 'mob.' Bache had complained that Hamilton's report to Washington on conditions in the trouble zone read 'like a lawyer's summing up to a jury.' [2] The Federalist papers traced the trouble to the Jeffersonians because they had opposed the enactment of the Excise Law, denounced the Democratic Societies for inciting the people to insurrection, and satisfied the moron-minded that a demand for a law's repeal is the same as urging its violation. These were the days when the high-flying Federalists, under the shadow of Washington on horseback, were meditating the Sedition Law. Yes, and the Alien Law as well, for they were pointing to the 'foreigners' as the ringleaders in the 'plot to overthrow the Government.' The Irish, now numerous in Pennsylvania, were mostly Jeffersonians. That was enough. Fenno warned of 'the refuse of Europe that will swarm to our shores' if laws were not rigidly enforced.[3] Wolcott wrote his father that the insurrection was 'a specimen of what we are to expect from European immigrants' and that 'Pennsylvania need not be envied her Irishmen.' [4] 'Down with the Democrats!' 'Down with the critics of public men and measures!' 'Down with the foreign devils!' On these themes the Federalists harped through the summer and autumn. Their persistence was so persuasive that Muhlenberg, the Speaker, narrowly escaped defeat for renomination because he had voted against the Excise Law.[5] The Hamiltonians made the most of the situation.

Before this fusillade the Jeffersonians and Democratic Societies handled themselves well. Never had these societies done more than denounce the excise and demand its repeal, and under the fierce fire they made their position plain. One after another they gave public expression to their views. The Excise Law was reprehensible, but as long as it remained a law it should be obeyed.[6]

[1] Jefferson's *Works*, IX, 293–97.
[2] *Philadelphia Daily Advertiser*, September 1, 1794.
[3] *Gazette of the United States*, October 21, 1794.   [4] Gibbs, I, 156.
[5] *Philadelphia Daily Advertiser*, October 13, 1794.
[6] Philadelphia Democratic Society, *Gazette of the United States*, August 7, 1794; German

The Democratic press took a similar stand. 'The question is not whether the excise is a proper or improper mode of collecting revenue,' wrote Bache. 'It is constitutional . . . and it becomes the duty of every citizen to give his aid, if called upon, to enforce its execution. If the opposers should triumph . . . the axe is laid to the root of all national government.' [1] Greenleaf in the 'New York Journal' was quite as direct: 'The excise, however obnoxious, is the law of the Union; constitutional measures only therefore ought to be adopted.' [2] Jeers of derision from the Federalists greeted these resolutions and editorials. The insurrection, they contended, 'is the natural result of these Democratic clubs.' Honest men among their members had been deceived and the rioting in the West would open their eyes. 'Down with the Democratic Clubs!' 'Down with the critics of governmental measures!' [3] This aroused the wrath of the Jeffersonians, who now took the offensive. Bache summoned the Jeffersonians to join in the suppression of the insurrection to 'give the lie to the bawlers against the Democratic Societies.' [4] The response was instantaneous. Members of these societies and enemies of the excise rushed to the colors. The Irish Democrats of Philadelphia in an advertisement urged the Irish to 'stand to their arms,' and they formed a volunteer company.[5] The Federalists found themselves in a brisk competition for places in the army. With the Philadelphia aristocrats eager to follow Hamilton, and with the Democrats demanding places, the city's quota was soon doubled. 'Let those who derive the most benefit from the revenue laws be the foremost to march,' wrote Bache gleefully. 'Let the stock-holders, bank directors, speculators and revenue officers arrange themselves immediately under the banner of the Treasury, and try their prowess in arms as they have in calculation.' [6] But the jubilant Bache was soon to sing another tune.

Republican Club, Philadelphia, *ibid.*, September 1, 1794; Democratic Society, Washington, North Carolina, South Carolina, *Philadelphia Daily Advertiser*, October 6, 1794; Democratic Society, Canaan, New York, *New York Journal*, September 4, 1794.

[1] *Philadelphia Daily Advertiser*, September 10, 1794.   [2] September 13, 1794.
[3] *Gazette of the United States*, September 5, 1794.
[4] *Philadelphia Daily Advertiser*, September 15, 1794.
[5] *Ibid.*, September 24, 1794.
[6] *Philadelphia Daily Advertiser*, August 20, 1794.

VI

On the last day of September, three spirited horses stood in front of the President's house on Market Street. Three men emerged from the house and mounted, Washington in the center, Danbridge, a secretary, on one side, and on the other — Alexander Hamilton. They turned their horses toward the camp at Carlisle. So Hamilton was going to enforce his law with the sword. Well did the Democrats know the spirit in which he rode to his task. Under the signature of 'Tully,' he had not been able to conceal his identity in a series of articles in the summer designed to prepare the country for forceful measures. These had bristled with partisan invective. The Excise Law was defended and its opponents were charged with playing 'with passions and prejudices.' And it was not without passion and prejudice that he himself rode forth that September morning.[1] It was at this time that Bache began to sing another tune. In response to what constitutional duty was the head of the Treasury usurping the functions of the Secretary of War? he asked. 'Pray, where is the Secretary of War? Is he superintending the operations of the Treasury department?'[2] He knew at the time that Knox was on a mission of private business in Maine, for more than two months before he had sternly taken him to task for his absence in a crisis.[3] But Washington was going — why Hamilton? It was whispered about that he had intruded without an invitation, and some felt 'that his conduct is a first step in a deep laid scheme.'[4] Madison was convinced that Hamilton planned to use the insurrection as a pretext for the creation of a standing army,[5] long before the dynamic young leader rode forth with Washington to join the army. A cry of rage went up from the Democrats everywhere. 'Malignant — malevolent — uncandid — spiteful — envious — pitiful — mean,' responded Fenno — and so throughout the summer and autumn the epithets were hurled, the war in the East more venomous than that on the western front.

Meanwhile, Hamilton rode on, close to Washington's ears, con-

[1] Hamilton's *Works*, VI, 420–21.
[2] *Philadelphia Daily Advertiser*, November 10, 1794.
[3] *Ibid.*, September 8, 1794.   [4] *Ibid.*, November 6, 1794.
[5] Madison's *Writings* (to Jefferson), II, 18–19.

temptuous of the attacks. Never had he had less respect for democracy. 'It is long since I have learned to hold popular opinion of no value,' he wrote Washington after the President had returned to Philadelphia, leaving him in actual command.[1] 'Without rigor everywhere,' he wrote King at the same time, 'our tranquillity will be of very short duration.'[2] It was the tone of Federalist society in Philadelphia that led Bond, the British Consul, in a letter to Grenville, to comment that 'the establishment of a national force to strengthen the hands of the executive party can alone secure the existing form of government.'[3] As the brilliant young leader rode along the wood-lined roads, aflame with the colors of the fall, his plans for the capitalization of the insurrection for his party were made. The Executive should have more power, with an army of some pretensions to enforce the laws. The Democratic Societies that had awakened the political arrogance of the masses should be crushed. Attacks on governmental measures should be associated with disloyalty to the State. Perhaps on this trip Albert Gallatin, the one financial genius among the Jeffersonians, could be ruined — even indicted.[4] But the insurrection faded at the army's approach. Nowhere was opposition offered. Everywhere the soldiers met with cordial receptions, albeit the liberty poles literally lined their way. Only an occasional frontiersman in his cups made a weak show of hostility by hurrahing for the Whiskey Boys.[5] The ringleaders and many who should have been unmolested were arrested and sent to jail in Philadelphia under military guard. They who fell to General White were brutally treated, confined in damp cellars, tied back to back, kept in confinement from Thursday until Sunday morning with scarcely anything to eat or drink. Most of them were misguided youths who were redeeming an empire, and not a few had fought in the war for independence. Most of these were acquitted on trial. But when they reached the ferry at Schuylkill, they were forced to decorate their hats with a paper bearing the inscription, 'Insurgent.' Thus denounced, they were subjected to the humiliation of a march down Market Street, like slaves at the chariot of a

---

[1] Hamilton's *Works*, VI, 457.   [2] *Ibid.*, X, 77.
[3] Bond's *Letters*, 558.   [4] Stevens, *Gallatin*, 90.
[5] *Gazette of the United States* (letter from a soldier), October 16, 1794.

Roman conqueror, for the amusement of fashionable ladies at the windows.[1]

A pitiful spectacle — that march — and more significant than many realized. The soldiers were of the first Philadelphia families in wealth, gorgeous in their blue uniforms made of the finest broadcloth, all mounted on magnificent bay horses so nearly uniform in size and color that 'any two of them would make a fine span of coach horses.' A proud show they made with their superb trappings, their silver-mounted stirrups and martingales, their drawn swords glistening in the sun. Patrician conquerors, these. And their captives, mounted on nondescript plough and pack horses — old men who had fought for American independence, young men, all bronzed by the weather, some pale and sick, some sad, others flushed with fury that they should be used to make a show for the rich Philadelphians who looked upon them with complacent smiles. It was the East and the frontier — it was Aristocracy with drawn sword and Democracy with the insulting paper in its hat. The insurrection was over — a tempest in a teapot. A small army of twenty-five hundred was left in the western country like an army of occupation. Two men were found guilty of treason and pardoned by Washington. The law was vindicated — now for the crushing of the Democratic Societies.

VII

Foremost among the reasons for the virulence of the Hamiltonians toward these societies was that they were interfering with the Federalist plans for the political suppression of the 'mob.' Many 'men of no particular importance' were, by combining, making themselves a force to be reckoned with at the polls. Meeting regularly throughout the year, they were teaching the mechanic, the clerk, the small farmer, to think in terms of politics. Worse still, they were manifesting an uncomfortable disposition to pry into the proceedings of their representatives in Congress. No one saw this more clearly than Jefferson, who, in his retirement, was observing their growing power with complete approval. Throughout the summer of 1794, politicians were constantly driving up the hill to Monticello. It was determined to force the fight

[1] Biddle's *Autobiography*, 262.

in that year's elections. Candidates were brought out in most of the districts, and wherever there was a Democratic Society, the fight was a hard one for the Federalists. For the first time they faced an organization, disciplined, practical, aflame with enthusiasm.

This was especially true in Massachusetts where a herculean effort was made to defeat Fisher Ames with Dr. Jarvis in the Boston district. The Titan of the Federalists in debate was kept on the defensive, with charges that he had speculated in the funds and was in English pay. The men in the streets made merry with Ames's solemn assurance that England was 'amicably disposed.' He was an 'aristocrat,' and had 'no faith in republican institutions' — a close guess. His friends mobilized for his defense. What if he had speculated? — so had Jarvis.[1] Alarmed at the rising sentiment for Jarvis, the friends of Ames resorted to modern methods of propaganda, with business men signing an appeal published as an advertisement.[2] This, described by the 'Independent Chronicle' as 'a new practice,' was turned upon the Federalists. 'How many of the poor seamen or Captains are there among the signers who have lost their all? Not one — are they of no account in the estimate?'[3] Election day found at the polling-place 'the greatest collection of people ever at a Boston election.' The polls opened at eleven and closed at one. The hall was so crowded 'it was difficult to receive the votes with any degree of order.' Half an hour before the polls closed, it was discovered that many non-residents and non-taxpayers were in the room, and thereafter these were challenged by the Jeffersonians. The Democrats afterwards charged that Ames had been the beneficiary of 'voters consisting of foreigners from on board vessels at the wharf, and persons from other towns.'[4] Ames carried Boston by a majority large enough to overcome his notable losses outside the city. Madison wrote Jefferson that Ames owed his victory to 'the vote of negroes and British sailors smuggled in under the loose mode of holding elections' in Massachusetts. Even so, he found a ray of sunshine in the close calls of Sedgwick and Good.[5]

[1] *Centinel*, October 25 and 29, 1794. [2] *Ibid.*, November 1, 1794.
[3] November 3, 1794. [4] *Independent Chronicle*, November 6, 1794.
[5] Madison's *Writings*, II, 29.

In New York City the Federalists moved heaven and earth to defeat Edward Livingston with the cry that 'Livingston is an aristocrat, his opponent a plebeian'; but this appeal to the masses fell flat with the exposé of the questionable patriotism of this 'plebeian.' Tammany, the Democratic Society, and Jeffersonians generally fought energetically for their young orator, and the exhortation to 'let Edward Livingston, the poor man's friend, and the uniform asserter of the Rights of Man return to Congress,' was not made in vain.[1] The severity of this blow to the Federalists was acknowledged in Ames's admission that 'the election of Edward Livingston almost gives me the hypo.'[2] In North Carolina a spectacular fight was made to crush the Federalists under the leadership of Timothy Bloodworth, directed by the cunning Willie Jones, who continued to make history with his whittling knife and pipe, and, with the resulting Waterloo, the Hamiltonians began to entrench themselves in Federal jobs.[3] There the country-squire type rose on the shoulders of the people under leaders who 'could not have obtained entrance to Lady Washington's parlors, but who knew the difference between the demands of popular institutions and special interests.'[4]

Even in Philadelphia the Jeffersonians won a sensational victory by defeating Fitzsimons, one of Hamilton's lieutenants, with John Swanwick, who had led the fight in the merchants' meeting for the Madison Resolutions. In Charleston, William Smith narrowly escaped defeat through the intervention, according to Madison, 'of British merchants . . . and their debtors in the country.'[5] All in all, Madison felt that great progress had been made. It was the first real challenge the Federalists had met, and they had not enjoyed the experience. Surveying the field in search of the cause, they pointed accusing fingers at the Democratic Societies.

VIII

Before passing on to the mass attack on these societies, let us pause for a hasty review of other happenings of that eventful

---

[1] *New York Journal*, December 10, 1794.   [2] Ames (to Dwight) I, 158.
[3] Dodd, *Macon*, 77.   [4] *Ibid.*, 78–79.
[5] Madison's *Writings* (to Jefferson), II, 19–20.

summer and autumn. Madison was in a tender mood. A little before he had fallen under the spell of a merry widow whose glance was coquettish and whose tongue was nimble. The early autumn found him married to Dolly Todd; the early winter, cozily ensconced in the house the Monroes had occupied before they went to France.[1]

In the house on the hilltop, Jefferson was living a quiet life. He was little more than fifty, his hair touched with gray, his form erect, his step elastic, his strength undiminished. With his daughters about him, all was gayety about the blazing hearth in winter and on the lawn in summer. The supervision of the plantation was to his taste. There were fences to be repaired, trees to be planted. He was interested in the growth of potatoes. He rode about ordering the uprooting of weeds here and bushes there. His correspondence was light. In acknowledging a book from John Adams, he wrote that his retirement had 'been postponed four years too long,' and that his present happiness left him nothing to regret. That fall Washington had sought again to entice him back into the Cabinet, but he had been untempted. Though happy in his retirement, he was the old war-horse, sniffing the battle from afar.[2]

And things were happening over the land. Dr. Joseph Priestley, the English liberal, driven from England by persecution, had been given an uproarious greeting in New York and had replied to addresses from Tammany and Democratic Societies with severe strictures on the repressive measures of Pitt; and an exotic creature, who had been living obscurely in Philadelphia as a teacher, startled the country with a pamphlet reply in a vein of sarcasm and satire worthy of the masters of the art. England was glorified, France crucified, Democratic Societies excoriated, the Irish in America damned — and the Hamiltonians rejoiced. Many were shocked. Since William Cobbett was to work under the encouragement of Hamilton,[3] we shall become better acquainted with him by and by.

Otherwise life was moving along in Philadelphia much the same as usual. Society was still in the saddle. Blanchard, who was

[1] Madison's *Writings*, II, 27; Goodwin, *Dolly Madison*, 26.
[2] Randall, II, 245; *Domestic Life*, 231.   [3] *Intimate Life*, 69.

thrilling the people with balloon ascensions, was postponing one
of his ascents 'because of the marriage of a person of distinction.' [1]
The French madness was unabated, and on July 11th a French
victory was theatrically celebrated. 'La Carmagnole' was danced
in the streets. Public officials marched with the populace to the
French Minister's house where orations were heard and 'La
Marseillaise' was sung. At Richardet's five hundred sat down to
a noisy feast, after which they danced around a liberty tree, set off
fireworks, and burned a British flag.[2] Even Rickett's Circus was
so fashionable that Fenno hoped he would begin his performances
an hour earlier to permit citizens to enjoy the dare-devil feats before repairing to the House of Representatives to hear the debates.[3]
Bache, educated abroad, was a lover of the play and interested
in seeing democratic features introduced — say, an occasional
'simple air' interspersed with the classics for the delectation of the
'gallery gods who pay their money like other folks.' [4] But the time
was to come when even Bache was to make sad grimaces at democratic manners in the theater. This was when the 'gallery gods'
hit upon a novel mode of entertainment, of selecting some in-
offensive 'aristocrat' in the pit and demanding that he doff his
hat to the gallery. Naturally ignored, 'a hundred stentorian voices
would call out for his punishment.' Thereupon the gods would pelt
the unfortunate victim with apples and pears, sticks, and even
stones, and assail him 'with scurrillity and abuse.' Throughout
the evening the persecution would continue. Spitting, and empty-
ing beer-bottles upon him increased his misery. It was bad
enough, thought Bache, to spit upon the men 'aristocrats,' without spattering the delicate dresses of the aristocratic ladies with
beer. One night most of the orchestra was driven out of the house.
'It is time to stop this growing evil,' wrote Bache, 'which has been
on the increase ever since the opening of the house.' [5] The Federalists were delighted at his embarrassment. Here was the rabid
editor's 'democracy.' These people in the galleries were his 'sovereign people.' And all this was due to the leveling influence of
the Democratic Societies. They must go!

---

[1] *Philadelphia Daily Advertiser*, April 10, 1794.
[2] *Gazette of the United States*, November 1, 1794.   [3] *Ibid.*
[4] *Philadelphia Daily Advertiser*, May 7, 1794.   [5] *Ibid.*, October 24, 1794.

IX

When, in his Message to Congress, Washington made his amazing attack on the Democratic Societies, the influence of Hamilton and the Federalist leaders, who had received not a few scars in the recent elections, was evident. Here was a proclamation that the masses of the people in private life had no right to organize for political purposes. That the Hamiltonians had no interest in the mass of the people was generally understood.[1] They were impressed with petitions from the Cincinnati, or Chambers of Commerce, but frankly contemptuous of those signed by mere citizens 'of no particular importance.' When these people organized into Democratic Societies, things were going too far. If this continued, the ordinary mechanic might get the impression that he counted in governmental affairs. There was too much of this democratic virus in the body politic.

The Jeffersonians were momentarily stunned by Washington's denunciation, but quickly rallied. Madison, calm, composed, courteous, but grimly determined, sat on the House committee to frame the Reply to the President's Address, and he planned to ignore that feature of the Message. He was not deceived as to its purpose or inspiration. 'It was obvious that a most dangerous game was playing against the Republicans,' he wrote Jefferson. 'The insurrection was ... deservedly odious. The Democratic Societies were presented as in league with it. The Republican part of Congress was to be drawn into an ostensible patronage of those societies, and into an ostensible opposition to the President.' The sponsorship of a purely partisan attack by Washington pained Madison, but it did not intimidate him. He considered it an assault on the citadel of liberty, and it was, in truth, the forerunner of the infamous Sedition Law.[2] In a letter to Monroe, he described the attack as the 'greatest error in his [Washington's] political career.'[3] That it was 'an attack on the essential and constitutional right of the citizen,' he had no doubt.[3] Jefferson characterized it as 'one of the extraordinary acts of boldness of which we have seen

[1] Professor Morse, in *The Federalist Party in Massachusetts*, makes this point.
[2] Madison's *Writings*, II, 21–23.   [3] *Ibid.*, 23–27.
[4] *Ibid.* (to Jefferson), 28–30.

so many from the faction of monocrats' — an attack 'on the freedom of discussion, the freedom of writing, printing and publishing.' And what of the Cincinnati, 'self-constituted,'[1] whose members met behind closed doors, maintained a system of secret correspondence, while 'carving out for itself hereditary distinctions?'[2]

Even so, the Jeffersonians would have taken no notice of the
attack had not the Federalists forced the issue by proposing an
amendment to the Reply commendatory of the assault on the
societies. That Hamilton was the inspiration of this move there
can be no doubt. When the debate began, we find him hurrying
around to Fitzsimmons's house with 'proof' of the connection between the societies and the insurrection; and, finding the mover
of the amendment absent, leaving a memorandum. The Hamiltonian proof was that the Mingo-Creek Society was 'sometimes
called the Democratic Society'; that some of the insurrectionists
were on its membership rolls; that one of its members had led one
of the attacks and another a second. Quite enough, he thought,
to damn all the societies in America, albeit almost all had denounced the insurrection, and many of their members had marched
under arms against the rebels.[3] This was the reasoning of all the
extreme Federalists.

Into the debate both parties dragged their heavy artillery.
Madison, Giles, and Nicholas on one side, Ames, Sedgwick, Smith,
and Tracy on the other. 'Stand by the President!' — from the
Hamiltonians. 'Stand by the Constitution!' — from the Jeffersonians. 'Plunge these societies into contempt — sink them into
abhorrence and detestation,' shouted Sedgwick, still smarting
from the pummelling they had given him.[4] 'The people have a
right to speak and to think,' protested Venable of Delaware. 'The
fact that the President thinks them guilty is enough,' thought
Murray of Maryland. 'I refuse to surrender my opinions to the
President where a matter of fact is involved,' retorted Nicholas.
'No,' thundered Giles, 'the fiat of no person in America should
ever be taken for truth.' 'Infamous creatures!' snorted Smith of
Charleston who had felt their blows. Nonsense, exclaimed Christie
of Maryland, the members in Baltimore 'were not the fair weather

---

[1] Washington's phrase. [2] Jefferson's *Works* (to Madison), ix, 293–97.
[3] Hamilton's *Works*, x, 78–79. [4] *Annals*, November 25, 1794.

patriots of the present day, but the patriots of Seventy-five.' Yes, added Carnes of Georgia, citing the case where one of these societies 'turned out as volunteers against the rioters,' and expressing the hope that the time 'will never come when the people of America shall not have leave to assemble and speak their mind.'

Giles and Madison closed against the amendment in powerful constitutional arguments on the rights of citizens to have opinions on men and measures or to express them by voice or pen, individually or collectively; and Ames closed for it, making much of the burning of Jay in effigy by the society at Lexington, and picturing the people on tip-toes on all the post-roads to learn whether Washington or the societies had triumphed in the House.[1] Dexter foreshadowed the Sedition Law, toward which the Federalists were feeling their way, with the declaration that the Constitution did not give the people 'the precious right of vilifying their own Government and laws.' Madison warned of the tendency, the vote was taken, and in the end the Reply of the House went to the President without a reference to his attack on the clubs.

But in the press the fight went on throughout the year. 'Are men's principles among the subjects of public concern which you are to discuss?' asked the incredulous Noah Webster of the 'American Minerva.' 'If so, your society bears a resemblance to the Spanish Inquisition, destitute only of its power.'[2] One of Fenno's scribes was moved to hilarity at the absurdity of the defense that the societies had uniformly denounced the insurrection. Had they not at the same time denounced the excise law and asked for its repeal?[3] Republican societies checks and balances? sneered the 'Centinel.' 'So are lanthorn posts and guillotines.' The same journal neatly condensed the entire Federalist line of attack in a satirical 'book of the generations and downfall of Jacobinism,' from the hour 'Brissot begat the Jacobin club of Paris.' Genêt — Democratic Societies of America — the Pittsburgh rebellion — the armament of fifteen thousand men — an expense of two million dollars — ran the argument.[4] Thus it was reduced to a matter of dollars and cents.

[1] *Annals*, November 25–27, 1794.   [2] January 24, 1794.
[3] *Gazette of the United States*, December 11, 1794.
[4] *Ibid.*, October 14, 1794.

Meanwhile, the societies, recovering from the shock of the attack, stood to their guns, and issued statements setting forth in moderate tone principles, then jeered, which no one would care to challenge publicly in America to-day. The German Republican Club of Philadelphia concentrated the defense in a few words: 'Are we the abettors of insurgents for supposing that Government can do wrong, and for disapproving the excise? Then is the freedom of opinion at an end.' [1]

But the shadow of Washington fell darkly on the clubs and their power as organizations rapidly diminished. Many who refused to antagonize Washington openly were deeply resentful, and from that hour the popular impression grew that he had aligned himself as a partisan of the Federalists. From that hour, too, the high-flying Federalists began to move with greater confidence and celerity toward the Sedition Law. The erstwhile members of the societies fell back into the body of citizenship, but more keenly and intelligently interested in politics than ever before, and more than ever determined to make their influence felt. They were not to forget what they had learned of tactics, organization, and propaganda, and very soon the Jeffersonian Party would be the beneficiary of the Washington assault.

If this congressional session foreshadowed the Sedition Law, it also foreshadowed the Alien Law in a Naturalization Act reflecting the Federalist distrust of the immigrant. The Catholics were attacked in the debate, and Madison indignantly replied that 'there is nothing in their religion inconsistent with the purest republicanism.' [2] When the Jeffersonians created a diversion by offering an amendment that no titled foreigner could be admitted to citizenship until he had renounced his title, the Federalists stupidly fell into the trap and were instantly on their toes with indignant protests. Instead of accepting the amendment as a joke, they were soon pleading that titles were not so bad, and it did not matter if titled gentlemen voted and held office. 'You may force a man to renounce his title,' said Smith of Charleston, 'but you cannot prevent his neighbor from calling both him and his wife by the title.' Great must have been the merriment in the taverns at the spectacle of the Federalist leaders fighting with desperation and in-

[1] *Gazette of the United States*, December 29, 1794.   [2] *Annals*, January 1, 1794.

dignation against the proposal to prevent Lords, Dukes, Barons, and Viscounts from becoming American citizens without leaving their titles outside the door. What matter if Sedgwick did explain that the acceptance of the amendment would be a justification of the charge that there was a monarchical party in the country? — the better psychologists among the Jeffersonians knew that with the man in the street nothing could have been more conclusive on that point than the unification of the Hamiltonians in opposition to the amendment.[1] They had been maneuvered into standing up and being counted against the renunciation of titles — and the 'mob' shouted with joy.

[1] *Annals*, January 1, 1794.

CHAPTER XII

THE MARCHING MOBS

I

DURING the remainder of the short session of Congress, feeling ran high. The Jeffersonians made a second foolish attempt to trace some act of official turpitude tò Hamilton, and signally failed. The latter was now ready to go. His great work had been achieved with the establishment of public credit. His official honor had been vindicated. Never had he stood so high in the esteem of the commercial interests, the only class whose good opinion he coveted. He was the leader of the leaders of his party. With the rank and file he had never been popular, though always admired, but he sought no popularity with the multitude for whom he had a certain contempt. After years in the public service, he found himself in poverty, confronted with obligations to an increasing family. Early in December he wrote of his plans to Angelica Church: 'You say I am a politician, and good for nothing. What will you say when you learn that after January next I shall cease to be a politician at all? Such is the fact. I have formally and definitely announced my intention to resign and have ordered a house to be taken for me in New York.' [1] A little earlier he had hoped to take a vacation in Europe. He was 'heartily tired' of office. Only the opportunity to quit 'with honor and without decisive prejudice to public affairs' held him at all. Now political conditions seemed favorable for an early retirement for the elections promised 'to prove favorable to the good cause.' [2]

When Jefferson retired, Fenno announced the event in two lines, but he heralded the resignation of Hamilton in a glowing eulogy, double-spaced, of the man who had made 'two blades of grass to grow where none grew before.' [3] This was too much for Bache. 'America will long regret that his work lives after him,' he wrote. And why the fawning rhapsody? Had Washington done nothing?

[1] *Intimate Life*, 230.   [2] Hamilton's *Works*, x, 78.
[3] *Gazette of the United States*, February 9, 1795.

— nor Congress? — nor the natural advantages of the country? — nor the Constitution? 'No, the Secretary was the life, the soul, the mind of our political body; the spirit has flown — then we are a lifeless mass, dust, ashes, clay.'[1]

But the sneer of Bache and the contemptuous fling of Madison, because it was 'pompously announced in the newspapers that poverty drives him back to the Bar for a livelihood,'[2] could not rob the daring innovator of his triumphs. The Lancaster Troop of Horse, dining, toasted him, — 'May his domestic felicity be equal to his public services.'[3] The day the story of this toast was printed, a hundred and fifty of the leading merchants, capitalists, and social leaders of Philadelphia sat down to a farewell dinner in his honor. Judges of the Supreme Court and governmental functionaries were in attendance. When the project was suggested, merchants 'crowded to the subscription paper,' and many were excluded for lack of space. Toasts were mingled with convivial songs, and wine, we may be sure, flowed like water. After Hamilton had toasted the Philadelphia merchants, he withdrew, and he himself was toasted. 'May he enjoy in private life that happiness to which his public services have so justly entitled him' — and the rafters rang.[4] Two nights later, the fashionable Dancing Assembly, celebrating Washington's birthday with a dance and dinner, took note of Hamilton's departure with a toast.[5] When he reached New York, he found another dinner awaiting him, when more than two hundred people in his honor sat down at Tontine's Coffee-House 'at the expense of the merchants of the city.' There among the guests were the Chancellor, the Judges, the Speaker of the Assembly, the Recorder of the City, the President of Columbia. More convivial songs and stories, more wine and cheers and laughter, and again Hamilton toasted the merchants — of New York. And again he retired to permit the toastmaster to propose 'Alexander Hamilton' with nine cheers. Reporting the affair honestly enough, the 'New York Journal' could not omit the observation that 'few of our best citizens and genuine Republicans were present.' The editor had never ques-

---

[1] *Philadelphia Daily Advertiser*, February 10, 1795.
[2] Madison's *Writings* (to Jefferson), II, 35.
[3] *Gazette of the United States*, February 18, 1795.
[4] *Ibid.*, February 20, 1795.   [5] *Ibid.*, February 22, 1795.

tioned Hamilton's 'financial abilities,' but he doubted 'the propriety of his political principles.' However, 'in the language of the play bills it was a great dinner, Mr. Hodgkinson,[1] one of the managers of the farce being present.'[2]

Having been thus wined and dined, toasted and roasted, Hàmilton retired with his family to the Schuyler mansion in Albany for relaxation and rest. Perhaps he could not afford the coveted trip to Europe — it did not materialize. In April, Justice Iredell wrote his wife that Hamilton had 'already received more than a year's salary in retainer fees' and that a 'number of mechanics here [New York] have declared that they will build him a house at their own expense' — a promise unredeemed.[3] Hamilton had hoped to open his New York office in May, but autumn found his family lingering under the hospitable roof of the Schuylers.[4]

Such, however, was his insatiable craving for power that he was unable to forget, even for a month, the familiar field of battle. Enraged by a triumph of his political foes on a measure in the House, he wrote furiously to King that 'to see the character of the country and the Government sported with . . . puts my heart to the torture.'[5] Events were not moving with the felicity of old under the successor of his own choosing, and he turned spitefully upon some of his most faithful followers. 'So,' he wrote King, 'it seems that under the present administration of the department, Hillhouse and Goodhue are to be ministers in the House . . . and Ellsworth and Strong in the Senate. Fine work we shall have. But I swear the nation shall not be dishonored with impunity.'[6] Clearly he had determined to keep his hand on the driving wheel from afar. The Cabinet was composed largely of his followers, only Randolph remaining to plague him, and his days were short and full of trouble. The Federalists in Congress could be directed by correspondence — and should be; Washington not only could, but would be kept constantly advised. Hamilton retired from office in January, 1795, but he was not to retire from power until Adams, repeatedly betrayed, should drive the Hamiltonian stool-pigeons from his Cabinet some years later. Meanwhile, a party crisis was

---

[1] A favorite actor.
[2] *New York Journal*, February 28 and March 4, 1795.
[3] McRee, *Iredell*, ii, 442.
[4] *Intimate Life*, 205–06.
[5] King's *Works*, ii, 5–6.
[6] King's *Works*, ii, 7.

approaching that would require all Hamilton's genius to save his party from destruction.

II

We speak of the 'Jay Treaty'; the Jeffersonians called it the 'Grenville Treaty'; as a matter of fact it was more nearly the Hamilton treaty, and it was certainly a Federalist Party treaty.[1] Jay had arrived in London, to be so graciously received and so lavishly entertained that he had cautiously refrained from mentioning this unusual cordiality in official reports. Thomas Pinckney, the regular Minister, who had stoutly fought for American rights, was shunted aside. 'If I should say that I had no unpleasant feelings on the occasion I should be insincere,' he wrote his brother.[2] But he accepted the situation with good grace.

In time, after receiving attentions from the King not previously accorded America's diplomats at the court, Jay sat down with Lord Grenville to the negotiation of a treaty. The latter, a favorite of Pitt's, comparatively young, but rising rapidly because of an abnormal capacity for hard work rather than brilliancy, was in no sense the intellectual superior of Jay. In the first days of the negotiations, the prospects were bright enough for the Federalist emissary. England had previously faced and accepted the necessity for the abandonment of the western posts, and she was not, at the moment, in position vigorously and persistently to protest the other outstanding American claims. The conditions on the Continent were far from satisfactory, with the coalition apparently verging toward disruption. England was not seeking another open enemy, and she could not afford the loss of the American trade. But there was another danger threatening that was causing Grenville no little distress — and this is where Jay held the high card in the gamble.

The neutral nations of Europe had grown tired of the arrogant sea policy of the English, and steps were taken for the unification of neutrals in defense of neutral rights. Sweden and Denmark had ratified an Armed Neutrality Convention on March 27, 1794,

---

[1] Beard, *Economic Origins*, 295; Bemis, 271.

[2] Pinckney, *Life of Pinckney*, 123–24.

agreeing to join their fleets for the protection of their peoples. Pinckney had been approached by the Swedish Minister in London with an invitation to the American Government to join. He had received the invitation with frank enthusiasm, and thought his country would agree.[1] This was all known to Grenville, who was painfully impressed with the possibilities. He had put his spies to the task of opening diplomatic mail and keeping him informed of developments. Instructions had been sent to Hammond, the Minister at Philadelphia, to exert all his ingenuity to prevent the United States from joining the Scandinavian combination.[2] The day that Grenville sat down with Jay, the former had been informed by Count Finckenstein, the Prussian Minister of Foreign Affairs, that the position of America was doubtful, and that Jefferson had left the Cabinet to go to Denmark to assist in the organization and consolidation of the neutrals.[3] It was Grenville's cue to procrastinate on the treaty until he could ascertain to a certainty just what the United States contemplated in reference to the Armed Neutrality. Impatient over the delay, Jay submitted a complete draft of a treaty on September 20, 1794, which was, in many respects, an admirable document. When the treaty which was finally signed was submitted with the other papers to the American Government, the draft of September 20th was conspicuously absent — for the actual treaty was an almost complete surrender of the claims of the first draft, and its publication would have had a disastrous effect on Jay's reputation and on his party.

Ten days before Jay submitted his draft, Grenville was in possession of a curious report from Hammond. The latter had been informed by Hamilton, 'with every demonstration of sincerity,' that under no circumstances would America join the Armed Neutrality. This, Hammond understood, was secret information on Cabinet action.[4] Thus, through the amazing indiscretion of Hamilton, Jay was deprived of his high card at the critical moment of the negotiations. Hamilton was standing behind Jay, to be sure, but he was holding a mirror, however unconsciously, which reflected the American negotiator's cards to the enlightenment of the suave and smiling Grenville. From that moment Grenville

[1] Bemis, 224.   [2] Ibid., 225.   [3] Ibid., 226–27.   [4] Ibid., 246.

stiffened his opposition to Jay's demands, and thenceforth the latter was in a continuous retreat.[1]

The result was a sweeping victory for England and the most humiliating treaty to which an American has ever put his signature.[2] It provided for the abandonment of the western posts after June 1, 1796, but there was to be no remuneration for stolen negro slaves and no provision for ending the impressment of American seamen. The principle that 'free ships make free goods' was surrendered and the contraband list was extended. British claimants could appeal to the Mixed Debts Commission without first exhausting their resources in American courts, while the American claimants had to exhaust the resources of the British courts before appealing to the Commission. The Mississippi was to be opened to British trade; and the West Indian trade, which Jay was specifically instructed to secure, was granted to American ships of seventy tons burden only, and then on condition that the West Indian trade should be wholly free to British vessels and that American vessels should not carry molasses, sugar, coffee, cocoa, and cotton to any ports in the world except their own. The East Indian trade was opened to Americans provided no further restrictions should be laid on British commerce. And Jay agreed to provisions — despite specific instructions to enter into no obligations incompatible with our treaty obligations to France — which amounted to an alliance with England against America's ally in the Revolution.[3]

All in all, it was a rather disreputable performance which even Hamilton admitted to Talleyrand, in a social moment, to be an 'execrable one' on the part of 'an old woman.'[4] By a queer coincidence, Jefferson described the treaty with the same adjective, as 'an execrable thing,' in a letter to Edward Rutledge.[5]

However, Hamilton, familiar with the treaty long before it reached the Senate, was willing to accept the 'execrable thing' provided the twelfth article, forbidding American vessels from

---

[1] Bemis, 232–51. [2] Ibid., 261.

[3] Bemis, 267, quotes a French scholar, R. Guyot, as describing the Jay Treaty as 'almost equivalent to a treaty of alliance.'

[4] Related by Talleyrand to Volney, who told it to Jefferson, Anas, 336–37. Senator Lodge, in his biography of Hamilton, accepts this characterization as not improbable.

[5] Jefferson's Works, IX, 313–14.

carrying cotton, among other articles, to the ports of Europe, should be suspended. He wrote William Bradford, the Attorney-General, in May, of his distress over this article,[1] and Rufus King about the middle of June.[2] But he was sternly set on ratification, against a renewal of negotiations, and that was enough to determine the course of the Senate. There was no other way. It was a Federalist negotiation. The negotiator had been chosen in a Federalist caucus. The instructions had been determined upon in a Federalist conclave. They were practically written by the great Federalist leader, and the purpose served was in line with Federalist economics.[3]

Thus, when the Senate met in extraordinary session, its work was cut out for it. For eighteen days the Senators debated in secret. The American people knew that the treaty was under consideration, but they did not have the most remote idea what it was all about. For eight days the discussion was general; then the Federalists, acting under Hamilton's inspiration, submitted a form of ratification conditioned on the suspension of that portion of Article XII which enumerated the articles American ships could not carry to Europe. Meanwhile, the commercial interests in New York were becoming apprehensive over the delay. Hamilton was bombarded with anxious inquiries on the report that the treaty had been rejected, and was able to deny it, writing at the same time to Rufus King of the 'disquietude.'[4] Two days after Hamilton wrote King, Senator Aaron Burr moved to postpone ratification and to institute new negotiations, but this, with other hostile motions, was voted down. At length the Federalist programme was pushed through, Senator Gunn of Georgia voting to ratify. Ten Senators remained in opposition. And then the Senate, with a keen appreciation of the humiliating nature of the treaty, solemnly voted to 'not countenance the publication' of the document.[5] Such a high-handed proceeding, predicated upon the theory that the people had no right to know to what they had been bound, made an unpleasant impression

---

[1] Hamilton's *Works*, x, 98–99.   [2] *Ibid.*, x, 101–02.

[3] See Beard's illuminating chapter on the economics of the treaty, *Economic Origins*, 268–98.

[4] King's *Works*, ii, 14; Hamilton's *Works*, x, 109.

[5] Wolcott's phrase in letter to Mrs. Wolcott, Gibbs, i, 199.

even on Hamilton, who wrote Wolcott that it was 'giving much scope to misrepresentation and misapprehension.' [1]

But there was one Senator who refused to be bound in a conspiracy to conceal from the people the people's business. Stevens Thomson Mason of Virginia had crowded into his thirty-five years as much patriotic service as any of his colleagues. Although but sixteen when the Declaration of Independence was signed, he had served as a volunteer aide on the staff of Washington at Yorktown, and had been made a brigadier-general in the militia of Virginia. In the few years that remained to him, he was to earn an appreciation that partisan historians have denied him by his militant challenge to the Sedition Law. Ardent and courageous, he felt that the people had a right to know the contents of the treaty, and, while the Federalist Senators were congratulating themselves on having bound the Senate to secrecy, Bache's paper came out with the full text of the treaty. Mason had deliberately, openly, defiantly taken a copy to the office of the 'Aurora.'

Then something like a cyclone swept the land.

III

The injunction of secrecy and Bache's sharp comments upon it had prepared the public for something startling. 'A secrecy in relation to a law which shall rival the darkness of a conclave of a seraglio.' [2] 'Secrecy is the order of the day in our government — charming expedient to keep the people in ignorance.' [3] 'What are we to infer from this secrecy' but that 'the treaty will be unacceptable to the people?' [4] 'This imp of darkness,' he had written, referring to the treaty.[5] When Mason's copy reached Bache's paper, it was eagerly seized upon by the people, and copied in all the papers of the country. The people all but rose *en masse*.

July 3d found the Philadelphia streets littered with a handbill urging an attack on a British vessel at Goldbury's wharf. That night the streets leading to the wharf were packed with people, most of them from the section of the laborers, with a sprinkling of the curious. The Governor had ordered out some soldiers who

[1] Hamilton's *Works*, x, 107.
[2] *Aurora*, June 16, 1795. [3] *Ibid.*, June 18, 1795.
[4] *Ibid.*, June 20, 1795. [5] *Ibid.*, June 26, 1795.

prepared to meet the emergency with stern methods. Until eleven o'clock the crowd stood in sullen silence waiting for something to happen, for some one to lead the assault. Darkly outlined in the night loomed the British ship, in front the silent soldiers, behind them the angry crowd. Slowly this dwindled, and before midnight the danger was over, but the sight of the ship had not worked a conciliatory spirit in the people.[1] It aroused the mob spirit for action on the Fourth.

Throughout that day — an ominous quiet. Out in the suburb of Kensington, the ship carpenters were planning a demonstration. This was postponed till night because the troops were out in honor of the Nation's natal day. Eleven o'clock found five hundred men, mostly workmen, moving from the suburb on the city. By the lights they carried could be seen an effigy of Jay. This, according to rumors that flew over the town, was to be burned before Washington's house on Market Street. Then a feverish summoning of the light-horse, little Paul Reveres hurrying from door to door summoning soldiers to the saddle. Long before the marching mob reached the heart of the city, the cavalry was drawn up on Market Street waiting. On moved the mob in uncanny silence. Most of the people were asleep, and only the bobbing lights of the marchers indicated that something was stirring. No attempt was made to reach Washington's house. Through other streets tramped the mob in orderly procession, then back to Kensington where Jay was burned in effigy. Just for a moment a pause in the jubilation, when Captain Morrell and some of his men dashed into the glare of the lights to disperse the mob and to be pelted with stones and forced to precipitate flight. Only that, and an advertisement in the papers the next day announcing the finding of 'an elegant horseman's sword' which could be recovered by 'producing his muddy regimentals.' Little damage had been done. Some one had hurled a stone through the window at Bingham's house, but that was all, aside from the bruises of Captain Morrell, who had fought neither too wisely nor too well.

The next morning the curious strolled toward Kensington, where they found the ashes, and a board stuck in the ground bearing the words: 'Morrell's Defeat — Jay Burned July 4, 1795.'

[1] *Aurora*, July 3, 1795.

There, unmolested, it stood for days. 'I think an attempt to take it down without considerable force would be attended by serious consequences,' wrote a Philadelphian to a friend in New York.[1] The story of the burning spread rapidly over the country, carrying its inevitable suggestion.[2] While the ship carpenters were nursing their plans at Kensington, the Philadelphia County Brigade was celebrating the Fourth with a dinner in the woods along Frankfort Creek, where the French Treaty was toasted, and those seeking to supersede it were denounced as traitors. The ten Senators who voted against ratification were praised for having 'refused to sign the death warrant of American liberty,' Mason was eulogized, and the woods reverberated with shouts and laughter over the toast: 'A Perpetual Harvest to America — but clipped wings, lame legs, the pip and an empty crop to all Jays.'[3] Three weeks later a throng assembled in the State House yard to take formal action, with men of the first distinction in the community on the platform. A memorial of denunciation was read, adopted without debate, and the treaty was thrown contemptuously to the crowd, which pounced upon it, stuck it on the end of a pole, and marched to the French Minister's house where a ceremony was performed, albeit Adet denied himself to the mob; thence on to the British Minister's house where the treaty was burned while the mob cheered lustily; then on to the British Consul's and Bingham's for a hostile demonstration.

The Federalist leaders observed these demonstrations with misgivings, whistling the while to keep up courage. Somewhere on the outskirts stood Oliver Wolcott, who instantly wrote Washington at Mount Vernon that the crowd was composed mostly of 'the ignorant and violent part of the community.' Nothing shocked him more than the introduction to the mob of Hamilton Rowan, the Irish patriot, and the swinging of hats in token of welcome. Judge M'Kean swung his, Wolcott supposed, 'because he expected the honor soon of having the fellow to hang for some roguery in this country.'[4] Even more shocking to Wolcott was

[1] *Argus*, July 15, 1795.

[2] Gibbs (Wolcott to Mrs. Wolcott), I, 209; *Philadelphia: the Place and People*, 310; Hiltzheimer, 215; *New York Argus*, July 8, 1795; *Charleston City Gazette*, August 22, 1795.

[3] *Aurora*, July 7, 1795.

[4] Gibbs, I, 217. Rowan was a patriot, tried by a packed jury, and defended by John

the invitation of the colorful Blair McClenachan, as he threw the treaty to the crowd, to 'kick it to hell.' [1] Pickering assured Washington that there 'were not probably two hundred whom Chief Justice M'Kean would deem qualified to sit on a jury.' [2]

But it was not to be so easy to belittle the protest or to confine it to Philadelphia. It spread — like an epidemic. In New York City, the home of Jay, the feeling was virulent. The Fourth of July celebrations disclosed the sharp divisions between the commercial interests and the body of the people. With the merchants dining at the Tontine with Jay, the Democrats at Hunter's with the French Consul were shouting approval of the toast: 'May the cage constructed to coop up the American eagle prove a trap for none but Jays and King-birds.' [3] The 'Argus' published a scathing open letter to 'Sir John Jay.' [4] With the advertisement of a town meeting, Hamilton and King sought to organize the opposition of the merchants at a meeting at the Tontine when it was decided to contest the issue at the mass meeting. An address, protesting against the method of the proposed meeting, written by Hamilton, was given to the papers, and circulated in handbills. The stroke of twelve found from five to seven thousand people assembled, and the plans of the Hamiltonians were instantly surmised. There, on the stoop on Broad Street stood Hamilton himself, with King and a few others grouped about him. At the stroke of the clock, Hamilton, without waiting for the organization of the meeting, began to speak impassionedly. 'Let us have a chairman!' cried the crowd. A chairman was chosen and took his station on the balcony of Federal Hall. Instantly Peter Livingston began to speak. Hamilton interrupted. Cries of 'Order! Order!' from the people. 'Who shall speak first?' asked the chairman. 'Livingston,' shouted the greater part of the crowd. But when he sought to comply, he could not raise his voice above the confusion, though he managed to reach the swaying mass with the suggestion that all favoring the treaty go to the left, and those opposed to the right. A goodly portion of the crowd passed to the right to Trinity Church, and Hamilton, assuming that only friends of the treaty remained, be-

---

Philpot Curran in his classic defense of the freedom of the press. He was convicted, escaped, and came to this country.

[1] Gibbs, I, 217.   [2] Pickering, III, 183.   [3] *Aurora*, July 10, 1795.   [4] July 6, 1795.

gan to speak. Hissing — hooting — coughing — his voice was drowned. The orator paused, consulted his supporters, and a resolution prepared by King was passed to the chairman to read. A momentary lull, and then, finding it commendatory of the treaty, an angry roar — 'We'll hear no more of that, tear it up.'

Meanwhile, a stone struck Hamilton, without injuring him severely. With a derisive smile, he called on 'all friends of order' to follow him, and the Hamiltonians deserted the field. That afternoon at Bowling Green a cheering crowd could have been seen burning the treaty, while in the Fields another crowd was screaming its delight as Jay's effigy went up in smoke.

The next day the meeting reconvened and unanimously adopted resolutions against the treaty, and the Hamiltonians called a meeting of the merchants to protest against the action. This meeting of the merchants is more impressive in books than it was in reality. The 'Minerva' announced that the treaty had been endorsed by a practically unanimous vote; while the 'Argus,' more specific, reported that among the seventy present, ten had opposed the treaty, and that these ten 'own more tonnage than the other sixty put together.' [1] The minority of ten publicly denounced the majority as 'either inimical to this country in the late war, or have immigrated to this country since that period.' Having made the charge, they entered into details. Of the sixty merchants favoring the treaty, only eighteen had been outside the British lines in the Revolution, eight had actually joined the British, six came to the country from England during the war and located in sections held by the British army, and ten entered the country after the war.[2] At any rate, there were seven thousand people in the mass meeting and but seventy in the meeting of the merchants.

The ferocity of the protest had a depressing effect on Hamilton, who could imagine nothing less than 'Jacobins meditating serious mischief' to 'certain individuals.' Instinctively he thought of mobs, and meditated on soldiers to put them down. He was afraid the New York militia was sympathetic toward the mob. Time would be required for the Federalists to 'organize a competent

[1] July 23, 1795.
[2] Beard, *Economic Origins*, 290; Alexander, 79; *Argus,* July 6, 20, 21, 23; *Aurora,* July 10, 22, 23, 1795.

armed substitute.' He had thought of the 'military now in the forts,' but understood they were 'under marching orders.' Would not Wolcott confer confidentially with the Secretary of War and 'engage him to suspend the march?' [1] The majority were against the treaty — time to summon the soldiers. Nor was Hamilton alone in this thought of force. Ames could see no other way and was ready to 'join the issue tendered.' The moment was favorable for the Government to show its strength. Then action — 'Washington at the head, Pittsburg at its feet, pockets full of money, prosperity shining like the sun on its path.' [2] Within two weeks Hamilton, in the Assembly Room on William Street was denouncing the rabble, declaring the situation meant a foreign or civil war, and expressing his preference for the latter. Meanwhile he was proposing a house-to-house canvass through the wards for the treaty.[3]

If Hamilton was alarmed in New York, and Pickering chagrined in Philadelphia, the Federalist leaders in Massachusetts were stunned by the intensity of the feeling of the mob. A protest meeting was held at Faneuil Hall, with the venerable Samuel Adams participating with spirit. Without a dissenting vote resolutions were passed denouncing the treaty and praising Senator Mason for 'his patriotism in publishing.' [4] The aristocratic leaders of the Federalists in Boston knew the futility of challenging the throng. Declining the issue, they busied themselves with the merchants and wrote explanatory letters to their friends. 'Men of reputation would not attend the meeting,' Stephen Higginson, the merchant-politician, wrote Pickering, 'being opposed to the town's taking up the subject. They were left wholly to themselves; no attempt was made to counteract them, though nine merchants out of ten reprobated the procedure.' The people, to be sure, were excited, for had not Bache been to Boston 'with a large collection of lies of riots in Philadelphia and New York to create a flame here.' [5] Cabot, more truthful, was lamenting about the same time that 'some of our most respectable men have on this occasion joined the Jacobins and very many of them acquiesced in their

[1] Gibbs (to Wolcott), I, 218.   [2] Ames (to Dwight), I, 173–75.
[3] *Argus*, August 13, 1795.   [4] *Centinel*, July 15, 1795.
[5] Pickering, III, 177.

proceedings.'[1] Ames could not restrain his disgust because many of the rich had participated. Even so, these clever, tireless Massachusetts leaders were not inactive. After all, what were the farmers, artisans, and lawyers compared with the merchants? One merchant was more influential with them than a thousand tillers of the soil. Thus, they summoned the Chambers of Commerce to action, and resolutions were passed endorsing the treaty. 'The proceedings are to be transmitted to the President,' wrote the complacent Cabot to Wolcott.[2]

But that did not end the treaty fight in Boston, for throughout the summer the indignation of the people simmered and occasionally boiled over. The 'rabble' had to have its fling. On the walls enclosing the home of Robert Treat Paine were chalked the words: 'Damn John Jay! Damn every one who won't damn John Jay! Damn every one who won't put lights in his windows and sit up all night damning John Jay!'[3] Then, early in September, a great crowd marched through the crooked, narrow streets with a figure representing Jay; and the next day it reappeared with another effigy of Jay with a watermelon head, and marched noisily through the principal streets to the home of Samuel Adams who appeared and smiled approvingly upon the scene. A few days later, Jay was burned in effigy at Oliver's Wharf, and the home of the editor of the 'Federal Orrery' was attacked with bricks and stones.[4] The non-participants observed that the Federalist leaders were more outraged at the burning of the effigy than over the action of a British man-of-war that sailed into the harbor and helped itself to anything it wanted.[5]

Fisher Ames ascribed the mob spirit to 'a few young men who have lost property by British captures.' Just a few, he said — mostly boys with fifes and drums. 'The anti-treaty men were ashamed of the business.'[6] The Boston Federalists preferred to fight the mob with merchants' resolutions and their barbed wit. 'The reason given by the Jacobins for not reading the treaty,' wrote Russell in the 'Centinel,' 'is that no person ought to read what he knows to be bad.'[7] Meanwhile, the leaders were busy as

---

[1] King's *Works*, II, 18–20.   [2] Lodge, *Cabot*, 84.
[3] Pellew, 282.   [4] *Federalist Party in Massachusetts*, 154–55.   [5] *Ibid.*
[6] Gibbs, I, 229.   [7] August 15, 1795.

swarming bees all over Massachusetts, drumming up the merchants, soliciting resolutions, exerting influence to prevent town meetings. 'At Salem the respectable people are all acquiescent; and many of them approve but think it inadvisable to act,' wrote Cabot to Wolcott. 'At Newburyport, the principal merchants are also well satisfied; and some steps have been taken to bring them to express their opinions.' [1] With the merchants acquiescent, and the principal merchants satisfied, need any one worry over the marching multitudes?

But alas, in commercial Charleston, home of the Pinckneys and William Smith — there, too, the marching mobs, and mingling with them some of the rich and aristocratic. Here was the most bitter disappointment of all. It began in the Senate when the patrician South Carolina Senator Pierce Butler, cousin of the Duke of Ormond, refused to vote for ratification. Nothing of the rabble about him or his charming wife. When the treaty reached Charleston, the flags of the city were lowered to half-mast. The treaty was burned 'amidst shouts of abhorrence' — nor was there anything clandestine about the burning. It was duly advertised in advance. 'This evening at 8 o'clock,' read the notice, 'will be burned by the public executioner near the old Market in Broad street, the treaty proposed to be established between Great Britain and America to show the disapproval of the citizens of Charleston. Also an effigy of Jay will be burned.' Taking cognizance of rumors of possible interference, the 'satellites of anarchy,' were promised 'tar and feathers.' These took the hint and both the treaty and Jay crackled in the flames.

Then followed a formal meeting of protest in the Exchange — a great crowd — many veterans of the Revolution — an adjournment to Saint Michael's Church to accommodate the throng. Then rose a figure familiar to the generation of the Revolution, and then Chief Justice of the Supreme Court of the United States, John Rutledge. An able man was Rutledge, with a luminous career. Speaking with vigorous eloquence, analyzing the treaty as he proceeded, he denounced it as a betrayal of American interests and an insult to American manhood.[2] At a subsequent meeting condemnatory resolutions were adopted, Butler was lauded, and

[1] Lodge, *Cabot*, 84.   [2] *Aurora*, July 29, 1795.

Senator Read, who had voted to ratify, was denounced as 'unworthy of any further public trust.'[1] In the midst of this meeting there was a stir of anticipation when the popular orator Charles Pinckney, just arrived from his country place and covered with dust, strode into the room and claimed recognition. His was one of the fiercest excoriations of the year, and a few days later this speech, revised, appeared in the 'City Gazette,' to be copied by all the papers inimical to the treaty in the country. A master of the philippic, he poured oil upon the flames.[2] In parish after parish, meetings were called and the treaty denounced. The Federalists were appalled at the action of Rutledge, and he who had been numbered among 'the wise and the good' became a symbol of unspeakable depravity over night. It was suddenly discovered that he whom Washington had deliberately chosen for Chief Justice was 'insane.'[3] In the 'Centinel' of Boston appeared an open letter to him declaring him unfit to sit upon the Bench — because of his hostility to the document of Jay.[4] The private correspondence of the Federalist leaders bristled with abuse, and plans were immediately made to reject his nomination in the Senate.

In North Carolina the opposition was even more bitter, partly because of the absurd surrender in Article XII, and partly because of the provision which threw the property rights of Americans into jeopardy.[5] This one provision was said to affect half the lands in the State, and there was wild talk of resisting it by force.[6] Even Senator Johnson, Federalist, was shocked and disgusted. 'A hasty performance' at best, and one which greatly lowered his opinion of Jay's ability.[7] William R. Davie, however, was outraged at the opposition and thought the treatment of Jay measured 'the baseness of human nature.'[8]

In Virginia the people were infuriated. They, too, were affected by Article IX, and on the day the treaty was signed, Grenville presented Jay with papers which began the long litigation over the Fairfax estate; and more than any other State she was a sufferer from the loss of negroes carried away by the British troops. In 1791, Cornwallis had taken thirty thousand slaves, of whom all

---

[1] *Charleston City Gazette*, August 1, 1795.
[2] Thomas, *Reminiscences*, 1, 35.
[3] *Independent Chronicle*, August 17, 1795.
[4] August 26, 1795.
[5] Article IX.
[6] Giles, 42.
[7] McRee, *Iredell*, 11, 450.
[8] *Ibid.*, 11, 459.

but three thousand had died of smallpox and fever. When a mass meeting was convened at Richmond, the Federalist leaders had another shock when the celebrated Chancellor Wythe, a powerful figure at the American Bar, took the chair — 'a circumstance,' wrote Madison to Jefferson, 'which will not be without its weight, especially as he presided at the former meeting in favor of the Proclamation.' [1] Here the treaty was denounced as 'insulting to the dignity, injurious to the interests, dangerous to the security, and repugnant to the Constitution, of the United States.' [2] Patrick Henry thought it 'a very bad one indeed.' [3] And so thought the Virginians generally. At Petersburg a tribute was paid Senator Mason and Jay was burned in effigy.[4]

Still another blow fell to the Federalists when Senator John Langdon of New Hampshire, who had supported Hamilton's financial policies, deserted on the treaty. The merchants of Portsmouth — a sacred class with the Hamiltonians — shared in the general protest. A mass meeting was called at the State House. 'Your only hope is in the President,' ran the handbills. 'Assemble, then, to a man; shut up your shops; repair to the State House; remonstrate.' [5] And never had Portsmouth seen so great a throng. The treaty was denounced, Langdon approved, Mason praised for giving out the document 'unduly withheld by the Senate from the people.' When Langdon returned, he was given a public dinner at the Assembly Room with practically every merchant and tradesman gathered about the board. Stinging toasts, patriotic songs, a stirring speech from Langdon — who at this time aligned himself with the Jeffersonians and became their leader in New Hampshire.[6]

Even so, the Federalists held the line fairly well in New England. In Vermont, where the treaty was the sole topic of conversation, there were no public meetings. The Democratic Societies of the State had fallen under the frown of Washington, and rough-and-ready Matthew Lyon had not assumed the leadership. As late as September, 'Vermont Farmer,' complaining of non-action, urged that meetings be called in every town and county — but nothing

---

[1] Madison's *Writings*, II, 43.   [2] Giles, 38.
[3] Henry, *Henry*, II, 568–71; letter to Mrs. Aylett.
[4] *Argus*, July 30, 1795; *Gazette of the United States*, August 14, 1795.
[5] *Argus*, July 24, 1795.   [6] *New Hampshire Gazette*, July 21, 1795.

was done.[1] In Connecticut, where the preachers, professors, and politicians had the people cowed, there was scarcely a whimper. 'I have heard little said by our people about the treaty,' wrote Governor Wolcott to his son. 'Our people are calm and hard at work.'[2] In New Jersey a mass meeting was held at Trenton in the State House and the treaty denounced — with numerous township meetings following in its wake.[3] The sentiment generally was hostile. Another meeting at Newport, Rhode Island, and another sweeping denunciation.[4] In Delaware the opposition was overwhelming, even the Cincinnati at its Fourth of July dinner at Newcastle drinking heartily to the toast: 'John Jay, may he enjoy all the benefits of purgatory,'[5] while the diners at a more popular dinner drank, 'His Excellency, John Jay . . . may he and his treason be forever politically damned.'[6] In August the people of Wilmington crowded the Upper Market House in protest, with men like Cæsar Rodney and John Dickinson participating.[7]

In Georgia, where the popular sense had been betrayed by the ratification vote of Senator Gunn, the bitterness was sizzling. One day the people gathered about a poster in the Market at Savannah inviting them to meet the next day at the Court-House and join in the burning of John Jay in effigy. Most of the town responded. There they found the effigies of Jay and Gunn on a cart. Forming in procession, with the cart in front, they paraded through the numerous streets, along the Bay and back to the Court-House, and thence to the South Common where the gallows stood. Halters were put about the necks of Jay and the offending Senator, solemnly the accusation of treason was read to them, and they were given to the flames.[8]

In Maryland the Federalists whistled hard to sustain their courage, and made a brave effort to close their eyes to the situation. Representative Murray wrote encouragingly to Wolcott that among the men gathered for the General Court 'nine tenths . . . from all the counties approved the treaty.'[9] In Baltimore the merchants rallied and sought to intimidate Sam Smith, their Representative, by the circulation of a paper of instructions. He

[1] *Spooner's Vermont Journal*, September 11, 1795.   [2] Gibbs, I, 215.
[3] *Independent Chronicle*, August 13 and 27, 1795.   [4] *Ibid*., September 3, 1795.
[5] *Argus*, July 15, 1795.   [6] *Aurora*, July 13, 1795.
[7] *Argus*, August 14, 1795.   [8] *Ibid*., August 8, 1795.   [9] Gibbs, I, 249.

hastened home to suppress it, and failing, had a set of counter-instructions started. But there was no magic in pretense, and soon Murray, himself intimidated, was writing of his decision to retire with the admission that on the Eastern Shore there 'had been more agitation than I had imagined.'[1]

IV

These marching mobs, mass meetings, resolutions and petitions, and burning effigies give no conception of the popular ferment. Never had the people been more agitated or outraged. Whenever two men met, whether bankers or bakers, the treaty was the topic of their talk. In taverns, where travelers were promiscuously packed like sardines in a box, the quarreling made night hideous and sleep impossible. In the bar-rooms, men, in their cups, disputed and fought. The stage-coaches were a forum, the crossroads store a battle-ground. An English tourist, finding himself in a wayside tavern, was driven to distraction by the noise of combat. The farmers were against the treaty, the lawyers for it, and they debated with passion, with more heat than light. Assigned to a room with five or six beds, the forlorn foreigner was forced to listen to the continuance of the struggle until at length 'sleep closed their eyes and happily their mouths at the same time.'[2] The Duc de la Liancourt, journeying through upper New York, was swept into the maelstrom of controversy and had to record his own opinions in his 'Travels.'[3] When the messenger from the Boston mass meeting reached New York, hurrying to Philadelphia, Greenleaf stopped his press to print the story of the incident.[4] Soon the anti-treaty press was publishing statistics on public sentiment — the mass meetings against the select gatherings of the merchants. Fifteen thousand people had met and denounced the treaty, and seven hundred had approved it, according to the 'Independent Chronicle.'[5]

Meanwhile, Washington was causing the Federalists some uneasiness. As late as July 31st, he had written Pickering evincing a desire to know public sentiment. Had the Jacobins captured Washington? Wolcott was painfully depressed lest America lose

[1] Steiner, 194–95. [2] Weld, I, 102–03. [3] Liancourt, II, 79.
[4] *Argus*, July 16, 1795. [5] September 3, 1795.

the respect of England. What would she think with their 'Minister's house insulted by a mob, their flag dragged through the streets as in Charleston . . . a driveler and a fool appointed Chief Justice' by Washington? [1] Only the day before, Washington was writing of his alarm lest France resent a treaty she had some right to resent.[2] Clearly Washington required some attention.

V

The President held the treaty seven weeks before signing, and this put the Federalist leaders to the torture. Among themselves they made no concealment of their chagrin and indignation. Cabot, writing to King, confessed that the President's hesitation 'renews my anxiety for the welfare of the country.' He would suggest to the Boston merchants that they make 'a manly declaration of their sentiments' to Washington. He had 'too much respect for the character of the President to believe that he can be deterred from his duty by the clamor or menaces of these city mobs,' but he realized that something should be done to counteract their influence.[3] If Cabot kept a rein on his patience, it was not true of all. In a great house known as 'Elmwood' at Windsor, Connecticut, surrounded by elm trees and filled with books and religion, a stern and forceful master was literally walking the floor, and tossing restlessly on a sleepless bed, for Oliver Ellsworth was doubting Washington's firmness and courage. In bitterness he was writing that 'if the President decides right or wrong or does not decide soon his good fortune will forsake him.' [4] In commercial circles in New York many were already turning upon the man they made a virtue of pretending to worship. About the middle of July, Washington and his family left Philadelphia for Mount Vernon, he in a two-horse phaëton for one, his family in a coach with four horses and two servants, another servant leading a saddle horse — and without giving the slightest intimation of his intention.[5]

Then came the scandal involving Randolph and the French Minister Faucet. There was infinite joy in the Federalist camp. Pickering and Randolph hastened a summons to Washington to return. There was a dramatic scene, in which Washington is

[1] Gibbs, i, 219–20.   [2] Pickering, iii, 185.   [3] King's *Works*, ii, 20–21.
[4] Brown, *Ellsworth*, 219–20.   [5] Hiltzheimer, 215.

described as winking at Pickering, and setting a trap for his Secretary of State, who was the sole member of his original Cabinet chosen by the President to please himself. Randolph was dismissed — and Washington signed the treaty. The merits of the treaty were in no wise affected by anything Randolph may have done, and it is fair to assume that there was no connection between the disgracing of the Secretary and the signing.[1] The strategy of the Federalist now outlined itself, and Washington became the treaty and the treaty became Washington, and to oppose the treaty was to insult Washington. The popular President was literally pushed to the front line in the fight. Pickering was writing Jay suggesting that Washington be persuaded to issue 'a solemn public declaration ... of the principles of his Administration,' appealing to the record of his life 'for the purity and patriotism of his conduct'; [2] and Jay was replying that while 'in many respects useful,' he doubted the wisdom.[3] Christopher Gore was writing King inquiring if it were not 'possible for Col. Hamilton and yourself to induce the President to adopt some measures that would decidedly express his sentiments in favor of the treaty.' He was positive that 'in New England the word of the President would save the Government.' [4]

This plan of using the prestige of Washington for a party measure was not made for this particular occasion. Pickering and Gore wrote on the same day,[5] one from Philadelphia, and the other from Boston. It had long been a favorite feature in the party strategy. Ellsworth regained his composure and wrote Wolcott that 'the current I believe is turning in Massachusetts, though you may perhaps hear of some obscure town meetings.' [6] Senator James Ross, writing to Pickering from Pittsburgh, thought that after all it was well that Washington had taken his time. 'His sanction after hearing all the objections will quiet the minds of the thoughtful.' [7]

All that was required to make Washington the issue in the treaty fight was a stupid attack upon him from the Democratic press, and that was instantly forthcoming. When Fenno's paper

---

[1] For Randolph incident, Pickering, III, 213–14 and 216–19; Lodge, *Cabot*, 91–94.
[2] Pickering, III, 196.   [3] *Ibid.*, 197.
[4] King's *Works*, II, 24.   [5] August 14.
[6] Brown, *Ellsworth*, 220–21.   [7] Pickering, III, 199.

announced that the treaty had been signed, Bache wrote that since 'no information has been filed for a libel on the Executive . . . it may be fairly presumed, the character of the President for patriotism and republicanism notwithstanding, that the assertion is well founded.'[1] And when a great crowd attended the next presidential levee, Bache capped the climax of asininity with the comment that 'it was certainly necessary to let the public know that the just resentment of an injured and insulted people had not reached the purview of Saint Washington.'[2] These bitter expressions convinced the Federalists that the fight was not yet over. The public had too bitterly and generally resented the treaty to be so quickly won. Instinctively the friends of the treaty thought of Hamilton and the prowess of his pen. 'Mr. Hamilton might do great good,' wrote Murray of Maryland to Wolcott, 'by giving the public his luminous pen.'[3] Even as Murray wrote, Hamilton sat in his office writing 'Camillus' for Noah Webster's paper. His health was failing at the time, but King and Jay had promised to assist. For weeks and months the papers appeared, thirty-eight in all, in the most effective argumentative style, covering every possible phase. 'It is to pass for Hamilton's,' wrote John Adams to his wife, 'but all three consulted together upon most.'[4] Two months after the series began, the enemies of the treaty were circulating the story that Hamilton and Webster had quarreled because of the latter's decision to limit the number of papers. 'More than a hundred columns have already been run, to the exclusion of news, and the people are tired, no doubt,' suggested an editor.[5]

Unhappily, while Hamilton wrote, England was up to her old tricks upon the sea again. Scarcely had the treaty been ratified, when Pickering was officially protesting against an outrage on the United States by the British ship of the line *Africa*, and by the British Vice-Consul in Rhode Island,[6] and was writing complainingly to John Quincy Adams in London that 'if Britain studied to keep up the irritation in the minds of Americans . . . some of her naval commanders appear perfectly qualified for the object.'[7]

[1] *Aurora*, August 21, 1795.
[2] *Ibid.*, August 22, 1795.
[3] Gibbs, I, 222.
[4] King's story.
[5] *Aurora*, November 17, 1795.
[6] Pickering, III, 231–39.
[7] *Ibid.*, III, 239.

The enemies of the treaty made the most of these affronts. 'A Loyalist of '75' was urging Hamilton to 'discontinue his laborious work of defending the treaty' to give some attention to the justification of Captain Home of the *Africa*, and to the defense of the other sea captain who stole a peep 'at Mr. Monroe's despatches.' 'Camillus' could resume on the treaty after quieting 'the minds of the swinish multitude' on these later outrages.[1] Thus Hamilton's efforts were being constantly neutralized in effect by the conduct of the English, and the 'swinish multitude' chortled not a little over the doggerel:

> 'Sure George the Third will find employ
> For one so wise and wary,
> He'll call "Camillus" home with joy,
> And make him Secretary.'[2]

In truth, even as he wrote, Hamilton was raging not a little over these stupid insults to America, and was writing Wolcott proposing that the exchange of ratifications be refused until the order to seize our vessels with provisions be rescinded.[3]

Far away on his hilltop, Jefferson was observing Hamilton's literary efforts with real concern, if the rank and file of his party were not. 'Hamilton is really a colossus to the anti-republican party,' he wrote Madison, apropos of the defense of the treaty. 'Without numbers, he is a host within himself. They have got themselves into a defile where they can be finished; but too much security on the republican part will give time to his talent . . . to extricate them. . . . When he comes forward there is no one but yourself who can meet him. For God's sake take up your pen and give a fundamental reply to Curtius and Camillus.'[4] But neither 'for God's sake,' nor for Jefferson's, did Madison comply. He was enjoying his vacation with Dolly. Even so, the Federalists were still in the woods on the treaty — and there was yet a memorable fight ahead.

---

[1] *Argus*, August 15, 1795.
[2] *Ibid.*, August 27, 1795.
[3] Hamilton's *Works*, x, 113–14.
[4] Jefferson's *Works*, ix, 309–11.

CHAPTER XIII

THE DRAMA OF '96

I

EXUBERANT over their success in capitalizing Washington's consent to the treaty, the Federalists returned to Philadelphia in an ugly mood. With celerity and *éclat*, the Senate threw down the gauntlet with the rejection of the nomination of John Rutledge because of his hostility to the treaty. The motive was unescapable. He was an able jurist, an erudite lawyer, a pure patriot with a superb record of high public services — but he had denounced the Federalist treaty. That was enough. The leaders were delighted with their action, Senator Johnson thinking it would have been unfortunate to have permitted Rutledge to remain upon the Bench 'after what had appeared.' Of course, the opposition would 'endeavor to impress it upon the minds of the people that the majority were influenced by improper motives,' but that was unavoidable.[1] Jefferson viewed the incident from his hilltop with the vision of a prophet. 'A bold thing,' he thought, 'because they cannot pretend any objection to him but his disapprobation of the treaty.' It meant that the Federalists 'would receive none but Tories hereafter into any department of the government,' and it would not be surprising were Monroe recalled from Paris because 'of his being of the partisans·of France.' Monticello was remote, but its master could see a long way.[2]

The Senate still seemed safe to the Federalists on their return, but there were grave misgivings as to the House. Young Livingston had caused trouble enough and he was back to give more than Ames 'the hypo,' but more ominous was the appearance there for the first time of Albert Gallatin. He had been thrown out of the Senate as speedily as possible, but not before he had given proof of his financial genius. There, the Jeffersonians had been weak in leadership. It was characteristic of the inner circle of the Federalists to hate any opponent they could not despise — and they

[1] McRee, *Iredell*, II, 459.   [2] Jefferson's *Works* (to Giles), IX, 314–18.

dare not despise this young man from Geneva. Even in private
life he had been denounced and damned in the spirit of the pot-
house, and Hamilton had ardently hoped for his indictment in connection with the Whiskey Insurrection. When his election had
seemed probable, an effort had actually been made to disfranchise
his district as a region of sedition — but here was Gallatin. A duel
between Gallatin's father-in-law, Admiral Nicholson, and Hamilton had been narrowly averted in the autumn; but Gallatin, rising
serenely above his detractors, had refused to be ruffled, and had
advised his wife not to express her sentiments on the treatment
accorded him too hotly lest it 'lead to consequences you would
forever regret.' [1] Since these two brilliant, bitterly hated, and
violently abused men, Livingston and Gallatin, were to play conspicuous parts in the drama of the House, it is worth while to pause
for a more intimate impression of them.

II

'Edward Livingston now lives here in the style of a nabob,'
wrote Wolcott during this session.[2] It was a style to which he had
been accustomed from birth, for he was of the baronial aristocracy
of New York. He was but thirty-two at the time, tall, handsome,
dashing and daring, witty and eloquent, and with a luminous background of wealth, culture, tradition, and personal achievement.
Even the most inveterate snob among his political opponents must
have envied him his advantages. Born in the mansion of the Livingstons at 'Clermont,' on the Hudson, he had passed his winters
in the town house in New York, which swarmed with slave servants. From boyhood, his society had been eagerly sought. With
his fleeing mother he had witnessed from a hilltop his loved home
given to the flames by British soldiers; and to his dying day he
carried a poignant memory of the parting of his sister with her
hero husband, Richard Montgomery, when he set forth for his
final fight. Lafayette had been so captivated by the charming
youth while visiting his home that he had vainly importuned his
mother for permission to take him to France; and when the young
man attended the Marquis a way on the Boston road, so romantic
was the attachment that the latter had urged the youth to make

[1] Adams, *Gallatin*, 152.   [2] Gibbs (to Goodrich), I, 303.

the journey, nevertheless, with the promise to conciliate the family. His was a unique charm, a fascinating personality.

Graduating from Princeton, in the class with Giles, he had his choice between a life of laborious accomplishment and one of leisurely elegance. Society, the gayest, giddiest, most entrancing, held forth its arms to him. His mother's drawing-room was always crowded with brilliant and beautiful women and clever men, attracted partly by the exquisite charms of the widow of Montgomery. He had an income, a town and country house, slaves to do his bidding, and he turned from the enticing prospect to bury himself in the assiduous study of the law. Now and then he laid his books aside to flirt with Theodosia Burr, to dance with the pretty belles, to play for stakes with women at the gambling-table inseparable from the more fashionable houses — but only as a diversion.

Scarcely had he begun the practice of his profession when he took a commanding position. Hard work, a noble ambition, and native talent made him a success. But he could not have been a Livingston and indifferent to politics. Very early his capacity and popularity swept him into the fight. Strangely enough, he immediately became the idol of the masses. This aristocrat was a democrat who was able to move in the crowd with a distinction that commanded respect while compelling affection. Perhaps the artisans, the clerks, the lowly were flattered by his smile and condescension, perhaps captivated by his fighting mettle — whatever the cause, they loved him, gathered about and sustained him. The Tammany of his time marshaled its forces for him, and all the wit and wiles of Hamilton could not harm him. But the Federalists hated him. What moral right had a man of wealth and intellectual distinction and social prestige to affiliate with the 'mob'? They hated him as deserters are hated — he was an American Égalité to Mrs. Bingham's drawing-room, and Wolcott hated him less because he 'lived like a nabob' than because he fought like the devil.[1]

[1] The second phase of his remarkable career is treated in the author's *Party Battles of the Jackson Period.*

III

Quite a different type was Albert Gallatin — and yet both were born aristocrats. From the beginning of the republic at Geneva in the sixteenth century, his family had been second to none in prestige and power. The governmental system was aristocratic; his people were uncompromising aristocrats, and five Gallatins had been, at one time or another, head of the State. Into this reactionary atmosphere he was born, and in it he passed his youth. At the home of his grandmother, a domineering but clever old autocrat, who believed in the divine right of the aristocracy to rule, he often met Voltaire. Strange couple, that old woman worshiping tradition, and that cynical old philosopher sneering it away. And yet in his family Gallatin was an exotic. Instinctively he despised the system his people thought sacred. Rousseau may have influenced him, but he was probably born with democracy in his blood. When his grandmother arranged to get him a commission in the mercenary army of her friend the Landgrave of Hess, and he scornfully refused on the ground that he would 'never serve a tyrant,' the old woman boxed his ears — but without jarring his principles.[1] He was a grave disappointment in the family circle. It is a notable coincidence that like Hamilton he was remarkably precocious. He graduated from the Academy of Geneva in his seventeenth year, first in his class in mathematics, natural philosophy, and Latin translation. There, too, he had studied history under Müller, the eminent historian, and in the facts and philosophy of world history he was to have no equal in American public life. Nothing contributed more to his desertion of his country than his hatred of its petty aristocracy, its autocratic rule.

He was a dreamer in his youth. Was it Rousseau who planted in him a dislike of cities and a passion for the wilderness? Secretly he left Geneva and came to America, landing in Boston. He carried a letter of introduction from Benjamin Franklin to his son-in-law, the father of the editor of 'The Aurora' at Philadelphia. A few dreary months in Boston, a happier winter in a cabin in the wilderness of northern Maine, a year at Harvard as a teacher of French, a short time in Philadelphia in a boarding-house with

[1] Adams, *Gallatin*, 17.

Pelatiah Webster, the political philosopher, and the lure of land speculation led him to Virginia. There, in Richmond, some of his happiest days were passed. Society was courteous, kindly, and there he came in contact with great minds. John Marshall invited him into his office with the prediction that he would distinguish himself at the Bar, and Patrick Henry advised him to go West, with the observation that he was intended for statesmanship. At this time he was a youth of twenty-one with a pronounced foreign accent. Washington met him, and, impressed with his keenness, offered to make him his land agent — an honor happily declined. Then into the wilderness of Pennsylvania; a house on a hilltop which he called 'Friendship Hill'; a domestic tragedy — the death of his young wife; and soon the Whiskey Boys, keen of vision as Marshall, Henry, or Washington, literally swept him into public life.

He was primarily a democrat and an opponent of strong government. Fascinated by the work of the Constitutional Convention, he thought the Executive had been given too much power. But he was opposed to tinkering with constitutions once adopted.[1] As a member of the convention to revise the Constitution of Pennsylvania, he worked as earnestly as had Madison in the greater convention, fighting with moderation, but persistence for a popular government, for the freedom of the press, and popular suffrage. It is significant that when the subject of courts was reached he sought the advice of John Marshall — and received it.[2] His views on the French Revolution were those of Jefferson. He recognized the many excesses, the greed of demagogues for power, and he did not expect 'a very good government within a short time,' but he knew 'their cause to be that of mankind against tyranny' and that 'no foreign nation has the right to dictate a government to them.'[3] One glance at Genêt revealed to him the naked man — 'totally unfit for the place he fills,' his abilities 'slender.'[4] Yet, like Jefferson, despite the massacres in Paris and the Genêt excesses in Philadelphia, he clung to France because, 'if France is annihilated, as seems to be the desire of the combined powers, sad indeed will the consequences be for America.'[5] If he opposed the Excise Law,

[1] Adams, *Gallatin*, 80.   [2] *Ibid.*, 81.   [3] *Ibid.*, 103–04.
[4] *Ibid.*, 111.   [5] *Ibid.*, 113.

as was his right, he had a reason, and it was sane.[1] The charge the Federalists were to make, that he had incited the hard-pressed pioneers to violations of the law, was maliciously false. Throughout that insurrection, his part was hard, and he met it with sanity and courage.

This was the background of this remarkable man when, at the age of thirty-five, he stepped forward with the confidence of a veteran to assume the intellectual leadership of the Jeffersonians in the House. A shy man in social relations, he was utterly fearless in debate. There was no mind in that body so well stocked with facts, and none with a broader vision or deeper penetration. There was no one more masterful in logic, more clear, downright, incisive in statement, and none more impervious to abuse. His was the dignity of a superior mentality. If his foreign accent was still pronounced, and members, priding themselves on their refinement and taste, sneered openly, he remained the perfect gentleman, indifferent to such jeers. In the midst of excitement, he was calm. When others were demoralized, he kept his head. No greater figure ever stood upon the floor of an American Congress than when Albert Gallatin appeared, to force notable reforms in the fiscal system, and to challenge the Federalists to an intellectual combat that would call forth their extreme exertions.

IV

One of the most important and brilliant debates in American history, surpassing that on the Foote Resolutions, was precipitated early in March when Edward Livingston threw a bomb into the complacent camp of the Federalists with resolutions calling upon the President to lay before the House the instructions and papers pertaining to the Jay Treaty. There was some maneuvering in the beginning to feel out the position of the enemy, and then the members settled down to a month of memorable debating. On the whole, the discussion was pitched upon a high plane, for the question was one of constitutional interpretation. Throughout, there was scarcely a touch of personalities, albeit Tracy, described by his admirers as the 'Burke of Connecticut,' and by his enemies as the 'Burke of Connecticut without his intelligence,' could not

[1] Adams, *Gallatin*, 88; *Writings*, I, 3–4.

restrain a stupid sneer at the accent of Gallatin who led for the enemies of the treaty. A Pennsylvania member denounced Tracy's vulgar conduct as 'intolerable,' and there were many cries of 'order.' With the brazen effrontery of his school, Tracy asked Speaker Dayton to decide, and that rather disreputable speculator, if not peculator, held it in order to insult Gallatin with impunity.[1] But this incident was happily unique.

The Livingston Resolutions were based upon the theory that the House was a party to the treaty in that it would be asked to make appropriations to carry it into effect, and that the facts were necessary to the determination of its course. This was in perfect accord with the position of Jefferson.[2] The Federalists contended that the President and Senate alone were officially concerned, and that the House was obligated to carry out any financial arrangements entered into in a treaty. Did not the Constitution specifically say that the treaty-making power was lodged in the President and the Senate? Conceded, replied the opposition, but the Constitution also said that money bills must originate in the House, and in making appropriations for any purpose the popular branch of Congress is constitutionally bound to use its own discretion. Both sides could, and did, appeal to the Constitution. There was nothing merely factious or obstructive in the fight of the opposition, and it is impossible to peruse the seven hundred and nine pages of the debates without a realization of the complete sincerity of the participants. Into the debate dashed all the leaders of the first order. The galleries were packed. The discussion was the sole conversational topic in streets and coffee-houses. The newspapers printed the leading speeches in full. Even the Federal courts injected themselves into the controversy, and one jurist introduced a denunciation of the enemies of the treaty into his charge to the grand jury.[3] Fenno stupidly stumbled into the blunder of proving the opponents of the treaty a 'Robespierre faction' by quoting the London 'Morning Chronicle,' [4] and Cobbett, the Englishman and Federalist pamphleteer, selected this particular time to outrage the Philadelphia 'rabble' by filling

---

[1] *Annals*, April 27, 1796.   [2] Jefferson's *Works*, IX, 328–29; to Monroe.

[3] Judge Jonathan Elmer, Cumberland, New Jersey, *Gazette of the United States*, March 12, 1796.

[4] *Gazette of the United States*, March 26, 1796.

his windows with pictures of kings, queens, princes, dukes, Pitt, Grenville, and George III. With studied insolence, he added some portraits of American Revolutionary heroes, and 'found out fit companions for them.' Thus he 'coupled Franklin with Marat' and 'M'Kean and Ankerstrom.'[1]

The burden of the debate was borne by Gallatin, Madison, Livingston, and Giles for the Resolutions, and by Sedgwick and Griswold against them. Livingston spoke with spirited eloquence and with that power of reasoning which was afterward to compel his recognition as one of the foremost political thinkers of his time.[2] Giles sustained his reputation as a fluent, forceful, slashing debater. Madison spoke with moderation; but the honors of primacy fell to Gallatin. He was a revelation, and the Federalists were beside themselves with rage. Tall, and above medium size, his fine face aglow with intelligence, his black eyes burning with earnestness, his profile resembling in its sharp outlines that of a Frenchman, his accent foreign, his delivery slow and a little embarrassed, he spoke with a clarity and force that made the Federalists wince. Livingston was more showy, Giles more boisterous, Madison more academic. This new man was another Madison with greater punch.[3] He did not wander a moment from his argument — the constitutional rights of the House in the case of treaties involving appropriations.

'The House has a right to ask for papers,' he said, 'because their coöperation and sanction is necessary to carry the Treaty into full effect, to render it a binding instrument, and to make it, properly speaking, a law of the land; because they have a full discretion to either give or refuse that coöperation; because they must be guided in the exercise of that discretion by the merits and expediency of the Treaty itself, and therefore they have a right to ask for every information which can assist them in deciding that question.' Whence led the argument of the foes of the Resolutions? 'The Constitution says that no money shall be drawn from the Treasury but in consequence of appropriations made by law. But treaties, whatever provisions they may contain, are law; appropriations may therefore be made by treaties. Then the short-

---

[1] Melville, *Cobbett*, I, 101–02. [2] *Annals*, March 11, 1796.
[3] *Familiar Letters*, 108; Twining, *Travels*, 51–52.

est way to carry this treaty into effect would have been to add
another article appropriating the money.' Turning to the power
of the House of Commons in the case of treaties involving an appropriation, he found an analogy to the constitutional power of the
President and the Senate, in the power of the King to make treaties. But no one in England challenged the right of the Commons
to appropriate or not in putting the provisions of a treaty into
effect — and the speaker cited instances where the Commons had
rejected treaties by refusing appropriations. 'Are we in a worse
situation than Great Britain?' he asked. 'Is the House of Representatives . . . the immediate representatives of the American
people ranked below the British House of Commons? Shall the
Legislative power be swallowed up by the Treaty-making power
as contended for here, though never claimed even in Great Britain?' The issue raised by the opposition to the Resolutions was
clear, and their rejection would be 'tantamount to saying that the
House abandons their share in legislation, and consents that the
whole power shall be centered in the other branches.'

Such, in general, was the tenor of the argument for the Resolutions; while the Federalists insisted that the House possessed no
power to refuse any appropriation called for by a treaty — and
thus the discussion went round and round like a wagon wheel
in motion. Sedgwick, in justifying the Senate's power, made a
blunder on which the supporters of the Resolutions seized and
with which they played throughout the discussion. The Senators
were safer than the Representatives, he thought, because the
former were not chosen by 'an ignorant herd, who could be cajoled, flattered, and deceived.'

At length the vote was taken, and the Resolutions adopted by
61 to 38. Gallatin and Livingston, chosen by the House, personally presented the call for the papers to Washington, who promised an answer after consideration. An answer, sneered Bache,
which sounds like that which the King of France used to give to
his subjects.[1]

V

When Livingston introduced his Resolutions, Hamilton, in New
York, was momentarily at sea. His first impression was that they

[1] *Aurora*, March 28, 1796.

were 'of doubtful propriety.' [1] Within a few days, after discussions with 'those who think,' he was persuaded that the papers should be refused — possibly on the ground that no purpose could be served unless impeachment proceedings against Washington were in contemplation.[2] Here we have, in a flash, the political strategy outlined — to convince the people that the Jeffersonians were planning the expulsion of Washington from office. Again the Federalist war-cry — 'Stand by the President!' But a week later, Hamilton wrote King that the papers should be refused on the ground that the House had nothing to do with treaties, and that they were laws of the land to which the House had to conform.[3] Learning of the adoption of the Resolutions, Hamilton wrote Washington to refuse compliance and to await suggestions that would be sent the next day.[4] Two days later, he was mortified at his inability to send the promised papers, but he was at work upon them. Meanwhile, the papers should not be sent because the instructions to Jay would 'do no credit to the Administration.' Some would disappoint and inflame the people.[5] Two days after this, Washington sent his reply to the House, following Hamilton's instructions and using some of his phraseology, even to the convenient suggestion of an impeachment.[6] The House, with equal firmness and with a dignified moderation, responded with resolutions reaffirming its right — and the issue was made.[7] Almost immediately the introduction of a resolution providing the appropriation threw the House into another month's battle, on the treaty itself.

VI

Up to this time the congressional struggle had caused little excitement among the people. Now the idea that the Union itself was at stake was assiduously put out by the Federalist leaders. The Senate practically ceased to function. When Senator Tazewell called attention to the accumulation of business and urged action, King bluntly told him it was purposely held back, and that if the House failed to appropriate for the treaty, the Senate would

---

[1] Hamilton's *Works* (to Wolcott), x, 145.　　[2] *Ibid.*, 145–46.　　[3] *Ibid.*, 151.
[4] *Ibid.*, 152.　　　[5] *Ibid.*, 152–54.　　[6] *Annals*, March 30, 1796.
[7] *Annals*, April 6, 1796. The vote was 57 to 36.

consider all legislation at an end, and he would assume the Union dissolved. The next day Cabot expressed something of the same sentiment. In important commercial circles there was much loose talk of the dissolution of the Union.

The action of Washington, on the other hand, had aroused resentment and disgust. Jefferson, with his usual prescience, had foreseen it while hoping against it. 'I wish that his honesty and his political errors may not furnish a second occasion to exclaim, "curse on his virtues, they have undone his country,"' he had written of Washington to Madison three days before the refusal was sent to Congress.[1] Madison thought the tone and temper of the presidential letter 'improper and indelicate,' and suggested that Jefferson compare it with 'one of Callimus' last numbers . . . and the latter part of Murray's speech.'[2] It was reserved to Bache, as usual, to strike the harsh note. 'Thus though his decision could not be influenced by the voice of the people, he could suffer it to be moulded by the opinion of an ex-Secretary,' he wrote. 'Thus . . . though he has apparently discharged the nurse, he is still in leading strings.'

Meanwhile, the attacks on the Treaty were spreading consternation in all commercial quarters and infuriating the Federalist leaders. 'A most important crisis ensues,' wrote Hamilton to King a week after the debate opened; and he outlined a plan of action in the event the appropriations were refused. The President should send a solemn protest to the House and a copy to the Senate. That body should pass a resolution strongly commending the protest and advising the President to proceed with the execution of the Treaty. Then the merchants should meet in all the cities, adopt resolutions commendatory of the position of the President and Senate, and invite their fellow citizens to coöperate with them. Petitions should be circulated throughout the country. The Senate should refuse to adjourn until the terms of the members of the House had expired. Washington should send a confidential apology to England. 'The glory of the President, the safety of the Constitution depend upon it. Nothing will be wanting here.'[3]

Hamilton immediately set his machinery in motion, and thus,

---

[1] Jefferson's *Works*, IX, 330–31. [2] Madison's *Writings*, II, 89–91.
[3] Hamilton's *Works*, X, 157.

while the debate was at high tide in the House, the political leaders were busy with the country. King had written of the alarm of the merchants in Philadelphia. 'Our merchants here are not less alarmed and will do all they can,' Hamilton replied. Arrangements had been made for the insurance people to meet that day; the merchants and traders would meet the next. A petition would be put in circulation.[1] Two days later, he wrote jubilantly of the action of the merchants. 'Unexampled unanimity,' he said. And more — 'persons to-day are going through the different wards' — presumably with petitions.[2] That very day he was writing Wolcott that 'the British Ministry are as great fools or as great rascals as our Jacobins, else our commerce would not continue to be distressed as it is, with their cruisers.'[3]

The very day that Hamilton was writing of the distress of the New York merchants, Madison was writing to Jefferson of the plans of the Democrats. While a merchants' petition had been circulated in Philadelphia, he promised that 'an adverse petition will be signed by three or four times' as many people. In New York and Boston similar petitions would be put out. In Baltimore little could be expected, for there, while originally against the treaty, they had been won over 'by the hope of indemnification for past losses.'[4] Five days later, he reported progress. The Philadelphia petition against the treaty greatly outnumbered that for it, and petitions were being circulated in Delaware and New Jersey. The insurance companies in Philadelphia and New York were seeking to intimidate the people by stopping business. The banks had been active peddlers of petitions in the cities where there was 'scarce a trader or merchant but what depends on discounts.' A hateful picture, thought Madison. 'Bank Directors soliciting subscriptions are like highwaymen with a pistol demanding the purse.'[5]

Boston found the Federalists triumphant in a town meeting dominated by the eloquence of Otis, who played upon the horrors of war, and thus gave Ames and the other party leaders their cue. It was on this occasion that the orator, who had studied French under Gallatin at Harvard, and been treated kindly, referred to the

---

[1] Hamilton's *Works*, x, 160.　　　[2] *Ibid.*, 161.　　　[3] *Ibid.*, 161–62.
[4] Madison's *Writings*, II, 95.　　　[5] *Ibid.*, 98.

latter sneeringly as a nobody who had come to America without a second shirt on his back. Later, to the disgust of his Federalist co-workers, he had the decency to apologize to Gallatin.[1] Everywhere the latter was being deluged with billingsgate. There was not contempt here — there was hate. Noah Webster, in the 'Minerva,' was sneering at his foreign birth, while taking his cue from Hamilton, born in the West Indies; attacking his position on the excise with falsehoods and innuendoes; charging him with being an agent of France. Adams, of the 'Independent Chronicle,' replied with a parody, substituting Hamilton for Gallatin and England for France and making as good sense.[2] Wolcott was writing his father that it was 'neither unreasonable nor uncandid to believe that Mr. Gallatin is directed by foreign politics and influence.'[3] Nothing could have pained the sensitive Wolcott more than the feeling that he was being uncandid.

Meanwhile, the fight in the House went on — Gallatin in the forefront. The Federalists were thoroughly frightened over the prospect, resorting to every device to gain votes. Dreadful pictures of war if the treaty failed, appeals to 'stand by Washington,' and intimidation — these were favorite devices. 'I am told,' wrote Wolcott, with evident pleasure, 'that if Findlay and Gallatin don't ultimately vote for their [treaties'] execution, their lives will be scarcely spared.'[4] But frightened and afraid of a vote, they decided 'to risk the consequences of a delay, and prolong the debates in expectation of an impulse from some of the districts on their representatives.'[5] However, a vote could not be indefinitely delayed. Public business was at a standstill. Everything possible had been done. The bankers had been sent out with petitions to their creditors. The insurance companies had stopped business. The merchants had passed resolutions. Petitions had been circulated. Washington's glory had been pictured as in jeopardy. And the horrors of war had been described. The time had come to close the debate. The greatest orator in the country was their spokesman, and he had been held back for the last appeal. The time had come for Fisher Ames to make the closing plea.

[1] Morison, *Otis*, I, 56–57. [2] April 21, 1796.
[3] Gibbs, I, 327. [4] *Ibid.*, 325–26.
[5] *Ibid.* (Wolcott to his father), I, 331.

Fisher Ames was not only the premier orator of his party; he was one of its most brilliant and captivating personalities. He had a genius for friendship and was good company. Nature had blessed him with her richest intellectual gifts. His precocity equaled that of Hamilton or Gallatin — he was a prodigy. At six he was studying Latin, at twelve he had entered Harvard, and there he was conspicuous because of his scintillation. His powers of application were equal to his natural ability, but he found time for relaxation when his animation, wit, and charm, combined with modesty, endeared him to his fellows and won the affection of his instructors. Even at Harvard he was ardently cultivating the art of oratory, and the style then formed, while strengthened by age and experience, never greatly changed. Cicero was his model through life. During his preparation for the Bar, his appetite for good literature was not neglected, and he delved deeply into ancient history and mythology, natural and civil history, and he pored over the novelists and lived with the poets — Shakespeare, Milton, Virgil. These were fruitful years and the Federalists were to get the harvest. At the Bar he instantly took rank as a pleader, but he found time to write articles on the political affairs of the time. In the convention called to ratify the Constitution, he disclosed the political prepossessions that were to govern his career. While not hostile to a republican experiment, he was skeptical of republics, fearing the domination of popular factions. These factions he considered the rabble. Democracy, he despised. He was an aristocrat by instinct and this guided his political conduct.

He would have distinguished himself in literature had he devoted himself to it. He wrote, as he spoke, out of a full mind, and his first draft of an article required no polishing or revision. This made him an amazingly brilliant extemporaneous orator. Although the slow processes of logical argumentation were not beyond him, he depended more on illustration. His mind fairly teemed with images. The poets had endowed him with their gift. There was something Shakespearean in the fertility of his fancy, and he delighted his hearers or readers with his rapidly changing pictures. These came spontaneously, and, leaving an indelible impression on his audience, they were lost to him with their utterance. He scattered gems as though they were grains of the sea, and he the owner of the sands of the shore. Remarkably enough, this did not lead him to rhetorical flamboyance or over-elaboration. He was a master of the short sentence, and he possessed rare powers of condensation.

In social relations he was lovable, but he carefully selected his intimates, having no stomach for the commonplace person. His companions were of the élite. Among them he was simplicity itself, and generosity and kindness, but no man had a more brutal wit or sarcasm for a foe. Above middle height and well proportioned, he held himself erect. There was little in his features to distinguish him, for they were not strongly marked. His forehead was neither noticeably high nor broad; his blue eyes were mild and without a suggestion of the fire of domination; his mouth was well formed, but not strong; but his voice was melody itself. One who often heard him found that 'the silvery tones of his voice fell upon the ear like strains of sweetest music' and that 'you could not choose but hear.' [1] There was more than a touch of aristocratic cynicism in his nature, and his favorite weapon in attack was sarcasm, but he was ordinarily considerate of the feelings of a foe in combat. No other member of the House could approach him in the eloquence of persuasion.[2]

VIII

Happily married to a beautiful woman, Ames had built himself an elegant home at Dedham where he lived and was to die, but in the fall of 1796 he had little expectation of lingering long to enjoy it. Nothing had enraged him more than the popular agitation against the Jay Treaty, and in the midst of the fight he suffered a physical collapse. In September, he was unable to ride thirty miles without resting for a day.[3] He had consulted various 'oracles' and found that he was bilious, nervous, cursed with a disease of the liver, and he had been 'forbidden and enjoined to take almost everything' — meat — cider — a trotting horse —

[1] Thomas, *Reminiscences,* 53.
[2] Kirkland, *Life of Ames;* Thomas, *Reminiscences; Familiar Letters,* 24–25.
[3] Ames (to Dwight), I, 173–75.

and to refrain from excess of every kind.[1] In October, with the
congressional battle approaching, he had a relapse — 'extreme
weakness, want of appetite, want of rest.' Faint hope then of
reaching Philadelphia at the first of the session, 'if ever.' Still, the
cool weather might restore him. Philadelphia, perhaps, by December.[2] But December found him at Dedham, with King writing him of the desperate prospects in the House and urging his
presence,[3] and in January Ames was writing Jeremiah Smith of his
resolve to go on to Philadelphia. 'Should this snow last, I am half
resolved to jingle my bells as far as Springfield.' At any rate, on
the morrow he would go to 'my loyal town of Boston in my covered
sleigh by way of experimenting of my strength.'[4]

February found him on the way. At New Haven where he
lodged, the snow grew thin, and 'there was great wear and tear of
horse flesh.' At Stamford it was gone and he took a coachee. At
Mamaroneck, twenty-five miles from New York, he slept, and
awoke to find the snow 'pelting the windows.' Back with the
coach, and a wait for the sleigh. Even so, he wrote, 'to-morrow I
expect to hear the bells ring and the light horse blow their trump-
ets' on reaching New York. 'If Governor Jay won't do that for
me, let him get his treaty defended by Calumus, and such under-
strappers.' Two days in New York — three more — and Philadelphia. 'Do not let me go down to the pit of the Indian Queen,'
he had written a colleague. 'It is Hades and Tartarus, and Peri-
phlegethon, Cocytus, and Styx where it would be a pity to bring
all the piety and learning that he must have who knows the afore-
said infernal names. Please leave word at the said Queen, or if
need be at any other Queens where I may unpack my weary
household gods.'[5] The day before this letter was written, Bache's
paper said that the 'ratification is not to arrive until Mr. Ames
has recovered,' because 'the subaltern officers of the corps not
being supposed sufficiently skilled in tactics to be entrusted with
the principal command.'[6] Six days later, he announced Ames's
arrival in New York.[7] Thus, like a warrior borne to battle on a
stretcher, Ames entered the capital.

---

[1] Ames (to Dwight), I, 175–76.   [2] Ibid., 177.   [3] Ibid., 180–81.
[4] Ibid., 183–84.   [5] Ibid. (to Jeremiah Smith), 184–85.
[6] Aurora, February 2, 1796.   [7] Ibid., February 8, 1796.

All through March he sat in silence listening to the debate on Livingston's Resolutions, groaning under his physical disability. 'I am not a sentry, not in the ranks, not on the staff,' he wrote in disgust. 'I am thrown into the wagon as part of the baggage.' [1] With the debate on the treaty itself about to begin, he wrote that he was 'not fit for debate on the treaty and not able to attend through a whole sitting.' [2] Thus he watched the swaying fortunes of the fight, sick and feeble, but expected to save the day in a pinch. When he rose that April day to make the final effort for his party, there was drama in the general appreciation of his condition. That Ames enjoyed it, we have no doubt. It was so much like Chatham carried into the House of Peers wrapped in his flannels.

IX

Ames was a consummate actor that spring day. Not without art did he begin with a reference to his frailty. Here was a man ready to die for a cause. Impassionedly he pleaded against passion. The treaty, he said, had 'raised our character as a nation.' Its rejection would be a 'violation of public faith.' It had 'more critics than readers,' and 'the movements of passion are quicker than those of understanding.' Lightly he touched upon the constitutional question, and then hastened to his purpose — to discuss the consequences of rejection, to play on fear. With this he expected to win his fight — with this he won. Reject the treaty and leave the posts in the hands of the British and invite war?

'On this theme,' he said in his most thrilling tones, 'my emotions are unutterable. If I could find words for them . . . I would swell my voice to such a note of remonstrance, it would reach every log house beyond the mountains. I would say to the inhabitants, wake from your false security, your cruel dangers, your more cruel apprehensions are soon to be renewed; the wounds yet unhealed, are to be torn open again; in the day time your path through the woods will be ambushed, the darkness of midnight will glitter with the blaze of your dwellings. You are a father — the blood of your son shall fatten your corn field. You are a mother — the war whoop shall waken the sleep of the cradle . . . By rejecting the posts we light the savage fires, we bind the victims. This day we

[1] Ames (to Dwight).   [2] *Ibid.* (to Minor), I, 190–91.

undertake to render account to the widows and orphans whom our decision will make; to the wretches who will be roasted at the stake; to our country; and I do not deem it too serious to say, to our conscience and God. The voice of humanity issues from the shade of the wilderness; it exclaims that while one hand is held up to reject this treaty, the other grasps a tomahawk. It summons our imagination to the scenes that will open . . . I can fancy that I listen to the yells of savage vengeance and the shrieks of torture; already they seem to sigh on the western wind; already they mingle with every echo from the mountains.'

How the frontiersmen in the gallery must have stared at this solicitude for them from a Federalist of New England!

Then, in closing, a perfect piece of art. 'I have perhaps as little personal interest in the event as any one here. There is, I believe, no member who will not believe his chance to be a witness to the consequences greater than mine. If, however, the vote should pass to reject, and a spirit should rise as it will, with the public disorder to make confusion worse confounded, even I, slender and almost broken as my hold upon life is, may outlive the governments and Constitution of my country.' He sank into his seat. 'My God,' exclaimed a Federal Judge, 'did you ever hear anything like it?' Crusty old John Adams wiped his eyes. Accept, said Ames, or England will turn the savages upon you; accept, or your Constitution will be overthrown; accept, or the Republic will be destroyed.

The Federalists were jubilant — as was Ames, none the worse for the speech. Soon Christopher Gore was writing him from London that he knew his speech was 'in the hands of Mr. Pitt, Mr. Dundas and Lord Grenville.'[1] The Jeffersonians were alarmed. Madison was bitter because of the summons to 'follow Washington wherever he leads.'[2] Soon he was to find that 'the name of the President and the alarm of war' had done mischief.[3] When the roll was called, several enemies of the treaty had been frightened from the firing line. Patton of New Jersey had a convenient illness. Varnum was unavoidably absent. Freeman of New Hampshire had obtained leave of absence, and a newly elected Democrat from Maryland discreetly withheld his credentials until after the

[1] Ames, i, 199–200, note.
[2] Madison's *Writings* (to Jefferson), ii, 100–01.   [3] *Ibid.*, 103–05.

fight was over. By a majority of three the House decided to appropriate. Even so, it was the most expensive victory the Federalists had won, for the majority in the country was on the other side. Out of the struggle had emerged a new great leader to serve the Jeffersonians, Albert Gallatin. Jefferson had been so delighted with his speech that he wrote Madison that it deserved a place in 'The Federalist.'[1] During the remainder of the session, he was to cause much mental distress with his fiscal reform plans and his attacks on the Treasury.

x

Jefferson had followed the fight on the treaty from his mountain, making no personal effort to influence the result. It had not been so easy as he had hoped to forget politics in the cultivation of his peas, and when Congress met he had subscribed for Bache's paper.[2] He divided the friends of the treaty into two classes; the honest who were afraid of England, and the dishonest who had pecuniary motives. At no time did he question the honesty of Washington. In his letters to Madison he poured forth his innermost thoughts, but beyond this his correspondence had not been extensive.

It is the fashion to set down as a pose his pretended indifference to the Presidency in 1796, but there is evidence enough that he was deeply concerned over his health. He had begun, as he thought, 'to feel the effects of age,' and was convinced that his health had 'suddenly broken down.'[3] In a letter to Washington touching on political topics, he wrote that he would 'put aside this disgusting dish of old fragments and talk . . . of peas and clover.'[4] In July, with the Federalist press, in expectation of his candidacy, intemperately denouncing his letter to Mazzei, he was writing a friend his estimate of the height of the Blue Ridge Mountains, explaining his plan for a moulding-board, and expressing his indignation because of the silly attacks on the memory of Franklin.[5]

Fenno and Webster were working themselves into a frenzy over

[1] Jefferson's *Works*, IX, 330–31.   [2] Randall, II, 273.
[3] Jefferson's *Works*, IX, 335–37.   [4] *Ibid.*, 339–43.
[5] *Ibid.* (letter to Williams), 346–48.

the letter to Philip Mazzei, the Italian, in which Jefferson had frankly discussed American politics. It contained nothing that Jefferson had not repeatedly said to Washington's face. 'An Anglican aristocratical-monarchical party' — this the theme. But he had hinted that Washington had been captured by the aristocrats and monarchists — and here was treason. Webster said so with all his vocabulary, and there was some ridiculous talk of impeaching the author of the letter after his election to the Vice-Presidency, but throughout it all Jefferson made no public comment, no denial, no explanation. He was ever the consummate politician.[1] The announced decision of Washington to retire made Jefferson's candidacy a certainty, whether he willed it or not. Three years before, the Democrats had decided. All through the summer and autumn that was the understanding.

To the Hamiltonians the retirement of Washington was peculiarly distressing. On most controversial subjects he had ultimately adopted their view. More than one of their unpopular measures had been saved with their war-cry, 'Stand with Washington.' With Washington eliminated, it was vitally important to Hamilton and his leaders to find a successor who would be more or less subservient. Hamilton himself was out of the question for the reason that Hamilton had given — he did not have the confidence of the people. Jay, who would have been the second choice, would have been a red rag to the 'rabble' in 1796. Few of the other leaders, with all their brilliancy and personal charm, could have made a popular appeal; and Adams was thoroughly distrusted and disliked by the Hamiltonians because of his independence.

Under these circumstances, Hamilton and King, consulting, conceived the idea of persuading Patrick Henry to be a candidate. Just what appealed to them has never been satisfactorily explained, for Henry had been among the most bitter and brilliant enemies of the ratification of the Constitution. With the acquisition of wealth, great changes had occurred in the old patriot's manner of thinking, and he had come to lean strongly toward the Federalists.[2] Fear of Jefferson and a desire to break the solidarity of Virginia's vote may have been a determining motive. That an effort was being made to find a candidate who would appeal to the

[1] Jefferson's *Works* (Mazzei letter), IX, 335–37. [2] Beveridge, *Marshall*, II, 156.

South and West appears in King's letter to Hamilton.[1] Whatever the motive, the decision to offer Henry the support of the Hamiltonians was reached, and John Marshall was asked to approach him.

The old orator was living quietly and happily at 'Red Hill,' his home in the country, where he liked nothing better than to drag his chair out under the trees, tilt it against one of the trunks, and, with a can of cool spring water beside him, look out lazily across the green valley. There, with his family and friends about him, he asked nothing better than to be let alone.[2] Motives of discretion and the limitations of a letter dissuaded the chosen emissary from writing to 'Red Hill,' but Henry Lee, who knew Henry more intimately, was asked to write him an intimation of what was in the air. No answer was forthcoming. Very soon, however, the old patriot would be in Richmond and Marshall would then sound him, and, discovering an indisposition to embark on the enterprise, would 'stop where prudence may direct.'[3] Thus Henry was cautiously approached, without being given any intimation of the source of the suggestion, and was found 'unwilling to embark in the business.'[4] Thus ended the flirtation with Patrick Henry, with the friendly conspirators hidden behind the fan.

Anticipating a declination, Hamilton and King had canvassed the availability of Thomas Pinckney, the American Minister in London. 'It is an idea of which I am fond in various lights,' wrote Hamilton to King. 'I rather wish to be rid of Patrick Henry that we may be at full liberty to take up Pinckney.'[5] This was due to the feeling that 'to his former stock of popularity he will now add the good will of those who have been peculiarly gratified with the Spanish treaty' — which he had negotiated.[6] Thus the inner circle of the Hamiltonians settled the matter for themselves without reference to the rank and file of the party.

XI

Thomas Pinckney was one of the finest gentlemen of his time. Tall, slender, erect, with handsome features and a princely bear-

[1] King's *Works*, II, 46.   [2] Henry, *Henry*, II, 515.   [3] Beveridge, II, 157.
[4] King's *Works*, II, 48; Beveridge, II, 158.
[5] Hamilton's *Works*, x, 163; King's *Works*, II, 47.
[6] King's *Works* (to Hamilton), II, 46.

ing, he was a superb figure of a man. His manners were those of the natural aristocrat; he was courteous, dignified, and charming. A perfect self-control was reflected in the repose of his features and the tone of his voice. Though of ardent temper, he kept a tight rein upon it, and he became a master of persuasion and conciliation. A man of artistic temperament, with a touch of architectural genius, he planned his own houses, all imposing, and his town house in Charleston was the first to have self-supporting stairs four stories high. His library was one of the most extensive in the country. While lacking luster, there was a charm in his personality and a solidity in his character that appealed to men of conservative disposition. Born of wealthy parents, he had been educated in England, at Westminster, Oxford, and the Temple, and he had attended the fencing and riding school of Angelo in London. He had been trained as one destined to command. Through his English experiences he passed without yielding one jot of his robust Americanism, and he fought in the Revolution and was once left wounded on the field of battle.

As Governor of South Carolina, he had served with distinction; as Minister to England, he had stubbornly maintained positions that Jay was to yield; and as Minister to Spain he had electrified the country with a signal triumph. Matching wits with the celebrated Godoy, he had secured a treaty establishing our southern limits from the Atlantic to the Mississippi, making the river our western boundary, and throwing it open to our navigation with an outlet to the Gulf and the privileges of the port of New Orleans. It was this achievement, hailed with enthusiasm in sections where the Federalists were weak, that led to his selection by Hamilton and King.

XII

The campaign of 1796 was one of scurrility, albeit both Jefferson and Adams, favored by the rank and file of the Federalist Party, comported themselves becomingly. The party press teemed with silly attacks and personalities. Adams was a monarchist, an aristocrat, a panter after titles, an enemy of the masses, the defender of the red-coated assassins of the Boston massacre; and Jefferson was a French tool, a friend of anarchy, the inciter of the Whiskey Insurrection, a foe to public credit, an atheist, an enemy of the Constitution,[1] an incompetent in office, and a plagiarist who had stolen his essay on weights and measures from a pamphlet with which Noah Webster was familiar.[2] Worse still: Adet, the French Minister, 'better supplied with money than Faucet,' was distributing it liberally in an effort to elect Jefferson, and had sent agents into the western country in his behalf. Had not Gallatin been seen 'in frequent conferences with Adet?'[3] A grave disappointment, this Adet who had such a 'handsome wife' and had seemed 'mild tempered, well educated and no Jacobin.'[4] Then came Adet's letter to Pickering reviewing the complaints of France against the American Government, and mentioning Jefferson pleasantly in connection with his official acts — and the Federalists had an issue. France was trying to dictate a President to America. Her Minister was electioneering. Fenno and Noah Webster were hysterical, Hamilton was pleased, Pickering, the new Secretary of State, was frothing so furiously as to disgust the Federalist leader in New York.[5] Madison was disgusted too,[6] and the notorious Judge Chase was demanding the jailing of editors who had dared publish the Adet letter which had been given to the press.[7] What though Bache did point out that the letter was written on instructions from Paris given before the announcement of Washington's retirement — it was a campaign screed![8] Soon it was the paramount issue, and the 'Aurora,' accepting it, was urging Fenno to spare some of his indignation for 'the scourging of an American at a British gangway as Captain Jessup was scourged,' and the shooting of a brother of a member of Congress trying to escape from a British press gang.[9] Meanwhile, strange things were happening behind the screen in Federalist circles.

XIII

Hamilton was planning a repetition of the scheme he engineered in 1789, to bring Adams in second, with Pinckney first.

[1] *Gazette of the United States*, November 3, 1796.   [2] *Aurora*, September 1, 1796.
[3] Gibbs, I, 332; (Wolcott to his father), I, 350-52.
[4] *Ibid*. (Wolcott to his wife), I, 209.
[5] Hamilton's *Works* (to Washington), x, 198-200; 200-01.
[6] Madison's *Writings* (to Jefferson), II, 103-05.   [7] Steiner, *McHenry*, 203.
[8] *Aurora*, November 24, 1796.   [9] *Ibid*., December 27, 1796.

He had never cared for the downright Puritan of Quincy, and the latter had never forgiven him the reduction of the Adams vote far below that of Washington in the first election. During the first Administration, Adams's vote was indispensable to Hamilton's policies on several occasions, and it had never failed. Thus there was no opposition to his reëlection. But the Presidency — that was different. It was evident that Adams was not a man to be led around by the nose by any man or clique, and Hamilton had never been a god of his idolatry. Thus, during the summer and autumn of '96, Hamilton was busy with a subterranean plan to substitute Pinckney for Adams in the Presidency by arranging for Federalist electors, scattered over the country, to vote to a man for Pinckney, while throwing a few Adams votes away on other men. As the high man was elected President and the second Vice-President, he expected to carry his point by management.

It does not appear, however, that all his followers were in on the secret. His ever-faithful servitor, Oliver Wolcott's father, either knew nothing of it or disapproved, for he feared that the juggling would result in the election of Jefferson, to the Vice-Presidency at least.[1] In the event of his election to the Presidency, Wolcott hoped 'the northern States would separate from the southern.'[2] As fate would have it, the suspicious Adams anticipated some such attempt to trick him, and his friends decided quietly to offset any possible Adams losses by dropping a few Pinckney votes to a third party. The result was a Jeffersonian sweep in the West and South, with the exception of Maryland, where Adams had a majority of three. Of the thirty-nine New England votes, Pinckney received but twenty-two, while all went to Adams. Such was the result of Hamilton's strategy. Adams was elected with 71 votes, and Jefferson, with three votes less, had eight more than Pinckney.

Thus the hated leader of the Democrats became Vice-President. Then, too late, the Hamiltonians realized their mistake. Wolcott groaned that Jefferson in the Vice-Presidency 'would be more dangerous than as President.'[3] His very willingness to accept the position was 'sufficient proof of some defect of character.' Chauncey Goodrich was in accord. 'We must expect him to be the nu-

[1] Gibbs, II, 386–88. [2] Ibid., I, 408–09. [3] Ibid., I, 400–03.

cleus of a faction,' he wrote, 'and if it will give him some greater advantage for mischief, it draws him from his covert.'[1] Ames dreaded his election as 'a formidable evil.'[2] Hamilton buried his chagrin in a cynicism. 'Our Jacobins say they are pleased that the Lion and Lamb are to lie down together,' he wrote King. 'Mr. Adams's personal friends talk a little the same way. . . . Skeptics like me quietly look forward to the event, willing to hope but not prepared to believe. If Mr. Adams has vanity 'tis plain a plot has been laid to take hold of it.'[3] These hints at the possible seduction of Adams were not without some justification.

Madison had urged Jefferson to accept the Vice-Presidency on the ground that 'your neighborhood to Adams may have a valuable effect on his counsels. . . . It is certain that his censures of our paper system, and the intrigues at New York for setting Pinckney above him have fixed an enmity with the British faction.'[4] Before receiving this letter, the incomparable strategist at Monticello had written Madison that in the event of a tie he should 'solicit on my behalf that Mr. Adams may be preferred.'[5] Could he, by any chance, have expected this admonition to reach Adams in any way? A few days later, we find him writing directly to Adams expressing regret that they had been put in opposition to one another. It seemed, he said, that Adams had been chosen. Of course he might be 'cheated' by 'a trick worthy of the subtilty of your arch-friend of New York who has been able to make of your real friends tools to defeat their and your best wishes.' Personally, he asked no happier lot than to be left 'with the society of neighbors, friends, and fellow-laborers of the earth' rather than with 'spies and sycophants.'[6] Four days later, we find him writing Madison of his willingness to serve under Adams. 'He is perhaps the only sure barrier against Hamilton's getting in.'[7] Other letters probably phrased for Adams's eye went out from Monticello, referring to their 'ancient friendship.' But he wanted no place in the counsels of the Administration — and that was significant enough.[8]

Meanwhile, the Jefferson letter to Adams, sent to Madison to be delivered or withheld according to his judgment, was put aside.

[1] Gibbs, I, 411–13.   [2] Ames (to Dwight), I, 208.
[3] King's *Works*, II, 148.   [4] Madison's *Writings*, II, 108.
[5] Jefferson's *Works*, IX, 352–55.   [6] *Ibid.*, 355–57.
[7] *Ibid.*, 355–57.   [8] *Ibid.*, 367–69.

There was a 'general air' in the letter indicative of the difficulty under which it was written. Adams might resent the reference to Hamilton. Again he might interpret Jefferson's expressed preference for the simple life as a reflection on his own ambition. 'You know the temper of Mr. Adams better than I do,' wrote Madison, 'but I have always conceived it to be a very ticklish one.' The Jeffersonian press had begun to speak in kindly tones of Adams to·the disgust of the Federalists.

Then, one bitter cold day, the family carriage appeared at the door of Monticello, and the master carefully supervised the packing of the bones of a mastodon which he had recently acquired and wished to present to the Philadelphia Philosophical Society, of which he had been elected president. Thus he reached the capital on March 2d, to be received, against his expressed wishes, with gun-fire and a procession flying a flag inscribed: 'Jefferson, Friend of the People.' He went at once to Francis Tavern to pay his respects to Adams.

Thus the new Administration began, Bache sending a brutal parting shot at the old — an insult to Washington.[1] But the star of Hamilton had not set, for Adams had foolishly retained the Washington Cabinet, hand-picked by his 'arch-friend of New York,' and the congressional leaders were still under the magic spell of the old Federalist chief. That was the cloud on the horizon, small that day, but destined to grow bigger and blacker until the storm broke, leaving much wreckage behind.

[1] *Aurora*, March 6, 1797.

CHAPTER XIV
AN INCONGRUOUS PORTRAIT GALLERY

I

IT is a pity that in the days of the Adams Administration it was not the fashion to paint group portraits of the President and his Cabinet. Had it been the custom, a purely commercial artist might have left us a conventional picture of no special interest; but had the task fallen to a great artist of intuitive penetration, capable of seizing upon the salient characteristics and the soul of his subjects, the result would have been a fascinating study in incongruities and clashing spirits. The suspicion on the round, smug face of Adams; the domineering arrogance on the cold Puritan countenance of Pickering; the suave and smiling treachery in the eyes of Wolcott; and the effeminate softness and weakness in the physiognomy of McHenry would have delighted a gallery through the generations.

Ali Baba among his Forty Thieves is no more deserving of sympathy than John Adams shut up within the seclusion of his Cabinet room with his official family of secret enemies. No other President has ever been so environed with a secret hostility; none other so shamelessly betrayed by treachery. The men on whose advice he was to rely were not even of his own choosing. He inherited them — that was his misfortune; but he meekly accepted them — and that was his weakness. Where Washington had begun with at least two advisers of transcendent ability, he was to undertake his task with the assistance of an official family that exceeded mediocrity only in the field of treachery and mendacity. Not only were they to disregard his wishes — they were to conspire against him. Not only were they to ignore his leadership — they were to take orders from a private citizen who was his political rival·and personal foe. Years later, the relative of one was solemnly to justify their disloyalty with the remarkable statement that, having been appointed by his predecessor, 'they owed him nothing'; and to defend their retention of place despite their indisposition to serve him honestly with the astounding assertion that 'the interest of their party and the wishes of their friends prevented them.'[1]

We are interested in the personalities of these men primarily because it was not only not 'in the interest of their party' for them to remain, but ultimately destructive. The taxes, the standing army, the Alien and Sedition Laws would have weakened, and might have destroyed, Federalism; the party treachery within the Cabinet would have wrought its ruin without them.

II

John Adams was a very great man and a pure patriot, with many fatal temperamental weaknesses. Like Dr. Samuel Johnson, whom he strongly suggests, he would have thrived in an atmosphere of admiration. Had he been surrounded by incense-throwers and idolatrous disciples applauding his every utterance, forgiving his bursts of temper and smiling at the pinching of their ears and the kicking of their shins, with a worshiping Boswell jotting down his conversations, he would have been supremely happy and probably at his best. Like the genius who spread his tail feathers so proudly at Streatham, he was vain, domineering, ponderous, at times tempestuous in his bursts of passion, disdainful of finesse, given to intemperate expressions, learned, prejudiced, often selfish — and a little fat. But he had played a noble part in the Revolutionary struggle, a dignified rôle in the diplomacy of the Old World, and he was entitled to something better than he received.

There was nothing thrilling in the appearance of Adams to captivate the crowd. Below the medium height and rather full, he looked the stolidity of the English country gentleman [2] and invited the sobriquet of the sharp-tongued Izard of 'His Rotundity.'[3] His fat round face would have been less offensively smug had it not been so cold,[4] and his dignity more impressive had it been less aggressive. The top of his head was bald as a billiard ball, and, while he carefully powdered the remnant of his hair, nothing could have made this solid gentleman of the Quincy farm the glass of fashion. Unlike many of the public figures of the time, he affected no foppery, and, while he dressed with conventional propriety, his

---

[1] Gibbs, II, 213.   [2] Twining, 38.   [3] Maclay, 30.   [4] Twining, 37.

garb was so little a part of himself that most of the chroniclers of his time ignore it. We know that he appeared one day for dinner at Mrs. Francis's boarding-house in a drab-colored coat [1] and at his inauguration in 'a full suit of pearl-colored broadcloth.' [2] Even the saturnine Maclay, who poked fun at all his peculiarities of appearance, could find nothing objectionable but the sword he affected when he first presided over the Senate.[3]

Of his manner in company we must reach a conclusion from a composite of contradictions. Thanks to the Adams spirit of self-criticism, we have a confession of the manners of his youth when he was prone to make a display of his intellectual wares, and to prove his parts with sneering sarcasms about his elders.[4] Years later, an English tourist was impressed with his 'somewhat cold and reserved manner' and with 'the modesty of his demeanor.' [5] In neither picture do we have an attractive personality, and are safe in assuming that it was not pleasing, without drawing on the honest prejudices of Maclay. On the first attempt of the latter to establish social relations, he found Adams 'not well furnished with small talk,' and he was particularly struck with his 'very silly kind of laugh.' [6] This interested the sour democrat from the Pennsylvania frontier, and, critically observing his manner of presiding over the Senate, he complained that 'instead of that sedate easy air I would have him possess, he will look on one side, then on the other, then down on the knees of his breeches, then dimple his visage with the most silly kind of half smile.' [7] This smile was evidently aggravating to the Senator's gout, for we hear of it again at a dinner at Washington's where he was clearly angered when he caught the great man 'ever and anon mantling his visage with the most unmeaning simper that ever mantled the face of folly.' [8] 'Bonny Johnny Adams,' snorts the Senator, more than once.[9] Thus, painfully self-conscious, and without capacity for the appealing levity of banter, he was temperamentally incapable of that personal approach that makes for the intimacy of friendship. In the parlance of the day, he was a 'poor mixer,' and this had the same effect on political fortunes then as now.

This alone would have made men indifferent, but he had a

[1] Twining, 37.   [2] *Familiar Letters*, 116.   [3] Maclay, 44.   [4] *Diary*, II, 25.
[5] Twining, 37.   [6] Maclay, 14.   [7] *Ibid.*, 30.   [8] *Ibid.*, 206.   [9] *Ibid.*, 145, 206.

vanity that drove them away. If we are to believe the common comment of friend and foe, he was inordinately vain. With that strange, penetrating insight into his own character, he appreciated this weakness in his youth, and no doubt sought to uproot a vice that was in the very fiber of his being. In the musings of his diary we have the frank admission: 'Good treatment makes me think I am admired, beloved, and my own vanity will be indulged in me; so I dismiss my guard and grow weak, silly, vain, conceited, ostentatious.' [1] On another page he promises himself 'never to show my own importance or superiority.' [2] But the weakness increased with age. 'I always considered Mr. Adams a man of great vanity,' wrote the father of one of his Cabinet to his son two weeks after the inauguration.[3] This quality was so predominant that both friend and foe sought to turn it to advantage. Hamilton, in his ill-advised attack, was able to refer to 'the unfortunate foibles of vanity without bounds,' without fear of contradiction.[4] After his election to the Vice-Presidency, this vanity became 'ridiculous.' [5] Strangely enough, there is some evidence that this very weakness was responsible in part for his election to that post. Referring to the part played in the event by Dr. Rush and himself, Maclay wrote that 'we knew his vanity and hoped by laying hold of it to render him useful among the New England members in our schemes of bringing Congress to Pennsylvania.' [6] But stranger still — and this is something to be kept in mind throughout — it was reserved for his greatest political opponent to predict to one of his lieutenants that, while Adams was 'vain' and 'irritable,' 'he is so amiable that I pronounce you will love him.' [7] The general effect, however, was far different from love. It unquestionably played into the hands of his enemies and neutralized the effect of both his ability and militant patriotism.

III

Because of his inordinate vanity, he was susceptible to flattery, and they who knew him best approached him accordingly. We have an illustration of it at the time of the decision to dismiss

---

[1] *Diary*, II, 57.   [2] *Ibid.*, 25.   [3] Gibbs, I, 455–57; Wolcott, Sr.
[4] Hamilton's *Works*, VII, 734.   [5] Morse, 242.   [6] Maclay, 86.
[7] Jefferson's *Works* (to Madison), VI, 63–67.

Genêt. There was some question as to the attitude of Adams, and, knowing of his secret jealousy of Washington, George Cabot, to whom was assigned the task of guiding him favorably, called upon him one morning at an early hour.

'Mr. Adams, this French Minister's conduct seems to me to be the most objectionable,' ventured Cabot casually.

'Objectionable? It is audacious, sir,' stormed Adams.

'I think if you were President you would not permit him to perform his office very long,' said the cunning Cabot.

'Not an hour, sir. I would dismiss him immediately.'

'I wish you would allow me to say to the President that such are your views,' said Cabot.

'Certainly, sir; I will say so to the President myself when I see him.' [1]

Thus the danger of Adams's opposition was cleverly removed by conveying the impression that the suggestion of a dismissal had come from him. So thoroughly were his enemies imbued with the idea that he could be led by subtle flattery that the apologists for the traitors in his Cabinet, taking note of his later harmonious relations with Marshall, explained that these were due to the genius of the latter in insinuating his own ideas into Adams's head. However that may be, there was one thing that flattery could not do — it could not coax him from a principle or from the performance of a patriotic duty. When the royal Attorney-General of Massachusetts undertook to flatter him into the service of the King in the fight against the people eight years before the Declaration of Independence, he failed utterly.

The violence of his temper made him difficult even to his friends, and he had but few. He had a genius for embroilment, and dwelt perpetually on a battle-field, sometimes real, often imaginary, but always genuine to him. Liancourt, calling upon him at Quincy and finding his conversation 'extremely agreeable,' noted, however, that it was 'tinged with a sort of sarcasm.' [2] Madison, we have seen, referred to his 'ticklish' temper.[3] If a political opponent could give a moderate description of his weakness, and a Frenchman one so mild, the members of his Cabinet felt no compulsion for restraint. Franklin had done him a grave

---

[1] Lodge, *Cabot*, 65.   [2] Liancourt, II, 124.   [3] Madison's *Writings* (to Jefferson), II, 111.

disservice in a brief but altogether friendly characterization carrying the suggestion that he sometimes appeared mad. This was a hint on which his enemies were to play as long as he lived. They took Franklin literally and called Adams 'crazy.' 'What but insanity' could have led him to this or that? asks the biographer of Wolcott.[1] 'No sane mind could have imagined such a thought,' he says again.[2] 'A weak and intemperate mind,' writes one of his Cabinet to another.[3] Even Jefferson, who was more considerate of him than others, thought his French war message 'crazy.' But it was reserved for McHenry to sum up his enemies' case against him. 'Whether he is spiteful, playful, witty, kind, cold, drunk, sober, angry, easy, stiff, jealous, cautious, confident, close, open, it is almost always in the wrong place or to the wrong person.' [4] All of which means that he was super-sensitive, irritable, the victim of an ungovernable temper which drove him into spluttering rages on ridiculously slight provocations. Men shrank from conferences with him on subjects involving a difference of opinion. Then he could be as insulting as Dr. Johnson without the advantage of having obsequious idolators on whom to vent his rage. What a joy it would have been to have pitted these two men against each other on the question of colonial rights! What a picture Boswell could have made of the encounter!

Adams was difficult in conference, too, because of his suspicious disposition. He could never quite persuade himself of the sincerity of his conferee, and he carried a chip upon his shoulder. This suspicion of his fellows had been a curse of his youth; it followed him to the grave. He felt himself surrounded by envy, hatred, malice, and was inclined to suspect that a good-natured smile was in derision. In youth he fancied that his neighbors were anxious to retard his progress. He was miserable in London, where his reception, while cool, was not half so bad as he imagined. The British Minister in Paris could not disabuse him of the notion that in London he would be looked upon 'with evil eyes.' [5] His worst fears were realized in 'the awkward timidity in general' and the 'conscious guilt' and shame in the countenances of the people.[6] This feeling that he was in the midst of enemies made him more

---

[1] Gibbs, I, 468. [2] *Ibid.*, II, 215. [3] *Ibid.* (McHenry to Wolcott), 395.
[4] Steiner, 477. [5] *Diary*, III, 392. [6] *Ibid.*, III, 393.

than ever tenacious of his rights. He knew the privileges and
civilities to which his position entitled him, and keenly felt his
failure to receive them. It was something he was never to forgive.
The begrudging or withholding of a right was always, to him, an
affront instantly to be met with a stormy challenge. 'I am not
of Cæsar's mind,' he wrote, soon after becoming Vice-President.
'The second place in Rome is high enough for me, although I have
a spirit that will not give up its right or relinquish its place.' [1]
This sense of his deserts, because of ability and services, goes far
to explain his relations with Washington and Hamilton.

The evidence is abundant that he resented the fame and popularity of Washington. Like Pickering, he did not share the enthusiasm over the great man's military genius. During the war
he had sometimes found fault with his military tactics.[2] Later,
when he became the second official of the Republic, he secretly
resented the distance that separated him from the chief. He had
played the patriot's rôle long before Washington had shown a
marked interest in the quarrel of the colonies; had been one of the
makers of the Revolution; had served with distinction in diplomacy; and, unlike Washington, had studied politics and statecraft
all his life. Why should he, with such a record, be so completely
overshadowed, and why relegated to the end that upstarts like
Hamilton — 'the bastard brat of a Scotch pedlar' — might be
pushed to the front? This, the reasoning of his jealousy which was
to destroy his perspective and lead him into trouble.

IV

This was due in some measure to the distance between reality
and the dream world in which he lived. As he grew older, he became more and more impressed with the pomp of power. The son
of a Yankee shoemaker was covetous of the ribbons of distinction.
The masses receded to a respectful distance. In the forefront
were the gods, and he among them; and among these he claimed
a right to the front rank. Ceremony became important. Titles
were safeguards of organized society. An order of nobility sprang
up in his imagination. 'You and I,' he wrote Sam Adams, 'have
seen four noble families rise up in Boston — the Crafts, Gores,

[1] Adams, *Works* (to James Lovell), VIII, 493–94.   [2] *Autobiography*, II, 438.

Dawes, and Austins. These are really a nobility in our town, as the Howards, Somersets, Berties in England.' His feet lost contact with the earth — he soared. 'Let us do justice to the people and to the nobles; for nobles there are, as I have proved, in Boston as well as in Madrid.' [1] Many things, he thought, can make for nobility — even matrimony. 'Would Washington have been Commander of the Revolutionary army or President . . . if he had not married the rich widow of Mr. Custis? Would Jefferson have been President . . . if he had not married the daughter of Mr. Wales?' Thus he challenged John Taylor of Caroline. [2]

Infatuated with such views, he was naturally in harmony with his party in its contempt for democracy. [3] 'If our government does well I shall be more surprised than I ever was in my life,' he said one day, standing by the stove in the Senate Chamber before the gavel had fallen. Carroll ventured the opinion that it was strong enough. 'If it is, I know not whence it is to arise,' Adams replied. 'It cannot have energy. It has neither rewards nor punishments.' [4] This distrust of democracy was ingrained. We find it outcropping in his early life, as toward the end. When he was summoned to go over the reply of the Massachusetts Legislature to the pretensions of Hutchinson, the royal Governor, in 1773, he found 'the draught of a report [5] was full of very popular talk and of those democratical principles that have done so much mischief to this country.' [6] Even Paine's 'Common Sense,' which was tonic to the Revolution, was spoiled for him because 'his plan was so democratical.' [7] Haunting the bookstalls in London he thought 'the newspapers, the magazines, the reviews, the daily pamphlets were all in the hands of hirelings,' and was convinced that the men who 'preached about . . . liberty, equality, fraternity, and the rights of man' could be hired 'for a guinea a day.' [8] It was after this that he wrote the 'Discourses of Davilla' — an onslaught on democracy. And fourteen years after his retirement he wrote from his library at Quincy to John Taylor: 'Remember, democracy never lasts long. It soon wastes, exhausts, and murders itself. There never was a democracy that did not commit suicide.' [9] This distrust and dis-

[1] Adams, *Works*, IV, 420.   [2] *Ibid.*, VI, 462.   [3] Morse, 247.
[4] Maclay, May 28, 1789.   [5] Written by Samuel Adams.
[6] *Autobiography*, II, 310.   [7] *Ibid.*, 508.   [8] Adams, *Adams*, I, 404.
[9] Adams, *Works*, VI, 484.

taste for the masses weakened him as much with the people as his temperamental defects with his party associates. I have dwelt on these weaknesses because they explain the tragedy of his failure. There were other qualities that entitled him to a happier fate.

V

Chief among these were the fervor and the disinterestedness of his love of country. Had he died the day after the signing of the Declaration, he would have been assured a permanent place in history. No man played a more heroic part in the fight for independence. The struggling young lawyer who refused a position under the Crown that he might not be embarrassed in supporting his countrymen in their inevitable struggle;[1] who, awakened by the sinister drum-beats of the red coats every morning, 'solemnly determined at all events to adhere to [his] principles in favor of [his] country';[2] who defended Hancock in the courts on the charge of smuggling with stubborn tenacity until the case 'was suspended at last only by the battle of Lexington';[3] who, when the crisis came, prepared to immolate himself and family upon the altar of liberty;[4] and who had the audacity to base an argument against the Stamp Act on the principles of the Revolution itself, and, standing four square against more petitions to the King, won the lasting gratitude and admiration of Jefferson when, as 'the Colossus of the Debate,'[5] he bore the brunt of the battle for the Declaration — that man could well hold his head high in the presence of Washington himself. 'Politics,' he wrote Warren, 'are an ordeal path among red-hot plough shares. Who then would be a politician for the pleasure of running about barefooted among them. Yet some one must.'[6] And again: 'At such times as this there are many dangerous things to be done which nobody else will do, and therefore I cannot help attempting them.'[7] Nor was he blind to his fate in the event of the failure of his cause. 'I go mourning in my heart all day long,' he wrote his wife in dark days, 'though I say nothing. I am melancholy for the public and anxious for my family. . . . For God's sake make your children hardy, active and industrious.'[8] This intense Americanism did not moderate with

---

[1] *Autobiography*, II, 210.   [2] *Ibid.*, 214.   [3] *Ibid.*, 215.   [4] *Ibid.*, 232, 311.
[5] Jefferson's tribute.   [6] Morse, 59.   [7] *Ibid.*, 60.   [8] *Ibid.*, 61.

time. As a politician he was all too often open to censure; as a
patriot he was above reproach. Jefferson never doubted his ab-
sorption in his country; and Hamilton, temperamentally unable
to get along with him, wrote him down as 'honest, firm, faithful,
and independent — a sincere lover of his country.'[1] Because he
had more enemies than friends, and more detractors than admirers, one might conclude from the opinions of his contemporaries that he had but mediocre ability. There is no question as to
the fallibility of his judgment where his prejudices were enlisted
and the characters of men were involved. Again we find Jefferson
more friendly than the Federalists. 'A bad calculator of the force
and probable effect of the motives which govern men,' he wrote;
and then added, 'This is all the ill that can possibly be said of him;
he is profound in his views and accurate in his judgment except
where knowledge of the world is necessary to form a judgment.'[2]
Hamilton thought him 'a man of an imagination sublimated and
eccentric,' and was not impressed with his intellectual endow-
ments.[3] The father of Wolcott thought him 'of a very moderate
share of prudence, and of far less real abilities than he believes
he possesses.'[4] And McHenry, having been expelled from the
Cabinet for his disloyalty, declared 'the mind of Mr. Adams like
the last glimmerings of a lamp, feeble, wavering and unsteady,
with occasionally a strong flash of light, his genius little, and that
too insufficient to irradiate his judgment.'[5] The Adams who
emerges from these opinions is a man of ability often reduced to
impotency by the lack of judgment. This is, no doubt, the whole
truth about his intellect. The sneers from men who could not
forgive him for the wrong they had done him, and from others
who could not control him, cannot stand in the light of what he
did, and said, and wrote.

As a writer, he suffers in comparison with Hamilton and Madison, and his more ambitious productions, like the 'Discourses of
Davilla,' while showing much erudition and some ingenuity, are
heavy and pompous. But in the earlier days when he was writing
shorter papers for the press, he did better. Whether he could
write or not, he loved to do it. The author of the earlier period

---

[1] Hamilton's *Works* (to John Steele), v, 25.   [2] Jefferson's *Works* (to Madison), vi, 63–71.
[3] Hamilton's *Works*, vii, 314.   [4] Gibbs, i, 475–77.   [5] Steiner, 569.

was more interesting and attractive than that of later times.

However much the critics may quarrel over his capacity to write, the evidence is conclusive as to his ability to speak. As an orator he was the Patrick Henry of New England. His argument against the Writs of Assistance in 1761 fired the heart of Otis and swept him into the ranks of the active patriots. Jefferson bears testimony to the power of his eloquence in the fight for the Declaration. Given a cause that appealed to his heart and imagination, he never failed to find himself by losing himself in the fervor of the fight.

Nor can there be any question of his courage. It required temerity to step forth from the patriots' ranks to face the representative of the Crown with the most audacious denials of his pretensions; courage, too, to lead the fight against further attempts at conciliation with the King. But the most courageous act of his career was his defense in court of Captain Preston, the British officer charged with murder in the Boston massacre. Not only physical courage was here demanded, for he invited personal attack, but moral courage at its highest. He was dependent for clientage on the Boston public and the victims of the massacre were Bostonians. He was an American, and he was standing between a hated redcoat and an American revenge. He gambled with his career, for he armed his enemies with ammunition, and he was charged with selling his country for an enormous fee. The fact that he received but eighteen guineas would have been the answer, but he maintained a dignified silence. There is nothing finer or more courageous in the records of a public man.[1] This courage was to stand him in good stead when he defied his party for his country in the French negotiations, and played for the verdict of history.

This courage could only have sprung from the consciousness of an honest intent — and his honesty, personal or political, has never been questioned. Sedgwick recommended him to Hamilton for the Vice-Presidency as 'a man of unconquerable intrepidity and of incorruptible integrity,' and Hamilton was to find to his chagrin that the compliment was not given in a Pickwickian sense.[2] And yet he was not a Puritan of the intolerant sort. In

[1] *Autobiography*, ii, 230–32.   [2] Adams, *Adams*, i, 446.

early life he was given to the reading of sermons and at one time confessed to an inclination to the ministry — but it did not last long. In early manhood, we find him 'moralizing in his diary against card-playing, but not on moral grounds. 'It gratifies none of the senses . . . ; it can entertain the mind only by hushing its clamors.' [1] Even the scurrility of his times spared him the charge of immorality. 'No virgin or matron ever had cause to blush at sight of me,' he wrote in his 'Autobiography.' [2] And while Franklin and Morris appear to have taken advantage of the moral laxity of Paris, we are quite sure that Adams, packed in tight among fashionable ladies watching the Queen eat soup, never gave a flirtatious glance, and are more than half persuaded that his declination to join Madame du Barry in her garden was due to her none too spotless reputation. But if he was not given to women or to song, it appears that he consumed his full share of wine. We have his own story of the fashionable dinners in the Philadelphia of the Continental Congress, when he would sit at the table from three until nine 'drinking Madeira, claret and burgundy.' [3] We get a glimpse of him in a New York Club before the Revolution with 'punch, wine, pipes and tobacco.' [4] And on another occasion he records with boastful pride that he 'drank Madeira at a great rate and found no inconvenience in it.' [5] Even so, we may be sure that he seldom drank to excess.

Such the man who sat facing the Cabinet he did not choose — stubborn, suspicious, vain, jealous, courageous, honest, irascible, tempestuous, patriotic, and rising above its members in ability and public service as a mountain above the pebbles at its base.

VI

No student of physiognomy, familiar with the character of Adams, could have glanced at the stern, cold Puritan face of Timothy Pickering, his Secretary of State, without a premonition of certain estrangement. The long, thin, super-serious features were as uncongenial and unresponsive as though carved from granite. The thin, silvery locks and the spectacles combined to create an unpleasant impression of asceticism; and the cold eyes that peered through the glasses spoke of the narrow, uncompromis-

[1] *Diary*, ii, 62.　[2] Vol. ii, 145.　[3] Morse, 79.　[4] *Diary*, ii, 179.　[5] *Ibid.*, 381.

ing mind of a follower of Cromwell. There, too, he could read the insatiable ambition, the audacious courage, the relentless will of the Roman conqueror. Seldom did that face soften with a smile; for he had no sense of humor. His portrait, by Stuart, as a frontispiece to a volume of old New England blue laws would have symbolized the spirit of the book. No Indian stoic ever presented a countenance less revealing in repose, or more stone-like in composure. The resemblance to the Roundhead fanatic was accentuated in the extreme simplicity, the Quaker-like plainness of his garb.

Here was clearly a man to whom joyous frivolity was indecent dissipation; with whom the scrutiny of suspicion was a duty; and to whom duties were the sum total of life. But beneath the repellently cold, metallic exterior there were volcanic fires of passion, and when he emerged from the deadly calm of composure it was to storm. It was not in his nature to confer, but to lay down the law. So lacking was he in a sense of humor that he honestly persuaded himself that he always stood at Armageddon and battled for the Lord. Even when he was moved to treachery by an ambition wholly incongruous to his capacity, he really felt that he was detached from all personal considerations and was fighting for the abstract principle of right.[1] Never once in his long life, even when he was a cheap conspirator planning the destruction of the Union, did he think himself in the wrong. Never once in his voluminous correspondence does he hint at a possible mistake. He was, in his political views and his personal relations, impeccably pure — and he admitted it. Not only did he admit it — he impassionedly proclaimed it, and this alone made him an impossible adviser for John Adams. He was the smug, self-righteous type that would remake the world in its own image. They who disagreed with him were hounds of the devil to be thrown without pity into the uttermost darkness. And he was sincere in it all. He was fond of hymns and psalms, in church devout, at prayer most fervent, and he read the Bible habitually without discovering the passage about the throwing of stones.[2]

This temperament made him difficult in even ordinary conversation. He had an excellent command of language, but he preferred the harsher words. There was no twilight zone for him. Things

---

[1] Lodge, *Studies in History*, 201.   [2] Pickering, IV, 386, 391.

were white or black. He was violent in his opinions and violent in the gesticulation with which he tried to force them on his hearers. So little could he see himself as others saw him that, when he once exclaimed, 'I abhor gesticulation,' with a powerful sweep of his muscular arms, he could not understand the smile of his auditor.[1] But for this intemperance, all too much like that of Adams to make harmony possible, he would have been a great conversationalist. He used words with accuracy, was interesting in narrative, and had read widely and wisely; but too frequently to converse with Pickering was to quarrel. This unhappy quality, along with his poverty, explains why he did not figure in the social life of the Federalist capital. His tactlessness and bluntness, which he confused with honesty, were intolerable. In a letter to a friend who had given an acquaintance a note of introduction, he wrote that he should 'not put myself to the expense nor my family to the trouble of a splendid exhibition at table.' [2] It must have caused some mirth in the home of the elegant Binghams to read his reply to an invitation to dinner: 'Mrs. Pickering and I are constrained to forego many pleasures of society, because we cannot persuade ourselves to enter on a career of expenses, which, being far beyond our income, would lead to ruin. For this reason, Mrs. Pickering chooses to dine abroad only at Mrs. Washington's, as a consequence of my official station; and this as seldom as decency will permit. . . . But Mrs. Pickering is aware that as a public man I cannot seclude myself . . . and therefore often urges, on my part singly, an intercourse which is useful as well as agreeable. I shall, then, with pleasure, dine with you occasionally, but without promising to reciprocate all your civilities.' [3]

Here we have one of several traits that make him stand out among the other Federalist leaders as an exotic. He was poor, but not so poor as the letter indicates; nor was he so completely shut off from society, despite his frugality. If he gave no fashionable entertainments, his was a home of hospitality, and he who promised no reciprocation for the entertainments of the Binghams was able to entertain at his board a future King of France.[4] But, unfashionable, and plain as a Yankee huckster, he found the

---

[1] Pickering, II, 156.　　[2] Ibid., III, 170.
[3] Ibid., III, 171.　　[4] Louis Philippe; Pickering, III, 284–85.

ways of fashion irksome and offensive. Writing his wife disgustedly of the enormous head-dresses of the Philadelphia ladies, he added: 'But you know, my dear, I have old-fashioned notions. Neither powder nor pomatum have touched my head these twelve months, not even to cover my baldness.' [1] And the 'extravagance of the prevailing fashions,' suggested by the introduction of 'the odious fashion of hoops' convinced him that many families would be ruined.[2] Verily such a creature would have been grotesquely out of place among his fellow Federalists in the gay drawing-rooms of Mrs. Bingham.

He differed from them, too, theoretically at least, on a more vital point. They were thorough aristocrats; he was instinctively a democrat — though he seemed to prefer it as an ideal rather than as a reality. Lodge recognizes this difference and explains that 'he had all the pride of the Puritan who gloried in belonging to the chosen people of God.' [3] We can well believe the assertion of his son and biographer that he liked the common people because among them he belonged. Then, too, he inherited a respect for them from his father who ardently espoused the cause of equal rights for all men, and was prone to apologize for the weaknesses of the poor, and to criticize people of wealth and power.[4] With this inheritance he was to enter the field of controversy at twenty-five in a newspaper battle with the Tories of Salem with a letter which might have been written by Jefferson. 'For whom was government instituted?' he wrote. 'Was it solely for the aggrandizement of the few, who, by some fortunate accident, have been bred in a manner which the world calls genteel? or to protect the lives, liberty and property of the body of the people? Is government supported by the better sort? On the contrary, has not every attack on the laws and constitution proceeded from that class? The very phrase, "friends of government" is invidious and carries with it an impudent insinuation that the whole body of the people, the pretended friends of government excepted, are enemies to government; the suggestion of which is as ridiculous as it is false.' [5]

The tall, gaunt figure in plain garb, seated in company with the fashionable Hamilton or Morris, was not more incongruous than

---

[1] Pickering, I, 215.   [2] *Ibid.*, 351.   [3] *Studies in History*, 219.
[4] Pickering, I, 5.   [5] *Ibid.*, I, 23–30.

the mind, capable even in youth of such heretical and 'demagogic' thoughts. Stranger still, this liking for the common herd never wholly left him. Thus his experiment in pioneering in the western wilderness — where democracy thrived best. A wholly admirable figure, this Pickering of the frontier, applying brain and brawn to the conquering of the woods, organizing civil government, battling at the peril of his life for law and order, kidnaped and carted away. His own story of this adventure is as thrilling as a dime novel.[1] Even then his faith in the people was not destroyed.

Thus Pickering finally entered public life — a 'friend of the people,' farmer, frontiersman, unsuccessful merchant. About him there was no glamour of success. He had been a failure. At Harvard he had made a fair record, and his meager career as a lawyer was unsuccessful. He had failed as a farmer, failed as a pioneer, failed as a Philadelphia merchant because unfit for commercial life. He had played a spinet and a violin and given lessons in sacred music at Salem and Marblehead, but that could scarcely be deemed success;[2] and in the army, where he was capable as a trainer of raw recruits, his courage, energy, and promptness might have taken him far but for the handicap of short-sightedness and glasses.[3] Thus, when he entered the public service at forty-six his career had been one of failure, and he was to get this new chance through importunate applications to a man he little respected — for he had a poor opinion of the ability of Washington. Here again he differed from other Federalists holding a similar opinion; he did not simulate admiration.[4] The naming of a child after Washington called for his sarcasm.[5] He was disgusted during the war when a rustic was heard to say, 'I suppose he [Washington] is the greatest man in the world.'[6] He criticized Washington as overcautious[7] and refused to hail him as a hero because he thought him lacking in 'eminent military talents.'[8] He thought the army suffered through his procrastinated decisions.[9] Serving on the committee at the close of the struggle to formulate the answer of the officers to the 'Farewell Orders to the Armies of the United States,' he referred sarcastically to the word 'Orders,' and wrote

[1] Pickering, ii, 381–90.   [2] Ibid., i, 14.   [3] Ibid., ii, 66.   [4] Lodge, Studies in History, 221.
[5] Pickering, ii, 71.   [6] Ibid., ii, 74.   [7] Ibid., 78.   [8] Ibid., 80.   [9] Ibid., 81–85.

his wife: 'Though it is rather modest, or in other words does not abound in panegyric, I think it (the reply) will be graciously received.' [1] To another he boasted that the reply was marked 'as the Italians do some strains of music — moderato.' [2]

But land poor, and a failure, he was quite willing to serve under the man he did not appreciate. From the organization of the government, he was an office-seeker, looking, not for a career, but for a job. There was no demand for his services — he urged them. His brother-in-law, a member of Congress, became his broker. He applied to Hamilton for an assistant secretaryship of the Treasury, to find it promised.[3] In August his broker wrote him of a prospective vacancy in the postmaster-generalship and suggested that he see Washington at once.[4] A month later, Pickering made application,[5] but his interview with the President only resulted in a temporary position as a negotiator with the Indian tribes. In May, 1791, he asked Washington for the Comptrollership of the Treasury, to be refused,[6] and it was not until August, after more than a year of persistent wire-pulling, that he was recognized with the then comparatively unimportant post of Postmaster-General, which was not at that time a Cabinet position.

Thus he came into close contact with Hamilton, entered into his plans, made himself useful, and slowly ascended, finally reaching the State Department with some misgivings, and only after many others had declined the place. He owed everything to Hamilton, nothing to Adams, and, as he sat in sphinx-like silence at the Cabinet table, it was to Hamilton, not to Adams, that he looked as chief.

VII

The same was true of Oliver Wolcott, Secretary of the Treasury, albeit these two men were, in most respects, the antitheses of each other. There was nothing of saturnity and brooding silence in Wolcott — he smiled. Both wore masks — one that of a stoic, the other that of a smiling epicurean. They resembled in a common capacity for uncommon treachery. In this, they both excelled. Both were professional feeders at the public crib and passionate panters after office.

[1] Pickering, I, 483–84.   [2] *Ibid.*, 487.   [3] *Ibid.*, II, 442 and 445.
[4] *Ibid.*, 451.   [5] *Ibid.*, 452.   [6] *Ibid.*, 488.

The handsome Wolcott had infinitely more finesse in the art of double-dealing. He had read his Machiavelli to better advantage. If he was to conspire with the enemies of the chief, he was to present an ever-smiling face to Adams in the conference room. He was too exquisite a conspirator to seem one. He had early learned the advantage of smiling through; and leaving Adams, with his face wreathed in friendly smiles, he could sit down to the writing of a letter to Hamilton with the same smile still on his face. Life was altogether lovely and interesting to this happy warrior who delivered his sword thrusts through curtains.

The son of an idol of Connecticut Federalists who was repeatedly elected to the governorship, Wolcott passed his boyhood in and near Litchfield, ministering to a frail constitution by tending cattle and working on the farm. He did not permit the war to interfere with his career at Yale, felt no sentimental call to Valley Forge, and found that the rattle of musketry need not interfere with his preparations for the Bar. Almost immediately on the conclusion of these preparations, he found a job as a clerk in the office of the Committee of Pay Table, and such was his industry and methodical efficiency that he rose in that line of the civil service to be Comptroller of Public Accounts before the formation of the National Government.

This opened a new and fairer vista for an efficient bureaucrat, and the moment the department of the Treasury was established he was 'induced by his friends' to offer himself for a position.[1] Even then, professional office-seekers merely yielded to the importunities of admirers. The congressional delegation for Connecticut pressed hard for an appointment, and he was offered the post of Auditor of the Treasury at fifteen hundred dollars a year. We can scarcely conceive that he hesitated, though it is of record that his sponsors urged him to accept, and that Hamilton expressed the hope that he would not refuse. He had hoped for the Comptrollership — but that might follow. The fact that Hamilton had favored him for the better place was promising.[2] Meanwhile, on the salary, he could 'live cheap and snug as you please.'[3] Thus he went upon the Federal payroll. Thus he came under the observation and supervision of the genius at the head of the Treasury,

---

[1] Gibbs, I, 18.   [2] Ibid., 21.   [3] Ibid., 20; Wadsworth to Wolcott.

Sir

It is with pleasure I am able
to inform you that you have been appointed
Auditor in the Department of the Treasury.
The Salary of this office is 1500 Dollars.
Your friend having expressed a doubt of
your acceptance, I cannot forbear saying
that I shall be happy to find the doubt
has been ill founded; as from the character
I have received of you, I am persuaded
you will be an acquisition to the Department.
I need scarcely add that your
presence here as soon as possible is essential
to the progress of business.

I am Sir

Your obedient Servant

Alexander Hamilton
Secretary of the Treasury.

New York Sept. 13. 1789

Oliver Wolcott Esqr

then the most powerful dispenser of patronage. Thus he was able to practice his ingratiating arts on one worth while. In little more than a year he was made Comptroller on the recommendation of Hamilton, and when that statesman retired to private life, it was he who lifted the faithful servitor into the Cabinet as Secretary of the Treasury. There Adams found him; there, unhappily for him, he let him remain.

It would be unjust to leave the impression that Wolcott was without merit. He was not brilliant, but he possessed an infinite capacity for taking pains. Even in college, where he failed to sparkle, he was a hard student with 'the strong reasoning faculties of the Wolcott family' a little neutralized by 'some eccentricities in reasoning.' [1] In the Treasury, in subordinate positions, he had shown good judgment, much practical sense, a comprehensive acquaintance with business and business needs, exceptional power of sustained application, no imagination, and a dog-like devotion to Hamilton. The latter found this combination of virtues had not only made his conduct good, 'but distinguished.' More, he had 'all the requisites which can be desired,' and these were 'moderation with firmness; liberality with exactness, indefatigable industry with an accurate and sound discernment, a thorough knowledge of business, and a remarkable spirit of order and arrangement.' [2] In brief, he was the perfect bureaucrat, the indispensable man Friday. If he brought no political strength to the Administration, he could, with dependability, do the drudgery and register the will of others who could.

If he was not a friend of the people, nor the electorate of him, he was the courtier and friend of the powerful, and thus his was one of the first careers created by the social lobby. If he did not cultivate the voters, he selected his friends with fine discrimination with the view of his own advancement. At Yale he cultivated Noah Webster and Uriah Tracy, a potent writer and a powerful politician; he early profited by the popularity and prestige of his father, and through his father's and his family's influential friends; and socially, he made himself the 'bonny boy' of the Hamiltonian circle, and smiled and joked himself into the affections of the

[1] Noah Webster's impression, Gibbs, II, 11.

[2] Gibbs, I, 65.

Bingham set. A beautiful and brilliant sister brought him the championship of the clever Chauncey Goodrich and his associates. A charming wife threw wide all the doors of the capital. While he was earning the grateful appreciation of Hamilton and the Essex Junto, this attractive wife was winning and deserving the tender affection of Mrs. Washington, with whom she was on terms of intimacy, and she was corresponding regularly with Nellie Custis.[1] When Washington left public life, his wife gave the wife of Wolcott a lock of the General's hair and one of her own. The social lobby looked after its own — and Wolcott was its very own.

For this cultivation of the social lobby, he was well adapted, for he had a genius for society, with his cheerful disposition, his playful manner, his conversation, which, while sometimes sober, was usually gay. The 'small talk' that Adams lacked, Wolcott had in full measure running over. A master of the art of banter, no one with entrée to Mrs. Bingham's could tell a joke better or more noisily enjoy one. His laugh was hearty, frequent, and infectious. Living in a world of statistics, he at least affected a love of literature, was fond of quoting poetry, and interested in the personalities of distinguished writers. His conversation after office hours could be light and graceful. Gracious, smiling, ingratiating, this bureaucrat — one of the first — created and sustained by the social lobby as one of its first exhibits. He differed from Pickering as day from night, but like his sphinx-like colleague of Salem, he owed everything to Hamilton, nothing to Adams; and as he sat, suave and smiling, at the Cabinet table, it was to Hamilton, not to Adams, that he looked as chief.

VIII

If Pickering was a conspirator against Adams and did not care who knew it, and Wolcott a conspirator trying to conceal it, James McHenry, the Secretary of War, was a conspirator and scarcely knew it. The simplicity of this Irish immigrant is most disarming. Left alone, he would have been harmless. His was only another instance of loving, not wisely, and too well. Born in comfortable circumstances in Ireland, the impairment of his health through intensive application to his studies in an academy

[1] Gibbs I, 449.

in Dublin brought him to America on a recuperative voyage. So favorably was he impressed that his family soon followed and his father opened a general store in Baltimore. A year later, we find him in an academy in Newark, Delaware, and then in Philadelphia studying medicine under the celebrated Dr. Rush. But he took as little to his profession as to the prosaic duties of the counting-room, and, thanks to inherited property, lived through the greater portion of his life as a gentleman of leisure. In nothing that he ever undertook did he attain distinction. The practice of his profession was limited to a brief period as surgeon in the army; his career in commerce was almost as much curtailed; and he employed his leisure as a dilettante in politics and literature.

Had McHenry remained in Ireland, it is easy to imagine him as a young blade about Dublin, affecting the fashions, a bit dandified in dress, over-fond of society, given to verse. A searcher of souls might have discovered in him an ambition — to write poetry. Even in his academy days at Newark he was an inveterate verse-maker, and he thought enough of his effusions to send them to the papers. It was a weakness he never overcame, and at his death they found a great portfolio full of rhymes. It is possible — and it is this pathetic touch that makes one almost love him — that he hoped for a posthumous volume as a memorial and monument.[1] Some of these lyrics are clever, light and graceful, reminders of the sort that even Curran liked to make for the amusement of his friends — thoroughly Irish. He could never have become a poet, but there is evidence in his letters that had he turned his attention to the humorous essay, he might have produced things worth while. These epistles are charming in their playfulness, sprightly, witty, glowing with humor. No one among the public men of the period could have made posterity so much their debtor with letters on men, women, and events — not even Morris, Ames, or Goodrich. He was really made for an observer, rather than participant, in the harsh conflicts of life — more of a Horace than a Robert Walpole, more of a Boswell than a Johnson. Dinners, dances, routs, these, and the writing of light verses, were enough to make him happy.

And yet he was not effeminate. If he did not play his part in

[1] Steiner, 2.

the affairs of men with brilliancy or even efficiency, he did with
courage and to the best of his ability. We have few references to
his services as surgeon in the army. It was when he became one of
Washington's secretaries that he fell completely under the fascination of Hamilton. Even before his resignation from the army, he
had entered politics as a member of the State Senate in Maryland,
a rather important body consisting then of but fifteen members.
Here he was the representative of the commercial class. In the
Constitutional Convention he was obscure, and strangely enough
his views were the very opposite of Hamilton's. Speaking seldom,
his voice was raised in warning against too much centralization.[1]
He was even favorable to a mere amendment to the Articles of
Confederation,[2] and his chief interest was in the provisions for the
regulation of commerce.[3] When the work was over, he signed
with avowed reluctance, and solely on the ground — which was
characteristic — that he distrusted his own judgment, that amendments might be made, and he was willing to take a chance.[4] In
the bitter fight over ratification in the Maryland Convention, he
took but little part.

Even so, the confidence and friendship of Washington and
Hamilton were not weakened. To him they looked from the beginning for advice on Maryland patronage, and Washington found
it convenient to use him as an agent in matters of this sort.[5]
Hamilton thus employed him frequently.[6] Taking seriously his
rôle as the Federalist boss and distributer of the loaves and fishes,
he resented the disregarding of one of his recommendations, and
even the long explanatory letter of Hamilton failed to smooth his
ruffled feathers.[7] More than two years were to elapse before his
woman-like affection for his idol gained the ascendancy over his
resentment. 'I have not ceased to love you nor for a moment felt
an abatement of my friendship,' he wrote impulsively after the
long silence.[8]

Like Pickering and Wolcott, McHenry was persistent in his
hints for place. Six years before the Constitution went into effect,
we find him soliciting the influence of Washington to get him a
diplomatic post in Europe, and the great man tried and failed.[9]
Among the first letters Hamilton received on entering the Cabinet

---

[1] Steiner, 97. [2] *Ibid.*, 100. [3] *Ibid.*, 99. [4] *Ibid.*, 107. [5] *Ibid.*, 124.
[6] *Ibid.*, 129, 132. [7] *Ibid.*, 140–41. [8] *Ibid.*, 156. [9] *Ibid.*, 51.

was one from McHenry. 'I am not wholly lost to ambition,' he wrote, 'and would have no objection to a situation where I might indulge and improve at the same time my literary propensities, with, perhaps, some advantage to the public. Would you, there-fore, be good enough to feel . . . whether the President has thought of me, or would, in such a case, nominate me. I wish you would do this for me as a thing springing entirely from yourself.' [1] Nothing came of it, and the faithful party hack continued to run the er-rands of the Administration in Maryland. Three years later, he took his courage in both hands and wrote directly to Washington asking to be sent to Paris and Vienna to attempt to secure the re-lease of Lafayette. He wanted a change of air. It would be no use, the President replied.[2] It was not until near the close of Washington's eight years in office — and only then because many others had declined — that he was finally summoned to Phila-delphia to become Secretary of War. Would he have felt so much elated had he read Hamilton's comment on his capacity? 'McHenry, you know,' wrote the leader. 'He would give no strength to the Administration but he would not disgrace the office. His views are good.' [3] But happily he did not know, and jubilantly he gave up all private enterprises as incompatible with public office — for in such matters he was meticulously proper — and, mounting his horse, he rode to Philadelphia. He carried the conviction with him that he owed his honor to the earnest persist-ency of his idol. To the extent indicated, this was true. The great genius of Federalism, now planning to continue his domination of the Government from his law office in New York, had reasons to believe that whoever might be President, McHenry would be his own faithful servitor. When Hamilton had married Betty Schuyler, his friend had journeyed to Albany with some verses for the event. Was it with an indulgent smile that the bridegroom acknowledged the poem? 'You know I often told you you wrote prose well, but had no genius for poetry. I retract.' [4] Six years be-fore the first inauguration of Washington, this ardent friend had written Hamilton: 'Were you ten years older and twenty thousand pounds richer, there is no doubt but that you might obtain the

[1] Steiner, 123.   [2] *Ibid.*, 145.   [3] Hamilton's *Works*, x, 129–31.
[4] Steiner, 30.

suffrages of Congress for the highest office in their gift.'[1] Verily it was not without an eye to the future that Hamilton found a place for such an idolater and political valet in the Cabinet.

There is something a bit wistful and pathetic about McHenry that persuades forgiveness for even his treachery to Adams. His were the sins of a lover, and love covers a multitude of sins. Nature intended him for a snug harbor, and fate pushed him out upon tempestuous seas. His own best epitaph has been written by himself: 'I have built houses. I have cultivated fields. I have planned gardens. I have planted trees. I have written little essays. I have made poetry once a year to please my wife; at times got children, and at all times thought myself happy.'[2] Like Pickering and Wolcott, he owed everything to Hamilton — nothing to Adams; and as he faced Adams in the Cabinet room, it was to Hamilton — not to Adams — that he looked as chief.

The other member of the Cabinet, the Attorney-General, was a political cipher. Knowing what we now know of the characters and factional affiliations of the President and his advisers, it will not be difficult to follow the serpentine trail of the next four years, nor to understand one of the forces that worked with Jefferson for the utter destruction of the Federalist Party.

---

[1] *Life of Hamilton*, by his son, II, 241.   [2] Steiner, 159; letter to Hamilton.

CHAPTER XV

COMEDY AND HEROICS

I

SCARCELY had Adams entered upon his office when he found himself confronted with the possibility of a war with France. Some time before, Gouverneur Morris, the American Genêt in Paris, had been recalled, none too soon, and James Monroe had been sent to smooth the ruffled feathers of the French. Because he had followed his instructions too enthusiastically and failed to understand that 'a diplomat is a person sent abroad to lie for his country,' he had been recalled in disgrace, as Jefferson had foreseen, and Charles Cotesworth Pinckney, a Charleston Federalist, had been sent as Minister. Not only had the French Government refused to receive him, but he had been ordered from the soil of France. All this seems wicked perversity on the part of France without a hasty glance at the antecedents of the story.

Primarily nothing could have been more unfortunate than the appointment of Morris. No more charming or clever diplomat than this bosom friend of Hamilton has served America abroad. Born to the purple, he was an aristocrat by nature, with a blatantly cynical and contemptuous conception of the masses of mankind. His was the shimmer due to generations of polishing. As a young man in the society of New York and Philadelphia, he was enormously popular because he was. handsome, dashing, witty, eloquent, a bit *risqué*, and in consequence of his fashionable and gilded background. In the Constitutional Convention no one spoke with greater fluency or frequency — or with less effect. He sought the establishment of an aristocratic state, and made no secret of his hostility to democracy. To an even greater degree than Hamilton he foreshadowed the extreme policies of the Federalist Party. He was, in truth, its personification, able, brilliant, rich; socially delightful, cynical, aristocratic, masterful, and disdainful of the frontier.[1] Like Hamilton, he failed in the Conven-

[1] Roosevelt, *Morris*, 127.

tion, but his was the hand that fashioned the phrasing of the fundamental law.

There was more than a hint of the fashionable *roué* in this handsome fellow when he went to Paris. Women and their pursuit was ever an engrossing game with him. Even his graduation essay was on 'Wit and Beauty,' and for his Master's Degree he wrote on 'Love.' He was the sort of beau that Congreve would have cherished, elegant in dress and manner, given to levity and light banter, eagerly sought. The loss of a leg through an accident in 1780 did not sour him nor diminish his appeal to women. On 'a rough oak stick with a knob at the end,'[1] he hobbled on to his triumphs.

Such was the man sent to succeed Jefferson, the philosopher of democracy, at the moment the Revolution was breaking on the boulevards — a bitter, outspoken partisan of the old régime, a sarcastic enemy of the Revolution, a champion of privilege less compromising than the nobility itself. While Genêt was intriguing against the Government in America, Morris was intriguing against the Government in France. But his love flowers were still thrown over the garden wall of politics. Jefferson had been shocked at his reactionary opinions in Paris. Madame Lafayette had chided him on being an aristocrat.[2] Quite early he began his affair with Madame de Flahaut, the novelist, a pretty, winsome woman who effectively used her marriage to an old man as a lure for lovers, and his diary teems with references to the frail beauty. There were evenings at her home, sneering at liberty and democracy; teas in her salon; drives and dinners, when he was entranced by the 'spirituel and delicate repartee' of his friend.[3] Then walks in the Gardens of the Tuileries and about the Champs Élysées, afternoons at Madame's house reading 'La Pucelle,' while she rode about Paris in the well-known carriage of the American Minister,[4] and finally, when danger came, he took her into his house. The Minister aimed high, and even the Duchess of Orleans was not above his amorous expectations, thinking her beautiful enough 'to punish the duke for his irregularities,' and we find him writing poems to her, and buying her a Newfoundland dog in London.[5] No young blade ever found Paris more seductive.

---

[1] Morris, *Diary*, I, 14.   [2] *Diary*, I, 35.   [3] *Ibid.*, 133.   [4] *Ibid.*, 181.
[5] *La Belle Pamela*, 217, note.

On swept the Revolution, on came the Terror, with Morris openly and defiantly sneering at the former and its principles. The coldness of the crowds in the streets when the Queen rode by enraged him.[1] In the terrible August days of 1792 he drove the reactionary Madame de Flahaut through the Bois de Boulogne,[2] and when the nation imprisoned the King he was soon neck-deep in intrigues to effect his rescue.[3] Messages were exchanged with Louis, plans perfected, and only the King's courage failed. Later Louis made him the custodian of 750,000 livres to be used in bribing those who stood in the way of his escape. America's Minister was paymaster of the King seeking to join the allied monarchs in the crushing of the Revolution.[4] Much of this was known in Paris, and much of it known and approved by Federalist leaders in America, Ames objecting to the publication of certain papers because they would disclose Morris's intolerable activities.[5]

II

Monroe was the antithesis of Morris. Where Morris was brilliant, Monroe was dull; where Morris was bubbling with a sense of humor, Monroe had none at all; where Morris was a lover of dinners and dances, Monroe was indifferent; where Morris was a Cavalier, Monroe was a Puritan in his relations with women; where Morris was an aristocrat, Monroe was a democrat; Morris was a monarchist at heart, Monroe, a robust republican; Morris an enemy of the French Revolution, Monroe, a friend. But if Monroe was not scintillating, he was sincere, and if not brilliant, he was industrious.[6] Soon he was as popular in Paris as Morris had been unpopular — so popular that Jay thought it not beneath his dignity as an American Minister to England to exchange belittling letters with Grenville about him. He had ironed out old differences when the Jay Treaty compromised his position.

No diplomat ever worked under more disheartening handicaps, for the Federalists in Philadelphia hated him, and months went by without a line of instructions or news from the State Depart-

---

[1] *Diary*, I, 75. [2] *Ibid.*, 572. [3] *Ibid.*, 556.
[4] Roosevelt, *Morris*, 221–23. [5] Ames (to Gore), I, 134.
[6] *Familiar Letters*, 356–57.

ment. Meanwhile, Washington was being poisoned against him by Federalist politicians who had his ear, and in the spring of 1796 Madison wrote Monroe that his enemies had 'been base enough to throw into circulation insinuations that you have launched into all the depths of speculation' and 'purchased the magnificent estate of the late Prince of Condé.' [1] Pickering and Wolcott were planning his recall that spring and writing Hamilton about it.[2] The latter was easily persuaded.[3] Some one else should be sent — some one not so friendly to the French. That the leaders of the English party were not averse to giving offense to France is shown in the astounding suggestion that William Smith, spouter of pro-English speeches, written by Hamilton, that had been printed and circulated in England, should be sent.[4] It required no blundering by Monroe to pave the way for his recall — the politicians were sparing him that trouble.

He had officially informed the Minister of Foreign Affairs that Jay was not to negotiate a commercial treaty, and would sign none that was in conflict with the Franco-American Treaty — because those were his instructions. Then, with rumors to the contrary flying over Paris, on the completion of the treaty, he had, on the strength of a solemn and utterly false assurance from Jay, reiterated that there was no conflict. When the document reached Paris, the French were bitterly resentful and Monroe was discredited and crippled. Even so, he probably prevented a declaration of war by representing that such a course would throw America into the arms of England — and this was charged against him by those Federalist leaders who sought war. Then he was recalled; and at the farewell audience an offensive speech by the French official, which Monroe unpardonably failed to resent, gave his enemies more ammunition.

III

With the refusal to receive Pinckney, the crisis came. To the war hawks it was a golden hour — war and no negotiations. Pickering and Wolcott fumed over the suggestion of an extraordinary mission. Hamilton, the sanest and most prescient of them all,

---

[1] Madison's *Writings*, II, 91–92.
[2] Gibbs, I, 359.   [3] *Ibid.*   [4] *Ibid.*, 366–68.

realizing the importance of a united country in case of war, proposed sending an embassy of three, including one Jeffersonian of distinction. For almost five months a spirited debate of the leaders continued. In January, Hamilton had written Washington urging an extraordinary mission, including Madison, to conciliate the French, with Pinckney, who was not distasteful to them, and George Cabot, to moderate the Gallicism of the other two, to supply commercial information, and to represent the friends of the Administration.[1] Two months later, in a similar recommendation to McHenry, he proposed Jefferson instead of Madison, and Jay in the place of Cabot. Then he would have a day of fasting and prayer for the opening of Congress, an embargo, an increase in the revenue, the use of convoys, and qualified letters of marque for merchantmen to arm and defend themselves.[2] The same day he wrote the same suggestion for Pickering.[3]

It was at this juncture that Hamilton began to run foul of the pro-English war craze of Pickering, who questioned the plan because the Democrats favored it. All the more reason for it, replied Hamilton. Unhappily, there was a prevalent feeling that the Administration wanted war and this should be counteracted.[4] To Wolcott, he wrote in the same strain the next day.[5] Even the usually pliant Wolcott was in rebellious mood and replied with an attack on Madison as a frequenter of M. Adet's parties, whom that Minister wished sent, and who would wreck the negotiations, and 'throw the disgrace of failure on the friends of the Government.'[6] Clearly it was time for Hamilton to assume his imperial manner, and he did, in a sharp rebuke to his protégé against 'passions that prevent the pliancy to circumstances which is sometimes indispensable.' Then 'what risk can attend sending Madison, if combined, as I propose, with Pinckney and Cabot,' he added.[7] Realizing now the importance of bringing up his congressional reserves, he wrote to William Smith by the same mail.[8]

The insurgency against the plans of the Federalist chief was now in full blast. Tracy was writing Wolcott — 'No man will be

[1] Hamilton's *Works*, x, 234.   [2] *Ibid.*, 241.   [3] *Ibid.*, 243–46.
[4] *Ibid.*, 246–47.   [5] Gibbs, I, 484–85.   [6] *Ibid.*, 486–87.
[7] *Ibid.*, 489–90; Hamilton's *Works*, x, 251–52.   [8] Hamilton's *Works*, x, 253.

sent on this business but a decided Federalist.'[1] Jeremiah Smith having informed Cabot of the dispute, the latter wrote Wolcott that he could see no possibility of finding new messengers 'with the expectation that they will not be kicked.'[2] The same day — less circumspect outside Administration circles — he wrote Jeremiah Smith that a new embassy 'would be disgraceful.'[3] Ames had been won over by Hamilton, but the day after the extra session began, Cabot wrote Wolcott that his mind was 'still as unsatisfied as at first.'[4] Four days before the session opened, Hamilton was bringing pressure to bear on Pickering, declaring the mission 'indispensable to silence the Jacobin criticism and promote union among ourselves.' But by this time he had changed the personnel of his mission — Rufus King, rabidly pro-English, should be sent with Pinckney and Jefferson.[5] Meanwhile, McHenry was receiving letters from Maryland Federalists urging war,[6] but Hamilton's masterful methods had won the Cabinet, and when Adams took the opinions of the Ministers he received replies that had been dictated, and, in the case of McHenry, written in large part, by the Federalist chief.[7]

All the while Adams had been receiving volunteered advice, though it does not appear that Hamilton thought it worth while to communicate with him direct. He had received a letter from Knox urging Jefferson because of the compliment that would be implied in his rank. This touched Adams where he was ticklish. 'The circumstance of rank is too much,' he replied. 'What would have been thought in Europe if the King of France had sent Monsieur, his eldest brother, as an envoy? What of the King of England if he had sent the Prince of Wales? Mr. Jefferson is in a sense in the same situation. He is the first prince of the country, and the heir apparent to the sovereign authority.'[8] Ah, 'Bonny Johnny,' lucky that this letter did not fall into the hands of Bache with its references to the 'prince' and the 'heir apparent'!

However, in a discussion of the mission with Jefferson, the President had suggested Madison. The wary Democratic chief received the suggestion with caution, for the experience of Monroe

---

[1] Gibbs, i, 537.
[2] Lodge, *Cabot*, 129.
[3] *Ibid.*, 130–31.
[4] *Ibid.*, 137.
[5] Hamilton's *Works*, x, 261–65.
[6] Steiner, 208–09.
[7] *Ibid.*, 213.
[8] Adams, *Works*, viii, 532–34; 535–36.

offered little inducement to a Democrat to subject his reputation
to the mercies of the man-eating Pickering. Certainly the suggestion received no encouragement. The President and his most
dangerous opponent had a friendly chat and parted friends —
not soon to meet in conference again. The sage of Monticello had
never been more courteous or courtly, the man from Braintree
never calmer nor more kindly, but the hour had passed for a coalition. Jefferson was out for scalps, not olive branches.[1]

Thus the time came when Adams had to take the bit in his
mouth in the naming of the envoys. One day Fisher Ames had a
long talk with him in urging Cabot, as a compliment to the
Northern States, and the next day the envoys were named —
with Cabot out. He was eliminated because Adams knew that
Talleyrand was familiar with Cabot's bitter hostility to France,
and the President refused thus to 'gratify the passions of a party.' [2]
That was ominous enough; but when he disregarded the almost
unanimous protest of the Hamiltonians and named Elbridge
Gerry along with Pinckney and Marshall, the gage of battle was
thrown down. From that hour, the high-flying Federalists knew
that John Adams would be no man's man and no man's parrot.
Thus early, the small cloud on the horizon widened and darkened.

The proud old patriot of Braintree had been given a shock on
the opening day of the extra session when Senator Tracy spread a
lengthy letter before him on the table in the *ex-cathedra* manner
of one disclosing the tablets of Moses. The squat little President
read it with rising wrath. It was a letter from Hamilton, setting
forth in detail 'a whole system of instructions for the conduct of
the President, the Senate and the House of Representatives.' He
read it through and returned it to Tracy. 'I really thought the
man was in a delirium,' Adams wrote afterwards.[3] And the cloud
on the horizon grew more ominous.

IV

The opening of the session found the New England Federalists
in high glee over the prospects. The correspondence of their
leaders discloses their grim determination to have war with France;

[1] Gibbs, I, 463.   [2] Lodge, *Cabot*, from Adams's letters in the *Boston Patriot*.
[3] Gibbs, I, 483.

and if they had failed in their efforts to prevent a renewal of negotiations, they could use the extra session for the spreading of
war propaganda. Upon this task they entered with unprecedented
arrogance and intolerance.

The Message of Adams was dignified and calm, reviewing the
situation, announcing the plans for a new attempt at negotiations,
and urging the adoption of defensive measures in the meantime.
The first fight came in the framing of the Reply to the Address in
the House — and two young brilliant new members forged to the
front to assume the aggressive leadership of the war party. The
persuasive, polished eloquence of Ames could not be heard, for he
was nursing himself in his fine new house at Dedham; nor, on the
other side, could the lucid, convincing logic of Madison appear, for
he was in retirement in Virginia. Sedgwick had been sent to the
Senate, Fitzsimons had been defeated, Murray of Maryland was
on his way to The Hague as Minister. On the Democratic side,
Gallatin, Giles, and Nicholas of Virginia were to bear the brunt of
the battle, and the two new men were to lead the Federalists with
an audacity seldom equaled and never surpassed. These two
young blades, Harrison Gray Otis of Boston and Robert Goodloe
Harper of South Carolina, were in their thirty-second year. The
former was strikingly handsome, tall and well proportioned, with
coal-black hair, eyes blue and sparkling with vivacity, nose thin
and patrician, complexion rosy — his presence in any assembly
would have been felt had he remained silent, and he was seldom
silent. In dress fastidious, in manners affable, in repartee stinging,
in the telling of a story a master of the art: a devotee to pleasure,
dinners, dances, and women carried for him an irresistible appeal.
His eloquence was of a high order. A thorough aristocrat, he
prided himself on having no illusions as to liberty and democracy,
and he made no secret of his contempt for the masses. The rising
of the French against the ineffable cruelties of the nobility and
monarchy merely meant to him an attack of beasts upon the
homes and rights of gentlemen. Speedily he became an idol of his
party, and he enjoyed the bitter conflicts of the House as keenly
as the dinners where he was the life of the party.

Robert Goodloe Harper had much in common with Otis. Like
him, Harper was a social lion and a dandy in dress. Of medium

height, and with an uncommonly full chest which accentuated his pomposity, he had a handsome head and features, creating withal an impression of physical force and intellectual power. In eloquence he made up in force what he lacked in ornament. He had all of Giles's bumptiousness without his consistency, and no member of the House approached him in insolence. Coming upon the scene when the conditions seemed ripe for bowling over the Democrats with abuse and intimidation, he fitted into the picture perfectly. Thus he became the outstanding orator against the French. True, four years before, in Charleston, he had paid court to the Jacobins with an assiduity that should have made him blush in later life — but did not. Appealing for membership in an extreme Jacobin society, he had worn the paraphernalia, spouted his harangues on the rights of man, paid his tribute to the Revolution, become the vice-president of the organization — and all he lacked to make him a Camille Desmoulins was a table on the boulevards and a guillotine.[1] Now a convert to 'law and order,' he outstripped the most rabid enemies of the French. From 'dining almost every day' in 1793 at the table of the French Consul in Charleston, he passed without embarrassment four years later to the table of Liston, the British Minister.[2] The rabid democrat had become a rabid aristocrat, and the society of the capital took him to its heart. In social intercourse, he was entertaining, amiable, and pleasing.[3] Fond of the epicurean feast, expansive in the glow of women's smiles, he became a social favorite, and his enemies broadly hinted that he was a master in the gentle art of intrigue.

Brilliant, charming men, these two young orators of the war party, and it is easy to imagine the homage of the fashionable ladies when, after their most virulent attacks on the Democrats, they found themselves surrounded in Mrs. Bingham's drawing-room.

Even before Congress met, the premonitions of the coming Terror were in the air. With the impatient Giles, this was intoler-

---

[1] Thomas, *Reminiscences. The Aurora*, March 21, 1797, printed his application for membership.

[2] *The Aurora*, June 17, 1797, asked whether he was 'spy or parasite' while dining with the French Consul.

[3] *Familiar Letters*, 107.

able, and he soon retired to fight elsewhere; but Gallatin determined to ignore insults, disregard abuse, and to fight for
moderate measures to keep the door open for negotiations. He
was of the rare few who can keep their heads in the midst of riots
and remain calm in a tempest. For a while he could count on Giles
for rough blows at the enemy, on Livingston for eloquence and
courage; he would have to rely upon himself for wisdom and
the strategy of statesmanship.

v

The Message received, the war party in the House set itself with
zest to the framing of a bellicose Reply calculated to compromise
the chances for a peaceful accommodation of differences. Nicholas
of Virginia, representing the Jeffersonians, proposed a substitute,
couched in more conciliatory language, promising a review of the
alleged grievances of the French — and this let loose the dogs of
war. In presenting his amendment, Nicholas deprecated the Reply
as framed because extreme, denunciatory, and provocative and
not calculated to assist the embassy the President was sending.
In negotiations it would necessarily follow that there would
be an examination of the charges made against America by the
French.[1] It irritated Smith of Charleston that the Virginian
should be 'so wonderfully afraid of using language to irritate
France,' albeit he had protested against language that would
irritate England when Jay was sailing on his mission.[2] Otis was
weary of references to England's offenses against American commerce. 'The English were stimulated to annoy our commerce
through apprehension that we were united against them, and the
French by a belief that we are divided in their favor.'[3]

Livingston followed with a brilliant five-hour address, pointing
out the flagrant violation of Article XVII of the treaty with
France. We had made that treaty upon the basis that free bot-
toms make free goods, and in the Jay Treaty we had abandoned
that ground in the interest of England. Of what was it that the
French complained? What but the adoption of the British Order
in Council which we had not resented? Even so, she was not
justified in her course. That she would recede in negotiations he

[1] *Annals*, May 22, 1797.   [2] *Ibid.*   [3] *Ibid.*, May 23, 1797.

had no doubt, provided we used 'language toward her suitable to that liberality which befits a wise and prudent nation.' He had no apology to offer for his devotion to the cause of France. 'I could read by the light of the flames that consumed my paternal mansion, by the joy that sparkled in every eye,' he said, 'how great were the consequences of her union with America.' [1] Giles followed, a little more severe on the Federalist discriminations for England against France; and Gallatin closed in a sober, dignified, dispassionate analysis of the phrasing of the amendment to show that it was firm without being offensive.[2]

Then Harper, with an elaborate speech laboriously wrought in seclusion, entered the debate. The French were intemperately denounced, the Democrats lashed, and Monroe treated with contempt. It was a war speech, prepared as war propaganda, the first of his war speeches to be published and widely circulated throughout the country, and printed and acclaimed in England. Like Smith and Ames before him, he was to have his triumph in Downing Street. The profits of one of his war productions, which had a 'prodigious sale' in England, were given to a benevolent society in that country.[3] The Democrats were infuriated by Harper's attack, and the 'Aurora' truly said that he had 'unseasonably unmasked the intentions of his party.' [4] When, about this time, Liston, the British Minister, was seen to tap the orator unceremoniously upon the shoulder while seated at his desk — for Liston was then a familiar figure upon the floor — and to whisper to him, Bache saw red. 'If the French Minister had acted thus familiarly with Mr. Giles or Mr. Livingston, we should have heard something about French influence.' [5] Pooh! sneered Fenno in the 'Gazette,' Liston was merely reminding Harper of a dinner engagement for that night. 'Having heard it whispered,' he added, 'that Mr. Harper has received an invitation to dinner from another British Agent, the Consul General, we think ourselves bound to mention it.' [6] Nothing could better illustrate the confident arrogance of the Federalist leaders at this time.

[1] *Annals,* May 24, 1797.   [2] *Ibid.,* May 25, 1797.
[3] Steiner, 301; Murray to McHenry boasting that Harper's pamphlet had gone through several editions in England.
[4] June 1, 1797.   [5] *Aurora,* May 31, 1797.
[6] *Gazette of the United States,* May 30, 1797.

'I am not for war,' said Smith of Charleston. 'I do not believe that the gentleman wishes for peace,' retorted Gallatin, who had written four days before that 'Wolcott, Pickering, William Smith, Fisher Ames, and perhaps a few more are disposed to go to war' and 'to carry their party any length they please.'[1] Thus the debate continued until Jonathan Dayton, the Speaker, proposed a substitute amendment that received the support of the Democrats. Seizing upon a passage in Adams's Message, this commended the President's decision to seek further negotiations and cherished 'the hope that a mutual spirit of conciliation and a disposition on the part of the United States to place France on grounds as favorable as other countries in their relations and connection with us, will produce an accommodation compatible with the engagements, rights, duties, and honor of the United States.'[2] With the Democrats joining the more moderate Federalists under Dayton, the contest was speedily ended to the disgust of the war party. The batteries of scurrility were turned upon the Speaker. 'A double-faced weather-cock,' screamed 'Porcupine' the Englishman. 'His duplicity has been too bare-faced for decency. He is, indeed, but a shallow, superficial fellow — a bawler to the galleries, and unfit to play the cunning part he has undertaken.'[3]

Then, after the heroics, the comedy. Matthew Lyon, a Vermont Democrat and a new member, shocked the formalists with a characterization of the practice of marching in stately procession to the President to present the Reply as 'a boyish piece of business.' The time had come to end the silliness. 'Blood will tell,' sneered a colleague, referring to Lyon's humble origin. 'I cannot say,' replied Lyon, 'that I am descended from the bastards of Oliver Cromwell, or his courtiers, or from the Puritans who punish their horses for breaking the Sabbath, or from those who persecuted the Quakers and burned the witches.'[4] Some chortled, others snorted with rage. Vulgar Irish immigrant! But their wounded culture was soon soothed by a salvo from 'Porcupine.' How society must have screamed its delight in reading that Lyon as a child 'had been caught in a bog, and when a whelp transported to America'; how he had become so 'domesticated' that

---

[1] Adams, *Gallatin* (to Nicholson), 183–84.
[2] *Annals*, May 30, 1797.
[3] *Porcupine's Gazette*, June 3, 1797.
[4] *Annals*, June 3, 1797.

Governor Crittenden's daughter (his wife) 'would stroke him and play with him as a monkey'; how 'his gestures bear a remarkable affinity to the bear' because of 'his having been in the habit of associating with that species of wild beast in the mountains.' [1] The majority of the House, lacking Lyon's sense of humor, continued for a while their pompous strut through Market Street to read solemnly the meaningless Reply that had consumed weeks of futile debate.

Then Congress proceeded to measures of defense, prohibiting the exportation of arms and ammunition, providing for the strengthening of the coast fortifications, creating a naval armament, authorizing a detachment of militia, and adjourned. But the atmosphere had been one of intense party bitterness which had ostracized the Democrats, from Jefferson down, from the 'society' of the 'best people.'

VI

Mounted, booted, and spurred, and swinging their sabers, the Federalists started out to ride roughshod over their opponents. It was their strategy to attach a stigma to Democrats, and treat them as political outlaws and social outcasts. No one was to be spared — Jefferson least of all. A year before he had written the confidential letter to his friend Philip Mazzei, stating his oft-repeated views on the anti-republican trend in Federalist circles, and saying that men who had been 'Samsons in the field and Solomons in the council . . . had had their heads shorn by the harlot England.' [2] Sent to an Italian paper, it was translated from Italian into French for a Parisian journal, as we have seen, and thence translated again into English for political purposes in America. The translators had unintentionally taken liberties with the text and in the final translation it was quite different from the original. At last, it seemed, the cautious Jefferson had delivered himself into the hands of his enemies, for had he not attacked Washington? At Alexandria, en route to Philadelphia, Jefferson first learned of the renewed attack in Fenno's paper. Reaching the capital, he found the vials of wrath let loose upon his head. A politician of less self-possession or finesse would have offered some

[1] *Porcupine's Gazette*, June 6, 1797.   [2] Jefferson's *Works*, IX, 335–37.

explanation or defense. None of the courtesies of warfare were to be shown him — he was to be mobbed, his character assailed, his reputation blackened, his personal honor besmirched, and he was to be rejected socially as unfit to associate with the Harpers, Sedgwicks, and Wolcotts. An open letter greeted him in Fenno's paper on his arrival. 'For the honor of the American name,' it read, 'I would wish the letter to be a forgery, although I must confess that your silence . . . leaves but little probability of its not having proceeded from you.'[1] Jefferson ignored it. 'You are the author of the abominable letter to Mazzei,' ran a second open letter. 'Your silence is complete evidence of your guilt.'[2] 'Slanderer of Washington!' 'Assassin!' 'Liar!' — and Jefferson was silent.

Knowing the curative powers of time and patience, it was not until in August that he consulted Madison and Monroe as to his course. 'Reply,' urged the impulsive Monroe, 'honest men will be encouraged by your owning and justifying the letter.' Madison advised against it as more apt to give a 'gratification and triumph' to his foes.[3] 'Character assassin!' 'Libeler of Washington!' 'Atheist!' 'Anarchist!' 'Liar!' — these characterizations buzzed through the streets and in the drawing-rooms — and Jefferson was silent.

Then an attack from a new angle. In his 'Notes on Virginia,' published years before, in paying tribute to the red men and the eloquence of Logan, an Indian chief, he had referred to a Colonel Cresap as 'a man infamous for the many murders he had committed on these much injured people.' When the mass attack on Jefferson was at its height, a long open letter to him appeared in 'Porcupine's Gazette' from the brilliant, erratic, and usually intoxicated Luther Martin, known as 'the Federalist bull-dog,' demanding Jefferson's authority in the name of 'two amiable daughters who are directly descended from that man whose character your pen . . . had endeavored to stigmatize with indelible infamy.' This had been preceded by no personal note and was manifestly a part of the political plot to wreck him — and he was silent.[4] Time and again Martin returned to the attack in long open letters, to be

<hr>

[1] *Gazette of the United States*, May 19, 1797.
[2] *Ibid.*, May 30, 1797.
[3] Madison's *Writings*, ii, 118.
[4] *Porcupine's Gazette*, July 17, 1797.

ignored utterly as though he were as inconsequential as a ragpicker instead of being the leader of the Maryland Bar.[1] 'The mean and cowardly conduct of Mr. Jefferson,' growled 'Porcupine.'[2]

An open season now for shooting at the Democratic leader, all the snipers were busy with their guns. At Harvard College, on Washington's Birthday, there was a toast to Jefferson: 'May he exercise his elegant literary talents for the benefit of the world in some retreat, secure from the troubles and danger of political life' — and the Federalist papers gloated over it.[3] Bache was seen entering Jefferson's rooms, and a Gallic conspiracy loomed before the affrighted vision of Fenno. 'The brat may gasp,' he promised, 'but it will surely die in the infamy of its parents.'[4] Jefferson a man of the people? snorted 'Porcupine.' 'So is the swindling bankrupt Charles Fox who is continually vilifying his own government and stands ready to sell his country to France.'[5] Nothing angered 'Porcupine' more than Jefferson's suggestion in his 'Notes on Virginia' that British freedom had crossed the Atlantic. Freedom would live in England, he growled, when Jefferson's 'head will be rotting cheek by jowl with that of some toil-killed negro slave,' and when nothing would be remembered of Jefferson 'save thy cruel, unprovoked, and viperous slander of the family of Cresap.'[6] And Jefferson was silent.

Philadelphia was a city of but seventy-five thousand people. The papers were generally read, or their contents were at any rate the talk of the town. They formed the topic for ladies at their teas. Their husbands were sulphurous in their attacks at the breakfast table. And Jefferson became, in the fashionable circles, a moral monster unfit to drink whiskey with a *roué* of the morally bankrupt French nobility at the table of the Binghams. He was ostracized. It was at this time that he wrote Edward Rutledge that 'men who have been intimate all their lives cross the street to avoid meeting, and turn their heads another way lest they be obliged to touch their hats.'[7] To his daughter Martha, he wrote

[1] *Porcupine's Gazette*, December 14, 1797, January 13, 1798. It was this Luther Martin who assailed Jefferson so bitterly in connection with his defense of Aaron Burr in the trial for treason.

[2] *Ibid.*, January 29, 1798.

[3] *Gazette of the United States*, March 6, 1798.   [4] *Ibid.*, April 18, 1798.

[5] *Porcupine's Gazette*, July 5, 1797.   [6] *Ibid.*, October 23, 1797.

[7] Jefferson's *Works*, IX, 408–11.

of his disgust with the 'jealousies, the hatreds and the malignant passions,' [1] and of the 'politics and party hatreds [that] seem like salamanders to consider fire as their element.' [2]

Under these conditions he dropped out of the social life of the capital. In the evenings he consulted with his political associates; during the day he presented a calm, unruffled complacency to his enemies in the Senate over whom he presided with scrupulous impartiality. Driven from society, he found consolation in the little rooms of the Philosophical Society, among the relics of his friends Rittenhouse and Franklin.

With such abuse visited on Jefferson, it is easy to imagine the fate of his less important friends. Sam Adams was the laughing-stock of the silk stockings. Franklin was considered as base as Jefferson. 'Some person left at my house this morning a copy of Old Franklin's works, or rather plagiarisms,' wrote 'Porcupine.' 'I look upon everything which this unclean old fellow had a hand in to be contaminated and contaminating,' [3] and the time was to come when a Federalist mob raging through the streets of Phila-delphia would throw rocks through Bache's windows and besmear Franklin's statue with mud. Tom Paine, always a fair mark, was written down in print as a libertine. 'Porcupine's Gazette,' which was the favorite journal in the cultured homes of the pure at heart, had a story that Paine had been 'caught on his knees at a lady's feet by her husband,' and had explained that he was 'only measur-ing your lady for stays,' at which the delighted husband 'kissed and thanked him for his politeness.' [4] Because John Swanwick, a popular young Philadelphia merchant, had cast his lot with the Democrats, blocked the plans at the meeting of the merchants on the Jay Treaty, and defeated Fitzsimons for Congress, he was venomously assailed. When he toasted 'The Rights of Women' at a Democratic banquet, 'Porcupine' sneered that he did well 'to turn out a volunteer,' for 'no lady will ever give a bounty for his services.' [5] That he was a conscienceless rascal may be inferred from 'Porcupine's' suggestion that his 'consummate wisdom and patriotism' had been shown, when, in the legislature, he had

---

[1] *Domestic Life,* 245. [2] *Ibid.,* 249.
[3] *Porcupine's Gazette,* December 4, 1797. [4] *Ibid.,* June 14, 1797.
[5] *Ibid.,* July 11, 1797.

'sought to procure a law preventing imprisonment for debt.'[1] Fatally ill at the time, 'Porcupine' followed him with indecent sneers to his grave.[2]

Nor were even the Democratic women spared, and the Federalists' favorite journal sneered repeatedly at the wife of Justice M'Kean. 'Why is Mrs. M'Kean like a taylor? Because she trims her good man's jacket.'[3] 'I have no objections to their toasting Judge M'Kean' — at a banquet — 'but the unmannerly brutes might have added his lady.'[4] Even the Judge's famously beautiful daughter was not spared, and during her courtship by the Spanish Minister, Don Carlos de Yrujo, the fashionable circles were snickering behind their fans over 'Porcupine's' comment that 'what were his motives in commencing the suit we shall leave our readers to divine.'[5] Giles was 'Farmer Giles,' who descended 'from the lowest grade of gentleman' — 'a gambler at heart' — devotee of the race-track, and 'the infamous faro table.'[6] Monroe was infamous, and even gentle, cultured old Dr. Logan, 'neath whose magnificent trees at 'Stenton' Mrs. Washington had passed delightful afternoons, became a cross between a clown and a rascal. No Democrat was spared.

The Democrats, overwhelmed, were comparatively tame, but the publication of Hamilton's pamphlet on his relations with Mrs. Reynolds, necessitated as he foolishly thought by the book of the notorious Callender, made him an easy mark for the Democratic scandal-mongers. In July he had appeared in Philadelphia to secure affidavits from Monroe and Muhlenberg — 'an attestation,' as Bache phrased it, 'of his having cuckolded James Reynolds.' It was understood that 'his man Oliver [Wolcott] had made out an affidavit as long as your arm,' but that others were desired 'to patch up the threads and fragments of his character.' Soon, said Bache, 'our ex-Secretary expects to be brought to bed of his pamphlet containing love-sick epistles.'[7] When it was printed three months later, Bache published a letter from New York to the effect that it had appeared in the morning 'and at six o'clock in the evening the town rings with it.' But 'the women

[1] *Porcupine's Gazette*, November 8, 1797.　　[2] *Ibid.*, November 10, 1797.
[3] *Ibid.*, August 8, 1797.　　[4] *Ibid.*, July 5, 1797.
[5] *Ibid.*, August 8, 1797.　　[6] *Gazette of the United States*, April 5, 1797.
[7] *Aurora*, July 19, 1797.

cry out against it as if its publication was high treason against the
rights of women.' [1]

It was impossible for the ostracism of Democrats, however, to
blur the social brilliancy of the season. Pinckney found his
evenings crowded 'with plays, public and private,' and his dinner
invitations 'abundant.' [2] Subscription dances, brilliant dinners
every night, elaborate entertainments, a giddy whirl. The diplomats were particularly lavish, none so much so as Liston, the
British Minister, at whose table Otis, Harper, Sedgwick, Wolcott
were frequent guests, and he was on terms of such familiarity with
the President that they sometimes strolled together in the streets.
But everywhere in the fashionable houses the Jeffersonians were
excluded, if not by lack of invitation, by the offensive coldness of
their reception. The play-houses were packed, albeit the entertainment was sometimes so vulgar and obscene that fathers indignantly left with their daughters.[3] Everywhere politics was on
a rampage, and even at the dinner table of President Adams the
passions seethed. 'By God, I would rather see this world annihilated,' shouted Blair McClanachan, 'than see this country
united with Great Britain.' [4] 'I dine next Tuesday at Court,'
wrote Gallatin to his wife, 'Courtland dining there the other day
heard Her Majesty, as she was asking the names of different members of Congress of Hindman, being told of some of the aristocratic party, say, "Ah, that is one of OUR people." So that she is
Mrs. President, not of the United States, but of a faction.' [5]

VII

This rabid spirit was not a little inspired by the press, which, in
turn, was encouraged by the politicians. A new Knight of Scurrility had entered the lists, encouraged by Hamilton, armed with
a pen that flowed poison. He had previously distinguished himself
by his brilliant and abusive pamphlets attacking Priestley, the
Democratic Societies, and the Irish, and by his exhibition in his
shop window of pictures of George III and Lord North, with
Franklin and Sam Adams coupled with fools or knaves. His un-

---

[1] *Aurora*, October 10, 1797.   [2] Pinckney, *Life of Pinckney*, 179.
[3] *Porcupine's Gazette*, March 10, 1798, has a letter quoting some of the filthy lines.
[4] Adams, *Gallatin*, 185–86.   [5] *Ibid.*, 184–85.

limited capacity for abuse, his insane fury against the French
Revolution, his unfathomable contempt for democracy, his devotion to England, fitted in with the spirit of society, and William
Cobbett launched his 'Porcupine's Gazette' under the most distinguished patronage. In his first issue, in an open letter to Bache,
he had described the 'Aurora' as a 'vehicle of lies and sedition.'
This was his keynote. Soon the Federalists were reading 'Porcupine' as a Bible, and the editors were making journalism a matter
of blackguardism, of black eyes and bloody noses. In blood and
breeding, Cobbett was inferior to Freneau, Bache, or Duane, but
he was a more consummate master of satire than any of them. He
could string chaste words into a scorpion lash that Swift would
have envied, or stoop to an obscenity and vulgarity that would
have delighted Kit Marlowe in his cups. None but a genius could
have risen from his original low estate, with so little education.
But a little while before a corporal in the British army, and still a
citizen of England, his English biographer makes the point that
the happiest days of his life were those when he edited the Federalists' favorite journal because 'he was fighting for his country.' [1]
Nothing pleased him more than to lash and lambaste the old heroes
of the American Revolution, Jefferson, Franklin, Paine, and Sam
Adams, and he could not only do it with impunity, but to the applause of society. Fenno sought to keep pace, in his weak way,
and Bache tried to match him in abuse. The fur flew. There were
physical assaults and rumors of assaults. The time was approaching when Bache would have to barricade himself with a few armed
friends in his office to protect his life and property from the destruction of a Federalist mob; when he would be set upon by
ruffians and beaten, and when he would exchange blows with
Fenno in the street. 'The white-livered, black-hearted thing
Bache, that public pest and bane of decency,' wrote 'Porcupine,'
and the ladies of Mrs. Bingham's circle agreed that Mr. Cobbett
was tremendously clever.[2]

It was a feverish summer, fall, and winter. Public dinners were
the fashion, bristling with fighting toasts. Through these the
Jeffersonians sought to keep up the courage of their party. Always toasts to the French Republic, and always toasts to the Irish

[1] Melville, I, 108.   [2] *Porcupine's Gazette*, August 4, 1797.

patriots — 'May the Irish harp be speedily torn from the British willow and made to vibrate to a revolutionary tune.' References to Jay's Treaty were followed by the playing of 'The Dead March.' Franklin, Jefferson, Monroe — these were invariably honored.[1] The Federalists penetrated the Jeffersonian stronghold of Philadelphia with a banquet at the Cameron Tavern, Southwark, with warlike toasts, and with Harper as the hero,[2] and a few days later the 'young men' of this district met to pass ringing resolutions endorsing the 'wisdom and integrity' of the Administration. One courageous soul moved to strike out the word 'wisdom,' and the crowd struck him out instead; whereupon a few gathered about and cheered for Jefferson.[3]

But the most notable banquet was in honor of Monroe in Philadelphia. Reaching the city, the former Minister to France left the boat with Mrs. Monroe, to be summarily ordered back by the health officers until he had 'undergone the usual formalities of examination.' Short shrift for Democrats was the order of the day, and the returning Minister of his Government to another nation returned with his wife to remain on board until 'examined.' Such was the morbid madness of the Federalists of this period that it was considered a triumph for the Administration to hold the former Minister and his wife with the immigrants. 'Porcupine' roared with glee in his best barrack-room manner.[4] When finally released, Monroe went into conference immediately with Jefferson, Gallatin, and Burr, and for two hours the leaders listened to a detailed story of his mission. Gallatin, who had refrained up to this time from expressing an opinion on Monroe's conduct, was convinced, from his conversation, 'manner, and everything,' that he was 'possessed of integrity superior to all attacks of malignity,' and had conducted himself 'with irreproachable honor and the most dignified sense of duty.' When the conference was over, Gallatin, at least, felt that the 'Administration have acted with a degree of meanness only exceeded by their folly.'[5]

This became the view of the Jeffersonians generally. A dinner was given at O'Eller's Hotel, with General Horatio Gates in the

---

[1] *Aurora*, April 14, July 11 and 13, 1797.
[2] *Gazette of the United States*, April 23, 1797.   [3] *Ibid.*, May 1, 1797.
[4] *Porcupine's Gazette*, July 1, 1797.   [5] Adams, *Gallatin* (to his wife), 186–87.

chair. There was Jefferson, and there, too, were Burr, Livingston, Gallatin, Tazewell, Judge M'Kean, the Governor, and fifty members of Congress. With enthusiasm they drank to the freedom of Ireland, and on the invitation of Gates they lifted their glasses with cheers to ʻCharles James Fox and the Patriots of England' — a frequently recurring Jeffersonian toast of the times. Livingston proposed — ʻMonroe, the virtuous citizen, who, to keep the peace of the country, refuses to do justice to himself.' Monroe responded in a brief speech, unexceptionable in every way, but Gallatin predicted, in a letter to his wife, that ʻPorcupine & Co. will roundly abuse us.' [1] And Gallatin was right, for that was ʻPorcupine's' business. ʻAt some tavern in the city,' ran the ʻPorcupine' account, ʻa most ludicrous farce called "The Welcome of Citizen Monroe" was performed. The principal characters were the Virginia Philosopher, Mrs. M'Kean's husband, and Monsieur Citizen Tazewell of the ancient dominion commonly called the Land of Debts.' [2] Livingston was wrong, however, in his notion that Monroe would remain silent. Urged on by the Jeffersonians, he prepared a defense which was given a nation-wide circulation through the exertions of his fellow partisans.[3] Jefferson was satisfied, the Federalists enraged. ʻA wicked misrepresentation of the facts,' though ʻmany applaud it,' wrote Wolcott.[4]

Meanwhile, the envoys were lost in the mists of the sea, and nothing had reached the public regarding their reception. In November, the atmosphere charged with the electricity of war, Adams returned to the capital from his seat at Braintree, to be escorted with military pomp into the city. The war propagandists were good psychologists sometimes. When Governor Mifflin, Democrat, ordered out the militia to parade in the President's honor, ʻPorcupine' graciously declared it ʻthe first decent act he had ever been guilty of.' [5] On the night of his arrival there was a dinner at O'Eller's in honor of ʻHis Serene Highness of Braintree,' as Bache put it, and so noisy was the demonstration that ʻsome ignorant people imagined a boxing match was on the carpet.' [6]

[1] Adams, *Gallatin*, 187; description of banquet, *Aurora*, July 1'/, 1797.
[2] *Porcupine's Gazette*, July 3, 1797.
[3] Jefferson's *Works* (to Mercer), IX, 421; (to Madison), IX, 405–07.
[4] Gibbs, II, 12.   [5] *Porcupine's Gazette*, November 6, 1797.
[6] *Aurora*, November 15, 1797.

This was the spirit of the hour when Congress met in November — the bitterness among the members fully as intense as among the loungers in the streets.

VIII

And yet it was not to be without its touch of comedy. Before the crisis came, two incidents had set the country roaring. Matthew Lyon, the Vermont Democrat, was a constant provocation to the Federalists. Hot-tempered, ardent, uncouth in his manners, but thoroughly honest at heart, he had outraged the clubby spirit of the Federalists. During the Revolution he had been shamefully cashiered for an act deserving of a medal, but almost immediately he had been vindicated. The vindication was thoroughly understood in Philadelphia, but it suited the purpose of his political foes to ignore the facts for the benefit of the slander.

The House was sitting, but in a state of confusion — every one including the Speaker talking — Lyon holding forth in conversation on the ease with which Connecticut could be converted to Democracy through a Democratic paper in that State. Roger Griswold, a Federalist leader, made a slurring reference to Lyon's 'wooden sword.' The latter, hearing it, preferred to ignore the insult. Whereupon Griswold, following him and plucking at his coat, repeated the slander. At this Lyon made an unpardonable blunder — instead of slapping Griswold's face, he spat in it. Instantly the Federalists were in ferment. The 'little beast' was unfit to associate with gentlemen, anyway, and should be expelled. There was an investigation, with denunciatory speeches as indecent as the act denounced. The purpose was clear — to get rid of Lyon's vote. The Jeffersonians thereupon rallied to his support. Neither condoning the act nor asking that it go unpunished, Gallatin opposed the expulsion resolution on the ground that Congress was not a fashionable club and had no right to deprive a district of its representation on the basis of manners. A two-thirds vote was necessary to expel, and this was lacking. It was a party vote.

A few days later, Lyon was seated at his desk buried in papers, oblivious to his surroundings, and Griswold, armed with a hickory stick, approached from the rear and began striking him on the head. Several blows were struck before the victim of the assault

THE GRISWOLD-LYON FIGHT IN THE HOUSE

could extricate himself from his desk. Then, grasping some coal tongs, he advanced on Griswold, who, finding his enemy also armed, gallantly retreated, striking wildly. They clinched, rolled on the floor, and colleagues intervened. Here was another insult to the dignity of the House, but the Federalists were delighted with it. Since nothing could be done to Lyon without doing as much to Griswold, the matter was dropped. The scribes fell upon the morsel with a zest, the first political caricature in American history resulted, the public shrugged its shoulders and laughed, Jefferson thought the whole affair 'dirty business,'[1] but Gallatin, quite as much of a gentleman as Otis, thought that 'nobody can blame Lyon for resenting the insult,' since there was 'a notable lack of delicacy in the conversation of most Connecticut gentlemen.'[2] Fenno called Lyon a 'filthy beast.' 'Porcupine,' who had rather urged that some one spit in the face of Bache, gloated over Griswold's assault,[3] dubbed those who voted against expulsion 'Knights of the Wooden Sword,'[4] and virtuously resolved 'to make the whole business as notorious as the courage of Alexander or the cruelty of Nero.'[5] Speaker Dayton, whom he had recently denounced as a 'double-faced weather-cock,' having voted for expulsion, became an ornament over whom 'New Jersey has indeed new reason to boast.'[6] The real significance of the incident was that the war party had fared forth, chesty and cocky, to intimidate the Jeffersonians and had met a check — but they were to have another chance at Lyon.[7]

---

[1] Jefferson's *Works*, x, 19–22. [2] Adams, *Gallatin* (to Mrs. Gallatin), 191.
[3] *Porcupine's Gazette*, February 16, 1798. [4] *Ibid.*, February 9, 1798.
[5] *Ibid.*, February 15, 1798. [6] *Ibid.*, February 14, 1798.
[7] Henry Adams says: 'Lyon, though a very rough specimen of democracy, was by no means a contemptible man, and, politics aside, showed energy and character in his subsequent career.' (Adams, *Gallatin*, 192.)

CHAPTER XVI

HYSTERICS

I

THE meeting of Congress in the early winter of 1797 found the war party in fine fettle and the Jeffersonians fighting desperately for peace. Early in the session, Adams called for the advice of his Cabinet on the policy to be pursued in the event of the failure of the envoys. The three Hamiltonian members had conferred and McHenry was instructed to write Hamilton for instructions. 'I am sure I cannot do justice to the subject as you can,' wrote the Secretary of War to the President's enemy in New York. Agreeing, no doubt, with the sentiment, the power behind the Cabinet speedily complied, and the response to the President of his advisers was the recommendations of Hamilton copied into the handwriting of McHenry.[1] These did not contemplate a declaration of war, but a resort to warlike measures. Merchant vessels should be armed, twenty sloops of the line built, an immediate army of sixteen thousand men recruited with provision for twenty thousand more, the French treaty abrogated, a loan authorized, and the tax system put upon a war basis. An alliance with England? Not improper, perhaps, but inexpedient; though Rufus King in London should make overtures to the British for a loan, the aid of convoys, perhaps the transfer of ten ships of the line, and, in the event of a definite rupture with France, he should be authorized to work out a plan of coöperation with England.[2]

All this while the debates in Congress were increasing in bitterness. Monroe was accused and defended, democrats denounced and damned, aristocrats and monocrats assailed. Orators were mobilized and paraded in war-paint spluttering their most vituperative phrases, and the most insignificant pack-horse of the war party attacked Jefferson's letter to Mazzei as 'a disgraceful performance.'[3] The chest of the flamboyant Harper was never so

[1] Steiner, 291, 295.　　　　　　　　　　[2] Adams, *Works*, I, 515-17.
[3] Coit, *Annals*, February 28, 1798.

protuberant as in those days when he strutted through the Dictionary hurling the most offensive words in the language at the Jeffersonians, rattling his sword, waving his pistol, and offering to meet gentlemen outside the House. All revolutions he thought the work of fools and knaves, philosophers, Jacobins, and *sansculottes*. The Jeffersonians were conspiring to prostrate popular liberty and establish tyranny by curtailing the power of the Executive and increasing the power of the House. It was all very simple. The President crushed, the Senate next destroyed, three or four audacious demagogues would dominate the House until the strongest cut the throats of the others and seized the scepter. The Federalists were delighted — what a wonderful man was Harper! [1] Day by day the violence increased. Harper snapped at Giles, who snapped back, and when Otis made a nasty attack on the Virginian and the latter dared him to repeat it 'out of doors,' there were loud cries of 'order.' Only Gallatin remained cool, in possession of his senses. He contented himself with the assertion that only on information that had not been given could war measures be excused.[2]

The superheat of the House cooled the passions of the people and remonstrances against the arming of merchant ships poured in. Even from New England they came, maddening to Cabot and Ames, reassuring to Jefferson, who made the most of them in his correspondence.[3] When the town meeting at Cambridge joined the remonstrators, the Boston 'Centinel' fumed over 'the indecent abuse of the merchants,' and the 'forestalling knavery' of the town.[4] Then, to revive the failing spirits of the war party, Adams came to the rescue with a Message announcing the failure of the envoys and recommending warlike measures. How the little patriot would have winced had he known that in adopting the recommendations of McHenry he was accepting the dictations of Alexander Hamilton! Jefferson wrote Madison that it was 'an insane message,' and the Jeffersonians, no longer doubting that war was the purpose, arranged to force a show-down.[5] Thus appeared the Sprigg Resolutions providing for purely defensive

---

[1] *Annals,* March 2, 1798.   [2] *Ibid.,* March 13, 1798.
[3] Jefferson's *Works,* IX, 437–39.   [4] April 14, 1798.
[5] Jefferson's *Works,* IX, 405–07.

measures for the coast and the interior, and declaring that 'under existing conditions it is not expedient for the United States to resort to war against the French Republic.' [1]

Momentarily taken unaware, the Federalists were stunned. Harper blundered into the admission that he could see no objections, but Otis, with keener insight, proposed to substitute the word 'declare' for 'resort to' war — and the cat was out of the bag. The Jeffersonians feared, not so much a declaration of war as warlike measures that would force a state of war, and to forestall that was the purpose of the Resolutions. Thus the debate proceeded, more bitter and personal, with Giles and Harper resembling the wenches of the fishmarket without their skirts.

Meanwhile, the Federalist leaders were familiar with the X Y Z papers of which the Democrats were kept in ignorance. Hamilton, private citizen of New York, knew their contents; Jefferson, Vice-President of the United States, did not. This was the trump card of the war party, and no one saw it so quickly as Hamilton, who immediately began to work secretly, through his agents in the Cabinet, for their publication. 'Nothing certainly can be more proper,' he wrote Pickering. 'Confidence will otherwise be wanting.' [2] In utter ignorance of their contents, the Jeffersonians began to demand their production. Only a few days before, the Jeffersonian organ in Boston was charging that Adams withheld the papers because they 'contain an account of some resentful expressions of the French respecting our Cabinet, and Mr. Adams does not expect any credit by publishing them.' [3] Thus, when the motion was made that the papers be produced, Gallatin, Giles, Livingston, and Nicholas supported it, and the next day they were sent with the request that they be considered in confidence until the effect of their publication could be discussed.

The galleries were cleared — the doors locked and guarded — and for three days and into the fourth the secret discussion continued. Then the doors were opened and the crowd in the galleries heard a brief discussion of the number of copies to be printed for circulation. 'One thousand, two hundred,' said Bayard of Delaware. 'Three thousand,' urged Harper. 'Seven thousand,'

---

[1] *Annals*, March 27, 1798.   [2] Hamilton's *Works*, x, 279.
[3] *Independent Chronicle*, March 26, 1798.

sneered the hot-headed Matthew Lyon, 'for the papers are so trifling and unimportant that no printer would risk the printing of them in a pamphlet.' Otis incredulously inquired if he had rightly understood the Vermont fire-eater. Lyon unblushingly repeated his strange assertion. The suggestion of Bayard was adopted, and, when the members filed out of the little room in which they deliberated that day, Harper and the war hawks could already hear the thunder of the guns.

II

Thus did the shadows close in on the Jeffersonians. The blow was staggering. On the appearance of the damaging documents, most of the Democratic papers were silent, while printing them in full. One made a brave show of satisfaction by criticizing Adams for withholding them so long, and suggesting that perhaps 'the most important papers' had been withheld.[1] Even the buoyancy of Jefferson suffered a momentary collapse. Writing Madison the day the papers were read, he did not have the heart to indicate the nature of their contents.[2] The next day he had recovered sufficiently to write that his first impressions were 'very disagreeable and confused,' and that this would be the first impression of the public. A more mature consideration, he thought, would disclose no new ground for war, but war psychology and fear of false imputations might drive the people to the war hawks.[3] Madison, equally astonished, thought Talleyrand's conduct 'incredible,' not because of its 'depravity, which, however heinous, is not without example,' but because of its 'unparalleled stupidity.'[4] Monroe, who had spent the night with Madison in Virginia, thought the incident 'evidently a swindling experiment,' which was clear enough on its face.[5] The public, in the meantime, was reading one of the most grotesque stories of political infamy and personal cupidity on record. The envoys had been treated with contempt, refused an audience, insulted by unofficial blackmailers sent by the unscrupulous Talleyrand to demand a loan for France and, more particularly, a bribe for himself. The envoys had conducted

---

[1] *New York Time Piece*, April 13, 1798.
[2] Jefferson's *Works*, x, 22–24.   [3] *Ibid.*, x, 24–26.
[4] Madison's *Writings*, ii, 133.   [5] *Ibid.* (to Jefferson), ii, 138.

themselves with becoming dignity and spirit. 'Millions for defense, but not one cent for tribute,' was a clarion call to battle. The pride of the people was touched, and overnight the political complexion of the country had been changed. A wave of hysterical patriotism swept over the Nation, and the war hawks set to work to turn it into frenzy. It was now or never.

III

For once John Adams was on top of the world. He who had so longed for popularity had found it. Everywhere, in cities, on Southern plantations, under the primeval forests of the frontiers, men were wildly waving flags and saluting the President. Addresses pledging life and fortune poured in to be prominently printed in the papers, and nowhere more than in the Jeffersonian States.[1] Most were the spontaneous expressions of an excited people, some were unquestionably engineered by the politicians.[2] But on the surface the country was aflame. Down the Philadelphia streets one day swung twelve hundred young men, keeping step to martial music, the streets lined with the cheering populace, and, as 'Porcupine' observed, with 'every female in the city whose face is worth looking at' gladdening 'the way with her smiles.'[3] At Adams's house the little man, who had always wanted to be a warrior, appeared on the steps to greet them, wearing a cockade, in full military regalia, his sword dangling at his side. Intoxicated by the adulation, he plunged impetuously into a denunciation of France and its Revolution.[4] Madison thought his language 'the most abominable and degrading that could fall from the lips of a first magistrate of an independent people, and particularly from a Revolutionary patriot.'[5] Aroused by the philippic of the President, the young men spent the day marching the streets, and in the evening wined and dined until ten o'clock, when they sallied forth to exercise their patriotism in deeds of violence. The Terror had begun. Reeling and shouting, they bore down upon the home of Bache. With only women and children in the house, they fell in right gallant fashion on the doors and

---

[1] *Centinel*, May 30, 1798. [2] *Independent Chronicle*, November 22, 1798.
[3] *Porcupine's Gazette*, May 7, 1798. [4] *Ibid.*, May 7, 1798.
[5] Madison's *Writings* (to Jefferson), II, 142.

windows and were making headway when the neighbors interfered and sent the drunken youngsters upon their way.[1] But with the war hawks, the attack on the home of Bache was not least among the virtues of the mob, and the Federalist press was unstinted in its praise.

Then, on May 9th, came the day of fasting and prayer, set by Adams in happy ignorance that when he yielded to the importunities of Pickering for a proclamation, he was again acting under the direction of the hated Hamilton.[2] The President had worked himself into a morbid state of mind. Some mysterious wag had sent him a warning that the city would be burned that night. The Jeffersonians smiled and shrugged their shoulders, and one editor suggested that, since the conflagration was promised for the fast day, 'the incendiaries meant political or ecclesiastical fire.'[3] But Adams, taking it seriously, saw conspirators all about, incendiaries, assassins. Determined to die resisting at his post, he had his servants carry arms and ammunition into the house by the back way to withstand a siege.

The day was quiet enough, with business suspended and the churches filled. Preachers pounced upon the Democrats and infidels with demoniac fury. But in the evening the Terror came — and even as an old man Adams could recall it only with a shudder. The Administration papers of the time, eager to paint the picture black, could find nothing serious to report, however. A few butcher boys, none the wiser for drink, exercised their lungs in the State House yard until the soldiers swept down upon them, arresting a few who were dismissed on the morrow, and frightening the others home.[4] But that was not the only mob that roved the streets that night. The patriots had their inning, too, smashing the windows of Bache's house and smearing the statue of that filthy Democrat, Benjamin Franklin, with mud from the gutters. The war propagandists fairly fluttered with activity. Hopkinson's new song, 'Hail Columbia,' was wildly cheered at the theaters, much to the disgust of the Democrats, who resented the com-

---

[1] Bache in a statement ascribed the incident to the intoxicated condition of the youths. *Time Piece*, May 14, 1798.

[2] Hamilton's *Works*, x, 275–79.

[3] *Independent Chronicle*, May 10, 1798.

[4] *Gazette of the United States*, May 10; *Porcupine's Gazette*, May 10, 1798.

plimentary reference to Adams,[1] and, when the author was soon
given a Government position, it was suggested that Hopkinson
had certainly 'written his song to the right tune.'[2] When Fox the
actor sang the song at the theater in Baltimore, it was observed
that 'some Jacobins left the room.'[3] Even this hysteria did not
satisfy the war hawks who stood in the wings beating tom-toms
and crying, 'War! War! War!' Hamilton was urging Washington
'under some pretext of health' to tour Virginia and North Carolina to give occasion for dinners and warlike addresses. From his
retreat at Dedham, Fisher Ames was writing nervously to Pickering that 'we must make haste to wage war or we shall be lost.'[4]
Hopkinson, the song-writer, observing the serenity of New York,
was wishing that he were a despot that he might 'order the whole
city to undergo the Turkish ceremony of the bastinado' and 'rouse
the lazy drones with a whip.'[5] In far-off Lisbon, William Smith
was nauseated with 'the old womanish whining about our reluctance to war.'[6]

Then John Marshall returned and the tired voices of the
shouters found a tonic. Out to Kensington they went to meet him,
sour-visaged Pickering in a carriage looking stern and warlike despite his spectacles, three companies of cavalry on prancing steeds,
citizens and Congressmen in conveyances or on horseback. Long
before the town was reached, 'the streets and windows, even the
housetops in many instances, were crowded with people.'[7] The
bells in the steeple of Christ Church began to peal, and peal they
did far into the night. The reverberations of cannon mingled with
the huzzas of the populace as the procession moved slowly on
through as many streets as possible to the City Tavern. 'All this
was to secure him to their views that he might say nothing that
would oppose the game they were playing,' Jefferson wrote Madison.[8] The next morning the war party thronged the tavern, a
dinner was given, and there was much satisfaction when Jefferson,
who had called, was unable to see the hero.[9] Livingston, who had
accompanied Marshall from New York, had been assured that

[1] *Aurora*, April 27, 1798.   [2] *Independent Chronicle*, May 21, 1798.
[3] *New York Commercial Advertiser*, October 19, 1798.   [4] Ames, I, 232–35.
[5] Gibbs (to Wolcott), II, 49.   [6] *Ibid.*, II, 117–20.
[7] *Porcupine's Gazette*, June 20, 1798.   [8] Jefferson's *Works*, x, 45–53.
[9] Beveridge, II, 346–47.

France had no thought of war, but soon stories were afloat through the city, as emanating from the envoy, of a contradictory nature.[1]

Again the prancing of cavalry in the streets when Marshall departed for Virginia — a series of ovations all the way.[2] Then Pinckney returned — and more pageants. Soldiers and citizens vied at Princeton and Trenton, and a dinner was given and the French damned.[3] All the time the country was being overwhelmed with propaganda such as it had never known before. Hamilton was writing his bitter invectives against the French,[4] in which France was 'a den of pillage and slaughter' and Frenchmen 'foul birds of prey.' These letters, running in Fenno's paper, alarmed Jefferson, who wrote to prod Madison from the lethargy of retirement. 'Sir, take up your pen against this champion. You know the ingenuity of his talents, and there is not a person but yourself who can foil him. For heaven's sake, then, take up your pen and do not desert the public cause entirely.'[5] But even more damaging than the pen of Hamilton was that of William Cobbett, 'Peter Porcupine.' As a manufacturer of horrors he makes the wildest propagandists of the World War pale like a candle held against the sun. Childishly happy was the 'Porcupine' of those days when he could fight, on American soil, 'for his country' and his King. Thus 'the sans-culottes' had 'taken vessels off the bar at Charleston' and the French had landed and were plundering farmhouses.[6] Thus a French invasion plot was discovered. 'Porcupine' had the particulars. The negro slaves were to be armed and used as allies against the whites. 'What a pretty figure Nicholas and Giles will cut,' wrote the jubilant Peter, 'when Citizen Pompey and Citizen Cæsar shall have tied their hands behind them. . . . Could its miseries be confined to these, I would say, God hasten it.'[7] 'Gaunt Gallatin' working hard all night? Useless, useless — 'war, frightful war there will be in spite of all his teeth and his nails too.'[8] And then again, the invasion. Rumor had it that the French were buying three thousand stand of arms

[1] Jefferson's *Works*, x, 45–53. [2] Beveridge, ii, 348.
[3] *New York Commercial Advertiser*, October 31, November 5, 1798.
[4] 'Titus Manlius,' Hamilton's *Works*, v, 259–301.
[5] Jefferson's *Works*, x, 22–24.
[6] *Porcupine's Gazette*, May 23, 1798. [7] *Ibid.*, May 24, 1798.
[8] *Ibid.*, May 26, 1798.

for the West Indies. 'That these arms were bought for Virginia and Georgia is much more likely,' commented 'Porcupine.' 'Take care, take care, you sleepy southern fools. Your negroes will probably be your masters this day twelve month.' [1] 'Extra!' 'Extra!' 'Startling News from Virginia' — 'these villains have actually begun to tamper with our negroes.' An 'ill-looking fellow on horseback' had been seen talking with some slaves. It was understood he had come from Philadelphia, and the ruffian was a refugee from English justice in Ireland. [2] And then, another lurid article on 'Horrors of a French Invasion,' with bloodcurdling pictures of the outraging of American wives and daughters. [3]

The French invasion at hand — slaves armed — masters murdered in their beds — churches burned — women outraged — girls kidnaped — horrors piled on horrors, and all because of democracy. Little wonder that the apprehensive Adams, who temperamentally sniffed treachery in every breeze, all but trembled as he turned the pages of his 'Porcupine' that year. In Boston the presses were kept busy turning out Harper's war speech, [4] and Cabot was spurring Harper on to greater efforts. There, too, the rabid war speech of a Harvard professor made on Fast Day in Brattle Street was being published as a pamphlet, [5] and the clergy were urging the hate of French democracy as a Christian duty, and converting their pulpits into pedestals of Mars. Dr. Tappan of Boston was making political harangues that Federalist politicians were praising, [6] and Father Thayer was clamoring for slaughter in pious accents. [7] Sometimes Democratic members of congregations who sought Christ instead of Cæsar in the temples indignantly left, and on one occasion an audacious and irreverent Jeffersonian paused on his way out to exclaim in Latin, 'Why so much anger in the heart of a divine?' [8] Nor were some of the war propagandists on the Bench to be outdone·by those in the pulpit. Judge Rush was thundering vituperative phrases at the French in a charge to a jury. [9] Chief Justice Dana of Massachusetts phrased one of his charges like a participant in a congressional party scrim-

---

[1] *Porcupine's Gazette*, June 7, 1798.
[2] *Ibid.*, June 8, 1798.
[3] *Ibid.*, June 12, 1798.
[4] Lodge, *Cabot* (to Wolcott), 153–54.
[5] *Independent Chronicle*, April 9, 1798.
[6] Gibbs, II, 46.
[7] *Independent Chronicle*, August 9, 1798.
[8] *Ibid.*, December 6, 1798.
[9] *Centinel*, September 29, 1798.

mage.[1] Much earlier, Chief Justice Ellsworth of the United States Supreme Court made a grand jury charge the occasion for an amazing attack on the Jeffersonian Party.[2] As early as May, Jefferson was utterly disheartened by the 'war spirit worked up in the town.'[3] By June he was writing Kosciusko that he thought war 'almost inevitable.'[4] In August he felt that 'there is no event however atrocious which may not be expected,' and was promising to meet the Maratists 'in such a way as shall not be derogatory either to the public liberty or my own personal honor.'[5]

The country was rushing toward the Terror, with the war party rattling sabers and threatening their opponents with violence. 'Porcupine' was predicting gleefully that 'when the occasion requires, the Yankees will show themselves as ready at stringing up insurgents as in stringing onions.'[6] It was an open season for physical assaults on Jeffersonian editors and Bache was being attacked in his office,[7] and another assailant who had sought to murder him found his fifty-dollar fine paid by the politicians when he proffered the money, and Adams sent him on a mission to Europe.[8] The Federalists, for the moment, were cocks of the walk, and even Hamilton was rushing into print with a letter that would have endeared him to the Three Musketeers. A nondescript had referred in the press to his ambition and his affair with Mrs. Reynolds. Ludicrously interpreting it as a threat of assassination because of a reference to Cæsar, Hamilton lost his head and published a signed statement promising that the 'assassin' would 'not find me unprepared to repel attack.'[9] This childish boast played into the hands of the obscure assailant, who replied: 'Armed with a cane (whether with a sword therein I cannot say) you walk about, prepared, you say, to defy attack. By this you fall beneath resentment and excite my pity.'[10] A few days later he was writing of 'the declaration made in company' by 'a Mr. Patterson, a clerk to Alexander Hamilton,' that the writer would be murdered, and offering five hundred dollars reward for the apprehension of the prospective assassin.[11] Wild days, wild days!

[1] *Centinel*, December 15, 1798.   [2] *Porcupine's Gazette*, April 11, 1798.
[3] Jefferson's *Works* (to Madison), x, 33–36.   [4] *Ibid.*, x, 47–49.
[5] *Ibid.* (to Samuel Smith), x, 55.   [6] *Porcupine's Gazette*, June 1, 1798.
[7] *Gazette of the United States*, August 9, 1798.   [8] *Independent Chronicle*, May 21, 1798.
[9] *Time Piece*, May 25, 1798.   [10] *Ibid.*, May 28, 1798.   [11] *Ibid.*, June 11, 1798.

This was the temper in which Congress resumed its deliberations after the publication of the X Y Z papers. Jefferson advised his followers to seek an adjournment to permit the members to consult the people, and had this procedure been adopted the Federalists might have escaped the pitfalls to which they were reeling.[1] The Democrats in the streets were cowed and only the most audacious met threats with bravado or courage. The braves of Tammany at a public dinner drank to the toast: 'May the old Tories and all who wish to engage the United States in a war with any nation, realize the felicity they anticipate by being placed in the front of the first battle.'[2] The Boston 'Chronicle' was publishing letters from 'Benedict Arnold' offering his services in the war for England, and rejoicing 'to hear that so many of my countrymen have shaken off their delusion, as I predicted they would only eighteen years ago.'[3] Day after day it published Josiah Quincy's speech, made in 1774, against standing armies. Soon it was calling attention to profiteering of war patriots in Boston who had a monopoly on Raven's Duck which would be wanted for tents.[4]

III

But the Democratic leaders required all their courage to stand up before the fusillade — Jefferson most of all. With the Philadelphia streets filled with swaggering young men in uniforms, many nights he heard 'The Rogue's March' played beneath his windows. Bitter, threatening letters burdened his mail. Spies crept to his dinner table to pick up the stray threads of casual conversation that could be given a sinister twist, and he was forced to deny himself to all but his most intimate friends.[5] When forced to appear in company, he simulated an abstracted silence, ignored personal affronts, and talked calmly when at all. 'All the passions are boiling over,' he wrote in May, 'and he who would keep himself cool and clear of the contagion is so far below the point of ordinary conversation that he finds himself isolated in every society.'[6] Convinced that even his correspondence was tampered

---

[1] Jefferson's *Works* (to Madison), **x**, 16–19.
[2] *Time Piece*, May 18, 1798. [3] May 24, 1798. [4] October 15, 1798.
[5] Jefferson's *Works* (to Lewis), x, 36–37. [6] *Ibid.*

with, he no longer dared write freely in letters entrusted to the mails.[1] Spies dogged his footsteps and kept guard at his door.[2] When on a visit to Virginia he accepted an entertainment on Sunday, the floodgates were opened upon him, and his enemies boasted that 'this fact has been trumpeted from one end of the country to the other as irrefutable proof of his contempt for the Christian religion, and his devotion to the new religion of France.'[3] Sad that Rufus King and Christopher Gore had continued their English tour on Sunday, and too bad that the Federalists persisted in holding their political caucuses in Boston on Sunday evenings, retorted the 'Independent Chronicle.'[4]

No dinner of the war party was complete without an insulting toast on Jefferson. 'Jefferson — May he deserve better of his country than he has hitherto done.'[5] 'The Vice-President — May his heart be purged of Gallicism in the pure fire of Federalism or be lost in the furnace' — with groans.[6] 'John Adams — May he like Samson slay thousands of Frenchmen with the jaw bone of Jefferson.'[7] And in the midst of the mobbing, the self-contained philosopher kept his mouth shut and his feet upon the ground. With 'The Rogue's March' ringing in his ears he was able to write a long letter on the value of crop rotation;[8] another on a plough he had invented;[9] and in the midst of the Sedition Bill debate, learning that an acquaintance was going west of the Mississippi where wild horses roved the plains, he sent the suggestion that this was 'the last opportunity to study them in a state of nature,' and requesting him to prepare a report for the Philosophical Society.[10] Many days found him alone in the library of this Society, and once, during that hectic summer, he stole away from the turmoil and hate to the beautiful country home of the Logans where he could forget the bitterness of the battle browsing in its great library or lounging beneath its majestic trees.[11]

Everywhere the Democrats were fair game for persecution.

[1] Jefferson's *Works* (to Madison), x, 22–24; (to John Taylor), x, 63–67.
[2] *Ibid.* (to S. Smith), x, 53–59.
[3] King's *Works* (Troup to King), ii, 431–32.
[4] August 20, 1798.
[5] *New York Commercial Advertiser*, November 20, 1798.
[6] *Centinel*, July 18, 1798.   [7] *Ibid.*, July 14, 1798.
[8] Jefferson's *Works*, x, 13–14.   [9] *Ibid.*, 15–16.   [10] *Ibid.*, 53–54.
[11] *Porcupine's Gazette*, July 21, 1798, makes a sneering comment.

Matthew Lyon found a band playing 'The Rogue's March' in front of his tavern at Trenton and New Brunswick where crowds shouted imprecations.[1] In New York, only the appearance of fighting Irish friends prevented the war hawks from serenading Edward Livingston's home with the offensive March.[2] In Boston the 'patriots' expelled Thomas Adams, editor of the 'Chronicle,' from the Fire Society of which he had been a faithful member for fourteen years.

IV

In this atmosphere, the Federalist machinery in Congress was set in motion at high speed on war measures. Provisions were made for the strengthening of the coast defenses, a navy was created, an army provided, taxes levied, and through all this the Jeffersonians, under the calm, courageous leadership of Albert Gallatin, merely sought to exercise a moderating influence. If war was to come, provision had to be made. But that was not enough for the radicals among the Federalists — the conditions were ripe for the crushing of domestic foes as well as foreign enemies. Here was the opportunity to destroy the party of democracy.

The first manifestation of this intent came with the introduction of the Alien Bill in the Senate — aimed at the Irish more than at the French, if we may judge from the correspondence of the Hamiltonian leaders and the tone of the Federalist press. Both fairly bristled with hatred of the Irish immigrant who was beginning to make himself felt in American politics. This, in part a by-product of the Federalist partiality for England, was, in large measure, an expression of the Federalist abhorrence of insurrections against constituted authority everywhere. From the Ireland of that day, seething with rebellion, incoming vessels were bringing Irish refugees, most of whom were members of the revolutionary United Irishmen. Instinct and observation took them in a body into the Jeffersonian Party, of which they became the shock troops in many parts of the country. It was only at Jeffersonian dinners that glasses were drained to the Liberal leaders in England, Fox and Sheridan, and to the success of the Irish Rebellion; and only in Jeffersonian papers that sympathy

[1] *Porcupine's Gazette*, July 23, 1798.   [2] *Time Piece*, July 30, 1798.

was expressed. It was during this time that Irish patriots were being hurried to the gallows, and John Philpot Curran was making his incomparable orations, now classics, in their defense. His burning phrases were being punctuated by the rattle of the soldiers' musketry intended to awe him into silence. The patriot press was being crushed in Dublin. Castlereagh was busy with his dirty money buying members of the Irish Parliament where money would buy them, and finding renegades ready to cut their country's throat for a title, a place, or a ribbon to pin on their coats. Of these latter the most loathsome was Lord Clare, whose infamy has been embalmed in the eloquence of Curran.

It is not without significance that the Jeffersonian dinners in those days were toasting John Philpot Curran, and that his speeches were printed by the column in the Jeffersonian press,[1] while Cobbett was giving three full pages to Lord Clare's excoriation of his countrymen.[2] A month before the Alien Bill reached the House, Cobbett was devoting a full page to a weird story involving the Irish in America in a conspiracy with the French for the destruction of the Government of the United States.[3] 'That restless, rebellious tribe, the emigrated United Irishman,' snorted 'Porcupine,' the English citizen.

All this was on the surface, but it did not reveal half the story. With the Irish patriots, crushed by the soldiers of Cornwallis, seeking an asylum in America, Rufus King, the Federalist Minister in London, was writing Hamilton rejoicing over the suppression of the Irish Rebellion, and expressing the hope that 'our Government . . . will have the power and inclination to exclude these disaffected characters, who will be suffered to seek an asylum among us.'[4] It was King's aggressive protest to the British Government that delayed for four years the release of the Irish prisoners who had planned an extensive settlement in America. Ten years later, the most brilliant of these, Thomas Addis Emmet, who was to become one of the ornaments of the New York Bar and to sleep at length by the roaring traffic of Broadway in Saint Paul's churchyard, wrote King in bitter rebuke: 'I should have

---

[1] *Time Piece*, June 13, July 2, 11, 13, 1798; *Aurora*, November 7, 1798.
[2] *Porcupine's Gazette*, December 22, 1798.   [3] *Ibid.*, May 8, 1798.
[4] King's *Works*, II, 376.

brought along with me a brother [Robert Emmet] whose name perhaps will you even not read without emotions of sympathy and respect.'[1] The Ministry had been favorable to the release and migration until King's hot remonstrance against admitting such desperadoes as Thomas Addis Emmet! This Federalist hate of the Irish reeked in the sneers of its press, exposed itself in the 'wild Irish' speech of Otis, in the official actions of King, in the correspondence of the leaders, in the description by Gibbs[2] of the victims of Cornwallis's bayonets and Castlereagh's bribes as 'fugitives from the justice of Great Britain.'

Many thought, when the Alien Bill was introduced, that it was aimed at Gallatin, and it was boasted in the coffee-houses of New York that it would soon be easy to 'ship him off.'[3] Terrorized by the threat of the measure, many harmless Frenchmen, including Volney, hastily chartered a ship and sailed away,[4] but when a little later some emigrant French royalists came knocking at the door they were admitted.[5] Jefferson thought the bill 'detestable,'[6] and Madison, 'a monster that will disgrace its parents.'[7] Even Hamilton was shocked at the bill introduced in the Senate, and he hastened a letter to Pickering urging moderation. 'Let us not be cruel or violent,' he wrote.[8]

The purpose of the Sedition Bill was to crush the opposition press and silence criticism of the ruling powers. Among the extreme and dominant Federalists criticism had long been confused with sedition, and Fenno had long described attacks on Administration measures as treason. Scurrility in the press was all too common, but the worst of the Jeffersonian organs could be matched by the Federalists; and no one in 1798 imagined that a Sedition Law would ever be evoked against 'Porcupine' or Russell. The Hamiltonians were moving with such celerity toward repression that a Congressman's circularization of his constituents with comments on policies and measures was being denounced as seditious, and Judge Iredell, a narrow partisan, had actually called the attention of the Richmond Grand Jury to a letter from Representative Cabell. 'Porcupine' had published

[1] Randall, *Jefferson*, 400, note. [2] Volume II, 75, 77.
[3] *Time Piece*, June 1, 1798. [4] Jefferson's *Works* (to Madison), X, 33–36; 40–43.
[5] *Porcupine's Gazette*, July 11, 1798. [6] Jefferson's *Works* (to Madison), X, 40.
[7] Madison's *Writings* (to Jefferson), II, 142. [8] Hamilton's *Works*, X, 293.

this letter with abusive comments as though it were a treasonable correspondence with an alien enemy.[1] The next day he published with enthusiastic praise a letter that Otis the Federalist had written to a constituent in Boston.[2]

The moment these measures were introduced, every one knew that Gallatin was in danger because of his Genevese accent, but that 'Porcupine,' the English subject, had no fears. Men like Hamilton Rowan, Dr. James Priestley, and Volney could be sent away, but the putrid offal of the defunct court of Versailles could continue to count upon a dinner at the Binghams'. Cabell was subject to indictment for an action that was commendable in Otis, and the merest child knew that the Sedition Law would be applied to Jeffersonian papers alone.

V

Bad as was the Alien Law, it did not approach the viciousness of the Sedition Act; and the Sedition Bill as passed was mild compared with the one the Federalist leaders in the Senate originally framed. Albeit America and France were not at war, the bill declared the French people enemies of the American people, and that any one giving the former aid and comfort should be punishable with death. A strict enforcement of such an act would have sent Jefferson to the gallows. Under the Fourth Article any one questioning the constitutionality or justice of an Administration measure could be sent to herd with felons. It would have sealed the lips of members of Congress.

When this monstrous measure reached Hamilton, he was dumbfounded at the temerity and brutality of his followers. Grasping his pen, he hurriedly sent a note of warning to Wolcott. There were provisions that were 'highly exceptionable' that would 'endanger civil war.' He hoped that 'the thing will not be hurried through.' Why 'establish a tyranny?' Was not 'energy a very different thing from violence?'[3] Reeling drunk with intolerance, even Hamilton's warning only coaxed a slight concession to liberty, and it was a thoroughly vicious and tyrannical measure that was debated in the House. These debates were conducted under con-

---

[1] *Porcupine's Gazette*, April 30, 1798. [2] *Ibid.*, May 1, 1798.
[3] Hamilton's *Works*, x, 295.

ditions of disorder that would have disgraced a discussion of brigands wrangling over a division of spoils in a wayside cave. Gallatin, Livingston, and Nicholas were forced to talk against coughs, laughter, conversation, and the scraping of the feet of the apostles of 'law and order.' No personal insult too foul, no nincompoop too insignificant to sneer in the face of Gallatin. Despite these terrorizing tactics, the Jeffersonians stood firm and made their record. Even the customary courtesy of Gallatin deserted him, however, and when the sneering Harper darkly hinted at traitors in the House, he retorted sharply that he knew 'nothing in the character of [Harper], either public or private, to entitle him to the ground he so boldly assumes.'

On the last day of the debate on the Alien Bill, Edward Livingston closed for the opposition; and in discussing the constitutional phase, he anticipated the doctrine of the Kentucky and Virginia Resolutions, indicating probable conferences with the tall, silent man who was presiding over the Senate. 'If we are ready to violate the Constitution,' he said, 'will the people submit to our unauthorized acts? Sir, they ought not to submit; they would deserve the chains that these measures are forging for them.' The effect of such a measure? 'The country will swarm with informers, spies, delators, and all the odious reptile tribe that breed in the sunshine of despotic power. . . . The hours of the most unsuspected confidence, the intimacies of friendship, or the recesses of domestic retirement, afford no security. The companion whom you must trust, the friend in whom you must confide, the domestic who waits in your chamber, are all tempted to betray your imprudent or unguarded follies; to misrepresent your words; to convey them, distorted by calumny, to the secret tribunal where jealousy presides — where fear officiates as accuser, and suspicion is the only evidence that is heard. . . . Do not let us be told that we are to excite a fervor against a foreign aggression to establish a tyranny at home; that like the arch traitor we cry "Hail Columbia" [1] at the moment we are betraying her to destruction; that we sing, "Happy Land," when we are plunging it in ruin and disgrace; and that we are absurd enough to call ourselves free and enlightened while we advocate principles that would have disgraced the age of Gothic barbarity.' [2]

[1] A reference to Hopkinson's song.   [2] *Annals*, June 21, 1798.

The vote was taken and the Alien Bill passed, 46 to 40.

Livingston was to hear a few days later when the debate on the Sedition Bill was reached that he had been guilty of sedition in his speech on the Alien Bill. Not least among the grotesque features of the crazy times was the prominence, amounting to leadership, attained by John Allen of Connecticut — a tall, hectic, sour-visaged fanatic. It was reserved for him to indict the Jeffersonians generally for sedition. Had not Livingston been guilty of sedition when he proposed that Gerry be authorized to renew negotiations? Was not the 'Aurora's' explanation of the effect of the Alien Law upon the Irish treason? Were not members of Congress who dared write their views to their constituents traitors? From a want-wit like this fanatic such views were more ludicrous than depressing, but Harper rose to give his full assent to the buffoonery of Allen. 'What!' exclaimed Nicholas, 'is it proposed to prevent members from speaking what they please or prohibit them from reaching the people with their views?' And Harper, disclaiming any desire to curtail the freedom of speech upon the floor, bravely admitted a desire to prevent the speeches from reaching the people 'out of doors.' This astounding doctrine brought Gallatin to his feet with a scornful denunciation of Allen's criticism of Cabell's letter. It 'contained more information and more sense than the gentleman from Connecticut has displayed or can display.' Taking up every assertion in Cabell's letter and making it his own, he challenged a denial of its truth. Then, referring to the attack on Livingston's speech, Gallatin gave his full sanction to the New York states-man's doctrine of resistance to unconstitutional measures. 'I believe that doctrine is absolutely correct and neither seditious nor treasonable.'

On the last day Livingston spoke with his usual spirit and elo-quence, and Harper closed for the bill with an anti-climactic charge, apropos of nothing, that the Jeffersonian plan of govern-ment was in the interest of 'men of immoderate ambition, great family connections, hereditary wealth, and extensive influence' like Livingston. 'Great patrician families,' would walk over the heads 'of we plebeian people.' This touching appeal for the plebeians could hardly have been meant for Philadelphia where at that time 'the great patricians' were lavishly wining and dining the Harpers, and rigidly excluding the Livingstons and Gallatins from their tables. Thus the Federalists closed their case and the bill passed, 44 to 41.[1]

The press was peculiarly silent through the debates. Russell in the Boston 'Centinel' observed that 'Benedict Arnold complained bitterly of the treason bill,' [2] and his rival, Thomas Adams of the 'Chronicle,' announced the passage with the comment that 'we are now abridged the freedom of the press.' [3] Soon the 'Commercial Advertiser' of New York would be dubbing all men traitors who criticized the Sedition Law, and Jefferson would be inviting Hamilton Rowan to the sanctuary of Monticello with the assurance that the Habeas Corpus Act was still operative in Virginia.[4] Almost immediately the Reign of Terror broke upon the land.

VI

In the midst of political terrors the yellow fever stalked again into the haunts of men, striking in New York, in Boston, with special virulence in Philadelphia. By the first of October, fourteen hundred had died in New York City. Hamilton remained in town until persuaded by his family to go to the country, but he continued to visit the city daily to confer with his political friends.[5] In Philadelphia those who could afford it took to flight. Soon thousands were encamped in tents on the common on the outskirts and by October not more than seven thousand people remained in the stricken city. An English traveler, entering in September, found the theaters, taverns, drinking-houses, gambling-dens, and dance-halls closed, hospital carts moving slowly through abandoned streets, the casket-makers alone busy. Sitting one night on the steps of a house in Arch Street, where most houses were deserted, he could hear nothing but the groans of the dying, the lamentations of the living, the hammers of the coffin-makers, the dismal howling of deserted dogs.[6] Even the physicians took to their heels, but Dr. Rush, the head of his profession, remained to battle with the disease.[7] The health office was kept open day and night.[8]

[1] *Annals*, July 10, 1798.   [2] July 28, 1798.   [3] July 19, 1798.
[4] Jefferson's *Works*, x, 59–61.   [5] King's *Works* (Troup to King), ii, 431–32.
[6] Davis, 46–48.   [7] King's *Works* (Troup to King), ii, 431–32.
[8] *Gazette of the United States*, September 1, 1798.

But even in the midst of death the politicians fought with scarcely diminished ferocity. 'Porcupine' and Fenno were stooping to the ghastly business of maligning the methods of Dr. Rush in treating the disease. Standing heroically to his duty where others had fled, he was forced, day by day, to read the most scurrilous attacks upon him. The animus was due to the fact that Rush was a Jeffersonian; and even from Lisbon, William Smith contributed his slur in a letter to Wolcott manifesting sympathy with the attacks because he had 'always considered the Doctor a wrong-headed politician.' [1] Bache and Fenno clawed on, amidst the dying and the dead, until one September day the fever entered the Fenno house and struck down both the editor and his wife. When she died, the 'Gazette' was suspended, and the next day John Fenno ceased his attacks on Dr. Rush, for Death had intervened.[2] 'Alas poor John Fenno,' wrote Ames, 'a worthy man, a true Federalist, always firm in his principles, mild in maintaining them, and bitter against foes. No printer was ever so correct in his politics.' [3] A few days later, Benjamin Franklin Bache of the 'Aurora' fought no more. The Boston 'Chronicle' announced his death in a black-bordered editorial lamenting 'the loss of a man of inflexible virtue, unappalled by power or persecution, and who, in dying, knew no anxieties but what was excited by his apprehensions for his country and for his young family.' [4] The Jeffersonian press published long articles and poems of tribute. In New York the Democrats lost the services of Greenleaf of the 'Argus,' another victim of the plague.

John Ward Fenno took up the work of his father, and the widows of Bache and Greenleaf sought to continue the 'Aurora' and the 'Argus,' the former calling to her assistance one of the ablest controversial journalists of his time, William Duane. No Jeffersonian papers made an unfeeling reference to the death of Fenno; the passing of Bache was gloated over in ghoulish fashion by the Federalist press, and soon 'Porcupine' and young Fenno were making merry over 'the widows Bache and Greenleaf.' It was part of the Reign of Terror — and the fight went on.

[1] Gibbs, ii, 55.
[2] *Gazette of the United States*, September 6, 1798.
[3] Ames (to Dwight), i, 240.
[4] September 17, 1798.

VII

It went on because there was a congressional election pending and both parties were putting forth their utmost effort. The Federalists were hoping that under the influence of war hysteria the Jeffersonians could be annihilated; the Jeffersonians were fighting desperately to hold the line. The most sensational feature of the campaign was the emergence as an avowed party man of Washington, whose aristocratic viewpoint made democracy offensive. He went the full length, finding nothing objectionable in the Alien and Sedition Laws. When, on his persuasion, Patrick Henry entered the campaign as a candidate for the Assembly, he too defended these wretched measures with the silly and insincere statement that they were 'too deep' for him and were the emanations of a 'wise body.' [1]

But more important than the emergence of Washington was the congressional candidacy of John Marshall, who entered the fight on Washington's insistence. The Hamiltonian Federalists were delighted with his candidacy until the publication of his letter opposing the Alien and Sedition Laws, when they turned upon him with bitter scorn. 'His character is done for,' wrote Ames.[2] Noah Webster commented that 'he speaks the language of true Americanism except on the Alien and Sedition Laws.' [3] 'Porcupine' added an editor's note to the letter in his paper: 'The publication of these questions and answers will do neither good nor harm. I insert them as a sort of record of Mr. Marshall's character. If I were a voter, however, I would sooner vote for Gallatin than for Marshall.' [4] The New England Federalists were wrathy among themselves over Marshall's apostasy. 'Mr. Marshall,' wrote Cabot to Pickering, 'has given us great uneasiness here by his answers ... Mr. Marshall, I know, has much to learn on the subject of a practical system of free government for the United States ... I believe, however, that he will eventually prove a great acquisition.' [5] It was at this juncture that Cabot proved his superior political perspicacity by taking up his pen in defense of Marshall

[1] Henry, *Henry*, ii, 612.   [2] Ames (to Gore), i, 246.
[3] *Commercial Advertiser*, October 17, 1798.
[4] *Porcupine's Gazette*, November 30, 1798.   [5] Lodge, *Cabot*, 179–81.

for the Boston 'Centinel.' [1] The struggle in Virginia was bitter. The Jeffersonians, long prepared for Washington's action, were undismayed, and they fought with increased vim. The result was that, while Marshall won by 108 majority, the Jeffersonians elected all but eight of the Representatives, carried the Legislature, and elected a United States Senator.

The Federalists were chagrined with the general result. Cabot was disappointed with Massachusetts [2] and Maryland.[3] A Senator had been lost in North Carolina, and from South Carolina the Jeffersonians had sent to the Senate their most resourceful leader, Charles Pinckney. Theodore Sedgwick, surveying the field, and writing his observations to King in London, could find no improvement in the Senate and but a slight 'amelioration' in the House. The Jeffersonians had won six out of ten seats in New York, gained two in New Jersey, and eight out of thirteen in Pennsylvania.

But Giles was gone — retiring in disgust to the Legislature of Virginia. The election was over — and the Reign of Terror was beginning.

VIII

It began in the summer of 1798 and extended through the autumn of 1800. The growing sentiment for democracy and the increasing popularity of Jefferson were maddening to the Federalists, who fared forth to destroy both with a club. The Alien and Sedition Laws were to be used for the purpose. Democrats, from the highest to the most lowly, were to be proscribed and treated with contempt. The New England clergy, for the most part, entered heartily into the plan. The colleges joined. So openly partisan became the institutions of learning that the Jeffersonian press opened their batteries upon the 'arbitrary spirit which has been exposed in the eastern seminaries.' [4] With much ceremony Doctors' Degrees were being bestowed upon Federalist politicians, and Pickering and Wolcott were made Doctors of Law. 'Except Timothy's vulgar diplomacy who ever heard of the qualifications in him?' asked the irreverent Duane, and while 'Oliver has dab-

---

[1] Lodge, *Cabot*, 147.　　　[2] *Ibid.* (to Pickering), 179.　　　[3] *Ibid.*, 172.
[4] *Aurora*, February 12, 1800.

bled in politics and glittered in prose' 'he would never have been discovered by the savants had he not been in the Cabinet of a New England President.' [1] Other Federalist politicians were thus given the disguise of scholarship, but Jefferson, President of the Philosophical Society, and friend of Franklin and Rittenhouse, received no degrees.

Very early, gangs of self-proclaimed patriots sallied forth into the country to tear down the liberty poles erected by the Democrats, armed with pistols and swords, and clattering over the country roads like Cossacks on a rampage. One of these gangs under the leadership of a Philip Strubling, operating in Berks County, Pennsylvania, had a triumphant career, except where armed men showed fight, when the gallant band found discretion the better part of valor.[2] This sort of outrage was being committed all over the country. Plans were made to wreck the printing plant of Duane until it was found that his friends had armed for defense, and the editor warned the conspirators that an attempt at violence 'would carry public vengeance to their firesides.' [3]

When thwarted in their plans against the leaders, the terrorists turned upon the weak and lowly, demanding the discharge of Jeffersonian artisans employed in the manufacture of war material. Out with them! 'It is a notorious fact,' complained Fenno, 'that a number of artisans . . . are of politics destructive of the Constitution.' [4] Everywhere, in the pulpits of political preachers, from the Bench of Federal Judges, through the press and on the streets, men were beating upon the tom-toms arousing the apprehensions of the people; and when, one night, some pirates, sentenced to execution, escaped from the Philadelphia jail, the clatter of the mounted soldiers in pursuit was enough to fill the streets with affrighted people. The Germans of Northampton were marching on the city with pitchforks. The soldiers were out after Duane, whispered others, and armed Democrats rushed to the rescue. At length the fever subsided and order was restored. 'Nothing more serious than the disturbance of love-making,' said the

[1] *Aurora*, February 22, 1800.
[2] In *Porcupine's Gazette*, February 2, 1799, Strubling attempts to explain his failure to fight when resistance was offered.
[3] *Aurora*, May 20, 1799.   [4] *Gazette of the United States*, April 15, 1799.

MAD TOM in A RAGE

A CONTEMPORARY CARTOON TYPICAL OF THE FEDERALIST ATTACKS ON
JEFFERSON

'Aurora.' [1] These were minor incidents — the background for the real terror to come. Judges were terrorizing the people with wild charges to grand juries.[2] The Right Reverend Bishop White of Philadelphia was preaching piously and patriotically from the text: 'Let every soul be subject to the higher powers. For there is no purpose but of God. The powers that be are ordained of God. Whoso therefore resisteth the power, resisteth the ordinance of God. And they that resist shall receive to themselves damnation.'[3] The Administration organ in New York was laying down the dictum: 'When a man is heard to inveigh against the Sedition Law, set him down as one who would submit to no restraint which is calculated for the peace of society. He deserves to be suspected.'[4] And Timothy Pickering was nervously peering through his spectacles over Jeffersonian papers seeking some phrase on which a prosecution for sedition could be brought, and prodding the district attorneys to action. 'Heads, more heads!' screamed Marat from his tub. 'Heads, more heads!' echoed Pickering from his office.

[1] April 29, 1800.
[2] Judge Alexander Addison, *Gazette of the United States*, February 15, 1799; Judge Iredell, April 9, 1799.
[3] *Gazette of the United States*, May 10, 1799.
[4] *New York Commercial Advertiser*, December 29, 1798.

CHAPTER XVII
THE REIGN OF TERROR

I

IT is not surprising that the first notable victim of the Terror was Matthew Lyon whom we have seen insulted at various points when homeward bound from Philadelphia. Bitter though he was, he had sound sense and realized his danger. When the Rutland 'Herald' refused to publish his address to his constituents, he launched his own paper, 'The Scourge of Aristocracy,' with a defiant challenge: ' When every aristocratic hireling from the English Porcupine . . . to the dirty hedge-hogs and groveling animals of his race in this and neighboring States are vomiting forth columns of lies, malicious abuse and deception, the Scourge will be devoted to politics.' How Pickering must have stared through his spectacles at that defiance! But patience! If speeches and papers offered no case, there still were letters, and one was found. Here surely was 'sedition.' Had Lyon not referred to Adams's 'continual grasp for power,' to his 'unbounded thirst for ridiculous pomp, foolish adulation, and selfish avarice'? Had he not charged that the President had turned men out of office for party reasons, and that 'the sacred name of religion' was 'employed as a state engine to make mankind hate and persecute one another'? Had he not printed a letter from Barlow, the poet, referring to 'the bullying speech of your President and the stupid answer of your Senate'? It was enough. True, the letter had been published before the Sedition Law was passed, but this was the Reign of Terror. The trial before Judge Peters was a farce, and the culprit was found guilty. 'Matthew Lyon,' said Peters in fixing the sentence, 'as a member of the Federal Legislature you must be well acquainted with the mischiefs which flow from the unlicensed abuse of Government' — and Lyon was sentenced to four months in jail and to pay a fine of a thousand dollars.

Then the Terror began to work in earnest. There was a fairly respectable jail at Rutland where the trial was held, but not for

Lyon. There was something worse at Vergennes, forty miles away, a loathsome pen in a miserable little town of sixty houses, and thither he was ordered. Refusing his request to return to his house for some papers, he was ordered to mount a horse, and with two troopers with pistols, riding behind, the forty-mile journey through the wilderness was made. At Vergennes they pushed him into a cell, sixteen by twelve, ordinarily used for common felons of the lowest order. In one corner was a toilet emitting a sickening stench. A half-moon door opened on the corridor, through which his coarse food was passed. Through a window with heavy iron bars he got some light. There was no stove and the cold of autumn nights came in through the window. When it became dangerously chilly, the prisoner put on his overcoat and paced the cell. He was refused pen and paper until the indignation of the public forced a concession. A visitor peering through the half-moon of the door a little later would have seen a table strewn with paper, Volney's 'Ruins,' some Messages of the President.

Meanwhile the Vermont hills were aflame with fury. The Green Mountain Boys, the Minute Men, the soldiers who, with Lyon, had followed Ethan Allen, were talking of tearing the jail down. Then, from the filthy, foul-smelling hole, into which the Federalists had thrown a member of Congress, came letters from the 'convict,' brave, cheerful letters, exhorting these men to observe the law. One day, however, Lyon was forced to plead through the iron bars of his window for the furious mob without to seek redress legally at the polls. Thus popular resentment increased with the growth of the prisoner's popularity. Thousands of the yeomanry of Vermont signed a petition for a pardon and sent it to Adams, who refused to receive it. Aha, 'the despicable, cringing, fawning puppy!' exulted Fenno.[1] The indignation of the yeomanry of Vermont now blazed high. The Administration was amazed, almost appalled. When this 'convict' in a hideous cell was nominated for Congress, there were not jails enough in Vermont for the talkers of 'sedition.' He was elected overwhelmingly with 4576 votes to 2444 for his nearest competitor.

Again the terrorists consulted on plans to thwart the public will. His term was about to expire, but where would this pauper get a

[1] *Gazette of the United States*, January 2, 1799.

thousand dollars? True, the farmers, the comrades of the Revolution, were going into their pockets to get the money — but a thousand dollars! Still there was a chance. The Marshal summoned Federalist lawyers to go over Lyon's letters and find more sedition on which he could be arrested on emerging from the jail. His triumphant election was more than the terrorists could bear. 'Must our national councils be again disgraced by that vile beast?' asked their New York organ.[1] Meanwhile, the problem of the fine was being solved. The eyes of the Nation were on that dirty little cell at Vergennes. Jefferson, Madison, Gallatin, John Taylor of Caroline, Senator Mason of Virginia — he who had given the Jay Treaty to the 'Aurora' — and Apollis Austen, a wealthy Vermont Democrat, were solving the problem of the fine. On the day of Lyon's delivery, the Virginia Senator rode into the village, his saddle-bags bulging with a thousand and more in gold. There he met Austen with a strong-box containing more than a thousand in silver. Mason paid the money.

Before the jail had assembled a vast multitude. Out of the door rushed Lyon. 'I am on my way to Philadelphia!' — to Congress, he shouted. A roar went up, a procession with a flag in front was formed, and the 'convict' was on his way triumphantly. The school children at Tinmouth paraded in his honor, and a youthful orator greeted him with a welcome to 'our brave Representative who has been suffering for us under an unjust sentence, and the tyranny of a detested understrapper of despotism.' The woods reverberated with shouts. Then on moved the procession. At Bennington, another ovation, more speeches. Seated in a sleigh, his wife beside him, Lyon was escorted by the throng. At times the procession was twelve miles long. Through New York, New Jersey, Pennsylvania, the ovations were repeated. He had gone home to the tune of 'The Rogue's March'; he returned by the same route to the tune of 'Yankee Doodle.'[2]

II

The terrorists ground their teeth and sought revenge — with nothing too petty. The Reverend John C. Ogden dared to be a

---

[1] *Commercial Advertiser*, December 28, 1799.

[2] McLaughlin, *Lyon;* Wharton, *State Trials*, 333–44.

Democrat and to carry the petition for Lyon to Philadelphia. Thenceforth he was a marked man. He was in debt — and a debt would serve. Returning from Philadelphia, he was arrested at Litchfield, Connecticut, and thrown into jail. 'It is presumed,' sneered Major Russell of the Boston 'Centinel,' 'that Lyon when he goes from his jail to Congress will at least sneak into Litchfield to pay a visit to his envoy and take a petition from him to the Vice-President [Jefferson].' [1] But jail was too good for such a rascal. On his release a crowd of soldiers followed him out of Litchfield, calling him 'a damn Democrat,' abusing, insulting, collaring, shaking him. It was their purpose to take him back to Litchfield and scourge him in public. Whirling him around, the gallant soldiers started back. Meanwhile, the report had spread that the heroic remnant of the army had set forth on a mobbing expedition, and a party of Democrats and civilians mounted horses and rushed to the rescue. The courage of the soldiers, so splendid in the presence of one man, oozed out on the approach of the rescuers, and Ogden was released. [2]

III

But Ogden was not the only victim of the terrorists, among the friends of Lyon. Anthony Haswell, born in England, a man of education, who had seen service in the army of Washington and had narrowly escaped death at Monmouth, was editor of the 'Vermont Gazette.' A gentleman of amiability and integrity, his popularity was great in Vermont — but he was a Jeffersonian. One day the sleuths of the Terror, scanning the pages of Democratic papers, found an appeal in Haswell's 'Gazette' for funds to pay the fine of Lyon. It referred to the 'loathsome prison,' to the marshal as 'a hard-hearted savage, who has, to the disgrace of Federalism, been elevated to a station where he can satiate his barbarity on the misery of his victims.' It was a faithful portrait. But in concluding, the article charged that the Administration had declared worthy of the confidence of the Government the Tories 'who had shared in the desolation of our homes and the abuse of our wives and daughters.'

Thus, one night there was a hammering on the door of Haswell's

[1] *Centinel*, February 27, 1799.   [2] *Aurora*, June 20, 1799.

house, and he was confronted by petty officials and notified to prepare for a journey to Rutland in the early morning. In feeble
health, and unaccustomed to riding, he was forced to mount a
horse for the sixty-mile ride to the capital. Through a cold October
rain the sick man jolted along in misery through the day, and it
was near midnight when the town was reached. With his clothing
soaked, he begged permission to spend the night at a hotel where
he could dry it. This was curtly refused. At midnight they pushed
the sick man in wet clothing into a cell. Responsible men of Rutland begged permission to go security to the end that the editor
might spend the night in decent quarters — it was denied. The
next morning he was hurried to trial at Windsor before Judge
Paterson who, on the Bench, continued to be a New Jersey politician. The defense introduced evidence to prove the charge of
brutality against the marshal, and asked the Court for permission
to summon McHenry and General Drake of Virginia to prove that
on one occasion the Administration had acknowledged the policy
of occasionally appointing Tories to office. The Court refused permission; and having refused, Paterson declared in the charge that
'no attempt had been made at justification' of the reference to
Tories. The jury was probably packed. The verdict was promptly
rendered — guilty of sedition. And Haswell was sent to jail for
two months. On the day of the expiration of his sentence, a great
throng assembled at the prison to testify to their regard for Haswell and their contempt for the Sedition Law and its sponsors.
When the editor appeared at the door, the band played while the
crowd sang:

> 'Yankee Doodle, keep it up,
> Yankee Doodle dandy.'

It was all too evident that, despite the Sedition Law, there were
'Yankee Doodles' to 'keep it up' too numerous for the jails.

IV

The enforcement of the law in Massachusetts offered comedy,
tragedy, and farce — with at least one hero among the victims.
There was something of pathos even in the farce. An illiterate and
irresponsible soldier of the Revolution, David Brown, was wander-

ing about the country reading and distributing some foolish compositions of his own that were incomprehensible in their incoherency. It was possible to detect some dissatisfaction with the Administration, however. His was the grievance of many others of the ragged Continentals of the ranks. He was a Democrat. Fisher Ames, who was not a soldier, though old enough to have been one, was outraged and alarmed over the foolish fellow's activities, and pretended to believe that he was one of the Jeffersonian 'runners sent everywhere to blow the trumpet of sedition.' He wrote Gore, who had grown rich buying up the paper of the private soldiers, of this 'vagabond ragged fellow, who lurked about in Dedham telling everybody the sins and enormities of the government.' Ames understood that he 'knew of my speculating connection with you;[1] and how I had made my immense wealth.'[2] Finally he participated in the erection of a liberty pole at Dedham bearing among its inscriptions the sinister words, 'No Stamp Tax, No Sedition.' The authorities pounced upon him as legitimate prey.

The next scene was laid in the courtroom in Boston. On the Bench sat the fat, red-faced Chase, like an avenging angel who looked too often on the wine when it was red. It was solemnly proved that Brown had writings of his own hostile to the Administration policies; that he had paid to have the inscription painted for the pole at Dedham; and that in the presence of forty or fifty dangerous farmers he had been seen holding the ladder while another ascended to nail the board on. There was no defense. Chase glowered on the miserable illiterate, and, reminding him that he was at the mercy of the Court, demanded the names of the miscreants who had subscribed to his writings. Brown refused to betray the imaginary men higher up, and Chase fined him four hundred dollars and sent him to jail for a year and a half. Working entirely on his own initiative, the unhappy wretch was buried in a cell and all but forgotten. The Federalist papers recorded his conviction with gusto, albeit with sorrow that such things could be. After sixteen months, he sent a pitiful petition to Adams asking for a pardon, but it was refused. In February, 1801, he sent a second petition, which was ignored. After spending two

[1] This connection was real.
[2] Ames, I, 247.

years in a cell, he was pardoned by Jefferson.[1] This trial was a farce.

V

Followed then the comedy. Among the desperate characters who had assisted in the pole-raising at Dedham was Richard Fairbanks. A thoroughly decent citizen, he was arrested and dragged tremblingly into court. Most of the victims of the Sedition Law were unrepentant and defiant, but Fairbanks was full of remorse. There may have been a bit of cunning in his confession of past wickedness and his profession of conversion. At any rate, the scene in court was not so threatening. True, the stern-faced Chase looked down from the Bench, but there in the room, ready to plead for mercy, was Fisher Ames. The charge was read, confessed, and up rose Ames. Not, however, as a paid attorney did he appear, but there was something to be said in extenuation for Fairbanks. He realized 'how heinous an offense it was.' He had promised to be a good citizen in the future. 'His character has not been blemished in private life,' the orator said, 'and I do not know that he is less a man of integrity and benevolence than others. He is a man of rather warm and irritable temperament, too credulous, too sudden in his impressions.' He had been seduced by the 'inflammatory sophistry' of the illiterate Brown. 'Besides,' continued Ames, in his most virtuous tones, 'men in office have not been wanting to second Brown and to aggravate the bad opinion of the government and the laws. ... The men who had Mr. Fairbanks' confidence and abused it are more blameable than he. A newspaper has also chiefly circulated there which has a pestilent influence.' Thus he had bad advice. 'Although Mr. Fairbanks was influenced like the rest and was criminal in the affair of the sedition pole he had no concern in the contrivance. He ... has freely confessed his fault and promised to be in future a good citizen.' Having attacked the Jeffersonians in Congress and out, and denounced 'The Aurora' or 'Independent Chronicle,' and implied that Fairbanks would vote and talk right in the future, Ames sat down; and

---

[1] *Independent Chronicle*, June 17, 1799; *Gazette of the United States*, June 17, 1799; 'Enforcement of the Alien and Sedition Laws,' by Anderson, American Historical Association *Report*, 1912.

just as solemnly Chase, commenting that 'one object of punishment, reformation, has been accomplished,' fined him five dollars and sent him to jail for six hours. Whereupon we may imagine Chase and Ames felicitating themselves on having scared the Democratic and Jeffersonian devils out of one sinner.

This was comedy.

VI

The tragedy in Massachusetts was reserved for a more important person — the editor of the 'Independent Chronicle,' Thomas Adams, who was printing one of the most powerful Jeffersonian papers in the country. He had published an attack on the denunciation of the Virginia Resolutions by the Massachusetts Legislature.[1] The Essex Junto had been seeking a chance at the throat of the editor. His paper had been keenly searched for some excuse for action under the Sedition Law. In the autumn of 1798 he had been arrested and the effect had been provoking. In announcing his arrest, Adams had promised his readers a full report of the trial, and pledged himself to 'always support the rights of the people and the liberty of the press, agreeable to the sacred charter of the Constitution.'[2] When, four days later, he reported the postponement of his trial, he was able to 'thank our new subscribers whose patriotism has led them to support the freedom of the press since the late persecution.'[3]

The political persecution of Adams had in no wise intimidated him. Every issue of his paper was a clarion call to the faithful. If anything, he raised his banner a little higher. The public, looking upon his arrest as tyrannical and outrageous, rallied around him as never before. Eleven days after his arrest, he reported an 'unprecedented increase in circulation,' and pledged himself to carry on the fight. Not without point did he quote, 'A free press will maintain the majesty of the people,' for, as he explained, 'this was originally written by John Adams, President of the United States, for Edes and Gill's Boston Gazette when British Excises, Stamp Acts, Land Taxes, and Arbitrary Power threatened this country with poverty and destruction.'[4] Courageous though he was, the

[1] *Independent Chronicle*, February 18, 1799.
[2] *Ibid.*, October 25, 1798.
[3] *Ibid.*, October 29, 1798.
[4] *Ibid.*, November 5, 1798.

persecution drained the editor's weakened vitality, and he was confined to his bed in a country house near Boston when the attack on the Massachusetts Legislature was published. Though too ill to be dragged into court, he was not too ill to announce the second phase of the persecution in the language of defiance. Doublespacing the announcement to make it stand out like a challenge, he said: 'The Chronicle is destined to persecution. . . . It will stand or fall with the liberties of America, and nothing shall silence its clarion but the extinction of every principle which leads to the achievement of our independence.' [1] Because the editor could not be dragged from a sick bed, Abijah Adams, the bookkeeper, was arrested on the ground that he had sold the papers and therefore published the 'libel.'

Chief Justice Dana presided at the trial — as intolerant, politically, but not as stupid and coarse as Chase. The prosecution based its action on the common law of England, which the defense declared inconsistent with the Constitution of Massachusetts, and hostile to the spirit of the American Government. Dana rose to the occasion, not only attacking Adams's lawyers from the Bench, but assailing them through the press. [2] The result was inevitable. A verdict of guilt was promptly reached, and Dana made the most of his opportunity in sentencing the criminal. The defendant's lawyers were denounced for 'propagating principles' as 'dangerous as those of the article on which the indictment was based.' Since the editor would not give up the name of the author of the offensive article, Adams would have to suffer, and he was sentenced to jail for thirty days, ordered to pay costs, and to give bond for good behavior for a year. So shocking was the spirit of Dana in passing sentence that he was challenged in the 'Chronicle' to publish his speech. [3] Adams editorially denounced the application of the common law of England as 'inconsistent with republican principles contemplated and avowed in our Constitution, and inapplicable to the spirit and nature of our institutions,' [4] and promised 'a regular supply of the papers.' 'The Editor is on a bed of languishment, and the bookkeeper in prison, yet the cause of liberty will be supported amid these distressing circumstances.'

---

[1] *Independent Chronicle*, February 25, 1799.   [2] *Ibid.*, April 11, 1799.
[3] March 28, 1799, from 'A Friend.'   [4] *Ibid.*, March 7, 1799.

The 'convict' was hurried off to jail, and into a damp, unhealthy cell where his feeble constitution threatened to succumb, until an indignant protest from without forced the jailer to transfer him to a better. The friends who flocked to see him were forced to convey their consolations through double-grated doors. Day by day the paper went to press, its spirit not one whit diminished. With the editor sinking under disease and the anticipated wreckage of his property, and the bookkeeper sick in jail and distressed over the condition of his wife and children, the fight was waged with un-diminished vigor.[1] One day old Samuel Adams, his Revolutionary spirit ablaze, flaunted his respect for the editor and his contempt for the persecutors, by stalking to the jail and expressing his ad-miration through the bars.[2] That day Adams's prison doors were opened and he passed out to freedom; and the next day the readers of the 'Chronicle' knew that 'Abijah Adams was discharged from his imprisonment after partaking of an adequate portion of his "birth-right" by a confinement of thirty days under the operation of the common law of England.'[3] Within three weeks, Thomas Adams, one of the bravest champions of democracy and the free-dom of the press, was dead — his end hastened by the persecution to which he had been subjected. Like Benjamin Franklin Bache, he sank into his grave with an indictment under the Sedition Law hanging over him.

VII

When Bache thus escaped the vengeance of his enemies, they turned to his successor, William Duane, who soon proved himself a more vigorous controversialist than his predecessor. A remarkable character was Duane, entitled to a monument for his fight for the freedom of the press. Born in America of Irish parentage, he was taken to Ireland on the death of his father, and there he grew to manhood. His career previous to his return to America was color-ful and courageous. For a time he had been a reporter for the London 'Times' in the press gallery of the House of Commons, before establishing a newspaper in India which he edited with such signal ability that the East India Company found it advisable to

[1] *Independent Chronicle*, March 28, 1799.
[2] *Ibid.*, April 25, 1799.   [3] *Ibid.*

resort to force and fraud to destroy his property and send him out of the country. At length in sheer disgust he returned to America, and soon became the editor of 'The Aurora.' [1]

One Friday night before the Monday on which the question of the repeal of the Alien Law was to be considered in Congress, a number of citizens, including some foreign-born, met in Philadelphia to arrange for a memorial to Congress. On Sunday morning, Duane and three others, including Dr. James Reynolds, appeared during services in the churchyard of Saint Mary's Catholic Church with the memorial and a few placards requesting natives of Ireland in the congregation to remain in the yard after the services to sign the petition. Some of these placards were placed on the church and on the gates leading into the yard. Some belated worshipers of the Federalist persuasion tore these down, and, entering the church, warned the priest that seditious men were in the yard planning a riot. The four men in the yard conducted themselves with perfect decorum. When the congregation was dismissed, Duane and his party had the memorial spread upon a tombstone. A few approached and signed. Almost immediately, however, the terrorists among the members of the church closed in upon the group, centering their attacks mostly upon Reynolds, who was knocked down and kicked. Struggling to his feet, Reynolds drew a revolver and prepared to defend himself, at which moment officers reached the scene and the four men were hurried off to jail on the charge of creating a seditious riot.

Before a great crowd at the State House, the trial was held, with Hopkinson, the author of the war song, as special prosecutor, and the men in the dock brilliantly defended by A. J. Dallas. The testimony showed that there had been no disturbance until the mob charged upon the men with the memorial; that the memorial itself was unexceptionable in every way; that Reynolds had been warned a week before of a conspiracy to murder him and had armed himself on advice of a member of Congress; that none of the others carried a weapon of any sort; and it was shown by the testimony of a priest that it was then the custom in Ireland to post notices in churchyards, and for members of the church to transact such public business in the yards after services. Members of the con-

[1] Hudson, *Journalism*, 211–13.

gregation testified that they had wanted to sign; the priest that the posting of the notice was not considered disrespectful to the church. In a brilliant speech of sarcasm and invective, Dallas riddled the prosecution, calling attention to attempts to intimidate lawyers from appearing for the defense, charging the prosecution with being inspired by partisan hate, and denouncing the Alien Law. Hopkinson replied lamely, attacking immigrants and Democrats. The jury retired, and in thirty minutes returned with a verdict of acquittal. The State House rang with cheers. The case, however, had not been tried in a Federal Court.[1]

That, however, was only the beginning of the attempt to wreck and ruin the leading Jeffersonian editor. John Adams and Pickering had been planning to reach him by hook or crook. The latter wrote Adams that Duane, though born in America, had gone to Ireland before the Revolution; that in India he 'had been charged with some crime'; and that he had come to America 'to stir up sedition.' More — he was 'doubtless a United Irishman,' and in case of a French invasion the military company he had formed would join the invaders. The picture was as Adams would have had it painted. 'The matchless effrontery of Duane,' he wrote, 'merits the execution of the Alien Law. I am very willing to try its strength on him.' This trial was never made, but two months later the Federal Courts began to move against him. At Norristown, Pennsylvania, with Bushrod Washington and Richard Peters on the Bench, an indictment was brought against him for sedition.[2] The case was continued until June, 1800 — and Duane went full steam ahead with his attacks on the Federalist Party. The trial was again postponed, and in October, 1800, he was indicted again — this time for having published a Senate Bill of a peculiarly vicious if not criminal character which its sponsors for sufficient reasons wished kept from the public. But it was of no avail. He would not cringe or crawl or compromise or be silenced. The cases against him were dismissed when Jefferson became President. Many historians have belittled him; he fought brilliantly for fundamental constitutional rights when men high in office, who are praised, were conspiring to strike them down.

---

[1] Wharton, *State Trials*, 345–91; Hudson, *Journalism*, 213–14.
[2] *Aurora*, October 22, 1799.

VIII

One day the Sedition snoopers fell upon an article by Dr. Thomas Cooper, an Englishman by birth, a scientist and physician by profession, a man of learning and culture, and a Jeffersonian. It referred to the early days of Adams's Administration when 'he was hardly in the infancy of political mistake.' It charged Adams with saddling the people with a permanent navy; with having borrowed money at eight per cent; referred to his 'unnecessary violence of official expression which might justly have provoked war'; to his interference with the processes of a Federal Court in the case of Robbins. And that was all. Adams had made mistakes, had established a permanent navy, had borrowed money at eight per cent; and many thought at the time that he had unduly interposed in the Robbins case. But this was sedition in 1800.

Hustled into the Federal Court at Philadelphia, Cooper found the red-faced Chase glowering upon him from the Bench — the same Chase who had been charged by Hamilton with speculating in flour during the Revolution. There was no denial of the authorship of the article. The evidence in, Chase charged the jury in his most violent partisan manner. There are only two ways to destroy a republic, he said: one the introduction of luxury, the other the licentiousness of the press. 'The latter is more slow but more sure.' Taking up the Cooper article, he analyzed it in the spirit of a prosecutor. Here, thundered the Judge, we have the opinion that Adams has good intentions but doubtful capacity. Borrowed money 'at eight per cent in time of peace?' What — call these times of peace? 'I cannot suppress my feeling at this gross attack upon the President. Can this be true? Can you believe it? Are we now in time of peace? Is there no war?' [1] The jury promptly returned a verdict of guilty. The next day Cooper appeared for sentence. Asked by Chase to explain his financial condition as that might affect the sentence, he replied that he was in moderate circumstances, dependent on his practice, which would be destroyed by imprisonment. 'Be it so,' he continued. 'I have been accustomed to make sacrifices to opinion, and I can make this. As to circumstances in extenuation, not being conscious that I

[1] It was true, of course.

have set down aught in malice, I have nothing to extenuate.' Chase became suspiciously unctuous and oily. If Cooper had to pay his own fine, that would be one thing; if his party had arranged to pay the fine, that would be another. 'The insinuations of the Court are ill founded,' Cooper replied with indignation, 'and if you, sir, from misapprehension or misrepresentation, have been tempted to make them, your mistake should be corrected.' Judge Peters, who had been squirming through these amazing partisan comments of Chase, here impatiently intervened with the comment that the Court had nothing to do with parties. Whereupon Cooper was fined a thousand dollars and ordered to jail for six months.[1]

Duane instantly announced an early publication in pamphlet form of the trial in full. 'Republicans may rest completely assured,' he wrote, 'that they will have every reason to be satisfied with the effect of this most singular trial on the mind of the public.'[2] The pamphlet appeared, and, as Duane had foreseen, the public was aroused. A man of decent character and high professional standing was languishing in a jail in the capital of the country for having told the truth and expressed an opinion on a constitutional question. There were rumblings and grumblings in the streets, and some uneasiness in Administration circles. The hint went forth that an appeal for a pardon might receive consideration, and one was put in circulation, when out from the 'convict's' cell came a letter of protest. He wanted and would have no petition for pardon. He believed with Adams that repentance should precede pardon [3] and he had no feeling of repentance. 'Nor will I be the voluntary cat's-paw of electioneering clemency,' Cooper continued. 'I know that late events have greatly changed the outward and visible signs of the politics of the party, and good temper and moderation is the order of the day with the Federalists now, as it has always been with their political opponents. But all sudden conversions are suspicious, and I hope that Republicans will be upon their guard against the insidious or interested designs of those who may wish to profit by the too common credulity of honest intention.'[4]

[1] Wharton, *State Trials*, 658–81.   [2] *Aurora*, April 25, 1800.
[3] Adams's answer in the case of Lyon.   [4] *Aurora*, May 17, 1800.

The petition was dropped. Cooper remained happily in his cell.
His incarceration was making votes for Jefferson.   When, on the
expiration of his sentence, Cooper stepped into the daylight, he
found a deputation of his friends awaiting him at the door. He
was escorted to a fashionable hotel where a public dinner had been
arranged to honor him and express contempt for the Sedition Law.
Two long tables were set, with Dr. James Logan presiding over
one, Thomas Leiper over the other. That night, as the wine flowed,
the men who would not be silenced drank to Cooper — to Jefferson — to a Democratic victory.[1]

IX

Having distinguished himself as an American Lord Clare in the
case of Cooper, Chase proceeded southward, boasting along the
way that he 'would teach the lawyers in Virginia the difference between liberty and licentiousness of the press.' He was going to
try James Thomas Callender for sedition on an indictment based
on his pamphlet, 'The Prospect Before Us.' This unsavory creature was hated quite as much for the truths he told as for the lies
he circulated, and there was nothing in the section of his pamphlet
on which he was indicted to shock any one to-day. It was an attack
on Adams in connection with the French war hysteria, the navy,
the army, the Robbins case. The only phrase that startles one to-
day is the reference to the hands of Adams 'reeking with the blood
of the poor friendless Connecticut sailor.' [2] The scenes in the little
Richmond courtroom were scandalous to excess. It was understood that Chase had instructed the marshal 'not to put any of
those creatures called Democrats on the jury,' and his boasts
concerning Virginia lawyers had preceded him. The most brazen
tyranny presided in the case of Callender, and the lawlessness of
the Judge was more threatening than the licentiousness of the
culprit. It was a political inquisition, not a trial. The courtroom
was thronged. The case was the sole topic of conversation in the
streets and taverns. The Democrats had no misapprehensions of
the nature of the trial, and three extraordinarily able lawyers were

[1] Scharf, I, 505.
[2] Robbins was turned over to the British, who claimed him as a national, and was exe-
cuted for murder on the seas. Even Gallatin thought this an outrage until Marshall made
his memorable speech in Congress in defense of the President's action.

there for the defense — John Hay, who was afterwards to prosecute Burr, Nicholas, and William Wirt, already well advanced toward that professional eminence which he so long enjoyed. There was a dignity and courage in the aspect of these three men that Chase could only interpret as a challenge. He had made his boasts. He would teach these Virginia lawyers — and there was nothing apologetic or fawning in the manner of Hay, Nicholas, or Wirt. The fact that neither was there anything of insolence made matters worse. Feeling himself on the defensive, Chase sought to conceal his embarrassment in the brutality of his conduct.

The shameful story of that travesty of a trial has been often told, and it played a part in the impeachment proceedings against Chase a little later. He stormed, fumed, spluttered, and injected Federalist stump speeches into the ludicrous proceedings. He refused the defense permission to ask a prospective juror if he had formed and expressed an opinion on the Callender pamphlet. 'The question is improper and you shall not ask it,' he thundered. When John Taylor of Caroline was put on the witness stand, Chase nervously demanded what the defense intended to prove by the witness. He was told. 'Put the question in writing and submit it to me,' he demanded. But why, asked Nicholas, when nothing of the sort in required in questioning witnesses for the prosecution? 'It's the proper procedure,' fumed the Court. Keeping a firm rein on both his temper and his contempt for the Court, Nicholas submitted three questions in writing. One glance, and Chase ruled them out. The Virginia lawyers showed their amazement. Even Chase could see it. 'My country has made me a Judge,' he shouted, 'and you must be governed now by my opinion.'

William Wirt rose to submit an argument on the admissibility of the evidence. He began with observations on the embarrassments of the defense because Callender had been 'presented, indicted, arrested, and tried during this term and had not been able to procure testimony essential to a proper defense.' He even hinted at the precipitancy of the Court.

'You must not reflect on the Court,' shouted Chase.

'I am prevented from explaining to you [the jury] the causes which have conspired to weaken our defense, and it is no doubt right that I should be prevented, as the Court has so decided.'

Chase saw at once that he was not going to care much for this 'young man,' as he contemptuously called him repeatedly. Wirt proceeded to an attack on the constitutionality of the Sedition Law.

'Take your seat, sir,' stormed the livid-faced Chase. 'Ever since I came into Virginia I have understood that sort of thing would be urged, and I have deliberated on it.' Whereupon he produced a long manuscript and prepared to read. 'Hear my words,' he admonished, glaring around the courtroom. 'I wish the world to know them — my opinion is the result of mature reflection.'

Wirt undertook to argue the point — Chase gesticulated, stormed, insulted — and William Wirt folded his papers, and resuming his seat declined to continue. Hay took up the argument, to be met constantly with barking interruptions, until he, too, in sheer disgust, folded his papers and sat down.

'Please to proceed,' urged Chase, wondering perhaps if he had gone too far with these Virginia lawyers, 'and be assured that you will not be interrupted by me, say what you will.' Hay refused to continue the farce.

Thus, throughout, the mobbing of Callender and his attorneys went on. The result was conviction and a jail sentence.[1]

X

Meanwhile, a serio-comedy in New York State which was working effectively for the Democrats. In the early spring of 1800, John Armstrong, author of the 'Newburgh Letters,' and until this time an ardent Federalist, outraged by the brazen attempt to suppress free speech and the freedom of the press, prepared a powerful and vituperative petition for the repeal of the Sedition Law and sent it into several counties to be circulated for signatures. In Otsego, then a new and undeveloped part of the State, it was entrusted to Jedekiah Peck, an eccentric character known to every man, woman, and child in the county. Poor to poverty, he had combined the work of an itinerant surveyor with that of a preacher, and was popular as both. Wandering through the country surveying land by day, night found him in some settler's

[1] Wharton, *State Trials.*

home preaching and praying, and, in the intervals between, he talked politics. He had baptized the infant, preached the funeral sermons for the dead, married the young, prayed for and with the old. His sincerity was apparent, his innate kindliness manifest. Many smiled at the diminutive old man, but most men and all children loved him. Burr, who had a genius for using the right man in the right place, took him up and had him sent to the Legislature as a Federalist.[1]

Right joyously the little old man started on his rounds with the petition. When his activity was made known to Judge William Cooper, father of the novelist, and temperamentally as unfit for the Bench as a large number of the Judges of the time,. he boiled with rage. Instantly he wrote the District Attorney of Peck's heinous sedition. Immediately a grand jury was empaneled in the city of New York. A bench warrant for Peck's arrest was issued. At midnight he was dragged from his bed, placed in manacles like a dangerous criminal, and the two-hundred-mile march to New York began. The roads were bad, progress was slow, the news spread, and in every village and at every crossroads crowds poured forth to look upon the pitiful spectacle and to sympathize with the victim. Jefferson could not have planned a more effective campaign tour. The plain people of the countryside knew Peck — and they turned away with a sense of personal outrage. For five days the march continued — it was a triumphant march for democracy.

Thus the uneducated, itinerant preacher and surveyor of Otsego County made his contribution to the election of Jefferson, marching in manacles to illustrate the Federalist conception of liberty.[2]

Merrily the Terror sped along.

XI

The New London 'Bee,' under the editorship of Charles Holt, a Jeffersonian, had greatly annoyed the Federalists of the surrounding States, and a remedy was now at hand. Had it not attacked the French war — and therefore tried to prevent enlistments? Here was sedition. The editor was arrested, his own brother summoned as a witness against him. There was more than one War

[1] Hammond, I, 123-24.　　[2] *Ibid.*, 131-32; Alexander, 89.

of the Roses in those days. The paper on which he was indicted
was furnished by two Federalist editors, one of whom had two
brothers on the jury that brought in the indictment. The foreman
of the grand jury was an Amos Bull who had been a British commissary in New York during the Revolution.[1] Bushrod Washington presided at the trial. The defense undertook to show the Sedition Law unconstitutional and the charges of the 'Bee' true. The
friends of Holt 'had collected from Dan to Beersheba to hear the
trial and afford aid and comfort to their brother.' When he was
quickly convicted and sentenced to jail for three months and to
pay a fine of two hundred dollars, a Federalist paper smugly commented upon the 'mildness of the punishment' and 'the humanity
of the Judges.' [2] Like the other victims of the Terror, Holt took
his punishment standing up, with shoulders thrown back. A few
days before his trial he wrote boldly of the things he had refrained
from saying — 'the insults and threats offered to peaceable inhabitants and helpless women in the neighborhood, and the alarm
and disturbance excited by firing in the streets and under the
windows at all hours of the night.' [3]

During the two years of the Terror the press was sprinkled with
brief reports on arrests, mostly of Democratic editors. One at
Mount Pleasant, New York, was arrested 'in the name of the
President for reprinting a paragraph from the New Windsor
Gazette supposed to be a libel against the President,' and he was
forced to give bond for four thousand dollars.[4] By November,
1798, it was announced that twenty-one 'printers' had 'fallen
victims to the . . . Sedition Law.' [5] In enumerating the arrests
that month, the 'Chronicle' commented that no Federalist editor
was included 'because they vilify none but Jefferson, Livingston,
and Gallatin.' [6] Everywhere men were being intimidated into
silence. Sometimes there was a touch of comedy to the Terror.
One poor wight was dragged into court because of a comment,
when a salute was fired in honor of Adams, that it was a pity the
ball did not find lodgment 'in the seat of his pants.'

Strangely enough, there was no serious attempt to make use of

[1] Carey's *Diary; Aurora*, January 17, 1800.
[2] *Commercial Advertiser*, April 23, 1800.   [3] *Aurora*, April 9, 1800.
[4] *Independent Chronicle*, August 9, 1798.   [5] *Ibid.*, November 1, 1798.
[6] *Ibid.*, November 26, 1798.

the Alien Law. We have seen that about the time of its passage many Frenchmen chartered a boat to escape its operations, and America thus rid herself of the peril of Volney. General Victor Collot, an officer in the army of Rochambeau, escaped deportation by leaving voluntarily. The only appeal to the Alien Law was by indirection in the case of John D. Burk, editor of the 'Time Piece,' a democratic paper in New York City. He had left his native Ireland to escape the terror there under Pitt, and finally ran foul of the law here by charging that a letter of Gerry to Adams, which the latter had sent to Congress, had been tampered with. The terrorists were not slow to act. When the offensive article stared at Pickering through his spectacles, he wrote the District Attorney: 'If Burk is an alien no man is a fitter object for the operation of the Alien Law. Even if Burk should prove to be an alien it may be expedient to punish him for his libels before he is sent away.' He had already been arrested for sedition, however, and the prosecution was finally dropped on condition that he would leave the country. Instead of leaving, he went into hiding, only emerging from his obscurity with the inauguration of Jefferson.[1]

Many of the terrorists were infuriated by the failure to use the Alien Law for wholesale deportations. 'Why in God's name is the Alien Law not enforced?' wrote the intolerant Tracy to McHenry.[2] Everywhere the Sedition Law was keeping men 'on the run.' E. S. Thomas, learning that Thomas Adams, of the 'Independent Chronicle,' had been arrested for the publication of an article by the former, fled to South Carolina just in time.[3] In the capital at Philadelphia, the Jeffersonians, fearing an attack, met in secret and made plans for defense. Moreau De Saint Merys, a scholarly Frenchman who kept a bookstore, was given keys to two houses where he could take refuge should his own be attacked. He was quite incapable of anything that would have made him amenable to the law, and President Adams had not only lounged in his bookstore frequently, but the two had exchanged copies of their books. Hearing that Adams had written him down among the proscribed, Moreau appealed to Senator Langdon for the reason.

[1] 'Enforcement of the Alien and Sedition Laws,' by Anderson, American Historical Association *Report*, 1912.

[2] Steiner, 436.   [3] Thomas, *Reminiscences*.

'No reason,' grunted Langdon, 'beyond the fact that you are French.' Finally, thanks to the courtesy of Liston, the British Minister, Moreau secured a passport and left the land of liberty with his books, maps, and papers.[1]

Drunk with hate and a sense of power, the terrorists were running amuck. At a banquet at Hartford in July, 1799, they thrilled to the toast: 'The Alien and Sedition Laws: Like the Sword of Eden may they point everywhere to guard our country against intrigue from without and faction from within.'[2] And every Democrat knew that 'faction' was the Federalist name for party, and 'party' meant the Jeffersonians. Armed with the sword, the Federalists no longer bandied idle words. When George Nicholas of Kentucky challenged Robert Goodhue Harper to a debate through the press on the Sedition Law, the latter was merely amused. 'The old proverb says, let them laugh who win; and for the converse of the maxim the consolation of railing ought to be allowed to those who lose,' jeered Harper.[3] Why argue? The courts were busy silencing and jailing the Jeffersonians, suppressing free speech, striking down the liberty of the press.

With the Democrats partly intimidated in the Eastern States, the honor of leading the fight against these laws was reserved for Virginia and the frontier States of Kentucky and Tennessee. Here mass meetings were held throughout the autumn of 1798. In Woodford County, Kentucky, it was declared 'the primary duty of every good citizen to guard as a faithful sentinel his constitutional rights and to repel all violations of them from whatever quarter offered.'[4] Four hundred gathered in Goochland County, Virginia, and, with only thirty opposed, denounced the laws and called upon the next Assembly to protest to Congress.[5] At Charlottesville, at the foot of Monticello, the people of Albemarle County, Virginia, met to adopt resolutions of denunciation, and at Lexington, Kentucky, they added their protest.[6] Richmond — Knoxville — followed. These resolutions were dignified and forceful protests, sponsored by men of the first ability in the communities acting. But in the House of Representatives at Phila-

---

[1] *The Nation*, July 18, 1912; Moreau's *Journal*.
[2] *Gazette of the United States*, July 10, 1799.   [3] *Aurora*, November 4, 1799.
[4] *Independent Chronicle*, September 27, 1798.   [5] *Ibid.*   [6] *Ibid.*

delphia, when Jeffersonians spoke in favor of the repeal of the obnoxious measures, their voices were drowned by loud conversation, coughs, laughter, the scraping of the feet of the Federalists. 'Livingston, however, attempted to speak,' wrote Jefferson, 'but after a few sentences the Speaker called him to order. . . . It was impossible to proceed.' [1] From 1798 until 1801, liberty was mobbed in America with the zealous support of the Federal Courts, to the applause of the church — and out of these conditions came the Virginia and Kentucky Resolutions.

XII

On the adjournment of Congress in 1798, Jefferson returned to his Virginia home profoundly impressed with the significance of the obnoxious laws. He had supposed that the freedom of speech and the liberty of the press had been guaranteed by the Constitution. That the fundamental law was outraged by these measures he had no doubt. It was his firm conviction that they had been enacted 'as an experiment on the American mind to see how far it will bear an avowed violation of the Constitution,' and that if it succeeded 'we shall immediately see attempted another act of Congress declaring that the President shall continue in office for life.' [2] He was not alone in this belief.

One day in the late summer a memorable conference was held at Monticello. There, in the center of the group, was Jefferson. There, too, was W. C. Nicholas, one of the foremost Jeffersonians of Virginia, and John Breckenridge of Kentucky, who had returned on a visit to his native State. It does not appear that Madison participated in this conference, although he was in complete accord with its purpose. There the plan was perfected to launch a movement of protest against the Alien and Sedition Laws through the Legislatures of the various States in resolutions pronouncing them violative of the Constitution and void. While Jefferson, recalling the occasion a quarter of a century later, thought that he had been pressed to frame such resolutions, it is unlikely that the plan did not originate in his own mind. He had an uncanny faculty for calling forth suggestions from others to meet his views.

[1] Jefferson's *Works* (to Madison), x, 119–21.
[2] *Ibid.* (to Senator Mason), x, 61–62.

On one point his memory was clear — there was to be the utmost secrecy as to the part he played. That he did prepare a draft is thoroughly established; that the draft finally submitted to the Kentucky Legislature, while based on the Jeffersonian draft, was the work of John Breckenridge has been convincingly maintained.[1]

This dashing young leader of the Kentucky Democracy had been a marked figure from his earliest youth. More than six feet in height, spare and muscular in build, with the strength and grace of carriage born of his wilderness training, he looked the leader of men. His hair, a rich chestnut tending to auburn, disclosed something of his ardent temperament and was not unlike that of his idolized chief. His brown eyes could be stern or tender. His address was easy and dignified, and his manner not without that touch of gravity which creates confidence in the follower. There was much of tenderness and everything of generosity in his nature to explain the love which enveloped him wherever he went.

Born of Scotch-Irish stock in Virginia thirty-eight years before, his had been an extraordinary career. Scarcely was he out of college when, without any effort on his part, he was elected to the Virginia House of Delegates at the age of nineteen. When the House refused him his seat because of his age, his loyal constituents elected him again. Again refused his seat, he was elected for the third time, and seated. During the next five years he distinguished himself by his industry and ability no less than by the charm of his personality. It was about this time that the young man ascended the hill to Monticello to sit at the feet of the god of his idolatry. Jefferson was impressed by 'the large scope of his mind,' his great store of information, and 'the moral direction' of his ideas.[2] There had to be something extraordinary in the man to whom Gallatin looked a little later as the man best qualified to continue the work of Jefferson, Madison, and himself.[3]

At the bar Breckenridge distinguished himself by his erudition, his industry, and the fluency and force of his arguments, which were notably free from the floridity then so popular in the South. Elected to Congress when thirty-three, he had abandoned his seat to remove to Lexington, Kentucky, where he acquired a large

[1] Warfield, *The Kentucky Resolutions*, 133–65.
[2] *Ibid.*, 55.   [3] *Ibid.*, 70.

plantation and settled down to the practice of his profession. Almost immediately he was deeply engaged in politics. He was made President of the Democratic Society of Kentucky and became one of the most engaging of the Democratic leaders of the pioneer State. Returning to Kentucky with the Jefferson draft, he made some changes, and on November 8th presented the Resolutions to the Legislature. The debate was brief, and on the 10th they were adopted.

The Virginia Resolutions, written by James Madison after conferences with Jefferson, were introduced in the Legislature of that State by the celebrated John Taylor of Caroline. These, too, were speedily adopted after a brilliant debate in which their sponsor and Giles crossed swords with the eloquent George Keith Taylor.

The primary purpose of these Resolutions was to concentrate attention on the Alien and Sedition Laws. They were to be sent to the Legislatures of all the States where they would be thoroughly discussed. Jefferson was too wise to have expected a favorable response from Legislatures dominated by the Federalists. But there would be debate, agitation, newspaper controversy — the hated laws would have the searchlight turned full upon them. Historians have been interested in these Resolutions because they set forth in the most impressive manner the compact theory of the Union on which the nullificationists and secessionists were to seize much later as justification for their course. We are interested here in the contemporary view and the political aspect. The reader of to-day is apt to overlook the fact that they were primarily intended as a protest against interference with the freedom of speech and the liberty of the press, and only 'incidentally they gave expression to a theory concerning the nature of the federal union.' [1] That this was the general contemporary interpretation is shown in the actions of the other Legislatures. Thus Maryland, Federalist, rejected the Resolutions as 'highly improper' because 'a recommendation to repeal the Alien and Sedition Laws would be unwise and impolitic.' [2] Thus Delaware, Federalist, dismissed

[1] Frank M. Anderson, 'Contemporary Opinion of the Kentucky and Virginia Resolutions,' *American Historical Review*, October, 1899; January, 1900.

[2] Professor Anderson calls attention to the fact that in Maryland the endorsement of the Alien and Sedition Laws was made more prominent than the condemnation of the proposed remedy.

them as a 'very unjustifiable interference with the general government.' Thus New Hampshire, Federalist, declared the obnoxious laws 'constitutional and . . . highly expedient.' The Federalists of Rhode Island pronounced them 'within the powers delegated to Congress and promotive of the welfare of the United States.'

Only in Massachusetts did the Federalists make a comprehensive and argumentative reply to the effect that the constitutionality of measures could only be passed upon by the Supreme Court. The Alien and Sedition Laws were defended as in no wise interfering with the liberty of the press. And here, strangely enough, Democrats were found to support the Resolutions in speeches of no mean merit. In John Bacon of Berkshire the Jeffersonians had their sole representative in the State Senate. Formerly a minister of the Old South Church, and a speaker of some ability, he delivered a carefully prepared speech assailing the constitutionality of the oppressive laws, and gave it to the press.[1] Dr. Aaron Hill of Cambridge, a Jeffersonian in the House, acted similarly in that body — and on both Hill and Bacon the floodgates of falsehood and abuse were opened. In an open letter to Bacon in the 'Centinel,' he was charged with having been a Tory, with having quarreled with the congregation at the Old South, with having owned, as slaves, a married couple, and with having sold the husband into a distant State.[2] When Bacon proved the charges shamelessly false, the 'Centinel' took no notice.[3] Dr. Hill fared quite as badly when students from Harvard exercised their learning by smashing the windows and casements of his home.[4] And it was at this juncture that Thomas Adams, of the 'Independent Chronicle,' was indicted and Abijah Adams was thrown into a cell for criticizing the action of the Legislature.[5]

Everywhere the Federalist papers made the Resolutions the occasion for a justification of the Alien and Sedition Laws; everywhere the Jeffersonians, usually refraining from a discussion of the

[1] *Independent Chronicle*, February 14, 1799.   [2] *Centinel*, February 27, 1799

[3] Professor Anderson comments on this unfairness.

[4] Anderson, *op. cit.*

[5] Professor Anderson says: 'The imprisonment of Adams indicates that the Federalists were ready on the slightest provocation to treat opposition to the policy of the Administration, whether federal or state, as crime. That case certainly does much to explain why Jefferson and other Republican leaders could fear that Republican institutions were about to be overthrown.' *American Historical Review*, January, 1900, p. 229.

theory of the Federal Union advanced, made them the pretext for a denunciation of the laws. And significantly enough, it was reserved for the favorite Federalist organ of 'Porcupine' to preach and all but urge secession. Replying to a correspondent who had denied the right of secession, 'Porcupine' said: 'Does he imagine that the industrious and orderly people of New England will ever suffer themselves to be governed by an impious philosopher or a gambling profligate imposed upon them by Virginia influence? If he does, he knows very little of New England. The New Englanders know well that they are the rock of the Union. They know their own value; they feel their strength, and they will have their full share of influence in the federal government, or they will not be governed by it. It is clear that their influence must decrease; because . . . the Middle and Southern States are increasing in inhabitants five times as fast as New England is. If Pennsylvania joins her influence to that of New England the balance will be kept up; but the moment she decidedly throws it into the scale with Virginia the balance is gone, New England loses her influence in the national Government, and she establishes a Government of her own.' [1] This reflects the spirit of the times when the two parties faced each other for the decisive battle of 1800. The Alien and Sedition Laws and the Terror were issues; the Kentucky and Virginia Resolutions played scarcely any part at all.

[1] Anderson, *op. cit.*

CHAPTER XVIII
ADAMS PULLS DOWN THE PILLARS

I

MEANWHILE, the Federalist leaders, having, as they thought, cowed and crushed the Democrats, were engaged in an internecine strife for control. There was to be war — at all hazards a war. It was to be a Federalist war, with Jeffersonians rigidly excluded from all places of command. But more than that, it had to be a war personally conducted by Alexander Hamilton — with no unseemly interference from John Adams. This was the grim determination of the radical Federalists everywhere, even the Essex Junto, in the President's own State, sharing it with the three leading members of the Adams Cabinet. Thus, when Adams one day casually asked Pickering who should be made Commander-in-Chief of the army, and the spectacled Puritan unhesitatingly answered, 'Colonel Hamilton,' there was an ominous silence. When, on another occasion, the same question elicited the identical answer, with a similar silence, even Pickering must have sensed the situation. But when, after a third question had brought the same answer, and Adams, a little annoyed, had rejected the suggestion with the sharp observation, 'It is not his turn by a great deal,' Pickering might have dropped his plans without disgrace.[1] But nothing was more remote from his intentions. It was at this time that the conspirators, including the three members of the Cabinet, put their heads together to devise ways and means of forcing the appointment of their idol. The chief command would naturally be offered to Washington, who would accept the position in an honorary sense, but old age and infirmities would make his activities and authority but perfunctory. The important thing was to secure the second position for Hamilton — and even there was a rub. Adams was prejudiced.

Then, one day, Adams ordered McHenry to Mount Vernon to proffer the chief command to Washington, with a request for ad-

[1] *Intimate Life*, 323–24.

vice in the formation of the officers' list. The names of several eligibles for the leading posts, enumerated by Adams, might be mentioned. Hamilton was among them, but he was fourth on the list. That day McHenry hastened to Pickering, and the conspiracy against the President in his own household began to unfold. It was agreed that Pickering should send a personal letter on ahead urging Hamilton for second place, McHenry should reënforce Pickering's plea in person, Hamilton should be instantly notified and a letter from him should be delivered to Washington along with the commission from Adams. Thus, when the smug-faced little War Secretary, more familiar with the pen of the rhymester than with the sword of the soldier, bade his chief adieu and set out upon his mission, he was the messenger of his chief's dearest enemy, prepared to exhaust his ingenuity in thwarting the plans of the man of whom he was a subordinate and on whose mission he went forth.

As early as June, Washington had planned to make Hamilton Inspector-General, but without placing him ahead of Pinckney or Knox, both of whom outranked him in the old army.[1] Just what treachery McHenry practiced as he sat on the veranda at Mount Vernon those July days will never be positively known. That he pleaded the cause of Hamilton against the wishes of his chief there can be no doubt. That it was he who suggested that Washington should make his own acceptance conditional on having absolute power in the selection of his subordinates is more than probable. At any rate, when he returned to Philadelphia he carried in Washington's handwriting the names of the three Major-Generals — Hamilton, Pinckney, and Knox, in the order given. In this order Adams, who assumed that their relative positions would be determined by himself, sent them to the Senate and they were confirmed.

Soon the Federalist camp was in fermentation as to whether Knox, favored by the President, or Hamilton, preferred by the party bosses, should be second in command. Pinckney, who accepted slights with the same contrite spirit with which his brother had stepped aside for Jay in London, agreed to serve under the Federalist leader, but Knox, not so humble, refused, and the crisis

[1] Hamilton's *Works*, x, 287.

came. Personally fond of Knox, the quarrel was embarrassing to Washington, but it had never been the habit of the Hamiltonians to spare him where their wishes were involved. Soon Hamilton was bombarding Mount Vernon with letters strikingly lacking in the spirit of humility. His claims were superior to those of Knox or Pinckney, and the Federalists preferred him to the former.[1] 'If I am to be degraded beneath my just claims in public opinion, ought I acquiesce?' he wrote the sympathetic Pickering.[2] To McHenry he wrote that he would not surrender the first place to which he 'had been called by the voice of the country';[3] to Washington that the Federalists of New England favored him over Knox.[4]

All the while the three leading members of the Cabinet were concocting plans for the humiliation of Adams, taking their orders from Hamilton, who, from his law office in New York, was directing the fight of the President's trusted advisers against their chief. One day the angels looked down and smiled through tears on the spectacle of McHenry writing a letter to Knox fixing his status, from a model in the handwriting of Alexander Hamilton.[5] As Adams stubbornly held his ground, one by one all the Hamiltonians of consequence were drawn into the conspiracy against him.

One evening the secretarial conspirators sat about a table phrasing a persuasive note to Adams which Wolcott, the most consummate deceiver of the three, should sign and send as his personal view. 'Public opinion' favored Hamilton, Washington preferred him, and 'Knox [has] no popular character even in Massachusetts.'[6] Having dispatched this cunning letter, Wolcott immediately wrote his real chief in New York that 'measures have been taken to bring all right,' and requesting Hamilton neither to do nor to say anything 'until you hear from me.'[7] Another little caucus of conspirators in Boston: present, Cabot, Ames, and Higginson; purpose, the framing of a letter to Adams that Cabot should sign, assuring the President of a 'remarkable uniformity of sentiment' in New England for Hamilton over Knox.[8] Having sent this letter, Cabot wrote confidentially to Pickering suggesting that General Wadsworth, who was 'accustomed to tell [Knox] his

---

[1] Hamilton's *Works*, x, 301.　　[2] *Ibid.*, 297–98.　　[3] *Ibid.*, 310.
[4] *Ibid.*, 311.　　[5] Hamilton's *Works* (to McHenry), x, 307.
[6] Gibbs, ii, 93–99.　　[7] *Ibid.*　　[8] Lodge, *Cabot*, 165–67.

faults,' should be enlisted in the cause.[1] Meanwhile Pickering, more sinister, if less deceptive than the others, was seeking to intimidate his chief by having Hamiltonian Senators declare that the officers had been confirmed with the understanding that Hamilton stood at the head.[2]

All this time, Iago-like letters were going forth from members of the Cabinet to Washington conveying the impression that Adams was contemptuously indifferent to the great man's wishes. The effect was all that could have been desired. In a surprisingly offensive note, Washington wrote peremptorily to the President demanding to know 'at once and precisely' what was to be expected.[3] Such a letter from a less popular idol would have elicited an answer sharp and decisive; but, taking discretion for the wiser course, Adams swallowed his pride and wrote a conciliatory note, not neglecting, however, to remind the man who had presided over the Constitutional Convention that under the Constitution the President, and no one else, 'has the authority to determine the rank of the officers.'[4] Thus the issue was closed, with Hamilton triumphant, but with Adams awaiting only an opportunity for revenge. The tiny cloud that had appeared in the beginning of the Administration was now dark and large and threatening.

II

Having won with Hamilton, the Federalist leaders now turned to another part of their programme — the rigid exclusion of Jeffersonians from commissions in the army. This was to be a Federalist war, nothing less. Even Washington, who had, by this time, become a partisan Federalist, was in sympathy with the view that the friends of Jefferson, Madison, Hancock, and Sam Adams should be proscribed. This appears in his consultations with John Marshall as to the personnel of the army,[5] and in a letter to McHenry referring to the 'erroneous political opinions' of an applicant.[6] This enlistment of Washington in the proscriptive policies of the Federalists is directly traceable to the Iagos who were writing him all the while. Hamilton was solemnly assuring him that the Democrats were 'determined to go every length with

---

[1] Lodge, *Cabot*, 170–71.   [2] Pickering, III, 432.   [3] Gibbs, II, 99.   [4] *Ibid.*, 100.
[5] Beveridge, II, 420.   [6] Steiner, 354. Here, however, he qualifies.

France' and to 'form with her a perpetual offensive and defensive alliance and to give her a monopoly of our trade.' [1]

Thus one day Adams sat in conference with Washington on the organization of the army. Knowing Aaron Burr as a brave and able officer anxious to fight, he wished to recognize the Democrats by giving him a commission. Washington, much under the influence of Hamilton, conceded Burr's capacity, but opposed his appointment because he was a master of intrigue. Through the mind of Adams, hampered in his plans at every turn, flashed the vivid memory of how his predecessor had forced him to humiliate his own friends in the appointment of Hamilton — 'the most restless, impatient, artful, indefatigable, and unprincipled intriguer in the United States.' But — as he afterward wrote — he was 'not permitted to nominate Burr.' [2] Here again the traitors in the Cabinet had played their part. [3]

But the war was not to be national, but Federalist. 'Every one of them [Democrats] ought to be rejected, and only men of fair property employed in the higher and more confidential grades,' wrote a Federalist Representative to Wolcott. [4] When Adams's son-in-law applied for a commission his application was held until he sent a certificate that he had not interfered in a gubernatorial election in New York. [5] So zealously did the minor politicians enter into this policy of proscription that some of the wiser leaders began to take alarm. Even a friend of McHenry at Baltimore was moved to protest. 'They seemed to imagine that nothing was left to be done but to exterminate every one who had been on the Democratic side' he complained. [6] Even Hamilton finally thought fit to call for a moderation of the programme. 'It does not seem advisable,' he wrote McHenry, 'to exclude all hope and to give to appointments too absolute a party feature.' [7] But there was no relenting in party circles, and no one had done more to arouse this fanatical spirit than Hamilton himself.

The climax of stupidity was reached in the case of Frederick A. Muhlenberg, former Speaker of the House, a leader and oracle among the Germans of Pennsylvania, but no blind follower of

[1] Hamilton's *Works*, x, 286.   [2] Parton, *Burr*, i, 235–36.
[3] Gibbs (Pickering to Wolcott), ii, 71.   [4] *Ibid.* (from Goodrich), 105.
[5] Steiner (McHenry to Tracy), 328.   [6] *Ibid.* (from James Ash), 333.   [7] *Ibid.*, 368.

Federalism. In a spirit of pure patriotism he had personally offered the service of his sword to Adams, whose wish to accept it
was again thwarted by Washington, acting under the inspiration
of the Federalist leaders. Whereupon Muhlenberg marched with
the Germans as a body into the Jeffersonian camp and enlisted for
another war.[1]

Under this proscriptive program the Jeffersonians remained
mute but for a few sarcastic comments in their press. 'General
Washington must have some very keen reflection,' said the
'Independent Chronicle,' 'in taking command of the army of the
present day, in seeing so many new friends who were his old enemies during the Revolution.'[2] When it was reported that Robert
Goodhue Harper had been made Commissioner-General, it
chortled, 'What lawyer would not plead for such a fee?'[3] And it
had reflected on Adams's 'pretence' for piety in connection with
his appointment of Hamilton, 'who published a book to prove
that he was an adulterer.'[4]

Bitter as were the reflections of Adams on reading such observations, it could have mattered little to Hamilton. Everything he
had started out to get he got. He wanted a war with France —
and got it. He wanted the command directly under Washington
as he had wanted nothing else in his life — and got it, by striding
to his sword over the humiliated pride of the President. He wanted
an army of fifty thousand men, and, if he fell short in this, he
nevertheless had an army. He was on the crest of the wave, the
most powerful man in America, and he was happy.

III

Feeling that supreme fortune was within his grasp, Hamilton
threw all his enthusiasm and vitality into the task of perfecting
the army and organizing the Nation for war. 'The law has abandoned him, or rather he has forsaken it,' wrote a friend to King.[5]
Preparing the plan for the fortification of New York Harbor, he
personally superintended its execution. He had worked out to the
minutest detail the organization of the army and all he lacked
was men and a declaration of war. But alas, he was confronted

---

[1] Adams, *Works*, x, 120–23.   [2] July 12, 1798.   [3] September 17, 1798.
[4] July 30, 1798.   [5] King's *Works* (from Troup), iii, 35.

on every hand by disheartening difficulties. The recruiting fell pathetically short of anticipations, the War Department under the Secretary of his own choosing was pitifully inefficient, and, while the army was woefully below the provisions of Congress, even the fragment was not adequately clothed or provisioned, and there was a deficiency of tents. In a rage, Hamilton wrote angrily to McHenry: 'Why, dear friend, why do you suffer the business of providing to go on as it does? Every moment proves the insufficiency of the existing plan and the necessity of auxiliaries. I have no doubt that at Baltimore, New York, Providence, and Boston additional supplies of clothing may promptly be procured and prepared by your agents, and it ought to be done, though it may enhance the expense. 'Tis terrible . . . that there should be wants everywhere. So of tents. Calls for them are repeated from Massachusetts where better and cheaper than anywhere else they can certainly be provided.' [1]

The truth is that the hysteria for getting at the throat of the French democracy was over almost as soon as it began, and the masses commenced to reflect on the cost, as the war measures grew apace. Jefferson, noting the increasing boldness of opposition in Pennsylvania, where petitions were signed by four thousand people protesting against the Alien and Sedition Laws, standing armies, and extraordinary war powers for the President, and observing similar unrest in New Jersey and New York, and 'even in New Hampshire,' was fearful of insurrection. 'Nothing could be so fatal,' he wrote. 'Anything like force would check the progress of public opinion.' [2]

When Wolcott tried to float a loan, he found the moneyed men cold to the regular legal rate of interest, for their patriotic passion had suffered a chill when it came to cash. After all, business was business, and why should the Federalist men of money fail to get in on the profits? It was not hard to persuade Wolcott, who had a sentimental weakness for the financiers, and he could see nothing unreasonable in a demand for eight per cent. The rates for stocks were good, commercial prospects were alluring, and after all, eight per cent would be but 'moderate terms.' Adams, sore from the un-

[1] Hamilton's *Works*, x, 354.
[2] Jefferson's *Works* (to Pendleton), x, 104–10.

merciful pummeling from his party, was outraged at such a rate,[1] but Wolcott persisted — it was the only way. War was war as business was business. Finally, in sheer disgust, Adams capitulated to necessity with the exclamation: 'This damned army will be the ruin of this country; if it must be so, it must; I cannot help it. Issue your proposals as you please.' [2] When Hamilton had urged that all the resources of revenue be seized upon, Adams thought him mad, but it soon became evident that something of the sort would be necessary.[3]

Aha, said the 'Independent Chronicle,' '"millions for defence but not one cent for tribute." This has been the language of those who are in favor of war. The patriotism of such persons is every day becoming more and more evident. A loan of five million has been attempted, but instead of the old legal rate of six per cent these modern patriots have required the moderate premium of Eight. At this rate we shall soon verify the first part of the motto, viz., "millions for defence," but whether the latter is not violated by the extra interest is left to the decision of those who are to bear the burdens.' [4] And they who were to pay the piper gave an acquiescent nod.

The taxes which the war party had levied with such patriotic abandon aroused bitter resentment. Among the Germans of Pennsylvania, the taxes on houses, lands, and windows were considered the beginning of a system which would extend to everything. The immediate outcome was an insurrection led by John Fries, an ignorant son of a German farmer, and the marching of the troops and the easy dissipation of the incipient rebellion against the assessors.[5]

About that time Hamilton arrived in Philadelphia. 'For what purpose?' inquired 'The Aurora.' 'Can it be to foment another insurrection and thereby to increase the energies of the Government? What distinguished citizen is there in the counties of Northampton and Bucks that he wishes to glut his vengeance

---

[1] Gibbs (Higginson to Wolcott), II, 177.
[2] Adams, *Works*, x, 126–31. [3] *Ibid.* [4] January 28, 1799.
[5] McMaster (II, 435) makes the statement that 'Republicans were fully determined that the direct tax should not be gathered.' There is abundant evidence, including the letter from Jefferson, previously quoted, that the Republicans thought an insurrection against the collection the worse possible thing for the party.

upon? Does he wish that Easton may be burned to afford him a pretext for military execution?'[1] If there were no executions, the people had a touch of military rule. A troop of horse from Lancaster committed outrages on citizens at Reading, and Jacob Schneider, a local editor, commented with severity upon their actions. On their return through Reading these troops went to the editor's office, tore his clothing from his back, dragged him to the Market House, and were preparing to give him twenty-five lashes when troops from Philadelphia interfered.[2] The brutality of the soldiers shocked the country. The prisoners taken on the expedition were treated with the same unnecessary cruelty which marked the treatment of the rebels in the Whiskey Insurrection. Ignorant or besotted with partisan passion, under a lax discipline, and contemptuous of the civil government, many soldiers strutting about in uniforms, insulting and attacking citizens, convinced the majority of the people that the Jeffersonians were right in their observations upon the evils of standing armies.

No one had denounced these excesses with greater vehemence than William Duane, editor of 'The Aurora.' One day some petty officers in uniforms, swords and pistols on their persons, said by Duane to have numbered thirty and by his enemies to have been fifteen, entered his office. With drawn pistols the compositors and pressmen were driven into a corner and kept at bay by a part of the assailants. Some grasped and held Duane's hands while others beat him over the head with the butt end of a pistol. Then with ten gallant soldiers participating in the assault on the one man, he was brutally dragged downstairs into Franklin Court, where the assault was repeated. He was knocked down and kicked. The editor's request to be permitted to fight any one of them was ignored, and had not his sixteen-year-old son thrown himself across his father's body, and a number of Democrats arrived to give battle, he would have been murdered in cold blood. That night armed Democrats went to the 'Aurora' office prepared to give shot for shot if an attempt should be made to destroy the plant.[3] 'Porcupine' chortled, and young Fenno declared that

---

[1] March 22, 1799. This refers to Hamilton's efforts to involve Gallatin in the Whiskey Rebellion.

[2] *Aurora*, April 14 and April 27, 1799; McMaster, ii, 438–39.

[3] *Ibid.*, May 16, 1799; Hudson, 214; McMaster, ii, 439.

'the punishment of this caitiff is of no more consequence than that of any other vagabond.' Besides, did not every one know that 'the infernal Aurora and the United Irishman who conducts it' were 'expressly chargeable with the Northampton Insurrection?' [1]

With such encouragement from the organs of the Administration, these outrages by soldiers soon became commonplace wherever they were assembled, with uniformed ruffians swaggering down the streets pushing civilians into the gutters, taking liberties with women, picking quarrels while drunk, and slashing and lunging with dirk and sword.[2] This bullying spirit affected the petty officers and reached a climax when civil officials, armed with a warrant for a thief who had escaped to the soldiers near Philadelphia, were literally kicked out of the camp, their warrant cursed and trampled.[3] With the tide rising rapidly against both the war and the army, the recruiting lagged. Adams in later years recalled that the army was as unpopular 'as if it had been a ferocious wild beast let loose upon the nation to devour it.' [4] With the recruiting officers putting forth their utmost efforts, 'with all the influence of Hamilton, reënforced by the magical name of Washington,' they were unable to 'raise one half of their ... little army.' [5] Duane wrote that before the law creating the army passed 'there were 15,000 applications for commissions — since the passing of the law there have been only 3000 soldiers.' [6] There is more than a touch of irony in the fact that while the Administration papers were vilifying the Irish, 'three fifths of the men enlisted were Irish immigrants.' [7]

But there was another reason for the failure in recruiting — the people soon concluded that some one had cried 'wolf' when there was no wolf. No one, including Hamilton, believed that France had the most remote notion of warring on the United States. The impression grew that the army was intended for purposes other than the protection of the country from a foreign foe. Meanwhile, the taxes were bearing hard, the national debt was mounting and the passion for peace returned. Right gallantly the war party sought to reawaken the fine frenzy of the hysterical days of the

[1] *Gazette of the United States*, May 16, 1799.
[2] *Aurora*, June 25, August 5, 1799.   [3] *Ibid.*, September 24, 1799.
[4] Adams, *Works*, x, 116–19.   [5] *Ibid.*
[6] *Aurora*, January 10, 1800.   [7] *Ibid.*, February 27, 1800.

X Y Z papers. The preachers were as distressed over the possibility of peace as the politicians, and a convention of ministers in Boston issued a war cry. 'You will see by these things that the clergy are not asleep this way,' wrote a Massachusetts man to Wolcott. 'They ought everywhere to be awake.'[1] From the New York 'Commercial Advertiser' came a pathetic attempt to sweep back the rising tide for peace: 'The necessity in times like the present in cherishing the war spirit . . . is evident.'[2] Apropos of the report that the French were ready to make every concession to our interest and pride, the 'Centinel' in Boston sent forth the warning, 'The trying time is now approaching';[3] but the rabble, as the masses were called, could see nothing distressing in winning a war without the loss of a drop of blood. Fenno's 'Gazette,' commenting on the business stagnation, promised that 'a war with France would within two months revivify every department of society, commerce would be invigorated, the funds would rise, and every employment of life would receive new vigor.'[4] This sordid note he was soon to strike again.[5] But it was all unavailing. The enlistments dwindled to nothing, common soldiers were actually cheering the Democratic Governor in the streets of Philadelphia, no one feared an invasion, and, as Wolcott confided to Fisher Ames, 'no one has thought it prudent to say that the army is kept to suppress or prevent rebellions.'[6] To make matters all the worse, desertions multiplied until the harassed McHenry was writing Hamilton urging executions. The little rhymester was far beyond his depths, scolded by Washington, kicked like a flunky by Hamilton in one or two letters a day. But the idea of shooting a deserter was a bit too high-toned for Hamilton. 'There must be some caution,' he wrote, 'not to render our military system odious by giving it the appearance of being sanguinary.'[7] Adams was prepared for extreme measures, but it was decided to leave the decision with Hamilton and McHenry — which meant with Hamilton. 'If the virtuous General Hamilton is determined upon shooting every soldier who deserts,' said 'The Aurora,' 'Billy Wilcox's court martial will be kept at pretty constant duty. In a Daily Adver-

---

[1] Gibbs, II, 241; Morse to Wolcott.
[2] May 14, 1799.
[3] June 1, 1799.
[4] May 16, 1799.
[5] July 18, 1799.
[6] Gibbs, II, 313–18.
[7] Steiner, 382.

tiser of last week no less than ten of these strayed gentlemen are advertised for apprehension at $10 a head.' [1]

But Hamilton was too wise to shoot.

IV

The war cry was sinking to a hoarse whisper when Dr. James Logan, who had entertained the Washingtons, and who was a follower of Jefferson, quietly slipped out of Philadelphia one day and sailed for France — and the war hawks were in a frenzy. When Logan, at his own expense and wholly on his own volition, went to Paris, it was to determine the state of the public mind there for himself. He was a leading citizen, his family familiar to society, his home one of the most cultured in the community, and, aside from being a friend of the French democracy, he was a Quaker and an enemy of war. He felt that the country had been deceived by war propaganda, and he determined to find out for himself.

The war wing of the Federalist Party knew that an investigation in Paris was the one thing they could not afford. No one knew better that war was unnecessary and that the French were ready if not eager to recede. Harrison Gray Otis knew it best of all because his fellow Federalist of Boston and classmate, Richard Codman, was writing him from Paris of the French disposition for peace and conciliation. But this was being carefully concealed from the American people. Thus, when Logan sailed it was clearly the cue for the war party to hint darkly of weird conspiracies with the French and a factional embassy from the Democrats. Soon Harper, who had a supersensitive nose for conspiracies and treason, was hinting mysteriously on the floor of the House of a traitorous correspondence between the French Directory and the Jeffersonian Party. The truth is that, when Logan foolishly made a mystery of his departure and almost surreptitiously stole out of Philadelphia, he carried letters from Jefferson and Governor McKean. Four or five days before his departure he had informed Jefferson of his purpose and asked for letters of introduction and a certification of his citizenship. It was not a secret that Jefferson was opposed to a preventable war, but no instructions were given the Doctor, no communication was sent by Jefferson, and there

[1] August 21, 1799.

was no conspiracy at all.[1] Thus, on his own volition Logan went to Paris, talked with Otis's Federalist friend Codman and other Americans, conversed with leading Frenchmen, dined with Merlin, met Talleyrand, and ascertained, as he had expected, that peace could be preserved with honor. A simple, honest man, with none of the crooked mental twists of the professional politician, he returned with the confident expectation that the President and his advisers would be glad to get the benefit of his observations. He reached Philadelphia to find himself the object of immeasurable abuse.

Not doubting that Pickering would be glad to have his impressions, Logan went first to him. This was, in truth, a ludicrous performance, and a Federalist paper was moved to mirth because he had 'actually unfolded his budget to Pickering' and 'needless to say' returned 'with a bug in his ear.'[2] Going on to Trenton, the temporary seat of government, he saw Washington, to be received with more than his customary coldness. He had a message from Lafayette to Washington. 'Aye,' said the General. And one from Kosciusko. 'Aye,' said Washington. Whereupon Logan courteously proffered him the use of his home, which the Washingtons had often found agreeable, while in Philadelphia, to have his offer curtly declined. Even Pinckney haughtily refused the use of Logan's carriage when the General was seeking a conveyance to the capital. 'This fellow Logan had the unparalleled effrontery to offer the General a seat in his carriage,' sneered a war paper.[3] Some historians insist that Adams treated him contemptuously, and this seems probable in the light of the latter's letter to Pickering,[4] albeit Gibbs records that Adams was much impressed with Logan's story and with his sincerity and candor.[5] The letter was written to Pickering, however, before the interview was granted.

When Congress met, Logan found himself the subject of a bitter debate brought on by the introduction of the so-called 'Logan Law' prohibiting unofficial meddling in international affairs. Harper had followed his cue and found his conspiracy. Logan had

[1] Jefferson's *Works* (to Madison), x, 49–53; (to Gerry), x, 74–86. All of which is borne out by the signed statement of Logan, whose veracity was more reliable than that of Harper.

[2] *New York Commercial Advertiser,* November 15, 1798.

[3] *Ibid.,* November 22, 1798.   [4] Adams, *Works,* VIII, 615.   [5] Gibbs, II, 195.

actually presented a paper to the Directory as from one having authority. The story was all too thin, the facts too badly twisted, and the Jeffersonians under the leadership of Gallatin showed their teeth. The climax came when Harper read the paper which Logan was presumed to have presented. Then, through frank letters in 'The Aurora,' Logan brought out the truth to the discomfiture of the war hawks. In view of the scurvy treatment he has received, his own statement is one of value. He had been met at Hamburg by Lafayette, who had furnished him with the means to proceed to Paris. There he found negotiations at an end. Knowing no law, 'moral or political,' that prevented him from serving his country, he had sought interviews with leading characters and found France anxious for peace. Whereupon he had suggested the lifting of the embargo on American shipping detained in French ports and the release of American sailors held prisoners. He had not gone to Paris 'at the direction or on the request or on the advice of any person whatever.' He went for his own pleasure, on his own views, and at his own expense.[1] Not only had the memorial Harper had read to the house not been presented by him, it had not been written by him, but by a good Federalist who was an intimate friend and correspondent of Harrison Gray Otis, and he had refused the request to present it on the ground of its 'having too much the appearance of an official act.'[2] The absolute veracity of this story was known to Otis, who was intimate with Harper, for he had a letter from Codman in verification, and to the effect that Logan had told Talleyrand that in the event of war all parties in America would rally around the Government 'and oppose all its enemies.'[3]

Thus there was a conspiracy, a peculiarly ugly conspiracy, of the war hawks to ruin an honest, patriotic, if Quixotic man because of his interference with their plans to manufacture a needless and therefore a criminal war.

But there was a special reason for the war party's rage over Logan. About this time Elbridge Gerry, one of the three envoys, who had stayed over in Paris on the invitation of Talleyrand, had returned with a similar story. The Federalists had been outraged by his failure to leave with his colleagues, and on his return to his

---

[1] *Aurora*, January 3, 1799.   [2] *Ibid.*, January 16, 1799.   [3] Morison, *Otis*, I, 168–71.

home in Cambridge he found himself socially ostracized. Adams, who was his friend, had severely condemned him for continuing his conferences in Paris.[1] So bitter was the feeling against him, that the war party did not scruple to terrorize his family in his absence. His wife received anonymous letters charging that a woman was responsible for his lingering in Paris. With only women and children in his house, their nights were made hideous with yells and bonfires under their windows; and one morning Mrs. Gerry looked out of the window on a miniature guillotine smeared with blood. On his return, Gerry had gone to Philadelphia and left his dispatches, which Pickering had published with his intemperate comments. The Federalists were well pleased with Pickering's excoriation.

And Jefferson? So different was his conception of public opinion that he was delighted. Seizing upon the Gerry correspondence as a complete answer to the X Y Z papers, he wrote Edmund Pendleton that it was too voluminous for the masses, and urging him to prepare 'a capitulation ... stating everything ... short, simple, and leveled to every capacity ... so concise, as, omitting nothing material, may yet be printed in handbills, of which we could print and disperse ten or twelve thousand copies under letter covers, through all the United States by the members of Congress when they return home.'[2]

Meanwhile, Gerry had hastened to Quincy, and in the rambling frame house of the President was going over the situation with him.

V

The restoration of peace with France would mean the end of the army created with so much expense and trouble. So determined were the Hamiltonians on war that they were ready to wreck the Federalist Party on the issue. Many explanations have been offered. Wolcott had hinted in his letter to Ames that an army was wanted for domestic use.[3] That was the common charge of the Democrats. That there was another and more portentous reason we may be sure, albeit the public, and even John Adams, was ignorant of it.

<hr>

[1] Adams, *Works*, VIII, 617.   [2] Jefferson's *Works*, X, 86–89.   [3] Gibbs, II, 313–18.

At that time a queer little Latin-American soldier of fortune, Francesco de Miranda, was living in London, playing about Downing Street, and conferring with Rufus King, the American Minister, who, next to Morris, was the ablest of Hamilton's lieutenants. There was a possibility that at any time England might be forced to war on Spain should that country enter into the struggle on the side of France. The United States was then engaged in a quarrel with Spain. It was the idea of Miranda to enlist England and the United States in a grand revolutionary scheme in South America. He had discussed it with the British Ministers and with King, who was in correspondence with Hamilton. It involved an alliance between the English-speaking countries. This had been hinted at, as we have seen, long before, by Hamilton in a letter to Pickering, who was in favor of entering into such an alliance without delay. It was the plan of Miranda for England to furnish the ships, not exceeding twenty, men and money; the United States to supply no less than seven thousand soldiers, two thousand of these being cavalry. The lure of Florida and Cuba was held out to the United States.[1] Here was a grand scheme of conquest that appealed irresistibly to Hamilton's ambition for military glory.[2] Entirely unknown to Adams or Washington, Hamilton had been in correspondence with the soldier of fortune, and in communication with him through King who was managing the London end of the affair. He made it plain to King that in the event of a successful issue he would want the United States to be the principal agency. 'The command in this case would very naturally fall upon me, and I hope I should disappoint no favorable anticipations,' he wrote. He thought the country not quite ripe for the enterprise, but 'we ripen fast, and it may, I think, be rapidly brought to maturity if an efficient negotiation for the purpose is at once set on foot.'[3] To Miranda he was writing that he would not embark in the affair 'unless patronized by the Government of this country.' An army of twelve thousand men was being raised. 'General Washington has resumed his station at the head of our armies, I am second in command.'[4] In the autumn of 1798, he was writing Senator Gunn on the importance of heavy

[1] Adams, *Adams*, I, 523–24.   [2] Lodge, *Hamilton*, 212.

[2] Hamilton's *Works* (to King), x, 314–15.   [4] *Ibid.*, 315–16.

cannon for fortifications and mortars in the case of a siege. 'If we engage in war our game will be to attack where we can. France is not to be considered as separated from her ally. Tempting objects will be within our grasp.' [1] In January, 1799, Hamilton was writing Otis in the same strain. 'If universal empire is still to be the pursuit of France, what can tend to defeat that purpose better than to detach South America from Spain. . . . The Executive ought to be put in a situation to embrace favorable conjunctures for effecting that separation.' [2] With all this Pickering was familiar and in sympathy, but Adams was in total ignorance. In time the subject was cautiously broached to him, to be rejected with the curt notation that we were not at war with Spain. But the record is too clear to leave the South American project out of consideration in seeking the reason for the intense desire for war — and a large army. Through all this period, Hamilton had visions of himself on horseback, at the head of troops in South America, with England as an ally.[3]

Never had Hamilton felt himself so near the top of the world. When Congress met in the fall of 1798, he had a plan ready for a complete change in the formation of the Nation. This provided for eighty United States District Courts; [4] the division of old States into new ones for any territory having as many as 100,000 people on the request of any considerable number — which would or could have made seven States out of Virginia; and for the extension and more rigid enforcement of the Sedition Law.

It was on this state of affairs that Adams, perplexed, harassed, worried by the serious illness of Abigail, aching under the humiliations visited upon him by the bosses of his party, meditated during the summer and early fall of 1798. And he thought seriously, too, on what Gerry had told him of the temper of France.

VI

This had almost persuaded him that a new mission to France was feasible, when a letter from Murray at The Hague, indicating uneasiness in Paris lest the United States be forced into an alli-

---

[1] Randall, *Jefferson*, II, 464.   [2] Hamilton's *Works*, x, 389.
[3] See King's *Works*, II, 649–66; III, 556, 565; Adams, *Works*, x, 145 and 147.
[4] At the rate of four for Connecticut with a population of 250,000.

ance with England, convinced him. Thus, about the middle of October, in a letter to Pickering, he submitted two questions for the consideration of the Cabinet. 'Should there be a declaration of war?' 'Could proposals for further negotiations be made with safety, and should a new envoy be named, prepared to sail on assurances that he would be received?'

That letter fell like a bomb in the camp of the war conspirators. How Pickering must have scowled, and McHenry grumbled, and Wolcott shrugged his shoulders with a cynical grin when they sat down to meditate on its meaning. That more important personages were informed we may be sure. To that note, however, the Cabinet did not deign to reply. Had not Adams declared that he would never send another envoy unless solemnly assured that he would be received? No such assurance had come. Then why discuss it — even on the request of the President? However, a Message would have to be sent to Congress, and with Adams in a conciliatory frame of mind it was imperative that something definite await him on his arrival. Thus the conspirators sat down to the framing of a Message that would defeat the very purpose the letter had indicated. Hamilton and Pinckney were summoned to the conference. The result was a paragraph putting it squarely up to France to take the initiative in the matter of a renewal of negotiations. Wolcott, who, better than any of the others, could hide his treachery behind an ingratiating urbanity, was put forward as the author. Reaching the capital, Adams summoned his Cabinet to go over the Message. All went well until the fateful paragraph was reached, and instantly the keen eye of the suspicious old man caught its full significance. That, he would not accept, and an open struggle began. With earnestness and even heat the obnoxious paragraph was urged upon him, but Adams planted his feet and stood. He would rewrite that paragraph to conform to his personal view of the proprieties.[1]

The Cabinet conspirators retired with the realization that there were dark days ahead. Adams in his substitute held forth the olive branch to the extent of declaring that no new envoy would be sent unless assurances were forthcoming that he would be properly received. Washington, Hamilton, and Pinckney, in uniforms, sat in

[1] Adams, *Adams*, I, 536.

the chamber when the Message was read. Two of these, at least, had grave forebodings. Then it was that the conspirators determined to override Adams by meeting his plan for negotiations with an immediate declaration of war. A caucus of the Federalists was called. The most brilliant and fiery orators were primed for the occasion. The proposal was made and supported with eloquence. The vote was taken, and by a small majority Adams triumphed over his foes. This was the most significant incident yet — it meant that Hamilton had lost control of the party councils.[1] With that knowledge, Pickering made no further attempt to conceal his bitter hostility to his chief. Ordered to prepare a treaty that would be acceptable, he ignored the request. Asked to moderate his report on the Gerry dispatches, he refused. Among his associates he was bitterly resentful, and all this was carried to the President, who cunningly simulated ignorance of what was happening. Then, at length, came the desired assurances from Talleyrand, that an envoy would be 'received as the representative of a great, free, powerful, and independent nation.' That was enough. Adams was ready for action.

Thus, without further warning to the Cabinet, a messenger from the President appeared in the Senate on February 18th with the nomination of Murray as Minister to France. The Federalists were paralyzed. Jefferson, equally amazed, managed to conceal his pleasure over the evident discomfiture of his foes.[2] Almost a week later he still suspected that the nomination had been sent 'hoping the Federalists . . . would accept the responsibility of rejecting it.'[3] But the Federalist Senators had no such suspicion. Their faces betrayed their indignation. That night they met in caucus with their war paint on, and the decision was reached to defeat the confirmation. They still had the whip hand. If Adams would modify in some way — At any rate, he should remain in no doubt as to their opinion of his action. A committee, consisting of Bingham, Read, Sedgwick, Ross, and Stockton, was named to wait upon him, and a note was sent requesting an audience. The reply left them in no doubt as to the fighting mood of the man they sought to intimidate. He would be very glad to receive them 'as

[1] Adams, *Adams*, I, 538–39.
[2] Ifferson's *Works* (to Madison), x, 110–13.   [3] *Ibid.* (to Madison), 119–21.

gentlemen, at his house, at seven in the evening.' At the appointed hour they were ushered into the audience room. No one was there. Then the door opened, and Adams, the picture of dignity on short legs, entered.

'Gentlemen, I am glad to see you as friends and Senators; but as a committee interfering, as I think you are, with my executive duties, I cannot consent to receive you, and I protest against all such interference. I have a duty to execute, and so have you. I know and shall do mine, and I want neither your opinion nor aid in its execution.'

At which he politely asked them to be seated.

Not a little nonplussed by his masterful manner, Bingham apologetically explained that there was no thought of interference, but merely a disposition to reconcile differences of opinion.

'Well, then, gentlemen,' snapped Adams, 'if you are determined to interfere in diplomatic matters, reject Mr. Murray. You have the power to do this, and you may do it; but it will be upon your own responsibility.'

As mildly as possible it was suggested that Adams's action, so soon after the insult, would be interpreted as a humiliation.

'I know more of diplomatic forms than all of you,' Adams hotly replied with perfect truth. 'It was in France that we received the insult, and in France I am determined that we shall receive the reparation.'

Forced to compromise, a commission was then suggested.

'Who would you have me send?' Adams demanded, an ugly expression on his face. 'Shall I send Theophilus Parsons, or some of your other Essex rulers? No, I will send none of them.'

At this the committee showed its teeth with the threat to defeat the confirmation. Adams, infuriated by the threat, replied that there was a party determined to rule him, but that they would fail.[1]

That night when the caucus met again, it was decided to reject the nomination. Meanwhile, the effect outside the Senate was quite as sensational. Duane announced the nomination the day after it reached the Senate, in large type. The next day 'Porcupine' fired a broadside.

[1] Pickering, III, 439. According to another version, Adams received the committee politely until Sedgwick angered him with a slurring remark on Gerry.

'For the last two days,' he said, 'there has been a most atrocious falsehood in circulation . . . that the President . . . has intimated by a messenger to the Senate that he has resolved on sending another plenipotentiary to treat with the French Republic. Every one must perceive the falsehood on the front of this; yet have audacious wretches dared to promulgate it without hesitation and they have even named the plenipotentiary, Mr. Murray. . . . I will not expatiate upon the consequences of such a step . . . because I cannot suppose the step within the compass of possibility; but I must observe that had he taken such a step it would have been instantaneously followed by the loss of every friend worth preserving.' [1] Encouraged by the applause of the Federalists, he recurred to it the next day with a denunciation of 'a mere fabrication intended to alienate the President's friends . . . at this momentous crisis and sink his character in the eyes of all Europe and America.' [2] But two days later, the ferocious 'Porcupine' had changed his tune and was singing low, with the absurd protestation that he had 'never published a word with regard to the President that could possibly be construed into disrespect.' [3] He had discovered he was amenable to the Alien Law he had so stoutly defended!

Adams had asserted himself and was happy, and when Pickering was writing Washington that his successor was 'suffering the torments of the damned,' Adams was writing cheerfully to his wife that he could hardly be chosen President a second time, and would be glad of the relief. 'To-night I must go to the ball; where I suppose I shall get cold and have to eat gruel for breakfast for a week afterwards.' [4] The determined little patriot was now on the top of the world, and now it was his enemies that were guessing. The senatorial committee had been an idea of Hamilton's, to whom Sedgwick had hastened the news of the nomination. The committee had failed. Even the suggestion of two more envoys had been scorned. Something might still be done through conciliation. Ellsworth, the Chief Justice, had Adams's confidence and he was sent to try his powers of persuasion, and succeeded. Thus, the nominations of Murray, Ellsworth, and Patrick Henry were sent to the Senate, and confirmed without even a whimper from 'Por-

[1] *Porcupine's Gazette*, February 20, 1799. [2] *Ibid.*, February 21, 1799.
[3] *Ibid.*, February 28, 1799. [4] Adams, *Adams*, I, 544–45.

cupine.' But beneath the surface, the passions were seething. Sedgwick wrote King that he had not 'conversed with an individual . . . who did not unequivocally reprobate the measure.'[1] Tracy, who had wanted to arm the women and children against the French, wrote McHenry that while he had sacrificed much 'to root out Democracy,' he thought it 'to be lost and worse.'[2] Cabot assured King that 'surprise, indignation, grief, and disgust followed each other in quick succession in the breasts of the true friends of the country,'[3] and informed Pickering that he had written 'a piece' about it for the Boston papers, but that 'the Boston press had been fixed by the President's friends and it had not appeared.'[4] To King, he ascribed Adams's action to jealousy of Hamilton and Washington.[5] Pickering wrote Cabot that 'the President's character can never be retrieved.'[6] Stephen Higginson, the merchant prince of the Essex Junto, found the world dark indeed. Why had not war been declared in the summer of 1798? Even the powers given Adams by the Alien and Sedition Laws had not been used![7] Jonathan Mason was furious because 'from being respectable in Europe, from having convinced Great Britain and from having associated with all the friends of Order, Property, and Society . . . we must again become soothers and suppliants for peace from a gang of pitiful robbers.'[8] Ames wrote that the new embassy 'disgusts most men here' because they thought 'peace with France . . . an evil.'[9] Even at Adams's table the jeremiads of the Federalists were heard, and the dinners were somber affairs. Bayard of Delaware was loud in his lamentations.

'Mr. Bayard, I am surprised to hear you express yourself in this manner,' said Adams. 'Would you prefer a war with France to a war with England in the present state of the world; would you wish for an alliance with Great Britain and a war with France? If you would, your opinions are totally different from mine.'

'Great Britain is very powerful,' Bayard replied mournfully. 'Her navy is very terrible.'[10]

When at the end of the session, Adams set forth for his seat at Braintree, Harper expressed the hope that his horses might run

[1] King's *Works*, III, 68.   [2] Steiner, 416.   [3] King's *Works*, IX, 249.
[4] Lodge, *Cabot*, 224–26.   [5] King's *Works*, III, 7–10.   [6] Lodge, *Cabot*, 221.
[7] Gibbs (to Wolcott), II, 229–30.   [8] Morison, *Otis* (to Otis), I, 171.
[9] Ames (to Dwight), I, 252.   [10] Morison, *Otis*, I, 174–75.

away and break his neck.[1] Only John Jay, among the outstanding
Federalists, could see no objections to the mission, but he was always bothered by scruples.

VII

It was unfortunate that Adams's love for Braintree caused him
to desert the capital in this crisis. The policy of the conspirators
was to wear out their chief's purpose through procrastination, and,
in the meanwhile, to bring all possible pressure to bear to restore
his secret enemies to his good graces. He had made the sailing of
the envoys conditional on a direct assurance from France as to the
reception they would receive. Under the most favorable conditions
this meant months of delay, and the treacherous policy of Pickering made it worse. On March 6th Adams instructed his Secretary
of State to inform Murray of the conditions, but it was not until
in May that the latter heard from Pickering. Talleyrand was immediately informed, and within a week Murray was in possession
of the required official assurances, but it was the last day of July
before they reached Philadelphia. Disappointing to the conspirators though these were, a careful study of the Talleyrand note
disclosed a touch of annoyance over the delay. The insolence of
the man! Another insult! The conspirators determined if possible to make this the occasion for further delay. If Adams could
only be persuaded to insist upon an explanation of the impatient
paragraph, more time would be gained, and Pickering strongly
recommended this in his note transmitting the Talleyrand letter
to the President. But Adams was too wary now to be easily caught.
Replying dryly that he could overlook the language for the deed,
he instructed Pickering that, while preparations for war proceeded,
the commission should be hurried to Ellsworth and Governor
Davie — for the latter had been named in the place of Henry, who
had declined — with instructions to prepare for embarkation at
any moment.

Meanwhile, with Pickering taking six weeks in the preparations
of the instructions, efforts were being made to coax Adams into
his enemies' camp. One day Cabot suavely presented himself at
the house at Braintree on a purely social neighborly visit. He went

[1] *Anas,* I, 351–52.

at the instance of the Hamiltonians to wheedle the old man back into their clutches. That the ablest politician of the Essex Junto was affectionately friendly, we may be sure, but his courtesy was matched by that of Adams and Mrs. Adams, and he stayed for dinner. But Abigail never left the room. The President occasionally went out, Abigail never. Though she was gracious to a degree. Thus the door of opportunity was closed and locked and Abigail had the key. Cabot found that 'every heart was locked and every tongue was silenced upon all topics that bore affinity to those which I wished to touch.' [1] Hamilton was in intimate touch with the leading members of the Adams Cabinet all the while — far more so than Adams; but the President knew of the movements of his dearest enemy through the Jeffersonian press. The latter part of April found Hamilton in Philadelphia with Gouverneur Morris, in close communion with Pickering, Wolcott, and Mc-Henry. Duane flippantly announced that they had 'kept the fast in Philadelphia,' and that 'a pair more pious, more chaste, more moral perhaps never mortified the flesh and the spirit since the days of David and the fair Shunammite.' [2] At Braintree Adams was keeping his own counsels, enjoying the serenity of domesticity, with occasional excursions into Boston to attend church or the theater, always accompanied by the Marshal of the district. When the Boston Troop went to Braintree to accompany him, with military pomp, to the Harvard Commencement, he was enormously pleased.[3] But he was on the alert. About the time Pickering's belated instructions reached him with a letter from the Cabinet suggesting the suspension of the mission for a time, he read a cautiously worded note from Stoddert, his Secretary of the Navy, hinting at the importance of his presence in Trenton, whither the Government had temporarily gone because of the prevalence of yellow fever again in Philadelphia. Adams was able to read between the lines.

The silent treatment to which the conspirators were being subjected annoyed them beyond endurance. They were by no means certain it was a hoax when they read in 'The Aurora' on August 15th that 'the Executive of the United States has ordered the

[1] King's *Works* (Cabot to King), III, 111; (to Pickering), 228; (to Wolcott), 229.
[2] *Aurora*, April 27, 1799.   [3] *Centinel*, June 8, June 17, 1799.

frigate "John Adams" to be prepared to carry our envoys without delay to Europe,' and the 'Centinel' in Boston was not able to deny it for several days.[1] In September, Pickering was urging Cabot to persuade Ellsworth to dissuade Adams from sending the mission. 'There is nothing in politics he despises more than this mission,' he wrote.[2] Ellsworth did as he was bid — with a difference. He asked that early notice be given him of the plans because of 'unusual demands upon his time on the official circuit.' [3] The real attitude of Ellsworth is not at all plain, for it was being whispered about that he hoped to reach the Presidency through the success of the mission. [4]

Then came another pretext for delay. There had come another shift in French politics, with some indications of the restoration of the Jacobins to power, and Talleyrand had resigned. Did this not call for further postponement? Adams replied in the affirmative, fixing the latter part of October as the limit, and promising to be in Trenton by the middle of that month. Rejoicing in this delay, Pickering began to meditate on the possible intervention of the Senate. With this in view he wrote Cabot for advice. The reply was wholly unsatisfactory. 'If the Senate should be admitted to possess a right to determine a priori what foreign connections should be sought or shunned, I should fear that they would soon exhibit the humiliating spectacle of cap and hats which so long and so naturally appeared in Sweden,' said Cabot.[5] Adams had the power, and he was silent. The conspirators began to mobilize for a desperate attempt at Trenton.

VIII

On October 6th, Adams drove down the road from Braintree on his way to Trenton with such secrecy that he was halfway there before Cabot knew he had gone.[6] The conspirators were there before him, Pinckney on the ground, Hamilton at Newark within easy call. Ellsworth had been summoned from Hartford. Governor Davie, having received a flattering address from his

---

[1] August 28, 1799.   [2] Lodge, *Cabot*, 237.
[3] Adams, *Adams*, I, 554.
[4] Stoddert was reported to have told General Sam Smith that this was in his mind; *Anas*, I, 349–50.
[5] Lodge, *Cabot*, 240–42.   [6] King's *Works* (Cabot to King), III, 114.

fellow citizens at Raleigh, was on the road, 'a troop of horse and a cavalcade of citizens escorting him four miles on his way.' [1]

Adams reached Trenton on Thursday, and on Friday night there was 'a handsome display of fireworks' in his honor, 'in which Mr. Guimpe, the artist, exhibited much skill and ingenuity.' The initials of Adams and Washington 'displayed in colored fires was received with shouts of applause.' On Saturday, Ellsworth arrived. Hamilton appeared upon the scene. Just at that juncture the conspirators were much elated with the news of the successes of the British army under the Duke of York in Holland, and the triumphant march of the Russians under Suwarrow in Switzerland. Might not the next report bring the news of the restoration of the Bourbons in France, and the end to the hideous nightmare of democracy? Here was a new club, and the conspirators laid eager hands upon it. Hamilton called to urge the point.

'Why, Sir, by Christmas Louis XVIII will be seated upon his throne,' he declared.

'By whom?' demanded Adams.

'By the coalition,' Hamilton replied.

'Ah, then,' said Adams, 'farewell to the independence of Europe.' [2]

When the President entertained the two envoys at dinner, he was amazed to find Ellsworth echoing the views of Hamilton.

'Is it possible, Mr. Chief Justice,' demanded Adams, 'that you can seriously believe that the Bourbons are, or will soon be restored to the throne of France?'

'Why,' said Ellsworth, smiling sheepishly, 'it looks a good deal so.'

'I should not be afraid to stake my life upon it that they will not be restored for seven years, if they ever are,' was Adams's retort.[3]

The coincidence in the views of the two men was not lost on Adams, who asked a member of his Cabinet if 'Ellsworth and Hamilton had come all the way from Windsor and New York to persuade me to countermand the mission.' [4] That was an ominous comment. The resulting excitement among his advisers did not

[1] *Centinel*, October 9, 1799.   [2] *Anas*, I, 349.
[3] Brown, *Life of Ellsworth*, 279.   [4] *Ibid.*

escape the watchful eye of Adams, who wrote Abigail that it left him 'calmly cold.'

On the night of October 15th Adams, calm, cold, thrice-armed, sat about the table with his Cabinet, no longer deceived by any of them save Wolcott. The purpose was the consideration of the instructions that had been prepared. Some changes were made. Adams asked advice on certain points. At eleven o'clock the instructions were unanimously approved. The Cabinet lingered, but Adams brought up no new subject. Out into the dark Trenton streets trooped the conspirators, almost hopeful. They were still at breakfast the next morning when orders were received from Adams that the instructions should be put in shape, a frigate be placed in readiness to receive the envoys who should sail not later than the first of the month.

The conspiracy had failed and John Adams was actually President.

The Jeffersonians were jubilant. Duane wrote that Adams had 'crossed the Rubicon,' but that the rumor that Pickering and Wolcott had resigned was groundless. 'They will never sacrifice their places to squeamish feelings.' [1] Hamilton had sought to deter the President, but to his honor 'he resisted every seduction and repelled every insinuation.' [2] The Hamiltonians were either furious or depressed. The Southern Federalists under Marshall approved, as did Jay, and the 'Centinel' commended the act, but the men who had made and maintained the prestige of the Federalist Party were in murderous mood. The mission would succeed — they knew it. There would be no war, and the army would have to go. With that would go the instrument for keeping down insurrections in America or for waging a war of conquest in South America. With one masterful effort, Adams had pulled down the pillars of the party temple and he could not escape in its fall. But it was the proudest and most masterful moment in his life, and he was content. Long after the débâcle he was to write that he asked no better epitaph than the sentence that he had taken upon himself the responsibility of the peace with France.

[1] *Aurora*, October 23, 1799.
[2] *Ibid.*, October 25, 1799.

IX

From that moment the Federalists were a house divided against itself, and the cloud burst and the rain descended and beat upon it, and the days were dark. Dreary, indeed, that winter of 1799. 'Porcupine' was driven from Philadelphia, and young Fenno, disgusted, gave up his paper with a farewell address so contemptuous of democracy and American institutions that the wiser leaders trembled at his temerity. M'Kean, the Democrat, had been swept into the gubernatorial office. Washington had died, and could no longer be used to advance the party interest. Even the dashing Harper, clever in political fight or social frolic, had despaired of the future in politics, resigned his seat, and made arrangements to move to Baltimore as the son-in-law of Carroll of Carrollton.[1] Duane was firing relentlessly at the scandals and finding flesh, and there was no 'Porcupine' to return the fire. The brilliant and audacious Charles Pinckney had appeared in the Senate to give a militant leadership to the Jeffersonians that the Federalists could not match. Into the House had come a giant, in John Marshall, to give to a later-day Federalism a sanity that came too late, but he was with Adams, not Hamilton.

The shadows even fell on the brilliant Federalist society. Hamilton was there that winter, to be sure, 'to keep the watch,' as Duane put it, and through an unhappy coincidence 'The Aurora' was able to add that 'Mrs. Reynolds, the sentimental heroine,' was back in town. But something like tragedy had fallen on the Holland House of Federalism, and weeping was heard in the rooms once given to gayety and laughter. One night Marie Bingham, not sixteen, slipped out of the home of her father, with Count de Tilly, age forty-five, a dissolute scion of the French aristocracy with an eye to the Bingham fortune, and was married at two o'clock in the morning. The couple were found in the home of a French milliner in the early morning, and physicians worked over the brilliant Mrs. Bingham, who was in hysterics. Money soon dissolved the union, but the lights were never quite so bright thereafter in the princely mansion of the cleverest hostess in Philadelphia. The rain fell even upon the House of Bingham.[2]

---

[1] *Aurora*, July 26, August 5, 1799.   [2] Morison, *Otis*, I, 137; McRee, *Iredell*, II, 571.

CHAPTER XIX
'THE GRAPES OF WRATH'

I

WHEN Congress convened in the winter of 1799, the Federalists thoroughly appreciated the desperation of their situation. The tide of public opinion was rising against them rapidly because of their measures, and they were divided against themselves. As the sun of the once brilliant party went down, there was one colossal figure of brilliant promise silhouetted against the darkening sky, but John Marshall, now a member of the House, was not in good odor with the Hamiltonians because of his opposition to the Alien and Sedition Laws. The irrepressible clash of contending policies and ambitions had been foreshadowed in the difficulties Marshall had encountered in framing a Reply to Adams's Address that could command the united support of the party, and he had succeeded measurably by giving the Reply a meaningless phrasing. For a moment it seemed that Marshall might regain the confidence of his fellow partisans when, in a speech of brilliancy and force, he had demolished the flimsy case of the Democrats against the President in the matter of Jonathan Robbins. With his characteristic readiness to concede the full strength of an enemy, Jefferson had written Madison that in the debate on Robbins 'J. Marshall [distinguished himself] greatly.' [1] But the Federalist cheers for their new leader were speedily turned to groans and hisses — and thereon hangs a tale of political infamy scarcely approached in audacity in American history.

Almost two years before, when the French war hysteria was at its height and the Federalists were cocks of the walk, the inner circle of the party in the Senate met one night about the table in the Bingham dining-room with the more moderate senatorial members. To assure party solidarity on all important party measures, it was proposed to bind all by the votes of the majority

[1] Jefferson's *Works*, x, 154–59.

in a party caucus. The extremists had a slight majority over the moderate element. Thus, for a season, the Government was, to all practical purposes, in the hands of a Senate oligarchy composed of a minority of the Senators. From the summer of 1799, the extremists entertained no illusions as to their popularity with the country. The election of Jefferson seemed imminent — provided a way could not be found to cheat him of his victory. From that moment on until the hour of his final triumph by the vote of the House in 1801, there was not a moment when the Federalist leaders were not ready to adopt any method, however disreputable and desperate, to accomplish their purpose. In this spirit they conceived the wicked scheme to rob Jefferson of his victory through an amazing measure prescribing the mode of deciding disputed elections for President and Vice-President. Senator Ross of Pennsylvania agreed to sponsor the bill.

Briefly and baldly, this provided that on the opening and reading of the certificates of the electoral votes in the presence of Congress, the papers should be turned over to a grand committee consisting of six members of each branch of Congress, with the Chief Justice as presiding officer. The members of the House and Senate committees should be elected by ballot. These, with the Chief Justice, were to go into secret session behind locked doors. They were to have the power to send for persons and papers, to pass on the qualifications of electors, and the manner in which they had cast their votes; to investigate charges that bribery, intimidation, persuasion, or force had been employed; and finally, to decide which votes should be counted and which cast out. This decision was to be final. In other words, it was a criminal scheme and an unconstitutional plot to steal the election. It had the support of the great majority of the best minds in the Federalist Party.

In keeping with the sinister nature of this monstrous measure, it was proposed to withhold it carefully from the public until the consummation of the crime. Happily there were members of Congress who did not consider themselves bound in honor to protect dishonor from the light, and almost immediately three copies of the bill found their way to the office of Duane. Two of these were personally delivered with permission to print and disclose the donors; one was mailed under cover.[1] The bill was immediately printed in full in 'The Aurora' with appropriate comments, and the conspirators were dragged into the light. 'The new electoral council or college may be very fitly compared with the secret Council of Ten at Venice of old,' wrote the editor.[2] Out of this exposure grew the proceedings culminating in the prosecution for sedition against Duane.

With the Federalists in control of both branches of Congress, it did not appear at first to matter much. The leaders of the party had never greatly concerned themselves with public opinion. They mustered their men in the Senate for a vote, leaving a discussion of the measure to the opposition. Behind the sorry smoke screen of the Duane prosecution they marched unblushingly to their purpose. The final protest was made by Charles Pinckney, the brilliant new leader of the Democrats in the Senate, in a powerful constitutional argument that no one cared to meet.[3] 'Equal in eloquence and strength of reasoning to anything ever heard within the walls of Congress,' said 'The Aurora.'[4] He sat down. No one rose to reply. The question was taken on the passage of the bill and it passed by a strict party vote of 16 to 12.

Meanwhile, the publicity given the rather brazen plan to steal the election was having its reactions on the people, and Federalist members of the House began to protest. There was no one in a more rebellious mood than Marshall, who thought the situation too serious to permit him to leave for home on the birth of his fifth child.[5] With a more far-reaching vision and a greater respect for public opinion than the veteran leaders of his party, he made his objections audible. On the floor of the House, on the street, at the boarding-house, he talked boldly and incessantly against the measure. The Federalists were amazed, disgusted. Some of the leaders who appreciated his ability observed his insubordination with sorrow. They had doubted his 'political judgment,' but had counted on swaying him to their views because of his companionable temperament. They took note of his 'very affectionate disposition,' his attachment to pleasures, his conviviality, his seeming 'indolence,' and they cultivated him on the side of his weak-

---

[1] *Aurora*, April 2, 1800.   [2] *Ibid.*, April 4, 1800.
[3] *Annals*, March 28, 1800.   [4] April 2, 1800.   [5] Beveridge, II, 453.

nesses. But they found him a difficult psychological problem. He had a timidity due to his tendency to 'feel the public pulse,' was disposed to 'erotic refinement,' and, worse still, to 'express great respect for the sovereign people.' With all this he possessed a persuasive power that worked with fatal effect on 'more feeble minds,' and he was exerting this power among the members with disastrous results.

Theodore Sedgwick, ponderous and pompous, and in politics insinuating, was apparently delegated to coax Marshall into the conspiracy. A number of heart-to-heart talks with the rebel followed. The Virginian doubted the constitutional 'power of the legislature to delegate such authority to a Committee.' After a long talk he 'confessed himself . . . to be convinced,' but shifted, according to Sedgwick, to the ground that the people had authorized the members to decide, each for himself, in the case of election disputes. In its nature this power was 'too delicate to be delegated.' To Sedgwick this was 'so attenuated and unsubstantial' as to be beyond his comprehension, and Marshall was persuaded to abandon this ground too. But 'in the meantime he had dwelt so much in conversation on these subjects that he had dissipated our majority,' Sedgwick wrote King.[1]

When the discussions opened in the House, Marshall questioned the propriety of the Senate naming the chairman of the committee and of making the decision final, and offered an amendment.[2] This was followed by other amendments and ultimately by the revamping of the whole measure. The Senate refused to accept the amendments, and thus the measure died between the two houses. Duane was jubilant. Here was evidence of the value of a free press. The 'odious bill was introduced for party purposes,' and a party in the Senate 'sought to overwhelm by terror and oppression the men who dared to publish the bill, which even after numerous amendments was found too abominable to be countenanced by the House of Representatives.'[3] The Federalists were downcast and indignant. Senator Tracy, who had no political scruples, declared that 'Marshall has spoiled all the fair hopes founded on Mr. Ross's bill.'[4] Thus Marshall saved the

---

[1] King's *Works*, III, 237–38.
[2] The nature of the amendment is not disclosed in the *Annals*, April 16, 1800.
[3] *Aurora*, April 28, 1800.   [4] *Ibid.*, April 30, 1800.

country from revolution and Jefferson from defeat regardless of the vote — as Hamilton was to save him later.

II

The campaign was now on, but from this time we shall hear little of the activities of Jefferson. His work was done. Back to his beloved hilltop he hurried on the adjournment of Congress, and there he remained, apparently less concerned with politics than with potatoes. But he had already created the machinery, trained the mechanicians, supplied the munitions of victory, found means for financing the enterprise — and he left the work with his lieutenants.

In the leadership of his party Jefferson had no rival, and he was the idol of his followers, 'the people's friend.' The persecution he had met had but endeared him more to his supporters. He was their Messiah. On New Year's Eve in 1799, a company of Democrats spent the evening in conversation and songs until the new year came. Then, headed by a regimental band, they marched through the dark streets of Philadelphia, past the homes of the rich and fashionable blazing with light, to pay their respects to Jefferson at his lodgings. On the way, they encountered another large group, who, unknown to the first, had conceived the same plan for declaring their allegiance. The two crowds fraternized and marched on together. With cheers and shouts they summoned their leader to the door. When the tall, familiar figure appeared, the welkin rang, the band played, and a song, written for the occasion, was sung.[1] The incident is significant of the common recognition of Jefferson's leadership.

During the two preceding years the consummate political genius of Jefferson had been planning the programme for the struggle of 1800. The congressional strategy of his party had been his work, and night after night he had gathered his lieutenants about him at the dinner table of the Indian Queen and given his orders for the morrow. If the party platform had not then been conceived, he had his programme, which met the purpose. Writing Madison in January, 1799, he proposed that all possible emphasis be put upon the Alien and Sedition Laws, the direct tax, the army and navy,

[1] *Aurora*, January 2, 1799.

'the usurious loan to set these follies on foot,' and on the picture of 'recruiting officers lounging at every court-house and decoying the laborer from his plough.' [1] About the same time he was expanding this programme in a letter to Gerry: The constitutional rights of the States should be asserted. The right of Congress to 'its constitutional share in the division of power' should be maintained. The Government should be 'rigorously frugal' and all possible savings should be applied to the discharge of the public debt. The multiplication of offices should be stopped. A standing army in time of peace should be attacked. Free commerce should be maintained with all nations, and there should be 'political connections with none.' The liberty of speech and the freedom of the press should be preserved.[2]

That same month he was writing Edmund Pendleton in the same vein — the 'direct tax,' the 'army and navy in time of peace,' the 'usurious interest,' the 'recruiting officers at every court-house to decoy the laborer from his plough.' [3] In these letters we have the first Jeffersonian platform — and on these points, from that time on, the Democrats harped constantly in Congress, in pamphlets and through the press. Not least, nor least effective, among the methods of propaganda were the congressional letters with which the Jeffersonian members flooded their constituents, setting forth in vigorous fashion all the counts in the indictment. As these letters fell upon the country like a snowstorm, the Federalists were infuriated. They summoned their Federal Judges to denounce them in charges to grand juries, and Iredell foolishly responded. In Congress they hinted darkly that these records of public affairs sent by public servants to the public they served were seditious. Many years afterward Adams recalled them with rage — these letters that 'swelled, raged, foamed in all the fury of a tempest at sea against me,' a flood so enormous that 'a collection of those letters would make many volumes.' Adams never forgave his party for finding no means for their suppression.[4]

These letters were part of the Jeffersonian plan to reach the people and set the tongues to wagging. Everywhere Jefferson was encouraging his followers to establish newspapers. Soon Noah

---

[1] Jefferson's *Works*, x, 70–74. [2] *Ibid.*, **74**. [3] *Ibid.*, 89–92.
[4] Adams, *Works*, x, 116–19.

Webster's paper was complaining that the irrepressible Matthew Lyon 'in the course of one year has established no less than four . . . presses.' [1] Was money needed for the publication of pamphlets or the distribution of newspapers? Jefferson made out a subscription list, put his friends down for a contribution, and informed them of his action without apology. Thus, to Monroe: An important measure is under contemplation which 'will require a considerable sum of money.' He had therefore put Monroe down for from fifty to a hundred dollars.[2] Thus, to Madison: 'Every man must lay his pen and his purse under contribution.' [3] Were articles required? He sent instructions to his friends to write. Thus, to Pendleton, asking him to prepare a pamphlet on the Gerry correspondence,[4] and to Madison asking him to 'set aside a portion of every post day to write what may be proper for the public.' [5] Were pamphlets printed and ready for distribution? Then a letter from Jefferson to men of the standing of Monroe ordering them to place them in the hands of 'the most influential characters among our countrymen who are only misled.' [6]

In every State he had men of political sagacity through whom he could work while maintaining the semblance of aloofness. In Massachusetts, Gerry; in New Hampshire, Langdon; in Connecticut, Bishop and Granger; in New York, Livingston and Burr; in Pennsylvania, Gallatin, M'Kean, and the Muhlenbergs; in Maryland, Mercer and General Sam Smith; in Virginia, Madison, Monroe, Giles, and Pendleton; in Kentucky, John Breckenridge and George Nicholson; in North Carolina, Macon, Jones, and Joseph Gales, the clever and daring editor of the Raleigh 'Register' who put the Federalists to the torture with the best paper in the State, which was sent free to prospective converts; [7] and in Tennessee, Senator William Cocke, an old Amelia County Virginian, and William C. C. Claiborne. In South Carolina, where the Hamiltonians were strong in the support of the Pinckney brothers, and through the commercial interests of Charleston, he was fortunate in having Charles Pinckney, more brilliant, daring, picturesque, and magnetic than his cousins, and Peter Freneau, brother of the

[1] *Commercial Advertiser*, February 13, 1800.
[2] Randall, II, 470.
[3] Jefferson's *Works*, X, 95–97.
[4] *Ibid.*, 86–89.
[5] *Ibid.*, 95–97.
[6] *Ibid.*, 97–99.
[7] Dodd, *Macon*, 157–59.

poet, and editor of the 'Charleston City News.' Nowhere did the Jeffersonians make better progress against stubborn resistance than in the Palmetto State. Thence Hamilton had long drawn for talent, but his party was being gradually undermined. William Smith, who recited speeches Hamilton had written, had retired to escape defeat to a berth in Lisbon; and Harper, noting the premonitions of a storm, had announced his retirement from Congress to seek consolation in the glamour of the Carroll wealth and in the charms of a Carroll daughter in Maryland.

This revolution was largely wrought through the management of a few Jeffersonians who met night after night in Freneau's office on George Street to plan the fight. Either of two participants in these conferences was a host within himself. There was Freneau — huge in frame, and, aside from height, bearing a striking resemblance to Charles James Fox in voice, conversation, and manners, with a literary style which a contemporary found to combine 'the beauty and smoothness of Addison and the strength and simplicity of Cobbett.' And there was Charles Pinckney, handsome, imposing, a favorite of fortune, dominating in leadership, eloquent and forceful in debate, conspicuous in the Constitutional Convention in his twenties and Governor of his State at thirty-one. There about the table, and over their cups we may be sure, they set their traps, and planned their propaganda. Freneau would take up his pen and literally dash off a powerful article with a facility and felicity that called for no revision or correction; and Pinckney would write an article to be signed 'A Republican,' or appear unexpectedly at a public meeting to sweep the audience with him by the fire and force of his eloquence.[1] These men sallied forth to battle with a gallant gayety suggested by their own facetious description of their conferences as 'The Rye House Plot.'

Thus everywhere Jefferson had men on whom he could depend, and his orders given, his work done, he could spend the summer and autumn of 1800 with his potatoes. There we must leave him and look elsewhere for the drama of the fighting. Only twice during the campaign did he wander farther from Monticello than Charlottesville. Mounted on his horse, he rode daily over his plantation. Every evening he made his customary notations in his

[1] Thomas. *Reminiscences*, II, 54–56.

farm account book. When Marie's pianoforte arrived, he might
have been seen tuning it himself while the battle raged on many
fronts. He wrote his daughter the details of a neighborhood murder, and of the prospects of the harvest, but nothing of politics.
His work was done. He had ploughed and sowed and tended —
but the work in the harvest-field was for others. In the early summer a strange tale traveled throughout the country, recorded in all
the papers, that he had died suddenly. The papers printed it
cautiously, however, and there was no political motive in its
circulation. At length it was explained. One of his slaves named
'Thomas Jefferson' had died at Monticello. Jefferson was never
more alive than that summer on his hilltop.

III

That a tidal wave toward Democracy had set in was shown in
the early spring in the elections in New York, Massachusetts, and
New Hampshire. By common consent New York was put down
as the pivotal State and both parties planned to put forth their
utmost efforts there. Jefferson, still in Philadelphia, was keeping
in intimate touch with the situation through his correspondents in
the State, and placing reliance on the sagacity of Aaron Burr. As
early as January, he was writing Monroe with the utmost confidence of the result 'on the strength of [his] advices.' [1] In March
he was assuring Madison, on the representations of Burr and
Livingston, that the State was safe if the city of New York could
be carried.[2] The Federalists, he found seriously alarmed. 'Their
speeches in private, as well as their public and private demeanor
toward me, indicate it strongly.' [3] Hamilton himself had seemed
so depressed that Henry Lee had written rallying him on his pes-
simism and urging him to 'be more like yourself and resist to
victory all your foes.' [4] He had replied with a touch of petulance
that he was not despondent and stood 'on ground which, sooner or
later, will assure me a triumph over all my enemies.' [5] But he was
then facing the most desperate fighting of his career, with Burr
leading the opposition with a smiling gayety that was disconcert-
ing.

[1] Jefferson's *Works*, x, 134–36. [2] *Ibid.*, 154–59. [3] *Ibid.*
[4] Randall, II, 538. [5] Hamilton's *Works*, x, 363.

The prevailing fashion of picturing Hamilton as a saintly soul sent to his death by a deep-dyed villain of the type once popular in the melodrama, cannot conceal the amazing resemblance of these two men. There were probably no other two men in the America of their day who were so much alike. Physically both were small, compactly built, of militant carriage, with penetrating eyes of different colors, and of persuasive voices. Both were dandies in their dress, the glass of fashion and the mould of form, courtly, Chesterfieldian, and dashing. Both had demonstrated their courage and military sagacity on the field of battle — Hamilton in the assault at Yorktown, Burr in carrying his beloved Montgomery from the battle-field on his back, wading knee-deep in snow, and amidst a rain of bullets. Burr, no less than Hamilton, had served in the military household of Washington, and both alike had resented their leader's rather imperious manner. At the New York Bar both had risen to eminence, and some hesitated to give the superiority to either. Here their methods were different — Hamilton relying on erudition where Burr depended on finesse, the former exhaustive in argument, the latter concise. Both were effective orators in different ways. Hamilton was declamatory, Burr conversational. Socially they had many points of similarity, and in a social sense they were not averse to one another's company at dinner. In conversation one was scarcely more scintillating than the other, and both were fond of badinage, and adept in compliments to the ladies. Both were gallants, attractive to, and attracted by, women of wit and beauty. Neither was above the intrigues of love, with ideas of morality that would have been appreciated in the London of the Restoration. If Burr kept his diary, which seems so shocking to some, Hamilton had his pamphlet on his affair with Mrs. Reynolds — but Burr did not publish his diary. Neither should be judged too harshly, for it was a day of rather loose morals, and the press made free with the gossip concerning Harper and Sedgwick. Both were inordinately ambitious for command, impatient under restraint, and wont to dream of leading triumphant armies. The ambition of neither was circumscribed by the boundaries of the country. If Burr wished to lead an army of conquest into Mexico, Hamilton longed to lead the same sort of an army into South America.

Hamilton and Burr were natural enemies because too much alike in temperament and ambition. Their hopes clashed. Both were deeply in love with their wives, notwithstanding their transgressions. There is something touching in Burr's letters to his sick wife, his anxiety, his consultations with physicians, his instructions to Theodosia. He was idolized by wife and daughter because they, in turn, were idolized by him. Unlike Hamilton, he was even tender with his servants. It is quite impossible to conceive of Hamilton writing friendly letters to his men and women domestics and slaves. To understand Burr's fascination for many, one thing must be borne in mind — he was loved because he was lovable in his personal contacts.

These two men faced each other for a finish fight in the spring of 1800.[1]

IV

In the early spring the surface indications were not favorable for a Jeffersonian victory in the election that was to determine the political complexion of the Legislature that would select the presidential electors. The Federalists were seemingly entrenched. Behind them, victories. Hamilton was openly active, Burr watchful like a cat. One of the latter's closest lieutenants wrote Gallatin of the situation developing in March. 'The Federalists have had a meeting and determined on their Senators; they have also appointed a committee to nominate suitable characters for the Assembly. . . . Mr. Hamilton is very busy, more so than usual, and no exertions will be wanting on his part. Fortunately Mr. Hamilton will have at this election a most powerful opponent in Colonel Burr. This gentleman is exceedingly active; it is his opinion that the Republicans had better not publish a ticket or call a meeting until the Federalists have completed theirs. Mr. Burr is arranging matters in such a way as to bring into operation all the Republican interests.' [2]

The purpose of Hamilton was twofold — to elect the Federalist electors, and to elect only such electors as he could control against

---

[1] Parton, *Life and Times of Aaron Burr;* Davis, *Memoirs of Aaron Burr; Familiar Letters,* 237; Oliver, *Hamilton;* Bradford, *Damaged Souls.*

[2] Adams, *Gallatin* (Matthew L. Davis to Gallatin), 232–34.

Adams. With this in view he called a secret caucus composed of his most pliant followers. Preferring tools to men of independence and capacity, the caucus selected men of no popularity and little weight. Burr, who had an incomparable system of espionage in this campaign, was instantly put in possession of the ticket. The brilliant black eyes of the little politician hastily and gravely scanned the list. Then, folding it and placing it in his pocket, he murmured, 'Now I have him hollow!' [1] Meanwhile, Burr had been busily engaged in the creation of a powerful, compact organization. Like most brilliant men of ingratiating manners, he had drawn about him a formidable array of the young men of the city prepared to execute any orders he might give. This was his purely personal following. He found the backbone of his organization in Tammany.

The potentialities of that organization, composed, for the most part, of men in the ordinary walks of life, the poor, the unimportant, he had instantly sensed. They were democrats by instinct. Their Wigwam, a one-story frame building, was so unprepossessing that the Federalists dubbed it 'The Pig Pen' — but that did not bother Burr. These men had votes, and influence among others of their kind who had votes. They met night after night to smoke their pipes and drink their ale, to tell stories and talk politics. It is not of record that Burr ever entered the Wigwam, but he was the Tammany boss notwithstanding, operating through his friends who were the ostensible leaders. It was he, seated in his law office, who moulded the policies. His suggestions whipped it into shape as a fighting political organization.[2] For weeks his home had been crowded night after night with the most daring, adventurous, and ardent members of his party. Most of them were young, fit, and eager for any enterprise. Because there had been factions in the party, he laid down the law on these occasions that personalities should not be discussed or mentioned. These were to be submerged for the campaign. Local considerations were to be ignored. Discipline was to be maintained. Compromises necessary to solidarity were to be effected. The all-important thing was to amalgamate every section of the party and appeal to the people through a ticket notably superior to that of the Federalists.

[1] Parton, *Burr*, I, 247. [2] Myers, *Tammany Hall*, 12.

With the audacity of genius he determined that General Horatio Gates should be a candidate for the Assembly. More daring still, that the venerable George Clinton, many times Governor, should stand, and that Brockholst Livingston, eminent as patriot and lawyer, should run. Samuel Osgood, a former member of Congress, and Washington's Postmaster-General, was slated. It was easy to put them down — the problem was to persuade them to accept. Here Burr's genius for leadership counted heavily. Time and again he labored without avail on Clinton, Gates, and Livingston. At length Livingston agreed to stand provided both Clinton and Gates would run. Straightway, Burr rushed to Gates. It was a hard struggle. Burr pleaded, cajoled, flattered, appealed to party pride. Finally Gates agreed to run if Clinton would make the race. And there Burr almost met his Waterloo. The rugged old war-horse was prejudiced against Jefferson. He had ambitions for the Presidency himself, and they had been passed over. Burr left the matter open, smiled, flattered, bowed, departed. Then, out from his office committees began to make their way to Clinton with importunities to stand. The personal friends of the stubborn old man were sent to persuade him. He was adamant. A scene at Burr's home at Richmond Hill: Present, the nominating committee and Clinton. A mass movement on Clinton — he would not budge. Then Burr's master-stroke. A community had a right to draft a man in a crisis — the crisis was at hand. Without his consent they would nominate him. The rebellious veteran, flattered, agreed not to repudiate the nomination. The victory was Burr's — and Jefferson's.

A little later, the press announced that a meeting of the Democrats had been held at the home of J. Adams, Jr., at 68 William Street, where the Assembly ticket had been put up. Spirited resolutions were adopted. The enthusiasm of the Jeffersonians reached fever heat. Hamilton and the Federalists were paralyzed with amazement. The impossible had happened. Against Hamilton's mediocre tools — this ticket, composed of commanding figures of national repute! [1] Immediately the frantic fears of the Federalists were manifest in the efforts of 'Portius' in the 'Commercial Advertiser' to frighten the party into action. Jefferson had become a

[1] *Commercial Advertiser*, April 26, 1800.

possibility — the author of the Mazzei letter! Clinton and Gates candidates for the Assembly! Old men laden with honors who had retired, in harness again! Clearly no office lured them — it must be the magnitude of the issue. And who were Clinton, Gates, and Osgood? Enemies of the Constitution! To your tents, O Federalists![1] A few days later the merchants met at the Tontine Coffee-House to endorse the Hamiltonian ticket because 'the election is peculiarly important to the mercantile interests.'[2] In the 'Pig Pen' the Tammanyites read of the action of the merchants, clicked their glasses, and rejoiced. Hamilton, now thoroughly alarmed, redoubled his efforts. The Federalist press began to teem with hysterical attacks on Jefferson, Madison, and Clinton — men who were planning the destruction of the Government.[3]

Meanwhile, Burr, calm, confident, suave, silent, was giving New York City its first example of practical politics. Money was needed — he formed a finance committee to collect funds. Solicitors went forth to wealthy members of the party to demand certain amounts — determined upon by Burr. It was a master psychologist who scanned the subscription lists. One parsimonious rich man was down for one hundred dollars.

'Strike his name off,' said Burr. 'You will not get the money and . . . his exertions will cease and you will not see him at the polls.'

Another name — that of a lazy man liberal with donations. 'Double the amount and tell him no labor will be expected of him.'

With infinite care Burr card-indexed every voter in the city, his political history, his present disposition, his temperament, his habits, his state of health, the exertions probably necessary to get him to the polls. The people had to be aroused — Burr organized precinct and ward meetings, sent speakers, addressed them himself. And while Burr was working, the lowliest too were working on the lowliest. One evening 'a large corpulent person with something of the appearance of Sir John Falstaff' was seen in the lobby of a theater 'haranguing an old black man who sells peanuts and apples to come forward and vote the Republican ticket.'

[1] *Commercial Advertiser,* July 26, 1800. [2] *Ibid.,* April 29, 1800.
[3] *Ibid.*

'You pay heavy taxes this year.'

'Yes, Massa, me pay ten dollars.'

'Well, if you vote the Republican ticket you will have little or no taxes to pay next year; for if we Republicans succeed, the standing army will be disbanded, which cost us almost a million of money last year.'

The peanut vendor promised to appear at the polls 'with six more free-born sons of the African race.' [1] Whereupon the campaigner had a tale to tell to the boys at the Wigwam that night.

The polls opened on April 29th and closed at sunset on May 2d. Days of intense ceaseless activity. Hamilton and Burr took the field. From one polling-place to another they rushed to harangue the voters. When they met, they treated each other with courtly courtesy. Handbills were put out, flooding the city during the voting. In the midst of the fight Matthew L. Davis found time at midnight to send a hasty report to Gallatin in Philadelphia. 'This day he [Burr] has remained at the polls of the Seventh ward ten hours without intermission. Pardon this hasty scrawl. I have not ate for fifteen hours.' [2] The result was a sweeping triumph for the Democrats. When the news reached the Senate at Philadelphia, the Federalists were so depressed and the Democrats so jubilant that the transaction of business was impossible, and it adjourned.[3]

Hamilton was stunned, and ready for trickery to retrieve the lost battle. The next night he was presiding over a secret meeting of Federalists where it was agreed to ask Governor Jay to call an extra session of the Legislature to deprive that body of the power to choose electors. Hamilton approached Jay in a letter. 'In times like these,' he wrote, 'it will not do to be over-scrupulous.' There should be no objections to 'taking of legal and constitutional steps to prevent an atheist in religion and a fanatic in politics from getting possession of the helm of state.' [4] Jay read the letter with astonishment, made a notation that it was a plan to serve a party purpose, and buried it in the archives. It was the blackest blot on Hamilton's record.

That victory elected Jefferson.

It destroyed Hamilton — and it made Burr Vice-President.

[1] *Commercial Advertiser*, April 29, 1800.   [2] Adams, *Gallatin*, 237–38.
[3] Adams, *Gallatin* (to his wife), 240–41.   [4] Hamilton's *Works*, x, 371.

Scarcely had the polls closed when Burr's friends, giving him the whole credit, as he deserved, began to urge on the leaders in Philadelphia his selection for the Vice-Presidency. Davis wrote Gallatin that the Democrats of New York were bent on Burr.[1] Admiral James Nicholas, the father-in-law of Gallatin, wrote that the triumph was a miraculous 'intervention of Supreme Power and our friend Burr, the agent.' It was his 'generalship, perseverance, industry, and execution' that did it, and he deserved 'anything and everything of his country.' He had won 'at the risk of his life.'[2] On May 12th Gallatin wrote his wife: 'We had last night a very large meeting of Republicans, in which it was unanimously agreed to support Burr for Vice-President.'

That was a bitter month for the Federalists. In the gubernatorial contests in New Hampshire and Massachusetts the Democrats had polled an astonishing vote. Painfully labored were the efforts of the Federalist press to explain these remarkable accessions. The 'Centinel' in Boston had previously sounded a note of warning under the caption, 'Americans, Why Sleep Ye?' The Democrats, it said, were 'organized, officered, accoutered, provided, and regularly paid.' They were 'systematized in all points.' In Pennsylvania a Jeffersonian Governor had thrown Federalist office-holders 'headlong from their posts.' In New Hampshire the Democrats were fighting 'under cover of an ambuscade.' In all States new Jeffersonian presses were established, 'from Portsmouth in New Hampshire to Savannah in Georgia,' through which 'the orders of Generals of the faction are transmitted with professional punctuality; which presses serve as a sounding board to the notes that issue through that great speaking trumpet of the Devil, the Philadelphia Aurora.' Did not Duane get the enormous salary of eight hundred dollars a year? 'Why Sleep Ye?'

Dismayed, disgruntled with Adams, but afraid to reject him openly, the Federalist caucus convened in Philadelphia and selected Charles Cotesworth Pinckney as his running mate with the idea of electing him to the Presidency through treachery to Adams.

V

When Adams learned of the Federalist defeat in New York, he momentarily went to pieces. His suspicious mind instantly saw

[1] Adams. Gallatin. 238-40.   [2] Ibid.. 241.

in his humiliation the hand of Hamilton and his supporters. He had long been cognizant of the treachery about him, in his official household. On the morning of May 5th, McHenry received a note from the house on Market Street: 'The President requests Mr. McHenry's company for one minute.' As the poet-politician walked up Market Street in response that spring morning, he could not have conceived of any other issue than a brief discussion of some departmental matter. Only a few weeks before he had, with Adams's knowledge, arranged for a house at Georgetown, and for the removal of his family thither.[1] As he had surmised, the subject which had summoned him to the conference was a minor matter relating to the appointment of a purveyor. This was satisfactorily disposed of. Was there something smug or offensive in the manner of Hamilton's messenger that suddenly enraged the old man, smarting under the sting of the defeat in New York? Suddenly he began to talk of McHenry's derelictions, his anger rising, his color mounting, his voice ringing with unrepressed rage. McHenry thought him 'mad.' Washington, said Adams, had saddled him with three Secretaries, Pickering, Wolcott, and McHenry. The latter had refused to give a commission to the only elector in North Carolina who had voted for Adams. He had influenced Washington to insist on giving Hamilton the preference over Knox — which was true. In a report to Congress, McHenry had eulogized Washington and sought to praise Hamilton — the President's enemy. He had urged the suspension of the mission to France. The old man was spluttering with fury, and his disloyal Secretary was dumb with amazement. It was time for him to resign. McHenry beat a hasty retreat, returned to his office, prepared his resignation, which in decency should have been voluntarily submitted long before, and sent it in the next morning.[2]

Having set himself to the task of ridding his household of his enemies, Adams bethought himself of Pickering. Five days after the stormy scene with McHenry, the austere Secretary of State received a note from the President inviting a resignation. This was on Saturday. On Monday morning, Pickering went to his

[1] Gibbs (McHenry to his brother), II, 246–48.
[2] Gibbs, II, 246–48; Steiner, 454.

office as usual, having been long accustomed to ignoring or thwarting the wishes of his chief, and sent a letter dealing, strangely enough, with his pecuniary embarrassments, and refusing to resign.[1] The letter had not been sent an hour before an answer was in his hands. It was curt and comprehensive. 'Divers causes and considerations essential to the administration of the government, in my judgment requiring a change in the department of state, you are hereby discharged from any further service as Secretary of State.'[2]

Hamilton, enraged at the dismissal of his servitors, hastened an astonishing letter of instructions to Pickering. He should 'take copies and extracts of all such documents as will enable you to explain both Jefferson and Adams.' No doubt Pickering was 'aware of a very curious journal of the latter when he was in Europe — a tissue of weakness and vanity.' The time was coming when 'men of real integrity and energy must write against all empirics.'[3] To McHenry he wrote that 'a new and more dangerous era has commenced'; that 'Revolution and a new order of things are avowed in this quarter'; and, with something of Adams's hysteria, that 'property, liberty, and even life are at stake.'[4]

The news that Adams had rid himself of his betrayers, and found in John Marshall and Samuel Dexter as successors men incapable of treachery, made a profound impression. To Duane of 'The Aurora' it was a vindication. Two months before he had divided the Cabinet into Hamiltonians and Adamsites, with Pickering and McHenry bearing the brand of Hamilton.[5] Announcing the dismissals under the caption, 'The Hydra Dying,' he described Pickering as 'an uncommon instance of the mischiefs that may be done in a country by small and contemptible talents and a narrow mind when set on fire by malignity.'[6] The Federalist papers were hard put to sugar-coat the pill. The 'Centinel' cautiously said that 'the best men here have variant opinions on the measure' of Pickering's dismissal.[7] Three days later, it rushed to the defense of the humiliated representative of the Essex Junto with the comment that the best eulogy on his official conduct was 'the chuckling

[1] Pickering, III, 487.   [2] *Ibid.*, III, 488.   [3] Hamilton's *Works*, x, 376.
[4] Steiner, 457.   [5] *Aurora*, March 6, 1800.   [6] *Aurora*, May 9, 1800.
[7] *Centinel*, May 21, 1800.

of the Jacobins over his removal' and the assurance that he carried into retirement 'the regrets of all good men.'[1] The Essex Junto made no attempt to conceal their disgust. Cabot, Ames, Gore, and Pickering were soon sending their versions to Rufus King in London. 'You are so well acquainted with the sort of sensibility for which our chief is remarkable, that you will be less surprised than most men,' wrote Cabot.[2] Gore wrote that the dismissal 'produces general discontent.'[3] The delicate moral sensibilities of all these politicians were much hurt because Adams had fallen into the habit of swearing and using 'billingsgate.'[4] He was even speaking with bitterness of the Essex Junto and the British faction, quite in the manner of Jefferson. It was even 'understood' among the Hamiltonians that the dismissals were the price of the alliance which had been formed between Jefferson and Adams.[5]

But Adams knew what he was about. He knew that a plan had been made to trick him out of his reëlection. The scheme was bald, bold, stupid. All the Federalist electors in the North would be urged to vote for Adams and Pinckney; in the South enough would be asked to vote for Pinckney, and not Adams, to bring the Hamiltonian Carolinian in ahead. Hamilton was writing frankly to his friends in this vein, ready to 'pursue Pinckney as my single object';[6] while Gore was writing King that 'the intention of the Federalists is to run General Pinckney and Mr. Adams as President and Vice-President.'[7] When, in July, Adams appeared in Boston at a dinner and toasted Sam Adams and John Hancock, the much-abused Jeffersonians, as 'the proscribed patriots,' the Hamiltonians groaned their disgust and the Democrats shouted with glee. 'This was well understood by the Jacobins whom it will not gain,' wrote Ames.[8] 'The Aurora' observed that 'he did not give the great orb [Franklin] around which he moved as a satellite.'[9] The rupture was now complete. When Adams was permitted to leave Philadelphia without a demonstration the latter part of May, 'The Aurora' was unseemly in its mirth. 'Did the Blues parade? No? What —

---

[1] *Centinel*, May 24, 1800.   [2] King's *Works*, III, 249.   [3] *Ibid.*, 250.
[4] King's *Works* (from Pickering), 262–63; (Ames to King), 275–76; (Goodhue to Pickering), 243–44.
[5] *Ibid.* (from Pickering), 248; (from Cabot), 249.
[6] Hamilton's *Works* (to Sedgwick), x, 375–76.
[7] King's *Works*, III, 250.   [8] *Ibid.*, 275–76.   [9] *Aurora*, July 17, 1800.

not parade to salute him "whom the people delight to honor" —
"the rock on which the storm beats " — the "chief who now com-
mands "? Did not the officers of the standing army or the marines
parade? The new army officers are not fond of the President; he
has dismissed Timothy.' [1]

Meanwhile, the most consummate of the betrayers, Wolcott,
unsuspected still, remained within the fort to signal to Hamilton.

VI

It was common knowledge early in the spring that Hamilton
would exert his ingenuity to defeat Adams by hook or crook.
'The Aurora' declared, March 12th, that 'the party with Alexander Hamilton at their head have determined to defeat Adams in
the approaching elections.' The watchful eye of the suspicious
Adams, who felt the treachery, unquestionably read the article
and heard the gossip. When, after the death of Washington, the
Cincinnati met in New York to select Hamilton as the head of the
order, Adams was informed that his enemy had electioneered
against him among the members. He heard particularly of the
action of 'the learned and pious Doctors Dwight and Babcock,
who . . . were attending as two reverend knights of the order, with
their blue ribbons and bright eagles at their sable button-holes,' in
saying repeatedly in the room where the society met, 'We must
sacrifice Adams,' 'We must sacrifice Adams.'

Thus, when in June, Hamilton, under the pretext of disbanding
the army in person, fared forth in his carriage on a tour of the New
England States, no one doubted the political character of his mission. His purpose was to prevail upon the leaders to give unanimous support to Pinckney and to drop a few Adams votes, or, that
impossible, to give Pinckney the same support as Adams. The
records of this dramatic journey are meager enough. It is known
that in New Hampshire he talked with Governor Gilman, who was
the popular leader, and 'took pains' to impress upon him 'the
errors and the defects of Mr. Adams and of the danger that
candidate cannot prevail by mere Federal strength.' He urged support of Pinckney on the ground that in the South he would get
some anti-Federal votes.[2] In Rhode Island he evidently encoun-

---

[1] *Aurora*, June 7, 1800.   [2] Hamilton's *Works* (to Bayard), x, 384–87.

tered a spirited protest from Governor Fenner. The Governor expressed the hope that all the electors would be Federalists, but clearly gave no encouragement to the Pinckney candidacy, according to Hamilton's own version of the conference.[1] There were other versions, however, indicative of a stormy interview. The 'Albany Register' advised Hamilton, in giving the story of his tour to the 'Anglo-Federal party which wishes to make Charles C. Pinckney President,' to 'forget his interview with the Governor of Rhode Island.' [2] 'The Aurora' followed in a few days with a more circumstantial story. Hamilton had 'warmly pressed Governor Fenner to support Pinckney' and 'the old Governor's eyes were opened and he literally drove the gallant Alexander out of the door.' [3]

But in Massachusetts, albeit the home of Adams, Hamilton could count upon a cordial reception for his views, since it was also the home of the Essex Junto. This was composed of the Big-Wigs of the party in that State, all ardently devoted to Hamilton, sharing in his hate of democracy and doubt of the Republic. For years these men had met at one another's homes and directed the politics of Massachusetts. They were men of intellect and social prestige, intimately allied with commerce and the law. There was George Cabot, the greatest and wisest of them all, and one of the few men who dared tell Hamilton his faults. He was a man of fine appearance, tall, well-moulded, elegant in his manners, aristocratic in his bearing, earnest but never vehement in conversation; a man of wealth, and a merchant.[4] There was Fisher Ames, brilliant, vivacious, smiling, cynical, eloquent, exclusive in his social tastes, and wealthy. There was Theophilus Parsons, learned in the law, contemptuous of public opinion and democracy, reactionary beyond most of his conservative contemporaries, more concerned with property than with human rights. Tall, slender, cold in his manner, colder in his reasoning, he stood out among the other members of the Junto because of his slovenliness in dress. Among his friends, at the dinner table, he was a brilliant conversationalist, for he liked nothing better than to eat and drink, talk and laugh, unless it was to smoke, chew tobacco, and use snuff.[5] He was the per-

---

[1] Hamilton's *Works* (to Bayard), x, 384–87.
[2] Quoted by *The Aurora*, July 30, 1800.   [3] August 5, 1800.
[4] *Familiar Letters*, 373; Lodge, *Cabot.*
[5] *Memoir of Theophilus Parsons*, 328–29; 336–42, 345, 418, 436.

sonification of the political intolerance of his class. There, too, was Stephen Higginson, one of the wealthiest and most cultured merchants of his day, a handsome figure of a man who took infinite pains with his toilet and always carried a gold-headed cane. Given to writing for the press, he made ferocious attacks on John Hancock under the *nom-de-plume* of 'Laco,' and the truckmen on State Street whom he passed on his way to business taught a parrot to cry, 'Hurrah for Hancock; damn Laco.' So intolerant and bigoted was his household that a child, hearing a visitor suggest that a Democrat might be honest, was shocked.[1] There also was John Lowell, able lawyer, cultured, ultra-conservative, disdainful of democracy; and there was Christopher Gore, who amassed a fortune in speculation, and held a brilliant position at the Bar. A striking figure he was, when he appeared at the unconventional meetings of the group, tall, stout, with black eyes and florid complexion, his hair tied behind and dressed with powder, courtly in his manners, eloquent in speech, utterly intolerant in his Federalism, and completely devoted to Hamilton's policies.[2] These and their satellites were Hamilton's Boston friends; more, they were the backbone of his personal organization, his shock troops. Thus, when he crossed into Massachusetts on his tour, he was going to his own with the knowledge that they would receive him gladly — and they did.

Reaching Boston on Saturday evening, he conferred with his friends, and on Sunday 'attended divine services at the Rev. Mr. Kirkland's.' On Monday a dinner was given in his honor, where, the party paper insisted, 'the company was the most respectable ever assembled in the town on a similar occasion.' General Lincoln presided. Higginson and Major Russell of the 'Centinel' were vice-presidents. Governor Strong, the Lieutenant-Governor, the Speaker of the House, Chief Justice Dana, Ames, Cabot, several members of Congress, and members of 'the Reverend Clergy' sat about the boards. 'The tables were loaded with every dainty the season affords and every luxury which could be procured.'[3] It appears that some Adamsites or Jeffersonians declined to do homage,

---

[1] Thomas, *Reminiscences*, I, 17; T. W. Higginson, *Stephen Higginson*, 137, 272, 280, 273–76.

[2] *Familiar Letters*, 370–71, 381.   [3] *Centinel*, June 21, 1800.

for we find the 'Centinel' commenting that 'had a certain citizen known that General Hamilton resembled his demi-god, Bonaparte, instead of refusing a ticket to the dinner he would have solicited the honor of kissing — his hand.'[1] The Hamiltonians were clearly delighted with the occasion; Hamilton himself expanded and talked with freedom in the friendly atmosphere. He talked for Pinckney and against Adams; and in an especially expansive moment, dwelling on the sinister presumption of democracy, said that within four years 'he would either lose his head or be the leader of a triumphant army.' The dinner over, the conference concluded, he made an inspection of Fort Independence on Castle Island, and was on his way, accompanied 'as far as Lynn by a cavalcade of citizens.'[2] Everything had been carried off with becoming *éclat*, for had he not stayed at 'the elegant boarding house of Mrs. Carter?'[3] Unhappily the carriage in which he rode with the 'cavalcade' broke down in the middle of the street,[4] to the delight of the Jacobins, but his composure gave his followers much satisfaction.

Had not the Adamsites implied that he had received the cold shoulder elsewhere in Massachusetts we might never have known his activities beyond Lynn. He was 'everywhere welcomed with unequivocable marks of respect, cordiality, and friendship.' He dined in Salem with Mr. Pickman, 'drank tea at Ipswich,' arrived at Davenport's late in the evening, departed early in the morning for Portsmouth, and reached Newburyport on Sunday. That is the reason there was no demonstration there. But there in the evening he stayed with Parsons 'in company with some of the most respectable gentlemen of the town.'[5]

But Hamilton and the Junto were not soon to hear the last of that tour. The Democrats harped incessantly on the promise to lose his head or be the leader of a triumphant army. 'We have often heard of a French gasconade,' said 'The Aurora,' 'but we have now to place alongside of it a Creole gasconade in America. Alexander Hamilton leading an army to effect a Revolution! Why, the very idea is as pregnant with laughter as if we were to be told of Sir John Falstaff's military achievements.'[6] 'Manlius'

---

[1] *Centinel*, June 21, 1800.
[2] *Ibid.*
[3] *Aurora*, June 21, 1800.
[4] *Aurora*, June 30, 1800.
[5] *Centinel*, June 28, 1800.
[6] August 9, 1800.

rushed to the attack, ostensibly in behalf of Adams, in the 'Chronicle.' Why this trip to 'disband the army'? Had Hamilton ever been in the camp before? Had he appeared 'to plant the seed of distrust in the bosom of the troops? against Adams?' And what a painful effect upon the great men of Boston! 'Your personal appearance threw poor Cabot into the shade. Even what had been deemed eloquence in the smiling Ames was soon reduced to commentary; and so petrifying was your power that our District Judge has scarcely since dared to report an assertion from his Magnus Apollo of Brookline, either on politics or banking.' And lose his head or lead a triumphant army if Pinckney were not elected? 'Your vanity was more gross than even your ignorance of the characters of the people of the eastern States.'[1] Two months later, the echoes were still heard. The Reverend Mr. Kirkland, flattered by Hamilton's cultivation and ingratiation, and young, not content with indiscreetly repeating Hamilton's observations made in company, rushed into the papers with an attack on Adams and a glorification of Hamilton. What a disgrace to the clergy, wrote 'No Politician,' for this flattered youth 'to vindicate the character of a confessed adulterer, and artfully to sap the well-earned reputation of President Adams.'[2] Even King heard from a Bostonian that Hamilton 'in his mode of handling [political themes] did not appear to be the great General which his great talents designate him.'[3] But Hamilton made his observations and reached his conclusions — that the leaders of the first order were in a mood to repudiate Adams, but that those of the second order, more numerous, were almost solidly for him. He merely changed his tactics.

[1] *Chronicle*, July 31, 1800. [2] *Ibid.*, August 18, 1800.
[3] King's *Works* (J. Hale to King), III, 270.

CHAPTER XX

HAMILTON'S RAMPAGE

I

FINDING that persuasion had failed to shake the fidelity of the second-class leaders, Hamilton bethought himself of coercion. The moment he returned to New York, he wrote Charles Carroll of Carrollton proposing to 'oppose their fears to their prejudices,' by having the Middle States declare that they would not support Adams at all. Thus they might be 'driven to support Pinckney.' Both New Jersey and Connecticut, he thought, might agree to the plan, since in both places Adams's popularity was on the wane. In any event, it was not 'advisable that Maryland should be too deeply pledged to the support of Mr. Adams.' [1] The effect on Carroll was all that could have been desired. Two months later, an emissary of McHenry's, sent to interview the venerable patriot, found that he considered Adams 'totally unfit for the office of President, and would support . . . the election of General Pinckney.' [2] Throughout the summer the leaders in the inner circle of the Hamiltonian conspirators were busy with their pens. Richard Stockton urged on Wolcott the wisdom of making a secret fight. 'Prudent silence . . . get in our tickets of electors . . . they will be men who will do right in the vote . . . and Mr. Pinckney will be the man of their choice.' [3]

No one was deeper in the business than Wolcott, who, holding on to his position, and presenting a suave, unblushing front to his chief, was writing feverishly to the leaders of the conspiracy. While Hamilton was receiving the homage of his New England idolaters in June, Wolcott was writing Cabot that 'if General Pinckney is not elected all good men will have cause to regret the inactivity of the Federal party.' [4] In July he was writing McHenry that if 'you will but do your part, we shall probably secure Mr. Pinckney's election,' [5] and to Chauncey Goodrich that good

---

[1] Hamilton's *Works*, x, 379–80.   [2] Gibbs (McHenry to Wolcott), ii, 414–15.
[3] Gibbs, ii, 374–75.   [4] Lodge, *Cabot*, 273–80.   [5] Gibbs, ii, 381.

men thought Mr. 'Adams ought not to be supported.'[1] He was receiving letters from Benjamin Goodhue, presumably Adams's friend, concerning 'Mr. Adams' insufferable madness and vanity,'[2] and from McHenry that 'Mr. Harper is now clearly of opinion that General Pinckney ought to be preferred.'[3] In August he was assuring Ames that 'Adams ought not to be supported,'[4] and in September 'The Aurora' was charging that during that month he had declared in Washington 'that Mr. Adams did not deserve a vote for President.'[5] Clasping Adams's hand with one of his, this consummate master of intrigue was using the other to wig-wag messages to Hamilton from the window of the fortress.

But Hamilton found much to disconcert him. Albeit Cabot rather boasted that in July he had not yet paid a visit of courtesy to Braintree, and probably would not,[6] he was writing Hamilton that to discard Adams at that juncture would mean defeat in Massachusetts.[7] He was opposed, however, only to an open rupture. Noah Webster, having made a New England tour of his own, and lingered a moment under the trees at Braintree, went over to Adams bag and baggage.[8] All but two of the Federalist papers were supporting Adams with spirit. To prod him more, the Jeffersonian press was pouncing upon Hamilton ferociously. 'Dictator of the aristocratical party!' 'Father of the funding system!' Working desperately for Pinckney, 'continually flying through the continent rousing his partisans by the presence of their chief, prescribing and regulating every plan,' was Hamilton, charged a Jeffersonian editor. Author of 'a little book' in which he 'endeavors to give an elegant and pleasant history of his adulteries,' he added.[9] Hamilton began to meditate a sensational stroke.

II

Meanwhile, the Jeffersonians, united, enthusiastic, thoroughly organized, confident, were waging war along the whole line. The mechanics who could vote, the small farmers, the liberals and Democrats, the private soldiers of the Revolution who felt they

---

[1] Gibbs, II, 382.   [2] *Ibid.*, 379.   [3] *Ibid.*, 384.   [4] *Ibid.*, 400–05.
[5] *Aurora*, September 11, 1800.
[6] Lodge, *Cabot* (to Wolcott), 282.
[7] Lodge, *Cabot*, 286–88.
[8] Gibbs (Phelps to Wolcott), II, 380.
[9] *American Mercury*, September 11, 1800.

had been tricked, the small merchants, the Germans because of taxes and the proscription of Muhlenberg, the Irish because the Federalists abused them and passed the Alien Law, were almost a unit behind their chief. All the cost of the army and navy, and the frequent outrages of soldiers with nothing to do, brought support. In North Carolina, Gales, in 'The Register,' was using the camp near Raleigh as a veritable recruiting point for Democrats. The eight per cent loan of that day and the Excise Law of the day before were bringing great accessions to the ranks. The growing indebtedness of the Nation, and Wolcott's admission that another eight per cent loan would be necessary, was making converts. The scandals in administration were creating havoc in Administration circles and driving Wolcott to distraction. The scandal of Jonathan Dayton, Federalist leader of New Jersey, broke, and the hailstones beat upon the head of Wolcott, who was the victim of his credulity alone. While Speaker, Dayton had made written application at the end of the session of 1798 for thirty-three thousand dollars as compensation for the House. That amount was not needed. Wolcott's plea that he did not know he had given Dayton more than necessary was greeted with jeers. His assertion that he had the right to expect the unexpended balance to be immediately refunded only met derisive laughter. Not until the winter of 1799 was the discovery made that Dayton had retained more than eighteen thousand dollars since July, 1798. Wolcott, discovering this fraud, summoned Dayton, wrote him a sharp letter, and recovered the money — but not the interest.[1] Meanwhile, Duane, in 'The Aurora,' was devoting pages to affidavits concerning Dayton's notorious land frauds.[2] Defalcations were numerous, due, according to the apologists of the Administration, to 'the difficulty of procuring men of standing and character . . . to execute their duties.'[3]

Then, to darken the picture for the Federalists, stories were afloat corroborative of the Jeffersonian charge that they favored aristocracy and monarchy. Again Adams appeared as the champion of kingly government. Senator John Langdon, a reputable man, personally vouched in a signed letter to the truth of the

[1] Lodge, *Cabot* (Wolcott to Cabot), 278.
[2] *Aurora*, July 26, 28, 1800.   [3] Gibbs, II, 162.

charge that, in the presence of himself and John Taylor of Caroline, Adams had said that 'he expected to see the day when Mr. Taylor and his friend, Mr. Giles, would be convinced that the people of America would not be happy without an hereditary chief and Senate — or at least for life.' [1] This was greatly strengthened from Federalist sources. 'The observations of the President when he went through town [New Haven] last, made more Democrats than any other thing beside,' wrote Timothy Phelps to Wolcott. 'He told Dr. Dana he did not believe the United States could exist as a nation unless the Executive was hereditary.' [2]

The lesser lights among the Federalists were likewise contributing to the Jeffersonian cause. Noah Webster was being vigorously assailed in the 'American Mercury' for saying that reading and observation had convinced him that republicanism was impossible unless the poorer classes were excluded from the vote.[3] But the climax came with the publication of the stupid pamphlet of John Ward Fenno, who, with his father, had been editor of the Federalist organ for years. In 'Desultory Reflections on the New Political Aspect of Public Affairs,' he clearly reflected the views of Hamilton, to whom he referred as having been pitched 'down the Tarpeian rock of oblivion, not for subsequent apostacy, but for the very deed of greatness itself.' It was a slashing assault on Adams for making peace with France. Glorious prospects had been opening 'the doors of the temple of Janus,' but Adams had acted in a 'puerile' fashion. The masses were denounced as 'the stupid populace, too abject in ignorance to think rightly, and too depraved to draw honest deductions.' The patriotic Federalists were, by Adams's action, 'by one sudden stroke in one short hour, beaten off their ground, overwhelmed with confusion, and left abandoned to all the ridicule and all the rage of their antagonists . . . and nauseating nonsense, meanness, abject servility, and the effeminacy of Sybaris now reign with a pomposity undisturbed even by any casual exertions of genius or common sense.' Pickering had been dismissed because he 'approached too near to holding a divided empire with [Adams] in the hearts of the people.' The time had come to 'repudiate the author of our evils.'

[1] *Aurora*, November 15, 1800; Langdon to Samuel Ringgold.
[2] Gibbs, ii, 418–19. [3] August 7, 1800.

More: the form of government should be changed. 'The continent [should be] divided into ten, fifteen, or twenty counties, to
be governed by a Lieutenant or Prefect appointed by the Executive; certain subaltern appointments should be in his gift. These
Prefects would constitute as proper an upper House for one
branch of the Legislature as could be devised.' The franchise
should be 'cut off from all paupers, vagabonds, and outlaws' —
the poor, the democrats — and 'placed in those hands to which it
belongs, the proprietors of the country.'[1] This from the man who
had edited the Hamilton Federalist organ in Philadelphia. Copies
were carried about in the pockets of the Jeffersonians and worn
out by readings in the taverns.

On top of this, Federalist leaders, writers, and papers began to
hint at secession in the event of Jefferson's election. It had become a habit. There had been talk of secession among them if the
State debts were not assumed: talk again if the Jay Treaty was not
ratified. Wolcott's father had written his son, long before, of its
desirability if Jefferson should be elected. Four years previously
the 'Hartford Courant,' the strongest Federalist paper in New
England, began to publish letters by 'Pelham,' paving the way
for the secession of the North. The South was bitterly assailed.
There were more interesting objects than the Union, thought
'Pelham.' The time had come to secede. A year later, 'Gustavus' began writing in the same paper on the same theme. Jefferson was denounced as an atheist and traitor.[2] In 1800, 'Burleigh' took up his pen to advocate secession in the event of Jefferson's election. In this case the author was known — it was the
fanatic John Allen, who, as a member of Congress, had charged
Livingston with sedition because of his attack in the House on the
Alien Law. In his initial letter he urged all Federalist papers to
copy, and some did. The election of Jefferson would destroy the
Constitution, result in anarchy, expel Federalists from office,
wreck the financial system, and lead to Revolution, for 'there is
scarcely a possibility that we shall escape a civil war.' This would
be bad, but 'less, far less, than anarchy or slavery.' Secession
would be almost certain. Where would the boundary be? At the
Potomac? — the Delaware? — the Hudson? New England might

[1] This pamphlet is in New York Public Library.   [2] Welling's *Lectures*, 274–75.

have trouble if New York and Pennsylvania were included in the Northern Confederacy. 'They are large, wealthy, powerful. They have many men of intrigue and talent among them, desperate in their fortunes, ambitious and unprincipled.' It would be hard to get them to join a peaceful body and keep them quiet.

These were the leading political articles in the leading Federalist paper in the most uncompromising Federalist State through the campaign of 1800.[1] In the 'American Mercury,' 'Rodolphus' replied with a stinging rebuke. 'He tells us,' wrote 'Rodolphus,' 'that if Mr. Jefferson is elected our towns will be pillaged, our inhabitants rendered miserable and our soil dyed in blood; that we shall have a Jacobin government, that the Constitution . . . will fall a sacrifice, and finally if the man of his choice is not elected, the Federal Union must be destroyed and that the Northern States must form a separate Government. The writer is a Federalist indeed.'[2]

The Jeffersonians made the most of 'Burleigh's' secession articles.

III

Nowhere were the Jeffersonian activities more annoying to the Federalists than in New England where Federalism thought itself permanently entrenched. It had reached its peak in 1798 during the war hysteria, and the next two years were marked by a notable decline. The activities of the defiant Democrats were intensified. Denunciations of the 'aristocracy' that governed, of the political meddling of the clergy, brought the fight personally home to the leaders. In Vermont, where Lyon had been persecuted and his followers aroused, the stamp tax and the extravagance in government made a deep impression on the small farmers. It was a scandal in the best regulated households that 'Matthew Lyon and his cubs' were prowling about the highways.[3] In Massachusetts, where Gerry had made a remarkable race for Governor in the spring, the fight was being made in every quarter, and Ames was wailing that 'on the whole the rabies canina of Jacobinism has

[1] *Hartford Courant*, June 23, 30, July 7, 14, 21, 26, August 4, 11, 18, September 1, 15, 22, 1800.
[2] *American Mercury*, July 10, 1800.
[3] Robinson, *Jeffersonian Democracy in New England*, 27.

gradually passed of late years from the cities, where it was confined to the docks and the mob, to the country.'[1] In New Hampshire, the Jeffersonians had made an astonishing showing in the gubernatorial contest in the spring, carrying a number of the towns, including Concord and Portsmouth. There, under the leadership of John Langdon, they had capitalized the refusal of the Federalist Legislature to grant a charter to a bank which proposed to loan money in small sums, and place credit within the reach of the farmers and the poor.[2] Their defeat, notwithstanding their heavy vote, encouraged them to persevere in their attacks on corporations and the 'privileged few.'

But it was in Connecticut that the Jeffersonians gave the Federalists their greatest shock by the audacity of their attacks. There the Democrats, though few, made up in zeal and ability for what they lacked in numbers. In the home of Pierrepont Edwards, a Federal Judge and a foremost citizen, they perfected their plans for the campaign. Aaron Burr spent some time in the State assisting in the creation of a militant organization. A Federalist complained in a letter to Wolcott that 'the Democrats spent all their time and talents for eight weeks endeavoring to persuade the ignorant part of the community that the Administration was endeavoring to establish a monarchy; and even good Mr. Edwards told them he had held an important office under government, but that he had found them so vile and corrupt, he was determined to resign the office.'[3] Nothing could have been more distressing to the aristocratic and clerical oligarchy which had long lorded it over the people. The 'Courant' piously prayed that Connecticut would not 'exhibit the distressing spectacle of two parties rending the State with their reproaches and whetting their swords for civic combat,' and held up 'the awful condition in Pennsylvania and Virginia' as a warning.[4] The 'New York Commercial Advertiser,' founded by a son of Connecticut, was disheartened at the effrontery of the Democrats. 'Jacobinism in Connecticut,' it said, 'has heretofore been confined to back streets and dark recesses; but in consequence of the successes in other States it begins to creep forth and show its hideous front in good company.'[5] In September the

[1] Robinson, *Jeffersonian Democracy in New England*, 27.
[2] *Centinel*, March 1, 22, 1800.   [3] Gibbs (Phelps to Wolcott), ii, 418–19.
[4] August 4, 1800.   [5] *New York Commercial Advertiser*, May 13, 1800.

'American Mercury' of Hartford was boasting through 'Gracchus' that 'in many towns where there was not a man who a few months ago avowed the cause of republicanism, the friends of liberty and the Constitution have now a majority,' although 'in most towns there was a fight.'[1]

To Abraham Bishop, the fighting leader of the Jeffersonians, was left the congenial task of whipping the Federalists to a frenzy. A graduate of Yale, of which Dwight, popularly known as 'the Pope of Federalism,' and a man of scholarly attainments, was President, he was invited to deliver the Phi Beta Kappa oration at the commencement. It was assumed that he would speak on some literary or scientific subject, but nothing was more remote from his intentions. Very carefully, and with malice aforethought, he prepared a scathing arraignment of Federalist principles and policies. At the last moment the clergy discovered the nature of the discourse and recommended its rejection. One indignant partisan wrote Wolcott that 'the Society discovered the cheat before it was delivered and destroyed its effect so far as was within their power.'[2] The 'Courant' explained that when the invitation was extended, the members of the fraternity were 'ignorant of his sentiments,' and of the fact that 'he had been once desired by a committee of the society to resign the presidency because of profanity.' The moment it was found that the wicked man had written 'a seditious and inflammatory libel on the religion and government of the country,' it was decided to dispense with the oration.[3] But the seditious and irreligious Bishop had no notion of being robbed of an audience. The 'Courant' reported that 'with an impudence and effrontery known only to weak or wicked men,' Bishop 'proceeded at seven o'clock to palm off on the public the production.'[4] More than fifteen hundred men, women, and children, including some members of the clergy, heard him,[5] but the 'Courant,' looking over the assemblage, solemnly declared it as 'a singular fact that every open reviler of religion was there and highly gratified,' but that the young ladies of New Haven 'refused to grace an audience thus collected and consisting of such characters.'[6]

[1] *American Mercury*, September 19, 1800.   [2] Gibbs (from Phelps), ii, 418.

[3] *Courant*, September 15, 1800.   [4] *Ibid*.

[5] *Connecticut in Transition*, 315–16.   [6] *Courant*, September 15, 1800.

No more slashing attack was heard during the campaign. The audience was sympathetic, jubilant. The orator in fine fettle, the subject to his taste. He attacked the extravagance in government, sneered at the ceremonious launching of war vessels, ridiculed the military pretensions of Hamilton. The army had not fought, but had 'stood their ground bravely in their cantonments.' The funding system had 'ruined thousands, but ... has also led up to an aristocracy more numerous than the farmers-general in France, more powerful than all others because it combined the men of wealth.'

But it was for the political preachers of Connecticut that Bishop reserved his heaviest fire. 'How much, think you, has religion been benefited by sermons intended to show that Satan and Cain were Jacobins?' Then a contemptuous fling at 'Pope' Dwight — 'Would Paul of Tarsus have preached to an anxious, listening audience on the propriety of sending envoys?' After all, 'the Captain of Salvation is not so weak as to require an army and navy and a majority in Congress to support His cause.' Then, falling into satire: 'Let no one imagine that I would represent the clergy as acting out of their sphere ... for is it not said unto them, "Go ye into all the world and preach politics to every creature. When men oppose ye, call them enemies of God and trample them under your feet." ... When the people are assembled, say to them that the Lord reigneth on the earth in the midst of men of power and wealth; that he delighteth in the proud, even in those who are lofty; that he will exalt the vain, and lay in the dust they who are humble in his sight; that the great are gods; but that the little men are like the chaff which he driveth before the wind; that in the day of his power he will shine mightily on those who are in power, and that he will make the people under them like the hay and the stubble and the sweepings of the threshing floor.'

Immediately the speech was published in pamphlet form and sent broadcast over the country. Editions were printed in numerous towns and States.[1] Within a week an answer had been published in a pamphlet, 'A Rod for a Fool's Back,'[2] but it failed to af-

[1] Original copies published in both Philadelphia and Newark are in New York Public Library.
[2] *Courant*, September 22, 1800.

fect the popularity of Bishop's 'Oration on the Extent and Power of Political Delusions,' and two months later, when he was at Lancaster during a session of the Legislature, he repeated the speech on invitation of Governor M'Kean.[1] It was a palpable hit.

IV

And it was a hit, primarily because it was an assault on the part the clergy was playing in the campaign. All over New England, and in New York and Philadelphia, ministers were preaching politics with an intemperance of denunciation and a recklessness of truth that seems incredible to-day. The game of the politicians to picture Jefferson as an atheist, a scoffer at religion who despised the Church and laughed at the Bible, was entrusted to the Ministerial Corps, which did the best it could. It was a line of slander that had followed Jefferson from the moment he forced religious liberty and toleration into the laws of Virginia. The only campaign canard of which Jefferson took cognizance was set afloat by the Reverend Cotton Smith, who proclaimed that the man of Monticello had accumulated his property by robbing a widow and fatherless children of their estate while acting as their executor. 'If Mr. Smith thinks that the precepts of the Gospel are intended for those who preach them as well as for others,' wrote Jefferson, 'he will some day feel the duties of repentance and acknowledgment in such forms as to correct the wrong he has done. All this is left to his own conscience.'[2] But if Jefferson was content to leave to their consciences clergymen bearing false witness, his followers were not. When the Reverend Dr. Abercrombie of Philadelphia gravely warned his congregation against voting for an atheist, Duane made a biting reply. 'He is the man who opposed reading the Declaration of Independence on 4th of July last,' he wrote. 'Need we wonder at his hatred of Mr. Jefferson?'[3] When the clergyman, stung by the attack, made a weak reply, Duane asked: 'During the prevalence of yellow fever ... in 1798 on a day in the house of Mr. Richard Potter in Germantown did you not provoke an argument in which you supported monarchical doc-

[1] *Courant*, November 17, 1800.
[2] Jefferson's *Works* (to Uriah McGregory), x, 170–73.
[3] *Aurora*, September 1, 1800.

trines and assert that the country would never be happy until it had a king?' [1] To another minister, fortunately 'the late Rev. Dr. J. B. Smith of Virginia,' was ascribed one of the most amazing stories of the campaign, that Jefferson on passing a dilapidated church had sneeringly said that 'it was good enough for Him Who was born in a manger.' [2]

When the Reverend John M. Mason published a political pamphlet under the cover of religion,[3] accusing Jefferson of being a Deist, and the Reverend Dr. Lynn of New York, actively electioneering for Pinckney against both Adams and Jefferson at the instance of Hamilton, printed another,[4] a Democratic pamphlet appeared declaring that 'Jefferson is as good a Christian as Adams,' and charging that 'Pope' Dwight, ten years before, had published a poem, 'The Triumph of Infidelity,' in which he named Pinckney as a Deist. In this pamphlet [5] Dr. Lynn was handled as roughly as the Philadelphia pulpit politician. Had he not called on a Democrat while electioneering for Pinckney and been forced to admit that Jefferson was a good man? Had he not, when pressed, been forced to concede that Pinckney was a Deist? Had not the wife of the Democrat indignantly taken the clergyman to task for his 'partiality to a self-confessed adulterer?'

If the Jeffersonians were attacking the political preachers with meat-axe and artillery, they were not without provocation enough. In Connecticut, these ministers were the backbone of the Federalist Party machine, with Dwight as their leader, than whom none more offensively intolerant ever breathed curses on a foe. In Massachusetts, when the Reverend Ebenezer Bradford espoused the cause of democracy, he was ferociously abused by his fellow ministers and the Federalist papers, ostracized in the name of Christ by his fellow clergymen, and refused a pulpit in Essex County. It was not a time when ministers in some sections were making much of the action of Christ in seeking his disciples among workers and fishermen.[6] The feeling of many of these was expressed by the Reverend David Osgood when, speaking of the masses, he said that 'they may know enough for the places and stations to

---

[1] *Aurora*, September 4, 1800.   [2] *Courant*, August 25, 1800.
[3] *A Voice of Warning.*   [4] *Serious Considerations.*
[5] *Serious Facts.*   [6] Morse, *Federalist Party in Massachusetts*, 133–34.

which Providence has assigned them; may be good and worthy members of the community, provided they would be content to move in their own sphere and not meddle with things too high for them.'[1]

In one pamphlet the case against Jefferson's religion was set forth in detail — he questioned the story of the Deluge; did not believe the Bible in its entirety was inspired; and was opposed to teaching the Bible in the public schools. 'No one, I believe,' wrote this distressed Christian, 'has openly and publicly asserted that Jefferson is a Christian.'[2] Soon a pamphlet in defense was in circulation.' 'Read, ye fanatics, bigots, hypocrites ... and you base calumniators whose efforts to traduce are the involuntary tribute of envy to a character more pure than your own — read and learn and practice the religion of Jefferson as displayed in the sublime truth and inspired language of his ever memorable "act establishing religious liberty." Read his views on slavery in his "Notes on Virginia" — "I tremble for my country when I reflect that God is just; that his justice cannot sleep forever."'[3] The 'Chronicle' was amused to observe 'the characters who are professed champions of religious zeal.' Who were they? 'What shall we say of a faction that has at its head a confessed and professed adulterer? ... In connection with this Saint we have a group of zealots, consisting of gamblers, bankrupts, Saturday evening carousers, or, to comprise the whole in one general appellation, a British Essex Junto intermixed with a few clerical hypocrites who have formed an alliance, offensive and defensive, to calumniate Mr. Jefferson.'[4] The 'American Mercury' dwelt on contributions made by Jefferson to the Church and to needy clergymen. 'Thus while Mr. Jefferson is ... practicing the blessed religion of Jesus Christ by acts of charity and benevolence ... these political parsons are abusing that holy religion and profaning the temple of God by fulminating lies and slander against Mr. Jefferson.'[5]

Thus through the summer and autumn and into the winter the

---

[1] Morse, *Federalist Party in Massachusetts*, 95, note.

[2] *The Claims of Thomas Jefferson to the Presidency Examined at the Bar of Christianity*, probably by Asbury Dickens in New York Public Library.

[3] *Address to the People of the United States*, etc., by John James Beckley, in New York Public Library.

[4] *Independent Chronicle*, June 30, 1800.   [5] *American Mercury*, October 2, 1800.

political preachers continued their assaults, and the Jeffersonians replied without undue reverence for the cloth. Everywhere the Federalist leaders were assuming a pious pose, even Sedgwick and Ames and Otis were becoming religious, and the Democrats greeted their pose with ribald mirth. Into an amusing imaginary diary of Jonathan Dayton of the soiled reputation, Duane was writing the notation: 'Went to church — must go to church — Federalists must be pious — 'twill do a great deal of good.'[1] When an appeal was made to Catholics to vote against Jefferson, Duane dryly commented: 'We presume the . . . reason to be that it was owing to Mr. Jefferson that the Catholic priest was saved from being hanged for going into . . . Virginia . . . and that to his toleration law it was owing that the Catholic can now build churches and adore God without incurring penalties of fine and imprisonment.'[2]

Thus religion in virulent form fought with politics in the campaign of 1800.

v

But this sort of fighting and sniping was not working to the disadvantage of Adams — and that was of some concern to Hamilton, who had concluded that he would be happier under the presidency of Jefferson than under a continuation of Adams. Scurrility there was in abundance, but Adams suffered little. Occasional references were made to his vanity, his love of pomp, his partiality to titles, and to his writings as evidence of monarchical tendencies, but these were mild enough. With the political preachers and editors abusing Jefferson, and with the Democrats attacking Hamilton, it was time for some one to assault Adams — and Hamilton delegated himself to the task. During the summer, Adams, smarting under the discovery of the treachery of his party associates, had been freely talking in unguarded conversation of an 'English party,' and naming Hamilton and his friends. This furnished the pretext.

On the first of August, Hamilton wrote a note to Adams asking a verification or denial of the report that he had said there was a British faction with Hamilton at the head. This was sent to Cabot for transmission to Braintree. The cunning leader of the Essex Junto, in acknowledging the receipt of the letter, suggested that perhaps the election of Jefferson would be necessary for the reunification of the Federalist Party. Were Pinckney chosen, he would encounter the venomous hostility of the Adamsites. How would it do for the Federalists to throw their support to Burr? Many Federalists favored such action.[1] Adams ignored the letter from Hamilton, as the latter unquestionably supposed he would. Two days after its transmission and before it could have possibly reached the President, Hamilton wrote Wolcott of his 'impatience' at the latter's delay in sending the 'statement of facts which you promised me.' The trusted member of Adams's official family had promised his chief's most bitter foe the ammunition for attack. It was plain, said Hamilton, working on Wolcott's fears, that unless something were done the Adams faction 'will completely run us down in public opinion.' Had not Wolcott's name been bandied about with Hamilton's as a member of the British party?[2]

Later in the month he wrote McHenry, then nursing his wrath in retirement, of his plan to publish a pamphlet defending himself and friends and attacking Adams. He was prepared to put his name to it, but this he could not do without 'its being conclusively inferred that as to every material fact I must have derived my information from members of the Administration.' To both McHenry and Wolcott he sent a copy of the letter.[3] At the moment he wrote, he was having difficulty with some of his advisers. Cabot and Ames had discussed the wisdom of Hamilton's putting his name to the pamphlet, and both agreed it would be indiscreet. It should be remembered that Adams might be reëlected. Hamilton's sponsorship of the pamphlet would give it force with men who needed no conversion, while with his enemies 'it would be converted into new proof that you are a dangerous man.'[4] A month later, Hamilton was still in doubt about affixing his name, but evidently anxious for encouragement to do so. Thus he wrote Wolcott that 'anonymous publications cannot affect anything,' but that 'some of the most delicate of the facts stated I hold from the three ministers, yourself particularly, and I do not count my-

---

[1] Lodge, *Cabot*, 283–84.   [2] Hamilton's *Works*, x, 383–84.   [3] *Ibid.*, 388–89.
[4] Lodge, *Cabot* (Cabot to Hamilton), 284–86.

self at liberty to take the step without your permission.'[1] On
October 1st, Hamilton sent a second letter to Adams, through
Cabot, who, ten days later, wrote that it had been transmitted,[2]
but no reply was made. Nothing could have suited Hamilton
better. Thus the pamphlet was written and sent to the editor of
the New York 'Gazette' to print. It bore the name of Hamilton.
It was to be guarded from general publicity and sent only to leading Federalists over the country.

And right here the uncanny cleverness of Burr again intervened.
The suave little black-eyed master of espionage had known
Hamilton's slate for the Assembly within an hour after the caucus
had adjourned; when Hamilton's caucus decided to ask Jay to
call an extra session of the Legislature to defeat the effect of the
election, the fact was heralded in the papers the next day; and
now Burr was to see a copy of the printed pamphlet before the eye
of its author had seen it. Just how he got possession of the copy
will never be known. His intimate political associate and authorized biographer merely says that he learned it was in the press and
'arrangements were accordingly made for a copy as soon as the
printing of it was complete.'[3] Parton has a more colorful story.
Burr was an early riser, and, walking in the street near Hamilton's
house one morning, he met a boy carrying a covered basket. He
always spoke to children.

'What have you there, my lad?'

'Pamphlets for General Hamilton.'

Whereupon he requested and received a copy, immediately
summoned Davis and two others to his house, where extracts were
copied and hastened with the utmost speed to 'The Aurora' and
the New London 'Bee.'[4] There is still another version of the
general circulation that neither biographer mentions — that of
the editor of the New York 'Gazette,' who was forced to an explanation in self-defense. The general circulation was 'contrary
to the expectation . . . that it would be restricted to particular
quarters. The editor of the Gazette thinks it his duty to exonerate
Mr. Hamilton by making it known that the thing has happened in
direct opposition to his views. He had given the most precise in-

[1] Hamilton's *Works*, x, 389–90.   [2] Lodge, *Cabot*, 293.
[3] Davis, *Burr*, ii, 65.   [4] Parton, i, 126–27; Davis, ii, 65.

structions that the circulation might be deferred; but the Editor, having been informed that by a breach of confidence or indiscretion somewhere it was likely that extracts might appear in some newspapers, communicated the intelligence to Mr. Hamilton, who ... being about to depart for Albany left a letter with a friend directing him that if such a thing should happen, then to permit the letter to be thrown into circulation.' [1] This explanation did not appear, however, until Hamilton found that the tremendous sensation the pamphlet created was not reacting entirely in his favor. And for a sensation there was cause enough.

VI

An amazing production this, for the middle of the campaign. Adams did 'not possess the talents adapted to the administration of government.' There were 'great and intrinsic defects in his character which unfit him.' Even during the Revolution, Hamilton had entertained doubts as to 'the solidity of his understanding.' When Adams had conducted Madame de Vergennes, wife of the Foreign Minister in Paris, to dinner, and been rewarded with her comment that he was 'the Washington of negotiation,' he had interpreted it as an illustration of 'a pretty knack of paying compliments,' when he might have said that it disclosed 'a dexterous knack of disguising sarcasms.' His vanity was so great that it was 'more than a harmless foible.' True, Hamilton had sought to elect Thomas Pinckney in 1796, but this was due to the 'disgusting egotism, the distempered jealousy, and the ungovernable indiscretion of Mr. Adams's temper, joined to some doubts of the correctness of his maxims of administration.' Adams's letter to Tench Coxe, charging the Pinckneys with being English toadies, was silly; his conduct in preventing the French war was infamous. This latter had come out of the vice of not consulting his constitutional advisers — meaning Wolcott, Pickering, and McHenry. He had thus fallen into the hands of 'miserable intriguers' with whom 'his self-love was more at ease.' With gay disregard of the truth, Hamilton denied that there was any conspiracy to interfere with Adams's plans at Trenton.

More amazing still, Adams was denounced for the dismissal of

[1] Copied in the *Commercial Advertiser*, November 27, 1800.

two traitors in his Cabinet, and this, despite the fact that another, who remained, had furnished the writer with much of the material for the pamphlet. There was no cause for the dismissals — none at all. It was only Adams's 'paroxysms of rage, which deprived him of self-command and produced very outrageous behavior.' Pickering had been driven out because he was 'justly tenacious of his own dignity and independence.' The Adams interview with McHenry called for both 'pain and laughter' — an incredible performance. Then followed more abuse because Adams had not given Fries and others to the scaffold. Then — a pitiful touch — for not appointing Hamilton commander-in-chief to succeed Washington. Here the author entered into more personal grievances. Having pictured Adams as an ingrate, a liar, and a fool unfit for high administrative office, the author concluded with the statement that because 'the body of Federalists, for want of sufficient knowledge of facts, are not convinced of the expediency of relinquishing him,' Hamilton would 'not advise the withholding from him of a single vote.' [1]

It was the most astounding political performance in American history — and the Nation rocked with mingled imprecations and laughter. Even Cabot was a little shocked. 'All agree,' he wrote Hamilton, 'that the execution is masterly, but I am bound to tell you that you are accused by respectable men of egotism; and some very worthy and sensible men say you have exhibited the same vanity in your book which you charge as a dangerous quality and great weakness in Mr. Adams.' [2]

Major Russell, of the 'Centinel' in Boston, was painfully embarrassed, and flopped about like a fish on the burning sands. In one issue he supported Adams, and denounced the author of an attack on Hamilton's action as 'as well qualified for the task as a Billingsgate oyster is to contemplate the principles of the Newtonian philosophy.' [3] In another issue he regretted Hamilton's 'ill-timed epistle,' and denounced 'an imported renegado of the name of Cooper' who had written Hamilton a 'saucy production' to the effect that if he would admit the authorship of the pamphlet he would ask for his indictment under the Sedition Law.[4] This is

[1] Hamilton's *Works*, VII, 309–64.
[2] Lodge, *Cabot*, 298–300.
[3] *Centinel*, November 15, 1800.
[4] *Ibid.*, November 26, 1800.

evidence enough that Russell had parted with his sense of humor, else he would have appreciated the shot. The Hartford 'Courant' contented itself by merely reprinting, without comment, the Jeffersonian New London 'Bee's' excoriation of Hamilton.[1] The New York 'Commercial Advertiser' was silent, but gave space to the advertisement of a pamphlet entitled 'A Letter to General Hamilton, occasioned by His Letter to President Adams — by a Federalist.'[2]

The Jeffersonian papers made the most of the opportunity. The 'American Mercury' of Hartford, announcing the arrival of the pamphlet, explained that, 'since General Hamilton has secured a copyright to his masterly production,' only extracts could be given. It was evidently written in the interest of Pinckney, who, having been 'educated at the University of Oxford' in England, 'was naturally' supported by the British faction.[3] 'I am sorry, sir,' wrote the author of an open letter to Hamilton in the 'Independent Chronicle' of Boston, 'that you have been persecuted in the manner you mention, . . . but does it show a man of fortitude and independence to be continually groaning, like some feeble old woman under her troubles? . . . Egotism is the mark of a weak and vain mind. Here, General, you descend from your usual greatness to the level with female vanity.'[4]

Duane, of 'The Aurora,' fell upon it with the zest of a kitten lapping cream: 'John Adams, Alexander Hamilton, and the Pinckneys are now fairly before the public,' he wrote, 'not in the partial drawings of their political rivals, the Republicans. Their claims and pretensions to public confidence are exhibited by themselves.'[5] The Portsmouth 'Ledger' struck the same note: 'If President Adams is what General Hamilton and the Essex Junto represent him, and if Charles Cotesworth Pinckney is what President Adams in his letter to Tench Coxe has represented him, viz., a British partisan — can any one hesitate to say that Mr. Jefferson is the most suitable of the three for President?'[6]

But the most telling reply appeared in a pamphlet ascribed to James Cheetham, the New York editor.[7] Of course Hamilton was

---

[1] October 27, 1800.   [2] November 4, 1800.
[3] October 30, 1800.   [4] December 1, 1800.
[5] October 29, 1800.   [6] Reprinted in *The Aurora*, November 13, 1800.
[7] *Answer to Alexander Hamilton's Letter Concerning the Public Conduct and Character of John Adams.*

a monarchist, it said. It had been 'a thousand times reiterated from New Hampshire to Georgia.' The Madame de Vergennes incident? 'Your references to a certain private journal of Mr. Adams was surpassingly brutal and low. They demonstrate the imbecility of your cause and point out the base malignity of your heart.' The Adams letter to Tench Coxe? 'Evidently written in some jocular moment.' The cause of Hamilton's hostility? 'Envy, ambition, and the loaves and fishes.' The French peace? 'If your intrusive advice had been received, what would have been the condition of your country? Embroiled in an unprofitable war, commerce would have been at a stand, and the cause of liberty on the decline. A standing army would have gluttonized on the substance of society.' Adams? True, the 'Duke of Braintree' had 'very slender pretensions to consistency of character,' and the Nation's hope was in Jefferson, 'who has walked with dignity in every public and private calling,' whose mind 'is illumined with science and whose heart is replete with good'; who 'has stood firm and unshaken amidst the venality of courts and the temptations of power.'

Under such lashings Hamilton writhed and was eager to make reply. 'The press teems with replies,' he wrote Pickering, 'and I may finally think it expedient to publish a second time. In this case I shall reënforce my charges with new anecdotes. My friends will, no doubt, be disposed to aid me. You probably possess some that are unknown to me. Pray let me have them without delay.' [1] But his friends had no such disposition. They had had enough. Ames wrote him scornfully of his critics, who were unworthy of notice. 'It is therefore the opinion of your friends that the facts stated must be left to operate on the public mind; and that the rage of those whom they wound will give them currency.' [2] The Federalist Party had been split in two with a battle-axe.

VII

Its leaders realized the hopelessness of their prospects. Many did not care. McHenry, smarting in Maryland, wrote Wolcott that the lack of courage and initiative on the part of the leaders, and their failure to fight Adams in the open, meant defeat. What

[1] Hamilton's *Works*, x, 391.   [2] Ames, i, 283–85.

did they do? 'They write private letters,' said the scornful poet-politician. 'To whom? To each other, but they do nothing to give direction to the public mind. They observe even in their conversation a discreet circumspection generally, ill calculated to diffuse information. . . . They meditate in private. . . . If the party recovers its pristine character . . . shall I ascribe it to such cunning, paltry, indecisive, back-door conduct?' [1] And for once in his life McHenry was wise and right. Unable to meet the issues, the Federalist Big-Wigs still hoped to win through sharp practice. They got their cue from the Jeffersonians, who, finding from the election of the year before that the selection of electors by districts would result in the loss of one or two in Virginia, changed the law and provided for their election by the Legislature. This was enough for the Federalists in Massachusetts, where district elections would have given Jefferson at least two votes. Otis and others wrote the Speaker of the House and the President of the Senate to change the law and have the Legislature choose. The change was made. Estopped from complaining by their own action in Virginia, the Jeffersonians denounced the change in Massachusetts as a trick of the Essex Junto to rob Adams and elect Pinckney,[2] and much bitterness was aroused. In Maryland the district system was favorable to the Jeffersonians and the Federalists there were importuned from without to have the Governor call an extraordinary session of the Legislature to give that body the power.[3] Owing to the almost equal strength of the parties in that State, however, the leaders were afraid to act, and a series of letters appeared, first in the Baltimore 'Gazette,' and later in pamphlet form, citing the action of the Democrats in Virginia and the retaliation in Massachusetts. 'Should the State of Maryland suffer itself to be bullied out of its rights . . . by the clamors of the partisans in Virginia?' demanded the author.[4] 'The Aurora' charged that James Carroll had said at Annapolis that the Governor should call the General Assembly together to deprive the people of the right to vote for electors.[5] But when it came to the test the courage of the Marylanders failed and no change was made.

[1] Gibbs, II, 384–86.   [2] *American Mercury*, June 19, 1800.
[3] Steiner (Hamilton to McHenry), 466; (Dickinson to McHenry), 471.
[4] *A Series of Letters on the Subject of 'The Legislative Choice' of Electors in Maryland*, by 'Bystander.'   [5] August 4, 1800.

Only in Pennsylvania did the Jeffersonians have a real grievance. The most sanguine of the Federalists could find no silver
lining to the cloud here. Fitzsimmons complained that in Philadelphia, 'a city of 60,000 inhabitants, not a man is to be found who
is fit for the station who will accept the nomination for Congress.' [1]
The envenomed Uriah Tracy, after traveling through the State,
thought the outlook hopeless. M'Kean had 'brought forward
every scoundrel who can read and write into office.' The Democrats, 'with the joy and ferocity of the damned,' were enjoying
'the mortification of the few remaining honest men.' Tracy had
seen 'very many Irishmen' throughout the State — 'the most God-
provoking Democrats this side of hell.' Then 'the Germans are
both stupid, ignorant and ugly, and are to the Irish what the
negroes of the South are to their drivers.' The Democrats were
'establishing presses and newspapers in almost every town and
county in the country and the Federal presses are failing for want
of support.' [2] Under these conditions the Federalists conceived
the idea of depriving Pennsylvania of any voice at all in the election — an idea not unreasonable, since no provision had been
made as to the method of choosing electors. In July, Senator
Bingham had written Wolcott that there was little probability
that the State would have 'any agency in the election,' but in any
event its vote would be 'equalized from the preponderance which
the parties reciprocally possess in the two branches of the Legislature.' [3]

In November, Governor M'Kean called an extraordinary session. In the Senate the Federalists had a small majority; in the
House the Democrats had the advantage; on joint ballot the
Democrats outnumbered their opponents. The Democrats urged
a joint ballot; the Federalists laughed the proposal to scorn. Excitement rose to fever heat. Charges were made that Liston, the
British Minister, was using money to affect the result. [4] The State,
at the moment, was Jeffersonian, and the legislators were deluged
with petitions for a joint ballot, but petitions from the people had
never impressed the Hamiltonians. These stood firm — holding

[1] Gibbs (to Wolcott), ii, 388–90.   [2] *Ibid.*, ii, 399.
[3] *Ibid.*, ii, 387–88.
[4] *Aurora*, November 11, 1800.

the power of veto. At length they made a concession to the end that the State might not be deprived of any voice. The Senate could select seven electors, the House eight. The Democrats writhed and raved without avail. The Federalists were relentless.

CHAPTER XXI

DEMOCRACY TRIUMPHANT

I

THE final contest was staged in the new capital at Washington. It was as though destiny had arranged a new setting for the new drama on which the curtain was now rising. In the glamorous days of Federalist supremacy, Philadelphia, with its wealth, its fashion, and princely houses, harmonized with the spirit of government. The aristocratic party thrived in an atmosphere of luxury. Consistency called for a stage setting of more simplicity, in a wilderness suggesting the frontier, when the curtain rose on the triumph of democracy.

When that charming philosopher of cynicism, Gouverneur Morris, just elected to the Senate, reached the new capital in the clearing, after days of bumping and hardships on the woodsy road through Maryland, he looked about him with a smile and chuckled. Writing the Princesse de la Tour et Taxis, he poked gentle fun at the new seat of government. 'We only need here houses, cellars, kitchens, scholarly men, amiable women, and a few other such trifles to possess a perfect city,' he said, 'for we can walk over it as we would in the fields and woods, and, on account of a strong frost, the air is quite pure. I enjoy it all the more because my room fills with smoke as soon as the door is closed. . . . I hasten to assure you that building stone is plentiful, that excellent bricks are baked here, that we are not wanting in sites for magnificent mansions . . . ; in a word, that this is the best city in the world to live in — in the future.' [1]

Ten days before Morris wrote, Mrs. Adams had reached the capital in the wilds looking older and graver, and without a ceremonious reception, due to jealousies among the socially ambitious over the choice of a master of ceremonies.[2] After the well-traveled roads to Philadelphia, the journey to Washington had been quite enough to add to both her age and gravity. On the way

[1] Morris, *Diary*, II, 394–95.   [2] Gibbs (Wolcott to wife), II, 456.

from Baltimore her party had been lost in the woods, wandering aimlessly about for two hours until rescued by a wandering negro. 'Woods are all you see from Baltimore until you reach this city, which is only so in name,' she wrote her daughter. 'Here and there, a small cot, without a glass window, interspersed amongst the forest through which you travel miles without seeing a human being.' Nor was the grandeur of the President's house entirely to her liking. From her windows she could see on the Potomac the 'vessels as they pass and repass.' But a rapid survey of the large mansion with its numerous draughty rooms, convinced her that it would require thirty servants 'to attend and keep the apartment in order, and perform the ordinary business of the house and stables.' Not a single apartment finished. 'The great unfinished audience [East] room I have made a drying room of to hang up the clothes in,' she wrote glumly. But — added the tactful Abigail — 'when asked how I like it, say that I write you the situation is beautiful, which is true.' [1] A few days later she wrote of the impatience of the ladies for a drawing-room, but 'I have no looking glasses but dwarfs for this house, nor a twentieth part lamps enough to light it.' [2] Had the disgusted Abigail fared forth for a peep into the living arrangements of others, she might have thought herself more fortunate. But surveying the city from her point of vantage she would have found little to tempt to a tour of inspection.

Even then, it was a 'city of magnificent distances,' the houses separated by miles of mud roads, not entirely free from stumps. Travel by night was precarious. Blackness impenetrable, except when the moon was at its full, settled down over the homes and the frog ponds. Morris, having made an evening call, was forced to remain all night, for the road was 'not merely deep but dangerous to drive in the dark.' [3] James A. Bayard and a party of Federalist leaders, venturing forth on a return to their lodgings from the home of a friend two miles from town, were caught in a storm, and the coachman losing his way, they drove about the waste lands throughout the night, threatened every moment by the ruts and ravines.[4]

[1] Adams, *Letters of Mrs. Adams*, ii, 239-41.   [2] *Ibid.*, **243-44**.
[3] Morris, *Diary*, ii, 396.   [4] Mrs. Smith, 9-10.

Pennsylvania Avenue, stretching from the President's house to the Capitol, bordered by miasmic swamps, did not at this time boast a single building; nor would it have been possible to have lived along this causeway 'without devoting its wretched tenant to perpetual fevers.' [1] From the steps of the Capitol one could count seven or eight boarding-houses, one tailor's shop, one shoe-maker's, one printing establishment, the home of a washwoman, a grocery shop, a stationery store, a dry-goods house, and an oyster market. And this was all. Three quarters of a mile away on the Eastern Branch stood five or six houses and an empty warehouse. At the wharf, not a single ship. From the President's house to Georgetown living conditions were better because of immunity from swamps, but the wretched roads made it all but prohibitive as a place of residence for members of Congress. Six or seven of the more fastidious braved the distance and found comfortable quarters; two or three found lodgings near the President's house; but the remainder crowded into the boarding-houses on Capitol Hill. In the best of these, by sharing a room one could have attendance, wood, candles, food, and an abundance of liquor for fifteen dollars a week. However, the fare was unsatisfactory, the beef not good, and vegetables hard to get. [2] Such was the hair-trigger delicacy of the political situation that this packing of the politicians might easily have led to altercations and bloodshed had they not seen fit to herd together according to their political views. There was some gambling, some drinking, but Gallatin observed that for the most part the members 'drank politics' instead of liquor. [3]

How the dandies of the Federalist circle must have missed the royal hospitality at Mrs. Bingham's! Pathetic efforts were put forth to create something that might pass for society, but so limited were the resources that the lone church at the bottom of Capitol Hill, which had previously served as a tobacco house, was found alluring, and women donned their finery for worship. [4] The Thomas Laws, who had one of the few pretentious houses, organized a 'dancing assembly' to which many subscribed. [5] Mrs. Law,

[1] Adams, *Gallatin* (Gallatin to his wife), 252–55.
[2] *Ibid.*, 255.   [3] *Ibid.*, 255.
[4] Mrs. Smith, 13–15.   [5] *Ibid.*, 4.

related to both Lord Baltimore and Mrs. Washington, who aspired
to the scepter of Mrs. Bingham, was a worldly woman, overfond
of admiration and company, and finally there was a divorce. But
at this time she drew the gayer element to her by her merry
hospitality. 'Lay down your hat, we have a fine roast turkey and
you must stay and eat it,' she would say to a caller, and soon
others would casually appear, and an informal party would result.[1]
Callers in the old houses in Georgetown where Southern hospitality held sway, found 'bread, butter, ham, and cakes set before them,' and on leaving they would likely as not carry away
cake and apples in their pockets, a bottle of milk in their hands.[2]
Great was the amusement of the fashionable men and women, who
had been so elegantly served at the Binghams' by the French chef,
on finding themselves jolting over the dirt roads to their lodgings
with their pockets crammed with cake.

This was the Washington into which Jefferson was carried in a
stage-coach for the decisive struggle of his career. Wishing to pay
his respects to Adams, for whom he felt more respect than did the
Hamiltonian wing of the President's own party, he wondered if the
inordinate vanity of his defeated rival would interpret the call as
an attempt to humiliate him. He determined to take the chance.
Entering the President's house, he found Adams alone — the old
man in those difficult days was all but isolated. One glance was
enough to justify the caller's fears. In great agitation, and neglecting first to offer his visitor a chair, Adams burst forth: 'You have
turned me out; you have turned me out.'

With the gentleness of an elder soothing a hurt child, Jefferson
replied, drawing on his familiarity with the workings of the minds
and hearts of men, 'I have not turned you out, Mr. Adams; and I
am glad to avail myself of this occasion to show that I have not
and to explain my views. In consequence of a division of opinion
existing among our fellow-citizens, as to the proper constitution
of our political institutions, and of the wisdom and propriety of
certain measures . . . that portion of our citizens that approved
and advocated one class of these opinions and measures selected
you as their candidate . . . and their opponents selected me. If
you and myself had been inexistent, or for any cause had not been

[1] Mrs. Smith, **3.**   [2] *Ibid.,* **5.**

selected, other persons would have been selected in our places; and thus the contest would have been carried on, and with the same result, except that the party which supported you would have been defeated by a greater majority, as it was known that, but for you, your party would have carried their unpopular measures much further than they did.' Suffering as he was under the treachery of the Hamiltonians, this softened the unhappy President's mood. Jefferson was offered a chair. The two men, who had been intimate in Revolutionary days and in Paris, engaged in a friendly discussion of the topics of the day, and parted with mutual expressions of respect.

Jefferson returned to Conrad's boarding-house, where he had taken a suite of rooms. It was a commodious house, standing on a hill, the precipitate sides of which were covered with grass and shrubs in a natural state. The windows of Jefferson's rooms commanded a beautiful view of the surrounding country — the level plain between the hill and the Potomac through which the tree-lined Taber wound its course; and the man of Monticello could look down from his windows on the tulip-poplar trees, the magnolia, the azalea, the wild rose, the hawthorn. Characteristically enough, he had gone to Conrad's because of the charms of the scenery. There the man of the hour lived like the other lodgers, with the exception of having a drawing-room for the reception of visitors; eating at the common table with the others, at the foot of the table nearest the door and most remote from the fire. When Mrs. John Brown, wife of the Kentucky Senator, insisted that he sit at the head of the table, as the oldest man if not as the Vice-President, he waved the suggestion aside with a smile of deprecation, and there, in the coldest part of the room, he continued until he moved into the President's house. But for Mrs. Brown and Mrs. Theodorus Bailey, wife of a Jeffersonian Congressman from New York, the mess table would have resembled 'a refectory of monks.'[1] Living under the same roof during the hectic weeks that followed were Gallatin who shared his room with Varnum, a Democrat from Massachusetts, Senator John Langdon, General Sam Smith of Maryland, Senator Abraham Baldwin of Georgia, Senator Wilson Carey Nicholas of Virginia, his brother, the

[1] Gallatin's expression; Adams, *Gallatin*, 252–53.

Virginia Representative, and the Browns and Baileys. In the impending crisis Jefferson could scarcely have surrounded himself with a better board of strategy. There we will leave him for a while to take up the threads of the Federalist conspiracy to prevent his election and thwart the public will.

II

While Jefferson was calmly observing the development of the conspiracy, and Gouverneur Morris was reflecting on the absurdity of the human comedy, Alexander Hamilton sat in his office in New York writing feverishly to the leaders of his party. If he wrote in bitterness it was because he was fighting for the last vestige of his prestige as a leader. It had been ominous enough when he lost control of the party caucus and the leaders of the second class deserted him for Adams, but now, to his horror, he found the leaders of the first class scheming for the election of Burr, his pet aversion, to the Presidency. This was too much. Through the latter part of December, the indignant sparks flew from his fast-flying pen as he sought desperately to dissuade the conspirators who had been his faithful servitors. On the 16th he wrote Wolcott of his hope that 'New England at least will not so far lose its head as to fall into this snare.' Jefferson was infinitely preferable, because 'not so dangerous a man' and because he had 'pretensions to character.' But Burr was a 'bankrupt beyond redemption except by the plunder of his country.' He was 'the Catiline of America.' Would Wolcott communicate these views to Marshall and Sedgwick and reply speedily? [1] The next day Hamilton and his erstwhile idolater, Otis, were both busy with their pens. The former, in an evident fever of anxiety, was writing again to Wolcott. It was incredible that Federalists should be considering Burr. Within the last three weeks at his own table he had toasted the French Republic, the commissioners on both sides who had negotiated the peace, Bonaparte and Lafayette. Could anything have been more monstrous? 'Alas, when will men consult their reasons rather than their passions?' he asked. Elect Burr merely to mortify the Democrats by the defeat of Jefferson? 'This disposition reminds me of the conduct of the Dutch moneyed man,

[1] Hamilton's *Works*, x, 392–93.

who, from hatred of the old aristocracy, favored the admission of the French into Holland to overturn everything. Adieu to the Federal Troy if they once introduce this Grecian horse into their citadel.' [1]

While Hamilton was writing thus to Wolcott, Otis, in Boston, was writing to Hamilton. 'It is palpable,' he wrote, 'that to elect Burr is to cover the opposition with chagrin and to sow among them the seeds of morbid division.' But how open communication with Burr? 'We in Massachusetts do not know the man. You do. Please advise us.' [2] Hearing a few days later that Sedgwick was deep in the plot, Hamilton wrote him with almost hysterical earnestness. 'For heaven's sake, let not the Federalist party be responsible for the elevation of this man [Burr].' [3] Two days more, and Hamilton was writing in New York; Harper, who had been his idolater, was similarly engaged in Baltimore. The former was writing Morris, seeking an understanding with Jefferson; Harper was writing Aaron Burr, proffering an alliance. 'Jefferson or Burr? The former without all doubt,' wrote Hamilton. 'Let our situation be improved to obtain from Jefferson assurances on certain points — the maintenance of the present system, especially on the cardinal articles of public credit — a navy, neutrality. Make any discreet use you think fit with this letter.' [4] Alas, the flimsiness of political friendship! At that very hour Harper was writing Burr that the contest would be settled in the House. 'The language of the Democrats is that you will yield your pretensions to their favorite. . . . I advise you to take no step whatever by which the choice of the House . . . can be impeded or embarrassed. Keep the game perfectly in your own hands, but do not answer this letter, or any other that may be written to you by a Federal man, nor write to any of that party.' [5]

No importunities from Hamilton were necessary in the case of Morris, who had taken the high ground 'that since it was evidently the intention of our fellow citizens to make Mr. Jefferson their President, it seems proper to fulfill that intention.' [6] Such was his response to Hamilton, who responded gratefully to the loyalty of

[1] Hamilton's *Works*, x, 393–97.
[2] Parton, *Burr*, i, 267.
[3] Hamilton's *Works*, x, 397.
[4] *Ibid.*, 393–97.
[5] McLaughlin, *Matthew Lyon*, 386.
[6] Parton, *Burr*, i, 270.

one follower. 'If there is a man in the world I ought to hate,' he wrote, 'it is Jefferson. With Burr I have always been personally well. But the public good must be paramount to every private consideration.' [1] The next day Hamilton was bearing down hard on James A. Bayard, a Federalist Representative from Delaware, with an excoriation of Burr as liable to overturn the government to extend his power. Was it possible that Federalists were thinking of arrangements with a man of Burr's character? 'No engagement that may be made with him can be depended upon. While making it, he will laugh in his sleeve at the credulity of those with whom he makes it; and the first moment it suits his views to break it he will do so.' [2] At the same time he was appealing to John Rutledge of South Carolina to assist in crushing the Federalists' conspiracy as 'a service to your country.' [3] That month, too, Senator Ross of Pennsylvania heard from New York. 'Mr. Burr is the last man in the United States to be supported by the Federalists,' he read. Why not seek an understanding with Jefferson? [4]

But as December faded from the calendar, the colossal genius of Federalism found himself in a position of pitiful impotency and isolation. Morris and Jay shared his views, but even the New York friends of his youth, like Troup, were unresponsive, and most of the leaders, who had once responded gladly to his nod, were ignoring his frantic efforts and proceeding with their plans. On the day he was writing Bayard, two men knocked at the lodgings of Morris, and Robert Goodhue Harper and Senator Henry Latimer of Delaware appeared to electioneer the delightful cynic whose cynicism held so much of wisdom. The voluble Harper was the spokesman. Burr, he said, was his 'intimate friend.' It was advisable, he thought, to elect Burr 'without asking or expecting any assurances respecting his future administration.' There was enough in Burr's temper and disposition to give ample security 'for a conduct hostile to the democratic spirit.' Morris listened patiently, and dryly suggested the wisdom of the House suspending its determination 'until they can have more light as to the merit and probable conduct of the candidates.' [5] Unable to see

[1] Hamilton's *Works*, x, 401.   [2] *Ibid.*, 402–04.   [3] *Ibid.*, 404–05.
[4] *Ibid.*, 405–07.   [5] Morris, *Diary*, ii, 397.

with the majority of his party, Morris, who had touched life at so many points and in so many places, did not share in Hamilton's rage. 'Indeed, my dear friend,' he wrote Robert Livingston about this time, 'this farce of life contains nothing which should put us out of humor.' [1] With Harper making a personal canvass for Burr, Judge Samuel Sewall, of the Essex Junto, was urging Otis to stand for 'a steady and decided vote of the Federal party for Mr. Burr,' because it might at any rate prevent an election — a consummation 'most desirable.' [2]

Meanwhile Burr, pretending preoccupation with the approaching nuptials of his brilliant Theodosia, was suavely simulating, if he did not feel, a distaste for the plan of his 'intimate friend' Harper. When the movement in his behalf was first launched, he wrote General Sam Smith that he would 'disclaim all competition' with Jefferson, that the Federalists 'could entertain no wish for such an exchange,' and that his friends would dishonor his views and insult his feelings 'by a suspicion that I would submit to be instrumental in counteracting the wishes and expectations of the United States.' But eight days later, Harper had written him an encouraging letter on the prospects and he appears to have followed the admonition not to reply. After that — silence.

At Conrad's boarding-house the calmest man at the long table in the dining-room was Jefferson. He knew the plans of the opposition to prevent an election or to elect Burr, and noted the gloom among his friends and the exultation of his enemies. He was quite calm.

III

January found Hamilton still feverishly busy at his writing-desk. His worst fears had, by this time, been confirmed. His bosom friends had smiled incredulously upon his protests against Burr. The conspiracy was spreading ominously. His voice had lost its potency, his sword its shimmer. Grimly he fought against fate. McHenry had been impressed with the propaganda for Burr. A number of the Federalist leaders had escaped from the frog ponds of the capital to enjoy Christmas festivities in Baltimore, and from these he heard but one opinion — Burr should be

[1] Morris, *Diary*, II, 404.   [2] Morison, *Otis*, I, 211–12.

supported. Burr's letter to Smith? These worldly Federalists laughed derisively. He would not resent being elected by Federalist votes. Even McHenry thought that with Burr elected 'we may flatter ourselves that he will not suffer the executive power to be frittered away.' Still, he had misgivings. 'Can we promise ourselves that he will not continue to seek and depend upon his own party for support?' [1] It was with these doubts in his mind that McHenry opened a letter from Hamilton, whom he worshiped. Here he found Burr denounced as 'a profligate,' as a 'voluptuary,' as 'an extortionist' in his profession, as insolvent and dangerous.[2] A word from Hamilton was enough, and McHenry joined his leader in combating the Federalist plans in Maryland — and not without effect. But with Senator William Hindman, who had been a supporter of Hamilton in the House, nothing could be done. He was aggressively for Burr.[3] In early January, Pickering, still pitying himself, was not shocked at the idea of Burr's election. The suggestion that 'the federalist interest will not be so systematically opposed under Mr. Burr as under Jefferson' impressed him. Then 'in case of war with any European power there can be no doubt which of the two would conduct it with most ability and energy.' [4]

Meanwhile Bayard had sent a non-committal reply to Hamilton. He had found 'a strong inclination of the majority' of the Federalists to support Burr with the disposition growing. He ought, therefore, to have strong grounds for separating himself from the others. While their action could not bind him, it would be a painful wrench to leave them. Still, 'the magnitude of the subject forbids the sacrifice of strong conviction.' As the pen of Bayard traveled over the page, the conspirators were moving about him, for he wrote in the House of Representatives.[5] In truth, all Hamilton's advices were disturbing. Former Senator Gunn of Georgia, in sympathy with him, was afraid 'some of our friends have committed themselves by writing improperly to Burr.' [6] Even John Rutledge, while disgusted at the idea of either Jefferson or Burr in the Presidency, found his party associates convinced that 'Burr

[1] King's *Works*, III, 363.   [2] Steiner, 485–88.   [3] *Ibid.*, 489–90.
[4] King's *Works* (Pickering to King), III, 366.
[5] Parton, *Burr*, I, 272–73.   [6] *Ibid.*, 274.

will be the least mischief,' and that his election would be 'prodigiously afflicting to the Virginia faction and must disjoint the party.[1]'

It is easy to imagine Hamilton laying down the letter of Rutledge with a frown, to open one which had arrived from Sedgwick in the same mail, to get a greater shock. It was a vigorous plea for Burr. The author found it 'very evident that the Jacobins dislike Mr. Burr as President' and that 'he hates them for the preference given to his rival.' He had 'expressed displeasure over the publication of his letter to General Smith.' Would not 'this jealousy and distrust and dislike . . . every day more and more increase and more and more widen the breach between them?' Would not the election of Burr by the Federalists cause 'incurable' wounds? Then again, 'to what evils should we expose ourselves by the choice of Burr, which we should escape by the election of Jefferson?' True, given an opportunity, Burr would be more likely to become a 'usurper' — but what of that?[2]

About this time, in the middle of the month, the Federalists met to determine on their course. The caucus was not entirely harmonious, but the Burr sentiment was overwhelming. Shocked and inwardly enraged at the disaffection of his friends, Hamilton now redoubled his efforts, and in a 'very, very confidential' letter to Bayard dissected the character of Burr, demolished the arguments of his Federalist supporters, and pronounced Jefferson far superior in real ability. To this he gave a personal touch — something he had hitherto held back. 'It is past all doubt,' he said, 'that he has blamed me for not having improved the situation I once was in to change the government; that when answered that this could not have been done without guilt, he replied, "Les grandes âmes se soucient peu des petits moraux"; and when told that the thing was never practical from the genius and situation of the country, he answered, "That depends on the estimate we form of the human passions, and of the means of influencing them." Does this prove that Mr. Burr would consider a scheme of usurpation as visionary?'[3] Four days after sending this letter to Bayard, Hamilton was writing Morris of the inability of the conspirators to get assurances from Burr, who complained that it would injure him with

[1] Parton, *Burr*, I, 274-75.   [2] *Ibid.*, 277-78.   [3] Hamilton's *Works*, x, 412-19.

his friends. 'Depend upon it,' he warned, 'men never played a more foolish game than will do the Federalists if they support Burr.'[1] But Hamilton was striving against the basest, lowest instincts of his party. One of his Boston followers was writing King at this very time that he favored Burr because 'his opposition heretofore' had 'arisen from ambitious motives,' and because he was 'not as honest in his politics as Jefferson.'[2] No one was a stouter contender against Hamilton's decent patriotic impulses than Sedgwick, who was moved by the motives just indicated.[3] No one knew it better than Hamilton, but he persisted. 'I never was so much mistaken,' he wrote Sedgwick, 'as I shall be if our friends in the event of their success do not rue the preference they will give to that Catiline.'[4] Fighting desperately, Hamilton looked clear-eyed upon the repudiation of his leadership of the party into which he had breathed the breath of life and given the dignity of power by the prestige of his genius. Among his friends he made no secret of his depression, admitting to them that his 'influence with the federal party was wholly gone' and that he 'could no longer be useful.'[5] Had he created a Frankenstein to destroy not only himself but his policies and country? he wondered.

All through that month there was only serenity at Conrad's boarding-house in Washington. Thoroughly informed of every move made by the enemy, Jefferson discussed the situation in the evenings with Gallatin, the Nicholases, and General Smith. Such was his imperturbable temperament that in the midst of the intense excitement he was able to write to one friend of a meteorological diary from Quebec, and to another on a similar one from Natchez.[6] His cause was in the keeping of Gallatin, who was quietly checking up on all members of the House, closing his own ranks, preparing for every possible contingency, and concluding that 'the intention of the desperate leaders must be absolute usurpation and the overthrow of our Constitution.'[7] Thus January passed, and February came with its fateful possibilities.

[1] Hamilton's *Works*, x, 419–20.
[2] King's *Works* (J. Hale to King), iii, 372.
[3] *Ibid.* (Sedgwick to King), 455.   [4] Hamilton's *Works*, x, 420.
[5] King's *Works* (Troup to King), iii, 391.
[6] Jefferson's *Works* (to Hugh Williamson), x, 188; (to William Dunbar), 191.
[7] Adams, *Gallatin* (Gallatin to his wife), 257.

IV

As the time for the contest approached, the village capital over-flowed with visitors of stern visage. The boarding-houses packed with members of Congress, these onlookers found lodgment in Georgetown and in Alexandria. Notwithstanding the bitterness of the fight there was no trouble — due to stern repression. A little spark would have caused an explosion. The American people had determined on Jefferson, and it was no longer a secret that forces were at work to defeat the public will. Some of the Federalist papers deprecated the attempt to elect Burr with Federalist votes. The New York 'Commercial Advertiser' made vigorous protest in denunciation of the conspirators. 'They are now taking the ground which the Democrats have occupied and descending to the baseness of supporting their cause by railing, abuse and scur-rility. Nothing can be less politic or honorable. It is the duty of good citizens to acquiesce in the election and be tranquil. It is proper that Mr. Jefferson should be made Chief Magistrate.' [1] The same note was struck by the New York 'Gazette.' 'Many advocate the support of Mr. Burr,' it said. 'In matters of such importance it is idle to suffer our passions to get the better of our reason; and in statesmanship it would be particularly culpable from such puerile motives to risk the welfare of the nation. . . . Bad as both these men [Jefferson and Burr] are, there is no com-parison between them.' [2] But the organ of the Essex Junto was openly advocating Burr's election. The 'Centinel' of Boston teemed with Burr propaganda. 'The people of New England have yet faith to believe that a good tree cannot bring forth bad fruit, nor vice versa,' it said. 'They think the stock from which Mr. Jefferson has sprung to be bad because his works are known to be so; and . . . that whatever Mr. Burr may be reported to be he will eventually turn out good; as he is the grandson of the dignified Edwards, the great American luminary of Divinity, and a son of President Burr who was also a burning and shining light in the churches.' [3] At times it fell into verse:

[1] *Commercial Advertiser*, January 17, 1801.
[2] Reprinted in Connecticut *Courant*, January 26, 1801.
[3] *Centinel*, January 28, 1801.

'Stop ere your civic feasts begin;
Wait till the votes are all come in;
Perchance amidst this mighty stir
Your monarch may be Colonel Burr.' [1]

A correspondent from Washington was quoted approvingly on the plan to support Burr — 'the expediency of which course is so palpable to common sense . . . that I am astonished any Federal man should hesitate upon the subject.' [2] And the 'Centinel' expressed the hope that it would be able 'by Saturday next to announce either that the people will have another opportunity to elect a Federal President; or that the House, rejecting a theoretical and experimental philosopher, will prefer, as a very respectable member of Congress describes Mr. Burr, "a practical gentleman who will have judgment, taste and genius enough to appreciate the usefulness of our federal fabric, and nerve enough to preserve its integrity."' [3]

There was no longer any doubt that the Federalist hot-heads were ready for usurpation and revolutionary measures. It was known to every Democrat of any consequence in the country. Gallatin, counting noses, had no fear of desertions from the Jeffersonian ranks. The real danger, as the little conclave at Conrad's saw it, was the prevention of an election, and Gallatin was certain that, to prevent this calamity, a Federalist from Maryland and Morris of Vermont would go over to Jefferson. A plan to meet this contingency was drawn up by Gallatin and accepted by the chief. More sinister still was the threat, commonly heard, that should the Federalists succeed in preventing an election, they would pass a law placing the Presidency in the hands of Marshall or some other official. This the Democrats were prepared to resist by physical force. To prevent this usurpation, the Jeffersonians notified Governor M'Kean of Pennsylvania and Governor Monroe of Virginia, who were prepared to march troops instantly upon the capital 'for the purpose, not of promoting, but of preventing revolution and the shedding of a single drop of blood.' [4] A careful survey convinced Gallatin that this scheme of usurpation would not have mustered more than twenty votes among the Federalist

[1] *Centinel*, January 7, 1801.   [2] *Ibid.*, February 11, 1801.   [3] *Ibid.*
[4] Adams, *Gallatin*, 248–51.

members. Only Henry Lee, 'a desperate character,' and Roger Griswold of Connecticut, a bigot, appeared to Gallatin to be really favorable to such a monstrous measure. Even so the rumor spread, and it was said that fifteen hundred men in Virginia and Maryland had agreed in the event a usurper were placed in the Presidency to move on Washington to assassinate him.[1]

Jefferson had other plans in view, which he conveyed only to Madison and Monroe — to call a convention to reorganize the Government and amend the Constitution, but he concealed this from Gallatin.[2] The Gallatin plan, with its military feature, leaked out, causing some uneasiness among the conspirators, who proceeded, however, with their plans. The 'Centinel' boasted that Federalists had no fear of Southern and Western fighters. 'Our General [Burr] if called upon can assure them that he has seen southern regiments in former times and knows what they are composed of.'[3]

Meanwhile the Federalists proceeded with their plans. Burr, concealing himself in Albany, was maintaining a discreet silence, and on February 1st, Jefferson wrote him a letter. At no time had he any confidence in Burr's political honesty or reliability. During the two Federalist Administrations he had observed that, whenever a great military or diplomatic appointment was to be made, Burr had hurried to Philadelphia and was 'always at market if they wanted him.' Jefferson had thought it wise to remain rather distant.[4] But he was too sagacious to reveal his distrust at this juncture. He had no thought of giving Burr any excuse for treachery, and enemies had been busy with a forged letter bearing Jefferson's signature setting forth uncomplimentary opinions. He wrote to call attention to the forgery and denounce it. 'It was to be expected,' he wrote, 'that the enemy would endeavor to sow tares between us that they might divide us and our friends.' If the letter was ever answered, the reply has been lost.

On the day Jefferson sat in his room at Conrad's writing Burr, Gouverneur Morris's morning slumber was interrupted by two

[1] Adams, *Gallatin*, 248–51.
[2] *Ibid.*
[3] *Centinel*, February 18, 1801, before the result of the election was known.
[4] *Anas*, I, 381.

visitors who wished to discuss with him the organization of Burr's Administration. 'Laughable enough under the circumstances which now exist,' chuckled the cynic.[1] Two days later, still serene, Jefferson was writing Dr. Caspar Wistar of some bones recently discovered which the Doctor wished for the museum. The candidate had taken the trouble to write Chancellor Livingston, and the reply was inspired by the latter's letter in answer. With the village capital crowded, with talk of revolution, usurpation, assassination, he wrote at length. Perhaps it would be better to ask only for the bones missing from the museum's collection, as the town where they were found would probably be loath to part with them at all. Even then the philosopher and scientist was not wholly lost in the politician.[2]

In New York, Hamilton, having gone his limit, was no longer writing letters. The indifference of his erstwhile followers had left him depressed and bitter. Then, one day at the Tontine Coffee-House, he had an opportunity to renew his warning in the most dramatic manner. Wolcott had resigned from the Cabinet, his treachery still unsuspected by Adams, to be wined and dined by the Federalist members of Congress in Washington, and toasted by the merchants of Philadelphia and New York. After the regular toasts had been given at the Tontine and volunteers were in order, Hamilton rose, and in his most impressive manner proposed: 'May our government never fall a prey to the dreams of a Condorcet NOR THE VICES OF A CATILINE.'[3] 'The vices of a Catiline' was the one expression remembered by the diners as they poured out into the streets.

The next day the balloting was to begin. On the day of the dinner at the Tontine the 'Commercial Advertiser' predicted the election of Burr on the second ballot; and that same day Representative William Cooper was writing a friend of the determination of the Federalists 'to run Burr perseveringly' and to 'leave the consequences to those who have hitherto been his friends.'[4] At Conrad's boarding-house all was serene.

[1] Morris, *Diary*, II, 403.
[2] Jefferson's *Works*, x, 196–97.
[3] Connecticut *Courant*, February 11, 1801.
[4] Parton, *Burr*, I, 288.

V

In a blinding snowstorm the lawmakers and spectators fought their way to the Capitol on Wednesday morning, the 11th. Nature spread a white mantle over the crudities of the village as though to dress it becomingly for the great day. The great plain between the foot of the hill and the river was covered with a spotless sheet, and even the shop of the shoemaker and the home of the wash-woman took on the appearance of beauty. No one minded the storm, not even Joseph H. Nicholson of Maryland, who, though bedridden with fever, insisted on being carried through the storm to cast his ballot for Jefferson. The electoral votes being counted in a joint session of the two houses, the members of the House re-tired to their own chamber to elect a President. The crowded gallery was ordered cleared. The visitors, grumbling loudly, filed out into the corridors. When Samuel Harrison Smith, editor of the 'National Intelligencer,' who had established his paper in the capital on the advice of Jefferson, insisted on remaining, he was angrily ordered out by Theodore Sedgwick, the Speaker. Ar-rangements were thereupon made by the Jeffersonians to keep Smith informed hourly of the fortunes of the fight. In a committee room off the chamber lay Nicholson on a bed, burning with fever, an anxious wife at his side to give him water and medicine. Even the conspirators could not restrain their admiration. 'It is a chance that this kills him,' wrote Otis. 'I would not thus expose myself for any President on earth.' [1] The stricken Democrat was not there, however, against the wishes of his wife, who had the fighting spirit of a Spartan woman.

The first ballot found Jefferson with eight States — Burr with six — nine necessary to a choice. Another ballot immediately — the same result. A third, fourth, fifth, sixth, seventh — no change. As each ballot was taken, a teller from Maryland entered the little committee room where Nicholson lay fighting the fever, his head supported by the arm of his wife. He was awakened from his fitful sleep, a pencil was put in his trembling fingers, and with his wife's aid in guiding the pencil the name of Jefferson was written. The pencil fell from his hand — he slept again.[2] At the

[1] Morison, *Otis*, I, 207–08.   [2] Mrs. Smith, 24.

end of the eighth ballot a motion to vote again in an hour prevailed. There was little electioneering — men's minds were made up. Only a buzz of conversation, some laughter.

The ninth ballot, the tenth, eleventh, twelfth, thirteenth, fourteenth, fifteenth ballots — and no change. Darkness had long since fallen on snow-covered Washington. Bed-clothing, blankets, pillows, had been brought in. The Federalists had determined to hold on without adjournment. At nine o'clock the sixteenth ballot brought no change. At ten o'clock the seventeenth, at eleven the eighteenth — and no change. The motion was made to adjourn until Thursday, only to be voted down. At midnight the nineteenth ballot was taken, with the lines unbroken. By this time the members were slipping off to cloak and committee rooms between ballots to sleep, and some slept in their chairs. As a ballot was called, it was 'ludicrous to see them running from committee rooms with night caps on.' [1] The crowd in the corridors dwindled, a few stubbornly held on. Every hour a messenger waded laboriously through the heavy snow to the home of the editor of 'The Intelligencer' with the results. No sleep in that house that night. When the knock at the door was heard, the editor's wife, her heart beating audibly, as she thought, could scarcely open to receive the paper.[2]

At one o'clock another ballot — then at two. Nature was beginning to claim its toll when it was agreed not to vote again until four o'clock. After that the ballots were taken hourly throughout the night. When the twenty-seventh ballot was taken at eight o'clock and the motion was made to vote no more until noon, there were no protests. The vote at noon found the opposing lines unbroken. The House adjourned until eleven o'clock on Friday — the next day.

Friday: larger crowds about the Capitol. Nicholson still on his bed. When the twenty-ninth ballot showed no change, an adjournment was taken until noon on Saturday.

Meanwhile the participants in the struggle were sending out meager reports on the results. While the first ballots were being taken on Wednesday, Jefferson had written Tench Coxe: 'For some time since, a single individual has said he would by his vote

---

[1] *Commercial Advertiser*, February 16, 1801.   [2] Mrs. Smith, 24.

make up the ninth State. On Saturday last he changed, and it stands at present eight one way, six the other, and two divided. Which of the two will be elected, and whether either, I deem perfectly problematical; and my mind has long since been equally made up for either of the three events.'[1] Otis, writing his wife, was more interested in the scene at the sick bed than in conjectures.[2] Gallatin wrote Mrs. Gallatin of the results without comment, other than that he had slept from eight o'clock until noon on Thursday morning.[3] Saturday found the lines still holding, but with the conspirators subjected to a heavy and disturbing fire from outside. An imposing petition from Federalists in Maryland had been sent John Chew Thomas declaring that two thirds of his constituents favored Jefferson. Gallatin did 'not know what effect they would have,'[4] and the thing that worried the Federalists was that they knew no better. Some of these were finding the backfire distressing. Others were openly disgusted with Burr. 'Had Burr done anything for himself, he would long ere this have been President,' wrote Cooper of New York.[5] It was clearly time to push the contest. Thus, on Saturday three ballots were taken without results, and the House adjourned until noon Monday.

Meanwhile, Jefferson, presiding over the Senate, surrounded by hatred and excitement, presented an unruffled front, an untouched temper. From time to time he could hear the angry discussions of his enemies, but he made no sign. His impartiality was beyond question. 'A spectator,' wrote a contemporary, 'who watched his countenance would never have surmised that he had any personal interest in the impending event.'[6] From the Capitol he walked like one unconcerned back to Conrad's, enjoying the snow. Some of the politicians sought to wring concessions from him to gain support, but he was adamant. General Sam Smith, without his authority or knowledge, entered into a negotiation, which had no effect beyond furnishing the groundwork for the charge of his enemies in history that he had made arrangements. As far as we know he was openly approached by but one — and he was acting on the suggestion of Alexander Hamilton.

[1] Jefferson's *Works*, x, 198–99.　　[2] Morison, *Otis*, I, 207–08.
[3] Adams, *Gallatin*, 260–61.　　[4] *Ibid.*, 261–62.
[5] Parton. *Burr*, I, 238.　　[6] Mrs. Smith, 23.

One day, as Jefferson was descending the steps of the Capitol, he met Gouverneur Morris and they paused to exchange compliments. Differing as widely as the poles, they had enjoyed their social contacts in Paris. The conversation turned naturally to the contest, and Morris observed, significantly, that the opposition to Jefferson's election on the part of some was the fear that he would turn all Federalists out of office, put down the navy, and wipe out the debt. All that was necessary to his election was the assurance that none of these steps would be taken. 'I must leave the world to judge the course I mean to pursue by that which I have pursued hitherto,' Jefferson replied. 'I believe it my duty to be passive and silent during the present contest. I shall certainly make no terms, and shall never go into the office of President by capitulation, nor with my hands tied by any conditions which will hinder me from pursuing the measures which I shall deem for the public good.' The two parted in the best of feeling.

The crisis was now approaching. Public sentiment was asserting itself unmistakably, and statesmen could hear afar off the cracking of the whips. The Jeffersonians would clearly not budge. Even Nicholson was recovering instead of sinking under the exposure and excitement. The Federalists in their caucuses were breaking up after stormy meetings. It was agreed that nothing was left but desperate measures, and, while but few urged their adoption, few openly disapproved. Burr was an ever-increasing torment. Only his coöperation was needed, said Bayard afterward, to have won. 'By deceiving one man (a great blockhead) and tempting two (not incorruptible), he might have secured a majority of the States.' [1] But Burr was in Albany, silent as the sphinx and inactive as a mummy.

Over Sunday the leaders caucused and cursed. When the House met on Monday, Gallatin understood that Bayard was going to vote for Jefferson and end the fight. But on the one ballot taken on Monday, he remained with Burr. 'But it is supposed,' wrote Gallatin to his father-in-law, 'that the cause of delay is to make an attempt on his party and some others to prevail on the whole Federal party to come over.' [2]

The conferences continued on Monday and by night a decision

---

[1] Parton, *Burr;* Letter to Hamilton.   [2] Adams, *Gallatin,* 262.

had been reached. Nothing could be gained by fighting for a man who would not fight. The public was in an ugly mood. Hamilton's friends, like Bayard, were feeling a little ashamed of themselves. On Tuesday a crowd was packed in the corridors of the Capitol and in front of the building. Weary men in petulant mood pushed their way through these farmers, mechanics, and politicians to the House. A vote was immediately taken. Morris, Federalist from Vermont, withdrew, permitting Matthew Lyon to cast the vote of the State for Jefferson. The Maryland Federalists cast blank ballots — permitting the Democrats to put their State in the Jefferson column. Bayard, after much meandering, finally satisfied Hamilton by casting a blank, which, being the only vote to which his State was entitled, left Delaware out entirely. And Theodore Sedgwick, in a rage, was forced formally to announce the election of Thomas Jefferson. The throng in the corridors and in front of the Capitol gave way to noisy rejoicing, and the conspirators hurried to their lodgings to escape the scowls of the populace.

VI

While most of them hurried home, three members of the House, including two of the vanquished, with Thomas Pinckney as spokesman, made their way with many jests, we may be sure, up the slushy Avenue, between the frog ponds, to the President's house to notify John Adams that his successor had been chosen. No record of their reception remains, but the imagination can supply the want. Nor is there any record that Adams sent a note of congratulation to the victor. Those were the days when 'The Duke of Braintree's' morbid vanity was suffering keenly the flings of outrageous fortune.

Two days later, the same committee formally notified Jefferson of his election and was asked to convey a gracious response to the House.[1] Meanwhile, unflurried and unhurried, he went his way, appearing in the Senate, as usual to preside, and continuing to occupy the foot of the table at Conrad's boarding-house. He had long since determined upon Madison for the head of the Cabinet and Gallatin for the Treasury, gigantic figures compared with those who had occupied these posts after Jefferson and Hamilton

[1] *Annals*, February 21, 1801.

had left them in the days of Washington. The other positions were filled during the two weeks intervening between the election and the inauguration.

On Saturday before his inauguration on Wednesday, Jefferson appeared for the last time in the Senate to withdraw from his post there in a farewell address. There before him sat men who hated him venomously, but the suave, serene victor took leave as though departing with sorrow from a cherished circle of congenial souls. Mistakes he had probably made, but he had sought to 'observe impartial justice,' and his measurable success had been due to the generosity and uniform courtesy of the members. Could he but carry to his new station such support as he had received from the Senate, he would 'consider it as commencing under the happiest auspices.' In tendering his 'cordial and respectful adieux,' he wished for all both health and happiness. With a courtly bow he descended from the rostrum, and passed out of the chamber.

On Monday, Gouverneur Morris, chairman of the committee named to make response, reported an answer matching the courtliness of Jefferson's farewell. It lamented 'the loss of that intelligence, attention, and impartiality' with which Jefferson had presided, and expressed appreciation of the kindly expressions on the Senate. Then, as Morris proceeded, there was a savage wagging of heads among the die-hards, as he read: 'In the confidence that your official conduct will be directed to those great objects [the honor and interests of the country] — a confidence derived from past events, we repeat to you, sir, the assurance of our Constitutional support in your future administration.' Instantly an irreconcilable was on his feet with a motion to strike out the words, 'derived from past events.' The roll was called. The motion was lost by a vote of 9 to 19. The intolerant Tracy and Ross voted with the nine, but Morris carried some of his party with him.[1] The next day Morris reported Jefferson's reply — a gesture of appreciation.

As the day of the inauguration approached, great crowds began to pour into the drab little capital from the surrounding country. In the President's house and in the Senate there was feverish activity. Early in the session, the Federalists, realizing that their

[1] *Annals*, March 2, 1801.

power was over in the executive and legislative branches, sought to maintain themselves and provide for their favorites through the creation of many Federal judgeships. The purpose was transparent. The Democrats had fought the measure without avail. All that now remained was for Adams to pack the courts with partisans as narrow and intolerant as those who had for ten years been delivering common party harangues from the Bench. With the joyous visitors wading the muddy streets in holiday mood, with Jefferson closeted with his friends at Conrad's, the Senate was busy confirming these partisan Judges, and in the Executive Department they were busy signing the commissions. Night came — and John Marshall remained in his office making them out.

To this drama of hate, Adams gave a touch of irony in selecting the beneficiaries of his generosity. Wolcott had left him but a little while before. Through four years he had played the game of Adams's enemies, presenting all the while a smiling countenance to his chief. We have seen him lingering on in the citadel after Pickering and McHenry had been thrown from the battlements, to wig-wag secret messages to the enemy in New York. But Adams had suspected nothing. Moved by an impulse of gratitude, he offered Wolcott a life position on the Bench, and that consummate actor, smiling still, sent the assurance that 'gratitude to benefactors is among the most amiable . . . of social obligations,'[1] and accepted. There is something of pathos to the Adams of the sunset. Something of pathos and inspiration, too — for, to the disgust of the inner circle of his party, he made John Marshall Chief Justice of the United States, and thus, unwittingly, saved the better part of Federalism from the wreckage of the temple, to fight on through many years to come.

VII

The morning of inauguration day found the entire nation marching in the streets, exultant Democrats following the fife and drum, singing and shouting hosannas. Merchants locked their doors, mechanics left their work-benches, clerks laid down their pens, farmers deserted their homes for the towns, and from Boston to Savannah men and women celebrated with an enthusiasm not approached since the celebration of the peace in 1783.

[1] Gibbs, II, 497.

In Washington, the thunder of artillery ushered in the day. As it shook the heavens, an embittered old man with a sour countenance sat far back in his coach as it bumped and splashed its way through the mire and over the stumps of the Baltimore road, for at four o'clock in the morning John Adams had slipped out of the house of the Presidents and hurried away, rather than remain to extend the ordinary courtesies to his successor. 'You have no idea,' wrote Gallatin to his wife, 'of the meanness, indecency, almost insanity of his conduct, especially of late. But he is fallen and not dangerous. Let him be forgotten.' [1] Somewhere in hiding, or in flight, was Theodore Sedgwick, Speaker of the House, who could not bear to witness the triumph of a foe.

That morning Jefferson remained quietly at Conrad's, receiving friends. As he entered the dining-room for breakfast, the wife of Senator Brown rose impulsively and offered him her seat. With an appreciative smile he declined and sat down as usual at the end of the table near the door.[2]

At ten o'clock there was a flurry among the men, women, and children standing reverently in front of Jefferson's lodgings, when, with a swinging stride, companies of riflemen and artillery from Alexandria paraded before the boarding-house. At noon, dressed plainly, with nothing to indicate the dignity of his position, Jefferson stepped out of Conrad's, accompanied by citizens and members of Congress, and walked to the Capitol. As he passed the threshold, there was a thunder of artillery. When he entered the little Senate Chamber, the Senators and Representatives rose, and Aaron Burr, now Vice-President, left his seat — all standing until Jefferson sat down in the chair he had occupied until a week before. On his right hand, Burr; on his left, Marshall. Only a little while, and Burr, arrested for treason at the instigation of Jefferson, would be tried by Marshall at Richmond.

After a moment, Jefferson rose and read a conciliatory address, in a tone scarcely audible in the tiny room.[3] 'We are all Republicans; we are all Federalists. If there be any among us who would wish to dissolve this Union, or to change its Republican form, let them stand undisturbed as monuments of the safety with which error of opinion may be tolerated where reason is left free to com-

---

[1] Adams, *Gallatin*, 265. [2] Mrs. Smith. 12. [3] *Ibid.*, 26.

bat it.' As he concluded, he turned to Marshall, his Hamilton of the future. The Chief Justice administered the oath. It was over. The festivities of '83 had celebrated the achievement of the right of the American people to form their own government and make their own laws. The roar of artillery as the new President emerged from the Capitol meant that the real American Revolution had triumphed, and definitely determined that this should be a democratic republic.

In the streets and public-houses that afternoon there was rejoicing, shouting, singing, laughing, drinking. Even the more tolerant of the vanquished fraternized with the victors, and the wife of the editor of the Jeffersonian organ [1] poured tea for Gouverneur Morris, Jonathan Dayton, and James A. Bayard. For the moment 'all were Republicans, all were Federalists.' That night Washington saw its first illumination.

Lumbering along the wretched mud roads in his coach rode Adams, the reverberations of the artillery peal of the morning still hammering on his nerves, meditating bitterly on the treachery of men. . . . Somewhere in hiding, Sedgwick — cursing the fates. . . . And somewhere in New York, Alexander Hamilton was tasting the bitter fruits of the victory he had fought to win for his greatest opponent. From his window he could see the marching men and he could hear the pæans of triumph. The brilliant party he had moulded was in ruins — his leadership scorned by the crawling creatures who had shone only in the reflected light of his brilliance. He was alone — isolated. . . . A little while and he would write Morris, 'What can I do better than withdraw from the scene? Every day proves to me more and more that this American world was not made for me.' [2]. . . A few months, and he would be describing himself as a 'disappointed politician' in a letter to Pinckney requesting melon seeds for his garden and parroquets for his daughter.[3] . . . Four years — and before Burr's pistol he would fall on the banks of the Hudson one tragic summer morning. . . . Some years more, and a visitor to the home of the retired sage of Monticello would see in the hall a marble bust of Hamilton — the tribute of one great man to another.

---

[1] Mrs. Smith.　　　　[2] Hamilton's *Works*, x, 425.　　　　[3] *Ibid.*, x, 444.

The eighteenth century witnessed their Plutarchian battles; the twentieth century uncovers at the graves at Monticello and in Trinity Churchyard — but the spirits of Jefferson and Hamilton still stalk the ways of men — still fighting.

BOOKS, PAMPHLETS, NEWSPAPERS, AND MAGAZINES CITED OR CONSULTED

ADAMS, ABIGAIL. *See* Charles Francis Adams.

ADAMS, CHARLES FRANCIS. *Diary and Autobiography of John Adams; Works of John Adams.* 10 vols. Boston, 1853; *Letters of Mrs. Adams, the Wife of John Adams.* 2 vols. Boston, 1840; *Life of John Adams* (with *Works*).

ADAMS, HENRY. *Life of Albert Gallatin.* Philadelphia, 1879; *Writings of Albert Gallatin* (editor). 3 vols. Philadelphia, 1879.

ADAMS, JOHN. *See* Charles Francis Adams, John T. Morse, Correa Moylan Walsh.

ADAMS, JOHN QUINCY. *See* Worthington C. Ford.

ALEXANDER, D. S. *A Political History of New York.* New York, 1906.

AMES, FISHER. *See* Seth Ames and J. T. Kirkland.

AMES, SETH (editor). *Works of Fisher Ames.* 2 vols. Boston, 1854.

AMORY, THOMAS C. *Life of James Sullivan.* 2 vols. Boston, 1859.

ANDERSON, DICE ROBINS. *William Branch Giles: A Study in the Politics of Virginia and the Nation from 1790 to 1830.* Menasha, Wisconsin, 1914.

AUSTIN, MARY S. *Philip Freneau: Poet of the Revolution.* New York, 1901.

BASSETT, JOHN S. *The Federalist System.* (The American Nation Series.) New York, 1906.

BEARD, CHARLES A. *Economic Origins of Jeffersonian Democracy.* New York, 1915; *An Economic Interpretation of the Constitution of the United States.* New York, 1919.

BECK, JAMES M. *The Constitution of the United States.* (Gray's Inn Lectures.) Printed in England, 1922.

BEMIS, SAMUEL FLAGG. *Jay's Treaty: A Study in Commerce and Diplomacy.* New York, 1923.

BENTON, THOMAS H. *Thirty Years' View; or, A History of the Working of the American Government from 1820 to 1850.* 2 vols. New York, 1861.

BEVERIDGE, ALBERT J. *Life of John Marshall.* 4 vols. Boston, 1916–19.

BIDDLE, CHARLES. *Autobiography.* Philadelphia, 1883.

BROOKS, NOAH. *Henry Knox: A Soldier of the Revolution.* New York, 1900.

BROWN, WILLIAM GARROTT. *The Life of Oliver Ellsworth.* New York, 1905.

BURDICK, CHARLES K. *The Law of the American Constitution: Its Origin and Development.* Philadelphia, 1922.

BURR, AARON. *See* James Parton and Matthew L. Davis.

CABOT, GEORGE. *See* Henry Cabot Lodge.

COBBETT, WILLIAM. *See* Lewis Melville.

COX, JACOB (editor). *The Diary of Jacob Hiltzheimer.* Philadelphia, 1893.

DAVIS, JOHN. *Travels of Four Years and a Half in the United States of America, 1798–1802.* New York, 1909.

DAVIS, MATTHEW L. *Memoirs of Aaron Burr.* 2 vols. New York, 1836.

DODD, WILLIAM E. *Life of Nathaniel Macon.* Raleigh, 1903; *The Statesmen of the Old South; or, From Radicalism to Conservative Revolt.* New York, 1911.

DRAKE, FRANCIS S. *Life and Correspondence of Henry Knox.* Boston, 1873.

ELLET, FRANCES S. *The Queens of American Society.* Philadelphia, 1867.

ELLSWORTH, OLIVER. *See* William Garrott Brown.

FORD, WORTHINGTON CHAUNCEY (editor). *Works of Thomas Jefferson.* 12 vols. 1904–05 (*Anas* and *Autobiography*); *Writings of John Quincy Adams,* 7 vols. New York, 1913.

FRENEAU, PHILIP. *See* Mary S. Austin.

FISKE, JOHN. *Essays, Historical and Literary.* 2 vols. New York, 1907.

GALLATIN, ALBERT. *See* Henry Adams and John A. Stevens.

GAY, SIDNEY HOWARD. *James Madison.* Boston, 1899.

GIBBS, GEORGE (editor). *Memoirs of the Administrations of Washington and John Adams.* Edited from the papers of Oliver Wolcott. 2 vols. New York, 1846.

GILES, WILLIAM B. *See* Dice Robins Anderson.

GOODWIN, MAUD WILDER. *Dolly Madison.* New York, 1896.

GORDY, J. P. *A History of Political Parties in the United States.* 3 vols. Athens, Ohio, 1895.

GRAYDON, ALEXANDER. *Memoirs of a Life, Chiefly Passed in Pennsylvania, Within the Last Sixty Years.* Edinburgh, 1822.

GRISWOLD, RUFUS W. *The Republican Court: or, American Society in the Days of Washington.* New York, 1867.

HAMILTON, ALEXANDER. *See* Henry Cabot Lodge, John C. Hamilton, F. S. Oliver, A. M. Hamilton.

HAMILTON, ALLAN MCLANE. *The Intimate Life of Alexander Hamilton.* New York, 1911.

HAMILTON, JOHN C. *Life of Alexander Hamilton.* New York, 1911.

HAMMOND, JABEZ D. *History of Political Parties in the State of New York from the Ratification of the Federal Constitution to December, 1840.* 2 vols. Syracuse, 1852.

HAZEN, CHARLES DOWNER. *Contemporary American Opinion of the French Revolution.* Baltimore, 1897.

HENRY, PATRICK. *See* W. W. Henry.

HENRY, WILLIAM WIRT. *Life, Correspondence, and Speeches of Patrick Henry.* 3 vols. New York, 1891.

HIGGINSON, STEPHEN. *See* Thomas W. Higginson.

HIGGINSON, THOMAS WENTWORTH *Life and Times of Stephen Higginson.* Boston, 1907.

HILL, FREDERICK TREVOR. *The Story of a Street; A Narrative History of Wall Street from 1644 to 1908.* New York, 1908.

HILTZSHEIMER, JACOB. *See* Jacob Cox.

HUDSON, FREDERIC. *Journalism in the United States from 1690 to 1872.* New York, 1873.

HUNT, CHARLES HAVENS. *Life of Edward Livingston.* New York, 1902.

HUNT, GAILLARD (editor). *First Forty Years of American Society, Portrayed by the Family Letters of Mrs. Margaret Bayard Smith.* New York, 1906.

IREDELL, JAMES. *See* Griffith J. McRee.

JACKSON, JAMES (editor). *The Thomas Jefferson Bible.* New York, 1923.

JAY, JOHN. *See* George Pellew.

JEFFERSON, THOMAS. *See* John T. Morse, James Jackson, James Parton, W. C. Ford, Henry S. Randall, Thomas E. Watson, David Muzzey, Sarah E. Randolph, and A. W. Lipscomb.

BIBLIOGRAPHY

KING, CHARLES R. *Life and Correspondence of Rufus King.* 10 vols. New York, 1888.

KING, RUFUS. *See* Charles R.

KIRKLAND, J. T. *Life of Fisher Ames* (with *Works*). Boston, 1854.

KNOX, HENRY. *See* Noah Brooks and Francis S. Drake.

LIANCOURT, DUC DE LA ROCHEFOUCAULD. *Travels Through the United States of North America.* London, 1799.

LIPPINCOTT, HORACE MATHER. *Early Philadelphia: Its People, Life, and Progress.* Philadelphia, 1917.

LIPSCOMB, A. W. *Works of Thomas Jefferson.* Washington, 1903. (*Works.*)

LIVINGSTON, EDWARD. *See* C. H. Hunt.

LODGE, HENRY CABOT. *The Works of Alexander Hamilton.* 12 vols. New York. *Alexander Hamilton.* Boston, 1899. *Life and Letters of George Cabot.* Boston, 1877. *Studies in History.* Boston, 1884.

LYON, MATTHEW. *See* J. F. McLaughlin.

MACLAY, EDGAR S. (editor). *The Journal of William Maclay.* New York, 1890.

MACLAY, WILLIAM. *See* E. S. Maclay.

MACON, NATHANIEL. *See* W. E. Dodd.

MCHENRY, JAMES. *See* B. C. STEINER.

MCLAUGHLIN, J. FAIRFAX. *Matthew Lyon: The Hampden of Congress.* New York, 1900.

MCREE, GRIFFITH J. *Life and Correspondence of James Iredell.* 2 vols. New York, 1857.

MADISON, DOLLY. *See* Maud W. Goodwin.

MADISON, JAMES. *See* William C. Rives, S. H. Gay.

MARSHALL, JOHN. *See* A. J. Beveridge.

MELVILLE, LEWIS. *Life and Letters of William Cobbett in England and America.* 2 vols. London, 1913.

MONROE, JAMES. *See* George Morgan.

MORGAN, GEORGE. *Life of James Monroe.* Boston, 1921.

MORISON, SAMUEL ELIOT. *Life and Letters of Harrison Gray Otis.* 2 vols. Boston, 1913.

MORRIS, ANNE CARY. *The Diary and Letters of Gouverneur Morris.* 2 vols. New York, 1888.

MORRIS, GOUVERNEUR. *See* A. C. Morris.

MORRIS, ROBERT. *See* E. P. Oberholtzer.

MORSE, ANSON DANIEL. *Parties and Party Leaders.* Boston, 1923.

MORSE, ANSON ELY. *The Federalist Party in Massachusetts to the Year 1800.* Princeton, 1909.

MORSE, JOHN T. *Thomas Jefferson.* Boston, 1899. *John Adams.* Boston, 1899.

MUZZEY, DAVID. *Thomas Jefferson.* New York, 1919.

MYERS, GUSTAVUS. *The History of Tammany Hall.* New York, 1917.

OBERHOLTZER, E. P. *Robert Morris, Patriot and Financier.* New York, 1903.

OLIVER, FREDERICK SCOTT. *Alexander Hamilton: An Essay on the American Union.* New York, 1907.

OTIS, HARRISON GRAY. *See* S. E. Morison.

PARSONS, THEOPHILUS. *Memoir of Theophilus Parsons.* Boston, 1859.

PARTON, JAMES. *Life of Thomas Jefferson.* 2 vols. Boston, 1874. *Life and Times of Aaron Burr.* 2 vols. Boston, 1892.

PAYNE, GEORGE HENRY. *History of Journalism in the United States.* New York, 1920.

PELLEW, GEORGE. *John Jay.* Boston, 1899.

PICKERING, OCTAVIUS. *Life of Timothy Pickering.* 4 vols. Boston, 1867.

PICKERING, TIMOTHY. *See* O. Pickering.

PINCKNEY, C. C. *Life of General Thomas Pinckney.* Boston, 1895.

PINCKNEY, THOMAS. *See* C. C. Pinckney.

PURCELL, RICHARD J. *Connecticut in Transition, 1775–1818.* Washington, 1918.

RANDALL, HENRY S. *The Life of Thomas Jefferson.* 3 vols. Philadelphia, 1871.

RANDOLPH, SARAH N. *Domestic Life of Thomas Jefferson.* New York, 1871.

REPPLIER, AGNES. *Philadelphia: The Place and the People.* New York, 1898.

RIVES, WILLIAM C. *History of the Life and Times of James Madison.* 3 vols. Boston, 1868.

ROBINSON, WILLIAM A. *Jeffersonian Democracy in New England.* New Haven, 1916.

ROOSEVELT, THEODORE. *Gouverneur Morris.* Boston, 1899.

SCHARF, J. THOMAS. *History of Philadelphia.* 3 vols. Philadelphia, 1884.

SMITH, MARGARET BAYARD. *See* Gaillard Hunt.

SMITH, THOMAS E. *The City of New York in the Year of Washington's Inauguration.* New York, 1889.

STEINER, BERNARD C. *Life and Correspondence of James McHenry.* Cleveland, 1907.

STEVENS, JOHN AUSTIN. *Albert Gallatin.* Boston, 1899.

STORY, JOSEPH. *See* W. W. Story.

STORY, W. W. *The Life and Letters of Joseph Story.* 2 vols. Boston, 1857.

SULLIVAN, JAMES. *See* T. C. Amory.

SULLIVAN, WILLIAM. *Familiar Letters on Public Characters and Public Events.* Boston, 1834.

THOMAS, E. S. *Reminiscences of the Last Sixty Years.* 2 vols.

TWINING, THOMAS. *Travels in America One Hundred Years Ago.* New York, 1893.

WALSH, CORREA MOYLAN. *The Political Science of John Adams.* New York, 1915.

WANSEY, HENRY. *The Journal of an Excursion to the United States of North America in the Summer of 1794.* London, 1796.

WARFIELD, ETHELBERT DUDLEY. *The Kentucky Resolutions of 1798.* New York, 1894.

WARVILLE, J. P. BRISSOT. *New Travels in the United States of America.* Bowling Green, Ohio, 1919.

WATSON, JOHN F. *Annals of Philadelphia and Pennsylvania in Ye Olden Time.* 2 vols. Philadelphia, 1857.

WATSON, THOMAS E. *The Life and Times of Thomas Jefferson.* New York, 1903.

WELD, ISAAC. *Travels Through the States of North America.* 2 vols. London, 1807.

WELLING, JAMES CLARKE. *Addresses, Lectures, and Other Papers.* Cambridge, 1904.

WHARTON, ANNE HOLLINGSWORTH. *Salons, Colonial and Republican.* Philadelphia, 1900.

WHARTON, FRANCIS. *State Trials of the United States during the Administrations of Washington and John Adams.* Philadelphia, 1849.

WILSON, JAMES GRANT. *The Memorial History of the City of New York.* 4 vols. New York, 1893.

Woodburn, James A. *Political Parties and Party Problems in the United States.* New York, 1914.

Contemporary Pamphlets

Anonymous. *Serious Facts Opposed to 'Serious Considerations' and the 'Voice of Warning to Religious Republicans.'* (Pamphlets attacking the religion of Jefferson.) New York, 1800.

Beckley, John James. *Address to the People of the United States, with an Epitome and Vindication of the Life and Character of Thomas Jefferson.* Philadelphia, 1800.

Bishop, Abraham. *An Oration on the Extent and Power of Political Delusions.* Newark, 1800.

'Bystander.' *A Series of Letters on the Subject of the 'Legislative Choice' of Electors in Maryland.* Baltimore, 1800.

Callender, J. T. *Sedgwick & Company: A Key to the 6 per cent Cabinet.* Philadelphia, 1798. *The Honorable Mr. Sedgwick's Last Will and Testament.* Newark, 1800. *The Prospect Before Us.* Richmond, 1800.

Cheetham, James. *An Answer to Alexander Hamilton's Letter concerning the Public Conduct and Character of John Adams.* New York, 1800.

Cobbett, William. *Observations on the Emigration of Dr. Joseph Priestley.* Philadelphia, 1794. *A Bone to Gnaw for Democrats.* Philadelphia, 1795.

Coxe, Tench. *Strictures upon the Letter Imputed to Mr. Jefferson Addressed to Mr. Mazzei.* Philadelphia, 1800.

Fenno, John Ward. *Desultory Reflections on the New Political Aspects of Public Affairs.* New York, 1800.

Hodgkinson. *Letters on Emigration.* London, 1794.

Smith, William. *Address to his Constituents.* Philadelphia, 1794.

Taylor, John. *An Examination of the Late Proceedings of Congress, Respecting the Official Conduct of the Secretary of the Treasury.* Philadelphia, 1793.

Contemporary Newspapers

Boston:
  The Columbian Centinel.
  The Independent Chronicle.
New York:
  New York Daily Advertiser.
  Commercial Advertiser.
  New York Journal.
  American Minerva.
  The Argus.
  The Time Piece.
  Gazette of the United States.
  Louden's Diary, or Register.
Philadelphia:
  National Gazette.
  Gazette of the United States.
  The General Advertiser.
  The Aurora.

Porcupine's Gazette.
Pennsylvania Daily Advertiser.
BALTIMORE:
   Maryland Gazette.
   Maryland Journal.
PORTSMOUTH:
   New Hampshire Gazette.
CHARLESTON:
   City Gazette.
WINDSOR, VERMONT:
   Spooner's Vermont Journal.
HARTFORD:
   The Courant.
   The American Minerva.
NEW HAVEN:
   Connecticut Gazette.

MAGAZINES

American Historical Review, October, 1899, January, 1900, 'Contemporary Opinion of the Virginia and Kentucky Resolutions,' by Frank M. Anderson.

American Historical Association, *Annual Reports,* 1912, 'The Enforcement of the Alien and Sedition Laws,' by Frank M. Anderson; 1896–97, 'Letters of Phineas Bond.'

The Nation, July 18, 1912, ' Extracts from Diary of Moreau de St. Mery'; September 5, 1895, 'The Authorship of the Giles Resolutions,' by Paul L. Ford.

INDEX

Adams, Abigail, New York house at Richmond Hill, 16; on removal of capital to Philadelphia, 116; on Philadelphia, 125; and Mrs. Bingham, 128, 129.

Adams, Abijah, bookkeeper for editor of *Independent Chronicle*, imprisoned for libel, 394, 395.

Adams, John, begins 'reign' as Vice-President, 3; troubled as to proper titles for the President and Vice-President, 3; on reception of President in Senate, 3; what is the Vice-President when the President is in Senate? 3; writer of 'Discourses of Davilla,' published in Fenno's *Gazette*, 17; on Hamilton, 37; Jeffersonians attempt to defeat for Vice-Presidency in 1792, 181; elected, but by small margin, 183; candidate for Presidency, in 1796, 310; suspects trickery, 312; retains Washington's Cabinet, 314; sketch of, at time of entering on Presidency, 316–26; Maclay on, 317; his vanity, 318; jealousy of Washington, 319; difficult in conference, 320; not in sympathy with democracy, 322; his love of country, 323; moral courage, 325, 326; war with France threatened, 339; sends special mission to France, 345; reports failure of envoys to France, and recommends Congress to authorize warlike measures, 363; is ignorant that Hamilton through McHenry is dictating policy, 363; action on publication of X Y Z papers commended, 366; pulls down the pillars, 412; is troubled about French situation, 412; offers command of army to Washington, 412, 413; conspiracy in Cabinet in favor of Hamilton, 412, 413; nominates Hamilton, Pinckney, and Knox as major-generals, 413; Federalist conspirators bombard him with suggestions that Hamilton should be second in command, 414; war plans all in Hamilton's hands, 418–28; is ignorant of much going on, 426; considers sending new mission to France, 428; submits questions to Cabinet, for new negotiations with France or a declaration of war, 429; Cabinet conspirators with Hamilton write war Message, 429; A. rewrites Message, 429, 430; is conscious of Cabinet conspiracy, 430; appoints Minister to France, 430; contest with Senate over confirmation, 430, 431; agrees to compromise, 432, 433; confounds his Cabinet conspirators, 436–38; depressed by Federalist defeat in New York election in 1800, 455, 456; suspects Hamilton, 456; dismisses McHenry and Pickering from Cabinet, 456, 457; defeated for Presidency, 486; relations with Jefferson, on quitting office, 489, 490.

Adams, John Quincy, on speculation by Congressmen, 47; on Madison, 57.

Adams, Samuel, defeated for Representative to First Congress by Fisher Ames, 1; looked to by Jefferson for aid in forming opposition party in Massachusetts, 144; chosen by Jefferson as lieutenant, 144; presides at meeting in Boston on Jay Treaty, 278.

Adams, Thomas, editor Boston *Independent Chronicle*, 152; prosecuted under Sedition Law, 393–94.

Adet, ——, Minister to United States, from French Republic, credited with efforts to influence election in 1796, 311.

Alien Bill, aimed at Irish immigrants, 374; French residents frightened and sail for France, 376; passed by close vote, 379.

Allen, John, Representative from Connecticut, 379.

American Minerva, on party feeling, 232.

Ames, Fisher, Representative from Massachusetts, elected over Samuel Adams, 1; cynical over prospect of improvement in form of government over old Confederation, 1; not impressed by his fellow Congressmen, 1; on cost of Federal Hall, 2; on titles, 6; Hamilton's defender in House, 47; on Madison, 51, 52; disgusted with contest for site of permanent capital, 65; on proposed amendment to Excise Bill, 73; defends doctrine of 'implied powers,' 76; elected director of Bank of United States, 90; on Giles's resolutions attacking Treasury management, 201, 203; on yellow fever epidemic in Philadelphia, 237; on Madison commerce resolutions, 240, 241; sketch of, 302–04; makes strong plea in House for appropriations to carry out Jay Treaty, 305, 306.

An Examination of the Late Proceedings of Congress Respecting the Official Conduct of the Secretary of the Treasury, pamphlet published in Philadelphia, 205; authorship attributed to John Taylor of Caroline, 206.

Assumption, favored by North, where most of State indebtedness was unpaid, 59; opposed by Virginia, whose debt was largely paid, 59; defended by Madison,

popularity of Washington, 41; from beginning under domination of Hamilton, 140; favored by commercial, intellectual, and professional classes, 140; leaders men of strength in most of the States, 140, 141; opposition to, inevitable, 144; denounce Democrats as conspirators, 151; attack Jeffersonian newspapers in Federalist organs, 203, 204; sympathies with royalists in French Revolution, 207, 208; enforce policy of neutrality in French Revolution wars, 216; force recall of Genêt, 231; avert war with England and send Jay to negotiate treaty, 247; leaders induce attacks on 'Democratic Societies,' 261; defend Jay Treaty, but with wry faces, 285–88; refuse to confirm nomination of Rutledge as Chief Justice, 289; pass Alien and Sedition Acts, 375–80; efforts of leaders to force war with France, 412–28; mean war to be a Federalist war, 412; Hamilton is to conduct war with no interference from Adams, 412; secure appointment of Hamilton as second in command, 415; conspire to prevent Jeffersonians from securing commissions in army, 416; war not popular among the people at large, 418; raising funds for war purposes difficult, 418; taxes for war arouse resentment, 419; recruiting slow, 421; public refuse to believe there is to be a war, 421, 422; Logan's visit to France upsets Federalist war plans, 423, 424; the war hawks disappointed, 425, 426; Federalists determined on war, 426, 427; Cabinet conspirators write war Message for Adams, 429; scheme to override Adams, 430; caucus, 430; friends of Adams's policy in majority, 430; losing ground politically in 1799, 440; plan for changing method of counting electoral votes in Presidential election, 441, 442; bill passes Senate, but fails in the House, 442, 443; spring elections of 1800 show tide running against them, 448, 451–55; under Hamilton's influence leaders plan to defeat Adams for Presidency, 455–58; hints at secession from Federalist leaders in case of Jefferson's election, 468, 470; party split hopelessly on publication of Hamilton's attack on Adams, 481, 482; defeated in election, leaders conspire to have electors vote for Burr, 491; Hamilton opposed to plan, 491–501; plan fails, after much balloting, 506.

Fenno, John, protégé of Hamilton, establishes *Gazette of the United States*, 4; his paper aspires to be the 'court journal,' 4; King and Hamilton interested in financing paper, 153, 154; patronage of government printing, 154; death of, from yellow fever, 381.

Fenno, John Ward, son of founder of Fenno's *Gazette*, continues publication, 381.

Fitzsimons, Thomas, Representative from Pennsylvania, speculator in certificates, 47; Hamiltonians meet at lodgings of, 58; and the Assumption Bill, 62; Hamilton's lieutenant in the House, 186; introduces resolution asking Hamilton to report plan for redemption of part of national debt, 186; resolution precipitates sharp debate, 186, 187; on Giles's resolutions attacking Treasury management, 201.

Florida Tea Garden, New York City, 10.

Ford, Paul Leicester, quoted, on Jefferson, 199.

France, revolution in, effect of, in United States, 207; asked to recall Genêt, 216; Adams sends mission to, 345; envoys unsuccessful, 363; publication of X Y Z papers, 364, 365; Adams recommends preparations for war with, 365.

Franchise, in 1789 limited in most of the States, 142; property qualifications, 142; Jefferson and, 142.

French Revolution, the, its influence in the United States, 207, 208; Hamiltonians instinctively hostile to purposes of, 208; denounced by leading Federalist Senators, 209; supported by Jefferson, 210; sympathy for, of the common people, 213; enthusiasm for the French, 213, 214; enthusiasm for, heightened by arrival of Genêt, 221, 222; liberty caps and liberty poles, 222; Democratic and Jacobin Clubs everywhere, 223; Federalists alarmed, 223; clubs denounced as vicious 'nurseries of sedition,' 223.

Freneau, Philip, 'Poet of the Revolution,' induced by Madison to establish newspaper, 154; appointed to clerkship in Department of State, 155; establishes *National Gazette*, 155; Jeffersonians aided, 155; at once assumes leadership, 155; paper recognized as Jefferson's organ, 155; arouses Federalist rage, 156; influence of paper felt in back country, 156; classmate of Madison, Lee, Burr, and Brockholst Livingston at Princeton, 157; rebel by nature, 158; his career in the Revolutionary War, 158, 159; *Gazette* carefully watched by Hamilton, 163; attacks Hamilton's policies, 164–68; attacked anonymously in Fenno's *Gazette*, 168; his dignified reply, 168; denies any connection of Jefferson with his paper, 169; renews crusade against Hamilton's financial policies, 195, 196; contrast of newspaper with Fenno's, 163; criticisms of acts of Administration, 163; 'Brutus' article, 164; 'Sidney' articles open attacks on Hamilton, 164, 165; controversy with Fenno, 166, 167; charges Hamilton with author-

necessarily offended sensibilities, 36, 37; lacked sympathy always with the 'common man,' 37; affectionate in his family relations, 38; with his equals socially delightful companion, 38; inordinately fond of women and their society, 38, 39; always of delicate rather than robust health, 39, 40; not a church member, but a believer in religion, 40; attitude toward his chief, 41; obsessed by idea of a strong government, 45; believed necessary to enlist propertied interest, 45; indifferent to unpropertied classes, 45; active in interest of Funding Bill, 49; bargains with Jefferson on location of new national capital, 66–68; at high tide of popularity, 69; considers himself Prime Minister, 69; offends other Cabinet members, by dictatorial manner, 69; indifferent to public opinion, 70; prepares Excise Bill, 70, 71; takes personal charge of Excise Bill in Senate, 73; National Bank Bill, 74; enunciates doctrine of implied powers, 75; breaks with Jefferson when J. advises Washington Bank Bill is unconstitutional, 78; Fenno's *Gazette* his organ, 154; *Report on Manufactures* filed with Congress, 161; interests capital in developing Passaic Falls, 162; portrait by Trumbull subscribed for, 162; attention attracted by Freneau's *Gazette*, 163; believes Jefferson responsible for attacks in paper, 166; attacks Freneau anonymously, 168; tries to drive Jefferson from the Cabinet, 169; in Fenno's *Gazette* attacks Jefferson, 172; denies his own unfriendliness to Constitution, 173; complains of Jefferson's interference with Treasury Department, 173; warns Adams of effort to defeat him in 1792 campaign, 181; possible candidacy of Aaron Burr for Vice-President maddening, 181; makes strenuous efforts in Adams's behalf, 181; urges Adams in dictatorial terms to his duty, 182; blackmailing of, by Reynolds, 187; tells complete story of relations with Reynolds's wife to deputation from Congress, 188–90; amazes House by reports, 198; his official conduct of the Treasury vindicated by Congress, 203; alarmed at enthusiasm for French Revolution, 214; urges Washington to return to Philadelphia, 214; takes matters into his own hands and decides on proper policy of Jefferson's Department of State, 215; prepares list of questions for Washington to submit to Cabinet, 215; his position on the reception to be given Genêt, 215; writes series of papers for Fenno's *Gazette* justifying policy of Neutrality in French Revolution struggle, 225, 226; is answered by Madison, 226; aided by Genêt's conduct, 227; is stricken

with yellow fever, 237, 238; sees risk of war with England, 245; is mentioned as special envoy to England, 246; declines to have his name considered, 247; goes in person to put down Whiskey Insurrection, 254–56; plans to crush the Democratic Societies, 256; is aided by Washington's attack on Societies, in Annual Message, 262, 264; prepares to leave Cabinet, 266; considers his work finished, 266; opens law office in New York, 268; plans to direct Federalist Party in Congress by correspondence, 268; dubs Jay Treaty an 'execrable thing,' 271; is injured in rioting in New York, 276, 277; consults with leading Federalists on campaign of 1796, 308; distrusts Adams, 308; H. and King decide to offer support to Patrick Henry, 308, 309; H. turns to Thomas Pinckney, 310; plans to bring in Adams second, 311; publishes pamphlet on relations with Mrs. Reynolds, 355; advises Adams through McHenry on French situation, 362; prepares to play trump card — X Y Z papers — to force war with France, 364; advises moderation in framing Alien and Sedition Bills, 376, 377; is nominated Major-General in prospective war with France, 413; schemes to be made second in command, 414; directs fight against Adams through his tools in Cabinet, 414; in correspondence with Miranda, South American adventurer, 427, 428; opposed by Burr in 1800 New York elections, 448–55; contrast between H. and Burr, 449; plans election of Presidential electors he can control, with view of defeating Adams, 451; power broken with defeat of Federalists in New York in 1800, 454; tour of New England in 1800, 459; schemes against Adams in contest for Presidency, 459–65; writes pamphlet attacking Adams, not intended for general publication, 477, 478; effect of pamphlet when published, 479, 480.

Hamilton, Mrs. Alexander, daughter of General Schuyler, 134.

Hamilton, William, and trees in Philadelphia, 117.

Hammond, George, British Minister to United States, 246; more friendly to Hamilton than to Jefferson, 246.

Hancock, John, Jefferson's aide in forming new party, 144.

Harper, Robert Goodloe, president of Jacobin Club of Charleston, 223; Representative from South Carolina, 346; sketch of, 347; on the Sedition Bill, 379, 380.

Harrowgate Gardens, Philadelphia, 121.

Hawkins, Benjamin, Senator from North Carolina, in conference with Jeffersonian leaders, 205.

Henry, Patrick, on Assumption, 60; Hamil-